Microsoft®
FrontPage® 2000 Bible

Microsoft® FrontPage® 2000 Bible

David Elderbrock and David Karlins

IDG Books Worldwide, Inc.
An International Data Group Company

Foster City, CA ✦ Chicago, IL ✦ Indianapolis, IN ✦ New York, NY

Microsoft® FrontPage® 2000 Bible

Published by
IDG Books Worldwide, Inc.
An International Data Group Company
919 E. Hillsdale Blvd., Suite 400
Foster City, CA 94404
www.idgbooks.com (IDG Books Worldwide Web site)

ISBN: 0-7645-3313-4

Printed in the United States of America

10 9 8 7 6 5 4 3

1B/RU/QZ/ZZ/FC-IN

Distributed in the United States by IDG Books Worldwide, Inc.

Distributed by CDG Books Canada Inc. for Canada; by Transworld Publishers Limited in the United Kingdom; by IDG Norge Books for Norway; by IDG Sweden Books for Sweden; by IDG Books Australia Publishing Corporation Pty. Ltd. for Australia and New Zealand; by TransQuest Publishers Pte Ltd. for Singapore, Malaysia, Thailand, Indonesia, and Hong Kong; by Gotop Information Inc. for Taiwan; by ICG Muse, Inc. for Japan; by Norma Comunicaciones S.A. for Colombia; by Intersoft for South Africa; by Le Monde en Tique for France; by International Thomson Publishing for Germany, Austria and Switzerland; by Distribuidora Cuspide for Argentina; by Livraria Cultura for Brazil; by Ediciones ZETA S.C.R. Ltda. for Peru; by WS Computer Publishing Corporation, Inc., for the Philippines; by Contemporanea de Ediciones for Venezuela; by Express Computer Distributors for the Caribbean and West Indies; by Micronesia Media Distributor, Inc. for Micronesia; by Grupo Editorial Norma S.A. for Guatemala; by Chips Computadoras S.A. de C.V. for Mexico; by Editorial Norma de Panama S.A. for Panama; by American Bookshops for Finland. Authorized Sales Agent: Anthony Rudkin Associates for the Middle East and North Africa.

For general information on IDG Books Worldwide's books in the U.S., please call our Consumer Customer Service department at 800-762-2974. For reseller information, including discounts and premium sales, please call our Reseller Customer Service department at 800-434-3422.

For information on where to purchase IDG Books Worldwide's books outside the U.S., please contact our International Sales department at 317-596-5530 or fax 317-596-5692.

For consumer information on foreign language translations, please contact our Customer Service department at 800-434-3422, fax 317-596-5692, or e-mail rights@idgbooks.com.

For information on licensing foreign or domestic rights, please phone +1-650-655-3109.

For sales inquiries and special prices for bulk quantities, please contact our Sales department at 650-655-3200 or write to the address above.

For information on using IDG Books Worldwide's books in the classroom or for ordering examination copies, please contact our Educational Sales department at 800-434-2086 or fax 317-596-5499.

For press review copies, author interviews, or other publicity information, please contact our Public Relations department at 650-655-3000 or fax 650-655-3299.

For authorization to photocopy items for corporate, personal, or educational use, please contact Copyright Clearance Center, 222 Rosewood Drive, Danvers, MA 01923, or fax 978-750-4470.

Library of Congress Cataloging-in-Publication Data

Elderbrock, David
    Microsoft FrontPage Bible / David Elderbrock and David Karlins.
        p.   cm.
    ISBN 0-7645-3313-4 (alk. paper)
    1. Microsoft FrontPage. 2. Web sites--Design.
    3. Web publishing. I. Karlins, David. II. Title.
TK5105.8885.M53E44   1999
005.7'2--dc21   99-11047
                                                          CIP

is a registered trademark under exclusive license to IDG Books Worldwide, Inc., from International Data Group, Inc.

ABOUT IDG BOOKS WORLDWIDE

Welcome to the world of IDG Books Worldwide.

IDG Books Worldwide, Inc., is a subsidiary of International Data Group, the world's largest publisher of computer-related information and the leading global provider of information services on information technology. IDG was founded more than 30 years ago by Patrick J. McGovern and now employs more than 9,000 people worldwide. IDG publishes more than 290 computer publications in over 75 countries. More than 90 million people read one or more IDG publications each month.

Launched in 1990, IDG Books Worldwide is today the #1 publisher of best-selling computer books in the United States. We are proud to have received eight awards from the Computer Press Association in recognition of editorial excellence and three from Computer Currents' First Annual Readers' Choice Awards. Our best-selling ...For Dummies® series has more than 50 million copies in print with translations in 31 languages. IDG Books Worldwide, through a joint venture with IDG's Hi-Tech Beijing, became the first U.S. publisher to publish a computer book in the People's Republic of China. In record time, IDG Books Worldwide has become the first choice for millions of readers around the world who want to learn how to better manage their businesses.

Our mission is simple: Every one of our books is designed to bring extra value and skill-building instructions to the reader. Our books are written by experts who understand and care about our readers. The knowledge base of our editorial staff comes from years of experience in publishing, education, and journalism — experience we use to produce books to carry us into the new millennium. In short, we care about books, so we attract the best people. We devote special attention to details such as audience, interior design, use of icons, and illustrations. And because we use an efficient process of authoring, editing, and desktop publishing our books electronically, we can spend more time ensuring superior content and less time on the technicalities of making books.

You can count on our commitment to deliver high-quality books at competitive prices on topics you want to read about. At IDG Books Worldwide, we continue in the IDG tradition of delivering quality for more than 30 years. You'll find no better book on a subject than one from IDG Books Worldwide.

John Kilcullen
Chairman and CEO
IDG Books Worldwide, Inc.

Steven Berkowitz
President and Publisher
IDG Books Worldwide, Inc.

Eighth Annual Computer Press Awards ≥1992

Ninth Annual Computer Press Awards ≥1993

Tenth Annual Computer Press Awards ≥1994

Eleventh Annual Computer Press Awards ≥1995

IDG is the world's leading IT media, research and exposition company. Founded in 1964, IDG had 1997 revenues of $2.05 billion and has more than 9,000 employees worldwide. IDG offers the widest range of media options that reach IT buyers in 75 countries representing 95% of worldwide IT spending. IDG's diverse product and services portfolio spans six key areas including print publishing, online publishing, expositions and conferences, market research, education and training, and global marketing services. More than 90 million people read one or more of IDG's 290 magazines and newspapers, including IDG's leading global brands — Computerworld, PC World, Network World, Macworld and the Channel World family of publications. IDG Books Worldwide is one of the fastest-growing computer book publishers in the world, with more than 700 titles in 36 languages. The "...For Dummies®" series alone has more than 50 million copies in print. IDG offers online users the largest network of technology-specific Web sites around the world through IDG.net (http://www.idg.net), which comprises more than 225 targeted Web sites in 55 countries worldwide. International Data Corporation (IDC) is the world's largest provider of information technology data, analysis and consulting, with research centers in over 41 countries and more than 400 research analysts worldwide. IDG World Expo is a leading producer of more than 168 globally branded conferences and expositions in 35 countries including E3 (Electronic Entertainment Expo), Macworld Expo, ComNet, Windows World Expo, ICE (Internet Commerce Expo), Agenda, DEMO, and Spotlight. IDG's training subsidiary, ExecuTrain, is the world's largest computer training company, with more than 230 locations worldwide and 785 training courses. IDG Marketing Services helps industry-leading IT companies build international brand recognition by developing global integrated marketing programs via IDG's print, online and exposition products worldwide. Further information about the company can be found at www.idg.com.   1/24/99

Credits

Acquisitions Editor
Kathy Yankton

Development Editor
Katharine Dvorak

Technical Editor
James P. Sally

Copy Editors
William F. McManus
Corey Cohen
Marti Paul

Production
Foster City Production Department

Proofreading and Indexing
York Production Services

Cover Design
Murder By Design

About the Authors

David Elderbrock has worked for over five years as a technical consultant and Internet developer for Silicon Valley start-ups, small businesses, and large corporations. He got his start as an Internet developer at the University of California, Berkeley, where he helped design an online reading and composition database for writing instructors while working on his Ph.D. in English. David has been instrumental in the design and implementation of over two dozen Web sites, and in addition to hammering out his share of Web pages in text editors, he has also done programming, mostly in Perl, JavaScript, and Java, with, more recently, a smattering of Visual Basic and C++. He has developed a number of online database applications, SQL and otherwise, on Macintosh, Windows, and Unix platforms. He is the principal author of *Building Successful Internet Businesses* and a contributing author of *Producing Web Hits*, both published by IDG Books Worldwide.

David Karlins has written or contributed to nine books on FrontPage and Image Composer. He teaches FrontPage and Web design classes and hosts the FrontPage Forum at www.ppinet.com.

Preface

Just a few years ago, the Internet was a sleepy cow-town on the virtual edge of reality, inhabited primarily by hard-core techie types. Then somebody (okay, several somebodies) built the information highway right down its main street, and behold, a new frontier was discovered. Go Web, young man!

Today, the Web has transformed itself into a global metropolis in which a broad range of people and institutions have staked out claims. A similar transformation has occurred within the walls of corporations, both large and small. Here, Web-based activity continues to become an increasingly important part of even the least technical employee's day-to-day activity.

FrontPage 2000 is designed for those people, technical and non technical alike, who inhabit this brave new world. Like its earlier incarnations, FrontPage 2000 is a remarkably easy-to-use tool for creating Web pages and managing Web sites. In its most recent release, FrontPage also joins the elite ranks of the other Office 2000 applications in melding Web content creation and development tasks with more traditional "business applications." Web-page authoring has grown up.

Why You Need This Book

FrontPage is easy to use. Without the slightest training, a novice user can start FrontPage and begin creating attractive Web pages almost immediately. So, if it's that simple, why do you need this book?

FrontPage puts a great deal of power in your hands — text searching, discussion forums, form submission, CGI scripting, Java applets, ActiveX controls, database access, and a host of other advanced, jargon-packed Web techniques. Sure, you can use FrontPage to add a host of whiz-bang effects without a stitch of programming or Web-development experience. But sooner or later (usually about the time something goes wrong), it's nice to know a little bit about what you are doing. That's where this book comes in. Here's why:

✦ **For new users:** The *Microsoft FrontPage 2000 Bible* offers plenty of carefully explained, step-by-step examples and tutorials. It's ideal for anyone who wants to create high-quality Webs without focusing on the technical side, whether you're planning to concoct your own personal Web site or have been tasked with adding content to your company's intranet.

✦ **For the pros:** The *Microsoft FrontPage 2000 Bible* pushes and prods FrontPage at every turn to take the application as far as it can go. This book is for developers fluent in the ways of the Web, looking for the tools to become *more* productive and expand their repertoire of technical expertise. It's also for Web project teams who need to coordinate the work of content editors, graphic designers, and programmers. This title offers sage advice on how to get the work done quickly, while ensuring quality results.

✦ **For all of us:** For the most part, the *Microsoft FrontPage 2000 Bible* is just good solid information presented in readable doses. It recognizes the serious nature of Web publishing yet, thankfully, retains the sense of fun — and occasional good-natured irreverence — that has characterized the Web since its inception.

How This Book Works

The *Microsoft FrontPage 2000 Bible* retains the fundamental wit and wisdom of its predecessor, the *FrontPage 98 Bible*. It has been revised to highlight new and altered features in FrontPage, and several sections have been added to cover advanced topics in even more depth. Whatever your level of interest, you can use the book as a cover-to-cover tutorial (along with the wealth of examples and applications on the book's CD-ROM) — beginning with the basics and proceeding to the advanced stages of FrontPage 2000 and beyond. Or you can use this book and the CD-ROM as a reference, dipping into them topic by topic as you deem necessary.

Here is a brief synopsis of what you'll find in the pages of this book and on the CD-ROM.

Part I: FrontPage Essentials

The first chapter provides a quick-start tour of FrontPage 2000, taking you through the basic steps of creating a personal Web. Only one chapter into the book, and already you've created your own Web site! Chapter 2 provides a more detailed overview of the FrontPage 2000 environment. Chapter 3 examines the ins and outs of publishing your FrontPage content, while Chapter 4 shows you how you can integrate FrontPage with other Office 2000 applications, such as Word, Excel, and PowerPoint.

Part II: Enhancing the Look and Feel

In Part II, we focus on ways to make your Web site more attractive and easy to navigate. Chapter 5 covers the essentials of creating effective site-navigation elements in FrontPage. Chapter 6 looks at the nitty-gritty of text-formatting issues.

The last two chapters in this part focus on graphics. After discussing Web-design fundamentals, we explore Image Composer, Microsoft's sprite-based image-creation tool, in detail. We show you how to use FrontPage 2000 to create image maps so painlessly, it would make a Web old-timer cry.

This is a Note icon. It's a signpost to call your attention to especially insightful or just plain interesting factoids of various types. For instance, when you see the ⇨ symbol in this book (as in "Select Edit ⇨ Current Color Fill"), it's telling you in shorthand what path you need to follow to find a command under a menu. You'll find lots of notes like these in the text.

Part III: Layout and Design

In Part III we turn to advanced page-layout topics — formatting with tables and frames, HTML editing techniques, and using style sheets. Although these chapters speak, at times, to the HTML power users, they also provide step-by-step examples that even the HTML-challenged can follow.

The Caution icon alerts you to the presence of a don't-say-I-didn't-warn-you comment. Cautions often call your attention to an ever-so-slight shortcoming in FrontPage's ability to perform. Ignore them at your peril.

Part IV: Activating the User Experience

Part IV explores the many ways FrontPage 2000 enables you to add interactive pizzazz to your Web pages without resorting to actual programming. Chapter 13 takes FrontPage Components through their paces, giving special attention to FrontPage's text searching and discussion forum components. Chapters 14 and 15 explore creating and activating HTML forms. The final chapters in this section explore several ways to add multimedia effects to your Web pages and the effects of discussion Webs and channels.

Part V: Programming Elements

Part V looks at the variety of programming languages for which FrontPage 2000 provides at least a modicum of support — VB Script, JavaScript, DHTML, ActiveX, and Java are all covered in detail. Special attention is given to the Microsoft Script Editor and the Visual Basic editor incorporated into FrontPage 2000. The last chapter in this section provides examples of the many ways FrontPage eases the process of connecting a Web page to a database.

The Tip icon indicates a pearl of wisdom that you could spend your life hunting for in vain. Tips are usually creative solutions to insoluble life problems — or at least sticky Web problems.

Part VI: Advanced Topics

The last part of this book examines a number of issues relating to managing and publishing your Web project and administering your Web site. We discuss the ins and outs of customizing the FrontPage environment to suit your purposes, and provide in-depth explanations of working with the FrontPage Server Extensions for Web server administrators. We also look at ways that FrontPage can be incorporated into team-based Web projects, including several new FrontPage 2000 features to facilitate (or at least enable) team development projects.

A Few Basic Concepts

Sidebars such as this one are a major feature of this book. They usually contain interesting technical asides and extra information to support step-by-step processes. This sidebar informs you of the following important concepts:

✦ We assume you have a copy of FrontPage 2000 and a Web server somewhere in the wings.

✦ Generally, you will glean the most from each chapter if you read it with FrontPage 2000 up and running on your computer.

✦ The book begins with the basics, works through Web-page design concepts, tackles the technical topics, and concludes with information aimed at Web administrators.

✦ The operating system that receives the most attention in this book is Windows 95. Windows NT issues are covered in the later chapters.

✦ Unix Web servers and other Windows servers, such as O'Reilly's WebSite and Microsoft's own Windows NT–based Internet Information Server (IIS), are mentioned only in passing.

What's on the CD-ROM

In the back of the book is a CD-ROM containing all of the examples described in the book, as well as a number of other goodies. The Appendix, "Using the CD-ROM," contains a detailed list of the contents of the CD and how to install each program.

Summary

At the end of each chapter, we pause to reflect on what we've learned and reveal what adventures the next chapter holds.

Acknowledgments

This is my second go-around on this FrontPage book, and I would like to thank IDG Books Worldwide for giving me the opportunity to revise and update the content for the Office 2000 series. Trying to write a book for software that is still in beta testing can present a number of special challenges, and it is due largely to the efforts of a number of talented and caring individuals that the process was as smooth and, dare I say, enjoyable as it was. I would like to thank acquisitions editor Kathy Yankton for her direction and skill in keeping this project on track. I am especially indebted to development editor Katharine Dvorak, who had the unenviable job of gently prying chapters out of me on deadline. My thanks as well to the technical editor, Jim Sally, who helped keep me honest and accurate technically, and to Bill McManus and Corey Cohen, who repaired the damage I not infrequently wrought on the English language. I owe a special thanks to my co-writer, David Karlins, for contributing his considerable FrontPage knowledge and authorial expertise to this book. — David Elderbrock

Thanks to David Elderbrock for the opportunity to contribute to this book, and to Katharine Dvorak, Kathy Yankton, and everyone at IDG Books Worldwide for making the whole process as fun as it was challenging. Thanks also to Denise Snaer-Gauder for her artistic contributions, and to all the participants in the FrontPage Forum (www.ppinet.com) for their ongoing help and input. — David Karlins

Contents at a Glance

Contents

Part III: Layout and Design   231

Part IV: Activating the User Experience   339

Chapter 13: Adding FrontPage Components 341

Part V: Programming Elements   517

Chapter 18: Scripting Languages 519

FrontPage Essentials

Getting Started with FrontPage 2000

If you are in a hurry to create a Web site, start here. The following chapters expand on and add to the concepts introduced in this chapter. You can use the rest of this book as a reference, looking up features as you need them. Or, you can work your way through the book section by section, explore the tutorials along the way, and acquire a complete set of skills for creating and managing FrontPage Web sites. But this chapter moves quickly through all the essentials necessary to create a Web site in FrontPage 2000. If you're familiar with Web design and Web page editing, you'll find this first chapter to be a quick roadmap to follow to apply your skills to FrontPage 2000. If you're brand-new to Web design, you'll find this chapter to be a good introduction and starting point.

Before diving right into the nuts and bolts of creating a Web site, the next section quickly defines some of the basic elements that you will be working with.

FrontPage Webs, Web sites, and Web pages

From the vantage point of a Web designer, when you create a Web site, you work on two basic levels: Web design and page design. Unless your Web site is simply one page, you have two related jobs. You need to design a Web structure that visitors can use to navigate from page to page, and you need to design the Web pages themselves. To use an analogy from architecture, your job is to design both a building (your site) and individual rooms or offices (your pages).

The streamlined interface in FrontPage 2000 makes all of this very intuitive. You can easily jump to views that enable you to see an overview of your entire Web site. Or, you can zoom into an individual page, and edit the content and look of that page.

While the FrontPage interface enables you to shift back and forth seamlessly between page view and site views, having a basic sense of what's happening "under the hood" will help you while you put your Web site together.

FrontPage Webs and Web sites

FrontPage Webs are organized collections of files that are associated with a Web site. The Internet has come to be known as the World Wide *Web*, and locations on that network are known as *Web sites*. Unless they are very simple, one-page sites, most Web sites are composed of many Web pages. To visit a Web site, you enter a *URL* or *Uniform Resource Locator* (a Web site address) into the browser, and that Web site is located by the browser.

Just to complicate things, FrontPage has its own use of the term *Web*. A *Web*, in FrontPage's lexicon, is a set of Web pages and associated files organized in a single folder or directory structure. *In general*, your FrontPage Web is your Web site, although multiple FrontPage Webs can be created on the same Web site. That is because FrontPage uses the term *Web* to refer to the folder or directory structures that hold Web site files. More than one of these *Webs* can be attached to a single URL or Web site.

The practical implication of all of this is that the first step in creating a Web site in FrontPage is to define a *FrontPage Web*. This chapter jumps right into that process, but first, take a quick look at the other main element of Web sites.

In most cases, a FrontPage Web and a Web site are the same thing. The two terms describe what is going on from different perspectives — *Web site* being the external appearance, and *FrontPage Web* being the underlying file structure. Unless it is necessary to make a distinction, this book refers to FrontPage Webs as Web sites.

Web pages

Web pages differ from other documents in that they are designed to be interpreted by Web browsers. Microsoft Internet Explorer (IE) and Netscape Navigator take text, graphics, and even interactive elements, such as input forms, sound, and video, and enable them to be accessed by visitors to your Web site.

Web browsers interpret and display Web page content by reading a programming language called *Hypertext Markup Language (HTML)*. FrontPage shields you from having to learn HTML, by translating the menu options that you select into HTML code. If you prefer to do your own HTML coding, you can (see Chapter 11).

Not only does FrontPage interpret your commands into HTML, it also generates programming scripts in other languages, enabling you to add content such as search boxes, input forms, interactive responses to visitors, and sound and video.

What's new in FrontPage 2000?

If you're a veteran of earlier versions of FrontPage, you'll find some pretty dramatic changes in FrontPage 2000. Most of these new features will be incorporated into the remaining sections of this book, but if you want a quick reorientation, this chapter previews some of the most significant new options.

The first thing that you'll notice is that there is now just one FrontPage! No more FrontPage Editor versus FrontPage Explorer. What used to be the FrontPage Editor is now the Page view of FrontPage. And what used to be the FrontPage Explorer is organized into the remaining views in FrontPage.

The other major structural change in FrontPage is that you can now work much more easily with *disk-based* FrontPage Webs. In earlier versions of FrontPage, you were pretty much out of luck if you needed to design a Web site but didn't have access to a Web server. You won't be able to use many of FrontPage 2000's Components without a server, but you can design a Web site and still use most of FrontPage's page editing tools.

New features in FrontPage 2000 include the ability to place interactive spreadsheets, charts, and pivot tables in Web sites. You'll explore those Components in Chapter 4 and Chapter 21.

Earlier versions of FrontPage came with nominally customizable *Themes* that added color schemes, font formatting, graphic elements, and other look-and-feel elements to an entire Web site. What's vastly improved in FrontPage 2000 is the ability to customize these Themes. Customizing Themes is covered in Chapter 5.

Finally, for Microsoft Office 2000 users, FrontPage 2000 is a closer match to the rest of the Office interface. You get nice touches such as background spell checking and the Format Painter tool, which were not included in previous versions. FrontPage's new Open File menu looks and acts like those in other applications. You'll find detachable submenus, menu bars that display only those features that you use frequently, and help icons that look just like the features that you're used to in other Office applications, such as Word, Excel, PowerPoint, or Publisher. Expert Web managers will find new features that enable you to manage subwebs and joint workflow on a site more easily. You'll examine the connection between Office 2000 and FrontPage 2000 in Chapter 4.

A quick tour of FrontPage

When you open FrontPage 2000, you see a Views list on the left side of the screen, which is where you select from many different ways to look at the files that you create in FrontPage, and you see a big open space on the right side of the screen, which is your workspace.

Even before you start creating Web pages and organizing them into a Web site, you can introduce yourself to the following different views in FrontPage 2000:

✦ **Page view**: If you are responsible for the *content* of a Web site, you will probably spend much of your time in Page view, which is where you edit individual Web pages. Figure 1-1 shows FrontPage's Page view. You can view or hide a list of your files by selecting View ➪ Folder List from the menu.

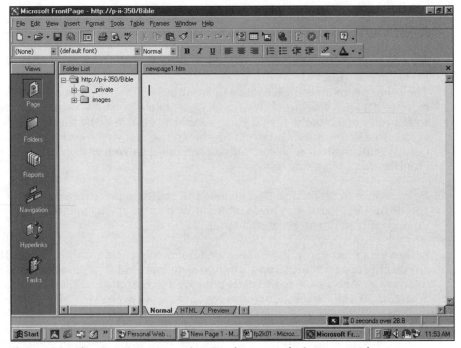

Figure 1-1: The FrontPage Page view is where you design your Web pages.

✦ **Folders view**: A directory of the files that you create in FrontPage. FrontPage creates two empty folders (_private and images) when you open a new Web site. When you save a Web page, or any other element of your Web site, you'll see files listed here.

✦ **Reports view**: FrontPage can generate reports that assess the status of your Web site. The default view that appears when you click the Reports icon in the View bar displays a summary of the different reports available. You can view any particular report by double-clicking it in the Site Summary spreadsheet, or by selecting a report from the View Reports submenu.

✦ **Navigation view**: Enables you to organize all of your different Web page files into an integrated Web site, and to define navigational links between pages.

✦ **Hyperlinks view**: *Hyperlinks* (or *links* for short) are text or graphics that, when clicked, connect a visitor to another Web page. Links can become corrupted or out of date when Web pages change, and this view checks up on them for you.

✦ **Tasks view**: FrontPage allows several members of a Web design team (or an individual Web designer) to create lists of things to do. Tasks can be assigned to different team members, who can in turn check off their progress as the Web is completed.

Creating a Web Site

Because Web sites are collections of Web pages, you can start either by designing the site structure or by creating the page content. If, for example, you are designing a site that will include many Web pages created in other Office 2000 applications, you might not need to do much with page content, and your entire task might be to orchestrate and organize all of these pages into a Web site. Or, in another scenario, you might be creating the entire Web site, including its content, from scratch.

In either scenario, your first task is to create a FrontPage Web, the underlying structure that holds together, coordinates, and manages all the files in your Web site.

 You may be tempted to start designing a Web page without first defining a Web site. Bad idea. Unless you are in a position to make a conscious decision to circumvent FrontPage's Web structure, stick with Web design. The only situation in which you would ever have a reason to create Web pages without creating a Web structure first is if you aren't going to use FrontPage to publish your Web to a server.

When you select File ➪ New from the FrontPage menu, you'll see two menu options, Page or Web. Again, unless you are consciously trying to short-circuit FrontPage's ability to keep track of and manage your site files, choose Web. After you do, you'll see the New dialog box, shown in Figure 1-2.

The New dialog box poses two decisions that determine the structure of your Web site. You can select a template to provide a design for your site, and you can select a location for your Web site. Both of these decisions require a little explanation, so they are explored next.

Where to save your new Web

As mentioned earlier, you have two basic options in creating a Web. You can create your Web on a Web server that is accessible to the Internet or an intranet. Or, you can create your Web on a local computer drive (your hard drive). Webs saved to your hard drive do not all have the advanced features available in FrontPage, such as the ability to collect data from input forms. And, of course, they can't be visited by anyone else. But you can use your local drive to design a Web, and then publish it to a Web server when one becomes available.

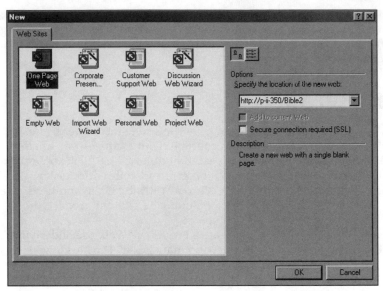

Figure 1-2: The New dialog box

Saving to a folder on your hard drive

To create your Web on your local hard drive, enter a drive and folder location in the drop-down box labeled "Specify the location of the new web" on the right side of the New dialog box. For example, in Figure 1-3, the folder is defined as C:\FrontPage Web Sites.

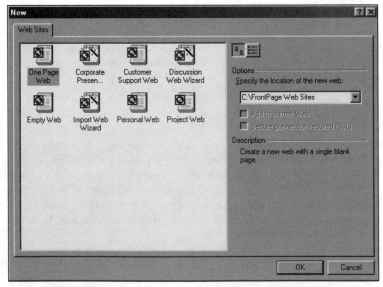

Figure 1-3: Saving a Web site to a local folder

After you select a template, you can click the OK button to generate a local Web for your FrontPage Web site. The next section of this chapter explores those templates, after the present section finishes discussing the remaining Web location options.

Saving to an intranet or Internet Web server

If you have access to an Internet or intranet Web server, you can publish your Web there. You need a URL (site address) from your Web administrator, and you need to be connected to the Internet or your intranet. Establishing these connections is the job of your Internet Service Provider (ISP) or your local intranet administrator. They should provide you with the URL address to which you are publishing, and a password.

If you have a Web server, enter the URL of the Web address in the drop-down box labeled "Specify the location of the new web" in the New dialog box. After you select a template and click OK, you'll be connected to your Web server, and prompted to enter a username and password.

Saving your Web site to the Personal Web Server

If you want to save your Web site to a Web server, but you don't yet have access to an Internet or intranet Web site, you can create your own Web site by using the Personal Web Server, included with Windows 98 and Office 2000. At the time of this writing, we are still lobbying to have the Personal Web Server included with every copy of the FrontPage CD-ROM, but if you don't find it there, you can install the Personal Web Server from your Windows 98 or Office 2000 CD-ROM.

After you install the Personal Web Server, run the FrontPage Server Administrator program (found in the Internet Explorer option from the Windows Start menu). Figure 1-4 shows the Personal Web Server Administrator.

Use the Check and Fix button in the FrontPage Server Administrator window to test your Personal Web Server, and to fix any problems. If you have an older version of the Personal Web Server installed on your computer, use the Upgrade button to add new files to your server.

After testing (and fixing or upgrading, if necessary) your Personal Web Server, launch the Personal Web Manager program (also found in the Internet Explorer area of your Start menu). The Personal Web Manager window is shown in Figure 1-5.

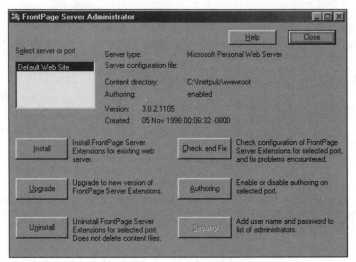

Figure 1-4: Installing the Personal Web Server

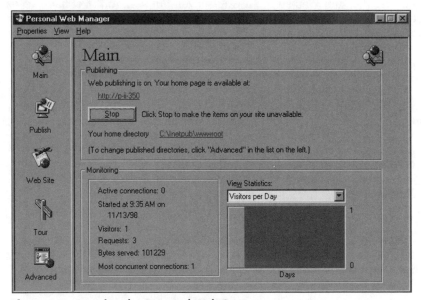

Figure 1-5: Running the Personal Web Server

The only option that you currently need to pay attention to in the Personal Web Manager window is the Start/Stop button. This button must be in Start mode (that is to say, it must say "Stop"), as shown in Figure 1-5. This means that the Personal Web Server is running, and that your local computer is functioning as a full-featured Web server with FrontPage Extension files that enable you to test all FrontPage 2000 Components.

The Personal Web Server includes features that help you to design Web pages, but you will be using FrontPage to do that. To use the Personal Web Server with FrontPage, you simply need to make sure that it is running. You should also note the location of your personal Web site in the section of the Personal Web Manager that says "Your home page is available at." This is the URL that you enter in the "Specify the location of the new web" drop-down box, in the New dialog box in FrontPage.

Do you need to select a location for your Web site?

If you just tore off the shrink-wrap from your copy of FrontPage and installed it, this discussion of where to save your Web site might seem a bit daunting. Put it in perspective, though: First of all, you're done! After you go through the process of deciding where you are going to save your Web site, you don't have to make that decision again. And, you can easily change the location of your Web site. As long as you've chosen one of the options previously discussed for saving your Web site, you can automatically publish your Web site to the Internet or an intranet, and FrontPage will handle all your file transferring automatically.

Tip

You can bypass the entire process of selecting a Web site location by choosing File ➪ New ➪ Page instead of File ➪ New ➪ Web when you start to create new Web pages. If you do that, you can still create individual Web pages, but you lose much of FrontPage's power to manage all of your files and transfer them from one Web location to another.

Choosing a Web template

After you select a location for your Web site, your next option is to choose from one of the eight Web templates provided by FrontPage, which include the following:

✦ **One Page Web**: A new Web with a single blank page.

✦ **Corporate Presence Web**: A complex Web with dozens of pages that can be converted into a Web site for a corporation.

✦ **Consumer Support Web**: A Web site that includes input forms for customer questions and feedback.

✦ **Discussion Web Wizard**: A wizard that leads you step by step through the process of creating a Web site in which visitors can post questions and get answers.

✦ **Empty Web**: Just a Web site, no pages.

✦ **Import Web Wizard**: A wizard that leads you through the process of assembling a Web from pages created outside of FrontPage.

✦ **Personal Web**: A nifty little four-page Web site that works well for sharing your interests.

✦ **Project Web**: A specialized Web site template for project managers only.

Some of these templates are quite complex, and require a pretty high level of experience with FrontPage to customize. The Corporate Presence Web, the Customer Support Web, the Discussion Web Wizard, and the Project Web include many Components that won't work unless you have saved your site to a Web server with FrontPage extensions (the Personal Web Server will work). The Empty Web, One Page Web, and Personal Web work well without FrontPage extensions on a Web server.

After you select both a location for your Web site and a template, click OK in the New dialog box. FrontPage generates a Web site for you and creates files and folders necessary for your Web pages.

Creating a home page

After you generate a Web, the next step in designing your Web site is to create a home page. If you used the Personal Web template or the One Page Web, your Web opens up with a home page. Figure 1-6 shows a new Web generated by the One Page Web template, with a lonely-looking home page in the middle of Navigation view.

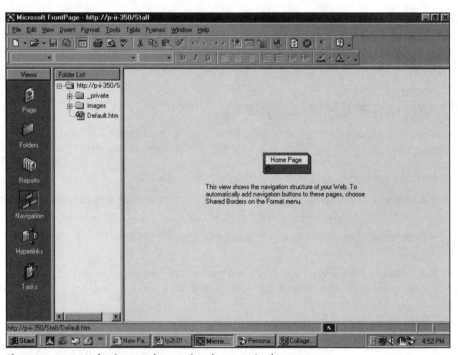

Figure 1-6: A Web site can be as simple as a single page.

If you created your new Web from the Empty Web template, you can click the New Page button in the FrontPage toolbar to create a new page. The first page that you create will be your home page.

Adding pages to your Web site

You can add Web pages to your Web site in Navigation view by clicking the New Page button in the toolbar. As you click the New Page button, new pages appear as "child" pages of the home page.

If you click one of your child pages and then click the New Page button, the new pages become child pages of child pages. You can construct many levels of Web pages in this manner. Figure 1-7 shows a Web site with three levels of pages.

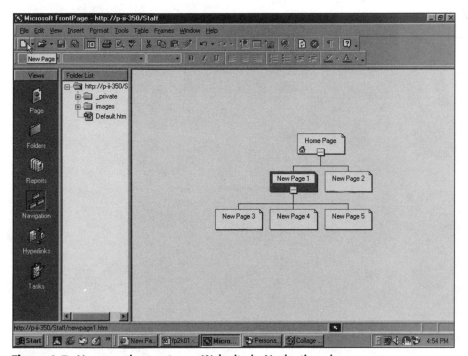

Figure 1-7: You can chart out your Web site in Navigation view.

Web structure strategies

As you design your Web site structure, put yourself in the shoes of someone visiting your Web site. One rule of thumb applied by many Web site designers (and programmers of all types) is to present visitors with between three and five options at each level of the Web site. So, for example, you might welcome visitors to your site at your home page, and present them with three options. Each of those options might have three, four, or five options.

Web design strategies are explored in much more detail in Chapter 2, and navigation options are discussed in depth in Chapter 5. For now, remember that your Web site can run many levels, but in general, you should keep the number of pages at each level of the site between three and five.

Changing site design

After you define a Web structure, you can easily change it. Just click and drag a page in Navigation view to move it to another location or level in the flowchart. Figure 1-8 shows a page being moved.

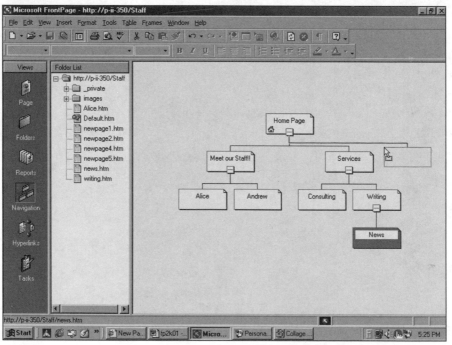

Figure 1-8: You can rearrange pages in Navigation view by clicking and dragging.

You can delete pages from your Web by right-clicking them in Navigation view and selecting Delete from the context menu. If your site is large, you can use the horizontal or vertical scroll bars to navigate within it.

You can collapse any section of Navigation view by clicking the minus symbol (-) on parent pages, to display only the parent page for that section of the Web. To expand the flowchart, click the plus sign (+) under a parent page.

Page titles and filenames

Web pages have both titles and filenames. The *filename* is used internally, for FrontPage to organize the Web. The *title* is the "public" name of the Web page, and displays in the visitor's browser when the Web page is opened.

New pages are generated with filenames that have titles such as New Page 6. You will want to change the page *titles* for these pages, so that something more descriptive and creative appears in a visitor's browser title bar.

Changing page titles

To change the page title in Navigation view, right-click a page in the flowchart and select Rename from the context menu. Type a new name and press Enter.

Tip A quick trick for renaming many pages is to use the Tab key to jump from one page to the other, which automatically allows you to rename pages. You can also change a page title by *slowly* double-clicking the page in Navigation view, or by clicking the page once and pressing the F2 function key.

Page titles are not restricted to eight characters, and can include spaces. However, you don't want to make them so long that they don't fit in your visitor's browser window.

Changing page names

Although page names do not appear in browser title bars or as generated navigation links, you still may want to rename them. One good reason is so that when you edit pages and keep track of files, you can associate a page filename with a page title.

As you generate new pages in Navigation view, they appear as HTML files in the Folder list on the left side of the Navigation view window. For now, the safest way to name a Web page is with an eight-character filename, with no spaces or non-ASCII characters, and with a filename extension of *.htm. You can assign a new filename to a Web page by right-clicking the filename in the Folder list on the left side of the FrontPage window, and selecting Rename from the context menu. Type a new filename (don't forget the .htm filename extension) and press Enter to change the filename.

Tip Sometimes, matching a filename with a page title can be difficult. After you rename your page titles in the flowchart area of Navigation view, your page filenames in Folder view will not match those titles. The solution is to right-click a page in the Folder list and select Find in Navigation from the context menu. The page associated with the file will be selected in Navigation view.

Adding Global Web Site Elements

Two global elements exist in designing a Web site: navigational structure, and look and feel. The two work together to create the overall flow and ambiance of your site. Think of an engineer and an interior decorator working together to make a building habitable.

You design the flow of your Web site by moving pages around in Navigation view. Unless you are aiming for the ultra-minimalist look, you will want to define a global atmosphere for your site. You do that by assigning global elements such as a global color scheme, global graphic elements, global text fonts, and global page backgrounds.

You can define and assign these global design elements by assigning a *Theme*. FrontPage comes with a large selection of Themes, each of which includes attributes such as fonts, colors, and icons. FrontPage supplies over a dozen Themes. Additionally, by selecting or deselecting options such as vivid colors or a background picture, you can define several variations on each Theme. Furthermore, you learn how to create your own custom Themes in Chapter 5. In the present section, you'll learn how to implement the Themes that come with FrontPage, starting with a discussion of how to select a site Theme.

Selecting a site Theme

Each Theme is a group of elements that can be applied to *every page* in a Web site. You can remove a Theme from a page, or even use different Themes for different pages in a Web site. But the purpose of selecting and applying a Theme is to use the same colors, icons, and other attributes throughout a site, to give the site a unique and consistent atmosphere.

To assign a Theme, follow these steps:

1. With your Web open, select Format ➪ Theme from the FrontPage menu. You can do this from any view.

2. To apply your Theme to all pages in your site, click the All Pages radio button. Alternately, if you have selected a single page (or pages) in Folder, Page, or Navigation view, you can click the Selected Page(s) radio button to apply the Theme to only the selected page(s).

3. Click one of the Themes in the list on the left side of the Themes dialog box. A preview of the Theme is displayed in the Sample of Theme area on the right side of the dialog box. Use the check boxes to experiment with Vivid Colors, Active Graphics, and a Background Picture, as shown in Figure 1-9.

4. When you settle on just the right Theme to suit your image, click the OK button to apply the Theme to your Web site (or selected pages).

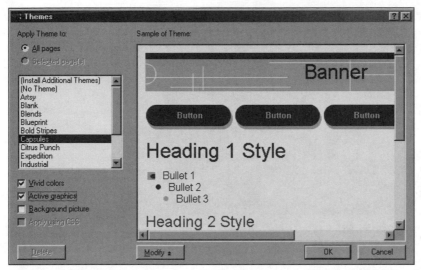

Figure 1-9: Themes provide color schemes, navigational icons, fonts, and colors.

You could sneak a peak at your Web pages now by double-clicking a page in Navigation view to open it in Page view. However, you will appreciate more the impact of Themes after you add shared borders in the next section of this chapter.

Note

Themes collect *many* elements of global page design, one of which is font and paragraph attributes. These attributes can *also* be applied through inline or Cascading Style Sheets. (Style Sheets are covered in Chapter 12.)

Adding shared borders

Along with Themes, you can apply universal characteristics to all pages in your Web site by applying shared borders. These shared borders can be placed on each page of your Web site, and are often used, at least in part, as navigational tools.

To apply shared borders to your Web site, follow these steps:

1. Select Format ➪ Shared Borders from the FrontPage menu (you can be in any view). The Shared Borders dialog box appears, as shown in Figure 1-10.

2. Select the All Pages radio button to apply the shared borders to the entire Web, or select the Selected Pages radio button to apply shared borders only to selected pages.

3. Select any combination of top and left shared borders that are the most widely used. Start experimenting by selecting them. Later, you can deselect one or both of these shared borders and apply bottom or even right shared borders.

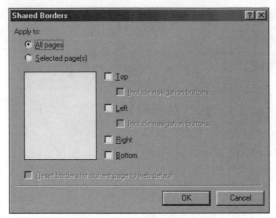

Figure 1-10: Up to four shared borders can be defined for a Web site.

Note   Most page designers put navigational guides at the top, left, or bottom of a Web page, and avoid right-side shared borders. The right side of a Web page is sometimes out of the browser window and can be viewed only if a visitor uses the horizontal scroll bar.

4. If you select top and/or left shared borders, you can select the Include Navigation Buttons check boxes for one or both of these shared borders.

5. After you select your shared borders, click the OK button.

Viewing Your Pages

Even if you have not placed any specific content on individual Web pages, you can generate many Web elements simply by applying Themes and Shared Borders. And, if you used a template, such as the Personal Web template, to generate your pages, you have some Comment text and other page elements.

To see how your Web site is shaping up, you can examine it in four ways:

✦ Page view, Normal tab

✦ Page view, HTML tab

✦ Page view, Preview tab

✦ A Web browser (such as Microsoft Internet Explorer or Netscape Navigator)

You can examine any page in Page view by double-clicking that page in the Folder list or in Navigation view. Page view is where you edit and view individual Web pages.

Normal tab

The Normal tab in Page view displays Web pages similar to how they will appear in a Web browser (see Figure 1-11). The Normal tab also displays page elements that don't appear in a browser, such as Comment text (also referred to as *purple* text), dotted lines to demarcate shared borders, and other editing marks.

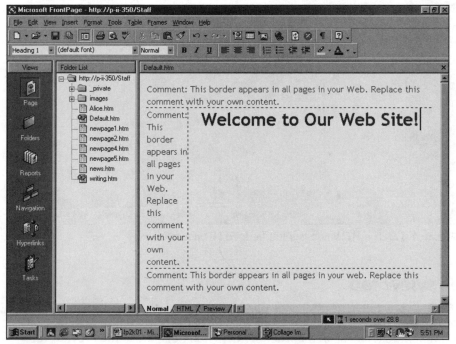

Figure 1-11: Comments and shared border dividers are visible in the Normal tab of Page view.

The Normal tab is discussed again shortly, because this is where you edit the content of Web pages.

HTML tab

You can see the HTML code that is generated by FrontPage for your Web page by clicking the HTML tab in Page view. If you are an HTML coder, feel free to edit the HTML code in this view. If not, you can simply admire the fact that you generated all of this code without knowing HTML, or you can study the generated code and use it to teach yourself some HTML. Figure 1-12 shows the HTML tab of Page view.

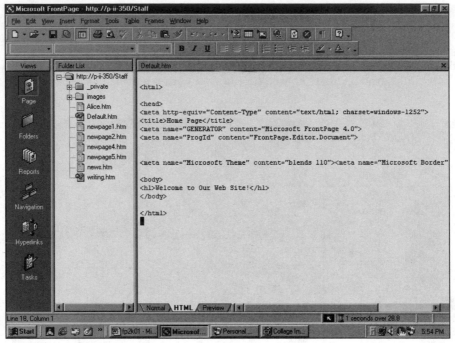

Figure 1-12: The HTML tab is a full-fledged HTML editor.

Preview tab

The Preview tab in Page view displays your Web page *closer to* the way that it will look in a browser (compared to the display in the Normal tab). Elements such as Comment text and shared border dividers don't display in the Preview tab. However, you cannot edit in Preview tab. Figure 1-13 shows a Web page displayed in the Preview tab of Page view.

Previewing in a browser

Preview tab roughly approximates how a Web page looks in a browser, but nothing can substitute for actually testing your pages by looking at them in Internet Explorer and/or Netscape Navigator.

Different browsers interpret Web attributes differently. *And* different screen resolutions display Web pages differently. You should periodically preview your Web pages in both Netscape Navigator and Internet Explorer, and it might be a good strategy to keep an older version of one of these browsers installed on your computer, so that you also can see how your Web pages look in those browsers.

To preview your Web page in a browser, select File ➪ Preview in Browser. The Preview in Browser dialog box allows you to select between any installed browser on your computer, and any screen resolution supported by your system.

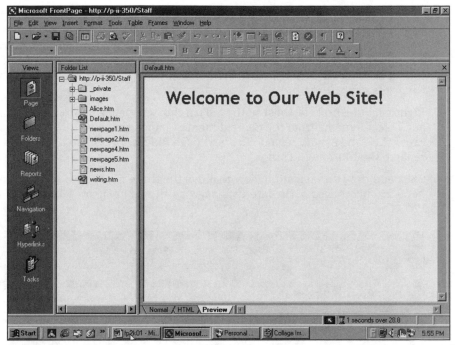

Figure 1-13: The Preview tab approximates the appearance of a Web page in a Web browser.

Before going forward in this chapter to explore the process of editing and formatting page content, you might want to experiment with the following tutorial to sharpen your Web design skills.

Deleting a Web

Deleting a Web is a bit unintuitive. In an attempt to make the FrontPage 2000 File menu compatible with the other applications in Windows 2000, this procedure has been moved to the Open dialog box.

You can delete this Web if you want by selecting File ➪ Open Web, right-clicking a Web file, and selecting Delete from the context menu.

The following tutorial reviews the process of generating a Web site, with the option to delete it after you create it.

Tutorial 1.1: Create a Web Site

1. Launch FrontPage 2000. Select File ➪ New ➪ Web to open the New dialog box.

2. Enter a location for your Web in the "Specify the location of the new web" drop-down list. This location can be a Web server or a file folder.

3. Click the Personal Web in the Web Sites list, and click the OK button in the dialog box.

4. Click the Navigation icon in the View bar to see your Web site in Navigation view. Click the Favorites page in Navigation view, and then click the New Page tool in the toolbar three times to create three "child" pages connected to the Favorites page.

5. Right-click the first (farthest to the left) of the new pages in Navigation view and select Rename from the context menu. Change the page title to **People**. Press the Tab key and rename the next page **Places**. Press Tab again and rename the third page **Things**.

6. Click and drag in Navigation view to move the three new pages so that they become child pages of the Interests page, as shown in Figure 1-14.

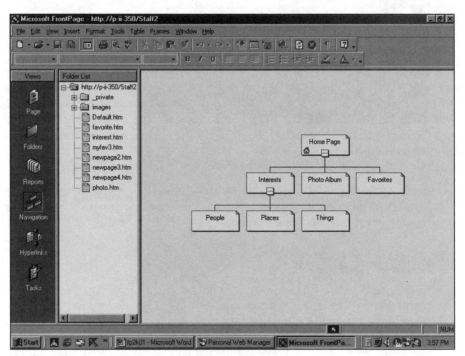

Figure 1-14: Rearranging pages in Navigation view

7. Select Format ⇨ Theme. Select one of the Themes from the list by previewing the list of Themes in the Sample of Theme area of the dialog box. When you find a Theme that you like, experiment with the three available check boxes in the dialog box. After you choose a Theme and select options that you like, click the OK button in the Themes dialog box.

8. Select Format ⇨ Shared Borders and note the default settings that are associated with your Theme. Close the Shared Borders dialog box.

9. Double-click the Home Page in Navigation view to open that page in Page view. Note the elements placed on your page by the Theme and Shared Borders. Click the HTML tab to see the HTML code that you generated.

10. If you have a browser installed on your computer, select File ➪ Preview in Browser and then double-click one of your installed browsers. Test your Web site in your browser by clicking underlined links in the navigation bars to move from page to page, as shown in Figure 1-15.

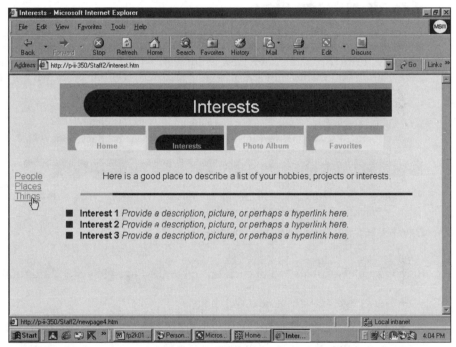

Figure 1-15: Testing navigation links in a Web browser

11. Select File ➪ Close Web to close your entire Web, including all the page files. You can delete this Web if you want by selecting File ➪ Open Web, right-clicking a Web file, and selecting Delete from the context menu.

Editing Pages in Page View

Chapter 6 is devoted entirely to an in-depth exploration of adding, editing, and formatting text in Page view. But, you can start here by entering and formatting text, and adding graphics. Because most of the work of designing Web pages and controlling Web page content takes place in Page view, you could say that the bulk of this book is about working in Page view. This first chapter can only scratch the surface of designing pages, but you don't really need to know much about Page view to edit and format text, and add pictures.

You'll find that Page view is very much like a word processor or desktop publishing program—or even a presentation program, such as PowerPoint. You enter, edit, and format text much as you would in any text program.

You can also insert, move, format, and edit graphics. All of this is explored in more detail in Chapter 6, but you can begin to work and edit in Page view without detailed preparation.

A look at Page view

You can open an existing Web page in Page view by double-clicking it in any other view, including in Navigation view. The tools in the Standard and Formatting toolbars at the top of the Page view window provide quick access to the most-used page editing and formatting features. The Standard toolbar is shown in Figure 1-16.

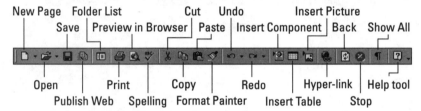

Figure 1-16: The Page view standard toolbar

Here is a quick explanation of each button in the Page view Standard toolbar:

✦ **New Page**: Creates a new Web page.

✦ **Open**: Accesses the Open Files dialog box to open existing Web pages.

✦ **Save**: Saves the open Web page.

✦ **Publish Web**: Publishes your Web site from your local computer to an intranet or Internet location.

✦ **Folder List**: Displays (or hides) a list of folders and files associated with your Web site.

✦ **Print**: Sends your Web pages to your printer.

✦ **Preview in Browser**: Displays your Web page in your default Web browser.

✦ **Spelling**: Checks your Web page for spelling errors.

✦ **Cut**: Cuts selected text or objects and saves them in the Clipboard.

✦ **Copy**: Copies selected text or objects and saves them in the Clipboard.

✦ **Paste**: Pastes contents of the Clipboard at the insertion point.

✦ **Format Painter**: Copies a selected format to apply with the (paintbrush) format cursor.

✦ **Undo**: Undoes your last command or keystroke.

✦ **Redo**: Cancels your latest Undo action.

✦ **Insert Component**: Opens the Insert Component submenu.

✦ **Insert Table:** Opens the Insert Table grid.

✦ **Insert Picture**: Opens the Image dialog box.

✦ **Hyperlink**: Opens the Create Hyperlink dialog box to define or edit a link to another Web page or a location on a Web page.

✦ **Back**: If you followed a link in FrontPage, you can move back to the previous Web page.

✦ **Stop**: Stops refreshing a page.

✦ **Show All**: Shows paragraph and line breaks.

✦ **Help tool**: Displays a help cursor — point and click to get help with any onscreen element.

Most of your Web page text formatting is controlled from the Formatting toolbar in Page view. You can see the Formatting toolbar in Figure 1-17.

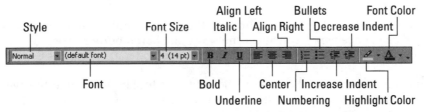

Figure 1-17: Page view's formatting tools act a bit differently than those in Word.

Here is a quick description of each tool in the Formatting toolbar:

✦ **Style**: The styles in the list are HTML styles, and can't be edited in the same way that you edit styles in programs such as Microsoft Word. You can elect to assign formatting without worrying about what HTML style is assigned to text. Styles are discussed in detail in Chapter 12.

✦ **Font**: Drop-down list from which you can assign fonts to selected text.

✦ **Font Size**: Drop-down list from which you can assign font size to selected text. The selection of sizes is constrained by those available in HTML.

✦ **Bold**: Assigns boldface to selected text.

✦ **Italic**: Assigns italics to selected text.

✦ **Underline**: Underlines selected text.

✦ **Align Left**: Left-aligns selected paragraph(s).

✦ **Center**: Centers selected paragraph(s).

✦ **Align Right**: Right-aligns selected paragraph(s). HTML does not support full justification.

✦ **Numbering**: Assigns sequential numbering to selected paragraphs.

✦ **Bullets**: Assigns indenting and bullets to selected paragraphs.

✦ **Increase Indent**: Indents entire selected paragraph(s).

✦ **Decrease Indent**: Moves selected paragraphs to the right (undoes indenting).

✦ **Highlight Color**: Adds a background highlight to selected text.

✦ **Font Color**: Assigns colors to selected text.

Editing text

You can type anywhere on a page in Page view to add text. You'll find that all standard text editing and navigation techniques used in other Windows applications can be used to edit text in Page view. You'll also find that FrontPage has spell checking as you type, underlining words not found in its dictionary in wavy red lines, so that you can correct spelling as you go. A detailed exploration of text editing is in Chapter 6, but for now, you can add and edit text by typing and deleting.

If you enter or edit text in a shared border (they are separated from the page by dotted lines in Page view), you affect the way that shared border appears on *each page* of your Web site. Shared borders are explored in detail in Chapter 5.

As you enter text on your Web pages, click the Save tool in the toolbar to save your changes. Changes to a Web are saved by saving individual pages (you don't "Save" a Web, you save pages in it to update files).

Formatting text

The tools in the Formatting toolbar can be used to apply formatting to selected text. For example, you can select text, click the down arrow next to the Font Color button, and select a font color to apply to selected text from the palette, as shown in Figure 1-18.

Adding images

The following are several ways to add images quickly to a Web page in Page view:

✦ Copy and paste images through the Clipboard.

✦ Insert an image from a file on your local drive or from the Internet.

✦ Use FrontPage's nice collection of clip art.

✦ Scan an image directly into FrontPage.

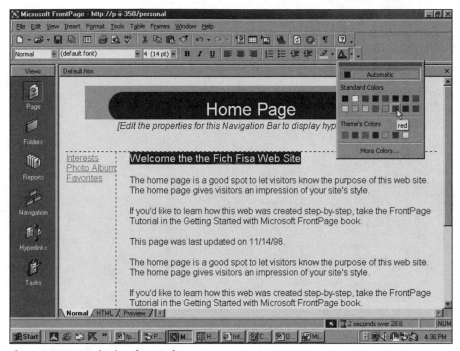

Figure 1-18: Assigning font color

To insert clip art, follow these steps:

1. Click the Insert Picture from File button in the Standard toolbar.

2. Click the Clip Art button in the Picture dialog box.

3. Click a clip art category to see a list of available pictures.

4. Click a picture that you want to insert, and select the Insert Clip button from the pop-up menu, as shown in Figure 1-19.

You can insert a graphic file in very much the same way:

1. Click the Insert Picture from File button in the Standard toolbar.

2. Click the Select a File from Your Computer button in the lower-right corner of the Picture dialog box.

3. In the Select File dialog box, navigate to the folder with your image file and double-click the file to insert that image in your Web page.

Flowing text around images

You can do many things to edit image properties in FrontPage's Page view. They are described in Chapter 7. But one of the most useful features is the ability to flow text around a graphic image.

Figure 1-19: Inserting clip art

To flow text around a graphic, right-click the graphic and select Picture Properties from the context menu. Click the Appearance tab in the dialog box and select Right or Left from the Alignment drop-down menu. Click OK and your picture is set to have text flow around it.

Making images transparent

Another of the most useful graphic features in FrontPage 2000 is the ability to assign transparency to one color in an image. To do that, click the image. When you do, the Picture toolbar, covered in Chapter 7, appears on the bottom of the page. Each of the Picture toolbar's buttons is a powerful editing tool.

To assign transparency, click the Set Transparency Color tool in the Picture toolbar, and point the Transparency cursor at the color in your image that you want to make invisible. Figure 1-20 shows the Transparency tool aimed at a background color.

Saving images

After you place a picture in a Web page, you can save that picture as an embedded image by saving the page. As you save a page with a new (or edited) image file, you are prompted to save the image as well, as shown in Figure 1-21.

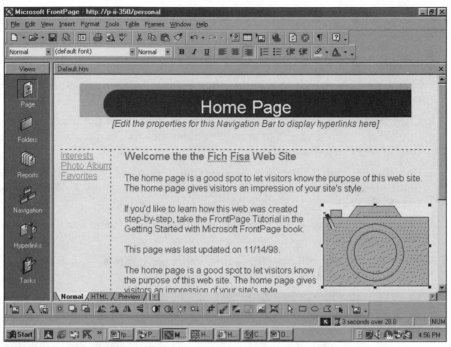

Figure 1-20: Assigning transparency

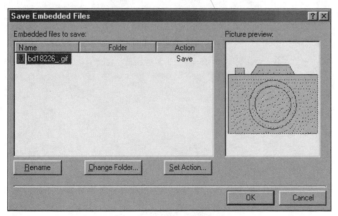

Figure 1-21: Saving an embedded image

As you save your page and its embedded graphic files, those graphic files are converted to a Web-compatible graphics format and saved to your FrontPage Web.

The following tutorial will walk you through the process of creating and editing a Web page in a Web site.

Tutorial 1.2: Edit a Web Page

1. Select File ➪ New Web and double-click the One Page Web template to create a new Web.

2. Click Navigation view in the View bar on the left side of the window, and double-click the Home Page in either Folder view or Navigation view to open the Home Page in Page view.

3. Because you didn't select a Theme or shared borders, your Web page is a blank slate. Click the page to set the insertion point, and type **Welcome to Our Web Site**.

4. Press the Enter key and type a paragraph describing what a visitor will find at your Web site.

5. Press Enter again and type three new, short paragraphs. Your Web page should look something like the one in Figure 1-22.

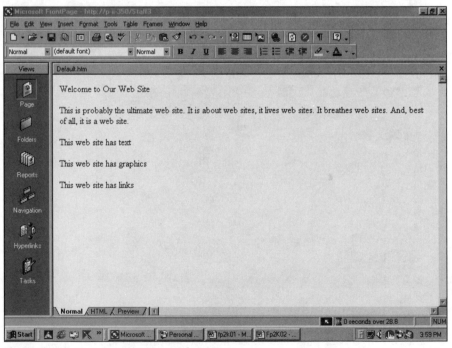

Figure 1-22: Entering text in a Web page

6. Click and drag to select the text in the three short paragraphs that you typed, and then click the Bullets button in the Formatting toolbar.

7. Click and drag to select the first line of text at the top of your page. Pull down the Font drop-down list and select Arial. Pull down the Font Size drop-down list and select 36 point. Click the Bold button in the Formatting toolbar. Pull down the Font Color palette and select red, as shown in Figure 1-23.

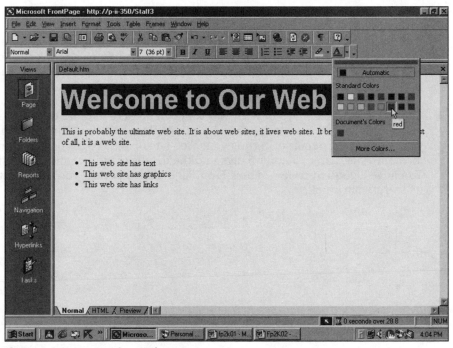

Figure 1-23: Formatting Web page text

8. Press Ctrl+End to move to the bottom of your Web page, and click the Insert Picture from File button in the Standard toolbar. Click Clip Art in the Picture dialog box.

9. Click the Conceptual category in the Clip Art Gallery to view several images. Click one, and then click the Insert Clip button in the pop-up toolbar.

10. Press Ctrl+End again to move to the bottom of your Web page, and type **Visit Microsoft at www.microsoft.com**. Press the spacebar to convert this to a hyperlink.

11. Click the HTML tab to see the HTML code that you have generated.

12. Click the Save button. You'll be prompted to save the clip art image that you embedded in your Web page. Click OK in the Save Embedded Files dialog box.

13. Select File ➪ Preview in Browser and then double-click an installed browser on your computer. If you are connected to the Internet, you can test your link to www.microsoft.com.

14. Select File ➪ Close Web. To delete this Web, select File ➪ Open Web. Right-click the new Web that you created, and select Delete from the context menu. Click OK in the dialog box that asks whether you are sure that you want to delete this Web.

Summary

In this fast-track introductory chapter, you learned to design a Web site, add and organize Web pages, and add content to those pages. You also took a quick look at adding content to your Web pages, formatting text, adding images, and including hyperlinks.

Chapter 2 explores much of what was touched on here in more depth, examining different Web design strategies and how to implement them. Chapter 3 then walks you through the details of getting your Web site or Web pages on the Internet or a local intranet. Later, Chapter 6 digs into the details of editing and formatting text. You have a good overview of how FrontPage works, so now you're ready to explore its features in detail.

✦   ✦   ✦

Working with FrontPage Web Sites

In Chapter 1, you learned to create a Web site with linked pages. You applied Themes and shared borders to give your site a sense of consistency and to allow visitors to navigate your site. This chapter explores in more detail the process of designing and adding content to a Web site.

Web Design Strategies

Web pages and Web sites have something of a chicken and egg relationship: no real answer exists as to which comes first when you design a Web site. As discussed in Chapter 1, you may create Web page content first and then organize the pages together into a Web site. Alternatively, you can design a Web site and then plug in page content. With either approach, however, your site design creates the framework for the display of all the content that you provide.

Why start with site design?

Theoretically, you could create a Web site that consisted of a single page. If your Web site has much content at all, this approach presents both technical and aesthetic problems. The page would take unnecessarily long to download in your visitors' browsers, and they would have to wait while some information downloaded that they didn't even want to access. Aesthetically, visitors would have difficulty finding and digesting information at your site. For these reasons, Web sites generally modularize information into many small pages. And, generally, many small, quick-loading pages with digestible bites of information are more helpful than a few long, slow-loading pages that mix together different kinds of information.

The following are the two main strategic decisions to make when you design your Web site:

✦ What kind of *navigational strategy* do you want to provide for visitors — what options to jump to other pages in the site do you want to make available at each page?

✦ What kind of *visual theme* do you want to apply to your site? Consistent visual elements — such as color schemes, navigational icons, page backgrounds, and fonts — provide coherence to your site and are part of the message that you project to visitors.

After an architect designs a building, and the beams are welded into place, the building can't easily be changed from a 48-story skyscraper to a sprawling, two-story campus. Luckily for Web designers, things are more flexible in cyberspace. You can modify the structure and design of a Web site fairly easily in FrontPage. But, you still need to make some initial decisions as to how to lay out your site. One of the strengths of FrontPage 2000 is the ability to change universally both the layout and design of an entire Web site. Chapter 1 explored the basic process of organizing a site in Navigation view and assigning Themes. The next section of this chapter investigates strategies for organizing your site structure.

Defining navigational links

The following are the two basic design approaches to laying out your Web site:

✦ **Linear design:** Takes visitors through your site in a straight line.

✦ **Hierarchical design:** Presents visitors with layers of options.

Figure 2-1 shows a Web site laid out in a linear design.

Most Web sites are organized in some version of a hierarchical structure, but both design strategies can be useful, depending on the kind of presentation you are preparing for visitors.

The important thing is to make conscious decisions regarding which kind of approach you want to take to your Web site design, and then stick to that approach. By doing so, visitors will feel comfortable at your site, and will be able to jump intuitively to the information that they want. By making conscious decisions about Web navigation strategy, a Web designer can frame the kinds of options available to visitors in conformity with the mission of the site. For example, if your goal is to introduce every product and service that your company provides, the linear structure illustrated in Figure 2-1 channels visitors into a tour of those products and services.

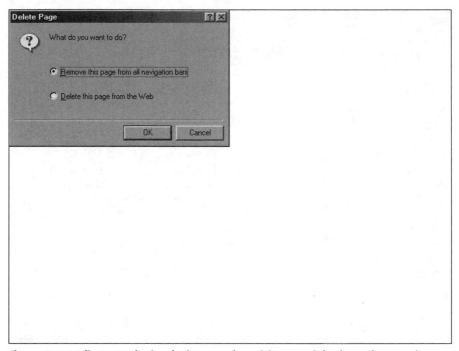

Figure 2-1: A linear Web site design marches visitors straight through your site.

Web sites with a linear flow

Orchestrating a linear flow in your Web site involves laying out your pages in Navigation view, and then assigning appropriate navigation bars in Web pages.

To create a Web site that provides a linear flow, start by either creating a new Web site or opening an existing one. You can review the section "Creating a Web site" in Chapter 1, if necessary, for all the information that you need.

With your Web site open, click and drag in Navigation view to arrange your Web pages in one or more lines. Selecting or deselecting the Folder list from the View menu shows (or hides) a list of Web pages in your site. If you have Web pages that are not connected to the navigational flow, you can drag them from the Folder list into the Navigation window, as shown in Figure 2-2.

With your site design defined in Navigation view, you can define navigation bars in your Web pages that apply the navigational structure in the form of navigational links. That process is explained in the section "Defining navigation bars in shared borders," a bit later in this chapter.

If you define a Web site with a long linear flow of pages, your site may be easier to view horizontally instead of vertically. To rotate the display of your Navigation view flowchart, right-click in the Navigation area and select Rotate from the context menu.

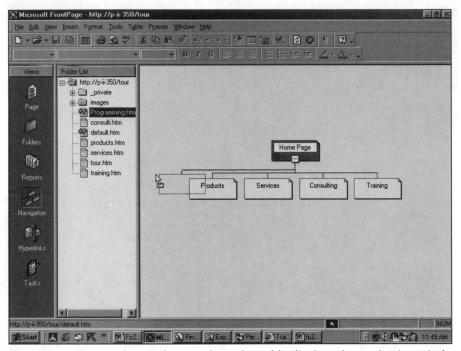

Figure 2-2: You can drag Web pages from the Folder list into the Navigation window.

Defining a hierarchical Web site

Hierarchical Web structures are used more frequently than linear site designs. Hierarchical structure allows visitors to make their own decisions about which pages they want to see, and in what order. Furthermore, hierarchical structures can be used to organize Web pages into groups, each with its own level of detail.

In Figure 2-3, for example, a visitor who is interested only in minidisc products can navigate to the Minidiscs "branch" of the Web site and choose between the different types of minidiscs, without being distracted by other options.

Defining navigation bars in shared borders

After you lay out your site in Navigation view, you can define the navigation bars for each page. Navigation bars can be inserted at any location in a Web page, but normally are inserted in *shared borders*, a special type of Web page that appears on *every* Web page. Shared borders can be attached to the top, bottom, left, or right side of a Web page. So, theoretically, you can define four navigation bars in your Web site that will appear on every page in the site.

Four navigation bars would clutter up a Web site, but providing navigation options at the top, bottom, and left (or right) side of a page might be appropriate in some cases.

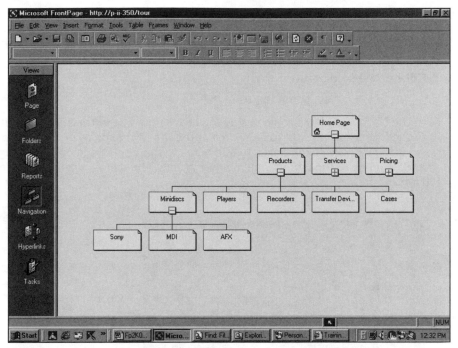

Figure 2-3: A hierarchical Web site design organizes options for a visitor.

Each navigation bar in a shared border generates links, depending on the logic that you define for that particular bar. For example, if you lay out your Web site in a linear structure, you can generate Next and Back buttons to help visitors travel from the beginning to the end of your page sequence. Or, if you design your site with a hierarchical structure, you have several options for allowing visitors to jump to parent and child pages.

Note   Shared borders are not *required* to place navigation bars on a particular page. You can place navigation bars in the body of a Web page. But, shared borders *with navigation bars* is a method by which you can create a navigational system for your entire Web site.

To assign shared borders to a Web site, follow these steps:

1. In any view, select Format ➪ Shared Borders from the menu.

2. In the Shared Borders dialog box, select the All Pages radio button to assign shared borders to every page in your Web site.

Note   After you define a shared borders design for your entire Web site, you can adjust it for specific pages by selecting a page and using the Current Page radio button.

To insert a navigation bar in a shared border, follow these steps:

1. Open any Web page in a Web site to which you have added at least one shared border.

2. Click in a shared border.

3. Select Insert ⇨ Navigation Bar from the menu.

4. In the Navigation Bar Properties dialog box, select one of the six radio buttons in the Hyperlinks to Add to Page area at the top of the dialog box. Use the Additional Pages check boxes to add a link to the home page on every page, and/or a link to the Parent Page on every page. The dialog box is shown in Figure 2-4.

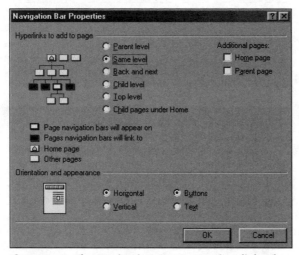

Figure 2-4: The Navigation Bar Properties dialog box provides six navigation options for your Web site.

5. Define the layout of the navigation bar links by selecting either vertical or horizontal, and by selecting either buttons or text. Then, click the OK button in the dialog box to insert (or revise existing) navigation links.

Note   The six radio buttons at the top of the Navigation Bar Properties dialog box break down basically into two different navigational strategies. The Same Level option and the Back and Next option allow visitors to navigate along a single row in the Navigation view, for a linear navigational approach. The difference between the options is that Same Level allows a visitor to jump to *any* page in a row, whereas Back and Next offers only two options, the pages to the right and left of a page in the Navigation view flowchart.

The other radio buttons offer variations on a hierarchical scheme. The most utilitarian hierarchical option is probably the Child Pages radio button, with the Home Page and Parent Page check boxes. This allows visitors to navigate up or down at any time, and always provides a link to the home page.

As you experiment with different navigational options, they are illustrated in the flowchart to the left of the radio buttons.

After you assign navigation bars to your shared borders, save the page in which you edited the links, and then select File ➪ Preview in Browser to test the links in your browser.

Customizing links

Automatically generated navigational links have a great advantage, which — at the same time — is their shortcoming: they apply the *same logic* to every single page. If you define a link to child pages in your navigation bar, *every* page (that has a child page) will have a link to that page. In that sense, navigation bars cannot be customized for particular pages.

However, other options are available that give you much more specific control over what links are available from your Web pages. Those options are introduced next.

Adding custom links to page content

You can insert a link (or *hyperlink*, as FrontPage calls them) anywhere in a Web page. You can either type the URL to which you are creating a link, or assign a link to an existing object, such as text or a graphic image.

To include a link, simply type the URL (or e-mail address) in the Web page. Press Enter to create a paragraph break; Ctrl+Enter to create a line break; or use a punctuation key followed by the spacebar. Your URL address automatically is transformed into a link.

To assign a link to existing text (or a picture), select the text (or picture) and click the Hyperlink button in the toolbar. The Hyperlink dialog box appears. Double-click a Web page in your Web, or enter a URL address outside of your Web in the URL drop-down list. Then, click OK to assign the link.

Adding custom links to a navigation bar

Shared borders can include generated navigation bars, but they can also be edited to include other text, or links.

Besides the links generated by navigation bars, you can add your own, specific links to a Web site or to any page. For example, you may want to include a link to a special page in your Web site from any page in the site. If that special page is your home page, you can do this by selecting the Home Page check box in the Navigation Bar Properties dialog box. If it isn't your home page, you can still add the link to a navigation bar.

Figure 2-5 shows a link to the What's New page in the top and left shared borders (which will appear on every page), and in the page itself (which only affects the page in which the link is inserted).

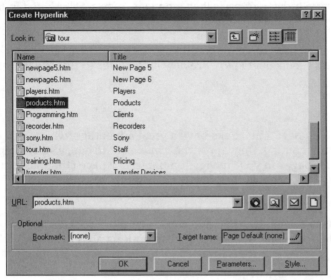

Figure 2-5: Custom links can be inserted into shared borders or into page content.

Adding navigation bars to page content

A final option for customizing links is to insert a navigation bar directly into the content of a page. Although this isn't a widely used feature in FrontPage 2000, it has some valuable uses. For example, a navigation bar with links to child pages can function as a miniature table of contents in a Web page.

Remember foremost that navigation bars inserted into page content appear only on the page in which they are inserted, whereas navigation bars placed in shared borders appear in every page.

Deleting pages from navigation bars

You can delete a page from the navigation structure by clicking the page in Navigation view and pressing the Delete key. The Delete Page dialog box appears, as shown in Figure 2-6.

The Delete Page dialog box has two options:

> ✦ **Remove this page from all navigation bars:** Doesn't delete the page from your Web site, but removes any link to this page from automatically generated navigation bars.

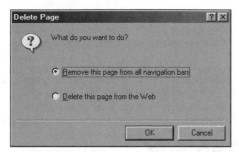

Figure 2-6: You can delete a page from navigation bars or completely remove it from your Web site.

> ✦ **Delete this page from the web:** Deletes the page *and its contents* from the Web site. This is a more drastic option and should be exercised with care, because after you delete a page from your Web site, it cannot be restored.

Changing navigation labels

You can redefine the labels that FrontPage generates for the home page, for moving up a page in a Web structure, and for Back and Next labels (used with a linear site design). To change label names, follow these steps:

1. Select Tools ➪ Web Settings and click the Navigation tab in the Web Settings dialog box. The tab is shown in Figure 2-7.

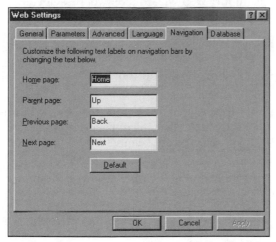

Figure 2-7: You can rename the labels generated in navigation bars.

2. Enter new label names for any of the four generated titles. For example, you can change the label assigned to a link to the previous page in a layout from "Back" (the default), to "Previous." Or, even something like "See previous slide."

3. After you change the generated label text, click OK. (Clicking OK in the Web Settings dialog box updates links in an existing site.)

Importing an Existing Web Site

You can organize existing collections of files into FrontPage Webs by using the Import Wizard, which imports files from two sources:

✦ An existing Web site that is not a FrontPage Web

✦ A folder on your local drive or network

After you import files, you can work with them as you would any FrontPage Web, organizing them in Navigation view, and adding Themes, shared borders, navigation bars, and so on.

Importing files into a Web

To import files into a new Web, follow these steps:

1. Select File ➪ Import. The Import Web Wizard icon will be selected, as shown in Figure 2-8.

2. Enter a location and name for the new Web in the "Specify the location of the new web" drop-down list. Then, click OK in the New dialog box.

3. Select the From a Source Directory radio button. Use the Include Subfolders check box to import files in subfolders. Click Next.

4. You can use the Edit File List dialog box to exclude files from your new Web. To remove one or more files from the list, select them and then click the Exclude button. The files you selected are removed from the list of those to be imported.

5. Click Finish in the final dialog box to generate a new Web from imported files.

Importing a Web site into a FrontPage Web

To import files into a new Web, follow these steps:

1. Select File ⇨ Import. The Import Web Wizard icon is selected, as shown previously in Figure 2-8.

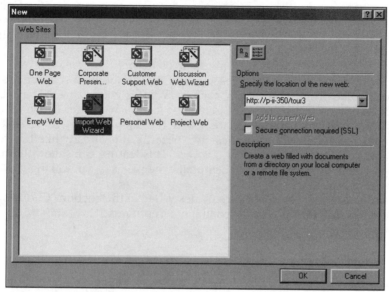

Figure 2-8: FrontPage provides a wizard to integrate existing objects into a new Web.

2. Enter a location and name for the new Web in the "Specify the location of the new web" drop-down list. Then, click OK in the New dialog box.

3. Click the From a Worldwide Web Site radio button and enter the URL for your Web page in the Location dialog box. The Secure Connection Required (SSL) check box is used only if your Web server uses SSL encryption programming to protect data. Click the Next button.

4. The Chose Download Amount box enables you to restrict the amount of disk space and files that you download. You can limit how deep into a Web site's structure the Import Web Wizard probes by checking the Limit to This Page Plus check box and selecting a number of levels from the Levels Below spin box. You can limit the size of files imported by checking the Limit To check box and entering a maximum file size for imported files. Finally, you can limit the types of files to text and graphics, thereby avoiding the long download times required for, say, a 20MB digitized file. The options in this dialog box protect you against filling your entire hard drive with files from a Web site of undetermined size.

5. Click Finish in the final dialog box to generate a new Web from imported files.

Using Web Templates and Wizards

In FrontPage terminology, a *Web template* is a set of predesigned Web pages collected into a single Web. In many cases, sample text is supplied, or Comment text is used to provide assistance in adding content to the Web. In Chapter 1, you used the Personal Web template to create the basic structure for a Web site.

A wizard is similar to a template, only smarter. Rather than create a Web with all generic content, the Corporate Presence and Discussion Web Wizards first ask you to answer some probing questions, such as "What is your name?" They also ask you what kinds of Web pages you want to include in your Web site. Those wizards then place your answer in the appropriate spot in the template. When you first open a Web that is generated by one of these two wizards, it is already filled with customized content based on your answers. This feature can save you time, although you are likely to want to customize the pages to your liking.

Some of the available templates briefly described in the section "Choosing a Web Template" in Chapter 1 are explored in more depth next.

One Page Web

Because the One Page Web template creates only a single Web page, you might wonder why you should bother using it. Actually, the One Page Web handles several important tasks that save time in generating a Web site. First, a Web folder is created on your server, ensuring that all of your files will be properly managed by FrontPage. This template also creates a Web page with the filename Default.htm, and the page title Home Page (for a full discussion of page names and titles, see the section "Page titles and file names" in Chapter 1).

The One Page Web template also generates two subfolders in your Web site, _private and images. The images folder can be used to organize picture files for your site, and the _private folder stores pages and other files that you don't want identified by searches or linked in navigation bars.

If your project is to develop a Web site from scratch, the One Page Web is a quick way to get started.

Corporate Presence Web

The Corporate Presence Web Wizard is a basic site for communicating information about a company. This is the most elaborate wizard included with FrontPage. The first dialog box in the wizard asks you which main pages you want to include in your Web site. This dialog box is shown in Figure 2-9.

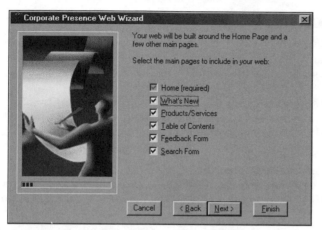

Figure 2-9: The Corporate Presence Web Wizard generates up to six main pages.

The pages available from the Corporate Presence Web Wizard are the following:

✦ **Home:** Not optional, because it anchors all the navigational links in the site.

✦ **What's New:** Lists links to other pages. If you select this check box, the wizard later provides a list of linked articles that you can generate.

✦ **Products/Services:** Can have any number of links to both products and services. If you select this check box, you later are asked how many products pages and how many services pages to generate, and what information you want on those pages. Some of these generated pages include input forms that collect data from visitors. The results of these forms are saved in files that are stored in the _private folder.

✦ **Table of Contents:** Generates a table of contents for the site on a separate page.

✦ **Feedback Form:** Generates a Web page with an input form that collects feedback from visitors. The data submitted to this form is collected in a file called inforeq.txt (located in the _private folder). Double-click that file in Folders view to display information in your word processor.

After you select the pages that you want to include in your Web site, the wizard prompts you for information related to generating those pages. When you complete the wizard, you are asked whether you want to see Tasks view after your site is generated. Select Yes to see a list of remaining tasks that you need to perform to complete your Web site.

Customer Support Web

The Customer Support Web template generates seven Web pages in a navigational flow, as well as additional Web pages that are used by those seven pages. The pages in the Navigation view generated by this template are the following:

✦ **What's New:** A list of links to pages with update documentation. To make these links functional, you need to edit their content, and then right-click them, select Hyperlink Properties from the context menu, and link them to actual pages that you create.

✦ **FAQ (Frequently Asked Questions):** Includes a list of six questions, with links to bookmarked answers in the body of the page. Bookmarks are discussed in "Inserting Bookmarks," later in this chapter. You need to edit the questions and answers.

✦ **Bugs:** Mainly an input form with which visitors can submit bug reports. When a visitor submits a bug report, the results are posted to a page called Buglist.htm. You can open that page to see the information submitted in the forms. Creating forms is discussed in detail in Chapter 14, and managing form input is explored in depth in Chapter 15.

✦ **Suggestions:** Mainly composed of an input form, too. Data entered into this form can be viewed by opening the Feedback.htm file.

✦ **Download**: Used to let visitors link to an FTP (File Transfer Protocol) download site. If you have files at an FTP site, you can edit the links at this page to send visitors to those files.

✦ **Discussion:** Links to a threaded discussion group, where visitors can post comments or questions, and respond to posted articles. Discussion Webs are examined in Chapter 17. (Jargon alert: a *thread* in an online discussion refers to a message in the discussion and any replies to that message.)

✦ **Search:** Includes a Search Box that visitors can use to find information at your site. For a full discussion of creating and modifying search boxes, see "Search Forms," in Chapter 13.

Discussion Web Wizard

The Discussion Web Wizard generates a fully threaded, searchable discussion group. This wizard is discussed further in Chapter 17.

Empty Web

The Empty Web template generates a Web folder and _private and images subfolders, just like the One Page Web template. The difference is that the Empty Web template doesn't generate a home page.

Import Web Wizard

The Import Web Wizard is generated when you select File ➪ Import. For a discussion of how this works, refer to "Importing an Existing Web Site," earlier in this chapter.

Personal Web

The Personal Web template generates a Web site with a home page and three other pages: Interests, Photo Album, and Favorites.

Project Web

The Project Web template generates a Web site specifically designed for displaying project-management information. The template generates six linked pages in Navigation view, some of which are connected to additional pages that don't display in Navigation view. The six accessible pages are the following:

✦ **Members:** Lists team personnel and provides hyperlinks to their e-mail addresses.

✦ **Schedule:** Posts tasks due this week and next week, and lists project milestones (important nodal points in the project).

✦ **Status:** Displays monthly, quarterly, and annual status reports.

✦ **Archive:** Includes hyperlinks to documents created by project members, to software programs, and to other elements of the project.

✦ **Search:** Includes a Search Box.

✦ **Discussions:** Includes links to two threaded discussion groups that are generated by the Project Web template — they are called the Requirements Discussion and the Knowledge Base.

In the following tutorial, you will use the Corporate Presence Web Wizard to generate a Web site.

Tutorial 2.1: Generate a Web Site from the Corporate Presence Web Wizard

1. Select File ➪ New ➪ Web from the FrontPage menu.

2. Enter a location and name for your Web in the "Specify the location of the new web" drop-down list.

3. Double-click the Corporate Presence Web Wizard icon in the New dialog box.

4. Read the first wizard option box and click Next.

5. In addition to the Home Page, select the What's New, Feedback Form, and Search Form check boxes. Click Next.

6. In the list of topics to appear on your home page, check all four check boxes and click Next.

7. From the list of topics for the What's New page, select all three check boxes and click Next.

8. In the list of options for the Feedback Form, select all seven check boxes and click Next.

9. For the Feedback Form format, select the option labeled "No, use web page format." This displays input in a Web page. Click Next.

10. In the dialog box that asks what should appear on the top and bottom of each page, accept the default check box settings and click Next.

11. In the Construction Icon options box, select the No radio button to omit the Under Construction icon from your pages. Click Next.

12. In the dialog box that collects information about your company, fill in the three fields and click Next.

13. In the dialog box that collects information on your phone numbers and e-mail addresses, fill in the four fields and click Next.

14. Click the Choose Web Theme button and select the Straight Edge Theme from the Choose Theme dialog box. Click OK and then click Next.

15. In the final dialog box, leave the one check box selected to show Tasks view after your Web is generated. Click Finish.

16. In Tasks view, right-click the first task, Customize Home Page, and select Start Task from the context menu.

17. Click and drag to select the Comment text, and then replace it with text of your own.

18. Close the page, saving your changes. You are prompted to mark this task as completed. Click Yes in the dialog box.

19. Return to Tasks view and complete the remaining tasks by replacing Comment text with your own text.

20. Open the Home Page in Pave view. Select File ➪ Preview in Browser to see your Web site in your browser.

21. Inspect your home page in your browser. Test the link to the Feedback page at the top of the page.

22. Fill in the fields in the Feedback form, as shown in Figure 2-10.

23. After you fill in the form, click the Submit Feedback button. Then, click the Return to Form link in the Form Confirmation page.

24. Return to FrontPage and view your site in Folders view. Double-click the _private folder to view files in that folder. Double-click the file Inforeq.htm to open that file in Page view. Examine the input that you collected.

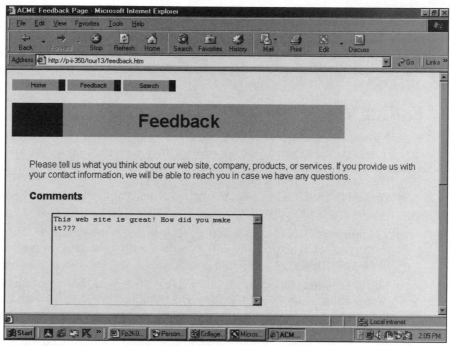

Figure 2-10: You can test the Feedback form in a browser if your site is published to a Web server with FrontPage extensions.

Note Input forms work only when your Web is saved to a server with FrontPage 2000 extensions. You can use the Personal Web Server that comes with Office 2000 for this. For a full discussion of server options, see Chapter 3.

25. Select File ➪ Close Web to close your Web after you finish experimenting with it. You can delete this Web by selecting File ➪ Open Web, right-clicking the Web, and then selecting Delete from the context menu.

Creating Basic Web Page Content

After you lay out the basic structure of your Web, you are ready to fill in page content, which includes text and many other Components, such as pictures. Chapter 6 explores in detail editing and formatting text; Chapter 7 covers inserting pictures. Other advanced elements are covered in the remaining chapters of this book. In fact, for the most part, the rest of this book is about how to place content on your Web pages.

In addition to text and pictures, FrontPage has many powerful elements, called *FrontPage Components* (examined in detail in Chapter 13). They range from search boxes to time stamps to hit counters. The present section briefly looks at editing Web page text, and then examines some other basic elements of Web page content: breaks, horizontal lines, Comments, and bookmarks.

Editing Web page text

Entering and editing Web page text is very intuitive. Click and type. You'll find most of the luxuries of a modern word processor, including red, squiggly underlining of words that are not found in the dictionary. Other editing help includes:

✦ **Format Painter:** Select text, click the Format Painter tool, and then click new text to apply the formatting of the original text to the target text.

✦ **Thesaurus:** Select a word and then choose Tools ➪ Thesaurus to see a list of synonyms. Find a good one in the Replace with Synonym list and click the Replace button.

✦ **Edit ➪ Find and Edit ➪ Replace:** Find text strings, with the option of designating replacement text. The Find and Replace dialog boxes don't have the option of locating (or changing) special characters, such as hard line returns, tabs, or paragraphs.

✦ **Tab key:** Use it (or the spacebar) to insert additional spacing between words.

Inserting breaks

The Break Properties dialog box enables you to insert a forced line break (as opposed to a paragraph mark). To create a forced line break, select Insert ➪ Break. The Break Properties dialog box appears, as shown in Figure 2-11.

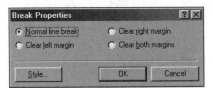

Figure 2-11: You can force line breaks with the Break Properties dialog box.

To create a forced line break (within the same paragraph), click the Normal Line Break radio button and then click OK. Use the Clear Left Margin, Clear Right Margin, or Clear Both Margins radio buttons to move the next line past any pictures, so that the Right, Left, or Both margins are cleared to the margin.

To toggle on and off forced line break symbols (nonprinting), click the Show All button in the Standard toolbar.

Adding horizontal lines

Before modern browsers and faster modems were able to interpret and download graphics quickly, older browsers recognized a graphic element called horizontal lines. New browsers still interpret these lines, and you can insert them as dividers between text or graphics. Select Insert ➪ Horizontal Line to place a horizontal line at your cursor point (no need to press Enter first).

Placing Comments

Comment text is visible in Page view, but doesn't appear in a browser window. As such, it is helpful for placing notes to yourself, or to a collaborator. For example, two Web developers can use Comments to leave each other messages about work that remains on a page.

To insert a Comment, follow these steps:

1. Click to place your insertion point where the Comment will appear in Page view.

2. Select Insert ➪ Comment.

3. Type text in the Comment window, as shown in Figure 2-12.

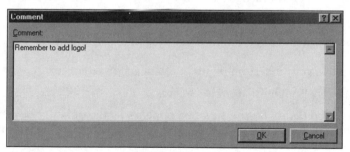

Figure 2-12: Comment text is not visible in a browser — unless the source HTML code is examined.

4. Click OK.

Caution

Although Comment text doesn't appear in a browser, it does appear if a visitor selects the View ➪ Source command in IE, or View ➪ Page Source in Netscape Navigator. When the underlying HTML code behind a Web page is displayed, Comment text is surrounded by the code:

```
<!--Webbot bot="PurpleText" PREVIEW="xxx" -->
```

whereby "*xxx*" is the Comment text.

So . . . don't put anything in Comment text that you don't want the world to read.

You can double-click Comment text to edit it. Comment text can be formatted like normal text, by selecting it and applying formatting attributes such as font color and size. However, formatting must be applied to an entire Comment; you cannot apply separate formatting to parts of a Comment.

Inserting symbols

Symbols include characters such as ©, ™, or ❤ that aren't available in normal keyboard keys. These symbols can be interpreted by most browsers.

To insert a symbol, follow these steps:

1. Place your cursor at the insertion point where the symbol will appear.

2. Choose Insert ➪ Symbol.

3. Double-click the symbol that you want to insert in the Symbol dialog box.

4. Click Close in the Symbol dialog box.

Inserting bookmarks

Bookmarks are locators in a Web page that can be the target of a hyperlink. Bookmarks can be used for navigation within a page, or as a locator for a link to a page.

To insert a bookmark in a page, follow these steps:

1. Click to place your insertion point on the page, or select text.

2. Select Insert ➪ Bookmark from the menu.

3. If you selected text in Step 1, that text appears as the default bookmark name, as shown in Figure 2-13. If not, the Bookmark Name box will be empty in the Bookmark dialog box, and you can enter a bookmark name. To avoid problems with older browsers, it is best to restrict the bookmark name to eight characters or less, with no spaces or punctuation.

4. Click OK to place the bookmark. If you assigned the bookmark to text, that text appears in Page view with a dotted line beneath it. If you assigned the bookmark to a blank space on your page, it appears as a small flag.

Bookmarks can be edited (or cleared) by right-clicking the bookmark, selecting Bookmark Properties, and then editing the properties in the Bookmark dialog box.

To create a link to a bookmark, follow these steps:

1. Select text (or a picture) that will be linked to the bookmark.

2. Click the Hyperlinks button. The Hyperlinks dialog box opens.

Figure 2-13: Bookmarks serve as targets for links within a page.

3. If you are linking to a bookmark on another Web page, enter that page in the URL box. If you are linking to a bookmark on the open page, you can leave that box blank.

4. From the Bookmark drop-down list, select the bookmark that is the target of your link.

5. The bookmark link target appears in the URL box, with the bookmark preceded by a # (pound sign).

6. Click OK. You can test your link in the Preview tab either by previewing your page in a browser or by holding down the Ctrl key and clicking the link in the Normal tab of Page view.

Using Page Templates

FrontPage 2000 comes with page templates, in addition to the Web templates explored earlier in this chapter. These page templates are of three types: General, Frames, and Style Sheets. Frames are covered in Chapter 10. Style Sheets are covered in Chapter 12. The options in the General tab of the New dialog box are explored here.

To utilize a page template, select File ➪ New ➪ Page. The General tab of the New dialog box displays icons for over two dozen page templates.

You can preview a page template by single-clicking it and viewing a sample of the page in the Preview area, as shown in Figure 2-14.

Some page templates are taken from the pages generated by Web templates. These include the Feedback Form page, the Form Page Wizard (that generates input forms), the Table of Contents page, and the User Registration page. You were introduced to these pages earlier in the chapter in the section "Using Web Templates and Wizards."

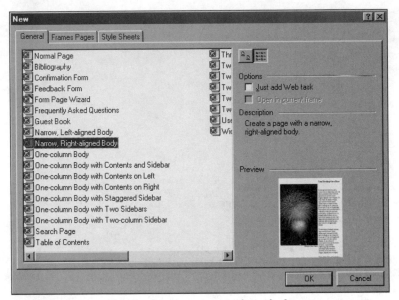

Figure 2-14: You can check out page templates before you generate a new page.

Other pages include sample graphics and content. Many of these pages are laid out in columns; these pages use tables. Using tables as layout tools is covered in Chapter 9.

Other Views

Up to now, the focus has been on Navigation view and Page view. These are the two most powerful views in FrontPage. Navigation view displays and controls Web structure, while Page view is used to edit individual pages.

Four other choices are available from the Views bar:

- ✦ Folders view
- ✦ Reports view
- ✦ Hyperlinks view
- ✦ Tasks view

All four of these views, described next, complement Navigation view as a way to manage your entire Web site.

Folders view

Folders view works like Windows Explorer, enabling you to view all of your files in folders. As in Windows Explorer, you can create a subfolder in your currently selected folder, by choosing File ➪ New ➪ Folder.

When a FrontPage Web is generated, some folders are created that hold files that only "advanced" users are supposed to know about. These folders include:

✦ **_borders folder:** Holds pages that serve as shared borders.

✦ **_fpclass folder:** Holds Java classes. These are files used for objects such as FrontPage-generated Hover buttons (see Chapter 13 for more on FrontPage Components).

✦ **_overlay:** Holds graphic images used with Theme elements.

✦ **_themes:** Holds files used with Themes.

To see these "advanced-level" hidden files, select Tools ➪ Web Settings, and click the Advanced tab in the Web Settings dialog box. Select the Show Documents in Hidden Directories check box to display hidden files, as shown in Figure 2-15.

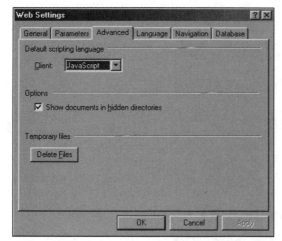

Figure 2-15: Hidden files include elements of Themes, and embedded shared border pages.

With hidden files displayed, you can open shared border pages (Left.htm, Right.htm, Top.htm, or Bottom.htm) and edit them as you would any other page.

Reports view

Reports view provides a list of many useful statistics in your Web site. Additional reports update you on the status of navigational links, slow pages, and new files. You can select a report by choosing View ➪ Reports, and then selecting one of the available reports.

The following is a list of the reports and descriptions of how you can use each of them:

✦ **Site Summary:** Gives you an overview of your site. The rows in the Site Summary are themselves links to other views. One of the most useful things about the Site Summary view is that you can get a quick idea of the size of your Web site, which is helpful when you look for server space for your site.

✦ **All Files:** Displays detailed information about each file in your Web site.

✦ **Recently Added Files**, **Recently Changed Files, Older Files**, **and Slow Pages:** Display files that are defined by selecting Tools ➪ Options and selecting the Reports View tab, as shown in Figure 2-16. Slow pages are calculated based on the modem speed that you enter in the Assume Connection Speed Of spin box.

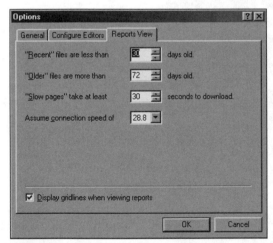

Figure 2-16: You can define which files to display as Recent, Recently Changed, and Older.

✦ **Unlinked Files:** Shows files in your Web site to which no links exist. These stranded Web pages are sometimes called "orphan pages."

✦ **Broken Hyperlinks**: Shows hyperlinks in your Web site that are either invalid or untested. You can right-click one of these untested hyperlinks and choose Verify from the context menu to test the link. If the link is to an Internet or intranet site, you must be logged on to the Internet or your intranet to test the link.

✦ **Component Errors:** Tests FrontPage Components (covered in Chapter 13) for errors.

✦ **Review Status and Assigned To:** Used for workgroups collaborating on a Web site. The Review Status report enables you to log pages that need to be reviewed, and track whether pages have been reviewed. The Assigned To report is similar to the Review Status report, but tracks who is assigned to which page.

✦ **Categories:** Sorts Components of your Web site by type, such as JPEG images, HTML pages, GIF files, CLASS Java files, and so on.

✦ **Publish Status:** Lists which pages have been published to your Web (and which haven't).

Hyperlinks view

Hyperlinks view displays all links leading into a Web page from other pages in the site, and displays the links out of a selected page. First, choose Hyperlinks view from the Views bar, and then click a Web page in the Folders list.

Figure 2-17 shows a page in Hyperlinks view, with links coming in and going out.

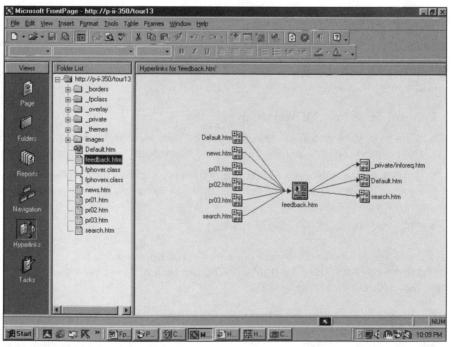

Figure 2-17: Viewing hyperlinks

If you are trying to track and test every hyperlink in a page or your Web site, the Broken Hyperlinks report discussed in the previous section of this chapter is much more efficient than looking for broken links in Hyperlinks view. Use this view only if you need to examine in detail all links in and out of a page. For example, before deleting a page, you can use this view to identify the Web pages with links to the page.

You can modify Hyperlinks view to do the following:

✦ **Display page titles instead of filenames:** Right-click in Hyperlinks view and select Show Page Titles from the context menu. Repeat the process to deselect page title display.

✦ **Include links that lead to graphic files:** Right-click in Hyperlinks view and select Hyperlinks to Pictures from the context menu. You can toggle off picture links in the same way.

✦ **Display multiple hyperlinks with the same target URL:** Right-click in Hyperlinks view and select Repeated Hyperlinks from the context menu. Repeat the process to uncheck this option, to turn it off.

✦ **Display hyperlinks to bookmarks on the same page:** Right-click in Hyperlinks view and select Hyperlinks Inside Page from the context menu. Deselect this option to hide hyperlinks in the page.

Tasks view

Tasks view contains a list of "things to do." Tasks are added to the Task view list by wizards that generate Webs, or you can add them yourself.

To add a task, follow these steps:

1. Select Tasks from the Views bar.

2. Select File ➪ New ➪ Task, or right-click in Task view and select New Task from the context menu. The New Task dialog box opens, as shown in Figure 2-18.

3. Enter a task name and a description. You also can modify the Assigned To box. Select one of the three priority buttons to assign a relative level of urgency to the task.

4. Click OK. The task appears in the task list.

Tasks that are created with a page open have that page associated with them. These tasks can be started by right-clicking the task in Tasks view and selecting Start Task from the context menu.

The context menu that opens when you right-click a task can be used to edit, mark as completed, or delete any task. However, only those tasks that were created with a page open (or generated from a wizard) can be started by right-clicking.

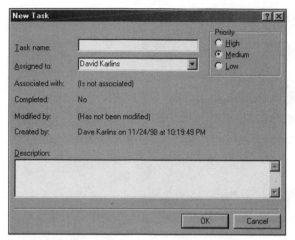

Figure 2-18: Defining a task

Global Site Editing

Most of the work that you do to edit the content of your Web site takes place in Page view, and is done on a page-by-page basis. But, some editing tools in FrontPage work across an entire Web. This section looks at two of these tools: spell checking, and search and replace.

Spell-checking your entire site

To spell check your whole Web site, select Tools ⇨ Spelling from a view other than Page view.

Note

If you select Tools ⇨ Spelling in Page view, or click the Spelling tool in the Standard toolbar, you spell check only your open page. When you select the Spelling dialog box (in a view other than Page view), the dialog box has two radio buttons: one to check Selected Page(s), and one to check the Entire Web. To spell check your entire Web site, use the Entire Web option.

You can also select the check box labeled Add a Task for Each Page with Misspellings. This creates a list of pages that need their spelling checked. After you select these options, click the Start button to begin checking your spelling.

FrontPage checks all of your pages for spelling errors and then creates a list in the Spelling dialog box, as shown in Figure 2-19.

If you selected the Add a Task option, you can click the Add Task button to add the marked pages to your task list. If you would rather correct your spelling immediately, double-click the page in the list in the site Spelling dialog box to check spelling on that page.

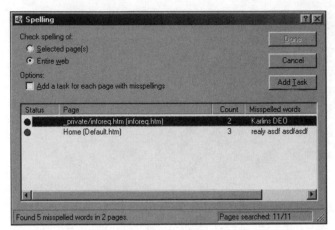

Figure 2-19: Checking an entire Web site generates a list of pages with spelling mistakes.

Replacing text throughout a site

To replace text throughout a site, select Edit ➪ Replace in any view. In the Replace dialog box, enter the text to find in the Find What box, and specify replacement text in the Replace With box. The Replace dialog box includes these options:

✦ Click the Entire Web radio button to replace in every page.

✦ The Up or Down radio buttons determine the direction that the replacing tool moves through Web pages.

✦ The Match Whole Word Only and Match Case check box options work like the Replace dialog box in Word or other Office applications.

✦ The Find in HTML check box allows you to search and replace HTML code.

After you define your replace options, if you are replacing in an entire Web, click the Find in Web button. FrontPage will generate a list of pages at the bottom of the Replace dialog box with the text to be replaced. Double-click a page to make the changes in that page. Or, click the Add Task button to add the task to your task list.

In the following tutorial, you will experiment with adding content to a Web page.

Tutorial 2.2: Edit Web Page Content

1. If you don't have a Web open, select File ➪ New ➪ Web. Enter a location for the new Web and double-click the One Page Web template icon in the New dialog box.

2. In Navigation view, double-click the home page to open it in Page view.

3. Type **Welcome to my Web site** and press Enter.

4. Click and drag to select the text that you typed. Select Arial Black from the Font drop-down list, 24. point from the Font Size list, Italics, Center, and Red from the Font Color Palette.

5. Click at the end of the text and select Insert ➪ Horizontal Line.

6. Under the horizontal line, select Insert ➪ Symbol and double-click the © symbol. Click Close. Type your name after the copyright symbol.

7. Select Insert ➪ Break, and with the Normal Line Break radio button selected, click OK to create a forced line break.

8. Select Insert ➪ Comment, and in the Comment window, type **This page needs to be finished!** Click OK.

9. Double-click the word "Welcome" and select Insert ➪ Bookmark. Click OK in the Bookmark dialog box.

10. Click to place your insertion point after the Comment text. Press Enter 12 times and then type **Go to top**.

11. Double-click to select the word "top," and then click the Hyperlink button in the toolbar. Pull down the Bookmark list and select Welcome. Click OK.

12. Select File ➪ New ➪ Task, and enter **Add Content** in the Task Name box. Click OK.

13. Click the Save button to save changes to the Web page.

14. Select View ➪ Reports to get an overview of your (rather small) Web site. How much server space would you need for this Web site? (Look at the All Files row of the report.)

15. Select Hyperlinks view. Right-click and select Hyperlinks Inside Page from the context menu. The links illustrate the bookmark link in the page.

16. Click the Tasks view. Right-click the task and select Start Task from the context menu. Add some text to your page and save it. Select Yes in the dialog box when prompted to mark the page as a completed task.

17. To delete this practice Web, select File ➪ Close Web. Then, select File ➪ Open Web, right-click the Web that you just created, and choose Delete from the context menu.

Summary

In the course of the first two chapters in this book, you learned to create rather complex Web sites. You still have more to cover! But, with the tools that you have available now, you can create a Web site with text, pictures, themes, navigation links, and other elements.

The process of publishing your Web to a Web server has been reviewed briefly. However, meshing your FrontPage Web with a Web server is one of the thorniest issues in FrontPage. The next chapter dives into publishing FrontPage Webs in depth.

✦   ✦   ✦

Publishing and Managing FrontPage Webs

This chapter shows you how FrontPage 2000 can assist you in publishing your Webs, managing a Web project, and maintaining your site. Whether you are working on your own or as part of a larger development team, you can profit from the many FrontPage features designed to help your project run smoothly. The chapter covers several common scenarios for developing, publishing, and maintaining a project using FrontPage.

Note   This chapter is primarily an introduction to the publishing and Web site maintenance functions in FrontPage 2000. To learn more about the Web server side of the publishing equation, turn to Chapter 23.

Publishing Your Web

FrontPage uses the concept of "publishing" a Web in a very specific way that can take some getting used to. You might suppose that publishing a Web means that you make it available for general viewing, in the same way that you might print out a Word document. This might lead you to believe that changes that you make to your Web are not visible until you publish them. This is not always the case.

When you work on your Web, you quite possibly may open it directly in FrontPage. If this is the case, then any time that you save changes to a page, you are effectively "publishing" your changes back to the Web for all to view. In this scenario, you never need to go through the steps of publishing your Web in the FrontPage sense.

The only time that you need to "publish" your Web is if you make changes to a copy of your Web rather than to the Web itself. For example, perhaps you have a development version of your Web, in which all changes are made and reviewed before being copied to your production Web server. Or, perhaps you have a Web site hosted by a Web hosting service, and you make changes to a local copy of your Web before you dial up your account and post your changes. These are all scenarios in which you may want to use FrontPage to help you publish your Web. As you can see, the notion of "publishing" a Web in FrontPage is really synonymous with copying your Web to another location.

The next section discusses in more detail some of the common methods of working with your Web. This section is intended for users contemplating the best way to set up their Web. If you already are working with an existing Web, you may want to skip to the next section, "Preparing to Publish a Web."

Web publishing options

At the most basic level, you can work with Webs in FrontPage in either of two ways:

✦ You can open and modify a "live" Web directly, in which case any changes that you save are immediately available to anyone who has browser access to your Web.

✦ You can work on a copy of your Web and publish changes to the "live" version when you are ready.

The latter method — publishing changes periodically — is a safer way to work. It is also somewhat more complicated and time-consuming. What method you choose depends on your circumstances.

Note   FrontPage 2000 enables you to publish only selected pages of one Web to another Web, making it much easier to maintain a development (or *test*) Web and publish the production-ready pages. Prior to its current version, FrontPage provided no easy way to create test pages that you did not want to publish.

Working on a "live" Web

Several years ago, it was common wisdom in the software development world that you build your product, test it thoroughly, and release it only when you are relatively confident that it is as close to being error-free as possible. The Internet has changed common wisdom. Now, releasing products in "beta" stage (a euphemism for incomplete) is fairly common, partly because of the increasing pressure to ship a product quickly, and partly because of the ease with which Web projects can be updated. Similarly, Web sites often don't hesitate to display their "under construction" areas.

In such an atmosphere, encountering people developing their "live" Web site directly isn't uncommon. In some ways, FrontPage invites this kind of updating, because it enables you quite easily to open a remote Web in FrontPage and make and save changes directly back to the remote server. Under any circumstances, this is easier than making a change and then later copying it to a live site.

Of course, making changes directly to a live Web site is risky. You can easily introduce an error that you may not immediately catch. You may also update a page that someone is accessing, causing them some consternation should they happen to reload the page and find it changed. Live updating tends to be most feasible under the following conditions:

✦ You are working on a small project.

✦ You aren't required to get authorization for changes from one or more people before the changes appear in public.

✦ Traffic on the Web site is low.

Even under these circumstances, operating in this way is more expedient than recommended.

Working with a local copy of your Web

A much better approach for developing and updating a Web site is to maintain a copy of the site on a server that is not "live." What makes a server not "live"? In some cases, this simply means that the Web server address, its *URL*, is not publicized — the Web equivalent of an unlisted phone number. Anyone who knows the URL (or is a very good guesser) can get to the unlisted site, but no one else can. In other cases, in addition to not publishing the URL, you might limit browse access to the local copy of your pages, by using FrontPage security (see Chapter 23 for details). Alternatively, you might maintain your local copy on a computer that typically isn't connected to the Internet, or maintain the local copy as a disk-based Web without a Web server attached to it. These methods also restrict the availability of your development Web.

In this scenario, you develop, update, and test your pages by using the development version. When you are ready, you publish one or more pages — even the entire Web — to the live, production Web server. A detailed description of how to do that is provided later in this chapter.

Working with a dial-up Web host

This scenario is really just a specific instance of the general cases previously described. If your Web is hosted on a commercial Web hosting service, you usually have the option either to dial up and open your remote Web directly in FrontPage or to make changes to a local copy of your Web and dial up only when you want to publish your changes. Depending on how you pay for your dial-up service, you may find that developing locally is more economical, as well as safer.

Working as part of a workgroup

As discussed later in the chapter, FrontPage 2000 includes many new features that are designed to help teams of people work together to develop a Web site. Many possible ways exist to set up your Web teams. One way is to make each group responsible for the upkeep of a certain portion of the Web site's content. This is how corporate intranets frequently are managed — organized by functional areas or departments.

This scenario is similar to the model of having a local copy of your Web, but in this case, each group has a local copy of only a portion of the live Web (usually, that portion corresponds to a subweb on the production Web server). Each group then makes changes to its portion locally and, when ready, publishes changes to the appropriate section of the live Web.

Preparing to Publish a Web

Before discussing how to publish your Web by using FrontPage, this section first looks at some of the tasks that you can perform before you publish your Web to ensure that you have an error-free site. These tasks include the following:

✦ Check the spelling of the content on your Web site

✦ Check for orphaned (stray) pages

✦ Validate links

✦ Validate Components

FrontPage 2000 includes features to help you check each of these aspects of your Web site prior to publishing. Even if you don't need to publish your Web, you should still use these features to check your current Web site for errors — and to fix them quickly — because those errors are already live! (If you are not sure whether you need to publish your Web, read the previous sections of this chapter.)

Checking your spelling

You can check the spelling of your Web pages on a per-page or a per-Web basis. Checking the spelling of a given Web page is discussed in Chapter 6.

Before you publish your Web for the first time, you should run a spelling check on the Web as a whole. To perform a multipage spelling check, follow these steps:

1. Open the Web to be checked in FrontPage and switch to Folders view.

2. If you want to check all documents in the Web, select Tools ➪ Spelling. To check only selected pages, either use the Shift key and the mouse to select a range of pages or use the Control key and mouse to select specified pages, and then select Tools ➪ Spelling.

3. In the Spelling dialog box, choose either Selected Pages or Entire Web (see Figure 3-1). If you haven't selected any pages, the Selected Pages option isn't available.

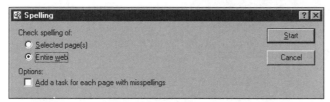

Figure 3-1: The Spelling dialog box

4. If you want to create a task item in the To Do list for each spelling error found, check the box labeled Add a Task for Each Page with Misspellings.

5. Click Start. FrontPage generates a list of spelling errors (see Figure 3-2). To edit all spelling errors, click the first error listed. FrontPage opens the page containing the offending word and prompts you to correct it with the standard page spelling check dialog box. After you edit all errors on the open page, FrontPage enables you to continue correcting errors with the next page in the list (see Figure 3-3). Alternatively, select one or more items and click the Add Task button to add the page to the task list.

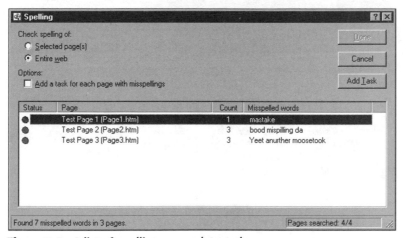

Figure 3-2: A list of spelling errors detected.

Caution   If you want to correct all pages listed, you need to start with the first page, because FrontPage currently stops at the last page. Thus, if you start the spelling check somewhere after the first page, any pages that precede the point at which you start are not reviewed for spelling errors by FrontPage.

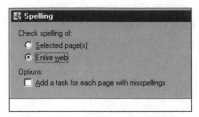

Figure 3-3: FrontPage prompts you
to continue checking spelling with
the remaining pages identified.

6. If you checked the Add a Task for Each Page with Misspellings option,
   FrontPage checks the page and adds a Fix Misspelled Words task to the list if
   it finds any misspelled words.

7. To view your new tasks, switch to Tasks view, as shown in Figure 3-4. See
   "Working with Tasks view," later in the chapter, for details on using the Tasks
   view window.

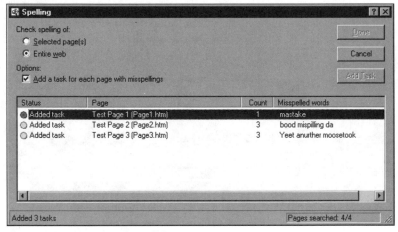

Figure 3-4: More work to do!

Removing orphaned files

In the Web publishing world, an "orphaned" file is one that has no references to it
from other files. In other words, no other pages in the Web contain a link to the
orphaned file. Typically, orphaned files are unused, forgotten files that you can
safely remove from your Web. (Of course, sometimes you may have good reasons
for why you have a file that is accessible on your Web server but not directly linked
to from any other files).

To find and remove orphans, follow these steps:

1. Switch to Reports view.

2. Select unlinked files from the Reports toolbar (see Figure 3-5). If the Reports toolbar is not available, select View ➪ Toolbars ➪ Reports to show it.

3. To delete a file in the list of unlinked files, right-click the file and select Delete from the option menu.

Figure 3-5: Tracking down orphaned files to remove

Validating links

Using FrontPage to insert hyperlinks can vastly decrease the number of broken or invalid links in your Web pages. However, you still might create a link to a nonexistent Web page, either on your own Web or elsewhere on the Internet. In addition, external links that are valid today may be nonexistent tomorrow, so rechecking your external links periodically is a good practice.

FrontPage has the capability to track down and list invalid hyperlinks, making it easy to correct or eliminate them from your Web pages.

Checking hyperlinks

To view the number of broken hyperlinks in your Web, follow these steps:

1. Open the Web in FrontPage.

2. Select Reports from the View menu.

3. To see summary information on the number of links in your Web, select the Site Summary report. This report lists the total number of hyperlinks, unverified hyperlinks (links that FrontPage hasn't yet checked), broken hyperlinks, external hyperlinks, and internal hyperlinks (see Figure 3-6).

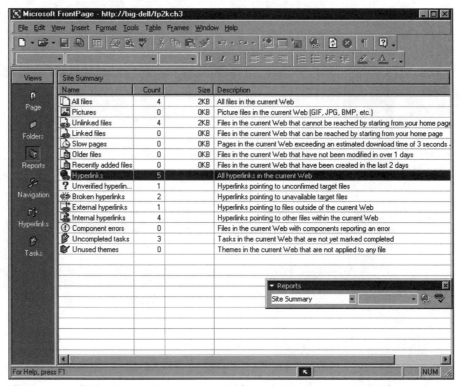

Figure 3-6: The Site Summary report provides information on your Web's hyperlinks.

4. To see a detailed list of broken hyperlinks, double-click the Broken Hyperlinks count in the Count column of the Site Summary report, or select the Broken Hyperlinks report from the Reports toolbar. A sample report is shown in Figure 3-7.

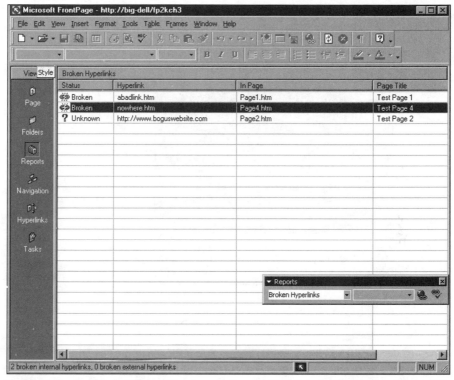

Figure 3-7: A sample listing of broken and unverified links in the Broken Hyperlinks report

5. To recheck any unverified links, select Tools ⇨ Recalculate Hyperlinks. Note that if you have a large number of external links, FrontPage may take several minutes to verify those links. To check only selected links, right-click the link item and select Verify from the option menu.

Note You must be connected to the Internet for FrontPage to verify any external hyper-links.

Editing invalid hyperlinks

After you identify broken links, you likely will want to fix them (at least we hope so. . .). From the Broken Hyperlinks report, you can choose one of the following methods of dealing with broken links:

1. To edit the hyperlink, double-click the list item, which opens the Edit Hyperlink dialog box, shown in Figure 3-8. Use this dialog box to change the hyperlink for the selected page or for all pages containing the same URL reference. Click the Edit Page button to open the selected page for editing.

Note You can't remove a hyperlink from the Edit Hyperlink dialog box. To remove a hyperlink, you must first open the page and edit it directly.

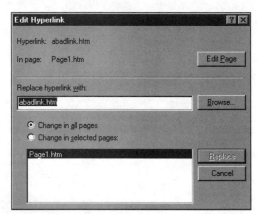

Figure 3-8: Use the Edit Hyperlink dialog box to fix broken hyperlinks.

2. To edit the page containing the hyperlink, right-click the item in the Broken Hyperlinks report and select the Edit Page option from the option menu.

3. To add the broken hyperlink to the task list, right-click the item in the Broken Hyperlinks report and select Add Task from the option menu.

Validating Components

If you are using FrontPage Components in your Webs, you can produce a report that lists any files that contain Components with errors. The procedure for locating and correcting nonfunctioning Components is very similar to that described in the previous section for validating hyperlinks.

Checking Components

To view the number of Components with errors in your Web, follow these steps:

1. Open the Web in FrontPage.

2. Select Reports from the View menu.

3. To see summary information on the number of Component errors, select the Site Summary report. This report lists the total number of errors.

4. If you have Component errors, you can double-click the summary item to view a detailed list of the files containing Components with errors. Alternatively, select Component Errors from the Reports toolbar to view this detailed report.

Editing non-functioning Components

From the Component Errors report, you can work with broken Components in one of two ways:

✦ Double-click an item in the report list to open the page and edit the Component.

✦ To add the broken Component to the task list, right-click the item and select Add Task from the option menu.

Validating HTML

To *validate* HTML means to check that all of your HTML code is written as directed by a certain HTML standard, such as HTML 2.0, HTML 3.2, or HTML 4.0. Although you can use the HTML Source and Compatibility tabs on the Page Options dialog box to control your HTML output, FrontPage 2000 does not include any direct means of validating HTML. If you want to validate your HTML, you must use an external tool.

Publishing a FrontPage Web

If you have determined that you need to publish your Web (see the beginning of this chapter for details), FrontPage offers a variety of ways to do so. The following sections describe each of the available options.

Publishing a Web using HTTP

You can use Hypertext Transfer Protocol (HTTP), the standard Web protocol, to publish pages to a Web server, if that Web server has the FrontPage Server Extensions installed. (For information on the FrontPage Server Extensions, see Chapter 23). If the Web server doesn't have the FrontPage Server Extensions installed, you can publish your Web by using FTP (see the upcoming section "Publishing a Web using FTP").

To publish the Web using HTTP, follow these steps:

1. Open the Web that you want to publish.

2. Select File ➪ Publish Web to open the Publish Web dialog box.

3. Specify the location of the Web to which you are publishing, either by typing its URL, by selecting it from the list of previously accessed Webs, or by clicking the Browse button to locate the Web.

4. Click the Options button to expand the dialog box, as shown in Figure 3-9.

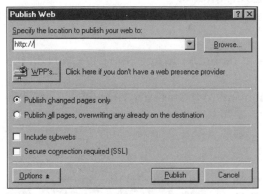

Figure 3-9: The Publish Web dialog box

5. Indicate whether you want to publish all pages or only the pages that have changed since you last published. (Note that any pages that you have specified as Don't Publish will not be published, regardless of which option you select here. See the next section for details on how to mark a page as Don't Publish).

6. If you want to publish subwebs as well as the main Web, check the Include Subwebs check box.

7. If you use a secure (SSL) connection to publish pages to your Web server, check the Secure Connection Required (SSL) check box.

8. Click Publish. FrontPage performs the updates and then displays the URL of the Web. You can click this link to verify that pages have updated successfully.

Caution   If you cancel the publishing operation before it has completed, those pages that have already been updated remain on the server (in other words, no rollback feature exists if you change your mind after you start to publish). You should always keep a backup of your Web so that you can restore any pages that you inadvertently change.

Specifying pages to publish

By default, when you publish a Web, FrontPage publishes all pages in the Web. You can elect to publish only changed pages. You can also specify exactly which pages to publish. This can be crucial if you are publishing from a development environment, in which you may have several versions of a test page in progress.

To exclude a page from being published, follow these steps:

1. Select Page Properties for the file. If you have the file open, either select File ⇨ Properties, or right-click the page and select Page Properties from the option menu. Alternatively, right-click the file icon in Folders view and select Properties from the option menu. Select the Workgroup tab, as illustrated in Figure 3-10.

Figure 3-10: The Workgroup tab in the File Properties dialog box. Note that this is the same Workgroup tab that appears in the Page Properties dialog box.

2. Check the box labeled Exclude This File When Publishing the Rest of the Web.

To change the publishing status of several files, follow these steps:

1. Select Reports view and the Publish Status report. This report lists all files and shows their publish status in the Publish column. The options are Publish or Don't Publish.

2. To change the publishing status of a file, click its publish status field. A drop-down menu appears. Select the desired option: Publish or Don't Publish.

Tip

If you want to delete a file from a published Web, you can first delete it from your local Web and then publish the Web. FrontPage notices that you have removed the file, and removes it from the publish site as well. (If you want to remove the file *only* from the publish site, you need to move the file out of the Web and then, after republishing, move it back.)

Publishing a Web using FTP

If the Web server to which you are publishing doesn't support the FrontPage Server Extensions, you can publish your Web pages by using File Transfer Protocol (FTP). The procedure is very similar to the procedure just described for using HTTP. The chief difference is that you may want to store the username and password information for your FTP account by adding an FTP location in FrontPage. The procedure for doing so is described at the end of this section.

To publish the Web using FTP, follow these steps:

1. Open the Web that you want to publish.

2. Select File ➪ Publish Web to open the Publish Web dialog box.

3. Specify the location of the FTP server to which you are publishing, either by typing its address, by selecting it from the list of previously accessed sites, or by clicking the Browse button to find the location. To publish to an FTP location that you have previously added, click Browse, select FTP Locations, and select the location from the list of available FTP sites. (See the next section for information on adding sites to the list of FTP locations.)

4. Click the Options button to expand the dialog box.

5. Indicate whether you want to publish all pages or only pages that have changed since you last published. (Note that any pages you have specified as Don't Publish will not be published, regardless of which option you select here. See the preceding section for details on how to mark a page Don't Publish).

6. If you want to publish subwebs as well as the main Web, check the Include Subwebs check box.

7. Click Publish. FrontPage performs the updates and then displays the URL of the Web. You can click this link to verify that pages have updated successfully.

Adding an FTP location

To set up an FTP location with username and password information, follow these steps:

1. Select File ➪ Publish Web and click the Browse button.

2. Select FTP Locations and double-click Add/Modify FTP Locations, as shown in Figure 3-11.

3. In the Add/Modify FTP Locations dialog box, shown in Figure 3-12, indicate the FTP server location and login information. Click OK to add a new item to the list of FTP locations.

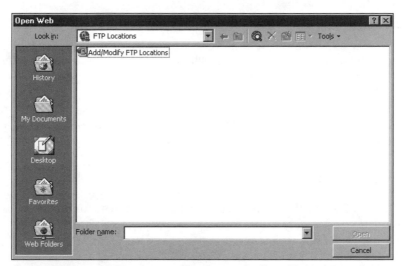

Figure 3-11: To add a new FTP location to the list of known FTP sites, select Add/Modify FTP Locations.

Figure 3-12: Adding a new FTP location to the list of known FTP sites

4. To publish to this location, select it from the list of FTP locations. FrontPage publishes your Web to this FTP site without prompting for login information.

Publishing to a disk-based Web

"Publishing to a disk-based Web" is FrontPage speak for making a copy of an existing Web on your local hard drive. Why would you want to do this? The following are some possibilities:

✦ To have a backup of your Web site.

✦ To make a version of your Web site that you can show to others without being connected to a Web server.

✦ To create a version of your live Web that you can use to test updates before republishing them.

The process of publishing a disk-based Web is the same as for other publishing operations:

1. Open in FrontPage the Web that you want to publish.

2. Select File ➪ Publish Web from the menu bar.

3. Click the Browse button and identify the location on your local file system where you want to publish the Web.

4. Click OK to return to the publishing dialog box. Click OK again to proceed with the publishing operation.

Caution   Any functionality in your Web site that requires a Web server and/or the FrontPage Server Extensions will not work in this disk-based Web.

Selecting a Web hosting service

Chances are, if you are planning to create a Web site, you probably have looked into the issue of where to put the site — before you get ready to click that Publish button. Just for the sake of argument, though, suppose that you haven't. You just figured, "Hey, I'll click that old Publish button and something will come to me..." Well, it's your lucky day, because Microsoft has thought to put a button on the publishing wizard that links directly to a list of FrontPage-enabled Web hosting services, or *Web Presence Providers (WPP)*.

To be honest, I do not recommend waiting until you are ready to publish your site to check out the list of WPPs. If you already have an Internet Service Provider (ISP) who provides you with a dial-up account to the Internet, you might want to inquire with it first to see whether it provides some Web site presence as part of that account, and if so, whether it supports FrontPage. An increasing number of ISPs do, even though they may not have made it onto Microsoft's list.

A wide range of services and prices are available, so be sure to check out your options carefully. Get each WPP to provide you with a list of references to speak to, and ask those references how satisfied they are with the service.

A Few Things to Consider

Your hardest decision in setting up a Web site is selecting a provider. Prices and services vary considerably. If you plan to use FrontPage exclusively, one of your main considerations is the level of FrontPage support provided. Many providers have added FrontPage Server Extensions because of customer demand, but they are not providing technical support for FrontPage. The list of providers with qualified, experienced support and technical staff to assist you with FrontPage questions is much smaller. You pay for the privilege, but if your budget permits it, you will not be sorry.

Another consideration is whether you need Internet access in addition to Web hosting. What is the difference? To publish your Web, you need to be able to connect your development computer to the Internet. If you happen to work for a company or institution whose internal network is directly connected to the Internet, then you have no problem. If you are operating from home or a small office, you probably have a dial-up connection to the Internet, via analog modem or possibly ISDN.

After you are connected to the Internet, you can publish your Web pages to any server where you have an account. Consequently, if you already have an ISP for dial-up access, you don't need to obtain dial-up access from your FrontPage hosting service. All you need is a Web account on its server that allows you to post your pages. If you don't yet have dial-up access, or if you prefer to have multiple dial-up accounts (not a bad idea if you can afford it, particularly if you can't afford to have your dial-up account busy when you need to publish your pages), then you may find some companies offering the full line of access services at reasonable prices.

Selecting a provider

First some definitions. In the beginning, the only Internet connectivity providers were Internet Access Providers (IAPs), more commonly known as ISPs. An ISP offers its customers connectivity to the Internet first and foremost. Secondarily, most ISP accounts come with e-mail, including some amount of online storage space for e-mail messages. Increasingly, ISPs also offer their customers other kinds of space, principally Web site space (and sometimes storage for anonymous FTP, as well). Typically, however, ISPs primarily (with notable exceptions) are in the connectivity business. They aren't as strong in the area of providing support and development services for business-oriented customers.

Enter a new breed of connectivity provider, the Web hosting company (sometimes called Web Presence Providers). These folks don't deal in providing Internet access for you. Instead, they focus on providing a safe and easily accessible home for your Web site on the Internet. In principle, this focus means that they can provide more expertise in the area of Web development, but they assume that you can find your own access to the Internet elsewhere.

Note   The divisions discussed in this section are not pure. Many ISPs offer Web hosting services. Some companies who focus on Web hosting also offer dial-up access, although their facilities are often less robust than those of the better ISPs.

So what do you do?

If you have a Web site with your current ISP, check with it to see whether it currently supports or has plans to support FrontPage. If it doesn't, you have three options (besides throwing in the towel on FrontPage, of course):

✦ Select a new service provider

✦ Keep your current provider and add a Web hosting provider

✦ Use FrontPage without the server extensions (as described earlier in the chapter)

Pricing and support

A survey of existing Web hosting facilities supporting FrontPage also demonstrates a range of pricing and support options. Here are some factors to consider:

✦ Most offer the FrontPage service at no additional charge. Some add an initial setup charge. However, pricing for Web hosting varies dramatically. The average range is roughly between $29 per month to $200 per month. Obviously, the features offered vary widely within this range, too.

✦ Options in the support category range from no support ("we do install the FrontPage extension for you, but you are on your own") to extensive (and expensive) on-site training options. A survey of Web sites also indicates a range of commitment to and expertise with FrontPage.

Working with Web Reports

Web Reports view, new in FrontPage 2000, is one of the most useful additions to the product. Open a Web and switch to Reports view to see the Site Summary report, which is described in more detail in the next section.

You can navigate through the reports in several ways. Double-clicking a summary item in the Site Summary report takes you to the detail report for that item. You can also view the Reports toolbar and select any Report from the drop-down menu.

Site Summary

The Site Summary report, shown in Figure 3-13, gives you a high-level overview of the health and status of your Web. For each summary item, this report indicates a count of the number of items, a file size total where relevant, and a description. Many, but not all, items have a detail page. To see the details for a line item in the

Site Summary report, double-click the line in question. The following list includes the Site Summary line items and a brief description of each. Those items with an asterisk have a detailed report, described in the next section.

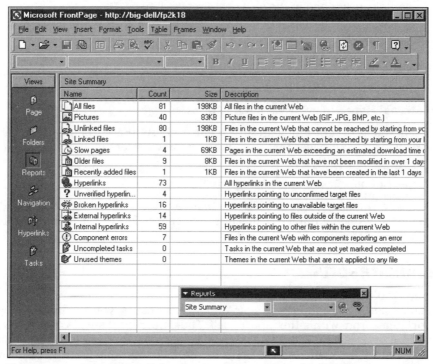

Figure 3-13: A snapshot of the Site Summary report, with the Reports toolbar toward the bottom of the window.

- ✦ **All Files*:** Indicates the total number of files in your Web and their total file size.

- ✦ **Pictures:** Indicates the number of graphics in your Web and their total file size.

- ✦ **Unlinked Files*:** Indicates the number of orphaned files in your Web.

- ✦ **Linked Files:** Indicates the number of files that are referenced by one or more pages in your Web.

- ✦ **Slow Pages*:** Estimates the page download time, based on the total number and size of the files associated with the page. The summary indicates the number of "slow" pages, based on a designated download time.

- ✦ **Older Files*:** Indicates the number of pages that have not been changed since a designated date.

✦ **Recently Added Files*:** Indicates the number of new pages added since a designated time. (The time designated for recent files is independent of the time designated for older files.)

✦ **Hyperlinks*:** The total number of hyperlinks, consisting of the four types of hyperlinks described in the next set of report items.

✦ **Unverified Hyperlinks*:** The number of hyperlinks that have not been checked.

✦ **Broken Hyperlinks*:** The number of hyperlinks that do not go to a valid URL.

✦ **External Hyperlinks*:** Valid URLs to external sites.

✦ **Internal Hyperlinks*:** Valid internal URLs.

✦ **Component Errors*:** Indicates the number of FrontPage Components that you are using in your pages that are not functioning correctly.

✦ **Uncompleted Tasks*:** Indicates any tasks in the task list that still need to be done. Double-clicking this item opens Tasks view.

✦ **Unused Themes*:** Lists any Themes that have been added to the Web and then abandoned. Double-clicking this item causes FrontPage to attempt to remove any existing Themes that are not in use.

Detailed reports

FrontPage 2000 includes over a dozen detailed reports that you can use to view information about the contents of your Web. In most cases, you can make changes to report items from within the report itself. Thus, the report serves as a powerful Find feature for problems when you are first preparing to publish or when you are doing periodic maintenance reviews of your site. The following lists the name and a description of each available report:

Note   You can sort any of the reports on a given column by clicking the gray column header.

✦ **All Files:** Provides details for the All Files summary item. It lists for each file the Name, Title, In Folder, Orphan, Size, Type, Modified Date, Modified By, and Comments. You can change the filename, its title, and add comments from this list. This is a great place to update titles, because you can see all of your titles simultaneously.

✦ **Recently Added Files:** Lists all files added within a definable date range. Includes for each file: Name, Title, Created Date, Modified By, Size, Type, and In Folder. You can edit Name and Title. Double-click a file to open it. You can configure the date that defines recent files in the Reports View tab of the Options menu or in the Reports toolbar.

Tip   Recently Added Files isn't a log of files changed. For that, if you have IIS, you need to enable author logging to retain a summary of author activity on the Web.

✦ **Recently Changed Files:** Lists all files added within a definable date range. Includes Name, Title, Modified Date, Modified By, Size, Type, and In Folder. You can edit Name and Title. Double-click a file to open it. You can configure the date that defines recent files in the Reports View tab of the Options menu or in the Reports toolbar.

✦ **Older Files:** Provides details for the Older Files summary item. Includes Name, Title, Modified Date, Modified By, Size, Type, and In Folder. You can edit Name and Title. Double-click a file to open it. You can define an older file date range in the Reports View tab of the Options menu or in the Reports toolbar.

✦ **Unlinked Files:** Provides details for the Unlinked Files summary item. Includes Name, Title, Modified Date, Modified By, Size, Type, and In Folder. You can edit Name and Title. Double-click a file to open it.

✦ **Slow Pages:** Provides details for the Slow Files summary item. Includes Name, Title, Download Time, Size, Type, In Folder, and Modified Date. You can edit Name and Title. Double-click a file to open it. You can define a slow page in the Report view of the Options menu or in the Reports toolbar.

✦ **Broken Links:** Provides file details for the Broken link summary item. Includes Status, Hyperlink, In Page, Page Title, and Modified By. You cannot edit fields. Double-click a file to open the Edit Hyperlink dialog box (see Figure 3-14).

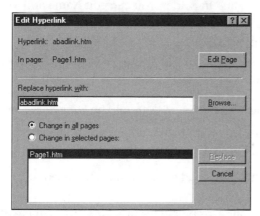

Figure 3-14: The Edit Hyperlink dialog box

✦ **Component Errors:** Provides file details for the Component Errors summary item. Includes Name, Title, Errors, Type, and In Folder. You cannot edit fields. Double-click the file to open the file.

✦ **Review Status:** Lists review information for each file in the Web. You can also use this report to modify review information. Includes Name, Title, Review Status, Assigned To, Review Date, Reviewed By, Type, and In Folder. You can edit Name, Title, Review Status, and Assigned To. Double-click a file to open it.

✦ **Assigned To:** Lists details about page assignments for each file in the Web. You can also use this report to modify assignment information. Includes Name, Title, Assigned To, Assigned Date, Assigned By, Comments, Type, and In Folder. You can edit Name, Title, Assigned To, and Comments. Double-click a file to open it.

✦ **Categories:** Lists category details about each file in the Web. Includes Name, Title, Category, Type, and In Folder. Oddly, you can't edit Category information in this report (presumably because you can select multiple categories per file?). You can use the Reports toolbar to select a specific category, to view files by Category.

✦ **Publish Status:** Lists publishing details for each file in the Web. It also enables you to enable or disable publishing for a file. This is a very handy report. Includes Name, Title, Publish, Modified Date, Review Status, Size, Type, and In Folder. You can edit Name, Title, and Publish.

✦ **Checkout Status:** Available only if you have enabled source control for the current Web. (See the next section for details on enabling and using FrontPage's built-in source control). Includes Name, Title, Checked Out By, Version, Locked Date, Type, and In Folder. You can edit Name and Title only.

Setting Reports view options

To configure various Reports view options, select Tools ➪ Options and choose the Reports View tab (see Figure 3-15). Options you can configure include:

✦ **Recent Files:** Indicate how many days a file should be considered recent.

✦ **Older Files:** Indicate how many days before a file should be considered old.

✦ **Slow Pages:** Indicate download time for a slow page.

✦ **Connection Speed:** Select a download connection speed used to calculate download times.

✦ **Display Gridline:** You can show or hide lines in your reports. (One of those cosmetic choices that probably resulted from a fight between two senior developers. If only I could change the color and width of the gridlines, too...)

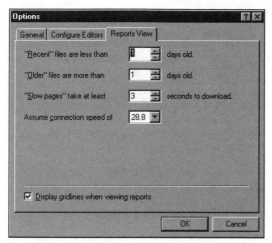

Figure 3-15: Configuration options for various reports

Managing a Web Project

In the last three or four years, the sum total of Web development talent and expertise has grown exponentially, in step with the feverish pace of increasingly sophisticated Web projects. Whereas a few years ago, a single person could have been counted on to design, develop, and maintain a typical Web site, now it takes a full team of people. Larger, more complex projects also equates to an increased need for tools that help keep a project running smoothly. FrontPage is designed to serve the needs of everything from small-business Web site development to large, coordinated projects in multidepartment corporations.

FrontPage 2000 includes the following utilities to help development teams collaborate effectively:

- ✦ **Tasks View:** Enables groups to assign and monitor tasks.
- ✦ **Workgroup Categories:** Enables groups to divide tasks into logical groupings.
- ✦ **Review Status:** Enables you to track pages and content files through the stages of publication.
- ✦ **Source Control:** Protects files from accidental overwriting in a multiuser environment.
- ✦ **Project Web Template:** A FrontPage Web for communicating among team members.

Working with Tasks view

FrontPage Tasks view is where you can keep track of the work that needs to be completed on your Web. This feature is neither a full-blown project management tool nor an incident tracking system. But, for average needs, it provides a convenient way to record and keep track of project tasks that need to be completed. You can use Tasks view to identify tasks, assign tasks, prioritize tasks, and update the status of tasks.

Creating a task

Several of the page checking utilities described in this chapter — for example, the spelling checker and the link checker — have the ability to create tasks automatically based on any errors that they detect. In addition to these mechanisms, you can add tasks manually, either associated with a particular page or just as a general-purpose task.

To create a general-purpose task, follow these steps:

1. From Folders view or Hyperlinks view, select File ⇨ New ⇨ Task to open the New Task dialog box, shown in Figure 3-16. Alternatively, from Tasks view, you can right-click the tasks list and select New Task from the option menu.

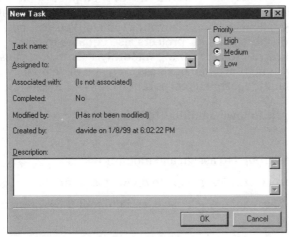

Figure 3-16: The New Task dialog box — without a file association.

2. In the New Task dialog box, give the task a name, assign it a priority (high, medium, or low), and assign the task to an authorized user, using the drop-down menu. Optionally, add a descriptive comment to explain the task.

To add a task and associate it with a particular file, follow these steps:

1. In either Folders view or Page view, select the file to which you want to add a task. You can do this either by opening the file and selecting Edit ➪ Task ➪ Add Task or by right-clicking a filename in Folders view and selecting Add Task from the option menu.

2. Complete the dialog box as described in Step 2 in the preceding list. Note that the selected filename is identified in the Associated With field in the dialog box. This item can't be edited.

Viewing and sorting tasks

To view current tasks, switch to Tasks view (a sample set of tasks is illustrated in Figure 3-17). You can adjust column widths and sort the task list for any of the available columns by clicking the column name. For example, to sort tasks by priority, click the Priority column heading. To reverse-sort the same field, click the column heading a second time.

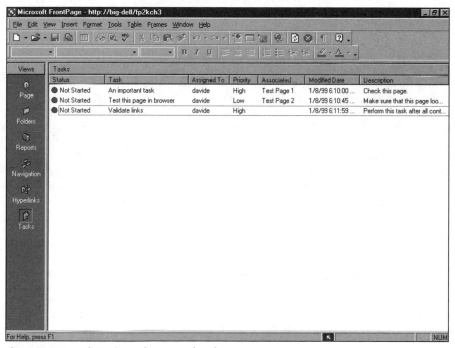

Figure 3-17: A list of newly created tasks.

Modifying tasks

You can make changes to task details by using the Task Detail dialog box. To view task details, double-click a task. This displays the Task Detail dialog box, which is identical to the New Task dialog box. Alternatively, right-click the task and select the Edit Task item.

In addition, you can edit any of the fields in the Task Detail dialog box directly in the Tasks view list. This includes the Task Name, Assigned To, Priority, and Description fields. To edit a field, select the field value and then either type a new value or select a new value from the menu of available options.

To delete a task, right-click the task and select Delete from the option menu.

Starting tasks

If a task is associated with a particular file or Web page, you can use Tasks view to start the task. In Tasks view, right-click the task that you want to perform and select Start Task from the option menu. Alternatively, select the task and choose Edit ⇨ Task ⇨ Start. Or (in case that isn't enough options for you), you can double-click the task to open its Edit dialog box and then click the Start Task button. Note that tasks that are not associated with any page have the start feature disabled.

Completing tasks

Sooner or later, all good tasks must be completed. After you complete a task, you should mark it as completed. To mark a task completed, right-click the task in Tasks view and select Mark as Completed from the option menu. Alternatively, select the task and then choose Edit ⇨ Task ⇨ Mark as Complete.

Tasks that have been completed can be removed from the list of Tasks that you view. To hide completed tasks, right-click inside the Tasks view window. If Show Task History is checked, all completed tasks will be displayed in Tasks view. To remove completed tasks from view, select Show Task History to uncheck this option. Alternatively, select Edit ⇨ Task ⇨ Show Task history and check or uncheck in the same fashion.

Working with categories

You can use workgroup categories to classify your files in groups. After you categorize your files, you can use the categories to manage your files or to insert a list of filenames of a given category into a Web page.

Assigning categories to a file

You can assign a category to a file when the file is open or closed. If the file is open, right-click anywhere on the open page in Page view and select Properties from the options menu. Click the Workgroups tab and select one or more categories from the list of Available Categories. To select a category, click the check box. To deselect a category, uncheck it.

If the file is closed, right-click the file icon in Folders view and select Properties from the options menu. Click the Workgroups tab and select one or more categories from the list of Available Categories. You can set the categories for several files simultaneously by selecting the files in Folders view and proceeding as you would for a single file.

Viewing pages by category

You can view your files by category by using the Categories report. Switch to Reports view and select Categories from the Reports toolbar. By default, the Category Reports lists all categories. To view files for a particular category only, select the category from the Reports toolbar. You cannot edit categories directly in this report. However, you can right-click one or more files to edit categories, as previously described.

Modifying the Category List

FrontPage 2000 comes with several preset categories. You can modify this list to suit your purposes. To modify the Master Category List, right-click a file in Folders view and select Properties. Select the Workgroup tab and click the Categories button. In the Master Category List, shown in Figure 3-18, type a new name in the New Category field and click the Add button. To delete an existing category, select it from the list and click the Delete button.

Figure 3-18: Master Category List

Inserting categories into a Web page

After you categorize your files, you can add a list of pages of a particular category to a Web page. For example, suppose that you have several pages that describe the various products that your company sells. You have added each page to the Products category. To add a list of product pages to a Web page, follow these steps:

1. Open the Web page where you want the list to appear.

2. Select Insert ➪ Components ➪ Categories to open the Categories Properties dialog box (see Figure 3-19).

3. Select one or more categories to include in the list by checking available categories in the list labeled Choose Categories to List Files By.

4. Optionally, select a sort method, either alphabetically by title or by modification date.

5. Optionally, select to include the file modification date and/or comments.

6. Click OK to insert the Categories Component into the page.

This Component updates dynamically any time that you add a new page to one of the selected categories in this list.

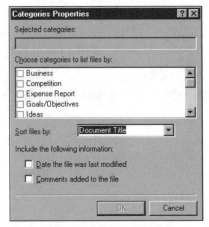

Figure 3-19: Adding a list of categories to a Web page using the Categories Component

Using Review Status

In addition to categories, development teams can assign a review status to their files as a way of tracking files through the development process.

Setting the Review Status

You can set the review status of a file in one of three ways:

✦ When the file is open

✦ When the file is closed

✦ From the Review Status Report

If the file is open, right-click anywhere on the open page in Page view and select Properties from the options menu. Click the Workgroup tab and select a Review Status code from the available menu.

If the file is closed, right-click the file icon in Folders view and select Properties from the options menu. Click the Workgroup tab and select a Review Status code from the menu of available options. To set the Review Status code for several files simultaneously, select the files in Folders view and proceed as you would for a single file.

You can also set Review Status codes for one or more files by using the Review Status report. Switch to Reports view and select the Review Status report from the Reports toolbar. Click the Review Status field of a given file and then select a Review Status code from the list of available options.

Tip   You can add a new Review Status code from the Review Status report. However, to edit or remove codes, you must use the Review Status Master List, as described next.

Modifying the Review Status Master List

By default, FrontPage includes a list of four Review Status codes: Code Review, Content Review, Legal Review, and Manager Review. You can modify this list to suit your purposes. To modify the Review Status list, right-click a file in Folders view and select Properties. Select the Workgroup tab and click the Statuses button. In the Review Status Master List, shown in Figure 3-20, type a new name in the New Review Status field and click the Add button. To delete an existing Review Status code, select it from the list and click the Delete button.

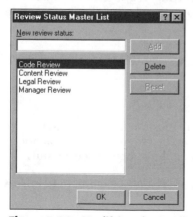

Figure 3-20: Modifying the Review Status Master List

Using source control

FrontPage 2000 includes a simple means of checking files in and out. You can use this feature to prevent two people from making changes to the same file and canceling out each other's work.

 Tip   If you need more advanced source control functionality, you can integrate Microsoft's Visual SourceSafe with FrontPage.

To use FrontPage's built-in source control, you must first enable it. To enable source control, you must have administrative-level privileges. Select Tools ➪ Web Settings and check Use Document Check-in and Check-out on the General tab.

Checking out a file

To "check out a file" means to open it to make changes. When you have source control enabled, only one person can make changes to a file at a time. When you check out a file, others can view the file but they cannot modify it.

To check out a file, switch to Folders view and right-click the file that you want to edit. Select Check Out from the option menu. Note that selecting this option does not automatically open the file for you.

If you attempt to open a file in the normal fashion, FrontPage alerts you that the file is under source control, and asks whether you want to check out the file. If you click Yes, FrontPage marks the page with the checked-out icon and opens it for you to edit. If you click No, FrontPage opens the file in read-only mode.

Checking in a file

When you are done editing, you must check in a file that you have checked out. First, save any changes that you have made to the file. Right-click the file in Folders view and select Check In from the options menu. This releases the file for another user to edit.

 Caution   It is possible (quite easy, actually) to close a file that you are done working with without checking it back in.

Viewing checkout status

When you enable source control on your Web, all files are marked to indicate their checkout status. Files with a small green bullet next to them are available for checkout. Files with a red check mark next to them have been checked out.

To view detailed information on the checkout status of files, switch to Reports view and select the Checkout Status report.

Caution The built-in source control has a few oddities. You can create a new page and continue to edit it without having it checked out. You can delete a file whether it is checked out or not. You can check out a file and then check it back in and still continue to make changes. I would like to believe that these are bugs, but I will believe it when I see them fixed.

Using the Project Web

The Project Web template that comes with FrontPage is designed to serve as a communication channel for a Web development team. It is relatively simple-minded, which is both a virtue and a shortcoming. Use this template if you want an uncomplicated, low-maintenance way to keep a group apprised of the status and progress of a project, and if you want to centralize implementation discussions, documents, and so forth.

The Project Web consists of a home page and the following six subsections:

✦ **Members:** This page provides an alphabetical listing of the development team members, including a placeholder for a photo, description, and contact information. This can be a handy reference, particularly if the development team is distributed remotely and you are trying to remember someone's fax number. On the downside, this page would be more convenient if its data could be sorted in various ways and searched like a phone directory.

✦ **Schedule:** This page lists upcoming events, such as meetings, review sessions, and so on, and milestones. It also provides for a priority listing of what is happening in the current and upcoming weeks. This page is organized as a generic text page. It lends itself to customizing, so that team members could, for example, schedule events using a calendaring-like feature.

✦ **Status:** This section lists monthly status reports, based on the assumptions that your project is going to last more than one month, and that you actually produce such reports. I am sure that they are a blessing to all involved if your project has them.

✦ **Archive:** This archive is really envisioned as something more like a library. It is a place to link documents produced by the project, software code developed by the project, and other tools and utilities that might be of interest to team members.

✦ **Search:** The standard FrontPage mechanism for searching HTML pages in a Web.

✦ **Discussions:** The Discussions, section is divided into two topic areas:

 • **Requirements:** The place to request, recommend, or dream about features for the project.

- **Knowledge base:** The place where general question and answer discussions are maintained.

After the archive, this is potentially the most valuable portion of the Project Web, assuming that it is used.

Tip   One element missing from the Project Web is a mechanism for incident tracking during development of the project. This could easily be implemented as a third discussion track, although ideally, one would like something a little more structured than just submitting a discussion item.

Summary

The first three chapters have introduced you to all the basic operations in FrontPage, and even to quite a few of the more advanced ones. This chapter has focused on publishing and general maintenance tasks in FrontPage. The main thing to take with you from this chapter is a working understanding of how FrontPage "publishes" its Web pages, whether to a Web server with the FrontPage Server Extensions installed, to a standard Web server, or just to your local, neighborhood hard drive. After you understand this process, you are ready for anything. If you are looking for information on how FrontPage fits into the bigger Office 2000 picture, then the next chapter is for you. If you are eager to learn more about creating Webs and Web pages with FrontPage, skip ahead to the next section, where you will learn how to create eye-catching, easy-to-navigate Web pages.

✦   ✦   ✦

Integrating FrontPage with Office 2000

Scenario: You have documents in Word, illustrations in PowerPoint, a brochure in Publisher, and a table in Excel, and you need to integrate them all into your Web site. This chapter explores the process of doing just that.

However, more is involved in the relationship between FrontPage and Office 2000 applications. Integration between FrontPage 2000 and other Office 2000 applications can be a two-way street. You can generate Web pages and other elements of a Web site from Word documents, Publisher publications, and Excel spreadsheets, but you can also collect data in FrontPage that you send to a mailmerge file in Word or an Excel database.

Finally, Office 2000 users can actually use working spreadsheets and PivotTables in Web browsers, attached to your Web site.

In Figure 4-1, a Web page is performing a calculation on data input by a visitor, and then collecting data that can be sent to an Excel or Word file.

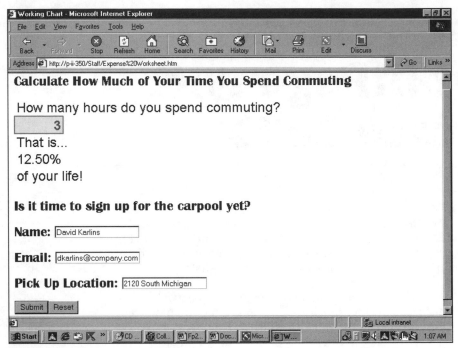

Figure 4-1: You can provide interactivity for visitors by using an Office 2000 spreadsheet component.

From Office to FrontPage

Office 2000 applications all have their own distinct methods for converting documents to Web pages. Excel automatically generates Web sites that look like spreadsheets. Publisher creates Web site folders full of files, with a separate Web page for each page of a publication. PowerPoint Web sites look like slide shows, and Word, too, generates Web sites.

That's all fine for folks using those programs who aren't demanding the ability to fine-tune their Web page display. However, as a FrontPage-empowered Web designer, you may want to pick and choose elements from Office applications to integrate into a Web site of your own design.

Importing components from Office applications requires understanding how they generate Web sites, where they stash the Web files, and how you can work around some of the automation routines to pull just what you want into your Web site.

Moving from Word to FrontPage

Actually, several ways exist to move text from a Word file into a FrontPage Web site. The quickest way is to copy text, although even this option presents several alternatives that affect how the text format gets translated to your Web page.

Other options include saving the file as a text file, or saving it as HTML. Each method has its advantages and drawbacks, which are explored in this section.

Note Most of the different ways of integrating Office documents into Webs involves using the Import dialog box, which is discussed later in this chapter, in the section "Importing files into Webs."

Attach text files to a Web site

If your Web design responsibilities include integrating many documents into a Web site, you will very likely want to import large blocks of text from Word (or another word processor) into FrontPage Web pages.

You have many options available for integrating word processing files into a Web site. If you are presented documents that don't need any formatting or Web design features, you can simply save your documents as text (.txt) files and import them into your Web site.

When you select File ⇨ Save As in Word (or other word processors), you have the option of saving to either of two different types of text files: with line breaks, or without line breaks.

If you save your text as a *.txt file without line breaks, the text appears in browsers as long, unbroken lines, with line breaks occurring only at paragraph marks. The advantage of saving a text file in this way is that it allows a visitor to copy the text back into his or her own word processor and then view, print or edit it easily. However, without line breaks, the text is difficult to read in a browser, and requires a visitor to scroll horizontally to see the ends of most lines of text. Figure 4-2 shows a text file with line breaks in a browser window.

The other option is to save you text as a text file with line breaks, which makes the text easy to read in a browser. The downside to forcing line breaks is that if the text is copied to a word processor, the paragraph breaks at the end of each line have to be removed for the text to be edited or formatted.

Copy and Paste

The easiest way to get word processing documents into FrontPage Web pages is simply to copy and paste the text. First, copy all or part of a document into the Clipboard. Then, open a page in FrontPage 2000 Page view and select Edit ⇨ Paste Special. The Convert Text dialog box appears, as shown in Figure 4-3.

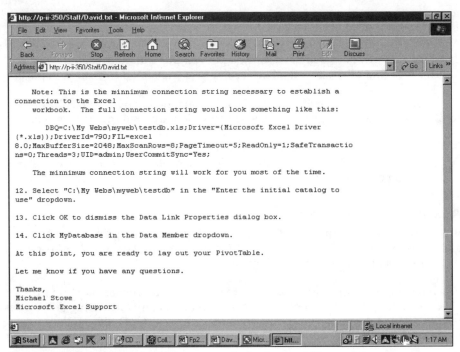

Figure 4-2: Including text files in your Web site is a no-frills way to make a document available to visitors.

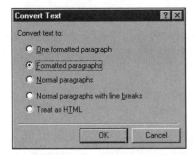

Figure 4-3: You have several options for pasting copied text into a Web page.

The following are the paste options:

✦ **One formatted paragraph:** Converts the text to one paragraph, replacing paragraph marks in the copied text with forced line breaks.

✦ **Formatted paragraphs:** Copies the text, preserving formatting and paragraphs.

✦ **Normal paragraphs:** Copies text, converting it to the Normal style defined for your Web site. If you assigned a Theme with a defined Normal style, or defined a Normal style yourself, those attributes are assigned to the copied text.

✦ **Normal paragraphs with line breaks:** Converts copied text to Normal style (like the preceding option), but substitutes forced line breaks for paragraph breaks.

✦ **Treat as HTML:** Interprets any HTML code within copied text. You are unlikely to use this option for imported Word text, unless you include HTML tags in your text. Use this option when you copy HTML code into a FrontPage Web page.

From Word to HTML files

The other main option for getting word processing files into FrontPage is to save your files as HTML in your word processor.

Using Word 2000's File ⇨ Save as Web Page option converts an open document to an HTML file. Or, in some cases, to several files, including image files. How good are the results? The resulting files often take some work to restore formatting and images. Publisher 2000 does a cleaner job of converting document files to Web pages. If you want to do complex page layout outside of FrontPage, Publisher is a better choice than Word. However, if you want to convert a 50-page Word document to a Web site, the Save as HTML option accomplishes the job in a hurry. And, of course, you can touch up the formatting in FrontPage Page view.

Word saves complex documents by generating several files. For example, long document footers have separate files generated for the footer(s). Similarly, separate files are generated for embedded image files. Word creates a new *folder* when these files are generated, to keep them all together. In that case, when you import a Word file that has been saved to HTML, you import the entire folder.

Creating Web sites from Publisher

Publisher 2000 provides a particularly smooth conversion from documents to Web pages by making many design decisions for you, including transforming some text into images when needed to preserve text flow around graphics.

When you save a Publisher 2000 publication as a Web page, a new folder is created with many files. Publisher creates a new Web page for each page in your publication, and saves all of them to a folder. So, when you save a Publisher publication as a Web site, you actually create and save to a *folder,* not to individual files.

To save your publication as a Web site in Publisher, select File ⇨ Save as Web Page. You need to do this even if you saved your file prior to converting it to Web pages. The Save as Web Page dialog box prompts you to select a folder to which your many Web site files will be saved. The Save as Web Page dialog box prompts you for a file folder, not a filename. Be careful to save only one single set of Web files in a folder.

Note Publisher converts all embedded pictures into GIF format and stores them in the folder generated for your saved Web site. Because not all images save well as GIFs, you can substitute JPEGs when necessary in the FrontPage Page view.

Sending Excel objects to FrontPage

Excel offers three options for sending spreadsheets and charts to FrontPage Web pages:

✦ Use copy and paste to transfer selected cells or charts to a Web page.

✦ Save selected cells, sheets, or charts as Web pages.

✦ Save an entire worksheet, including all tabs, as a set of Web files.

Copying and pasting works fine for quick and dirty transferring of cells into a FrontPage table. Copying charts works fine—you simply transfer the chart into Page view as a picture that can be edited or formatted using all of FrontPage's picture format tools. For example, you can copy a chart into FrontPage, assign a transparent background, save it as a GIF file, and make it into an image map with linked hotspots. For a full discussion of all of these picture editing features, see Chapter 7.

To preserve cell formatting or convert your entire spreadsheet (either one tab, or all of them) into a Web site, you can save your spreadsheet to an HTML file. All of these options are explored in detail next in this chapter.

Move tables into FrontPage

The quick and easy way to move a table into FrontPage is to copy the cells in Excel and paste them into an open Web page in FrontPage, using Page view. Copying and pasting cells does not preserve formatting, but you can use table formatting features in FrontPage to restore or add table and cell formatting.

You can send either a selected range of cells or an entire workbook to a Web page in Excel by selecting File ➪ Save as Web Page from the Excel menu. If you first select the cells that you want to convert, you can use the Selection radio button in the Save As dialog box, as shown in Figure 4-4.

The Add Interactivity check box in the Save As dialog box creates a page with an Office spreadsheet. For an explanation of how these interactive spreadsheets work in a Web page, see "Adding Office spreadsheets," later in this chapter.

Send charts to FrontPage

You can copy Excel charts into FrontPage Web pages through the Clipboard. However, we've found that the results are sometimes unsatisfactory, and chart attributes such as colors and fonts get lost or distorted.

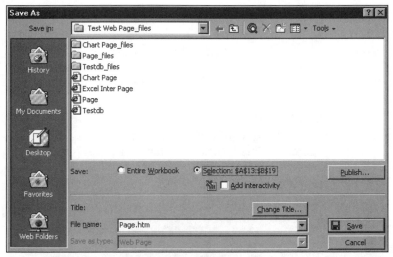

Figure 4-4: Selected cells in an Excel worksheet can be saved as a Web page.

A more reliable way to transfer an Excel chart into a Web site is to save the chart as a GIF file in Excel and then import it into FrontPage.

To save a chart as a GIF file, follow these steps:

1. Open the Excel workbook and select the chart that you want to save as a GIF file.

2. Select File ➪ Save as Web Page. The Save As dialog box appears, as shown in Figure 4-5.

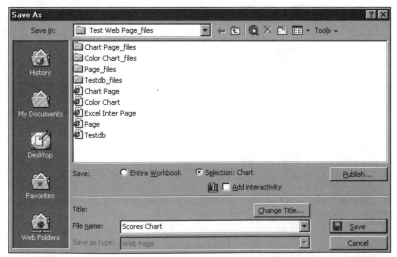

Figure 4-5: In the Save As dialog box, click the Selection Chart button, choose a filename and destination folder and then click save.

3. Click the Selection Chart option button in the dialog box.

4. Select a folder in the Save In box to which you want to save your file.

5. Enter a filename for your chart in the File Name box, and click Save.

You can now import the file into your FrontPage Web, and use it in Web pages.

Save Excel workbooks as folders

You can convert an Excel workbook with two or more tabs into a set of Web files. When you do, Excel simulates a tabbed workbook that can be used to create a familiar format for Web visitors who are used to looking up information in spreadsheets, as shown in Figure 4-6.

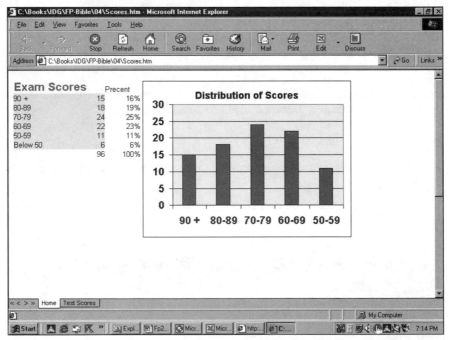

Figure 4-6: Excel can be used to generate framed Web pages that look like workbooks.

To generate an Excel-based Web, follow these steps:

1. Open an Excel workbook.

2. Select File ➪ Save as Web Page.

3. Select the Entire Workbook option button.

4. Navigate to the folder to which you want to save the generated Web files, and then click Save to save the entire workbook, or click Publish to save selected elements of the workbook.

As you save or publish your workbook as a Web "page," a set of files are generated in a separate folder, which uses the name of your file followed by an underscore and the word "files." So, for example, if you save a workbook called Scores as a Web "page," a folder is created called Scores_files. That folder includes several files required for a Web site that is based on your file. In addition, an HTM file is created in the parent directory (the one to which you saved your file in the Save As dialog box), with the name of the file (for example, Scores.htm).

When you import this generated Excel Web into FrontPage, you need both the HTM file generated in the folder that you specify in the Save As dialog box *and* all the files in the additional (_files) folder.

Moving from PowerPoint to FrontPage

PowerPoint in Office 2000 converts slide shows to HTML pages when you select File ➪ Save as Web Page. As with Excel, a whole batch of files, including HTML and image files, is generated when you do this conversion, and, in fact, rather than saving a "file" to a "page," you save many files to a folder filled with Web pages and other files.

The folders generated by PowerPoint don't mesh well with FrontPage Web sites. Basically, PowerPoint gives you a highly specialized Web site with complex page designs and links. Use PowerPoint's Save as Web Page option if you want a seamless slideshow on your Web site, as shown in Figure 4-7.

Figure 4-7: PowerPoint can generate animated Web sites.

You don't have to convert an entire PowerPoint slideshow to a Web site. If you want only a single slide, you can save that slide as a GIF or JPEG (or PNG) image. These picture files can then be added to a Web page just like any other image from a file.

To save a single slide as an image file, follow these steps:

1. Open the slideshow and the slide that you want to convert to a graphic file.

2. With the slide in view, select File ➪ Save As. The Save As dialog box opens.

3. From the Save as Type drop-down list, select an image file format, such as JPEG or GIF.

4. Navigate to a file folder and enter a filename in the File Name box.

5. Click the Save button.

6. When prompted with a dialog box that asks "Do you want to export every slide in the presentation" click No. You will save only the slide that you are viewing.

Importing Files Into Webs

Each of the applications in Office 2000 that hs been examined thus far can be used to generate HTML files, and other Web files as well. You can use FrontPage's Import menu to integrate these generated Web pages or Web sites into FrontPage.

In many cases, the examples discussed for different applications generated not just an HTML file or a GIF graphic file, but a whole folder full of Web files. In that case, you can use the Folder option in the Import dialog box.

To import a file or folder with Office Web files into FrontPage, follow these steps:

1. With a Web already created, select File ➪ Import. The Import dialog box appears.

2. Click the Add File button to import one or more files, or click the Add Folder button to import an entire folder with files.

Note   If you import a folder, that folder becomes a folder in your FrontPage Web, and the files within it are kept together in the folder.

3. You can use the Add File and/or the Add Folder buttons as often as you want, until you have selected all the files and/or folders that you want to import. The Import dialog box with both a file and a folder selected is shown in Figure 4-8.

4. After you select your files, click OK in the Import dialog box to copy files to your Web server or FrontPage Web folder.

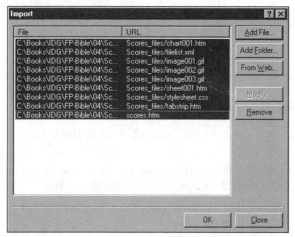

Figure 4-8: Many Office-generated Web sites are imported as entire folders.

If you are creating a *new* Web site from files generated by an Office 2000 application, you can select File ➪ New ➪ Web and double-click the Import Web Wizard in the New dialog box.

The Import Web Wizard walks you through the process of selecting a folder to import. You can also use the Import dialog box to add files to a Web generated from imported files.

The following tutorial requires a minimal knowledge of Word and Excel. If you can create a simple document in Word and a small spreadsheet and graph in Excel, you can test the ability of FrontPage to integrate these files into a Web site.

Tutorial 4.1: Bring Word and Excel Files into a Web Site

1. Create a document in Word with text at the top of the page that says **Welcome to My Web Site**. Add a line of text with your name.

2. Assign a Heading 1 style to the top line of text, and a Heading 2 style to your name.

3. Add a paragraph of text below your name. Assign formatting to the text, such as boldface, italic, font styles, and colors. Center all the text.

4. Select File ➪ Save as Web Page. Create a new folder called **Web Files**, and name the file index. Click Save.

5. Create a new Excel workbook. In cell A1, enter **Visitors this year**. In cells A2, A3, and A4, enter **January**, **February**, and **March**, respectively. In cells B2, B3, and B4, enter numbers.

6. Click and drag to select cells A2..B4 and click the Chart Wizard button in the toolbar. In the first Chart Wizard dialog box, click Finish to accept the default chart settings.

7. Leave Excel open. In FrontPage, select File ➪ New ➪ Web. Enter a filename for your Web in the "Specify the location of the new web" box of the New dialog box.

8. Double-click the Import Web Wizard icon in the New dialog box.

9. Select the From a Source Directory of Files option button in the Import Web Wizard dialog box.

10. Click the Browse button and navigate to the folder in which you saved your Word file (Index.htm). Click OK in the Browse for Folder dialog box.

11. Click Next. The Edit File List dialog box displays all the files in the folder, as shown in Figure 4-9. Click Next, and then Finish.

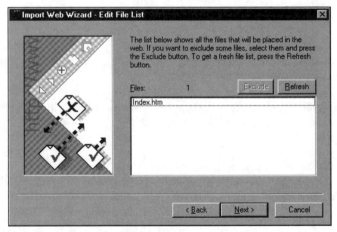

Figure 4-9: Selecting files to import

12. Switch to Navigation view. Your imported Word file has become your home page. Double-click it to open the page in Page view.

13. Switch back to Excel. Select cells A1..B4 and choose Edit ➪ Copy.

14. Switch to FrontPage, and in Page view, click to set the insertion point in your open Web page. Select Edit ➪ Paste to insert the cells.

15. Save the Web page. The embedded chart will be saved as an image file.

The copied spreadsheet cells became a table in FrontPage. Working with tables is explored in Chapter 9. The copied chart became an embedded image file, which is explored in depth in Chapter 7. Because you will lose some table and graphic formatting by copying, if you use these Office elements, you'll want to refer to those chapters so that you can format the copied table and image.

From FrontPage to Office

The discussion thus far has focused on how to create Web page content in Office and transfer it into FrontPage Web pages. You can also collect information in FrontPage and send it to text or spreadsheet files that will be stored at your Web server.

Collecting data from input forms requires some advanced FrontPage skills that are covered in Chapters 14 and 15. This section takes only a quick look at input forms from the perspective of collecting data that can be used in a spreadsheet or text file.

Even before you examine how to create your own custom input forms, you can begin to experiment with the Feedback Form page template, which contains a premade input form.

Sending data to Word mailmerge files

You can create an input form by using the page template with an input form (using the Feedback Form page template or the Registration Form template, for example). With a Web open, select File ➪ New ➪ Page and double-click one of the templates with an input form. The input forms are filled with different text and input fields, and are surrounded by a dashed line.

To create an input form that sends data to a DOC file, follow these steps:

1. With a form on your page, right-click anywhere in the form (within the dashed lines) and select Form Properties from the context menu. The Form Properties dialog box appears.

2. Click the Send To option button and enter a filename with a *.doc filename extension (for example, Registration.doc). Figure 4-10 shows the Form Properties dialog box.

3. After you name the target file (the DOC file is important), click the Options button in the dialog box and pull down the File Format list. Choose Text Database Using Tab As Separator.

4. Click OK.

5. Save your Web page.

You can test your input form by clicking the Preview in Browser button and entering information in the input form. After you do, click the Submit button.

You will see your DOC file in Folder view (you may have to press the F5 function key to refresh the Folder view). As data is saved to your DOC file, you can open the file in Word by double-clicking it. With fields separated by tabs, you can use this file as a mailmerge data file in Word.

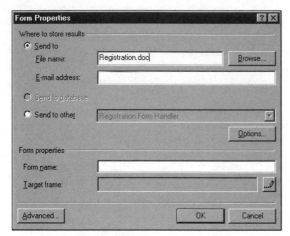

Figure 4-10: Sending input to a Word file

Sending data to Excel

You can save data to files that will open in Excel by using the same procedure previously outlined for saving to a Word file. The only difference is that your filename should have an *.xls extension (for example, Registration.xls). When you save tab-delimited text to an Excel file, you can open that file in Excel by double-clicking it.

Figure 4-11 shows an XLS file created from input data.

Adding Office Components to Web Pages

Spreadsheets, PivotTables, and graphs can be added to FrontPage Web pages as interactive elements. Visitors who have Office 2000 installed on their systems can come to your Web site, enter data in a table, see calculations made, and watch a graph display their input.

Interactive PivotTables can be placed in Web pages. PivotTables summarize information from spreadsheet or database tables and are somewhat complex. But, if your visitors want to synthesize data from a database live at your Web site, you can provide the tools to do that.

Office components are a new feature of FrontPage 2000. They hold intriguing potential for creating truly interactive Web sites, in which visitors enter data and see it calculated and graphed. At this point, however, access to these features is limited to the most recent versions of Internet Explorer *and* to visitors who have Office 2000 installed on their Web sites. Those constraints limit the usefulness of these features to closely defined environments, such as an organizational intranet where everyone has Office 2000 installed.

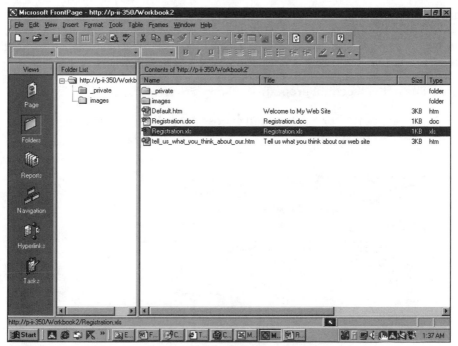

Figure 4-11: Double-click an XLS file in Folder view to open the file in Excel.

Caution   Office components can be used only by visitors who have Office 2000 installed on their computers. Office components do have a box in their Properties dialog boxes to allow you to divert other users to another Web page.

Adding Office spreadsheets

You can use an interactive spreadsheet element to let visitors to your Web site make all kinds of calculations. For example, you can create a worksheet on which a visitor can calculate the cost of his or her purchase, including sales tax. You can protect some cells, and leave others open for visitor input.

To place a spreadsheet on your Web page, follow these steps:

1. Open a Web page.
2. Select Insert ➪ Component ➪ Office Spreadsheet.
3. Click and drag on side or corner handles to resize the spreadsheet.

Define ActiveX control properties

Some attributes of your spreadsheet can be controlled in the ActiveX Control Properties dialog box. These properties include alignment (such as left or right), borders, and spacing around the spreadsheet.

To define ActiveX control properties, follow these steps:

1. Right-click the spreadsheet and choose ActiveX Control Properties. The ActiveX Control Properties dialog box is shown in Figure 4-12.

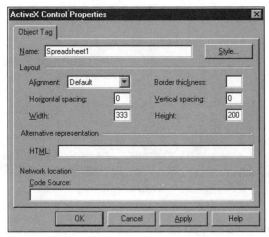

Figure 4-12: Use the ActiveX Control Properties dialog box to define how your spreadsheet will be displayed.

2. Use the dialog box to define any of the following attributes:

   ✦ **Name:** Relevant if you plan to link the spreadsheet to a chart (see "Adding Office Charts," later in this chapter).

   ✦ **Width** and **Height:** Use to define the size of the spreadsheet. This is an alternative way to size the spreadsheet (you can also resize in Page view by clicking and dragging sizing handles).

   ✦ **Left** or **Right alignment:** Use to let text flow around the spreadsheet. (For more on alignment, see the discussion of image properties in Chapter 7.)

   ✦ **Horizontal Spacing** and **Vertical Spacing:** Use to define buffer space between the table and page text.

   ✦ **Border Thickness:** Use to define the width of a border around the spreadsheet.

   ✦ **HTML:** Enter the URL of a Web page that displays if a visitor's browser doesn't support interactive spreadsheets.

3. After you define properties, click Apply in the dialog box.

Define spreadsheet properties

You can enter text, values, and formulas the same way that you do in Excel. Many other Excel functions are also available, using the collapsible Spreadsheet Property Toolbox. Some, but not all, of these property controls can be made available for visitors. For example, visitors can be allowed to enter data into cells and change cell formatting, but visitors cannot be given access to features such as Protection (a feature that defines which cells, if any, a visitor can change).

The Spreadsheet Property Toolbox, as it appears to visitors using Internet Explorer 5.0 and higher, is shown in Figure 4-13.

Figure 4-13: Most of the formatting attributes available in Excel are stashed in the Spreadsheet Property Toolbox and can be made available to visitors who have Office 2000 on their computers.

The General, Format, Show/Hide, Calculations, and Find sections of the Spreadsheet Property Toolbox are available in browser windows, while the Import Data, Protection, Title Bar, and Advanced sections are not. For example, you can elect to protect some cells in your worksheet from visitor entries, but defining protection is not available to visitors.

A detailed description of all the features of the Spreadsheet Property Toolbox would really require a book about Microsoft Excel, but here is a quick overview of the features available in each section:

✦ **General:** Has an Undo and a Help button.

✦ **Format:** Has a fairly full-featured Formatting toolbar for defining font type, style, size, and color. Other boxes in this section refine cell display. Of particular usefulness is the Number Format drop-down list that includes currency and date formats.

✦ **Show/Hide:** Enables you to display or conceal the toolbar, gridlines, the title bar, and column and/or row headings (the column numbers and row letters).

✦ **Calculations:** Enables you to define automatic or manual calculations for your spreadsheet. Automatic calculations recalculate whenever a relevant cell's contents are changed. Manual calculations recalculate formulas only when you (or a visitor) clicks the Calculate Now button.

✦ **Find:** Enables you or a visitor to search for a text string in the spreadsheet.

✦ **Import Data:** Enables you to import data from another Web site.

✦ **Protection:** Enables you to deny permission for visitors to change some or all cells. This is useful if you want to let a visitor plug information in *some* cells, but not all. The Allow Property Toolbox at Runtime check box lets you turn off access by visitors to the toolbox.

✦ **Title Bar:** Enables you to change the default title bar text (from "Microsoft Office Spreadsheet") and assign your own formatting.

✦ **Advanced:** Enables you to define spreadsheet properties, such as what happens when a visitor enters data in a cell and presses Enter, or whether to provide vertical and horizontal scroll bars in the spreadsheet display.

For an example of defining a spreadsheet component, see Tutorial 4.2 at the end of this chapter.

Adding Office charts

Office charts can be linked to embedded spreadsheets in FrontPage. These charts then interactively display spreadsheet content.

To link a chart to a spreadsheet, follow these steps:

1. Start by creating an embedded spreadsheet in a Web page (see instructions in the previous section).

2. Select Insert ➪ Component ➪ Office Chart. The Office Chart Wizard appears, as shown in Figure 4-14.

3. In Step 1 of the Office Chart Wizard, select a chart type. Then click Next.

4. In Step 2 of the Chart Wizard, select the name of the chart from which you are graphing data. (For an explanation of how to name a chart, refer to "Define ActiveX control properties," earlier in this chapter.) Then click Next.

5. In Step 3 of the wizard, click the Set this Chart's Data in One Step icon at the top of the wizard window. The Data Range dialog box appears, as shown in Figure 4-15.

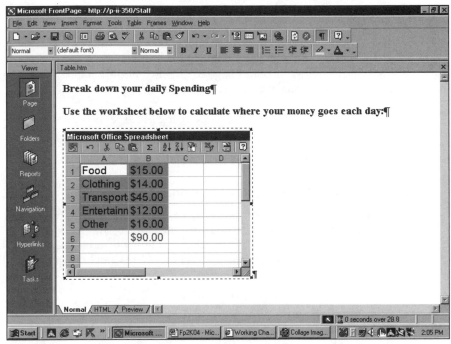

Figure 4-14: To create an interactive online chart, start by creating a graphable spreadsheet.

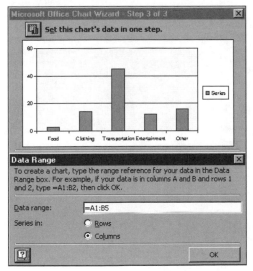

Figure 4-15: Selecting a range of cells to chart

6. In the Data Range field of the Data Range dialog box, enter a range of cells that you want to graph from the worksheet (for example A1:B5). Then, select the Rows or Columns option button to determine how your data will be graphed. The results are previewed in the wizard window.

7. Click OK to close the Data Range dialog box, and then click Finish to close the wizard and generate the chart.

You can resize a chart by selecting it and using the side or corner handles to change the size. Other chart properties are defined in the Chart Property toolbox.

To change chart properties, follow these steps:

1. Right-click in the chart and select Property Toolbox.

2. Click different parts of the chart to change the toolbox options interactively. For example, if you click the chart legend, the legend properties are displayed. Alternately, you can select an element of the chart from the drop-down list, just below the General section of the Chart Property Toolbox, as shown in Figure 4-16.

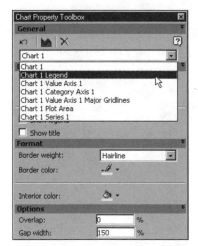

Figure 4-16: The Chart Property Toolbox can be used to format different elements of a chart.

3. Each chart element has its own array of formatting options and controls that you can explore and experiment with. The General section of the Chart Property Toolbox is always available. The three buttons located there are the following:

✦ Undo allows you to undo changes.

✦ The Delete button deletes a selected element of a chart.

✦ The Chart Type button opens a gallery of chart types (bar, column, pie, line, area, and so on) and allows you to change the type of chart.

4. To change the actual data displayed in the chart, change the entries in the charted spreadsheet cells.

After you create a linked chart, you — or visitors — can enter data in the spreadsheet and see it graphed in the chart. Figure 4-17 shows a chart working interactively in a browser.

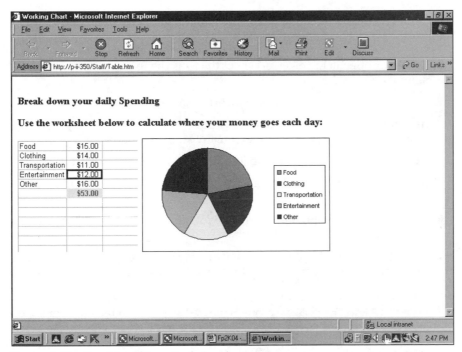

Figure 4-17: Graphing interactively in a browser

Caution   Again, remember that your visitors must have Office 2000 installed to enjoy the ability to use Office 2000 spreadsheets and linked charts.

Creating Office PivotTables

Of the three interactive Office components that you can use in a Web page, PivotTables are the most complex. First, PivotTables themselves are fairly complex. A full discussion of PivotTables is quite a bit beyond the scope of this discussion, but in short, *PivotTables* summarize data from a table. So, for example, if you have a list of 500 orders for 12 products, and the dates the orders were placed, a PivotTable could summarize how many orders had been placed for each of the 12 products. Or, the PivotTable could be used to total how many orders had been placed each day.

Assuming that you and your visitors are comfortable designing and manipulating fields in a PivotTable, you can create an interactive PivotTable that summarizes data in an Excel file or Access database table.

Connect a PivotTable to an Excel data source

Connecting a PivotTable to an Excel data source is no simple process, but we will walk you through it step by step. As we do, we have to acknowledge the help of Michael Stowe at Microsoft Tech Support in finding our way through the challenging maze of implementing an interactive PivotTable.

To generate an interactive online PivotTable from an Excel spreadsheet, follow these steps:

1. Create or open in Excel a worksheet that has the information you want to summarize in your PivotTable.

2. Select the data and then choose Insert ⇨ Name ⇨ Define.

3. Assign a range name (for example, "Data"). You might want to jot down the range name, because you'll need it many steps from now.

4. Save the Excel file and note the filename and folder to which it is saved.

5. In Page view, open the FrontPage Web page in which you will insert the PivotTable.

6. Select Insert ⇨ Component ⇨ Office PivotTable. A blank PivotTable appears in Page view.

7. Click the Property Toolbox button (the only active button in the PivotTable toolbar) to open the PivotTable Property Toolbox, shown in Figure 4-18.

Figure 4-18: Buried in the PivotTable Property Toolbox are the elements needed to connect your PivotTable to a data source.

8. Activate the Data Source panel in the toolbox. Click the Connection options button, and then click the Connection Editor button. The Data Link Properties dialog box appears, as shown in Figure 4-19.

9. Click the Provider tab in the Data Link Properties dialog box. Select Microsoft OLE DB Provider for OBDC Drivers.

10. Click the Connection tab.

11. Click the Use Connection String options button and then click the Build button. The Select Data Source dialog box appears. Select the Machine Data Source tab and click the Next button.

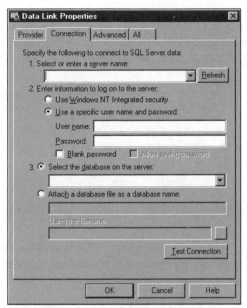

Figure 4-19: The Data Link Properties dialog box holds the key to connecting your PivotTable to data in a file.

12. In the Create New Data Source dialog box, select Microsoft Excel Driver (*.xls), and then click the Next button.

13. Click Finish. The ODBC Microsoft Excel Setup dialog box appears, as shown in Figure 4-20.

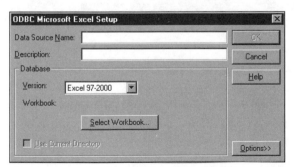

Figure 4-20: The final Create New Data Source dialog box displays your data source definition.

14. Click the Select Workbook button. The Select Workbook dialog box appears. Use the Browse button to navigate to your saved Excel workbook that has the named range that will be used in the PivotTable. Double-click the file. Enter a Data Source name (this can be any name that you make up). Then, click OK in the ODBC Microsoft Excel Setup dialog box.

15. Click OK. Your named data source file should be selected in the Machine Data Source tab of the dialog box. Click OK again to close the dialog box.

16. Click OK to return to the Connection tab in the Data Link Properties dialog box. Click the Use Data Source Name options button and then click the Refresh button.

17. Select Excel Files from the Use Data Source Name drop-down list and then click OK. You are now back at the PivotTable Property Toolbox, and almost ready to connect your spreadsheet to an online interactive PivotTable. Hang in there for just one more step.

18. Click the Command Text options button, and in the Command Text field, type **select * from [range name]**, where [range name] is the name that you assigned to the Excel workbook range in Step 3. Press Enter.

If you successfully linked your data to a database, you will see a blank PivotTable, like the one shown in Figure 4-21.

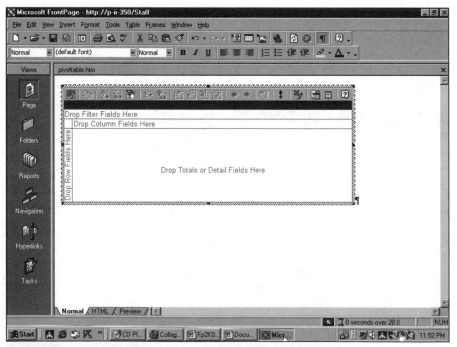

Figure 4-21: A PivotTable, ready for data fields to be assigned.

Define a PivotTable from source data

After your PivotTable control is connected to an Excel data source, you can use the Field List button in the PivotTable toolbar to add fields to the PivotTable display. Every PivotTable requires at least one Row or Column field, and at least one Total or Detail Field. If you're inexperienced with PivotTables, you can experiment.

The basic concept is to summarize data by sorting it into categories. For example, if you wrote books for a dozen publishers over the last four years, you could produce a PivotTable listing how many books you wrote for each publisher each year, by making Year the column field, Publisher the Row field, and Books Written the Detail field.

To add fields to a PivotTable, follow these steps:

1. Click the Field List button in the PivotTable toolbar to display a list of fields in your database.

2. Drag one of the fields into the Drop Column Fields Here area of the PivotTable, and drag one field into the Drop Row Fields Here area, as shown in Figure 4-22.

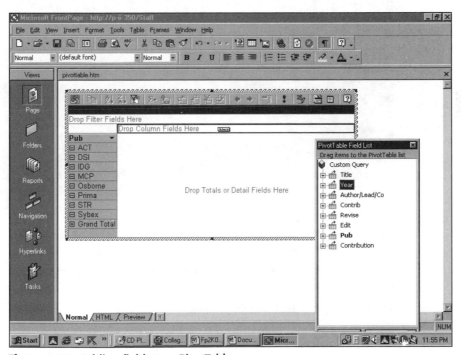

Figure 4-22: Adding fields to a PivotTable

3. You must have at least one field in the Detail area (in the middle of the PivotTable), so drag a field from the Field list into the middle of the PivotTable.

4. After you define your PivotTable, you can close the PivotTable Field List dialog box. Note that each field has a drop-down list associated with it. Use the check boxes in these drop-down lists to filter your PivotTable results, as shown in Figure 4-23.

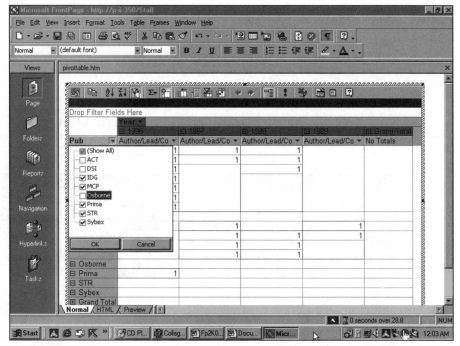

Figure 4-23: Filtering a PivotTable enables you to fine-tune your analysis of data.

5. You can remove fields by right-clicking them and selecting Remove Field from the context menu.

6. To calculate (count, sum, find maximum or minimum value), right-click a field in the Detail area and select Autosum.

7. To subtotal a field, right-click the Autosum.

8. Use the Show/Hide area of the PivotTable Property Toolbox to define which elements of the PivotTable to make available to visitors who use the PivotTable at your Web site. If you allow Expand Indicators, visitors can click the "+" and "-" symbols to expand and contract categories.

After you define your PivotTable, save your Web page and preview it in Internet Explorer to test it. Figure 4-24 shows an interactive PivotTable in Internet Explorer.

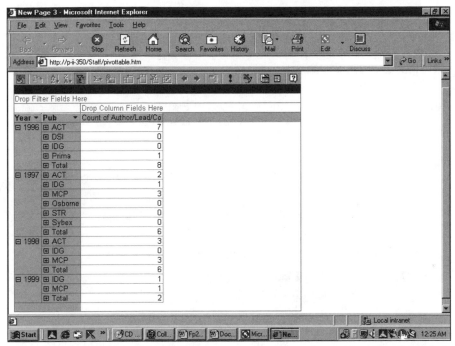

Figure 4-24: Visitors can do their own synthesis of your data with a PivotTable in Internet Explorer — as long as they have Office 2000 installed.

In the following tutorial, you'll add a spreadsheet to a Web page.

Tutorial 4.2: Implement an Office Spreadsheet Component

1. Open an existing FrontPage Web or create a new one. Open a Web page in Page view.

2. Enter the following title text on the page, **See How Much of Your time You Spend Commuting**, and then press Enter.

3. Select Insert ➪ Component ➪ Office Spreadsheet.

4. Click in cell A1 of the spreadsheet and enter **How many hours do you spend commuting?** Press Enter.

5. In cell A3 of the spreadsheet, enter **=A2/24**.

6. Click the Spreadsheet Property Toolbox button in the spreadsheet component. In the Format area, select Percent from the Number Format drop-down list.

7. In the Protection section of the Spreadsheet Property Toolbox, click to select the Enable Protection check box.

8. Click in cell A2 and deselect the Lock Cells check box.

9. Close the Spreadsheet Property Toolbox. Save the file, and preview it in Internet Explorer.

10. While testing the spreadsheet in Internet Explorer, attempt to enter text in cell A1. Try to enter a number in cell A3. You should see a warning like the one shown in Figure 4-25.

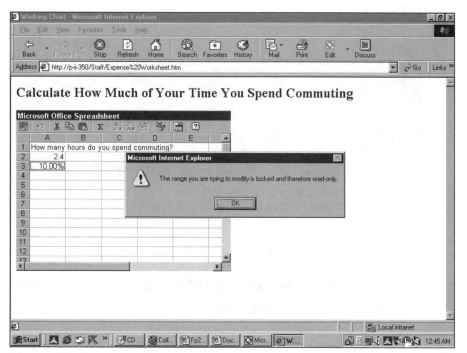

Figure 4-25: You can lock cells in a spreadsheet so that visitors can enter data only in cells that you designate to accept input.

Summary

In this chapter, you explored a variety of ways that FrontPage 2000 can interact with Office 2000. You saw that Web site elements created in Excel, PowerPoint, Word, and Publisher can be integrated into FrontPage Web sites. You also saw that data collected through input forms in FrontPage can be sent to files that can be opened in Word or Excel.

This chapter also explored the three Office components that can be added to Web pages. These components can be complex to define, and their recognition is limited to visitors to your Web site who have Office 2000 installed on their computers. Within those limitations, Office spreadsheets, charts, and PivotTables can provide an unusual amount of interactivity to your Web site.

This chapter concludes Part I of this book. In this part, you learned to create complex Web sites that integrate many page elements, and you learned to publish them to Web servers. In Part II of this book, you will explore many ways to enhance the appearance and usefulness of your Web site by customizing Themes, formatting text, editing pictures, and creating your own custom graphics.

✦　　✦　　✦

Enhancing the Look and Feel

Web Themes and Navigation

In Chapter 1, you learned to apply an instant, consistent look and feel to your Web site with a Theme. In this chapter, you learn to unleash the real power of Themes — the ability to create a custom Theme and apply a unique motif to your Web site. You also learn to control shared borders and navigation bars, two other tools that provide cohesiveness and coherence to your Web site.

Customizing FrontPage Themes

In Chapter 1, you learned to select a Theme and apply it to your Web site. This section outlines which elements are actually created by Themes, so that you can customize those elements. Theme elements are generally divided into three categories:

- ✦ **Colors**: Includes the color assigned to text and the colors assigned to graphic elements, such as buttons and horizontal lines.

- ✦ **Graphics**: Includes the images used for buttons, page background, horizontal rules, and bullets.

- ✦ **Styles**: Includes creating customized font styles in the Themes dialog box, which act in much the same way as styles in a word processing or desktop publishing program, with defined attributes such as font type, size, and color.

To define a customized Theme, select Format ➪ Theme from any view, and then click the Modify button in the Themes dialog box. The Colors, Graphics, Styles, and Save As buttons are displayed, as shown in Figure 5-1.

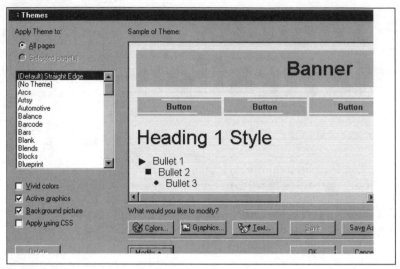

Figure 5-1: You can customize Themes by changing colors, graphics, and paragraph font styles.

Your list of available Themes depends on several factors, including whether you elected to install all the FrontPage Themes during installation, and whether you downloaded additional Themes from the FrontPage Web site. You can find links to those additional Themes (and to Themes sold by third-party vendors) at www.ppinet.com/resource.htm.

When you select a Theme from the list in the Themes dialog box, you see a preview of the Theme in the Sample of Theme window on the right. You can refine a selected Theme by making selections in the Vivid Colors, Active Graphics, and Background Picture check boxes, located in the lower-left corner of the Themes dialog box. As you select, or deselect, these check boxes, the Sample of Theme window reflects changes to the page attributes.

Below the three check boxes just described is the Apply Theme Using CSS check box, which enables you to attach an HTML-coded Cascading Style Sheet (CSS) file. (For a full discussion of Cascading Style Sheets, see Chapter 12.)

The first step in creating a custom Theme is to select a Theme that is close to the appearance that you want. After you select an existing Theme, click the Modify button in the Themes dialog box. Now, you're ready to start designing a unique set of colors, text styles, and graphic elements for your Web site.

Changing Theme colors

Before you start to modify your color scheme, you should decide whether you want to assign a page background color or image to your Web site. If you want to define a page background *color,* make sure that you deselect the Background Picture check box in the Themes dialog box before you begin to create a custom Theme. Figure 5-2 shows a Theme selected without a background image.

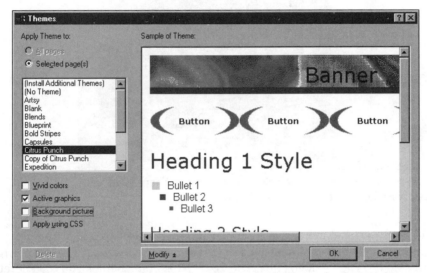

Figure 5-2: You can define a custom background color or background image for your Theme — but not both.

To modify a color scheme, click the Modify button in the Themes dialog box, and then click the Color button. A new dialog box appears with three tabs: Color Schemes, Color Wheel, and Custom.

The Color Schemes tab enables you to substitute the color scheme of a different Theme for the selected Theme. So, for example, if you like the graphics that come with the Citrus Punch Theme, but you prefer the color scheme in the Neon Theme, you can assign the Citrus Theme, but select the Neon color scheme. Figure 5-3 shows the Neon color scheme being grafted onto the Citrus Punch Theme.

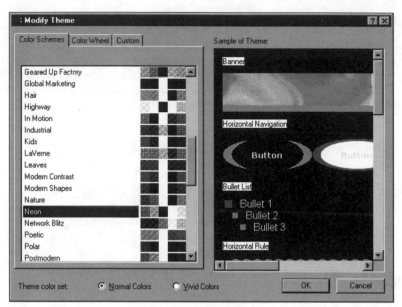

Figure 5-3: You can combine the color scheme of one Theme with the graphics of another to create a custom Theme.

Switching color schemes from one Theme to another gives you some ability to customize your Theme color scheme. For even more options, click the Color Wheel tab in the Modify Theme dialog box. The Color Wheel tab enables you to generate an aesthetically matched five-color color scheme to apply to your Theme. It's kind of like hiring an interior decorator for your home or office, and telling him or her that you want a color scheme for your location built around the color blue, aqua, orange, and so on. To generate a color scheme, click the Color Wheel tab in the Modify Themes dialog box. You'll see the Color Wheel, as shown in Figure 5-4.

To adjust the colors in your customized color scheme, change the setting of the Brightness slider. As you experiment with color schemes and brightness levels, you'll see the results previewed in the Sample of Theme area of the dialog box. You can also toggle between intense colors and muted colors by using the Normal Colors or Vivid Colors radio buttons, located at the bottom of the dialog box. Both options will be available after you complete your customized Theme.

For the most complete control over your Theme color scheme, you can use the Custom tab in the Modify Theme dialog box. The Custom tab is shown in Figure 5-5.

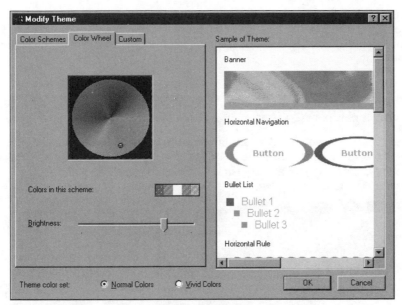

Figure 5-4: The Color Wheel generates a color scheme based on the selected color.

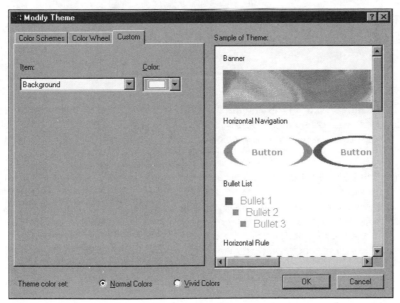

Figure 5-5: For total control over colors in your Theme, use the Custom tab of the Modify Theme dialog box.

With the Custom tab selected, pull down the Item drop-down list and select the page element (Background, for example) or the type of text to which you want to assign a color. Then, click the Color drop-down list and select a color to assign to that text element.

What About Custom Colors?

When you open the Color palette in the Custom tab of the Modify Themes dialog box, in addition to the 16 preset colors, you'll see a More Colors option. Click the More Colors option to open the Colors dialog box, shown in the following figure.

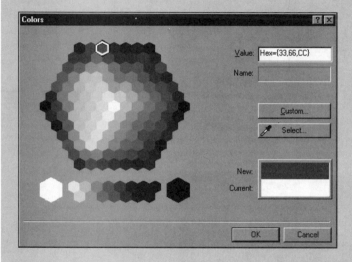

Assign a color by clicking a color in the palette. If you are an experienced professional Web designer working from your own palette of hexadecimal color values, you can select a color by entering a hexadecimal (six-character) color code in the Value field, in the format Hex={xx,xx,xx} (for example, Hex={FF,00,00} for bright red).

The colors in the palette in the Colors tab can be interpreted by the current generation of Web browsers. Sometimes, these colors are referred to as *browser safe*. If you mix up your own colors by using the palette that appears when you click the Custom button, browsers will do their best to reproduce these colors by mixing, or *dithering*, pixels of the 216 available colors to simulate your color, with varying degrees of success. In short, no guarantee exists that the custom colors that you mix up will be accurately displayed by browsers.

After you assign colors to your Theme elements, click OK in the dialog box. You'll return to the main Themes dialog box, and you can now define custom font styles and graphics for your Theme.

After you modify the color scheme of your customized Theme, click the OK button in the Modify Theme dialog box.

Modifying Theme graphics

Themes can be used to orchestrate several different graphic elements on your Web site, including the following:

✦ Background images

✦ Banners

✦ Bulleted list graphic icons

✦ Global navigation buttons

✦ Horizontal navigation buttons

✦ Horizontal rules

✦ Quick Home button

✦ Quick Next button

✦ Quick Previous button

✦ Vertical navigation buttons

These graphics (most of them navigation buttons) are generated in either your Web pages or your navigation bars. You can assign custom images for each of these elements in your Theme. You can also change the font of the text that is added to these images.

To customize Theme graphics, click the Graphics button in the Themes dialog box. A Modify Theme dialog box opens, as shown in Figure 5-6.

Most graphic elements include both images and text. Navigational buttons, for instance, consist of a graphical button and button text. Some graphic elements, such as the background page color, don't have text, so you don't need to define text fonts for them.

To define text for a graphic element, select the Font tab of the dialog box. In Figure 5-7, 24-point, Impact, bold font has been assigned to horizontal navigation buttons.

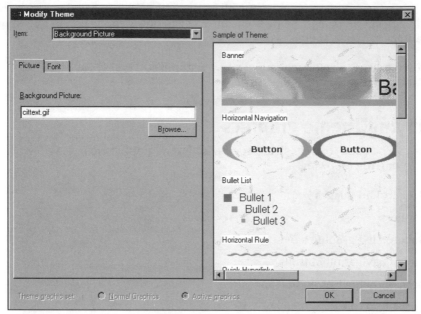

Figure 5-6: You can change the graphic images that are assigned with a Theme.

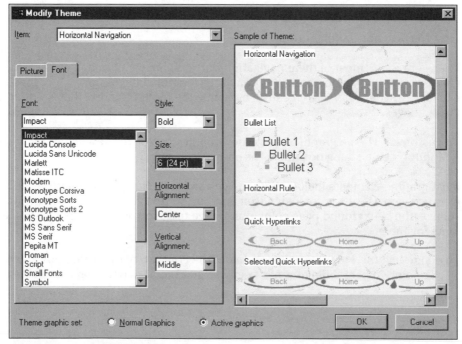

Figure 5-7: Defining a big, bold, brassy font for horizontal navigation buttons

Note Font sizes and types for navigation buttons are controlled in the Graphics Modify Theme dialog box, but font colors are assigned in the Colors tab.

Customizing Theme styles

You can create a customized font style sheet right in the Themes dialog box. The Modify Theme dialog box, opened by clicking the Styles button, lets you define font characteristics of standard HTML styles (such as Heading 1, Heading 2, and so forth) or define your own styles.

To define a style, click the Styles button in the Themes dialog box. The dialog box shown in Figure 5-8 appears.

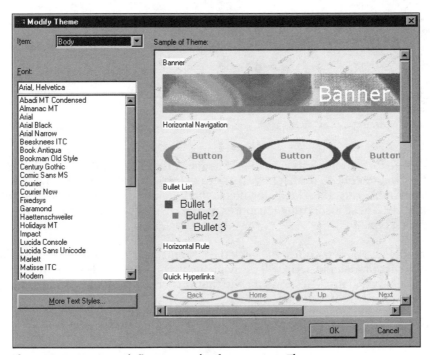

Figure 5-8: You can define text styles for a custom Theme.

Selecting a font for an existing style

You can define a font for a standard HTML style by first selecting that style (Heading 1, for example) from the Item drop-down menu in the Modify Theme dialog box. Then, click one of the fonts in the Font list. You can use the vertical scroll bar to see more fonts, if necessary.

Defining a new style for a Theme

You can also use the Styles button in the Modify Themes dialog box to define a new style and assign font type, size, color, and even paragraph formatting. To do this, click the More Styles button. Then, in the Style dialog box, click the New button. The New Style dialog box appears, as shown in Figure 5-9.

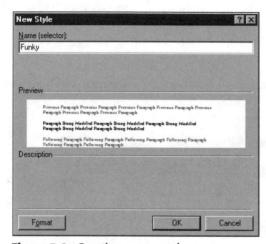

Figure 5-9: Creating a new style

Enter a name for your new style in the Name (selector) field, and then click the Format button to choose from four categories of formatting—Font, Paragraph, Border, or Numbering. Use the dialog boxes that open to define different attributes for your style. These formatting attributes will be displayed in the Preview window of the dialog box.

After you define your custom style, click the OK button in the New Style dialog box. Your new, custom-defined style will be available in the list of styles to edit in the Style dialog box. Figure 5-10 shows a style that was created as part of a custom Theme applied in FrontPage Page view.

After you assign custom fonts to different styles, click the OK button to close this dialog box and return to the Themes dialog box.

Figure 5-10: Custom styles are available whenever you apply a custom Theme to which they are assigned.

Saving a custom Theme

After you define a custom Theme, you can save it and reuse it on other Web sites. This is a powerful feature of FrontPage 2000 that enables you to do such things as create a Theme for your organization or corporation and then implement it on all of its Web sites.

To save a custom Theme and add it to the list of available Themes, click the Save As button in the Themes dialog box. The Save Theme dialog box appears, as shown in Figure 5-11. Enter a new, descriptive Theme name in the Enter New Theme Title field, and click OK.

Figure 5-11: Saving a custom Theme

After you save a Theme, it appears in your Themes list. You can apply that Theme to any Web site, and when you do, all the elements of that Theme, including customized styles, are available.

In the following tutorial, you will design your own custom Theme, including a custom background color, custom color scheme, and navigational buttons.

Tutorial 5.1: Design and Apply a Custom Theme

1. Open an existing FrontPage Web, or create a new one by using the Personal Web template.

2. Select Format ➪ Theme to open the Theme dialog box.

3. Click the Spiral Theme in the list of Themes, and click the Modify button in the dialog box to display the three modification buttons.

4. Click the Colors button, and click the Custom tab in the Modify Theme dialog box.

5. Click the Normal Colors radio button.

6. Choose Heading 1 from the Item drop-down list, and select Maroon from the Color palette, as shown in Figure 5-12.

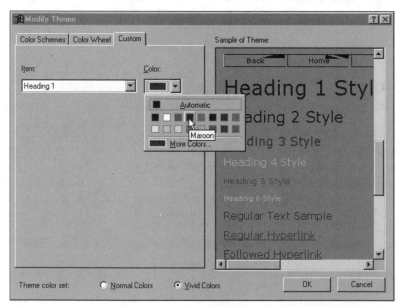

Figure 5-12: Assigning a color to Heading 1 for a custom Theme

7. In the same manner as Step 6, assign blue to hyperlinks and yellow to background.

8. Click the OK button in the dialog box.

9. Click the Graphics button. Select Global Navigational Buttons from the Item drop-down list, and click the Font tab in the dialog box. Select a font from the Font list, and 14 point from the Size list. Click OK.

10. Click the Styles button, and select Heading 1 from the Item drop-down menu. Click AdLib BT in the Font list, and note the display in the Sample of Theme window. Assign the same font that you assigned in Step 9 to Heading 2 and Heading 3. Click OK.

11. Click the Save As button in the Themes dialog box, and enter a new name for the Theme (make up your own name). Click OK.

12. Test your new Theme: Click OK in the Themes dialog box to apply your new custom Theme. Note the appearance of headings in your Web pages, the color of hyperlinks, and the page background.

13. If you don't want to save this custom Theme, select your new Theme in the Themes dialog box, click the Delete button, and then click Yes in the next dialog box.

Customizing Shared Borders

When you create a Web site from a template, FrontPage automatically generates *navigation bars*, which are placed in files called *shared borders*. Shared borders are separate Web page files (up to four per Web site) that are embedded in the top, right, left, and/or bottom of pages in a Web site.

Defining shared borders

To define shared borders, select Format ➪ Shared Borders. The Shared Borders dialog box, shown in Figure 5-13, has check boxes that enable you to assign shared borders to the Top, Right, Left, or Bottom of your pages. If you select Top or Left, and you haven't defined navigation bars, you can use the check boxes that appear to assign navigation buttons to either or both of these borders.

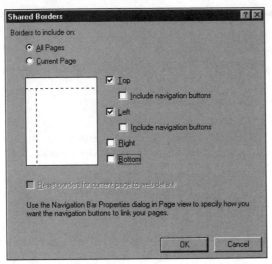

Figure 5-13: Shared borders can be on the side, top, or bottom of a page — or any combination thereof.

Adding navigation buttons to bottom and right borders

The Shared Borders dialog box enables you to assign navigation buttons to the top and left borders, but it doesn't enable you to assign navigation buttons to the bottom or right borders. However, you can add navigation buttons to the bottom and right borders by clicking the generated border and using the Insert ⇨ Navigation Bar menu command.

Shared borders can include any Web page element, including text and graphics. Shared borders act as a constant element of each page in your Web site. To edit the content of a shared border, click the border and then edit as you would any other Web page. When you save the open Web page, the embedded shared border page is saved as well.

To see shared border pages in Folders view, select Tools ⇨ Web Settings and click the Advanced tab (of all things!). Then, click the Show Documents in Hidden Directories check box, as shown in Figure 5-14.

After you elect to view hidden directories, you'll see that your Web page has a folder called _borders. This folder has page files for each of your shared borders. You can double-click a page file in that folder to open the page in Page view. You can edit attributes (such as background color) for a shared border page.

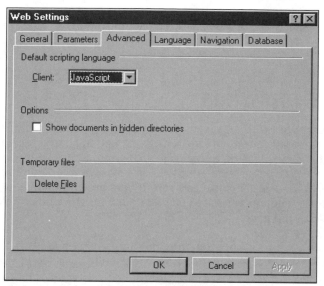

Figure 5-14: One of FrontPage's best hidden secrets is the ability to see shared border page files.

In the following tutorial, you'll create a new Web page from the Personal Web template, but you'll customize the shared borders and their content.

Tutorial 5.2: Customize Shared Borders

1. Select File ⇨ New ⇨ Web. Enter a Web name of **Personal**, and include a path to either a folder on your local computer or a Web server. Double-click the Personal Web template icon. If you are prompted to create a new folder, select Yes in the dialog box.

2. Select Format ⇨ Shared Borders.

3. In the Shared Borders dialog box, select the Top and Bottom check boxes. Deselect the Left check box.

4. Leave the Include Navigation Buttons check box checked for the Top border. Click OK.

5. In Page View, open the file Index.htm.

6. Scroll to the bottom of the page, and click and drag to select the comment text that identifies the bottom border. Type **Thanks for visiting my Web site!** to replace the comment text and then press Enter.

7. Click the top border. Press Enter, if necessary, to create a new line for text, and type **Thanks for visiting!**

The text that you added to your shared borders will be embedded in every page in the site. Leave your Web page open, or save it. You'll use it again in the next tutorial in this chapter.

Navigation Bar Properties

Navigation bars provide visitors with a convenient way to *navigate* to different pages within your Web site. Navigation bars are usually placed in shared borders, so that they appear in the same place on every page, providing visitors with a convenient and intuitive way to get around your Web site. Navigation bars differ from links that you insert manually, because navigation bars are automatically generated by FrontPage, depending on what logic you define for the kind of links that you want available on each page.

Navigation bars and shared borders work together, but actually they are two independent elements of a Web site. Navigation bars are usually included in shared borders. However, you can have shared borders without navigation bars, and vice versa. Shared borders are distinct embedded Web pages that can be edited. Navigation bars provide automatically generated links to other pages in your site.

Inserting navigation bars

You can insert navigation bars in a shared border or anywhere in a Web page. If you insert a navigation bar in a shared border, it will appear on every page in the Web site. If you place a navigation bar in a Web page (outside a shared border), it will appear only on that page.

The combination of placing navigation bars in, or out of, shared borders gives you more flexibility in creating convenient navigational links for your Web site visitors.

Changing navigation flow

To change the way navigation links are generated, select Insert ➪ Navigation Bars. The Navigation Bar Properties dialog box appears, as shown in Figure 5-15.

The links that you define in the Navigation Bar Properties dialog box correspond to the links that you defined (or got from a template) in Navigation view. These link options are described as follows:

✦ **Parent Level** links display only a link to the page in the Navigation view flowchart that appears just above the page being viewed.

✦ **Same Level** links display other Web pages on the same level of the Navigation view site flowchart.

✦ **Back and Next** displays Parent and Child level links from the current page.

✦ **Child Level** links generate links only to pages directly below the current page in the Navigation view flowchart.

✦ **Top Level** links display links to all pages in the top level of the flowchart.

✦ The **Home Page** check box adds a link to the site home page to every page in the site.

✦ The **Parent Page** check box adds a link to the parent page to each page.

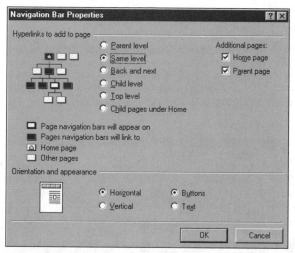

Figure 5-15: Navigation bar flow can be edited.

The navigation bars that you generate will apply the same link structure to each page. The links themselves will be *different* on each page, but the structure will be the same. This means that you have to choose which kinds of links to generate, and live with that choice throughout your site.

Note   What if you want to apply a unique, specific navigational logic to just one Web page? You can do this by assigning navigation bars to specific pages, placing them outside of a shared border. Similarly, you can use different navigation logic for different navigation bars in a Web site. For example, use Child Level for a top shared border, and Parent Level for a bottom shared border.

The two sets of two radio buttons in the Orientation and Appearance area of the Navigation Bar Properties dialog box enable you to choose whether to line up your links horizontally or vertically, and whether to use Buttons or Text. Your selections are previewed in the small preview page in the lower-left corner of the dialog box.

In the following final tutorial of the chapter, you'll use the Web page that you created in Tutorial 5.2 to customize navigation bars in the top and bottom shared borders that you created.

Tutorial 5.3: Create a Custom Navigation Bar

1. Double-click the navigation bar in the top shared border in any Web page in your Web site to open the Navigation Bar Properties dialog box.

2. Select the Child Level radio button, and both the Home Page and Parent Page check boxes in the dialog box.

3. Select the Horizontal and Text radio buttons in the Orientation and Appearance area, and then click OK.

4. Click and drag to select the text buttons that you just generated, and apply 14-point, AdLib BT font.

5. Save your page, and select View ➪ Refresh. Your top shared border should look something like the one in Figure 5-16.

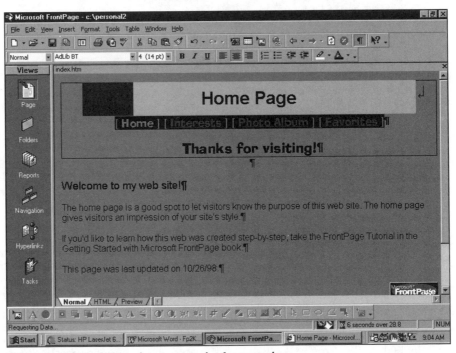

Figure 5-16: Navigation bar text can be formatted.

6. Scroll down to the bottom shared border and click inside of it.

7. Press Enter (if necessary) to create a new line, and select Insert ⇨ Navigation Bar.

8. In the Navigation Bar Properties dialog box, select the Back and Next radio button, both the Home Page and Parent Page check boxes, and the Horizontal and Text radio buttons.

9. Click OK in the dialog box. Not every link will be active—for example, if you selected a link to the home page, and you're at the home page, no link will appear.

10. Save your page, and preview your site in your Web browser. Test all the links in the top and bottom shared borders. Your links should look something like those in Figure 5-17.

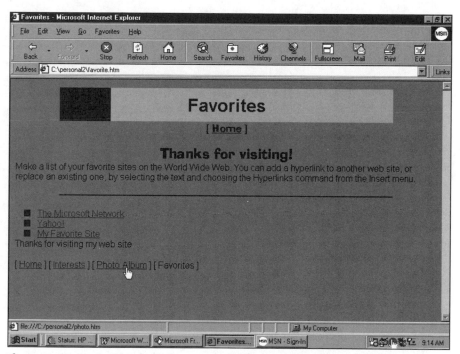

Figure 5-17: Navigation bars change, depending on what page is viewed in a browser.

11. You can delete this Web page by selecting File ⇨ Delete Web, and choosing the top radio button in the dialog box.

Summary

This chapter looked at three elements of site design: Themes, shared borders, and navigation bars. All three of these elements affect the content and look of your entire Web site. You learned how to apply, customize, and save Themes. You also learned to design customized navigation bars, both inside and outside of shared borders.

Up to now, most of the content and format of your Web pages have been automatically generated, using Themes, shared borders, and navigation bars. The task remains of creating content for these pages. In Chapter 6, you will explore the process of editing and formatting text in Web pages.

✦   ✦   ✦

Page Design with Text Appeal

In the previous chapters, you saw how easy it is to design an entire Web site by using FrontPage's Navigation view. Page relationships can be defined; shared borders with navigation bars can be assigned; and Themes can be applied. All that site design, however, still leaves you with the critical task of adding text content to your Web page. In this chapter, you'll learn how to add text to your Web page and how to edit and format Web page text.

Designing Web Pages in Page View

The specific content of distinct Web pages is controlled in Page view. This is where you will spend most of your FrontPage time. In Page view, you can add, edit, and format the actual content of your Web pages. You can also create new pages directly in Page view. These pages will not be automatically linked to your Web site, and won't have navigation bars included. But you can toggle between Page and Navigation view to create page content, and then link new pages to your Web's structure.

Web sites and Web pages

It's very helpful to envision and design your entire Web site first, and then create content for specific pages. After you chart out what your visitors will encounter at your site, you can "fill in the blanks" by adding content to each Web page.

Suppose all you want is a single Web page. Even if your Web site consists of just a single Web page, you should still start by creating a FrontPage Web site, as you learned to do in Chapter 1. That way, you can include more-sophisticated features of FrontPage, which you'll explore in the following chapter. And, you can rely on FrontPage to organize all your graphics and other embedded files, which makes transferring those files from one Web site to another much easier.

Caution

Our advice is to start with a FrontPage Web site, even if you only need one Web page. But, if you know how to manage Web site files, you can skip the step of creating a Web site and go straight to Page view to design a page. If you elect to do that, we've warned you of the risks, and assume that you'll take responsibility for overriding FrontPage's built-in features for keeping track of all the files associated with your Web page.

Exploring Page view

You can open an existing Web page in Page view by double-clicking it in any other view, including Navigation view. When you do so, you'll see your page open in Page view. If you assigned a Theme, shared borders, or navigation links to your Web page, you'll see those elements in Page view, as shown in Figure 6-1.

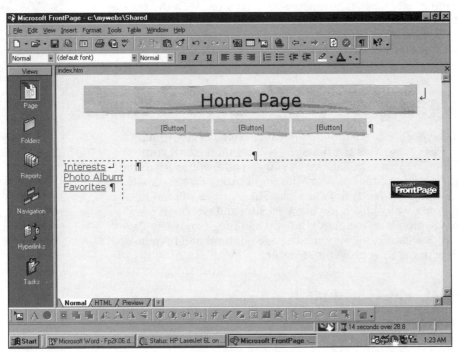

Figure 6-1: Even before you begin to edit page content, FrontPage may have assigned shared borders, navigation bars, and a color scheme.

The Standard and Formatting toolbars at the top of the Page view window will look somewhat familiar to you if you've used other Windows applications. Many tools (New Page, Copy, Cut, Paste, and others) do the same things in FrontPage that they do in other Windows applications, and they are very much like tools that you may be familiar with in other Office 2000 applications.

These toolbars are detachable, and can be moved off the top of the window by clicking and dragging on the toolbar (but not on a button). Detached toolbars can be re-anchored at the top of the window by dragging them back to the top of the screen. The Standard toolbar is shown in Figure 6-2.

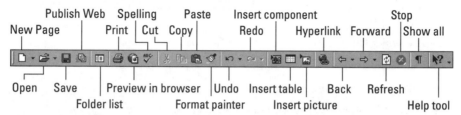

Figure 6-2: Page view's Standard toolbar handles basic editing tasks.

Although the Standard toolbar includes some buttons that you already know from other Office 2000 applications, many other buttons are unique to FrontPage. The following list explains what each tool does, and many of them are described in detail later in this chapter:

✦ **New Page**: Creates a new Web page with Themes and shared borders, but is otherwise blank.

✦ **Open**: Opens existing Web pages.

✦ **Save**: Saves your Web page.

✦ **Publish Web**: Publishes your Web site from your local computer to an intranet or Internet location.

✦ **Folder List**: Displays (or hides) a list of folders and files associated with your Web site.

✦ **Print**: Prints your Web pages to your printer.

✦ **Preview in Browser**: Displays your Web page in your default Web browser.

✦ **Spelling**: Checks spelling for your Web page.

✦ **Cut**: Cuts selected text or objects and saves them in the Clipboard.

✦ **Copy**: Copies selected text or objects and saves them in the Clipboard.

✦ **Paste**: Pastes contents of the Clipboard at the insertion point.

✦ **Format Painter**: Copies a selected format to apply with the (paintbrush) format cursor.

✦ **Undo**: Undoes your last command or keystroke.

✦ **Redo**: Cancels your last undo.

✦ **Insert Component**: Opens the Insert Component submenu.

✦ **Insert Table**: Opens the Insert Table grid.

✦ **Insert Picture**: Opens the Image dialog box.

✦ **Hyperlink**: Enables you to insert or edit a link to another Web page or a location on a Web page.

✦ **Back**: If you followed a link in FrontPage, you can move back to the previous Web page.

✦ **Forward**: Undoes the action of the Back button.

✦ **Refresh**: Reopens your Web page with any saved changes.

✦ **Stop**: Stops refreshing a page.

✦ **Show All**: Shows paragraph and line breaks.

✦ **Help Tool**: Displays a help cursor — point and click to get help with any onscreen element.

Most of your Web page text formatting is controlled from the Formatting toolbar in Page view, shown in Figure 6-3.

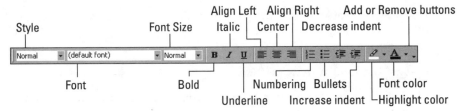

Figure 6-3: Many FrontPage formatting tools work differently than those in desktop applications.

The Formatting toolbar includes some tool buttons, listed next, that don't act like their twins in other Office applications:

✦ **Style**: The styles in the list are HTML styles, which are not customizable in the same way that styles are defined in word processors or desktop publishing applications. You can elect to assign formatting without worrying about what HTML style is assigned to text.

✦ **Font**: This drop-down list assigns fonts to selected text.

✦ **Font Size**: This drop-down list assigns font size to selected text. The limited selection of sizes reflects the limitations of HTML.

✦ **Bold**: Assigns boldface to selected text.

✦ **Italic**: Assigns italics to selected text.

✦ **Underline**: Underlines selected text.

✦ **Align Left**: Left-aligns selected paragraph(s).

✦ **Center**: Centers selected paragraph(s).

✦ **Align Right**: Right-aligns selected paragraph(s). HTML does not support full justification.

✦ **Numbering**: Assigns sequential numbering to selected paragraphs.

✦ **Bullets**: Assigns indenting and bullets to selected paragraphs.

✦ **Increase Indent**: Indents entire selected paragraph(s).

✦ **Decrease Indent**: Moves selected paragraphs to the right (undoes indenting).

✦ **Highlight Color**: Adds a background highlight to selected text.

✦ **Font Color**: Assigns colors to selected text.

✦ **Add or Remove Buttons**: Allows you to customize the Formatting toolbar.

Welcome to the world of HTML formatting

If you are an experienced HTML coder, you might be pleasantly surprised by how much control you have over text formatting in Page view. If you haven't formatted Web page text before, you might be a bit unpleasantly surprised by the reality that not as many formatting options are available in HTML (Web pages) as are available for printing.

FrontPage frees you from needing to learn HTML to design a Web page. While you work in a WYSIWYG environment, FrontPage works behind the scenes to translate your formatting into HTML code. However, you are not freed from HTML in two ways:

✦ You can still achieve greater control over the appearance of your page by tweaking and editing the HTML code generated by FrontPage. In later chapters, especially Chapter 11, you'll see how you can edit that HTML code in FrontPage

✦ You are still constrained by HTML insofar as your page formatting options are limited to whatever formatting the Web browsers can interpret, relying on the HTML code they read when they connect with your page.

The ability to create HTML as if you are formatting a printed document is pretty impressive. However, if you are transitioning from doing page layout and design for printed output, you might find the following aspects of text formatting somewhat disconcerting:

✦ HTML is more limited as a page description language than are most word processing languages. If you have spent any time doing even basic desktop publishing with a word processor, you'll immediately realize that FrontPage's capabilities are limited in comparison with those types of applications. The reason for this is mainly that HTML was not originally designed as a page description language, although it is evolving in that direction, pushed by demands for more control over document layout and formatting.

✦ FrontPage has a mixture of standard HTML formatting and word processor-like formatting, resulting in some redundancy of function. Even though FrontPage may seem limited in its formatting power, you will still find multiple ways to accomplish the same formatting task. This, too, is a product of the evolution of HTML. For example, select a string of text, and apply a Heading 1 style to it. Then, select a second text string, and increase the font size and assign boldface to that text. The results are about the same.

When you are designing your Web pages in FrontPage, you'll find that you can use the spacebar and the Tab key to insert spacing, and that you can control spacing with FrontPage's paragraph format features. But the control that you have in FrontPage over white space is restricted by the following:

✦ Many of the horizontal and vertical spacing controls in FrontPage, even things as basic as using the Tab key to separate words, are not widely recognized by other browsers.

✦ Because most monitor resolutions are a grainy 72 dots-per-inch (dpi), you can't get too fancy in your space formatting. Letters look grainy on Web pages, and being too tricky when fine-tuning line and word spacing often results in unreadable or unpleasant-looking text.

OK, that's enough warnings! The good news — and this is really the main news — is that you can easily apply all kinds of text and background formatting in FrontPage. Many formatting techniques are easier to apply to a FrontPage Web page than to a printed page, such as background colors, background images, and default colored fonts.

Text formatting in a hurry

The last half of this chapter explores text formatting in detail, but you need to learn the basics first. You can assign font attribute(s) to selected text by using the Formatting toolbar. First, select the text, and then click a toolbar button. For example, you can assign fonts from the Font drop-down menu, assign font size from the Font Size drop-down menu, and assign boldface by clicking the Bold button . . . you get the picture.

You assign colors to selected text by clicking the down arrow next to the Font Color button. This opens the (detachable) Font Color palette, shown in Figure 6-4.

After you assign a color to the Font Color button, you can assign that color to selected font simply by clicking the button. You can also assign default font colors for a page. You'll learn to do that in "Defining Page Properties," later in this chapter.

Figure 6-4: The detached Font Color palette assigns color to text.

Note

The one button that requires a bit of a disclaimer is the Styles drop-down list. As mentioned earlier, "styles" as used in this drop-down menu are an evolutionary holdover from the days when browsers did not interpret as many formatting commands as they do today.

Testing browser compatibility

The browser world remains divided, roughly equally, between the two browser superpowers, Internet Explorer and Netscape Navigator. The two interpret HTML somewhat differently. FrontPage allows you to assign formatting commands that will not be interpreted by Netscape Navigator. That's great if none of your visitors will be using Netscape, but that is unlikely in most cases.

How do you resolve this issue? You can tell FrontPage to display only formatting that both Navigator and IE interpret:

1. In Page view, select Tools ➪ Page Options and click the Compatibility tab in the Options dialog box.

2. Pull down the Browsers drop-down menu and select Both Internet Explorer and Navigator, as shown in Figure 6-5.

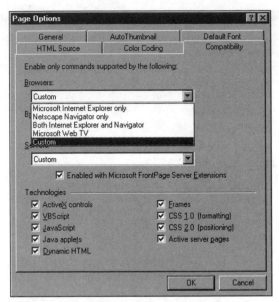

Figure 6-5: You can tell FrontPage to display only the formatting that can be read by both Netscape Navigator and Internet Explorer.

3. Click the OK button in the Options dialog box to apply your settings.

You can test your browser compatibility by pressing the Tab key. If you set your options to allow only Netscape-compatible formatting, you won't see tab spacing. Tab spacing is available if you set your options to show formatting available only in Internet Explorer.

Browser compatibility is, however, a moving target. It's one of the things that keeps Web designers on the edge, and sometimes pushes them off the deep end. New versions of Netscape Navigator and Internet Explorer add new formatting-interpretation features. Ultimately, the only real test of browser compatibility for your Web pages is to view them with the latest versions of Navigator and IE, as well as older versions of both browsers. In that way, you'll really know what visitors to your Web site see.

Defining page properties

Web page properties define the look of your page, including background colors or images, default font colors, margins, page titles, and other features that apply to an entire Web page. These attributes are available in the Page Properties dialog box.

Themes versus page properties

Because Themes define so many properties automatically, they rob you of the freedom to do your own page design. Aren't Themes supposed to be great formatting tools? Yes, they are, but they're prefabricated formatting tools, and even with the advanced Theme-control features that you learned in Chapter 5, you'll still find that if you want complete control over the look of your Web pages, you'll want to assign page formatting by hand.

To delete a Theme from an open Web page, follow these steps:

1. Right-click anywhere in a Web page in Page view.

2. Select Theme from the context menu.

3. Choose the Selected Page(s) radio button to delete the Theme only from your open page, or select the All Pages radio button to delete the Theme from every page in your Web site.

4. Select No Theme from the list of Themes on the left side of the Themes dialog box, as shown in Figure 6-6.

5. Click the OK button in the Themes dialog box.

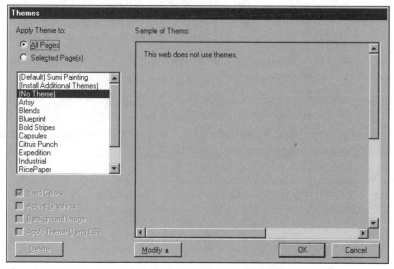

Figure 6-6: Select No Theme in the Themes dialog box to remove a Theme from your Web page.

After you remove your Theme, you can apply all the properties in the Page Properties dialog box. They are divided into five different tabs, but the page properties associated with page appearance are in the General, Background, and Margins tabs. Those tabs are described in detail here, followed by a brief look at the other two tabs, which have more esoteric page-property options. To access the Page Properties dialog box, right-click anywhere in an open page in Page view, and select Page Properties from the context menu.

Note   If you find that page properties described in the following sections are not available, first check to make sure that no Theme is assigned to the page, disrupting your normally available page properties.

Assigning page titles and background sounds

A couple basic elements of your Web page are the page title and a background sound. The *page title* displays in the title bar of a visitor's Web browser. Your Web page may be called index.htm or default.htm (these filenames designate home pages that open first when a visitor comes to your Web site). Or, your page's filename may be newpage4.htm. No matter, you can create a title such as "David's Web Site," and that page title will display when visitors come to your Web page.

Your FrontPage Web page can also have a sound file associated with it. The sound will play when your page is opened in a browser. Sounds can be overdone, and in general, the best idea is to think twice before adding a sound to your page. The downside of background sounds includes:

✦ Visitors get no warning that a sound is coming, and that can be disruptive in some work environments.

✦ Sounds slow down page download time considerably, with longer sound files being the worst offenders.

✦ Browsers don't come with the ability to turn off a background sound easily, leaving unhappy listeners quite annoyed.

Still, background sounds are appropriate in some situations. For example, you might have a link to a page that alerts visitors that they will hear music, voice, or other sound files at that page.

Both page titles and background sounds are defined in the General tab of the Page Properties dialog box, shown in Figure 6-7.

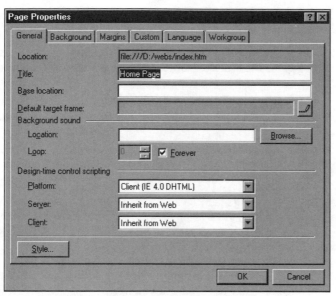

Figure 6-7: Add a page title and background sounds in the General tab.

The key features of the General tab are the following:

✦ **Title**: You can enter a page title such as "Home Page" or any other text that will display in the title bar of visitors' browsers.

✦ **Background Sound Location**: Use the Browse button to locate the sound files on your system that will play when the page is opened. WAV-format sound files are the most widely recognized by browsers.

✦ **Background Sound Loop**: The Loop spin box defines how many times the sound will play. The Forever check box plays a background sound over and over, as long as the page is open.

The Style button at the bottom of the General tab opens the Modify Style dialog box, in which you can use the Format button to define font, paragraph, numbering, and border defaults for your page.

Design-Time Scripting

What about the other options in the General tab of the Page Properties dialog box, the ones in the Design-Time Control Scripting area? These are very advanced features that you can ignore if you are relying on FrontPage to handle your HTML and scripting. If you're a coding daredevil and want to experiment with these features, here's our best advice to start you on your way:

A design-time control (DTC) is an ActiveX control that adds functionality to the development tool (in this case, FrontPage, but the model really comes from Visual InterDev), basically giving you a simplified way to configure certain elements of a Web page. In some ways, a DTC works like a FrontPage Component: It writes scripting code onto the HTML page. This code is interpreted at run time (when the page is loaded).

The Page Properties section for DTC Scripting enables you to define what scripting language FrontPage uses for DTC. The Platform option looks like it allows you to determine where the script is interpreted — either on the server side (as ASP) or on the client browser side (as DHTML). The other two options are analogous to the Default Scripting Languages properties in the Tools ➪ Web Settings ➪ Advanced dialog box. In fact, the default "Inherit from Web" means that the DTC scripting language will use the values set in this dialog box. Or, you can specify a scripting language on a per-page basis, if you like.

Defining page background

The Background tab of the Page Properties dialog box (shown in Figure 6-8) is where you control your page's entire color scheme.

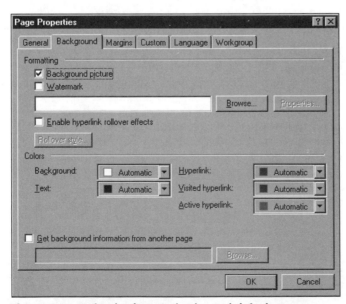

Figure 6-8: Assign background color and default text colors in the Background tab.

The Background tab lets you define both the page background and default text colors. Defining both simultaneously is handy. For example, if you create a dark-blue page background, you'll probably want to change your default text color to white, yellow, or another bright, light color that can be read against a dark background.

The features in the Background tab are the following:

✦ **Specify Background and Colors radio button**: Enables you to define a background color or image for your Web page.

✦ **Background Picture check box**: Enables you to define a graphic image to tile in the background of your Web page. Tiled images repeat horizontally and vertically, as necessary, to fill all the space behind your Web page.

✦ **Browse button**: You can locate a background image on your local computer or Web site by navigating to the image file.

✦ **Watermark check box**: Freezes a background image on the browser screen, so that as visitors scroll up and down your Web page, the background image stays in the same place.

✦ **Enable Hyperlink Rollover Effects check box**: Enables you to assign special font changes when a visitor moves his or her mouse over your hyperlinks. If you enable rollover effects, you can click the Rollover Style button to open the Font dialog box, in which you can assign special font attributes to display when a mouse is moved over a hyperlink.

✦ **Background drop-down list**: Enables you to select a color from a color palette to assign to your Web page background. Background images override background colors, so if you want the selected background color to work, deselect the Background Image check box.

✦ **Text drop-down menu**: Opens a color palette from which you can assign a default text color for your page.

✦ **Get Background and Colors from Page radio button**: Enables you to link the current page to another page's background and colors. For example, you can use the Browse button to select the home page for your Web site as a source of background and color for your page. Then, when you make changes to colors and background at your home page, the current page will change as well.

✦ **Hyperlink drop-down boxes**: Enable you to define colors for links on your page.

Defining margins

The Margins tab has two check boxes and two spin boxes, as shown in Figure 6-9. The Specify Top Margin check box enables you to define an area at the top of the page that will be clear (except for any page background).

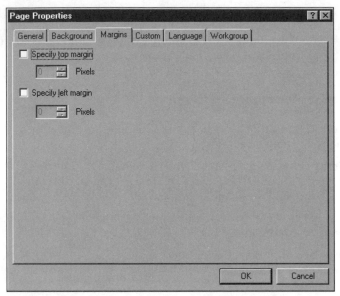

Figure 6-9: Margins are page design tools that create space to the top or left of your Web page objects.

The Specify Left Margin check box enables you to define a left margin. Both spin boxes are used to set the margin size in pixels. There are 72 pixels to an inch, so if you want to define an 1½-inch margin on the right side of your page, for example, you would define a 108-pixel left margin.

Other page properties

The Custom tab enables programmers to alter coding in the Web site. The Workgroup tab helps teams work together to design Web pages, or helps a Web designer organize pages into categories. When you assign categories by using the check boxes available in the Workgroup tab, you can then use those categories to generate reports in Reports view.

The Language tab enables you to set page defaults for Albanian, Zulu, or dozens of other languages.

Editing and Checking Text

The beginning of this chapter introduced you to text formatting. If you've gotten this far, you probably already figured out how to assign basic formatting to text and how to use the editing tools in the Standard toolbar. The Cut and Paste buttons work just as you'd expect, and click-and-drag editing is available in Page view.

Click the Spell Check button to check your spelling. FrontPage comes with a full-fledged spell checker. Not impressed? OK, but did you expect a Thesaurus in FrontPage? You got one. Select a word and press Shift+F7, or select Tools ⇨ Thesaurus when you're stuck for a missing synonym.

Another thing that you might not have expected is how easily you can import text, graphics, and even tables from other applications.

Getting text without typing

You can copy text from Word (or Excel, Access, and PowerPoint, for that matter) right into FrontPage's Page view. Select the text in another Office application, and click the Copy button in that application's toolbar to save the text to the Clipboard. Then, open or switch to FrontPage's Page view and paste the text at the cursor's insertion point.

Much — but not necessarily all — of your formatting will be saved when you paste text. You may be using formatting in your other applications that's not available in HTML pages. But FrontPage will do its best to keep your font type, size, color, and attributes when you paste text from other applications.

Editing text

The editing tools that are at your disposal in Page view include the following:

✦ Edit ⇨ Find and Edit ⇨ Replace enable you to find and/or replace text in Page view. Can you Find and Replace globally, for an entire Web site? Yes, you can — just select the Entire Web radio button in the Replace dialog box, as shown in Figure 6-10.

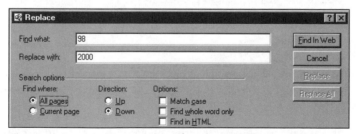

Figure 6-10: You can search and replace within an entire Web site.

✦ The Spelling tool in the Standard toolbar enables you to check spelling for the open page in Page view. But you can also spell check an entire Web site. To do that, click the Spelling tool while in any view except Page view, and you get the option of selecting the Entire Web radio button, as shown in Figure 6-11. The Add a task for each page with misspellings creates a link in Tasks view to each page that needs fixing.

Figure 6-11: You can spell-check an entire Web site.

Pushing the Limits of HTML Formatting

As alluded to at the beginning of this chapter, FrontPage is a bit schizophrenic when it comes to text and paragraph formatting. On one hand, the Style drop-down list in the Formatting menu displays a list of traditional, standard HTML styles. Old versions of Web browsers relied on these styles as the main way of identifying font and paragraph attributes. On the other hand, if you want to assign paragraph and font attributes to selected text, you have more freedom and control by using the Formatting toolbar buttons, and the Paragraph and Font Properties dialog boxes.

New in 2000

FrontPage 2000, for the first time, makes it easy to define customized styles that function very much like those in word processing or desktop publishing programs. You can explore that customization process in detail in Chapter 12. This chapter focuses on assigning paragraph and font attributes to selected text.

Formatting paragraphs

FrontPage enables you to indent selected paragraphs, using the Increase Indent tool. You can also left-align, center, right-align, or justify paragraphs by using the toolbar buttons.

Automatic numbering or bullets are assigned by selecting text and clicking either the Numbering or Bullets buttons. If you are adding to a numbered or bulleted list, each time that you press Enter, you create a new bulleted or numbered item. You remove bullet or numbering format from a selected paragraph by clicking the button in the Formatting toolbar.

By default, most paragraphs have a line of spacing between them. You can create line breaks without vertical spacing by holding down the Shift key and pressing Enter, to create a forced line break.

Note Paragraph formatting options have been expanded in FrontPage 2000. However, recall that vertical spacing between paragraphs and lines is not uniformly interpreted by Web browsers. While not all browsers recognize the additional formatting features available in the Paragraph dialog box, you can apply them, and visitors using IE 4 and higher will see these formatting effects.

You can apply paragraph formatting to selected paragraph(s) by selecting Format ⇨ Paragraph, or by right-clicking selected paragraph(s), and choosing Paragraph Properties from the context menu. The Paragraph dialog box, shown in Figure 6-12, gives you some ability to control line and paragraph spacing. The Preview area of the dialog box demonstrates the effect of the formatting that you apply, assuming that your page is viewed by a visitor with a browser version current enough to recognize these formatting features.

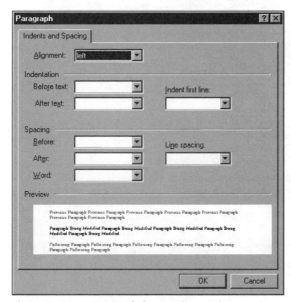

Figure 6-12: Paragraph formatting options are recognized by the latest generation of browsers.

The options in the Paragraph dialog box, shown in Figure 6-13, are the following:

✦ **Alignment drop-down list**: Enables you to left-align, right-align, center, or even full-justify text. Full justification displays in Internet Explorer version 4 and higher.

✦ **Before Text drop-down list**: Enables you to define horizontal indentation to the left of any selected paragraph(s).

✦ **After Text drop-down list**: Enables you to define horizontal indentation to the right of any selected paragraph(s).

✦ **Indent First Line drop-down list:** Enables you to define horizontal indentation for the first line of a paragraph.

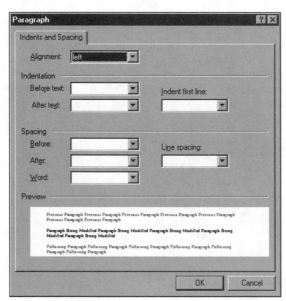

Figure 6-13: Indentation is assigned to the first line in a paragraph and to spacing before and after paragraphs.

Units of Measurement for Spacing

The default unit of measurement in spacing is points. However, paragraph spacing in FrontPage can be assigned in many units of measurement, including pixels (px), inches (in), centimeters (cm), ems (a unit of measurement the size of a letter *m*, often referred to as a pica), and percent (using the % symbol, such as 15%). The advantage of using percent as a spacing measurement is that it adjusts depending on the size of the browser window viewing your Web page.

The result of indenting the first line of paragraphs 5 percent and inserting 5-percent spacing above and below a paragraph is shown in Figure 6-14.

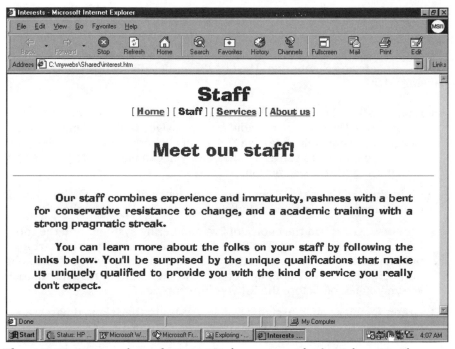

Figure 6-14: New versions of Internet Explorer support horizontal paragraph spacing attributes.

✦ **Before drop-down list**: Enables you to assign vertical spacing above any selected paragraph(s).

✦ **After drop-down list**: Enables you to assign vertical spacing below any selected paragraph(s).

✦ **Line spacing drop-down list**: Enables you to assign double, or 1.5 (line and a half) spacing between lines of text in a paragraph, as well as other more esoteric (and less widely recognized) measurements.

✦ **Word drop-down list**: Controls spacing between words in a paragraph.

✦ **Preview area**: Shows how your formatted text will look in browsers that interpret all the formatting commands available in FrontPage 2000.

Note

Remember, if you are designing for visitors who are using either Netscape Navigator or Internet Explorer, you can screen out formatting that isn't available in both by selecting Both Internet Explorer and Navigator from the Browsers drop-down list in the Compatibility tab of the Options dialog box. You get to that box by selecting Tools ➪ Page Options.

Formatting bullets and numbered lists

You can define bullets or numbering in more detail by using the List Properties dialog box. That box is accessed by selecting paragraphs and then choosing Format ➪ Bullets and Numbering. The List Properties dialog box has the following tabs:

- ✦ **Image Bullets**: Enables you to select images to use as buttons. The Use Images from Current Theme radio button assigns bullets from a Theme assigned to your Web page. The Specify Image radio button enables you to select any graphic to use as a bullet, and you can navigate to your graphic file by using the Browse button.

- ✦ **Plain Bullets**: Gives you a choice of three types of bullets. Or, by clicking the top-left icon, you can remove bullets from selected paragraphs.

- ✦ **Numbers**: Gives you the choice of five numbering systems, and the top-left icon removes numbering. The Start At spin box enables you to start a numbered list with a number other than one, which is helpful if you split up a numbered list with a paragraph of text and then want to resume numbering where you left off before the list was interrupted.

- ✦ **Other**: Enables you to assign HTML list styles to the selected paragraphs. For a complete discussion of HTML styles, see Chapter 12.

Formatting text

You can assign most text formatting from the buttons in the Formatting toolbar. But you can also control text formatting—and see and apply all text format options—in the Font dialog box. Open the Font dialog box by selecting text and then choosing Format ➪ Font. The Font dialog box is shown in Figure 6-15.

Formatting fonts

The Font tab of the Font dialog box provides menu options to assign Font, Font Style, Size, and Color. Those menu options work the same way as the buttons in the Formatting toolbar. In addition to formatting options available from the toolbar, the Font dialog box allows you to apply Effects. Many of these effects are features associated with HTML commands that have largely been made obsolete by the ability of browsers to interpret text formatting. Some text formatting features are still easier to assign by using Effects, including the often-annoying "blink" attribute that causes your text to flash on and off onscreen.

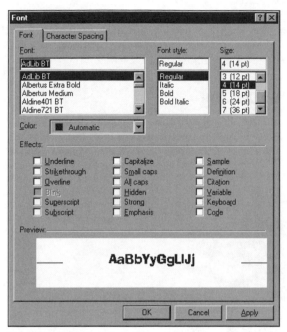

Figure 6-15: The Font dialog box

Text formatting available from the Effects check boxes includes the following options that are not available using font style options:

✦ **Strikethrough**: Draws lines through your text, ~~like this~~.

✦ **Overline**: Places a line above selected text.

✦ **Superscript**: Raises the selected text, and makes it a smaller font size.

✦ **Subscript**: Lowers the selected text, and makes it a smaller font size.

✦ **All caps**: Assigns uppercase to all selected letters.

✦ **Hidden**: Text is visible in the FrontPage Page view, but not displayed by browsers.

✦ **Strong**: Usually displayed by browsers as boldface.

✦ **Emphasis**: Usually displayed by browsers as italics.

✦ **Sample**: Usually displayed by browsers as typewriter (courier) font.

✦ **Definition**, **Citation, and Variable**: Usually displayed by browsers as italics.

✦ **Keyboard and Code**: Usually displayed by browsers as typewriter (courier) font.

Note   Why are Effects listed that are unreliably displayed as italics, boldface, or Courier fonts when these formatting features can more reliably be assigned from the Formatting toolbar? They are holdovers from earlier versions of HTML, when Web browsers did not always recognize those font attributes.

Formatting character spacing

The Character Spacing tab of the Font dialog box enables you to assign spacing between characters, or to define vertical spacing for superscript and subscript in a more-controlled way than is available using the Superscript and Subscript check boxes in the Font tab of the dialog box. The Character Spacing tab is shown in Figure 6-16.

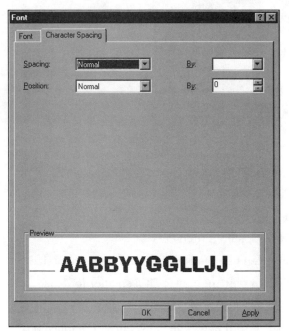

Figure 6-16: You can fine-tune character spacing in the Font dialog box.

The Spacing drop-down list enables you to choose between Normal, Expanded, or Condensed spacing, and the accompanying By drop-down list enables you to define how much you want to expand or condense spacing.

The Position drop-down list enables you to choose between Normal, Raised (superscript), or Lowered (subscript) vertical spacing for selected characters.

You can define how much you want to raise or lower characters in the accompanying By spin box.

Use the following tutorial to experiment with text and paragraph formatting.

Tutorial 6.1: Assign Text and Paragraph Formatting

1. Open an existing Web site, and open a Web page with a paragraph of text.

2. Select the paragraph of text, right-click, and choose Paragraph Properties from the context menu.

3. In the Paragraph dialog box, assign 5% to all three of the Indentation drop-down lists (Before Text, After Text, and Indent First Line).

4. In the Before and After drop-down lists, select 5% spacing.

5. In the Line Spacing drop-down list, select Double.

6. From the Alignment drop-down list, choose Justify. Then, click OK in the dialog box, and see how your paragraph looks in Page view.

7. Preview your page in your browser. Did all the paragraph attributes work?

Navigational Aid with Bookmarks

In Chapter 1, you learned the quick and easy way to create hyperlinks in a Web page. Simply typing a URL (Web site address) like `www.ppinet.com` and pressing the spacebar or Enter creates a link to that site in your page. You can create links to e-mail addresses the same way, by typing an e-mail address on your page.

In Chapter 1, you also learned to assign hyperlinks to selected text or graphics by clicking the Hyperlink button on the Standard toolbar and then selecting a Web page in your site, or elsewhere on the Web.

An additional tool for assisting visitors to your site is to provide bookmarks on your pages, with links to them. *Bookmarks* are target locations on Web pages to which a link can be directed.

To create a bookmark, follow these steps:

1. Click a location in your Web page that you want to function as a bookmark, and select Insert ➪ Bookmark.

2. If you have text selected, that text will be the default bookmark name. If you don't have text selected, you can type a bookmark name, as shown in Figure 6-17.

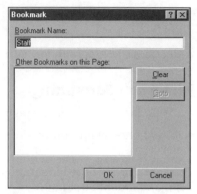

Figure 6-17: Defining a bookmark

3. Click OK in the Bookmark dialog box. The new bookmark is displayed as a small blue flag, or, if the bookmark is assigned to selected text, that text will be underlined with a dotted line, as shown in Figure 6-18.

Bookmark   Bookmarked text

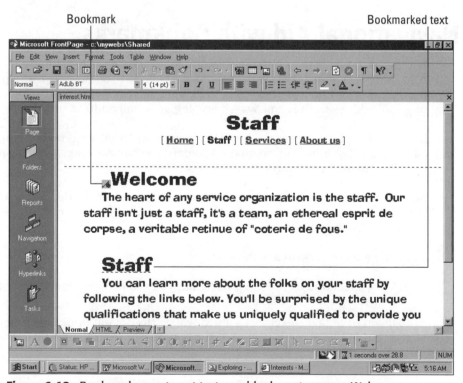

Figure 6-18: Bookmarks can target text or a blank spot on your Web page.

With bookmarks defined, you can create links to them from other locations on your page. One useful technique is to create a bookmark at the top of your page, and provide links to it from other places on the page.

To create a link to a bookmark on your Web page, follow these steps:

1. Select text or a picture that will serve as the hyperlink to the bookmark.

2. Click the Hyperlink button. In the Create Hyperlink dialog box, select your bookmark from the Bookmark drop-down list, as shown in Figure 6-19.

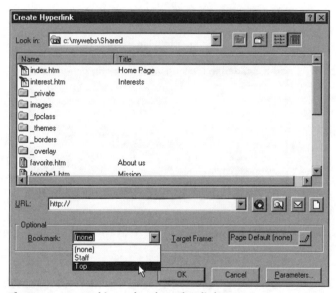

Figure 6-19: Making a bookmark a link target

3. You can test your hyperlinks to bookmarks by previewing your page in your Web browser, or in the Preview tab of FrontPage Page view, as shown in Figure 6-20.

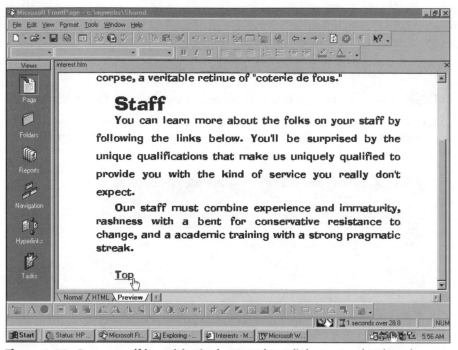

Figure 6-20: Put yourself in a visitor's shoes and test links to your bookmarks.

In the following tutorial, you will create a bookmark at the top of your page, and create several links to it:

Tutorial 6.2: Create Navigational Links with Bookmarks

1. Open a Web page with at least five paragraphs. If you don't have a Web page that long, open a shorter one, and use copy and paste to create more paragraphs.

2. Click at the top of the page and select Insert ⇨ Bookmark.

3. Enter a bookmark name, "top" and OK the Bookmark dialog box.

4. Scroll to the bottom of your page (or press Ctrl+End to navigate there quickly) and press Enter to create a new paragraph. Type **Top**, and format the word with boldface, red font.

5. Click the Hyperlink button. In the Create Hyperlink dialog box, select Top from the Bookmark drop-down list. Click OK in the dialog box.

6. Copy the linked text "Top" and paste it at several locations in your Web page, so that visitors can quickly get to the top of the page from anywhere on the page.

Summary

This chapter looked at some of the ways that you can format your Web pages in FrontPage, including page attributes such as background colors, default text color, and page margins. It also explored text formatting, such as font type, font color, font size, and paragraph attributes like alignment and spacing. You learned that, while FrontPage Themes are a powerful and quick way to assign color schemes and other page design features, you have more freedom in designing your pages if you remove Themes and apply your own page colors, text colors, and fonts.

In addition, this chapter discussed page formatting concepts, such as providing navigational links within your Web page by using bookmarks.

The next chapter explores how you can incorporate graphics into your page design. You may be surprised at how much control you have over the appearance of graphics from within Page view.

✦　　✦　　✦

Working with Graphics

◆ ◆ ◆ ◆

In This Chapter

How to add graphics
to your FrontPage
Web pages

How to control image
size and location

Managing image
attributes such as file
type and
transparency

Assigning image
map hotspot links to
sections of a graphic

◆ ◆ ◆ ◆

One of the most attractive, useful, and fun components of a Web page is graphics. Graphic elements can include icons, photos, navigational icons, drawings, maps...you get the *picture* (sorry!). Faster modems, large monitors, and the growing popularity of 256-color display are all working to make graphics an essential part of every Web page.

A Quick Look at Web Graphics in FrontPage

Whether you are a Web graphics guru who wants to personally tweak the compression ratio on your JPEG images, or you don't know a PNG file from a ping-pong ball, you'll find FrontPage a friendly way to manage your Web graphics. This section explores how you can quickly dump an image from your computer into your Web page. The rest of the chapter then examines in more detail how to control image properties.

FrontPage can insert any graphic in your Web page, regardless of the (original) format of the graphic file. FrontPage can handle the process of converting any image to a Web-compatible GIF file, and will save the image file so that it will be seamlessly embedded in your Web page.

The following are the two easiest ways to place an image in your Web page:

- ✦ Insert an existing graphic image file in your Web page.
- ✦ Copy a graphic from another application into a Web page.

You can insert a graphic image file by placing your insertion point and clicking the Insert Picture button in the Standard toolbar. The Image dialog box appears, as shown in Figure 7-1.

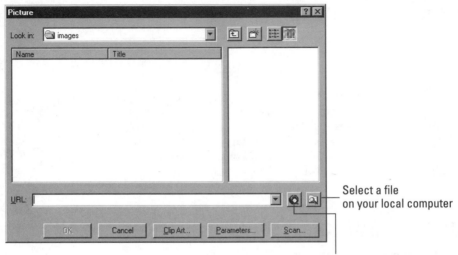

Figure 7-1: The Image dialog box

To insert clip art, click the Clip Art button on the bottom of the Image dialog box. You can search the Web for a graphic image by clicking the Use Your Web Browser button, or you can find a file on your local computer by clicking the Select a File on Your Computer button. Then, navigate to the file on the Web or your computer. When you locate your file, click OK in the dialog box.

After an image is saved to your Web site, it appears in a list of graphics in the Image dialog box. You can insert the image again by double-clicking the image file in the list.

Note   You can copy a graphic image by creating or opening it (or a file that contains it) in any application. Copy the graphic to the Clipboard, and then paste it into a Web page that is open in Page view.

Saving embedded Web graphics

When you save your Web page, FrontPage converts all the graphics on your page to Web-compatible formats and prompts you to save these embedded files. The Save Embedded Files dialog box appears, as shown in Figure 7-2.

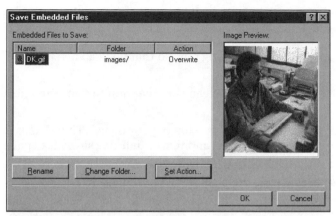

Figure 7-2: FrontPage prompts you to save new embedded graphics when you save a Web page.

Editing pictures in FrontPage

When you select an image in Page view, the Picture toolbar at the bottom of the window becomes active. The tools in the Picture toolbar let you adjust the appearance of your graphic image right in FrontPage.

Note FrontPage gives you quite a bit of editing and tweaking power for a page editing program, but if you want to design new images yourself, you need an image editor, such as Microsoft Image Composer. (Image Composer has its very own chapter in this book, Chapter 8.)

Figure 7-3 shows the tools located in the Picture toolbar.

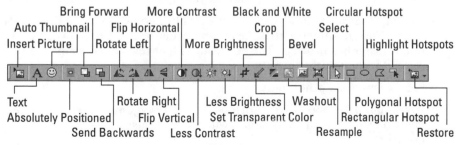

Figure 7-3: The FrontPage Picture toolbar

The picture tools enable you to add images and text, and change the appearance of a picture. The tool buttons on the Picture toolbar include the following:

✦ **Insert Picture**: Opens the Image dialog box, so that you can insert a new image.

✦ **Text**: Creates a text box in which you can enter caption text for the selected image.

✦ **Auto Thumbnail**: Generates a small version of your image. Thumbnails are often used as links to larger pictures, and their small size saves file space and speeds up page downloading.

✦ **Absolutely Positioned**: Locks the position of your image to any spot on your page.

✦ **Bring Forward**: Move selected images in front of other objects on the page.

✦ **Send Backwards**: Move selected images behind other objects on the page.

✦ **Rotate Left**, **Rotate Right**, **Flip Horizontal**, and **Flip Vertical**: Rotate your selected image.

✦ **More Contrast**, **Less Contrast**, **More Brightness**, and **Less Brightness**: Adjust the brightness and contrast of your image.

✦ **Crop**: Creates a cut with movable corner and side handles. Click and drag these handles to define crop marks for your picture, and then click the Crop button again to finalize your cut.

✦ **Set Transparent Color**: Displays an eraser tool. Point at and click any one color in your image to make that color disappear, allowing the page background to show through.

✦ **Black and White**: Converts images from color to black and white.

✦ **Washout**: Applies a watercolor-like effect to images.

✦ **Bevel**: Adds a 3D frame around an image, suitable for navigation buttons.

✦ **Resample**: Saves your image as a smaller file if you've reduced the size of your image. The advantage is that the file size is decreased, so that your Web page opens faster in a browser. The downside is that resampled images cannot be resized without losing quality.

✦ **Select**: Deselects other tools.

✦ **Rectangular Hotspot**, **Circular Hotspot**, and **Polygonal Hotspot**: Create clickable links called *image maps,* which are discussed in detail later in this chapter.

✦ **Highlight Hotspots**: Helps identify hotspots.

✦ **Restore**: Undoes editing changes to your picture, as long as you haven't saved the changes.

Importing Images Into a Web

When you save an embedded image, FrontPage automatically adds the graphic file to your Web. This means that the process of adding a graphic always involves two steps:

✦ An image is added to a Web page.

✦ The graphic is saved as part of the current Web site.

The order in which you perform these steps is entirely up to you. Probably the easiest and most intuitive way to add images is to first place them in a Web page, and then save the page — automatically saving the image as part of your Web site.

However, sometimes it will be faster and easier to import graphic files into your Web first, and then insert them in Web pages. For example, if you have dozens of photos that you want to use in your Web site, you can first import them, and then assign them to pages directly from the current Web site. You may have noticed when you created your Web that FrontPage created an empty folder called *images*, which is a convenient place to store your images.

To import images directly into your Web site before placing them on a Web page, follow these steps:

1. Select File ➪ Import. The Import File to FrontPage Web dialog box opens, as shown in Figure 7-4.

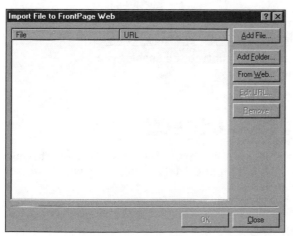

Figure 7-4: Importing images directly into your Web site.

2. Click the Add File button to add a file from your local computer or network, or click the From Web button to add a file from a location on the Web or an intranet.

3. Navigate to and select the image file that you want to add to your Web site.

4. Add more files if you want by clicking the Add File or From Web buttons.

5. After you add all the files that you want to the list, click all of those that you want to import (use Shift+click to select more than one). Then, click the OK button in the dialog box, and wait while the image files are imported into your Web site.

After you import images, they appear in the list of image files in your Web site when you click the Insert Picture button in the Standard toolbar, as shown in Figure 7-5.

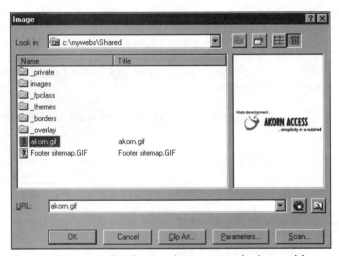

Figure 7-5: Importing images into your Web site enables you to add them to pages more quickly.

Working with Image Objects

After you insert an image into your Web page, it exists as a separate object on the page, allowing you to alter it in a number of different ways, which are detailed in this section.

Resizing images

Select the image by clicking it. Notice how little, black rectangles appear around it. These are its *handles*. You can resize the graphic any way you like by dragging these handles. If you drag from one of the corners, you can resize the graphic in two directions simultaneously. Figure 7-6 shows an image being expanded by dragging to the right with the right-side handle.

Figure 7-6: Graphically resize pictures by clicking and dragging.

Resizing by clicking and dragging is quick and easy, and graphical. But keep in mind that you can easily distort the dimensions of an image by resizing it in this way. If you *want* to distort a picture, this is a good way to do it. But if you want to maintain the same proportional sizing as the original image, you're better off resizing by using the Image Properties dialog box, discussed later in this chapter.

Positioning Images

You have two basic choices in positioning your image:

✦ Position it in relation to a paragraph: Enables you to flow text around an image, and to have the image move with the associated text. This option is explored later in the chapter, when image properties are defined.

✦ Position it at an exact spot on your Web page: Absolute positioning enables you to drag your image to the exact point on the page where you want it to display. If you display an image on top of text, or other page elements, you have the option of moving the image behind the other elements, or on top of them.

To assign an absolute position to an image, select it and click the Absolutely Positioned button in the Picture toolbar. Then, click the image, and move it to a location, as shown in Figure 7-7.

Figure 7-7: Images can be positioned at any location in a page.

Which Web Graphics Format Is Best?

Now that you've learned to control the basic appearance and location of images, you are ready to explore more-complex options for managing your graphics. One of those options is deciding what image format is best for your picture.

By default, FrontPage saves embedded images as GIF files. If you are adding an occasional icon to your Web page, that may be all you need to know. But FrontPage also makes it easy to save an image as one of the three widely recognized Web graphics formats (GIF, JPEG, or PNG). Which is best? Each of these formats has its advantages and disadvantages.

Graphics can be saved in a variety of formats, each of which has a slightly different method of storing the information necessary for a computer to render a bunch of 0s and 1s as a full-color image on your monitor. Until recently, almost all Web graphics were stored either as GIFs (GIF is variously pronounced "jiff," as in "I'll be there in a jiff," or "giff," as in "gift," but without the *t*) or as JPEGs (JPEG is always pronounced "jay-peg"). Recently, PNG (sometimes pronounced "ping") formats have come into wide acceptance, and are interpreted by recent versions of Microsoft Internet Explorer and Netscape Navigator.

These three formats are different, and each has its virtues in certain circumstances, but they share three characteristics that make them all well-suited to the Web:

✦ They are not proprietary formats.

✦ They are not specific to any computer platform.

✦ They use compression to create reasonably small file sizes (although this is no guarantee that Web images will download quickly).

GIF

GIF (short for *Graphic Interchange Format*) is a cross-platform graphics format invented by CompuServe to enable people to transfer graphic files easily over dial-up connections. This was the first graphics format used on the Web, and it continues to be the most prevalent — even though all the more recent Web browsers support both GIF and JPEG formats. Because of its compression techniques, the GIF format is particularly well-suited to graphics that have horizontal bands of color or large areas of similar colors. Thus, GIF works well for most banners, buttons, and basic illustrations.

GIF images also have two interesting characteristics:

✦ Any single color in a GIF image may be "transparent," allowing the background of your Web page to show through — these images are called *transparent GIFs*.

✦ A single GIF image can actually be composed of several individual pictures that are shown in sequence, giving the appearance of motion — these images are called *animated GIFs*.

Unfortunately, because of GIF's limit of 256 individual colors (called the *palette*, which is discussed in Chapter 5) and its compression technique, GIF images are not particularly well-suited to photographic images, which is where JPEGs come in.

JPEG

JPEG stands for *Joint Photographic Experts Group*, the name of the organization that created the format. The JPEG standard was devised as a method of compressing digitized photographs. Like the GIF format, it is a cross-platform standard. Although JPEG is used less frequently than GIFs on the Web, you will see it used for complex images and for larger background images. One interesting aspect of JPEG images is that they can be created with varying amounts of compression, whereas a GIF is just a GIF. This is because JPEGs, quite simply, are compressed by throwing out some of the information in the image — in theory, enough to make the file smaller but not enough that anyone would notice without a magnifying glass. The more information that you throw out, the smaller the file becomes, and the more degradation to the image quality that results. For the technical-minded, this is called *lossy* compression (because the image loses quality when compressed).

PNG

The PNG file format is a close (and younger) relative of GIF files. PNG images share the GIF format's attributes of supporting transparency and incremental downloading (interlacing). The main drawback of using the PNG file format — and it is an imposing one — is that older browsers will not interpret these images at all. For the time being, that disadvantage probably outweighs any small advantages PNG files have over GIF files.

Defining Image Properties

You've taken a basic course in image file formats. Now you are ready to control the properties of images in your Web pages, which you can do in the Image Properties dialog box. You can open this dialog box for a selected image in any one of three ways:

✦ Right-click the image and choose Image Properties from the context menu

✦ Select the image and choose Format ➪ Properties

✦ Select the image and then press Alt+Enter

Caution   Don't try to open the Image Properties dialog box by double-clicking an image. That opens the image in the assigned image editor (which, by default, is Image Composer).

The Image Properties dialog box gives you direct access to all the image properties in HTML. The dialog box is divided into three tabs: General, Video, and Appearance. The Video tab, which contains properties specific to video images, is discussed in Chapter 16. The options on the other two tabs are examined in detail now.

Defining General properties

The General tab of the Image Properties dialog box enables you to edit some basic characteristics of the image, including the name of the image file, its format type, alternative representations that can be presented to users, and any hyperlink associated with the image.

Image Source field

The Image Source field displays the filename of the currently selected image. You can use this field to replace the current image with another. Click Browse, locate a new image file, and click OK. When you close the Image Properties dialog box, the new image appears in place of the former one. You can also load the image into an editing application from this field. Click Edit, and the image file is opened in the designated image editor — by default, Image Composer. (You can also open Image Composer with the graphic loaded by double-clicking the image.)

Image Type

The Type option indicates the image format of the selected image. Click GIF, PNG, or JPEG to change the image format.

If the image is GIF format, two additional attributes of the image are indicated:

✦ **Transparent**: This enables you to designate one color in the graphic, typically the background color, that can be rendered transparent, allowing any background on the Web page to show through. Controlling transparency on a GIF image is explained in the next chapter. You cannot edit this property from the Image Properties dialog box. If the image contains a transparent color, the Transparent check box is checked. Otherwise, it is grayed out.

✦ **Interlaced**: This refers to an alternative way of storing the information about a GIF image. Some browsers are capable of displaying interlaced GIFs differently from non-interlaced images. By default, most Web browsers display images as they are downloaded. If the images are small, they appear to pop into the page. If they are larger, they draw in from top to bottom, which can be somewhat irksome if you happen to be the impatient type. Interlaced images can be displayed so that the entire image appears as the image is still downloading. The image at first appears blurry, and becomes increasingly focused as more of its information is downloaded. The effect is of an image materializing out of a haze of color. Interlacing was first introduced as a way of displaying the entirety of an image map quickly, so that the user could click some dimly recognized area in the image map without having to wait for the entire image to load. You can decide whether this really is a useful feature for your Web page. In practice, interlacing produces a pleasing effect for certain kinds of images, including photographs and illustrations. It can also be annoying, so use your judgment.

If the image type is JPEG, then two text boxes open, allowing you to specify more information:

✦ **Quality**: Adjust the quality of the image as a percentage from 0 to 100. The higher the number, the higher the quality of the image and the larger the file size. See the earlier discussion of the JPEG format for more information on how JPEGs work.

✦ **Progressive Passes**: This is essentially the same as "interlace" for GIF images. You do, however, have one advantage — you can specify the number of steps required to go from the extremely fuzzy version of your image to the full version. The number of steps can vary from 0 to 100.

Alternative representations

Several reasons exist for why HTML includes provision for designating alternative representations of images. One reason is that not all Web browsers are actually capable of displaying inline images. In addition, all Web browsers include an option to turn off the automatic display of images. This feature enables users with slower Internet connections, or users who might find the images distracting rather than useful, to browse the Web without waiting for images to download.

A more widely applicable use for alternative text is to function as an online caption for an image. Most modern browsers display alternative text when a visitor points his or her mouse cursor at a picture. Figure 7-8 shows alternative text displayed with an image in Microsoft Internet Explorer. To enter alternative text, just type the text in the Text field.

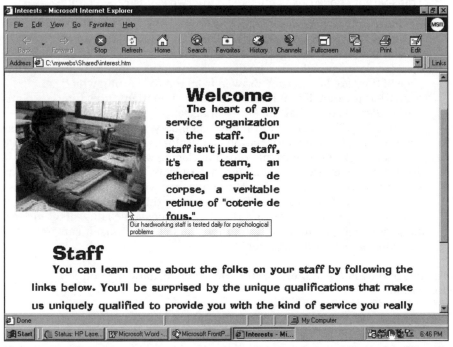

Figure 7-8: Alternative text appears next to an image when a visitor points his or her cursor over the image.

You can also define a low-resolution version of a graphic. This option is not universally supported, but it can be used to interesting effect. It enables you to designate a temporary, lower-resolution version of an image that is displayed first while the real image is still downloading. When the real image has completely downloaded, it replaces the temporary image. To make use of this feature, simply designate the image file to be used as the Low-Res version. Click the Browse button next to the Low-Res field in the Alternative Representations section to select an image for this purpose. (The Low-Res image and the main image must have the same dimensions.)

Alternative Low-Res images can be used to create interesting effects — the equivalent of a two-frame animation. One popular technique is to use a black-and-white version of an image as the low-resolution version. When the color version appears, it looks as if it is painting color into the image.

The default hyperlink

You can associate an image with a hyperlink in the same way that you associate a string of text with a hyperlink. For details on creating hyperlinks, refer to Chapter 2. When users click the image, they jump to the hyperlinked location. This is the standard method of creating graphical "buttons" on your Web page (unlike conventional computer interface buttons, though, these simple buttons do not change when you click them).

If you associate your image with a hyperlink, that information appears in the Image Properties dialog box as well. Alternatively, you can use the Image Properties dialog box to create and/or edit an image's hyperlink. To add a hyperlink to an image, click the Browse button next to the Location field in the Default Hyperlink section. Locate the file and click OK.

Controlling image appearance

The Appearance tab contains image properties that directly affect the way the selected image is displayed. The options in the Layout section of the Appearance tab are described next.

Alignment options

The alignment options affect how an image is aligned in relation to the text around it. The most powerful alignment options are left and right alignment. These options enable you to place text to the right or left of a paragraph, and to wrap text around the paragraph. Figure 7-9 shows text wrapped around a right-aligned image. The small arrow to the left of the paragraph indicates where the pictured is anchored, and the picture can be moved by clicking and dragging that anchor arrow.

Images can also be centered. The other alignment options control how images are positioned in relation to a line of text. These options are somewhat esoteric, and are used for fine-tuning the exact alignment of tiny graphics inserted into text. These alignment features are used when an inserted image is smaller (shorter in height) than the line of text within which it is inserted. For example, if you were using a tiny graphic image as a trademark or degree symbol, you could align those images with the top of a line of text.

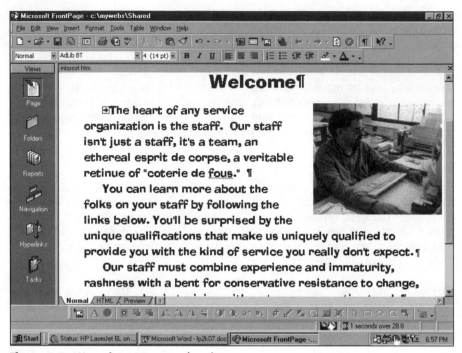

Figure 7-9: Wrapping text around an image

Horizontal and vertical spacing

Use the Vertical Spacing and Horizontal Spacing options to affect how much white space appears between an image and the surrounding text. These options are particularly useful when used in conjunction with the left- and right-alignment options to control how text wraps around an image.

Border thickness

If you associate an image with a hyperlink, by default, the hyperlink displays with a thin border that is the color of the other hyperlinks on the page around it. You can use the Border option to hide this border or control its width. In addition, you can use the Border option to add a border to nonhyperlinked images. To add a border to an image, simply designate its thickness, measured in screen pixels. The border displays in the color of the default text on the Web page.

Size options

The Size section of the Appearance tab indicates the width and height of the current image, designated in screen pixels. By default, these values are grayed out. You can alter them directly by first checking the Specify Size check box. This is the equivalent of resizing the image. Values for the size property can be given either in pixels or in percentages. If you select percentages, the size of an image changes in relation to the size of the Web browser window.

To maintain the same proportions between height and width as you resize, click the Keep Aspect Ratio check box. Then, when you change either the height or width, the other dimension will be reset automatically to keep the same aspect ratio.

Tip   You can speed up downloading by using this trick: Use the Size area of the Appearance tab to assign exact image size. To maintain the same proportions in your resized image, check the Specify Size check box, but leave the default values in the Width and Height text boxes (the original size of the image). This tells your visitors' browsers the size of the image before it's downloaded, so that your page doesn't redraw to accommodate the image's actual size each time an image is downloaded — this isn't a big thing, but it can make your pages easier to view.

Finding Images for Your Web Pages

You know how to work with an image once it is in FrontPage, but perhaps you are wondering how to fill your Web pages with beautiful artwork and interface elements like the ones you see on all the best professional Web sites.

The next chapter introduces Image Composer, the Microsoft image-creation application that comes with FrontPage 98. Image Composer makes creating your own professional-looking graphical compositions easy. But, you can also take advantage of resources for pre-made graphics.

Many ways exist to get images for your Web site, ranging from art that is free to take and use, to professional stock houses that provide images at prices that vary sharply but generally are well below the price of custom-designed graphics. This section briefly outlines some of the places you can look for images.

FrontPage sample art

FrontPage comes with its own library of clip art, which it installs in the FrontPage Clip Art folder. The Editor's Image dialog box has a special Clip Gallery that enables you to preview thumbnails of the images. To access the Clip Gallery, select Insert ➪ Clip Art. If you are already in the Image dialog box, you can also click the Clip Art button to access the Clip Gallery.

To add your own images to the clip art list, open the Clip Gallery, and then click the Import Clips button. Locate the image that you want to include in the gallery and click Open. A dialog box opens, asking which category or categories you want the image included in and a list of keywords that you can use to search for the image later. Click OK, and the image now appears in the Clip Gallery. (Note that the image is still in its original location, not in the Clip Art folder.)

In addition, FrontPage 2000 is shipped with an Image Composer CD that is loaded with more images. Located in the ImgComp folder is a subfolder called MMFiles that includes many media files in the default Composer format (.mic extension). These files can be opened in Composer and added to your Web site.

Note If you happen to be the owner of Office 2000, it too ships with a huge array of clip art, including links to the Web sites of the media companies who have provided royalty-free clips. One good way to browse the collection is by running a PowerPoint presentation called Overview.pps, located in the Valupack subfolder on the Office 97 CD.

Online resources

In addition to the clip art included with FrontPage, Microsoft maintains online resources that include sample media files and pointers to additional media resources. Two locations to check out are the following sites:

✦ **FrontPage Resources**: www.microsoft.com/frontpage/ documents/resources.htm

✦ **Image Composer resources**: www.microsoft.com/imagecomposer/gallery/gallery.htm

Of course, you need not rely on Microsoft for everything. The Web has a store of freely available art that is expanding all the time. To get a sense of the possibilities, enter **free Web graphics** into the search box of your favorite search engine, and explore the hundreds of sites offering free icons, pictures, logos, and designs.

Saving images from the Web

Some people think it is one of the Web's greatest virtues, others think it is downright criminal, but the fact remains that copying images from Web sites is astoundingly easy. (In fact, merely in the process of requesting a Web page, your Web browser automatically copies the images to a temporary location on your computer). If you have ever saved images from your Web browser, though, you know that you can save only one image at a time. What if you want to save all the images from a page? FrontPage makes this easy.

Note You already know this, but under no circumstances should you make use of images that you find on the Web for your own profit, either directly or indirectly, unless those images come with explicit permission to do so. Using images in this manner is illegal, and it threatens to undermine the whole spirit of the Internet.

To save images from a Web page:

1. Select File ➪ Open from the Editor menu.

2. In the Open File dialog box, choose the Other Location tab and check the From Location radio button.

3. Type into the From Location field the URL of the Web page you want to open. Note that this can be any publicly accessible URL.

4. Click OK. The Web page opens in Editor (don't worry, you can't make changes to the original).

5. Select File ⇨ Save. FrontPage prompts you to save the page to the current Web site, including the HTML file and any inline graphics.

Stock houses

You may notice that free images on the Web are of varying quality. In general, you can find lots of nice background textures (and some garish ones), and trinket art, such as ruled lines and bullets. You are harder pressed to find decent illustrative art. Even nice buttons and icons are a rare commodity. If you have some money to spare and want to add professional-quality illustrations to your Web pages, you might want to investigate some of the many stock photography and digital art companies. Here are two, large, representative examples of stock houses:

✦ **PhotoDisc** (www.photodisc.com): This service specializes in photographic images, and lots of them. These images are royalty-free, meaning that you pay for them once and then use them for their designated purpose as long as you like.

✦ **ImageClub** (www.eyewire.com/): Affiliated with Eyewire, this is a source for your clip art needs. They have line art, icons, and fonts, as well as photography.

In the following tutorial, you'll place in your Web page a sample graphic from the CD-ROM that accompanies this book.

Tutorial 7.1: Add Images to Your Web Page

1. Open a Web page with some paragraph text, or create a new one.

2. Place your cursor at the beginning of the first paragraph and click the Insert Picture button in the toolbar.

3. Click the Select a File on Your Computer button in the lower-right corner of the Image dialog box.

4. In the Select File dialog box, navigate to the CD-ROM that accompanies this book, and open the file Image Map.gif.

5. Right-align the image so that your paragraph text flows around it. To do so, right-click the image and select the Image Properties dialog box. Then, in the Appearance tab, select Right from the Alignment drop-down menu and click OK to close the dialog box. Your paragraph text should be wrapped around the image, as shown in Figure 7-10.

6. Make the image background transparent by clicking the Transparency tool in the Picture toolbar and then clicking the white image background, as shown in Figure 7-11. The effect is more obvious if you assign a page background other than white (right-click anywhere in the page, select Page Properties, and assign a background color from the Background tab).

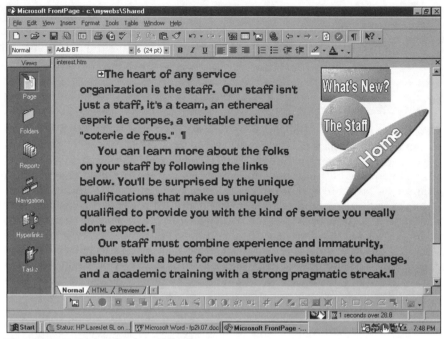

Figure 7-10: Right-aligning an image

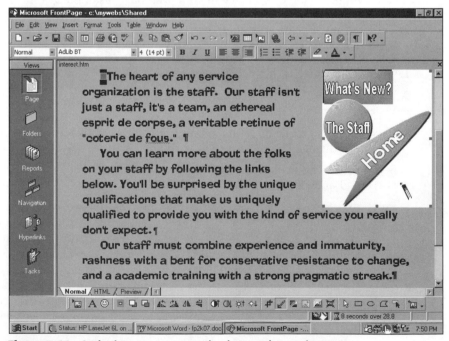

Figure 7-11: Assigning a transparent background to an image

7. Make the image a little smaller by clicking and dragging the image's bottom-left-corner handle up and to the right.

8. Add alternative text that says **Click to go places** by entering alternative text in the General tab of the Image Properties dialog box, shown in Figure 7-12.

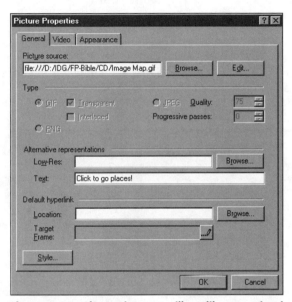

Figure 7-12: Alternative text will act like a caption in Web browsers.

9. Experiment with the Brightness and Contrast buttons. If you destroy the image, click the Restore button (and add transparency again).

10. Click the Save button to save your Web page with the embedded image. Note the default file name, folder, and the image preview, and then click OK to save the page with the image. Remember the name of your file; you'll use this at the end of this chapter to create an image map.

Creating Graphic Links and Image Maps

Any image can serve as a hyperlink. Hyperlinks are assigned to images in the same way that they are assigned to text — first select the object and then assign a link. *Image maps* are graphics with more than one link. With an image map, a visitor clicks one part of the image to go to one link, and another part of the image to go somewhere else. Well-designed image maps can provide an attractive and intuitive way for visitors to jump to a desired destination.

Assigning hyperlinks to an image

The easiest way to assign a link to an image is to click the image and then click the Hyperlinks button in the Standard toolbar. The Create Hyperlink dialog box opens, and you can assign a link to a page in your Web site from the list at the top of the dialog box. Or, you can enter a URL. After you define your target, click OK in the Create Hyperlink dialog box.

Note   When you test your link in a browser, the target displays in the status bar of the browser, not in the alternative text caption that appears when you point to the linked graphic, as shown in Figure 7-13. Keep that in mind when you decide what alternative text to assign to a graphic.

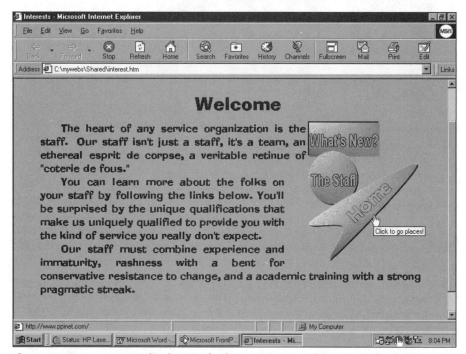

Figure 7-13: Your target displays in the browser's status bar, not in the link's alternative text.

Defining an image map

Defining an image map is as easy as drawing a rectangle, an oval, or a shape. First, click the image to which you are assigning links. Then, choose either the Rectangular Hotspot, Circular Hotspot, or Polygonal Hotspot tool from the Picture toolbar and (using the pencil cursor) draw an area on the picture that you want to associate with a link, as shown in Figure 7-14.

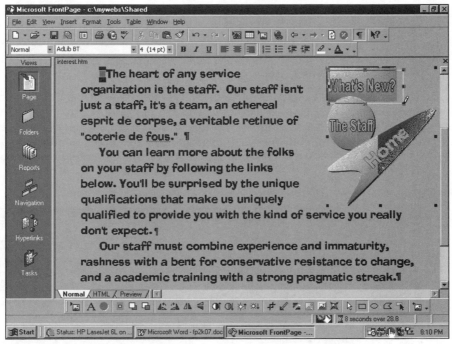

Figure 7-14: Defining a rectangular image map hotspot

If you are drawing a polygonal hotspot, click points to create the outline, and then double-click to complete the shape.

After you complete your hotspot, the Create Hyperlink dialog box will open, in which you can define the target for the hotspot link.

In the following tutorial, you will create an image map with three clickable hotspots. Each of these hotspots will serve as a link to a different page in your Web site.

Tutorial 7.2: Create an Image Map

1. Open an existing Web page; the one that you worked on earlier in this chapter will work fine. (If you open a new Web page, insert the picture Image Map.gif from the CD-ROM that accompanies this book.)

2. Click the image map picture and then click the Rectangular Hotspot tool in the Picture toolbar. Click and drag to draw a rectangle around the text "What's New?," as shown earlier in Figure 7-14.

3. As soon as you release your mouse button, the Create Hyperlink dialog box appears. If you have other Web pages in your Web site, click one of them to create a link, and then click the OK button.

4. Assign a link to the circle in the image map with the words "The Staff" on it. Use the Circular Hotspot tool.

5. With the image still selected, click the Polygonal Hotspot tool. Click several times around the outline of the shape with the text "Home" on it, as if you were playing a game of "connect the dots," but with an imaginary set of dots. When you've completed outlining the shape by clicking the points and spots on the lines (as shown in Figure 7-15), double-click to complete the hotspot. Define a target link in the Create Hyperlink dialog box.

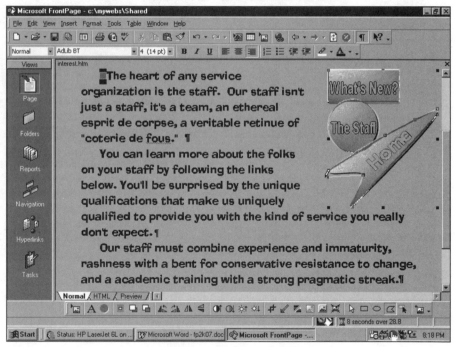

Figure 7-15: Drawing a polygonal hotspot in an image map.

After you complete your image map hotspots, save your Web page and test your links in a browser.

Summary

In this chapter, you learned to insert and format graphic images in your Web site. You found that FrontPage's Page view provides quite a few tricks that you can apply to an image, including assigning transparency. You also learned to control image properties, such as alternate text, size, and file format. A logical question is "When do I get to create my own images?" The answer is in the next chapter, which describes using Microsoft Image Composer — the graphics program bundled with FrontPage 2000.

✦   ✦   ✦

Creating Graphics with Image Composer

You can easily create nice-looking Web pages by using preexisting images, but sooner or later, you may feel the urge to create your own graphics. FrontPage 2000 includes Microsoft Image Composer, a friendly and useful tool for creating your own professional-quality Web graphics.

Many graphic design applications are available on the market, including the well-known Adobe Photoshop and Corel PhotoPaint, which are both professional commercial tools that you can use to create or touch up images. Another product is Paint Shop Pro, a shareware application that includes many of the same features as the more expensive products.

However, this book focuses on Microsoft Image Composer as the tool to use to create graphics for your Web pages, for the following reasons:

♦ It comes free with FrontPage.

♦ While not unfriendly, Image Composer is not exactly intuitive, even for those who have used other graphic design programs.

♦ Image Composer is unique in that it is designed to create graphics for *Web pages*. Other, more complex programs are loaded with features designed to facilitate hardcopy printing, but Image Composer's features are focused just on creating Web graphics.

Before diving straight into Image Composer, the next sections expand on what you learned in the previous chapter by discussing some of the basic rules and options available in creating Web-friendly graphics.

What's Unique About Web Graphics?

You already worked with Web graphics in FrontPage in the previous chapter in this book. You may have noted that a couple particularities distinguish Web graphics from graphics that are printed on paper, billboards, and so on. One is that Web graphics are restricted by the 72-dpi (dots-per-inch) resolution of most monitors. A really low-quality print job would print at least 600 dpi on paper, so you have to take the limitations of monitors into account when you design Web graphics. In short, fine details don't work well — broad strokes do.

The other constraint is that Web graphics must be created in one of the two (or three, depending on how you count) Web-compatible file formats. You're restricted to GIF (or its cousin, PNG) files or JPEG files.

Within these constraints, designing Web graphics has two principal challenges:

✦ Given the number of bandwidth-constrained users, the smaller and simpler the graphics, the happier the viewer. Unfortunately, it is much easier to create stunning, big graphics with lots of subtle color variations than stunning, little graphics with a limited number of colors, unless you know how to get more for less with your graphics.

✦ Because the Web is a cross-platform, multibrowser world, graphics that look gorgeous on one monitor can look dreadful on another, unless you know how to minimize differences.

When you design Web graphics, you should be aware of graphic file size and color compatibility. The larger the image file size, the slower your Web pages will download. And, both in file format and color, you need to be aware of the limitations of Web browsers, to ensure that your images will look good in browsers.

The following is an overview of some of the key concepts involved in creating great graphics for the Web.

File and image size

The three main factors that determine image file size are:

✦ The size of the image

✦ The number of colors used

✦ The quality of the image

In general, the larger the dimensions of an image, the larger the file size of the image. One way to decrease the file size of an image, then, is to decrease its physical dimensions. In other words, when you are creating large graphics, restrain yourself. Smaller is better, in terms of how long your Web pages take to open.

Smaller image sizes also have an aesthetic advantage. Your visitors may be viewing your Web page with monitor resolutions of 640 ⬜ 480, 800 ⬜ 600, or 1,280 ⬜ 1,024 pixels. Your task as a designer is to create images that look good on all three resolutions. An image that is wider than 640 pixels forces visitors with 640 ⬜ 480 monitors to scroll horizontally just to see your whole picture.

Note

Chapter 7 pointed to the Resample button in the FrontPage Picture toolbar. The Resample button can be used to reduce the file size of images that you shrink in FrontPage. This saves file size, but if you later try to enlarge a resampled image, you'll lose picture quality.

File types

When you create images in graphics programs, you can save them as GIF, JPEG, or PNG images to use in Web sites. Because GIF and PNG images have similar features, and GIF is more widely used, this book focuses on the relative advantages of GIF and JPEG images. You saw in Chapter 7 that after an image is brought into Page view in FrontPage, it can be saved as either GIF or JPEG (or PNG). However, when you design images, you'll want to save them in the most appropriate format.

In general, JPEG images work better for photographs, because they (theoretically) support an unlimited number of colors. This is *theoretical* because most Web browsers and monitor configurations restrict you to using 216 colors. But even restricted to 216 colors, JPEG often handles complex colors better than the GIF format. JPEG images also have variable compression. More compression causes JPEG files to download faster, but reduces quality. GIF images have the advantage of allowing interlacing (fading in to a browser window) and having a single transparent color.

Whole books are available on the science of selecting graphic file formats, but in the end, selecting a file format still sometimes comes down to saving your image as both a GIF and JPEG image, and seeing which file is smaller and looks better.

Colors and color palettes

Along with image size, the number of colors in an image contributes to the file size. GIF images have a limit of 256 colors, which corresponds to an 8-bit color depth (basically because it takes eight bits of data to define a color that is one of 256 possible colors). Not all graphics use 256 colors, but if the image is saved as an 8-bit GIF, it is still the same file size as an image that did use all 256 colors. Sophisticated Web graphic design programs (including Image Composer) allow you to save GIF files with smaller palettes (such as with 8 or 16 colors). Saving images with reduced color palettes often significantly reduces file size. Of course, reduced color palettes restrict how many colors you can use in an image. But if a graphic only needs eight colors, saving it with an eight-color palette will significantly improve download time.

JPEGs typically are saved with more than 256 colors, because they are often photographic images. You may be able to reduce the number of colors in your JPEGs without adversely affecting their appearance. Trial and error is a good method.

A Few Words on Palettes and Dithering

Many monitors can display only 256 colors. How, then, is a photo with an infinite range of colors, for example, displayed in 256-color monitors? *Dithering* is the art of substituting colors that are close to the actual colors, but within the range of colors that the computer has to work with. You know you are looking at a dithered image when you see little dots of color sprinkled around a graphic. This is the attempt to put several colors close to one another in order to fool your eye into seeing a different color. Dithering mixes color pixels to create the illusion of more colors than are available in the browser palette.

Dithering is useful because it allows more colors to be displayed than browser palettes support. The downside is that dithering methods vary, and the results are often unpredictable. Both Internet Explorer and Netscape Navigator's color palettes are restricted to 216 colors. Why 216 and not 256? Because the other slots are reserved for operating system colors — the colors that are used in your desktop graphical elements. Leaving some slots in the palette empty ensures that the computer has room for these colors, as well. So, if you want to guarantee that the colors you include in your image look good in those browsers, restrict your colors to those in the palettes for these browsers.

Modern Web-friendly graphic design packages (and Image Composer is in that class!) allow you to work with a palette of colors that is restricted to the 216 browser-friendly colors, and to choose whether to allow dithering to create additional colors.

Creating Web Graphics with Image Composer

Image Composer is a powerful, feature-loaded graphic design program. Several books are devoted entirely to Image Composer, including *Microsoft Image Composer For Dummies* (IDG Books Worldwide, 1998). Such books explore Image Composer's features, especially its wide and wild array of effects, in much more detail than can be covered in this chapter.

Still, you can create attractive, useful images quickly in Image Composer. This chapter shows you, through three tutorials, how to create your own custom icons, image maps, and background images.

Navigating in Image Composer

Image Composer must be installed from the FrontPage 2000 CD-ROMs. It opens in its own window, and really is a completely separate program from FrontPage.

When you open Image Composer, you see a large workspace in the center of the window, in which you create images. The workspace is where you design and manipulate graphic objects, called *sprites* in Image Composer terminology.

Sprites: The Building Blocks of Image Composer

The basic graphical object in Image Composer is called a *sprite*. A sprite is a self-contained graphical object that has its own properties. Put one or more sprites together, and you have a composition that can be converted to a GIF or JPEG file, and then transferred to your Web page.

The Image Composer workspace

Figure 8-1 shows the Image Composer window with a shape in the workspace, the Arrange tool selected, and the Arrange palette displayed. The window consists of four main elements — the toolbar at the top, the toolbox at the left, an open palette at the bottom of the window, and the workspace where you design sprites.

Image Composer's unique toolbar

The Image Composer toolbar is shown in Figure 8-2. You'll see some tools that look familiar, some that don't, and (surprise!) some that look familiar but act differently than they do in FrontPage.

Because the Image Composer toolbar has a few tools that are unfamiliar, or don't behave quite as they do in FrontPage, they are quickly introduced in the following list, along with some basic tips on editing in Image Composer (the notes in *italics* tip you off to particularly useful or unexpected features of the Image Composer toolbar):

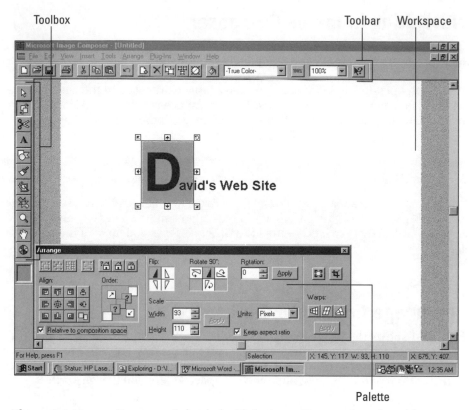

Figure 8-1: Image Composer is loaded with features. You can do quite a bit once you learn to manage the toolbox and palettes.

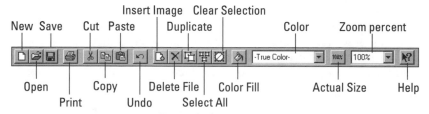

Figure 8-2: The Image Composer toolbar

✦ **New**: Opens a new, blank file *and closes your existing one.* Unlike most Windows applications, Image Composer 1.5 allows only one open window at a time. (Image Composer has a Window menu, but it only tiles or cascades views of the *same file.*)

✦ **Open**: No surprises here, this tool opens files.

✦ **Save**: Saves files, as you'd expect. *But in Image Composer, you are as likely to save selected objects* as you are to save an entire file.

✦ **Print**: Image Composer is built to create Web images, not hard-copy graphics, but it does have a Print command.

✦ **Cut**: Cuts selected sprite(s).

✦ **Copy**: Copies selected sprite(s).

✦ **Paste**: Pastes contents of the Clipboard.

✦ **Undo**: *Only works once in Image Composer*, which means a whole different thought process and working style. You'll want to use the Duplicate tool (discussed later in this list) often, to create safe backups of your images in the workspace.

✦ **Insert Image File**: Inserts graphics (your other option is to copy images through the Clipboard into Image Composer).

✦ **Delete**: Deletes selected object(s).

✦ **Duplicate**: Creates a duplicate of the selected sprite(s), which is *very useful for design and for backup.*

✦ **Select All**: Selects all sprites in the workspace.

✦ **Clear Selection**: Deselects whatever has been selected.

✦ **Color Fill**: Applies the color in the Color Swatch (at the bottom of the toolbox) to selected objects.

✦ **Color Format**: *This is where you select a color palette, discussed earlier.*

✦ **Actual Size**: Displays the workspace at 100 percent; *you must display the workspace at Actual Size to create or edit text.*

✦ **Zoom Percent**: *Ranges from a telescopic 10 percent to a bizarre 1,000 percent.*

✦ **Help**: You know how this works.

Image Composer's Power-Packed Toolbox

The heart of Image Composer's power lies in the toolbox (not to be confused with the toolbar), on the left side of the workspace. Many of the tools in the toolbox (all of them, except for the Selection, Zoom, and Pan tools, and the Color Swatch) open a palette on the bottom of the window. These palettes (not to be confused with color palettes) function something like dialog boxes in that they configure and apply toolbox tools and their effects.

The Image Composer toolbox is shown in Figure 8-3 with a composition in process. The toolbox contains all the tools that you need to create images, and hundreds of effects that you can use to alter those images. Each tool (except the Selection tool) opens a palette, and each palette, in turn, can contain dozens of effects. Therefore, an encyclopedic survey of all the buttons in each palette is beyond the scope of this chapter. But each palette is introduced, along with some advice on what each palette does. Later in this chapter, two tutorials introduce you to palettes in more detail.

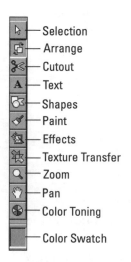

Selection
Arrange
Cutout
Text
Shapes
Paint
Effects
Texture Transfer
Zoom
Pan
Color Toning
Color Swatch

Figure 8-3: The bulk of Image Composer's power lies within the toolbox tools.

Selection

With the Selection tool, you can click a single sprite to select it, use Shift+click to select several sprites, or draw a Marquee, as shown in Figure 8-4, to select several sprites.

Arrange

After you select a single sprite, or a bunch of sprites, the Arrange tool enables you to manipulate it/them. The Arrange palette (shown in Figure 8-5) includes tools to do all kinds of stuff to your objects.

Combining sprites

One of the most useful features of the Arrange palette is the ability to combine sprites into (temporary) groups, or to flatten them permanently into a single sprite.

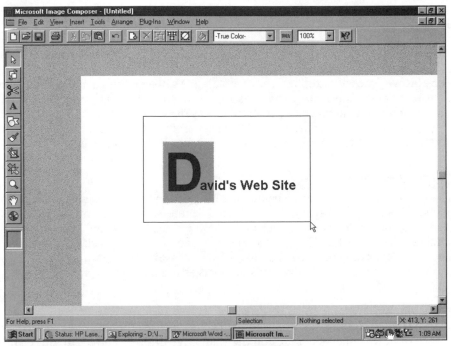

Figure 8-4: Selecting a bunch of sprites simultaneously

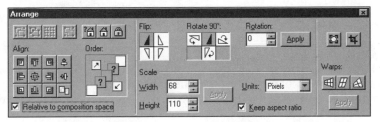

Figure 8-5: The Arrange palette acts like a sprite conductor, controlling the relationships of objects.

Grouping sprites makes them easy to move around or resize in your composition, while maintaining their relative positions and sizes. Grouped sprites retain their own identities, so that you can ungroup them later. To group several sprites, select them by using the standard Windows Shift+click combination, drag a Marquee box around them, or, to select all the sprites in a composition, press Ctrl+A and then press Ctrl+G (or select Arrange ⇨ Group). To ungroup a collection of sprites, select the group and press Ctrl+U (or select Arrange ⇨ Ungroup). You can even group several groups of sprites. To do this, select the groups as though they were individual sprites and press Ctrl+G. When you ungroup a group of sprites, the original groups are still intact. To return a group of groups to its individual sprites all at once, press Ctrl+E or select Arrange ➪ Explode Group.

Flattening, as opposed to grouping, a selection of sprites combines the individual sprites into one single sprite. (Users of vector graphics programs, such as CorelDRAW!, know "flattening" as "combining.") This can be advantageous if you want to create an intricately shaped sprite or need to paint all the sprites simultaneously. One downside to flattening sprites is that you can't unflatten them to get back the original sprites. To flatten several sprites, select them as just outlined and either press Ctrl+F or select Arrange ➪ Flatten Selection.

Aligning sprites

The Align area in the Arrange palette enables you to align the sides, centers, tops, and so on, of selected sprites. The Flip and Rotate areas flip or rotate a single sprite (the Rotation angle spin box doesn't work on groups of selected sprites, only on a single selected sprite). The Scale spin boxes can be used to resize a single sprite. The Fit to Bounding box strips sprites of unnecessary borders, and the Crop/Extend button manually trims or enlarges the border of a sprite.

Warping sprites

In addition to features that are used to arrange sprites, the Arrange palette has a couple of powerful effects stuck on the right edge of the palette. The three Warps options apply pretty wild distortion and perspective to a selected sprite. These features would be more at home in the Effects palette, but don't let that stop you from experimenting with them.

Cutout

The Cutout palette has two tabs: The Cutout Tools tab, which works like scissors, enabling you to cut shapes out of sprites, and the Select Color Region tab, which enables you to point at and click a selected color in a sprite, and cut out that color.

The Cutout tool makes it easy to cut and paste only certain areas of a sprite. The four main cutout tools are the Rectangle, Oval, Curve, and Polygon tools. The Rectangle and Oval tools enable you to copy simple geometric shapes, whereas the Curve and Polygon tools enable you to copy more-intricate shapes. In addition, you can select areas to copy based on their colors by using the Select Color Region tab of the Cutout palette.

To select an area to copy using the Rectangle or Oval tool, select either the Rectangle or Oval icon at the left side of the Cutout Tools tab. Click and drag the cursor over the sprite to define the area that you want to copy. You can constrain the shape to a square (or circle) by pressing either the Shift or Ctrl key while dragging. Release the mouse button when your shape is defined.

To select an area using the Curve or Polygon tool, select either the Curve or Polygon icon at the left side of the Cutout Tools tab. Click points on the sprite to define the outline of the shape that you want to copy. To edit the shape that you have defined, click one of the three icons in the Edit Curve or Polygon area of the palette. The icon with a plus sign in it adds points to your curve wherever you click it. To remove points from your curve (or vertices from a polygon), click the icon with a minus sign, and then click a point (the points are highlighted with small boxes when you move the cursor near them). To move a point or vertex, click the blank icon and then click the point and drag it to its new location.

To select an area by its color, click the Select Color Region tab. Set the "sharpness" of the selection's edge by using the Hard ... Soft slider. The further to the right this slider is located, the more "fuzzy" the edge of the selection becomes. Set the tolerance (or closeness of color) for your selection by using the Hue, Whiteness, and Blackness sliders — the lower these are set, the smaller the difference in colors that are selected. To select all matching colors within the sprite, check the Global radio button. To pick only those matching colors that are in direct contact with the point where you click, check the Local radio button. Click the Magic Wand icon on the left side of the palette and click the area of the sprite that you want to copy. You can add areas to your selection by checking the Add radio button and clicking another area within the sprite. Remove areas from your selection by checking the Delete radio button, tightening the Hue, Whiteness, and Blackness settings (making them closer to zero), and clicking the area that you want to remove.

To make the selection into a new sprite, click the Cut Out button (this button is on both the Cutout Tolls tab and the Select Color Region tab). The area that you selected now appears as a new sprite and is already selected. You can paint, copy, distort, or otherwise treat this new sprite just like any other. To cut the selection from the sprite, click the Erase button. The sprite now has a hole that is the shape of the selected area.

Figure 8-6 shows the letter *D* cut out of a sprite that originally combined the letter and a green background.

Text

The Text tool is used to create graphical text. Why not just use text in FrontPage? Good question, because FrontPage text can have colors and fonts assigned to it, just like graphical text. And, when you place graphical text from Image Composer into your Web site, you can't edit it. However, you can apply to graphical text all kinds of effects that you can't apply to regular text in FrontPage.

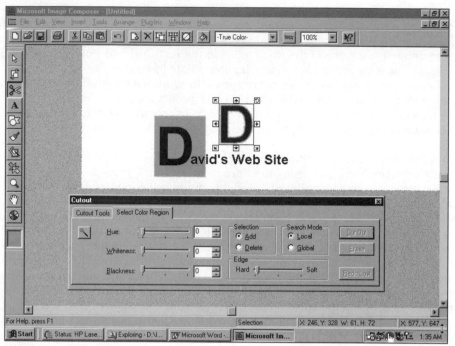

Figure 8-6: The Cutout tool works like scissors, and can be used to remove a color from a sprite.

Follow these steps to create a text sprite:

1. Select the Text tool, draw a text box with the crosshair cursor, and then type your text, as shown in Figure 8-7.

2. Select a font from the Font drop-down list in the Text dialog box.

3. Set the font size in the Size drop-down list.

4. Select a color for the text by clicking the Color rectangle in the lower-right corner of the dialog box. In the Color Picker dialog box, select the Custom Palette tab. Select a color by clicking a square in the color table. Click OK to accept the color.

5. The Smoothing check box applies a feature sometimes called "anti-aliasing" to your text sprite. Smoothing reduces the grainy, "step-like" look on diagonal lines in letters. The downside to smoothing is that letters look blurrier. The Underline check box adds underlining.

6. When you finish formatting and editing your text, click the Select Tool to create the letter sprite in the currently selected font and color.

Figure 8-7: Creating graphical text

Shapes

You can create rectangles, ovals, curves, or polygons with the Shapes tool. First, select one of the four shapes. Then, use the shape cursor to draw your shape. The Close and Fill check boxes turn those options on and off. Use the three Edit Curve or Polygon buttons to (from left to right) Move, Add, or Delete points. Figure 8-8 shows points being moved.

You can vary your shape edge from hard (tends to be jagged) to soft (tends to be blurry). The Lock Tool check box opens the Shapes palette with the selected tool the next time that you use it, which is handy if you're drawing lots of circles, rectangles, or polygons in a row.

After you tweak your shape, click the Create button in the Shapes palette — but think carefully first, because you can't edit shape points after you create a shape.

Note   One of the most universal techniques for creating buttons, icons, banners, and logos is to combine shapes with text. Right-click any sprite — text or shape — and select one of the order commands in the context menu (such as Bring to Front) to bring sprites forward or send them backwards.

Figure 8-9 shows a shape being moved behind a graphic.

Figure 8-8: Editing shape points

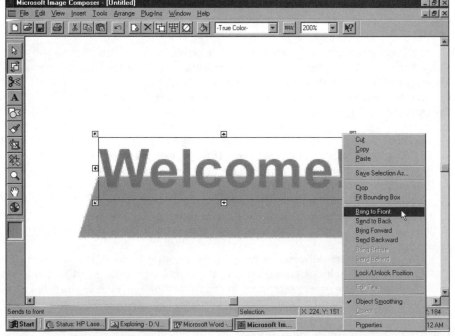

Figure 8-9: Many logos, buttons, and icons are made by combining shapes and text.

Paint

The Paint tool applies effects to *part* of a sprite. If you're familiar with paint programs (even Windows Paint, which comes with Windows), you're used to being able to select the Paint tool and begin drawing as soon as the program starts. This is not the way that Image Composer works. Instead, you can only paint on existing sprites.

While having to paint on sprites may seem like a totally bad thing, it is more of a mixed blessing — if you have a complicated image, the ability to work on a single sprite means that you don't have to worry about ruining sprites that you want to leave alone.

To paint on a sprite, select the sprite that you want to use and open the Paint palette by clicking the Paint Palette button in the toolbar. Select a paintbrush and begin painting on your sprite. If the tools in the Paint palette (see Figure 8-10) are gray, then you either haven't selected a sprite or have selected a group of sprites. The prior section, "Combining sprites," tells how to group, ungroup, and flatten (combine) sprites to make working with them easier.

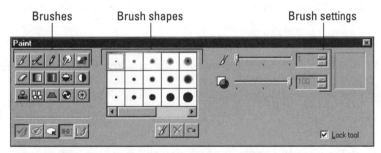

Figure 8-10: The Paint palette provides control over how you paint on a sprite.

Select the brush that you want to paint with from the left-hand table of brushes. The middle list, brush shapes, contains numerous preset sizes for the brushes — the fuzzy brushes in the top two rows indicate that these brushes paint with soft, more natural edges. The brush settings section contains several ways to customize each brush — these settings change depending on which brush you select.

The color shown in the Color Picker box at the bottom of the toolbar is the color that you'll be painting with. If you want to change the paint color, click the Color Picker and select the new color from the dialog box that opens.

As shown in Figure 8-10, the Paint palette contains 15 different standard brushes. Unlike some of the other paint programs, Image Composer includes various special effects brushes, in addition to the standard brush, spray gun, and pencil. All brushes can be used at various sizes, set by using the Brush Size slider in the brush settings (right) section of the palette. This lets you set brush sizes from 1 to 100 pixels in diameter.

Most brushes include the Opacity slider, which ranges from 0 to 100 — a setting of 0 means that the paint or effect being applied is nearly invisible, whereas 100 means that the effect obscures what's being painted over.

Here is a list of the brushes, with a short description of the capabilities of each one:

✦ **Paintbrush**: Works like the typical paintbrush. Lets you paint with solid colors.

✦ **Air brush**: Paints like an artist's air brush. The faster you move this tool, the lighter the paint is.

✦ **Pencil**: Makes a hard, solid line.

✦ **Smear**: Doesn't actually paint anything, but rather smears the paint already on the sprite.

✦ **Impression**: Adds an impressionistic "spottiness" when applied.

✦ **Erase**: Removes portions of the sprite, unlike the erase tool in most paint programs. You can't paint on any area that's been erased. Be very careful when using this tool.

✦ **Tint**: Tints the opaque areas of a sprite with the current color.

✦ **Color fill**: Applies the current color without affecting the brightness of the underlying paint (similar to tint).

✦ **Dodge/burn**: Darkens (dodges) or lightens (burns) the colors in the sprite. Use the Burn... Dodge slider to set the amount of darkening/lightening. If the slider is left in its default position, the tool has no effect.

✦ **Step contrast**: Changes the contrast of the painted area (the difference between the darkest and lightest areas). Low settings on the Low ... High slider bring the darkness levels closer together, while higher settings increase the contrast between dark and light.

✦ **Rubber stamp**: Duplicates small areas. Click the area to be duplicated and then click again in another area to "drop" a copy of it.

✦ **Pick source**: Similar to the rubber stamp brush, except that the source for the "paint" is another sprite. Select the sprite that you want to paint on and then select the pick source brush. Then, click the sprite whose paint you want to copy and click the original sprite where you want the copy placed.

✦ **Mesa**: Distorts the area on which it is used, by either pulling in or pushing out the center area. Set the amount of distortion in the Radius Factor % text box and the direction (in or out) in the Warp Direction area.

✦ **Vortex**: Distorts the area on which it is used, by swirling the colors to resemble a whirlpool. Set the "speed" of the whirlpool in the Angle text box.

✦ **Spoke inversion**: Distorts the area on which it is used, by pinching it toward the center. Set the amount of "pinching" in the Value text box.

Note We've created an online tutorial on working with the Paint palette, which you can visit at http://www.ppinet.com/paint.htm.

Effects

The Effects palette could really use a book of its own. The Categories list on the right side of the palette at least narrows down the options to various categories. For example, Figure 8-11 shows the five effects available when you select the Outlines category.

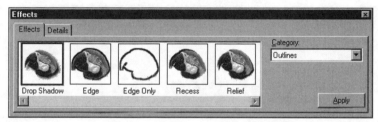

Figure 8-11: The Outlines category in the Effects palette includes drop shadows and outlines.

Many effects can be adjusted with the Details tab that appears in the Effects palette when they are selected. The selected effect in Figure 8-12 (and 8-11), Drop Shadow, has a Details tab that enables you to define the direction, distance, color, hardness, and opacity (opacity is the opposite of transparency — fully opaque shadows are solid; low opacity shadows allow objects beneath them to show through).

Figure 8-12: Drop shadows can be fine-tuned in the Details tab of the Effects palette.

Texture Transfer

The Texture Transfer tool transfers textures from one sprite to another. It comes with numerous, fairly complex options, but the most basic ones transfer the texture of one image into another image. To do that, select the Texture Transfer tool and follow these steps:

1. Move the "from" sprite and the "to" sprite on top of each other.

2. Select the "from" sprite first and then hold down the Shift key and select the "to" sprite.

3. Select the Transfer Full option in the Texture Transfer palette to transfer the full background of the "from" sprite into the "to" sprite. Or, select the Tile option in the palette to tile a smaller background into a larger sprite. Tile transferring is selected in Figure 8-13.

Figure 8-13: Tile transfers repeat an image as a fill for a second image.

4. Click the Apply button to transfer one image into another. The result will look something like Figure 8-14.

Figure 8-14: A tiled, transferred texture

Zoom

The Zoom tool doesn't open a palette; it transforms your cursor into a magnifying glass. Click to enlarge your view, as shown in Figure 8-15. Use Ctrl+click to zoom out.

Pan

The Pan tool transforms your cursor into a grabber hand, like the one shown in Figure 8-16. You don't have to click any sprites, or have any selected. Just click and drag any spot on your screen to scroll around in your window.

Color Tuning

Color tuning is a way to apply very subtle and complex adjustments to the colors in a sprite.

Click to zoom in

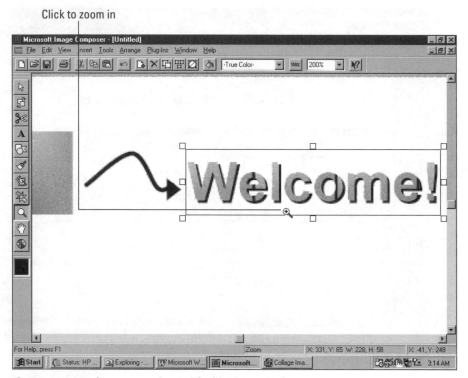

Figure 8-15: Enlarge your view with the Zoom tool.

You can use the Color Tuning palette to micromanage this process of adjusting color brightness, contrast, and intensity. Actually, you have three different Color Tuning palettes. They are available when you choose the Color Tuning tool in the Image Composer toolbox. The three palettes can then be selected by clicking one of the three tools that appear at the left edge of the Color Tuning palette. These three tools, listed next, are always visible, no matter which Color Tuning palette you are working with:

✦ **Color Tuning – Color Shifting**: Provides access to four sliders/spin boxes in the Color Shifting palette that enable you to adjust brightness and contrast for all colors in a sprite, or selectively to only Red, Green, or Blue pixels within a sprite. The Hue slider/spin box adjusts the color of each pixel around the Color Wheel. The Color Tuning – Color Shifting palette also enables you to change *saturation,* which alters a color by increasing or decreasing the gray pixels in the sprite. Unlike the other three slider/spin boxes in this palette, Color Saturation can't be applied to just one color. Lowering the degree of Color Saturation makes a sprite turn gray.

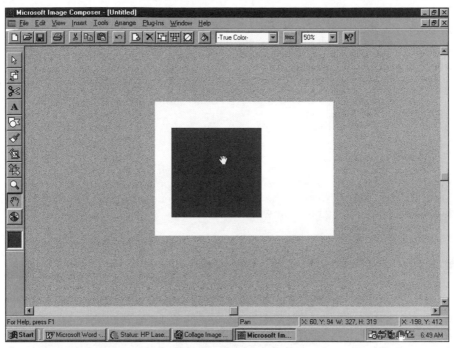

Figure 8-16: Dragging with the Pan hand cursor

✦ **Color Tuning – Highlights & Shadows**: Enables you to adjust the coloration of highlights and shadows in an image. When the graph line is straight at 45 degrees, the input equals the output, and the sprite coloring is not changed. When you tug on any of the three handles for a selected color (or all colors), you alter the ratio between input and output coloring. The top handle on each line changes bright pixels in the image. Moving the handle up brightens the already bright parts of the sprite. The lower handle affects the darker pixels in the sprite, and the middle handle affects midrange pixels. Dragging the top handle on a line up, for example, brightens the brightness of pixels of the selected color. The Highlight/Shadow graph does the same thing as the Brightness control on the Color Tuning – Color Shifting palette, except that the Highlight/Shadow graph gives you more control over how brightness is applied—enabling you to control individually the bright, midrange, and dark pixels of the selected color. For example, you can use the Highlights & Shadows tool to darken all the reds in a photo of a rose, while making the light-green pixels lighter, and the dark-green pixels darker.

✦ **Dynamic Range**: Enables you to control the range of color intensity in a selected sprite. Think of images as composed of high-intensity (bright) and low-intensity (dark) pixels. You can restrict the range of intensity in pixels with the Dynamic Range palette by cutting out either high- or low-intensity pixels in a selected sprite. When you select a sprite and then click the Dynamic Range tool in the Color Tuning palette, a histogram appears that reflects the range of intensity in the selected sprite. By moving the right, left, or both lines at the ends of the histogram, you can force pixels to a brighter or darker color. Moving the right bar to the left forces more pixels to be brighter. Moving the left bar to the right forces more pixels to a darker value. While color tuning requires quite a bit of experimentation, it does allow unequaled adjustment of color and brightness in imported color photos. For a tutorial and detailed discussion of color tuning, visit our Web site at `http://www.ppinet.com/color.htm`.

Color Swatch

The Color Swatch displays the color that will be applied to selected sprites when you click the Color Fill tool in the toolbar. Double-clicking the Color Swatch opens the Color Picker dialog box, shown in Figure 8-17.

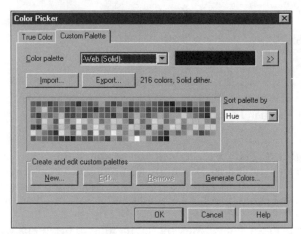

Figure 8-17: Picking colors from Image Composer's preset 216-color Web-browser palette

The Color Picker palette has the following two tabs:

 ✦ **True Color**: Enables you to apply an almost-infinite number of colors, and to mix up any exact color you want to use.

 ✦ **Custom Palette**: Enables you to use a predefined color palette, or define a new one.

The first of the following two tutorials shows you how to define a custom file space-saving eight-color palette. Click a color in either tab of the Color Picker dialog box to assign it to the Color Swatch.

In the following tutorial, you will create a logo for your Web site that can be used as an image map.

Tutorial 8.1: Create a Web Graphic

Cross-Reference See Chapter 7 for complete instructions on how to define image map hotspots in FrontPage.

1. Open a new window in Image Composer (if you have a window open, close it and save your work, if you want to keep it — remember, you can have only one image composer file open at a time).

2. Click the Actual Size button in the toolbar to view your workspace at 100 percent. (You can only edit text at 100 percent.)

3. Click the Text tool in the toolbox (on the left) and draw a square with the Text tool cursor, as shown in Figure 8-18.

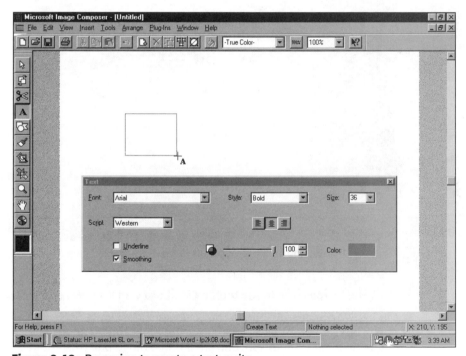

Figure 8-18: Preparing to create a text sprite

4. Type the first letter of your name. Click the Color Swatch in the Text palette and select a bright color (such as red). Check the Smoothing check box to remove jagged edges from your letter. Select a solid font (such as Impact) and set font size to 72. Make sure the Opacity slider is set to 100, so that your text is completely opaque (and not transparent). After you define your text attributes, click the Selection tool in the toolbox.

5. Click the Text tool again, and type the rest of your name (minus the first letter). Select a dark color, and 14-point Arial font. Click the Selection tool in the toolbox again.

6. Click and drag the small text and align it with the large letter, as shown in Figure 8-19.

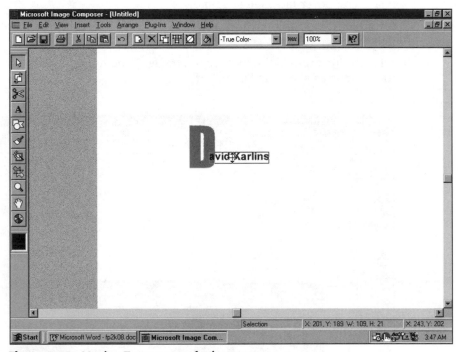

Figure 8-19: Moving Text on top of other text

7. Click the Shapes tool in the toolbox, and draw a rectangle of any size.

8. Click the Arrange tool, and in the Scale area, deselect the Keep Aspect Ratio check box. Set the Width at 400 pixels, and the Height at 40 pixels, as shown in Figure 8-20. Click the Apply button in the Arrange palette.

9. Double-click the Color Swatch at the bottom of the toolbox to open the Color Picker palette. Click the Custom Palette tab and select the Web (Solid) palette from the Color Palette drop-down menu. (These are colors supported by browsers.)

10. Click a bright-yellow square in the Color palette and then click OK in the Color Picker dialog box.

11. With the rectangle selected, click the Color Fill button in the toolbar to assign the selected color to the rectangle.

12. Draw a small oval with the Shapes tool.

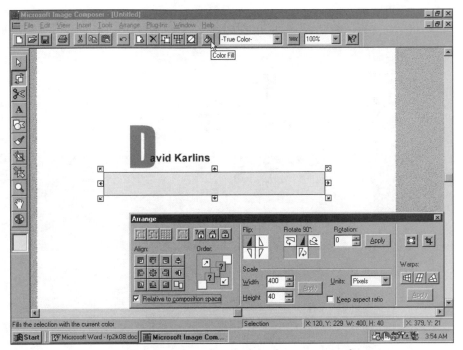

Figure 8-20: You can define size, to the pixel, in the Arrange palette.

13. Click the Effects tool in the toolbox. Select the Patterns category from the drop-down list on the right side of the Effects palette. Click the Hue/Whiteness effect, and then click the Details tab in the Effects palette. Set the Opacity slider to 60. Click Apply.

14. Select Outlines from the Category drop-down list in the Effects palette, click Relief, and then click the Apply button.

15. Size the button so that four buttons can fit on the rectangle that you created.

16. Click the Duplicate button three times to create more buttons. Move them all onto the rectangle that you created.

17. Create a text sprite with the word **Home** on it.

18. Resize the text so that it fits inside the oval buttons that you created. Duplicate the text sprite three times, and then double-click inside the duplicate buttons to change the text to **Back**, **New**, and **Next**.

19. Move each of the four text sprites so that they are roughly centered inside the four oval buttons. Select the Arrange tool. Draw a Marquee with the cursor around all four buttons and the large rectangle. Click the Center Horizontally tool in the Arrange palette, as shown in Figure 8-21.

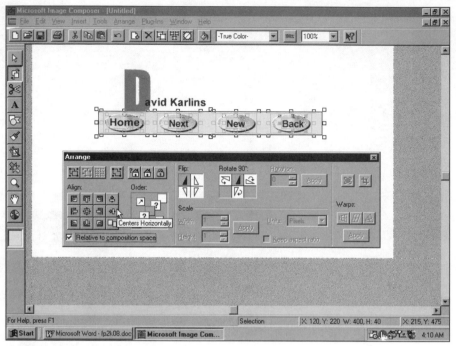

Figure 8-21: Centered sprites

20. Experiment with one more effect: Click the large capital letter (the start of your name) and click the Skew tool in the Warps area of the Arrange palette. Click and drag one of the corners of the text sprite, as shown in Figure 8-22.

21. Arrange your buttons and text sprites to create a banner for a Web page.

22. Save your file as an Image Composer file by clicking the Save button. Select Microsoft Image Composer as the file format, enter a filename, and navigate to a folder in which you want to save the file. Click the Save button.

Now that you've created a banner for a Web page and saved it in Image Composer format (*.mic), you can open this file at any time. The easiest way to transfer your banner to a Web page is to click and drag to select all the sprites (or click the Select All button in the toolbar), and copy the sprites into the Clipboard. Then, just open a Web page in Page view of FrontPage, and paste in the image.

Transferring Images to Pages

Tutorial 8.1 ended by explaining that you can easily copy any selected sprite(s) into FrontPage Page view. As described in Chapter 7, after you copy images into FrontPage, you can do quite a bit with them—add transparency, select a file format, resize them, and even adjust attributes, such as brightness and contrast.

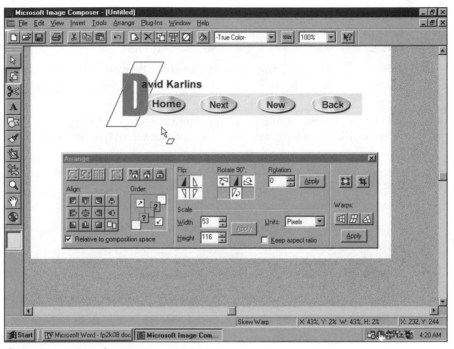

Figure 8-22: Warping text

That method of copying and pasting files from Image Composer to FrontPage works well. However, you can achieve even more control over your Web graphics by saving them to a Web-friendly graphic format in Image Composer. The reasons to save your images as Web-compatible graphics are the following:

✦ Web-compatible graphics can be used with any Web page creation program, including HTML coding.

✦ You can define custom, space-saving palettes in Image Composer to reduce file size (and download time).

✦ You can control transparency for GIF files in Image Composer.

✦ You can control the quality of JPEG images in Image Composer.

Creating custom color palettes

If you are going to save your image as a GIF file, you can often reduce file size by creating a custom palette. As with some other Web graphic concepts discussed thus far, the topic of reducing graphic file size has whole chapters of books written about it. But don't let that intimidate you, because Image Composer does a good job of reducing graphic file size, so you can simply use it to do the task. The following series of steps creates a custom palette for your Web graphic:

1. Select all the sprites that you want to save as a GIF file.

2. Double-click the Color Swatch to open the Color Picker dialog box, and then click the New button in the Custom Palette tab.

3. In the Palette Size drop-down list, choose the number of colors in your custom palette. (8- or 16-color images often are significantly smaller than 256-color images.)

4. Different methods of dithering are a bit beyond the scope of this chapter, but Error Diffusion generally works well. Click OK in the New Color Palette dialog box.

5. In the Palette Name field of the New Color Palette dialog box (shown in Figure 8-23), type a name for your palette. Then click OK.

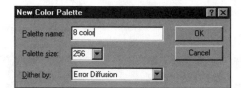

Figure 8-23: Naming a custom color palette

6. Click the Generate Colors button in the Color Picker dialog box, and select Selection in the Generate From drop-down list.

7. Click the Add button in the Generate Colors dialog box, and then click Close. Image Composer studies your selected sprites, and generates a limited-color palette that best covers the colors that you need for your image (using dithering to generate the illusion of additional colors, if necessary).

8. With your custom palette generated, you can click OK. Your palette is available to save files.

The next section discusses saving images as Web-friendly graphics, and explains how to implement a reduced-color palette.

Saving files as GIFs

Rarely does any reason exist to save an entire workspace as a GIF file. Instead, the first step in saving an Image Composer illustration as a GIF file is to select those sprites that you want to save. Even if all the sprites on your workspace will be part of your GIF image, you should still select them, to avoid saving unused parts of the workspace. With sprites selected, choose File ➪ Save Selection As. Choose CompuServe GIF from the Save File As Type drop-down list. The Saves the Current Selection dialog box offers you some options for your GIF image.

Adding transparency to images

You can save your selected sprites as a GIF file with built-in transparency by selecting the Transparent Color check box in the Saves the Current Selection dialog box. This works as long as you selected GIF (or PNG, which is a relative of GIF files) as your file type.

If the default color in the Transparent Color Swatch doesn't match the color that you want to make disappear, you can click the Color Swatch and select a new color from the Color Picker. The Threshold slider lets you tweak transparency; higher levels cause shades close to your transparent color to become transparent, lower values restrict transparency to a more exact match.

Saving with defined color palettes

If you created custom color palettes (discussed a bit earlier in this chapter), you can apply those palettes to your GIF file. To do that, pull down the Color Format drop-down list in the Saves the Current Selection dialog box, and select a palette.

Figure 8-24 shows selected sprites being saved as an eight-color GIF file.

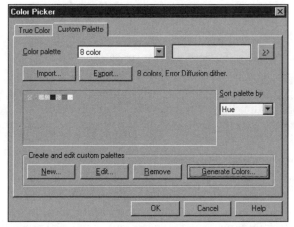

Figure 8-24: Saving selected sprites as a GIF file with an eight-color palette

Transparency, color palettes, and file format are all defined in the Saves the Current Selection dialog box. After you define these attributes, click OK.

Saving images as JPEG files

If your sprite has lots of colors, or a complex mix of colors (a scanned color photo, for example), JPEG file format may be the most efficient way to save your file. To save an image as a JPEG file, select sprites, choose File ⇨ Save Selection As, and choose JPEG in the Save As Type drop-down menu.

You can speed up your file by selecting the Compression check box. Higher values in the Amount slider cause your file to download faster, but reduce quality.

As with saving sprites as GIF files, you need to enter a filename in the File Name field, and then save your selected images by clicking the Save button in the Saves the Current Selection dialog box.

A Web page background works much like the wallpaper tiles on a Windows computer. A small image is repeated, horizontally and vertically, to fill the space defined by the window. Chapter 6 already discussed how to insert a background into a Web page by using the Page Properties dialog box. The following tutorial uses Image Composer to create two types of backgrounds: a tiled background, and a striped background.

Tutorial 8.2: Create a Tiled Page Background

1. Make a square approximately 80 ☐ 80 pixels.

2. Fill it with a color (use a light color, such as light yellow or beige).

3. Select the Effects tool in the toolbox. In the Effects palette, select Photographic in the Category drop-down menu and pick Grain from the list of effects. With the square selected, click Apply.

4. Save the image as a JPEG file with 50-percent compression.

5. Open a Web page in FrontPage's Page view. Right-click anywhere and select Theme. If a Theme is assigned to the page, select No Theme for the page (you can't apply your own background if you have a Theme assigned to the page). Then, right-click and select Page Properties. Click the Background tab and select the Background Image check box.

6. Click the Browse button and navigate to your saved JPEG background image. (If you didn't make one, you can use the background.jpg file on the CD-ROM that comes with this book.)

7. You can save your page with the background image. You'll be prompted to save the embedded background image as you save your page, as shown in Figure 8-25.

8. Back in Image Composer, create a rectangle 1,024-pixels wide and 40-pixels high (don't worry if the rectangle is wider than the white area of the workspace — it won't matter when you save the sprites). Assign a light color to the long, thin sprite.

9. Create a second rectangle sprite, 144-pixels wide and 40-pixels high. Align the bottom and left of the two rectangles. Assign a Gray Scale Right Gradient effect to the small rectangle (use the Details tab to find the Gray Scale Right Gradient). Use the Bilinear Warp effect to make the right side of the small rectangle a diagonal, as shown in Figure 8-26.

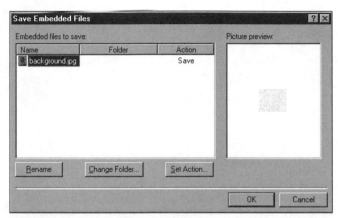

Figure 8-25: Embedded background images are saved with your Web page.

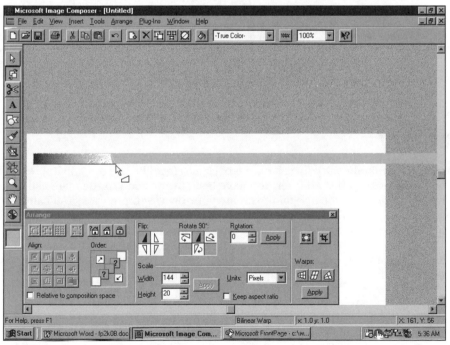

Figure 8-26: It's easy to whip up those fun wavy-stripe backgrounds in Image Composer.

10. Save the two sprites as a JPEG image, and assign that image to the background of a Web page. Look at the page in the Preview tab, or in your browser, as shown in Figure 8-27.

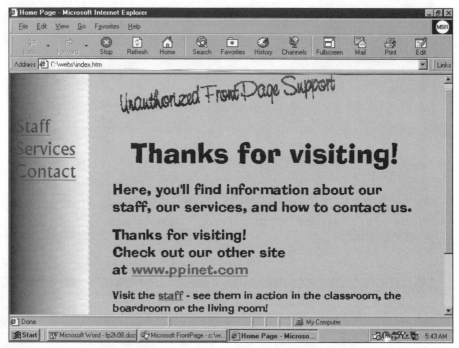

Figure 8-27: Checking out your striped background in a browser

Summary

You can justifiably pat yourself on the back and feel like the next digital Degas after you finish reading this chapter. You have been introduced to the main aspects of Image Composer and can begin to create your own Web pictures. You can also make image maps that let your visitors quickly and easily navigate your Web site. Furthermore, you can design custom background images.

You can use these custom images in more complex page designs if you employ tables as a design tool. You'll explore that technique in the next chapter.

✦   ✦   ✦

Layout and Design

Formatting with Tables

✦ ✦ ✦ ✦

In This Chapter

Creating a table

Editing table properties

Adjusting table structure

Using tables for page layout

✦ ✦ ✦ ✦

By now, you have learned to use FrontPage to create and edit your Web pages and to enhance them with Themes, office objects, formatted text, and graphic images. This chapter looks at more-advanced techniques for controlling the layout of information on your Web pages by using tables. Tables can be used to format tabular data or to arrange the layout of text and other objects on your Web pages.

Two Uses for Tables

Tables have two basic uses in Web design:

> ✦ **To display text and images in columns and rows**: If you have used spreadsheet applications such as Microsoft Excel, or created tables in Microsoft Word or Access, creating tables in FrontPage will be intuitive.

> ✦ **To design pages**: While Microsoft and its rivals continue to add new interpretive powers to HTML, including the ability to recognize exact locations for objects, tables are still the easiest and most effective way to lay out information at an exact location on your page, or in columns or rows.

Creating a Table

Whether you are creating a table to display shipping prices in neat rows and columns, or 3D animated graphics at different locations on your Web page, the process of defining a table is the same. To use tables as design tools or to display data, you first define the location of your table, and then define how many rows and columns you need. These attributes are easy to edit.

Three ways exist to create a table in FrontPage The simplest way is to use the Insert Table tool in the Standard toolbar. For the numerically oriented, the Insert Table dialog box enables you to define a table precisely. Finally, you can graphically draw a table and define columns and rows by using the Table toolbar. All three options are explored in the following sections.

After you create a table and place text or other objects in table cells, you can define table and cell properties. Fine-tuning the appearance of your table cells and rows is discussed in the sections "Editing Table Properties" and "Editing cell properties," later in this chapter.

Creating tables the quick and easy way

In many cases, you can use the Insert Table tool in the Standard toolbar to create a quick sketch of your table. Because you are likely to edit the size and features of your table anyway, the Insert Table tool is probably the most efficient way to add a table to your Web page.

With a Web page open in Page View, you can insert a table by following these steps:

1. Click to place your insertion point at the spot where you want the table to appear in your Web page.

2. Click the Insert Table button in the Standard toolbar.

3. Click and drag to the right in the Grid palette to add columns; click and drag down to add rows. Figure 9-1 defines a table that is nine-rows long and three-columns wide.

Inserting and defining a table

Inserting a table by using the Insert Table dialog box (shown in Figure 9-2) provides more initial control over the appearance of your table. While not every table option is available in this dialog box, enough options are there to make setting up your table easier. These options, as well as others, are explained in detail later in this chapter in the section entitled "Editing Table Properties."

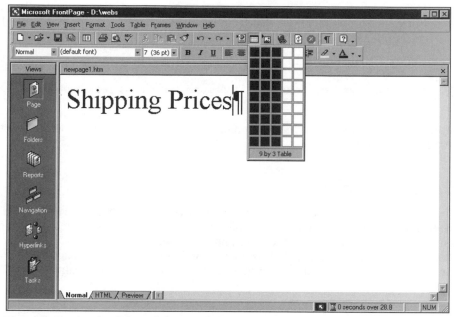

Figure 9-1: Simply click and drag to design a table.

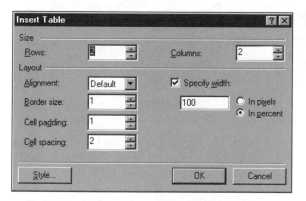

Figure 9-2: Use the Insert Table dialog box to define table properties as you create a table.

The main options of initial concern are located in the Size and Width sections of the dialog box. These options let you specify how many rows and columns your table has, and its overall width.

To insert a table, follow these steps:

1. Select Table ➪ Insert Table to open the Insert Table dialog box.

2. Set the Size, Layout, and Width options.

3. If you want to assign inline styles, click the Style button and use the Format button in the Modify Style dialog box to define local font, paragraph, border, or number styles for your table.

4. Click OK to insert the table.

Cross-Reference For a more complete discussion of styles and style sheets, see Chapter 12.

After the table is inserted, it can be manipulated in any of the ways detailed in the rest of this chapter.

Drawing a table

The Insert Table dialog box enables you to define many table properties digitally, by entering numbers in fields. The Table toolbar enables you to format your table in a more graphical form, using the tools shown in Figure 9-3. (The function of each of these tools is explained later in this chapter, in "Adjusting table structure," except for the Background Color tool, which is explained in the section "Editing Table Properties.")

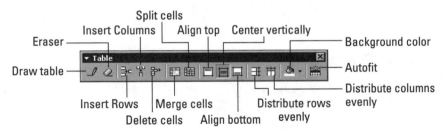

Figure 9-3: The Table toolbar

For the purposes of defining a new table, the important tool is the Draw Table tool. Appropriately named, this tool enables you to create a table simply by drawing its structure in your page. To create a table by using the Draw Table tool:

1. Select the Draw Table tool from the Tables toolbar, or if the toolbar isn't visible, select Table ➪ Draw table. The cursor changes to a pencil, and the Tables toolbar opens.

2. Click and drag the cursor to define the overall rectangular shape of the table that you want to create. When the table is the size that you want, release the mouse button.

3. Add rows and columns to your table simply by drawing them (see Figure 9-4).

4. After you finish creating your table, click the Draw Table tool in the toolbar again to deselect it. The cursor returns to normal.

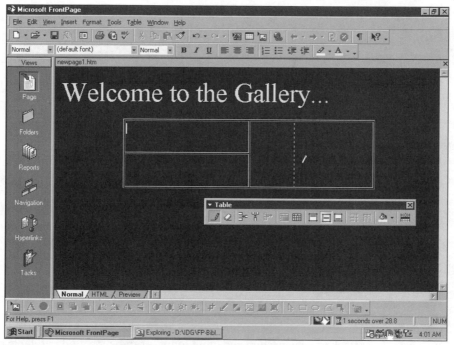

Figure 9-4: Adding cells by using the Draw Table tool

Placing text and other objects in a table

Adding content (text, graphics, form fields, videos, and what-have-you) is exactly the same as adding it anywhere else on a page. Click to place the insertion point at which you want to add content, and then type or insert the content. Voila! Figure 9-5 shows images and text placed in a table.

Resizing tables and rows

Table cells adjust in height and width as you place text and other objects in them. Inserting a large image in a cell enlarges that cell to accommodate the image. Typing unbreakable text strings (for example, long words) widens a column, as necessary. Typing additional text may lengthen your cell.

As you move your cursor over a row or column divider, a double-headed cursor appears, as shown in Figure 9-6. Click and drag to the right or left to change column width, and up or down to change row height.

Figure 9-5: Text, graphics—even video and input forms—can be inserted into table cells.

Figure 9-6: Click and drag row or column borders to change cell size.

Importing a table

Suppose you already have a carefully formatted spreadsheet full of data that you want to include in a Web page. Wouldn't it be nice if you could just copy and paste the table into FrontPage and have it automatically convert to HTML? Well, sometimes wishes do come true. You can either copy selected ranges or a worksheet into FrontPage, or import an existing spreadsheet file into a FrontPage Web page.

To copy spreadsheet cells into FrontPage:

1. Start Microsoft Excel, another spreadsheet program, or another program with a table (such as Microsoft Access or Word), and open the file with your table.

2. Highlight the cells that you want to include in your page and copy the selection either by selecting Edit ➪ Copy or by using the command-key shortcut, Ctrl+C.

3. Place the cursor where you want the table to be placed and either select Edit ➪ Paste or use press Ctrl+V to paste the table into FrontPage.

If a cell is empty and the table has a border (which an imported table does automatically), then no border appears around those cells.

When you copy a table into FrontPage that includes calculation cells, the calculation cell is replaced by its value before completing the copy. If you need to retain the calculation, you need to rewrite the calculation by using one of the client-side scripting languages discussed in Chapter 18.

Another option for placing a formatted table in a Web page is to insert an entire spreadsheet file in your Web page. This is appropriate for small files, in which you want to import an entire spreadsheet, not just a selected range of cells.

To insert a spreadsheet file into FrontPage:

1. Click to place your insertion point where you want to insert the spreadsheet.

2. Select Insert ➪ File.

3. In the Select File dialog box, select the file format for your spreadsheet from the Files of Type drop-down menu, and navigate to the folder with your spreadsheet files, as shown in Figure 9-7. Then, double-click the spreadsheet file to insert it in your Web page.

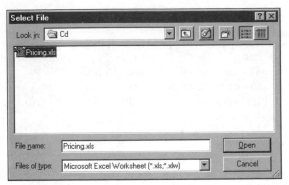

Figure 9-7: Spreadsheet files can be inserted directly into a FrontPage Web page.

In the following tutorial, you will import an existing spreadsheet into FrontPage.

Tutorial 9.1: Import a Table

1. Start with a new blank page: Select File ➪ New ➪ Page and select the Normal Page template.

2. Save this page as **Table1.htm** with the title **Prices**.

3. Type a heading for the page, **Shipping Prices**.

4. Select Insert ➪ File from the menu and choose Microsoft Excel Worksheet (*.xls, *.xlw) from the Files of Type drop-down menu.

5. Insert the CD-ROM that comes with this book and navigate to the files for Chapter 9. Double-click the file called Pricing.xls.

6. After you import the file into FrontPage, select File ➪ Delete Web, and choose the Remove this Web Entirely radio button. Click OK in the dialog box to remove this file from your hard drive.

Table Captions

A *caption* is a short phrase that is associated with a table. When you select the Insert Caption option, Editor automatically places the caption above the table. If you prefer that the caption be under the table, select the table caption and select Table ➪ Caption Properties to display the Caption Properties dialog box. This dialog box enables you to designate the location for the caption, either at the top or the bottom of the table.

Although you can format caption text normally, exactly how it displays is up to the browser (how far away from the table it is, how it's aligned to the table, and so on). For this reason, we suggest that you ignore captions.

Editing Table Properties

Some attributes of your table are defined in the Table Properties dialog box, while others are defined in the Cell Properties dialog box. Sometimes, it's not that intuitive which properties are defined where. Those table attributes assigned in the Table Properties dialog box apply to the *entire table*. So, for example, a table either has borders around cells, or does not. You can't assign border attributes to specific cells. On the other hand, you can define both a table background color and a cell background color (although older versions of Netscape Navigator won't recognize your cell background colors).

Definable table properties include:

- ✦ Table alignment
- ✦ Wrapping text around your table
- ✦ Border size (if any)
- ✦ Cell padding and spacing (the options that define how much space surrounds a cell and its contents)
- ✦ Background color
- ✦ Minimum table size (in pixels or percent)

Border width and color are perhaps the most basic of the formatting options available. Beyond that, you have (almost) complete control over how text aligns within cells, what color the cells are, and how much space exists between the cells.

Table Properties dialog box

The Table Properties dialog box, shown in Figure 9-8, provides quick access to all the formatting options available to the table as a whole. To open this dialog box, place the cursor within the table and select Table ➪ Table Properties, or right-click within the table and select Table Properties from the pop-up menu.

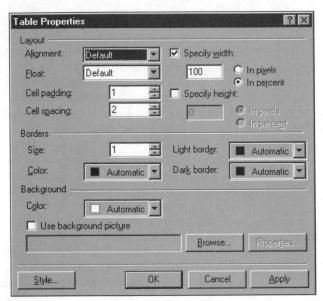

Figure 9-8: The Table Properties dialog box

Layout

The Layout section of the Table Properties dialog box provides settings for how other text interacts with the table and how individual cells are spaced within the table. The options in this area are the following:

✦ **Alignment**: Determines where the table is located. Left places the table against the left margin, right against the right margin, and center aligns the table between the left and right margins. The default option typically places the table against the left margin, but this placement is determined by the browser.

✦ **Float**: Enables you to wrap text next to the table, just as you can with an image.

✦ **Border Size**: Specifies the width of the outline placed around the table. A setting of 0 means that no border is displayed in a browser, though you can still see the dashed border when editing the page. Note that the thickness only applies to the outside border — when the border is active, only a thin line is placed between cells.

✦ **Cell Padding**: Specifies the space, in pixels, between the contents of a cell and the border around it. This option may be set regardless of whether the border is visible, and regardless of whether its size is greater than 0 (see Figure 9-9).

✦ **Cell Spacing:** Determines the spacing between individual cells (see Figure 9-9).

Cell Spacing   Cell Padding

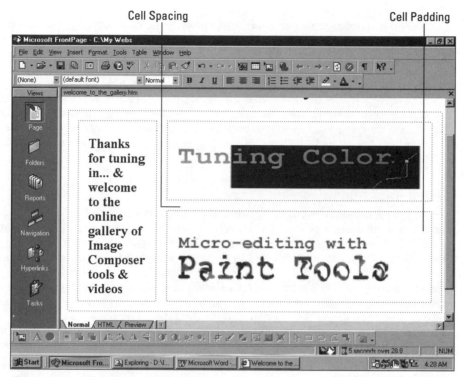

Figure 9-9: Cell spacing and padding specify how cells and their contents interact.

Minimum Size

The Minimum Size area of the Table Properties dialog box enables you to specify the overall height and width of a table. The height and width can be set in either pixels or as a percentage of the screen width. If the Width check box isn't checked, then the table typically is 100 percent of the browser window width. If the Height check box is not checked, then the table will be whatever minimum height is required to display everything in your cells.

Tip   If table width is not specified, then the table fills up as much space of the page as is needed to display the content, up to 100 percent.

Minimum is a very important word to notice in this area. If you set a table to be 50 percent of the height of the browser window, but the window is resized so that 50 percent of the height doesn't allow the entire contents to be displayed, the table will be larger than this setting.

Tip Should you define table minimum size in pixels or percent? Usually percent works best. It provides more flexibility for your table to be viewed with different monitor resolutions and different browser window sizes. If you define your table as 50 percent of the width of the browser window, your table will always take up half of a visitor's browser window. The downside to defining the minimum width as a percent of the browser window is that if a visitor's browser window is very small, your cells become very narrow. The alternative, defining minimum width in pixels, allows you more exact control over table size. Your table will always be the same number of pixels wide, but your visitors may need to use their horizontal scroll bar to see all the columns in the table.

Custom Background

Custom Background gives you the option of adding a background color or image to your entire table, much as you can add a background to an entire page. By default, the table is transparent, so that whatever background you have on your page shows through. Background images tile the same way that they do for entire pages.

To assign a custom background, click the Use Background Image check box. Choose a color from the Background Color drop-down menu, or use the Browse button to locate an image to tile as the background for the table. The Background Color palette for Tables in FrontPage 2000 includes a nice new feature: Custom-defined colors used in your Web page are available as background colors for your table.

Border Colors

In addition to setting the color of the table as a whole, you can set the color for the table's border in the Border Colors section of the Table Properties dialog box, which has three settings: border, light border, and dark border. The Border setting lets you set a single color for the entire border.

The Light Border setting enables you to specify colors for the top and left edges of the border, and the Dark Border setting enables you to specify colors for the bottom and right edges of the border. This can help you give your table a 3D look. Setting either of these overrides the Border setting for that area.

Tip If you set Light Border to a dark color and Dark Border to a light color, your table will look as though it's indented into your page rather than sticking out from it.

Note that if you leave all of these settings on Default, most browsers will display your table as though Light Border is set to silver and Dark Border is set to gray.

Assigning styles to a table

The Style button in the Table Properties dialog box opens the Modify Style dialog box. Use the Format button in the Modify Style dialog box to assign default font, paragraph, border, or numbering styles to your table.

Converting tables to text and text to tables

Before ending the discussion of what you can do to a table, you should know that you can easily convert a table into text. When you do, you don't lose any of the objects (text, graphics, and so forth) in the table. Those objects become normal page objects, laid out in paragraphs. To convert a table to text, click anywhere in the table and select Table ➪ Convert ➪ Table to Text. Conversely, if you have text that you want to convert automatically into a table, select the text and then choose Table ➪ Convert ➪ Text to Table. You'll be prompted to insert cells at paragraphs, tabs, commas, or a symbol of your choice (for example, a dash).

Editing Cell Properties

Cell properties can be assigned to individual cells, columns, rows of cells, or selected blocks of contiguous cells. You can select the cells that you want to format from the Table menu. The options include Select Cell, Select Row, Select Column, and Select Table. Or, you can click and drag to select cells.

Definable cell properties include:

   ✦ Horizontal and vertical alignment

   ✦ Text wrapping options

   ✦ Minimum cell size

   ✦ Background colors

If you move your cursor just to the left of a row, or just above a column, an arrow appears pointing to the row or column. By clicking, you can select an entire row or column, as shown in Figure 9-10.

The Cell Properties dialog box, shown in Figure 9-11, provides quick access to all the formatting options available to individual cells within the table. To open this dialog box, select the cells to which you will apply attributes, place the cursor within a cell that you want to edit, and then select Table ➪ Cell Properties or right-click within the cell and select Cell Properties from the pop-up menu. The following sections detail each portion of this dialog box.

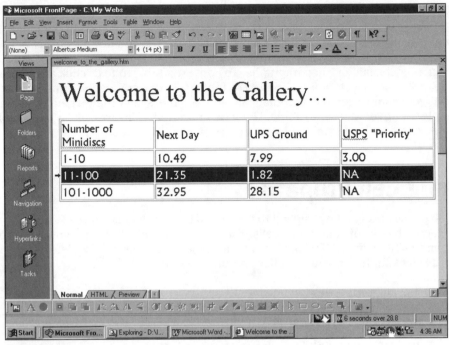

Figure 9-10: Many cell properties can be applied to an entire row.

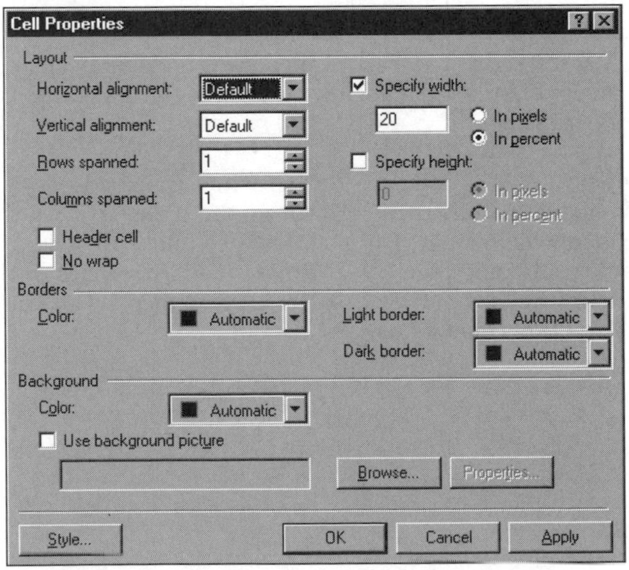

Figure 9-11: The Cell Properties dialog box

Tip

If you select several cells, some features in the Cell Properties dialog box may be grayed out. For example, you cannot define a minimum width for selected cells in different columns.

Layout

This section determines how text and graphics are placed within the cell. The four settings in this area are the following:

✦ **Horizontal Alignment**: Determines where the text or graphic is placed horizontally within the cell. The options are default, left, right, and center. Typically, browsers display the default setting as left. You can also perform this alignment by using the Align Left, Center, and Align Right icons on the toolbar.

✦ **Vertical Alignment**: Determines where the text or graphic is placed vertically within the cell. The options are default, top, middle, baseline, and bottom. Baseline makes the bottom of all letters in the row line up, no matter what the size. In general, most browsers display the default setting as middle. You can also perform these alignments (with the exception of default) by using the Align Top, Center Vertically, and Align Bottom icons on the Table toolbar.

✦ **Header Cell**: Makes the text within the cell bold (typically), although how it is actually displayed depends on the browser being used. This feature is a remnant of an earlier era when browsers were not able to interpret the same format commands that they recognize today. You probably won't find this feature too useful, because you can apply your own custom formatting to any cell in a table.

✦ **No Wrap**: Forces text to remain on one line. This setting overrides the minimum size settings for other columns. Minimum size is discussed in the next section.

Minimum Size

As with the overall table size, this area sets the *minimum* width and height for the cell. Note that the width setting applies to all cells in a particular column, and height applies to all cells in a row.

Caution

Some browsers can't display tables if the height and width settings don't make mathematical sense. For instance, if the overall width of the table is 500 pixels and the width of the individual columns (*plus* the cell padding and cell spacing for each column) is 510 pixels, then the browser may display the table erratically, or may even crash. A good rule of thumb is as follows: if you specify your table width or height in pixels, set the columns and rows in pixels as well. As mentioned earlier, using percent instead of pixels is a more foolproof way to define minimum table or cell size.

To quickly make a number of columns the same width, highlight cells in two or more columns and then either select Table ⇨ Distribute Columns Evenly or click the

Distribute Columns Evenly icon in the Table toolbar. To quickly make a number of rows the same height, highlight two or more rows and then either select Table ➪ Distribute Rows Evenly or click the Distribute Rows Evenly icon in the Table toolbar.

Cell span

Spanning cells are cells that take the space of two or more cells. Merging cells generally is easier and more intuitive by using the Table toolbar or the Table ➪ Merge Cells menu option.

Custom Background

As with the table and page, individual cells can have background images or colors. If you select more than one cell and apply a tiling background image, the image will tile seamlessly between the cells.

Border Colors

The three options in this section enable you to set the colors for the border of an individual cell, rather than the entire table. Light Border refers to the bottom and right edges of the cell, and Dark Border refers to the top and left edges of the cell — this is the opposite of their positions for the table's outline. If the table border is set to 0 width, then these settings have no effect.

Adjusting Table Structure

You can easily add or delete rows, columns, and cells with the Table toolbar. The Table toolbar also enables you to merge cells easily, to create irregular tables for design purposes. You can apply Table tools by selecting a table, and then displaying the toolbar (Table ➪ Draw Table).

Inserting rows, columns, and cells

To insert a row by using the toolbar, highlight the row *below* where you want to add the new row and then click the Insert Rows icon. A new row appears. Each cell of the new row has settings identical to the one below it (the one that you highlighted).

To insert a column by using the toolbar, highlight the column to the *right* of where you want to add the new column and then click the Insert Column icon. A new column appears. Each cell of the new column has settings identical to the one to its right.

To insert a row or column by using the menu options, select Table ➪ Insert Rows or Columns. The Insert Rows or Columns dialog box opens, as shown in Figure 9-12, which enables you to add additional rows and/or columns to the table. New rows or columns can be inserted above or below the selected row, and left or right of a selected column. You can insert one or more rows or columns at one time.

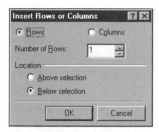

Figure 9-12: The Insert Rows or Columns dialog box

To insert a cell, highlight the cell to the right of where you want the new cell located and select Table ➪ Insert Cell. A new cell with the original cell's properties appears.

An alternative way to create new cells is to split a single cell in two. To split a cell, simply place the cursor inside the cell (or highlight several cells) and then either select Table ➪ Split Cells or click the Split Cells icon on the Table toolbar. This opens the Split Cells dialog box. Select the options that you want from this dialog box and click OK to split all the highlighted cells.

As discussed earlier in this chapter, you can also split cells by using the Draw Table tool, available on the Table toolbar. Select the tool and draw a vertical or horizontal line in the cell, or cells, that you want to split.

Removing cells, rows, and columns

Actually, this section should be called "*Reducing* the number of cells, rows, and columns," because a couple of the options presented remove the table's cells, but not the text or graphics inside of them. However, that title doesn't flow very well, so this one was used instead.

That said, the first thing to discuss is how to delete a row or a column. To do this, select the row or column to be deleted and select Table ➪ Delete Cells. All the highlighted cells are removed.

Merging cells is a nondestructive alternative to deleting cells. When this option is used, all the text or graphics from the merged cells is placed within the new cell. To merge cells, highlight the cells that you want merged and then either select Table ➪ Merge Cells or click the Merge Cells icon on the Table toolbar.

Designing Layout with Tables

Tables allow you to implement design features that are difficult or impossible to create with normal HTML formatting controls. The most widely used of these features is the ability to create column layouts on your Web pages. Many hardcopy layout designers suggest column layout for text to make it easier to read. With a creative use of columns, you can design a magazine-like appearance for your Web page. Columns can also be used to introduce two or more articles at the top of a Web page. Or, tables can be used to control a mix of images and text, as shown in Figure 9-13, which has a three-column layout that includes sidebar text, descriptive text, and matching images.

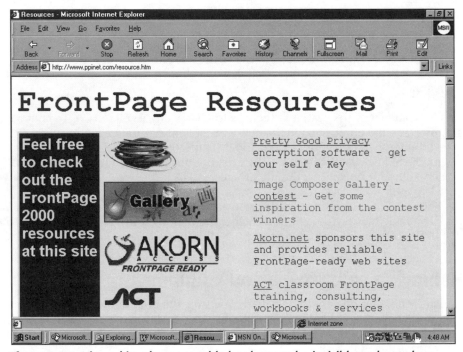

Figure 9-13: Viewed in a browser, table borders can be invisible and seamless.

How was this designed? Tutorial 9.2 shows you how. As you can see in Figure 9-14, the three columns are defined by table cells. The column on the left was created by merging all cells in the first column.

In the following tutorial, you will create a Web page that combines text, graphics, and a third column that functions as a sidebar to what appears as a table to visitors.

Tutorial 9.2: Design a Three-Column Layout

1. Start with a new blank page: Select File ➪ New ➪ Page and select the Normal Page template.

2. Save this page as **Table3.htm** with the title **3 Column Table**.

3. Type a heading for the page, **Meet our staff**.

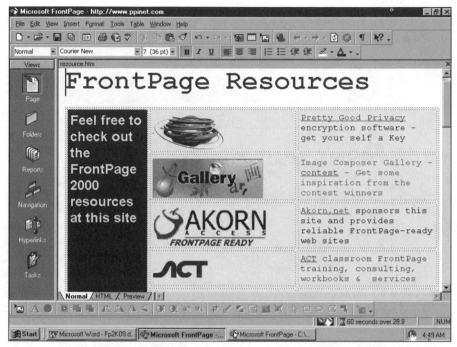

Figure 9-14: Underneath what appears to be a freeform layout are table cells.

4. Use the Insert Table tool to create a three-column, four-row table.

5. Select all the cells in the first column and then select Table ➪ Merge Cells.

6. Enter your name in the first (top) cell in the middle column. Then, enter the names of three of your associates or friends in the remaining cells in the second (middle) column. Ad lib descriptions of yourself and your friends or associates.

7. Place your cursor in the upper-right-corner cell and insert an image (you can use Insert ➪ Image ➪ Clipart to find pictures of people for this tutorial). If you have a picture of yourself on disk, use that; if not, improvise with clip art. Insert additional pictures for associates or friends.

8. In the first column, type **Thanks for visiting our Web page. Here, you'll have a chance to meet our staff.** (Or something along those lines.)

9. Select all the cells in the first and second columns, and assign top-vertical alignment to them (use the Cell Properties dialog box).

10. Assign a yellow background to the table and a light-blue background to the cell on the left side of the table. Assign top-vertical alignment to the cell on the left side of the table.

11. Use the Table Properties dialog box to assign a border size of 0 (no border), and then assign 6 pixels for cell padding and 0 pixels for cell spacing.

12. Add font attributes (color, font type, and size). Save and preview your table in a browser. Your table should look something like Figure 9-15 when you preview it.

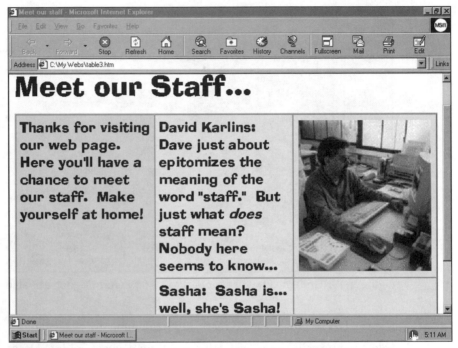

Figure 9-15: Use tables to organize text and graphics in a page.

Summary

Tables provide reliable and useful control for almost any aspect of page layout and design — you can use tables to create intricate columns and borders, and even to line up tabular data, if you're so inclined. With the completion of this chapter, you have learned all the basic tools for creating Web pages. Starting in Chapter 10, you'll learn how to use shared border frames, which give you even more control over your page layout.

✦ ✦ ✦

Designing Pages with Shared Borders and Frames

Both shared borders and frames enable you to design Web pages that combine fixed and changing elements. Shared borders and frames both enable you to "frame" Web pages with what are, basically, other Web pages. In this way, you can provide a consistent look to sections of your Web site and anchor your visitors with elements that provide navigational links.

You were introduced to shared borders in Chapter 1, when you created your first Web site. You saw that these borders are *shared* between different pages in your Web site. Frames allow two or more discrete, scrollable Web pages to be viewed simultaneously in a visitor's browser window. Frames are more complex than shared borders and allow for more design options.

Although both shared borders and frames involve complex HTML coding, FrontPage 2000 makes it easy to create these elements graphically. In this chapter, you'll first explore how to place, design, and fine-tune shared borders, and then learn how to create and link frame pages.

Working with Shared Borders

Chapter 1 introduced shared borders. The default shared borders contain only navigation bars. However, you can add much more than navigation links to your shared borders. In fact, a shared border can include all the objects of a regular Web page, such as formatted text, graphic images, or even interactive elements (for example, a Hit Counter or table of contents). Figure 10-1 shows a Web page with a navigation bar in the top shared border, and text and a graphic in the left shared border.

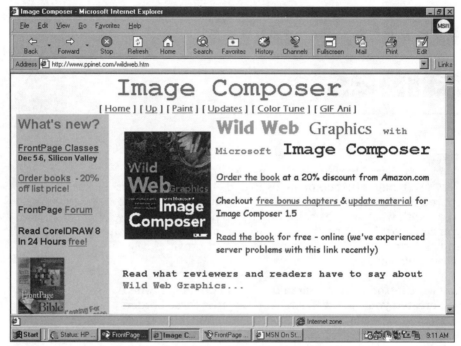

Figure 10-1: These shared borders provide navigation bars, text, and graphics.

Adding shared borders

In Chapter 1, you learned to add shared borders to a Web page by selecting Format ➪ Shared Borders. The defaults for the Shared Borders dialog box add shared borders to the right and top of your Web page. This chapter examines in detail how to define the location of shared borders on Web pages and throughout a Web site.

The Shared Borders dialog box opens when you select Format ➪ Shared Borders in Page, Folders, Navigation, Hyperlinks, or Tasks views. However, this dialog box functions a bit differently in Page view, in which you have the option of defining shared borders either for the page that you are editing or for the entire Web. In the other views, you have the option of defining shared borders either for selected pages or for the entire Web. In Folders view, you can choose which selected pages you want to control by holding down the Control key and clicking the page(s) in the

Folder list. The Shared Borders dialog box that appears in Folders, Navigation, Hyperlinks, or Tasks views is shown in Figure 10-2.

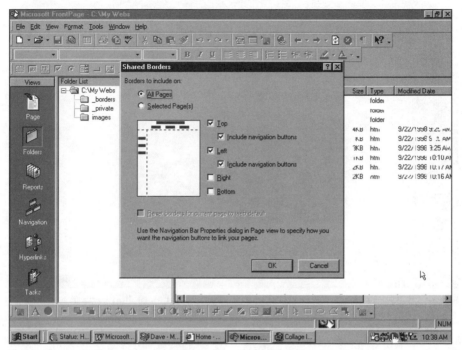

Figure 10-2: Defining shared borders from Folders view

The Shared Borders dialog box looks a little different when you select Format ➪ Shared Borders in Page view. The functions are the same, but you see the dialog box shown in Figure 10-3, with a radio button that enables you to apply shared border features to the *current* page — that is, the page that you are editing.

The top section of the Shared Borders dialog box enables you to assign shared borders to an entire Web or to the current (or selected) page(s) only. If you have defined shared borders for your Web and want to assign them to the particular page that you are editing, you can do so by clicking the check box at the bottom of the dialog box.

Click the Top, Left, Right, or Bottom check boxes to assign shared borders to the top, left, right, or bottom of the page(s), respectively.

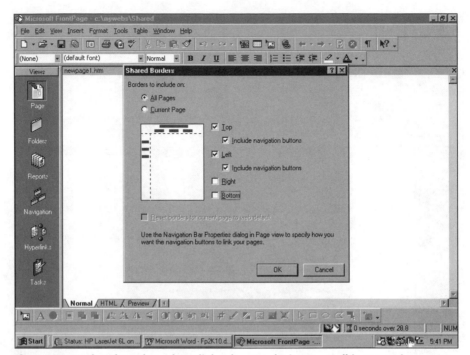

Figure 10-3: The Shared Borders dialog box works just as well in Page view.

Note   Usually, designers avoid shared borders on the right side of a Web page. From a functional perspective, the right side of a page may be beyond the browser window, requiring a visitor to scroll horizontally to see it. From an aesthetic standpoint, most visitors are used to looking to the top or left side of a page for anchoring elements. Bottom shared borders can be useful for shared navigational links or other objects that function as a page "footer."

When you click the OK button in the Shared Borders dialog box, you are actually creating or editing new HTML Web pages. These special shared border pages are embedded in the left, right, top, or bottom of each page in your Web site. You can define up to four of these shared borders for the *entire Web site*. In other words, you can have only one top shared border, one left shared border, and so on.

You can edit the content of shared borders, which is discussed later in this chapter, in "Changing shared border content."

Controlling navigation bars

The default shared borders that are generated with Web sites include navigation bars. If you want to insert navigation bars manually into a shared border, right-click inside the shared border and select Insert Navigation Bars.

The links generated in navigation bar are based on the structure of your Web site. If you plan to include navigation links in your shared borders, you must define a Web structure in the FrontPage Navigation view. You can define a Web structure in Navigation view by dragging pages from the Folder list on the left into the Navigation view area on the right. Figure 10-4 shows a page being dragged from the Folder list into the Navigation view, where it is being defined as a child of an existing page in the navigation structure.

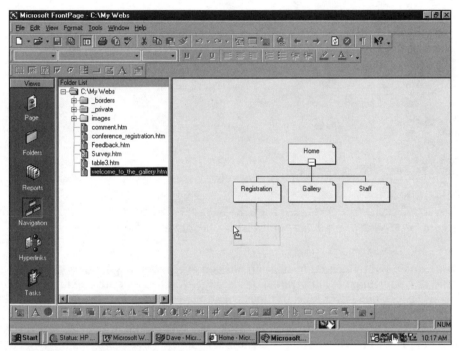

Figure 10-4: Adding a page to the navigation structure

New in FrontPage 2000

FrontPage 2000 includes a handy feature that helps you to locate a Web page in Navigation view. To locate a file in your navigation flowchart, right-click that file in the Folder list and choose Find in Navigation from the context menu. Figure 10-5 shows a Web page being located in Navigation view.

You can edit the structure of the navigation links in Navigation view by clicking and dragging Web pages in the flowchart. After you define navigation links in Navigation view, you can generate navigation bars for your Web site.

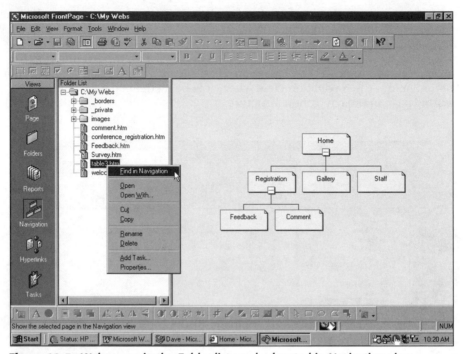

Figure 10-5: Web pages in the Folder list can be located in Navigation view.

You don't need to include navigation bars on every Web page, but you can have only *one navigation bar structure*. For instance, you can elect to use links to child pages (pages in a lower level of the Navigation view flowchart) in your navigation bars. Or, you can elect to place links to other pages at the same level of the flowchart. But, you can't do both in the same navigation bar. You can, however, have separate navigation bars in each shared border. For example, one page design strategy is to include a navigation bar with child page links in the top shared border, and same-level links in the left shared border.

The positive side of navigation bars is that you can instantly create a coherent and consistent series of navigational links in every or many pages of your Web site. The limitation is that they are applied in a uniform way to every page in your Web, and cannot be tweaked or customized for each page.

To insert (or edit) a navigation bar in a shared border, first view the page in Page view and click the shared border. With your insertion point in a shared border, select Insert ➪ Navigation Bar. The Navigation Bar Properties dialog box appears, as shown in Figure 10-6. Its two main areas are described next.

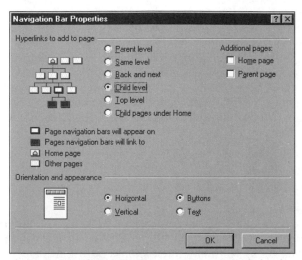

Figure 10-6: The Navigation Bar Properties dialog box governs the navigation bar for a selected shared border.

Hyperlinks to Add to Page

The Hyperlinks to Add to Page area of the Navigation Bar Properties dialog box determines what the structure of your hyperlinks will be. As noted earlier, you can select only one type of navigational organization, and it applies to all pages in your Web site. As you select a radio button in this section of the dialog box, the links that you select are illustrated in the flowchart on the left side of the dialog box. The following is a description of each of these radio buttons:

✦ **Parent Level**: Provides links to all pages on the level *above* the current page. The logic of using parent-level links is to encourage visitors to navigate up the flowchart of your Web site toward your home page.

✦ **Same Level**: Generates links to all pages on the *same* level of the navigation flowchart as the current page. This is useful if you have a Web structure in which related pages are on the same level of your navigation flowchart.

✦ **Back and Next**: Similar to creating same-level links, except that only two same-level links appear on each page — one to the same-level page to the right of the current page, and one to the same-level page to the left of the current page. This navigational strategy is useful for a slideshow-type series of links, whereby a visitor can move to the next page in a presentation, or back a page, but is restricted to those choices.

✦ **Child Level**: Enables a visitor to see all pages connected to, and one level *below,* the current page in the flow chart. When combined with the Home Page and Parent Page check box options, child-level links provide one of the most useful ways to let visitors move up and down the flowchart structure of your Web site.

✦ **Top Level**: This rather esoteric linking option allows visitors to jump from any page in your Web site to any page in the top level of the site.

The Hyperlinks to Add to Page area also includes the following two check boxes:

✦ **Home Page**: When checked, places a link to your home page on every page. Often, this is the single most useful option that you can add to your navigational links. In most Web site design, a quick link to the site's home page is appreciated by visitors.

✦ **Parent Page**: When checked, places a link to the page immediately above the current page.

Orientation and Appearance

The Orientation and Appearance area of the Navigation Bar Properties dialog box enables you to define the orientation of your links (horizontal or vertical) and the appearance of them (text or buttons). Normally, a left shared border has a vertically oriented navigational list, whereas a top shared border usually has a horizontal list of text or buttons.

If you have assigned a Theme to your Web page, you can click the Buttons radio button to generate graphical linked buttons automatically. With the Text radio button, you can choose to display your text in formatable text.

Figure 10-7 shows a page with a horizontal, text navigation bar in the top shared border, and a vertical, button shared border in the left shared border.

Changing shared border content

Shared borders can include much more than navigation bars. You can edit them in basically the same way that you edit any Web page. The following are two ways to edit shared borders.

Edit the shared borders in a Web page

Open a page incorporating shared borders in Editor and edit the shared border option(s) as you normally would. When you save the page, you are prompted to save the changes made to the shared borders. This is an excellent option if you don't plan to edit the borders very much. By editing in place, you can see exactly how the border will appear. Unfortunately, you have no control over the HTML code that makes up the shared border, which makes them difficult to fully "tweak."

Edit the shared borders individually

Open in Editor the pages that make up the shared borders and edit them as you would any other page. Before you can edit these pages, however, you have to give Editor access to them (the shared border pages are located in a hidden folder in your Web).

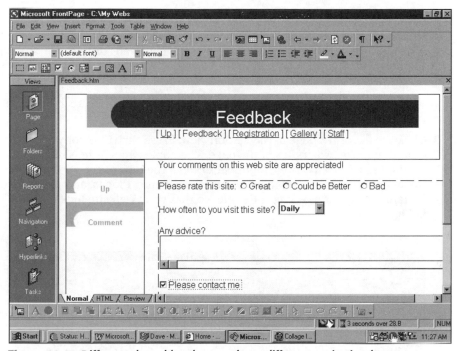

Figure 10-7: Different shared borders can have different navigation bars.

To allow direct access to your shared border pages:

1. View your Web in Folders (or Navigation) view.

2. Select Tools ➪ Web Settings to open the FrontPage Web Settings dialog box.

3. Select the Advanced tab and check the Show Documents in Hidden Directories check box.

4. Click OK to close the dialog box. Select View ➪ Refresh to see a new picture of your Web folders. Double-click to see the contents of the _borders folder. The shared border pages are included in this folder. Each file is named for the border that it represents.

You can now open and edit these pages in Editor. One downside to editing shared border pages in Editor, however, is that — unlike frames — you have no direct control over the size of your borders, so gauging whether your edits will look good in your Web's pages is difficult to do.

In the following tutorial, you'll create a new Web with shared borders on the bottom of your Web pages, with text and navigation bars that link to child pages, the home page, and the parent page in your Web site.

Tutorial 10.1: Create Shared Borders with Navigation Bars

1. Select File ➪ New ➪ Web. Click Personal Web in the New dialog box and select a Web location in the "Specify location of the new web" drop-down box. Name the new Web **Shared**. Click OK in the New dialog box to generate a new Web from the Personal Web template.

2. View the new Web in Navigation view and notice the structure: it contains one parent page (home page) and three child pages.

3. Click the Favorites page in Navigation view. Press Ctrl+C to copy the page, and Ctrl+V to make two copies of the page. The copies appear in Navigation view as child pages of Favorites. Right-click one of the new pages and select Rename from the context menu. Enter a new name, **Places**, and press Enter. Rename the other new pages **People**, so that your Web site looks like the one in Figure 10-8.

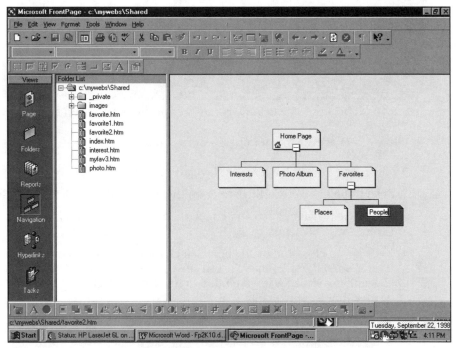

Figure 10-8: To create navigation bars, first define the Web structure.

4. Still in Navigation view, select Format ➪ Shared Borders. In the Shared Borders dialog box, click the All Pages radio button and deselect Top and Left. Select the Bottom check box and click OK in the Shared Borders dialog box.

5. Select Tools ➪ Web Settings and click the Advanced tab in the FrontPage Web Settings dialog box. Click the Show Documents in Hidden Directories check box and click OK. When prompted, click OK in the dialog box that asks

whether you want to refresh your directories. Note that the _borders folder is visible and contains your new shared border page.

6. Double-click the People page that you created in Navigation view, to open this page in Page view. Click and drag to select the Comment text that marks the shared border at the bottom of your page, and press the Delete key to get rid of it.

7. Type **Thanks for visiting my site** (or some other friendly note) in the bottom shared border. Press Enter to create a new line, and select Insert ➪ Navigation Bar.

8. In the Navigation Bar Properties dialog box, select the Child Level radio button, and click both the Home Page and Parent Page check boxes. Select the Horizontal and Buttons radio buttons in the Orientation and Appearance area. Because this Web site template came with a Theme, you can apply buttons to navigation bars. Click OK to add the navigation bar.

9. Just for fun, select Format ➪ Themes and pick a nice Theme for your Web site.

10. Save your changes, and preview your Web site in your browser. Note the navigation links that appear in each page. They will be different, depending on the page, but they will provide links to child pages (where they exist), parent pages (where they exist), and the home page on every page, as does the page in Figure 10-9.

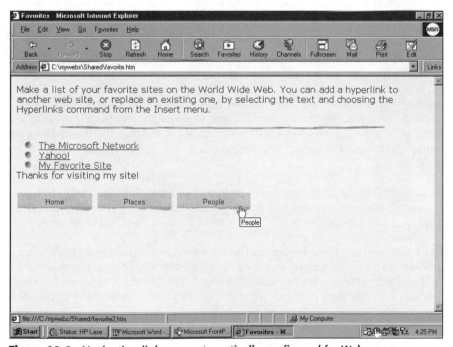

Figure 10-9: Navigation links are automatically configured for Web pages.

11. Save your Web before exiting FrontPage. You can use it again in Tutorial 10.2 at the end of this chapter.

Creating a Frame Set

Now that you understand how shared borders can be combined with Web pages, you can begin to explore the possibilities of combining more than one page within a browser window. Remember, the shared borders are actually separate Web pages. So, when a visitor sees what appears to be a single Web page with shared borders, he or she is actually seeing more than one Web page in the browser window.

With frames, you can exercise far greater control over this process of combining Web pages in a browser window. Pages designed with frames are called *frame sets*, because they are actually a *set* of HTML pages. Every frame page, or frame set, consists of at least three HTML files: the file that controls the frame structure, and at least two different HTML files that are displayed at one time.

One of the advantages of working with frame sets is that each page that displays within a frame set can be navigated independently. Each frame page that appears in the browser window can have its own scroll bar, and hyperlinks from one frame can jump a visitor to another Web page, while other parts of the frame set remain in place. One implementation of this ability to navigate frame pages independently is illustrated in Figure 10-10. Here, the top frame has links to articles in a forum discussion, while the bottom frame shows the actual article.

Figure 10-11 is a peek behind the scenes at this Web page. You can see that two different Web pages are actually displayed in Page view.

Normally, you shouldn't use both shared borders and frames in a single page, because they play a similar role in page and site design, and they both take up some of your available page space. The frame set in Figures 10-10 and 10-11 is an exception to this rule. The top frame includes a shared border, but the bottom frame does not.

Tip   You can include navigation bars within a frame set: Organize in the level below your contents frame page (using Navigation view) all the pages that you want displayed in the target. Then, add a navigation bar with the Child Level option set.

Designing with frames can be somewhat complex. But, one of the great features of FrontPage is the ability to put together frame sets in a graphical manner. FrontPage simplifies the technical side of creating frames. The biggest challenge for you as a FrontPage Web designer is to put together an effective combination of pages.

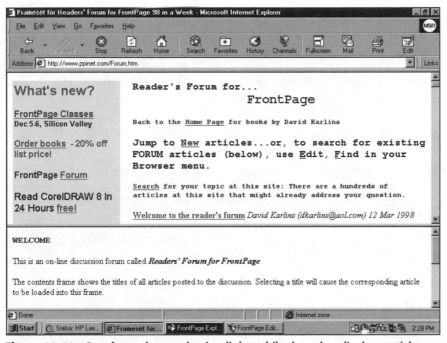

Figure 10-10: One frame has navigation links, while the other displays articles.

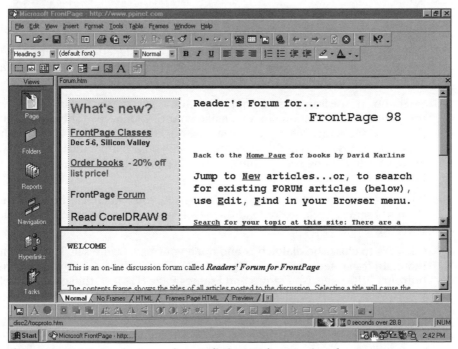

Figure 10-11: Page view reveals two distinct Web pages in a frame set.

Keeping Frame Hassles Under Control

Frames present a few unique challenges. One is aesthetic. A Web site crowded with complex frame sets can be distracting and annoying to visitors. Remember that most visitors are viewing your Web site with limited monitor space, and breaking that space into four or more frames divides that screen into unwieldy chunks.

One technical challenge is posed by the fact that not all browsers interpret frames. FrontPage makes this problem easy to solve by building in alternate Web pages for visitors who don't have frame-friendly browsers.

A third potential pitfall is that if links are not correctly designed, your visitors can find themselves wandering like Alice in Wonderland through a room full of increasingly smaller frames within frames within frames. "Creating Hyperlinks in Frame Sets," later in this chapter, examines in depth how to avoid this particular snag.

Each of these challenges can be met, if you decide that frames will enhance your Web site.

Creating a new frame set

If you're familiar with FrontPage 97, you'll really like this new approach to creating frame sets. With FrontPage 2000, all you need to do to create a frame set is to follow these steps:

1. In Page view, Select File ➪ New ➪ Page.

2. Click the Frames tab to display the available predesigned frame sets. Note that these are just a starting point; you can make changes to any of the frame sets after you create the new page.

3. Select one of the frame sets from the list at the left, noting the layout shown in the right Preview window. To help make your decision, read the description of the frame set in the Description area. The default way that links work within the frame set is noted in this description—if you are unfamiliar with the way links work in a frame set, see the section "Creating Hyperlinks in Frame Sets," later in this chapter.

4. If you are already editing a page in a frame set, you can check the Open in Current Frame check box to load the new frame set as a page, replacing the currently selected page.

5. Click OK to close the dialog box and open your new frame set. The Contents template frame set is shown in Figure 10-12. Notice the two new tabs at the bottom of the page, No Frames and Frames Page HTML—these tabs enable you to view attributes that are available only in frames pages. These tabs are explained in "The two extra view tabs" section later in this chapter.

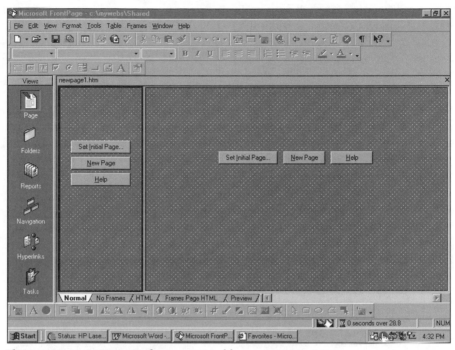

Figure 10-12: A Contents frame set awaiting your content

The new frame set looks a bit empty. Well, not for long. The next section shows you how to build or include pages in your set.

Adding pages to a new frame set

As you can see in Figure 10-12, each frame area in a new frame set contains three buttons: Set Initial Page, New Page, and Help. You will use these buttons to include an existing page or create a new page in the current frame (or to get help about either option).

The current frame is the one indicated by the dark-blue border around it. You can change the current frame by clicking in another frame to select it.

✦ **To create a new page to display in a frame, click the New Page button.** A clean, blank page appears. If you'd rather include a frame set within a frame (called a *nested frame*), select the frame and then repeat the steps involved in the last section, "Creating a new frame set," making sure to check the Open in Current Frame check box mentioned in Step 4.

Tip   FrontPage doesn't accurately display nested frames in Page view but instead shows a new View Frames Page button. Clicking this button changes Editor's view to display the frame set that's in the current frame. If you are editing a nested frame set, change the size of the Editor window to more accurately reflect the size of the frame in which the set is displayed in the main frame set. This will help you to picture how the frames will look in a browser. Also, Preview mode does display nested frames properly.

✦ **To include an existing page in a frame, click the Set Initial Page button.** Use the Create Hyperlink dialog box (shown in Figure 10-13) to pick the page to display in this frame. You can use any of the standard methods used to open a page, which are described in Chapter 1. (Don't worry that this dialog box is called Create Hyperlink; you clicked the correct button.) After you make your selection, the page is displayed in the frame.

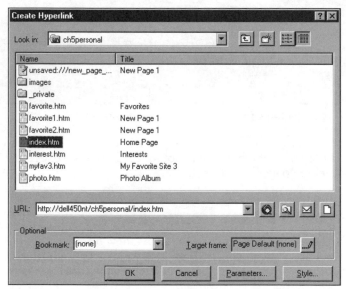

Figure 10-13: Use the oddly named Create Hyperlink dialog box to pick a page to display in the current frame.

After you create or add pages to your frame set, you can edit them as you would any normal page. Notice that when you select a different frame to edit, the dark-blue border shifts to that frame, and its filename appears in the FrontPage title bar.

Changing frame contents

The pages that you initially insert in your frame set are only the first pages to be displayed. The links in each frame can modify the contents of the frame, or any other frame. To learn more about the way that links operate in a frame set, see the section "Creating Hyperlinks in Frame Sets," later in this chapter.

To change the page that is initially displayed in a frame, select Frame ➪ Edit Initial Page. The (still oddly named) Edit Hyperlink dialog box opens. Select the page that you want to display in the current frame and click OK.

Editing Frame Set Properties

You can click and drag the border between frames to change frame sizes. Other frame properties can be changed in the Frame Properties dialog box, shown in Figure 10-14.

This dialog box (accessed by selecting Frames ➪ Frame Properties or by right-clicking within the frame and selecting Frame Properties from the context menu) also contains other options relating to the frame.

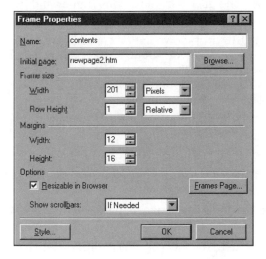

Figure 10-14: You can control many frame properties in the Frame Properties dialog box.

The following options are available in the Frame Properties dialog box:

✦ **Name**: The name given to the HTML file that defines the frame itself. Every frame set has at least three HTML files associated with it: at least two HTML files embedded in the frame, and the frame itself, which is that file that you are naming here. The name is important because it is used to indicate the "target" for any hyperlink that may be intended for this frame.

✦ **Initial Page**: The page that appears automatically when the frame set is opened. Earlier, you learned to make this link by using the Create Hyperlink dialog box. This is an alternative way to assign a page to a frame.

✦ **Frame Size Width and Height**: These two options determine the size of the frame. Changing the width or height of a frame affects other frames in the same row or column. Select units from the right list box and set the size in the left text box. Three units are available for frame sizing:

- **Percent**: Sets the frame's size as a percentage of the browser screen's height or width.

- **Pixels**: Sets the frame's size as a specific number of pixels.

- **Relative**: Sets the frame's size relative to the setting for other frames in the row or column, as long as they are using one of the other options. When using this option, set the amount in the left text box to 1.

By default, the leftmost frame in a row and the topmost frame in a column are set in pixels, while the other frames are set to relative.

✦ **Margins**: The Width and Height spinner boxes enable you to define margins for your frame set in pixels.

✦ **Resizable in Browser**: Used to allow users to resize the frame windows by dragging the divider bars. By default, all frames are resizable. Unless you have a real need to constrict your Web site guests from resizing frame windows, this option generally makes your site more visitor-friendly.

✦ **Show Scrollbars**: The choices in this drop-down list box are Always, which forces a scroll bar always to be present; Never, which forces no scrolling bar; and If Needed, which includes a scroll bar, if necessary, but doesn't show one if it's unnecessary. If Needed is the default option and is usually the most useful way to let visitors navigate your frame windows.

The bottom of the Frame Properties dialog box has the following two buttons that open up additional options:

✦ **Frames Page**: Opens the Frames tab in the Page Properties dialog box, which has two options:

- **Frame Spacing spin box**: Use to change spacing between frames in the frame set.

- **Show Borders check box**: Use to display (or hide) borders between frames.

✦ **Style**: Opens the Modify Style dialog box, in which you can click the Format button to assign inline style specifications for font type, paragraph alignment, and other default formatting.

Adding and deleting frames

If you need to add an additional frame to a frame set, you "split" an existing frame into two new frames. One of these two frames will contain the contents of the original frame, while the other will display the Set Initial Page, New Page, and Help buttons that are shown when the frame set is originally created. The following are the two ways to split a frame:

✦ Select the frame that you want to split and select Frames ⇨ Split Frame to open the Split Frame dialog box. Select either the Split into Columns or Split into Rows radio button and then click the OK button.

✦ Select the frame that you want to split and place the cursor over any border (including the four borders around the Editor window), so that the cursor changes to a two-headed arrow, and then use Ctrl+drag to create the new frame.

The two extra view tabs

As mentioned earlier in the chapter, the bottom of the Editor screen has two additional view tabs that provide additional control over your frame set: No Frames and Frames Page HTML.

The No Frames tab displays the page content that is shown on browsers that don't support frames. By default, this page contains only the rather perfunctory message "This page uses frames, but your browser doesn't support them," as shown in Figure 10-15. You can leave this somewhat unfriendly message as is, or you can use this page as the beginning of a nonframes version of the same information displayed in the frame set pages. The nonframes page can be edited exactly like any other page — remember, though, that browsers that can't display frames generally can't handle other "high tech" Web items, such as tables, Java scripts, shared borders, and ActiveX controls, so you will want to avoid or limit their use. An easy way to fill the No Frames page is to copy the contents of your main frame and paste it into the No Frames page.

The Frames Page HTML tab displays the HTML codes that define your frame set (see Figure 10-16). The No Frames page codes are also contained here, between the tags `<noframes>` and `</noframes>` — in this case, the No Frames page only has the default message.

Creating Hyperlinks in Frame Sets

Creating hyperlinks within a frame set poses some new challenges. You need to indicate both the page to link to and the frame in which the page should appear.

How it works

By default, FrontPage sets up each link in a frame to open a new page automatically in a different frame. For example, in the frame set Contents (see Figure 10-17), clicking a link in the contents frame changes the page shown in the main frame. Clicking a link in the main frame, however, only changes the contents of main frame.

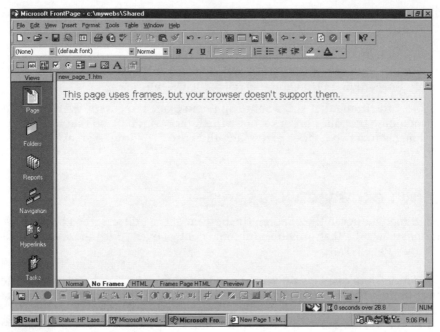

Figure 10-15: The No Frames page is displayed on browsers that don't understand frames.

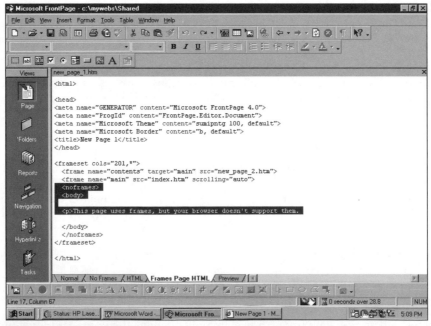

Figure 10-16: The typical HTML codes for a frame set

Contents frame   Main frame

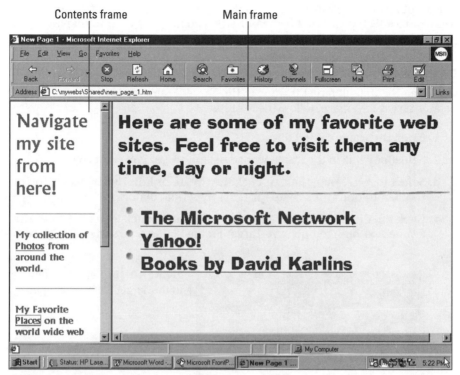

Figure 10-17: The link/frame relationship in a typical frame set

Note

This behavior calls attention to the fact that you don't need to create a frame set for every Web page. In fact, that is the whole idea behind frames: You create the frame set once, and then change the content frame only as needed.

Hitting the target

How does the frame set know to behave this way? An HTML code located in the frames page sets the default way for links to work. If you want to explore the HTML, look at the Frames Page HTML tab in Page view and note that the tags defining the banner and contents frames (`<frame name="banner"` ... and `<frame name="contents"` ..., respectively) each contain the code `target="..."`. The name inside the quotation marks indicates the frame that should be opened when you click a link. The target information is also placed in each page's HTML code — click the HTML tab and notice the tag that reads `<base target="...">` near the top of the banner and contents frames.

FrontPage automatically adds the base target tag to your pages, whether you created them from scratch when you made the frame set, or set them as initial pages later on. In the default links in the Contents frame set template, for example, links from the left (contents) frame open pages in the right, main window. However, that's not always desirable. For example, if you have links from the Contents window to a Web page outside of your site, you may *not* want to display that page in your frame set. In that case, you have the option to change the target of a link.

Changing the default target

Changing the default target is done in the Target Frame dialog box. To change the default target for a page, follow these steps:

1. Open the frame set in Editor.

2. Select any link in the frame whose default target you want to change.

3. Select Insert ⇨ Hyperlink, or click the Create or Edit Hyperlink button on the toolbar, to open the Create (or Edit) Hyperlink dialog box.

4. Click the Change Target Frame icon (the small pencil icon next to the Target Frame text box) to open the Target Frame dialog box, shown in Figure 10-18.

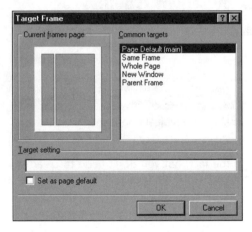

Figure 10-18: Set the default target in the Target Frame dialog box.

5. To open a link in one of the frames in your frame set, select the new target frame by clicking one of the frames in the left Current Frames Page area. To link to the default page for the frame set, choose the Page Default option from the Common Targets list. The Same Frame option in the list opens a link in the same frame as the link. The Whole Page option opens the linked page as a whole page. The New Window option opens the linked page in a new browser window. The Parent Frame opens the link in the parent frame of a nested frame set.

6. To assign this target to other links in the page, select the check box labeled Make Default for Hyperlinks on the Page.

7. Click OK in both the Target Frame and Edit Hyperlink dialog boxes to return to Editor.

8. Save your frame set. Notice that some extra time is taken to save — this is because FrontPage automatically changes the HTML code in the Frames Page.

Note Different frame-link options are used for different navigation and design strategies. If you want to "lock in" visitors, display links from a contents frame in a main frame, leaving the visitor operating within your frame set. Or, you can open links in a new browser window. That option allows visitors to roam the Web from your site, while your site remains open in a separate browser window.

Avoiding Frames Hate Mail

Frames can make a visitor's experience at your Web site more useful by providing helpful navigational tools and onscreen references. However, they can also be distracting or annoying. Visits to your Web site will not be pleasant or productive if visitors are using a browser that doesn't interpret, if the frames are not implemented properly, or if the use of frames makes navigating your Web more difficult than it would have been without the frames. Even if you create a perfect implementation of frames, some people just don't like to use them. Here are some of the ways that you can reduce complaints:

✦ Always have a no-frames alternative built into each page. Something more useful than the default "Your page doesn't display frames" page! Having a useful, full-featured alternative page should satisfy people whose browsers do not handle frames.

✦ Some people have frames-capable browsers, but they would rather not use frames. Consider giving users the option — at least from the home page, and potentially from other appropriate locations — to choose between a frames version and a no-frames version.

✦ Do not overdo the number of frames. The more that you break up the main window into little frames, the more cluttered your interface becomes. Remember the old saying, "two's company, three's a crowd." Reserve as much space as possible for the main content window of your frame set.

✦ Be sure that you have a better reason for using frames than the desire to show that you know how to use them. You should be able to explain why you have chosen to use frames rather than a simpler approach.

✦ Avoid multiple frame sets in a single Web. The whole point of using a frame set is to create a consistent interface. If you are using multiple frame sets, you are defeating the purpose.

✦ Be sure that all hyperlinks target the correct frame windows. Avoid any circumstances that might result in a frame set document being opened in a frame window.

In the following tutorial, you'll create a frame set with a header contents frame and a main frame.

Tutorial 10.2: Create a Frame Set

1. Open the Web site that you created in Tutorial 10.1. Select File ➪ New ➪ Page. Click the Frames Pages tab and select the Header template by clicking it once. Note that the Description area explains that links in the top frame control what is displayed in the bottom frame. Click OK in the New dialog box.

2. In Page view, you should see a top frame and a bottom frame. In the top frame, click the New Page button and create a page with a greeting line on top and links to pages in your Web site.

3. Click and drag the divider between the two frames so that your top frame text all fits in the frame window, as in Figure 10-19.

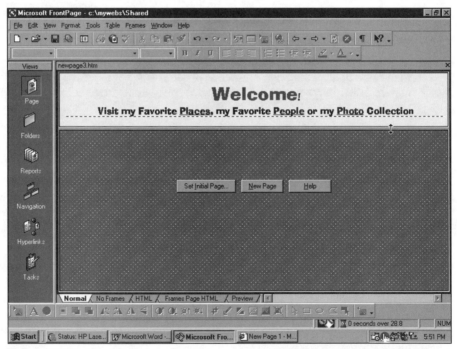

Figure 10-19: The top banner frame serves as a navigation tool for the bottom frame.

4. Click in the bottom frame, and click the Set Initial Page button. In the Create Hyperlink dialog box, double-click the home page for your Web site. Save the frame set (click Save in the Save As dialog box when prompted). Preview the frame set in your browser and test the links in the top frame.

5. Return to Page view and add a link in the top frame to a Web site outside of your page (www.ppinet.com takes you to the Web page for one of the guys who wrote this book). Right-click this new link and choose Hyperlink Properties from the context menu. In the Edit Hyperlink dialog box, click the Change Target Frame button (it looks like a pencil). Click New Window in the Target Frame dialog box, and click OK twice.

6. Save your frame set again and test your new link in a Web browser. Your new link should open a new browser window to display the target of the link.

Summary

This chapter detailed the construction and use of shared borders and frame sets within a FrontPage Web. If you ever had to do this with HTML code, you noticed how much easier and powerful these tasks are in FrontPage 2000. Now, you can create Webs that are extremely easy to navigate and maintain. Using these techniques, you can make large-scale changes to your Web's structure without having to duplicate a lot of effort to link your pages together.

The next chapter examines the ways FrontPage enables you to edit and extend HTML directly. It also looks at some relatively simple enhancements to frames and to page layout that necessitate making changes to the HTML of your Web pages.

✦   ✦   ✦

HTML Editing Techniques

As you have seen in the first part of this book, FrontPage enables you to create professional-looking Webs without having to learn or worry about HTML. However, some effects can only be achieved by directly editing the HTML code. This chapter examines the ways in which FrontPage enables you to edit and extend HTML directly. For those who are already familiar with HTML and would like to be able to use FrontPage in conjunction with other HTML editing tools, this chapter provides the basic information on how FrontPage deals with HTML.

Note   This chapter does not pretend to instruct you in the use of HTML. If you would like to learn more about HTML, several good books on this topic are available, for a wide range of audiences. If you are looking for an introductory-level book, one excellent choice is *Creating Cool HTML 4 Web Pages* by David Taylor (IDG Books Worldwide, 1998).

How FrontPage Handles HTML

FrontPage has always made creating Web pages possible, without requiring any knowledge of what HTML is or how it works. Previous versions of FrontPage, however, didn't always make it easy for those who *want* to work directly with HTML. In fact, FrontPage had a disconcerting habit of rewriting HTML to its own specification, which sometimes wrecked havoc with perfectly valid code that FrontPage just didn't happen to recognize.

Happily, one of the biggest improvements in FrontPage 2000 is that it no longer tampers with HTML. Not only does FrontPage let you control your own HTML destiny, it even allows you to tell it how you like to write HTML, and it will automatically

In This Chapter

How FrontPage handles HTML

Using the HTML Tab view

Cutting and pasting HTML

Inserting custom HTML tags

Working with Reveal tags

Setting HTML preferences

Configuring HTML compatibility

Handling special cases

format your HTML to your preferences! FrontPage 2000 has also improved the features of its built-in HTML editor, making it easier to write and edit code directly.

Note For the record, if you write improper HTML, FrontPage sometimes silently attempts to correct your error. For example, if you happen to put the text of your page *after* the final </HTML> tag, which marks the end of the page, FrontPage graciously puts it back where it belongs. But don't count on FrontPage to catch all of your HTML bloopers!

Do I need to know HTML?

If you bought FrontPage precisely because you don't want to have to know anything about this technical stuff, you may happily skip this chapter. Quite possibly, you will never need to edit — or even look at — the HTML that FrontPage produces. However, some of the following reasons might prompt you to reconsider your blissful ignorance:

✦ Your curiosity about how HTML works gets the better of you and you want to use FrontPage to help you learn what is going on behind the scenes.

✦ Try as you might, FrontPage doesn't quite get right the effect that you want to produce, and you are forced to take matters into your own hands.

✦ You happen upon a way-cool Web page with a feature that you want to reproduce on your own site, but FrontPage doesn't have direct support for it, so you roll up your sleeves and dig in.

✦ You read one of the later chapters in this book that describe advanced techniques that involve editing code directly, and you decide to take the plunge.

If none of these scenarios sounds mildly enticing, you are probably best served by skipping this chapter for the time being. If you are game, forge ahead. This chapter looks at the many ways that FrontPage gives you to work with HTML. The main questions addressed in this chapter are the following:

✦ Can I edit HTML directly, to take advantage of HTML elements or features not directly supported in FrontPage?

✦ Can I use FrontPage to *<name your favorite state-of-the-art HTML technique>*?

✦ Can I coordinate FrontPage with the other development applications that I already use?

✦ Can FrontPage help with compatibility and validation of HTML?

Using the HTML tab

Viewing the HTML source code of your Web page in FrontPage is as easy as opening a page in Page view and clicking the HTML tab (see Figure 11-1). The HTML tab functions like a glorified text editor. You can use it to insert or edit HTML tags and text directly or to make adjustments to the HTML that can't be made in Normal view. All the standard text editing features apply. You can insert and delete text, or cut, copy, and paste text selections. All of your favorite cut-and-paste shortcut commands work as well. Drag and drop does not work here, however. Also note that if you insert a space, tab, or paragraph return in HTML view, they don't appear in Normal view, because HTML ignores all whitespace after an initial space between words.

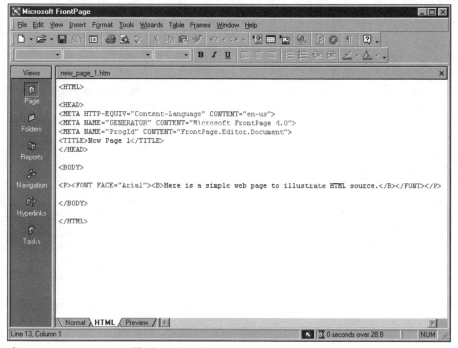

Figure 11-1: An HTML file in HTML view

 Tip If you select text in Normal view and then switch to HTML view, the text remains selected. This is a handy way to keep your place. Note that the same is not true when you go from HTML view back to Normal view.

Inserting tags

Having the ability to switch back and forth easily between Normal and HTML views is very useful in itself. You can make a change in Normal mode and then view the results in HTML mode, or vice versa. One of the new additions to FrontPage 2000 is the capability to insert HTML tags by using the menu commands even when you are in HTML view. This means that you can insert HTML without knowing the correct syntax, and see the results instantly!

To try this out for an image, switch to HTML view, place the cursor where you want to insert the image, and select Insert ⇨ Picture. Select a picture file, just as you would in Normal view, and click OK. FrontPage inserts the appropriate <IMG> tag into the HTML page. If you find it disconcerting to insert a picture and see only a string of text, you can quickly return to Normal view, where you will find the picture displayed as you would expect.

You can insert tags for the majority of the commands under the Insert menu, with the exception of Symbol, Database, Bookmark, and Hyperlink tags. Table and Frames functions are also available.

Caution   One caveat: FrontPage enables you to insert tags anywhere in HTML view. This means that you can insert an HTML tag accidentally into the middle of another HTML tag.

Editing Tag Properties

You may have noticed that when you are in HTML Tab view, you can't use the formatting menu commands. Perhaps this is to prevent people from inadvertently thinking that they can format the text in HTML view. At any rate, another way exists to access the formatting properties in HTML view: use the Tag Properties command in the HTML tab Options menu.

Tip   For what it's worth, even though most of the toolbar buttons are disabled in HTML view, Bold, Italics, and Underline buttons remain enabled. You can also use keyboard shortcuts to insert these HTML formatting tags. First, select the text to format, and then either click the toolbar button or press the equivalent keyboard shortcut.

To demonstrate how this works, create a standard paragraph of text in Normal view. Switch to HTML view. Your paragraph should have beginning paragraph (<P>) and ending paragraph (</P>) tags around it, something like the paragraph illustrated in Figure 11-2 (if not, you can always add them in HTML view!).

Now, right-click the beginning paragraph (<P>) tag (alternatively, you can select the tag and then click anywhere on the page). Select tag properties in the option menu. FrontPage displays the Paragraph properties dialog box, enabling you to format the paragraph as you want. For example, you might change the alignment from its default status to right alignment. Click OK to close the dialog box, and FrontPage updates the paragraph tag to (<P ALIGN=right>).

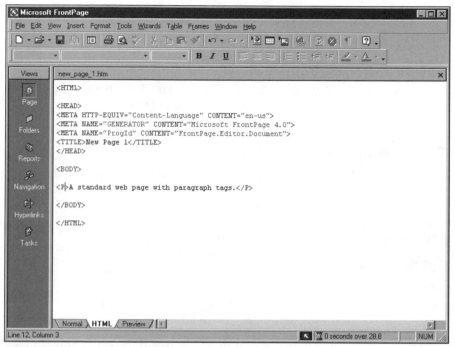

Figure 11-2: A standard paragraph in HTML view

Try the same technique with other HTML tags. In each case, FrontPage displays the appropriate properties dialog box, enabling you to specify tag properties from within HTML view.

Finding and replacing text

In addition to the other regular editing features, the Find and Replace features are active in HTML view, to help you quickly find or replace HTML code in your pages. These features work just as they do in Normal view:

✦ To use the Find dialog box, select Edit ➪ Find or press Ctrl+F, enter the text that you're looking for in the Find What text box, and then click the Find Next button. The text (if it exists on your page) is now highlighted.

✦ To use the Replace dialog box, select Edit ➪ Replace or press Ctrl+H, enter the text that you want to replace in the Find What text box, and then enter the text that you want it to be replaced with in the Replace With text box. To review each change before it's made, click the Find Next button to highlight the text that you're looking for, and then, if you want to change it, click the Replace button — Replace changes the text and then highlights the next instance of the text. To replace all instances of the text at one time, click the Replace All button.

✦ Both Find and Replace support matching whole words and case via the Match Whole Word Only and Match Case check boxes, respectively.

✦ If you enter **alt** and check Match Whole Word Only, `alternative` will not be found. Note that the whole word doesn't include punctuation or functions, such as the equals sign — in other words, entering **Bob** will return instances of `Bob`'s, and **alt** will return instances of `alt=`. This is both a blessing and a curse, and means that you must be very careful when using Replace All.

Controlling color coding

By default, HTML view color codes various HTML elements to help you distinguish them at a glance. The default color coding is as follows:

HTML Element	Color Code
Normal text	Black
Tags	Blue
Tag attribute names	Blue
Tag attribute values	Black
Comments	Gray
Scripts	Dark red

If you prefer, you can turn off the color-coding feature. In HTML view, right-click anywhere on the page and then select the Show Color Coding option to uncheck it and render all text in standard black.

You can also adjust the colors to your own liking. Select Tools ⇨ Page Options and click the Color Coding tab, as shown in Figure 11-3. Use the color-picker tool to adjust the display colors for any of the elements previously indicated. You can also use this tab to check or uncheck the Show Color Coding option. Note that you don't have to be in HTML view to adjust the colors, but it is useful for seeing the effects of your changes.

Finding a line number

One other useful feature in HTML view is the ability to jump to a particular line number. You access this feature by right-clicking the page in HTML view and selecting Go To from the options menu, which displays the Go To Line dialog box. Or, you can use the keyboard shortcut, Ctrl-G. Type the number of the line into the dialog box, as shown in Figure 11-4, and then click OK. This feature is especially useful when you are trying to locate a scripting error from an error message identifying the line that contains the error.

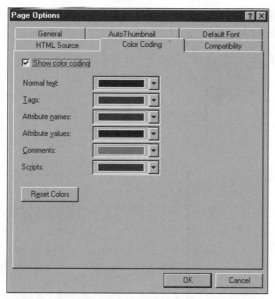

Figure 11-3: You can adjust color coding in the Color Coding tab in the Page Options dialog box.

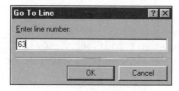

Figure 11-4: The Go To dialog box enables you to jump to a particular line number.

Tip

You can use the Go To feature as a quick way to find out the line number of a specific line in your page. Simply click to locate the cursor on the line in question, and then select Go To Line. The default line indicated is the line where your cursor is currently located.

Inserting HTML Text

Now, try a little experiment. Create a simple Web page. Open it in Notepad or the text editor of your choice. Select the HTML and copy the page onto the Clipboard. Now, return to FrontPage and open a New page. Try pasting the Clipboard normally into the new, blank page.

All the HTML shown on the page is translated into formatted text (refer to Figure 11-5). This is just fine, if that's what you want to do. However, sometimes you may want to have the text that you copy retain its HTML identity.

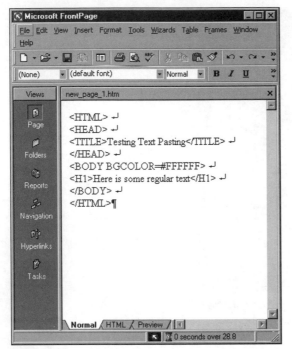

Figure 11-5: Formatted HTML text in Normal mode

One relatively simple solution to this problem is to switch to HTML view and then paste in the text. When you return to Normal view, everything is as it should be: a simple Web page.

But suppose that you are just a little bit lazy and would prefer to be able to accomplish this without ever seeing the HTML. FrontPage has a solution for you, too. Instead of doing a normal paste operation, use the Paste Special command:

1. Select Edit ➪ Paste Special to show the Paste Special dialog box.

2. Select the Treat As HTML option.

3. Click OK to paste the Clipboard contents into FrontPage as HTML. Compare the results in Figure 11-6 with the normal Paste operation results previously shown in Figure 11-5.

Caution   Note that FrontPage didn't correctly translate the <TITLE> element. In cases where you are copying complete HTML pages, you should do so in HTML view.

Note OK, if you are really lazy, you probably realized that this "shortcut" doesn't really save you any steps, because no shortcut command exists for selecting Paste Special, and you end up doing as much clicking as you would if you used the HTML view method. If you are concerned about saving time, you might want to consider customizing the FrontPage environment to save a few precious steps. (See Chapter 22 for details.)

Figure 11-6: Paste Special results

Inserting Custom HTML Tags

You may be wondering why you would ever need to create custom tags. Certainly, FrontPage has enough built-in tags to keep most people happy? True, but an increasing number of HTML-like markup languages are available that FrontPage neither knows nor cares about. Having a generic markup facility like FrontPage does helps it to deal with the unknown and the future.

One such language currently on the horizon is *Extensible Markup Language (XML)*. XML is essentially a means of writing customizable HTML, allowing you to create and use a set of markup tags that you define.

Opening a Web Page in a Different Editor

If you are accustomed to using a particular text editor to edit HTML, it would be nice if you could integrate this application with the HTML editor built into FrontPage. Unfortunately, no direct way exists to do this. You can always open the page twice and cut and paste HTML back and forth between your application and FrontPage, but this is an unwieldy alternative.

One option is to use the Open With facility in FrontPage to open Web pages in your editor. In either Hyperlink or Folder view, select a file. Then, select Edit ⇨ Open With or right-click and select Open With from the pop-up menu, either of which actions presents a list of editors that FrontPage recognizes.

The trick is to get FrontPage to add your editor to this list. To do this, select Tools ⇨ Options and then click the Configure Editors tab. Here, you see the list of editors that FrontPage recognizes, each one of which is associated with a particular file type. You might think that you could substitute your editor in place of FrontPage for files of extension type .htm/.html, but this would effectively disable your ability to open pages in FrontPage Page view.

In fact, which extension you associate with your editor doesn't matter, because you simply want to have your editor added to the list of options that FrontPage displays. One way to do this would be to make up an extension, (.xyz, for instance) and associate your editor with that. Alternatively, you could substitute your editor for Windows Notepad (unless, of course, your favorite editor *is* Notepad), which, by default, is associated with extension type (.)— in other words, no extension. Now, when you use the Open With function, your editor is one of the options, and you can open the file directly.

Recognize that this can get a little tricky. If you open the file in an editor and in FrontPage, you can make and save changes in the editor and then update FrontPage by using the Refresh command. However, because FrontPage only gives the editor a temporary copy of the file, and FrontPage does *not* update the temporary copy when you save a change, the editor isn't aware of any changes that you make in FrontPage.

Why would anyone want to do this? Take a simple example. Suppose that you want to create an application for reading poetry. You would like to be able to mark the structure of each poem: stanzas, verses, refrains, and so forth. In addition, to use your application as a learning tool, you would like to mark all the figures of speech contained in the poems: metaphor, simile, personification, synecdoche, and so forth. With XML, you could create a *document type definition (DTD)* for poems and then use that to mark up the structure of any poem that you come across.

XML provides a very powerful extension to HTML. In fact, for the genealogically inclined, HTML and XML are both offshoots of the same parent, *Standard Generalized Markup Language (SGML)*. Technically, HTML is really nothing more than an instance of an SGML DTD. XML is more closely related to SGML, simply lacking some of its sophistication.

Currently, XML editors and viewers are scarce (and current Web browsers aren't equipped to deal with XML markup yet). Microsoft has been instrumental in pushing the development of the XML standard, and XML support quite likely will be included in the next version of FrontPage. For now, the best that you can do is the HTML Markup command.

In HTML view, you can enter any HTML that you like, valid or invalid, and FrontPage doesn't object (for the most part). If you try entering some unorthodox HTML, such as an <ODDTAG> tag, and then switch back to Normal view, FrontPage inserts a yellow box with an embedded question mark <?>, as shown in Figure 11-7. This is the tag that FrontPage uses to represent HTML that it doesn't recognize.

In addition, FrontPage displays an exclamation point <!> icon whenever you insert a standard HTML comment.

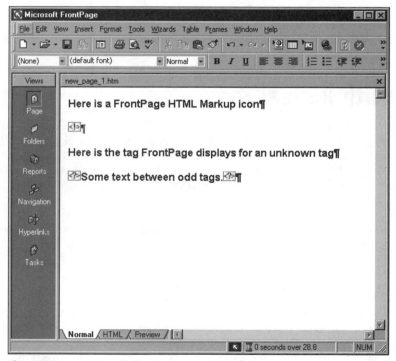

Figure 11-7: HTML Markup icons in Normal view

You can insert HTML markup from Normal view. Select Insert ➪ Advanced ➪ HTML to display the HTML Markup dialog box, shown in Figure 11-8. You can type anything that you want in this box. When you click OK, FrontPage displays your custom markup, using the HTML Markup icon.

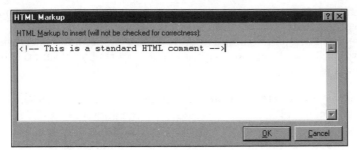

Figure 11-8: HTML Markup dialog box with a valid HTML comment

To edit a custom tag, you can double-click the markup icon to open the HTML Markup dialog box and display the current markup text.

Caution   Do not confuse the Advanced ➪ HTML Markup command with the Comment command. Selecting Insert ➪ Comment places a FrontPage Comment Component in the page. HTML Markup inserts HTML.

Working with Reveal Tags

In addition to HTML Tab view, FrontPage enables you to see the HTML tags that it is inserting as you work in Normal view. This feature is called *Reveal Tags*, which is roughly equivalent to the Show All icon that reveals other "hidden" symbols, such as line and paragraph breaks. However, with Reveal Tags, FrontPage turns on icons that represent the beginning and ending tags in your HTML document (see Figure 11-9).

To show Reveal Tags, select View ➪ Reveal Tags. To hide the codes, select View ➪ Reveal Tags again. (Yes, I know, this is counterintuitive, but what can I say?)

What can you do with Reveal Tags?

For the most part, Reveal Tags is just a convenience. If you are used to working with HTML and feel reassured seeing the tags as you work in Normal view, then Reveal Tags is for you. From a practical standpoint, Reveal Tags does have some limited value as shortcuts to the tag properties dialog boxes. If you double-click a Reveal Codes tag, for example, you bring up the properties dialog box that corresponds to that tag set, just as selecting Tag Properties (described earlier in the chapter) in the HTML tab does.

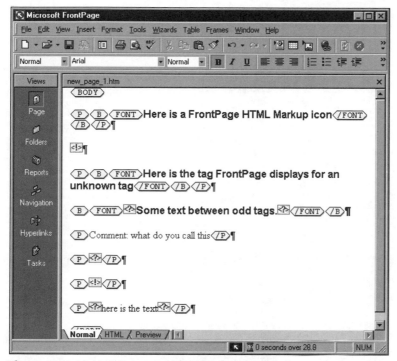

Figure 11-9: An HTML page with Reveal Tags turned on

Setting HTML Preferences

If you are accustomed to writing HTML by using a text editor, you probably have a set of conventions that you use to make your HTML more readable. Perhaps you use capital letters for all tags and attributes, to distinguish them from the content. You probably divide the lines of HTML and perhaps indent them, too, to make them easy to read. You may add comments internally to help you identify major sections of more complex pages.

One of the biggest improvements made on FrontPage in the FrontPage 2000 version is the fact that the page editor leaves your HTML alone. In previous versions, FrontPage's tendency to change HTML that you had created manually ranged from merely annoying to downright destructive. For those who want to have their HTML their own way, FrontPage 2000 is worth the price of the upgrade for this feature alone.

Not only did Microsoft decide to take a hands-off approach to HTML, it also added a handy mechanism that enables you to instruct FrontPage in how you want it to format HTML. Over the years, several HTML programming styles and conventions have evolved. You can now fine-tune FrontPage to write HTML to your preferences.

You set your HTML formatting preferences by using the HTML Source tab. To access this tab, select Tools ⇨ Page Options and click the HTML Source tab in the Page Options dialog box, shown in Figure 11-10.

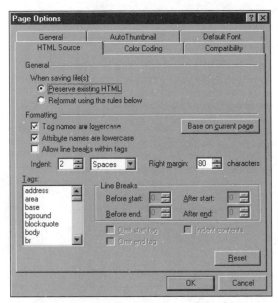

Figure 11-10: The HTML Source tab in the Page Options dialog box

The HTML Source tab contains multiple options. First, you must decide whether you want FrontPage to reformat its HTML to rules that you define or simply preserve the existing HTML. These options appear in the General area of the dialog box:

✦ **Preserve Existing HTML:** FrontPage makes no alterations to your HTML.

✦ **Reformat Using the Rules Below:** FrontPage revises the formatting of the current page and all subsequent pages. Basically, the way the reformat option works is that you designate formatting options and then specify for each and every tag how that tag should appear. (These options are reviewed in the next two sections.)

Caution
If you check any of the Formatting check boxes on this dialog box, FrontPage implements these changes to your HTML even if you have checked the "Preserve Existing HTML" option.

The following are the options available in the Formatting area of the Page Options dialog box:

✦ **Tag Names Are Lowercase:** Uncheck this option if you want HTML tags written in uppercase.

✦ **Attribute Names Are Lowercase:** Uncheck this option if you want HTML attributes within tags to be uppercase as well.

✦ **Allow Line Breaks Within Tags**: Uncheck this option to prevent tags from wrapping around to a second line (splitting a tag into multiple lines is perfectly valid HTML).

✦ **Indent:** Select a quantity and a unit (spaces or tabs) to indicate how much to indent the tags (in the Tags list at the bottom of the Page Options dialog box) that have the Indent Contents check box selected.

✦ **Right margin:** Select a number of characters to allow on a single line before wrapping occurs.

The remaining formatting options pertain to individual tags. To set these options for a specific tag, first select the tag by clicking it in the scrolling Tags list. Then, configure the following formatting options for that tag:

✦ **Line Breaks**: The options in this area determine whether a particular set of beginning and ending tags are placed on a separate line by themselves or are written on the same line with the content that they encompass. For example, by default, a `<BLOCKQUOTE>` tag is isolated on a line by itself, both before and after the text of the blockquote itself. This represents settings of 1 line break before and after both start and end:

```
Here is a paragraph of text
<BLOCKQUOTE>
     Here is a block quote.
</BLOCKQUOTE>
Here is another paragraph.
```

If you change the preferences to 1 line break before the start and after the start, you get the following:

```
Here is a paragraph of text.
<BLOCKQUOTE>Here is a block quote. </BLOCKQUOTE>
Here is another paragraph.
```

And, reversing the settings so that you have 1 line break after the start and before the start results in the following:

```
Here is a paragraph of text. <BLOCKQUOTE>
   Here is a block quote.
</BLOCKQUOTE>Here is another paragraph.
```

✦ **Indent Contents**: Check this to indent the contents between the beginning and ending tags.

✦ **Omit Start/End Tag:** In some cases, you can omit the start/end tags without creating an error. A good example is with table cells. Because the beginning of a new cell tag, by definition, coincides with the end of the previous cell tag, writing the end tag is unnecessary. If you prefer to write your table code this way, this is the place to stipulate your preferences. For a good use of this option, see the discussion of the list item tag (`<LI>`), later in the chapter.

One other important option in the Page Options dialog box is the Base on Current Page button. When you select this option, FrontPage analyzes the current page to determine how you like your HTML to appear. This assumes that your HTML stylistic practices on this page are consistent.

Tip

If you plan to configure your HTML preferences only once and you are specifying only a few changes, using the Page Options dialog box is the easiest method. If you use multiple configurations or specify options for several tags, you should consider making a "template" that includes a sample of each tag that you want to configure. Then, use the Base on Current Page feature of the Page Options dialog box to set all the preferences simultaneously. This way, you can make multiple templates and adjust them quickly and easily.

Configuring HTML Compatibility

One of the original notions behind HTML and the World Wide Web was to create a markup format that could be displayed consistently by any browser on any platform. Although to some degree this dream is realized in current browser practice, industry competition and the relatively slow (by Internet-time measurements) development of HTML standards have resulted in a proliferation of small, but sometimes debilitating, differences in browser behavior. This is only compounded by the frantic pace at which new versions of browsers are released.

The upshot of all of this is that creating even a mildly sophisticated HTML page can open up a rat's nest of compatibility problems. FrontPage 2000 tries to do its part to assist you in this regard by allowing you to dictate your compatibility preferences, using the Page Options dialog box Compatibility tab.

To access the HTML Compatibility tab (Figure 11-11), select Tools ⇨ Options ⇨ Compatibility.

Implementing a compatibility plan

The following are the two principal ways to use FrontPage's compatibility features when you are creating your site:

✦ Avoid all features not supported by one or more of the browser versions that you want to support

✦ Create multiple versions of the pages that contain potential compatibility problems

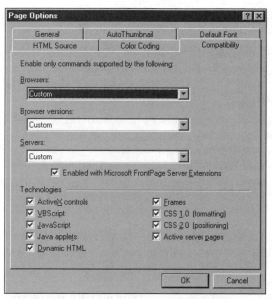

Figure 11-11: The HTML Compatibility tab in the Page Options dialog box

Implementing the first option is fairly simple. You simply need to use the Compatibility tab to disable any feature that might pose a problem. Depending on the complexity of your site, however, you may have to make some tough compromises. The question that you have to ask is whether eliminating features creates more difficulties for your users than would the possibility of dealing with an incompatibility.

If you choose the second route, you avoid the problem of potentially disappointing your users. However, unless you are prepared to resort to scripting to assist you in this endeavor, you have to set up your site to give your visitors the option of accessing pages that might contain "dangerous" features. Unless handled delicately, this can become almost as annoying to visitors as having a broken Web page.

Equally important is the amount of extra work this method involves for you. Of course, some features, such as frames and scripting, have built-in ways to handle browsers that don't support the feature, but maintaining these options still requires extra work. You have to develop multiple versions of key pages, and each time that you make a change to one of these pages, you have to make sure that the change is reflected in all versions. Doing this manually can become a nightmare if you have a large site.

Validating HTML

HTML *validation* refers to the process of checking the accuracy of your HTML to make sure that you haven't made any typographical errors or used tags and their attributes incorrectly. The strictest validation methods parse your HTML against the actual DTD that defines what elements are legal in various types of HTML.

FrontPage doesn't include any validation reporting capabilities for your HTML, although you can use FrontPage to verify internal and external links. On one hand, the lack of a validation feature isn't a big problem, because FrontPage is writing most of the HTML itself. On the other hand, the fact that you can still add your own HTML is reason enough to want to check your HTML for accuracy.

Tip   If you plan to use this method, you might explore the possibility of using the Include Page Component to help you manage the portions of pages that are identical for all.

Ultimately, if you have anything more than a small Web site and are serious about handling browser compatibility issues elegantly, you will want to investigate the use of scripting or programming to manage this task. Check out Chapter 18 for advise on this topic.

Handling Special Cases

This section concludes the chapter by looking at some of the finer points of FrontPage's HTML usage. The list of topics covered here is by no means exhaustive, but it is representative and should give you a feel for the kind of "gotchas" to watch out for if you plan to use FrontPage extensively.

Note   The HTML Tab view works adequately for most HTML editing purposes. For more advanced editing, particularly of client-side scripting, you will want to use the Microsoft Script Editor. See Chapter 18 for details.

Comments

FrontPage has a Comment feature that allows you to insert a comment into your Web page and view the comment in Normal view. The comment remains in the HTML, but it isn't displayed to users when the page is viewed in a Web browser.

To insert a FrontPage Comment, first locate the cursor on the page where you want the Comment to appear. Select Insert ➪ Comment and type the text of your Comment in the Comment dialog box. Click OK to return to the page and view the results.

FrontPage's Comment feature is really a FrontPage Component called PurpleText, alluding to the display style of the Comment. Because this Comment is embedded in a FrontPage Component, you can double-click the Comment text to bring up the Comment dialog box for further editing.

In addition to FrontPage's custom Comment feature, you can also insert standard HTML comments. These are indicated by using the following syntax:

```
<!— This is a standard HTML comment —>
```

You can insert a Comment manually in HTML view or by using the HTML Markup feature, described earlier in this chapter. Either way, FrontPage represents this Comment in Normal view with a highlighted yellow exclamation point.

Caution

If you insert an HTML tag by using the HTML Markup method, FrontPage inserts the tag. If you insert a string of text not enclosed in standard tag brackets, FrontPage places the text in an HTML Markup Component.

Meta tags

Whenever you add or edit a Web page in FrontPage, you are working primarily with the body section of the page. Web pages also contain a head section, which stores information about the page that typically does not display. (One exception is the Web page title. This tag appears in the head element and is displayed in the window title bar of the current Web page.)

Meta tags are one of the types of HTML tags that are located in the nondisplaying, head portion of an HTML Web page. Meta tags contain useful information about the HTML page, its creation date, the application that created it, the author, and so forth. This information is contained in the file, but is invisible to anyone who views the page in his or her browser.

By default, FrontPage adds the following meta tags to the header of every HTML document:

```
<META HTTP-EQUIV="Content-Type" CONTENT="text/html;
charset=windows-1252">
<META NAME="GENERATOR" CONTENT="Microsoft FrontPage 4.0">
<META NAME="ProgId" CONTENT="FrontPage.Editor.Document">
```

You can also add your own meta tag information in the Custom tab of the Page Properties dialog box. One common use of the meta tag is to create a list of keywords that text engines can use to index your Web pages. You can also include a short description of your site, which some search engines display with your URL when a search query matches your Web site.

To add keywords and a description to the meta tags of a page, select File ➪ Page Properties. Click the Custom tab in the Page Properties dialog box, shown in Figure 11-12, which shows options to Add, Modify, or Remove two kinds of meta tags: System Variables (HTTP-EQUIV) and User Variables (NAME). HTTP-EQUIV type tags are equivalent to standard HTTP headers. The NAME type tags can be user-defined, although some of these, such as the Keyword tag, are fairly standard. Next, you'll add the keywords and description meta tags to the User Variables section of the Custom tab in the Page Properties dialog box.

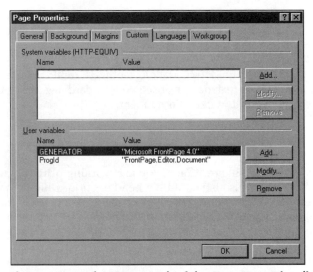

Figure 11-12: The Custom tab of the Page Properties dialog box. Use this tab to enter meta tags.

To add a meta tag, click the Add button next to the User Variables window. In the dialog box that appears, type **keywords** as the Name and a comma-separated list of keywords or phrases as the Value. Use Figure 11-13 for comparison. Click OK to add the keywords attribute. Repeat the process, using **description** and a short paragraph that describes your site. Click OK in the Page Properties dialog box to accept your changes. Save the page.

To check the results, select the HTML tab. You should see the new meta tags added to the header of the HTML file, as shown in Figure 11-14.

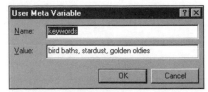

Figure 11-13: Adding keywords to an HTML page

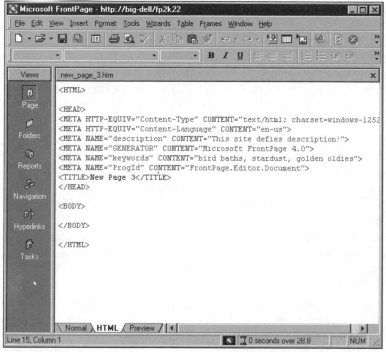

Figure 11-14: The results of adding user variables (meta tags)

If you want to add meta tags to a frame set page, select Frame ➪ Frame Page Properties and then the Custom tab.

Frame borders

In Chapter 10, you learned how to use FrontPage to create frame sets visually without having to write or understand the intricacies of HTML. However, FrontPage can't handle a few specialized features of frame sets, such as customizing frame borders and ensuring that frames appear consistently in both Internet Explorer and Netscape Navigator.

CSS <SPAN> tag

As discussed in the next chapter, FrontPage 2000 provides improved support for the creation and editing of style sheet elements. However, no mechanism exists for inserting a <SPAN> element. If you need to use this tag, you have to create it manually by using the HTML tab editor.

Customize Frame Borders

The frame and frame set HTML tags have several attributes that you can set to customize how the frame borders appear. These attributes can be added to either the <FRAMESET> tag or to individual <FRAME> tags. Adding border attributes to the frame set is generally easier, because it avoids "border conflicts" if, for example, you designate the border color of one frame to be purple and the color of an adjacent frame is green. Here are the attributes that you can use:

✦ **BORDERCOLOR=#rrggbb** Introduced by Netscape in version 3 of its browser and then inexplicably dropped in version 4. Just to keep things interesting, however, it is now supported in Microsoft Internet Explorer 4, though users of earlier versions will not see this color. You can designate a color by using either the standard, hexadecimal RGB value or, for more standard colors, an English equivalent (for example, "purple," "blue," "pink").

✦ **FRAMEBORDER="yes|no" or "0|1"** Used in conjunction with one or the other of the next two attributes to designate the presence or absence of a frame border. This attribute is supported by both Netscape and Microsoft as of version 3 of their respective browsers.

✦ **FRAMESPACING=number** Currently, the preferred method of designating the thickness of frame borders. It is equivalent to the CELLSPACING property of tables. It designates the distance between frames, in pixels, which effectively is the thickness of the border. Note that any change in the border spacing produces a flat borderline in older browsers, not the 3D beveled version that is the default.

✦ **BORDER=number** Used by Netscape 3.x and greater browsers to indicate border thickness. Internet Explorer simply ignores this attribute and uses the FRAMESPACING attribute instead. To create frames that look the same in both browsers, you need to use both attributes.

Entering the BORDER=number attribute in Editor's HTML view does a very interesting thing: it sets the FRAMEBORDER attribute to "0," effectively eliminating your border. This means that if you want a frame to have a border with a thickness different than the default, you need to enter the HTML code in an alternative editor, such as Notepad. This is a major annoyance and makes dealing with border widths extremely unwieldy. On the other hand, I can't really think of a reason to use different width borders.

List elements

Items in a bulleted or numbered list are indicated with a list item tag (<LI>). FrontPage also ends each list item with an end list tag (</LI>), which is unconventional, because it isn't necessary to determine where one item in the list ends and the next begins. This usage, though unorthodox, is harmless. You can alter it by using the HTML Source tab, described earlier in the chapter. The steps are as follows:

1. Select Tools ➪ Page Options and click the HTML Source tab.

2. Select Reformat using the rules below.

3. Select li, short for list item, from the scrolling Tag list.

4. Check the Omit End Tag check box.

5. Click OK.

Switch to HTML view (if you were already in HTML view, you need to switch to Normal view and then back—the Refresh option is disabled in HTML view) to see the effect of your changes.

Symbol entity references

HTML entity references are used to insert nonstandard ASCII characters into an HTML page. FrontPage correctly translates most typed characters, such as greater than and less than signs, or quotation marks, into their proper entity references. However, it doesn't translate any of the characters that it inserts as symbols. You can enter symbols by using the Symbol dialog box, shown in Figure 11-15, which is accessed by selecting Insert ➪ Symbol. This dialog box includes all the accented characters used in romance languages, as well as symbols such as the copyright and trademark signs. Using this mechanism simply inserts the symbol character. In practice, this means that browsers on Windows platforms may see the character that you intended, but results are unpredictable on other platforms

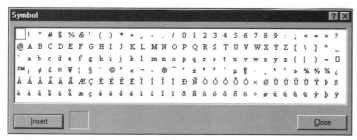

Figure 11-15: The Symbols dialog box

Nonbreaking spaces

You can indicate a nonbreaking space character in HTML by using the entity reference . This character can be inserted to force browsers to display space characters where they normally ignore them. However, not all browsers recognize this entity reference, so using it isn't always advisable. FrontPage uses it by default in a variety of circumstances.

FrontPage writes this symbol into blank paragraphs if, for example, you create two paragraph breaks in a row. It also often inserts this symbol into blank table cells. In addition, if you enter multiple spaces in Normal view, or attempt to insert a tab, FrontPage uses nonbreaking spaces to simulate this effect in HTML.

You can't prevent FrontPage from entering nonbreaking spaces. You can use the Replace feature in HTML view, as previously described, to eliminate these characters if you choose.

Summary

This chapter delved into the inner workings of FrontPage. In the process, you learned some simple techniques for viewing and editing HTML in your Web pages. This chapter also demonstrated the ways in which FrontPage 2000 enables you to control the HTML that it outputs, as well as some of its limitations. The next chapter introduces FrontPage style sheets, a powerful feature that lets you dictate exactly what you want your page to look like.

✦   ✦   ✦

Cascading Style Sheets

Chapter 6 showed you how to apply basic formatting styles to the text of your HTML pages. In this chapter, you learn how to use style sheets to gain better control over text formatting within a particular page or across an entire Web. This chapter explains how to create a style sheet and apply it to your Web pages. It also demonstrates some advanced features of Cascading Style Sheets (CSS), with a special emphasis on using CSS to position elements on the page.

Note   FrontPage 2000 adds the ability to create, edit, and link style sheets within Page view. It removes the Style buttons that were added to many formatting dialog boxes in FrontPage 98, and replaces them with a central Style dialog box. FrontPage 2000 also comes with a number of predefined style sheet pages, which you can either use as-is or customize.

Discovering Style Sheets

If you have poked around the features of your Web browser, you may have noticed that you can change the way the browser displays various elements of any Web page. Regardless of how the author of the page may have wanted you to see that Heading 1 text, if you want to render it as 8-point Script Italic, you can. The HTML standard was originally envisioned as a method of defining the structural elements of a document. It was left to the browser to decide how to display any particular element.

As the Web has increasingly become a media for publishing, developers have not been content to let viewers mangle their carefully designed Web pages. Likewise, as the size and complexity of Web publishing enterprises have increased dramatically, a mechanism was sorely needed to help control the consistency of pages within a site. The answer: the *Cascading Style Sheet (CSS)* standard.

What is a style sheet?

A *style sheet* is a collection of style definitions that can be applied to elements of an HTML page. You can use these styles to modify existing styles (say, Heading 1) or you can create your own styles.

Like Web pages, style sheets are simply text files that contain the appropriate formatting codes (see Figure 12-1). Of course, these formatting codes aren't the same as HTML code — that would be too easy.

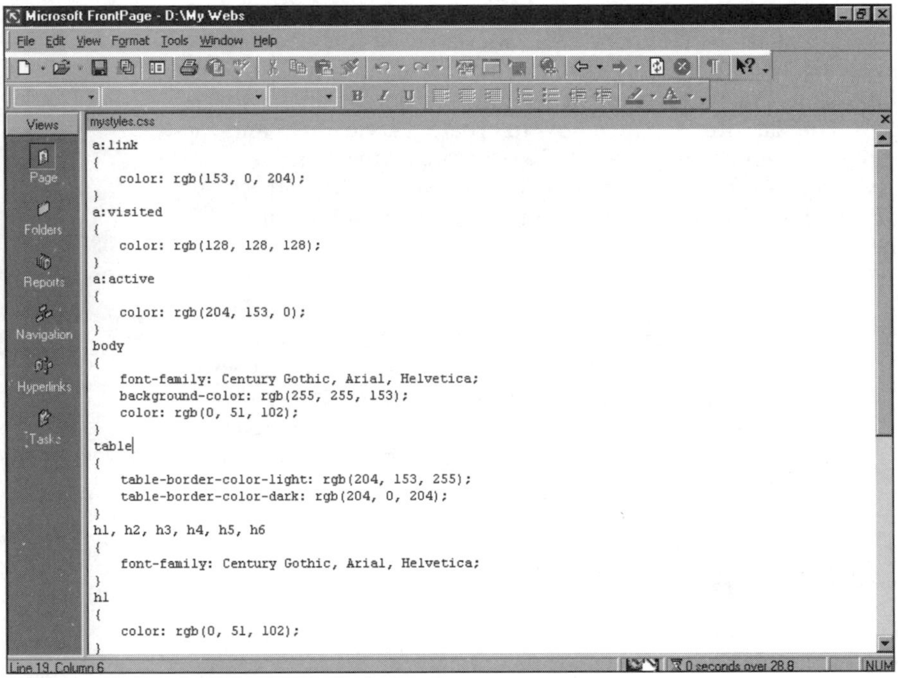

Figure 12-1: A style sheet contains commands for formatting Web pages.

These codes aren't identical to HTML for a reason: style sheet formatting is far, far more versatile than standard HTML, and you can use this versatility to make pages that you just couldn't make without styles. By using styles sheets, you can add background images to individual paragraphs, make text an exact size (rather than be restricted to the seven logical sizes available to HTML), add borders around text, and even adjust the spacing between lines of text.

The CSS standard

The standard that defines how to designate styles is called Cascading Style Sheets. Currently, the CSS Level 1 standard (CSS1) is accepted and implemented in the more recent browsers. CSS1 consists primarily of formatting properties of Web page elements. Most of this chapter focuses on creating and using style sheet formatting elements.

A CSS Level 2 standard (CSS2) has been proposed and, to varying degrees, implemented in both Netscape and Internet Explorer. CSS2 includes provisions for positioning elements on a page, which is an exciting prospect for anyone who has spent hours trying to lay out a complex page by using HTML tables. FrontPage 2000 includes support for the new positioning properties. (Positioning is addressed in the last part of the chapter.) See the sidebar "CSS Level 1 and Level 2" for details on the Level 1 and Level 2 specifications.

CSS Level 1 and Level 2

The Cascading Style Sheet standard is defined by the World Wide Web Consortium (W3C). Level 1 of the standard was approved in December 1996. It sets forth the basic concepts for style sheet notation and specifies the syntax for formatting elements of a Web page. Included in the specification are provisions for fonts, colors, text properties, alignment, margins, borders, and lists. You can read the complete W3C CSS1 Recommendation at `http://www.w3.org/TR/REC-CSS1-961217.html`.

In May 1998, the CSS Level 2 recommendations became an official W3C proposal. In plain English, this means that the Level 2 additions have been thoroughly discussed, resulting in enough agreement to present a formal proposal to the W3C. The proposal is not considered a standard until it is officially recommended by the W3C. In the interim, of course, the major browsers have already announced and begun to implement various aspects of the proposal (as well as some of their own variations). Don't count on consistent behavior from the browsers until the proposal is accepted.

The most highly touted feature of CSS2 is its support for absolute and relative positioning of Web page elements. After the specification has solidified, designers will be able to lay out page elements precisely. Gone will be the days of kludging page layouts with tables and frames. Also, when combined with a scripting language, positioning styles can be used to create Dynamic HTML (DHTML) animations and sophisticated page effects.

Less noticed, but equally valuable, are provisions in the Level 2 proposal for specifying how page elements should be represented by different media types, such as printed output, a Braille device, speech synthesizers, handheld devices, and so forth. These provisions will enable devices other than standard computers to access and present Web pages easier. For more information, and to peruse the latest version of the W3C CSS2 Proposed Recommendations, visit `http://www.w3.org/TR/REC-CSS2/`.

Do I need a style sheet?

Using FrontPage 2000, creating style sheets is so easy — and using them will save you so many headaches down the road as you develop your Webs — that, in a sense, you would be foolish not to use a style sheet under any circumstances. If any of the following circumstances apply to you, you would definitely be wise to implement style sheets:

✦ Your site has more than 20 Web pages with a similar look and feel.

✦ Your site's content is developed or maintained by multiple authors.

✦ You feel strongly that your viewers should see your pages as you designed them.

If you have an existing Web, adding a style sheet is fairly straightforward as well — which is demonstrated in a moment. Furthermore, you needn't worry about whether all of your users' browsers support styles. The styles are simply ignored by browsers that don't recognize them.

Caution   The original style sheet standard has been around for a few years. Still, only the more recent browsers actually support the standard, and even those don't offer complete (or consistent) support for all aspects of the standard. If you use style sheets, you should be prepared to handle browser-compatibility issues.

How styles work

Styles are relatively easy to understand and, by using FrontPage 2000, even easier to implement. A basic style declaration looks like this:

```
h1 {font-size: 12pt; color: red }
```

If you are familiar with HTML, you know that h1 in this style represents a Header 1 style tag. This portion of the declaration is called the *style name* or *selector*. This selector tells the browser to treat any Header 1 text in the designated manner. The rest of the style declaration — the part inside curly brackets — represents a series of *property:value* pairs. Each pair is separated by a semicolon. This style declaration says to render Header 1 text in red, using a 12-point font size.

Classes and IDs

Any valid HTML element can be used as a CSS selector (although, in practice, some elements lend themselves more readily to style sheet usage than others.) In addition, CSS permits the use of class and ID designators to give you more flexibility in how you assign styles.

In the style sheet syntax, a class is indicated by an initial period in front of the selector name. An ID is designated with an initial hash mark (#). You can also combine class names and/or IDs with selector names. The following code illustrates all the valid possibilities:

```
h1
.myClass
#myID
h1.myClass
h1#myID
h1.myClass#myID
.myClass#myID
```

To associate a particular HTML element with a class or ID identifier, simply add the class or ID identifier as an attribute of the tag. So, for example, to associate an HTML element with the selector, h1.myClass#myID, use the following:

```
<h1 class="myClass" id="myID">Some stylish text</h1>
```

In practice, you may never need to add these by hand to your Web pages (although the advanced example presented later in the chapter requires some manual labor). In most cases, FrontPage 2000 takes care of the dirty work. FrontPage does use, and assumes that you understand, the CSS terminology of selector, class, and ID.

Note   What is the difference between a class identifier and an ID? Basically, a class is reusable. So, for example, you might create a style class called ".bigred". You could then associate that class with as many different HTML elements as you want. An ID is guaranteed to be unique. It can only be associated with a single instance of an element.

Inline Styles

In earlier chapters (see Chapters 6 and 11), you used the Style button to format various elements of your HTML page. Little did you know that you were actually implementing an inline style using the CSS formatting standard. In FrontPage, you can easily create an inline style for the following page elements:

- ✦ Web pages
- ✦ Tables
- ✦ Form fields
- ✦ Bulleted or numbered lists
- ✦ Images
- ✦ Horizontal rules
- ✦ Java applets or plug-ins

For each of these elements, the process of defining an inline style is essentially the same, namely:

1. Select the page element to which you want to apply the style.

2. Right-click and select the properties dialog box for that element.

3. Click the Style button.

4. Optionally, define a class and/or ID tag for this style.

5. Click the Format button and select an option from the drop-down menu (Font, Paragraph, Border, Numbering — note that some options may not be available for a given element).

6. Make any desired style designations.

7. Click OK for all dialog boxes until you return to Page view.

In contrast to the standard method of setting an element's HTML properties, defining an inline style specifies the properties that you want by using the CSS language. If you care to know more about how this works behind the scenes, read on. If you just want to find out more about using FrontPage 2000's style sheet features, jump ahead to "Embedded Styles."

Inline styles behind the scenes

Now, take a peek at the HTML created by the steps described in the previous section. Figure 12-2 shows a bulleted list rendered using an inline style. The following shows the code added to the list to create the formatting:

```
<ul style="font-family: Arial; color: #CC0099; letter-spacing:
2pt; font-size: 12pt; font-weight: bold; list-style-type:
square" class="7wonders">
  <li>The Pyramids of Egypt</li>
  <li>The Hanging Gardens of Babylon</li>
  <li>The Statue of Zeus at Olympia</li>
  <li>The Colossus of Rhodes</li>
  <li>The Temple of Artemis at Ephesus</li>
  <li>The Mausoleum at Halicarnassus</li>
  <li>The Pharos (Lighthouse) of Alexandria</li>
</ul>
```

The key element to notice in the HTML listing is the "style" attribute added to the bulleted list element (`<ul>`). This attribute uses the same basic syntax as a CSS style sheet definition, minus the selector name and curly brackets (see "How Styles Work," earlier in the chapter, for details):

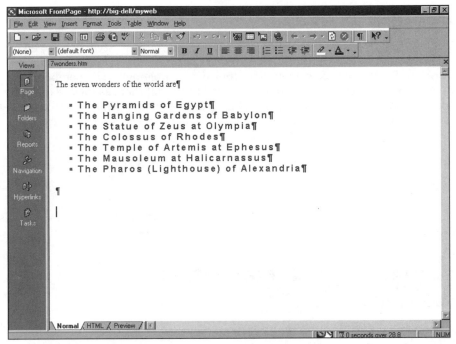

Figure 12-2: The Seven Wonders of the World formatted with an inline style

This local style operates only on this particular element. The only way to re-create the same style for another bulleted list would be to redo the step that you used to create this one (or cut and paste the style information directly into the HTML). In other words, inline styles don't help you to make your Web page styles more consistent. They merely provide an easy way to override temporarily any standard styles that you may have created. But read on, because the next section shows how to create a style that you can reuse.

Why Are They Called "Cascading" Style Sheets?

This chapter introduces you to several ways to incorporate styles into your Web pages. The "Cascading" in *Cascading Style Sheets* defines the hierarchy that specifies which styles receive higher priority in cases where several methods create conflicting style information.

The basic rule dictates that an author's style sheets override any styles that a reader has created, and the reader's styles override the default behavior of the browser. As for the different varieties of style designations, an inline style takes precedence over an embedded style, which takes precedence over a linked or imported style reference. In the case of multiple, linked style sheets, later references supercede earlier references.

Embedded Styles

Suppose that you want to be able to reuse the "7wonders" style developed in the previous section. One solution is to create an embedded style that can be associated with multiple elements on your page. Implementing an embedded style takes two steps: First, define and name the style; then, associate the style information with an HTML element. This section explains these two steps in detail, using the Seven Wonders list developed in the previous section as an example. To start the process, follow these steps:

1. Create a new Web page to contain your embedded style.

2. Select Format ➪ Style.

The Style dialog box (shown in Figure 12-3) enables you to create user-defined style classes or to alter the default appearance of any standard HTML tag.

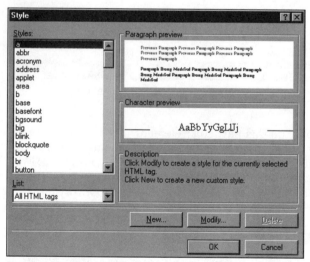

Figure 12-3: The Style dialog box enables you to create and edit embedded styles.

Creating a new style

To create a new, user-defined style, follow these steps:

1. In the Style dialog box, click the New button.

2. In the Name (selector) field, type a name for your style (for example, **7wonders**), as illustrated in Figure 12-4.

3. Click the Format button and define your style.

4. Click OK three times to return to Page view.

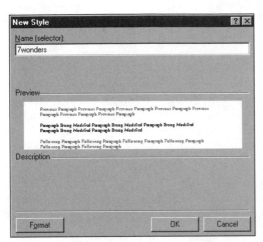

Figure 12-4: Creating a new, user-defined style

 Make sure that you restrict style names to single words (no spaces).

You now have a custom-defined style that appears in the drop-down list of available styles. Note that FrontPage puts a period in front of the name of the style that you defined. So, for instance, 7wonders appears as .7wonders in the style list, as shown in Figure 12-5. The dot indicates that the style is really a style class that can be applied to any HTML element. (More on style classes later in this chapter.)

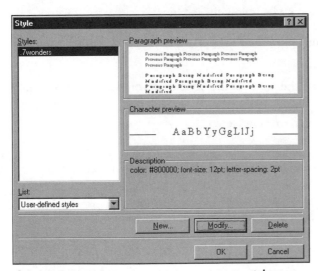

Figure 12-5: FrontPage 2000 converts your style name to a CSS class.

When you create a style in this fashion, FrontPage embeds the style definition in the HTML page. The following is the code for the style just created:

```
<style>
<!-

.7wonders    { font-family: Arial; color: #008000; font-size:
14pt;
          letter-spacing: 2pt; font-weight: bold }
->
</style>
```

An embedded style sheet is created by using the `<style>` and `</style>` tags with internal HTML comment tags to hide the style definitions from browsers that don't support CSS. The `<style>` tag is placed between the `<head>` and `</head>` tags in the HTML page. The syntax for a style definition, as discussed earlier in the chapter, is the following:

Applying a style

In many cases, you can use the Style drop-down menu on the toolbar to apply your user-defined styles in the same way that you would apply any standard HTML style to an element. This method doesn't work for your bulleted list, however. (If you try it, you discover that FrontPage applies the style to the text of a single item in the list, which is not the result that you want.)

To apply your newly created style, follow these steps:

1. Right-click the list and select List Properties from the drop-down menu.
2. Click the Style button.
3. In the Class field, type the name of the style that you want to apply (minus the period), as shown in Figure 12-6.
4. Click OK twice to return to Page view.

You should see your style applied to your list. If you look at the HTML source, you will see that FrontPage has added a class identifier to the bulleted list tag, such as the following:

```
<ul class="7wonders">
```

Notice that nothing about this style forces it to be associated only with lists. Try associating some normal text with this style. The effect should be the same.

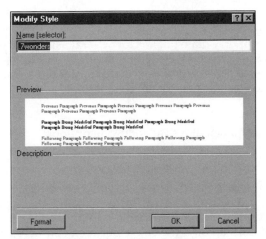

Figure 12-6: Applying a user-defined style to a list element

Tip

A quicker way exists to implement your user-defined style. When you name the style, give it a name beginning with **ul** and a period (for example, **ul.7wonders**). Doing this creates a new style called Bulleted List.7wonders in the drop-down menu. Apply this style to any bulleted list, and FrontPage takes care of the rest.

Modifying existing styles

Rather than create a new style for the Seven Wonders list, you might elect to modify the default style for the standard HTML list tag (<ul>). To do this:

1. Select Format ⇨ Style.

2. From the List drop-down menu in the Style dialog box, select either All HTML Tags, to modify a standard HTML tag, or User-Defined Styles, to modify a style that you previously created.

3. Select the tag, (for example, ul) from the Styles list.

4. Click the Modify button.

5. Click the Format button.

6. Make your Style selections, as desired.

7. Click OK on all dialog boxes until you return to Page view.

By using this method, all bulleted lists that you create on this page will inherit the style that you have defined for bulleted lists. Usually, you will create general-purpose style definitions for standard HTML elements and use class designations for more-specialized styles.

Style formatting options

FrontPage 2000 provides you with property dialog boxes for several aspects of style formatting. Note that not all styles apply to every element. Usually, FrontPage prevents you from using style properties inappropriately. But, you should always apply styles — like you would exotic spices when cooking — sparingly and judiciously.

The Modify button in the Style dialog box includes the following options:

Font

Use the Font property to select a font family, and then designate a color, size, style (bold, italics, or bold italics) and any special effects for the font family. You can also control a font's character spacing, both vertically (the position of the character relative to a line of characters) and horizontally (the space between characters).

Tip   CSS supports multiple font family references for a given style. A browser uses the first font in the list that it can find (this is the same behavior exhibited by the `<font>` tag). For example, you could create a style such as the following:

```
h1 {font-family: my_favorite_wacky_font, Arial,
Helvetica, sans-serif;}
```

The catch is that the FrontPage 2000 Style dialog box does not permit you to designate multiple fonts. You have to do it by hand.

Many of the style dialog boxes, including the Font dialog box, provide access to the new FrontPage 2000 Color Picker tool. You can either select a color from the default colors in the Color Picker's drop-down menu or select More Colors to access the Colors dialog box, shown in Figure 12-7. This dialog box shows a "beehive" of Web-safe colors that will display consistently in any Web browser. Click a color cell to update the New color swatch and to display the color's Hex values. For more information on Web-safe palettes and selecting colors for graphics, refer to Chapter 7.

Tip   One of the coolest parts of the new Color Picker tool is the eye-dropper tool. Click the eye-dropper tool (Select button), and your cursor changes to an eye-dropper icon. Pass this cursor across the screen, noting that it displays the color of every pixel that you cross. It even translates the color to the closest Web-safe equivalent.

Paragraph

The Paragraph dialog box, shown in Figure 12-8, enables you to control a block of text's alignment, indentation, and spacing.

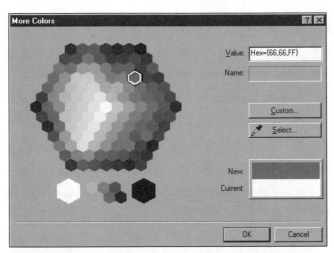

Figure 12-7: The FrontPage 2000 Color Picker dialog box features "Web-safe" colors.

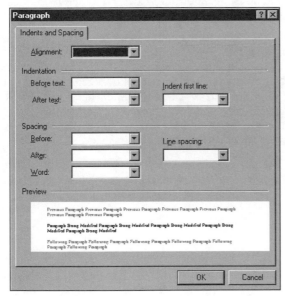

Figure 12-8: Set paragraph style options in the Paragraph dialog box.

All Units Are Not Created Equal

Many of the options available for styles involve distances (margins, line height, font size, and so on). While you may be used to having the units in a Web page forced on you (for example, table borders are always set in pixels), you have many options when you're using style sheets. You can choose from the following:

✦ **##px**: Specifies the distance in pixels.

✦ **##ex**: Specifies a height based on the height of the current font's uppercase *X*.

✦ **##em**: Specifies a height based on the height of the current font's lowercase letter *m*.

✦ **##in**, **##cm**, and **##mm**: Specifies a distance in inches, centimeters, or millimeters, respectively. Note that the dots-per-inch (dpi) setting on most monitors is different, so that the physical distances are different, too. A 15-inch monitor and a 17-inch monitor set to the same resolution have different dpi, which may not correspond to the dpi setting.

✦ **##pt** and **##pc**: Specifies a distance in points or picas, respectively. Both of these are typesetting measurements (you are probably familiar with setting font sizes in points). The same dpi considerations that apply for inches, centimeters, and millimeters come into play with point and pica measures.

Although it may not seem intuitive at first, I suggest that you always set font sizes in pixels rather than points. In addition, unless absolutely necessary, you should avoid all the "absolute" measurements (##in, ##cm, ##mm, ##pt, and ##pc) and stick with ##px, ##em, and ##ex. I say this because, as previously noted, you have no control over the dpi settings for your visitors' monitors, and thus text can display in sizes that are wildly different than what you intended. By using pixel measurements, you tell the browser exactly what size you want the text to be. Also, because the ex and em sizes are based on the font size, your display will be an accurate representation of what your visitors see.

WARNING: If you produce a page that you intend to print, ignore the preceding advice regarding setting text size in pixels. If you set text size in pixels, then the text will probably print amazingly small! (For example, on a 300-dpi printer, text that is 10-pixels high prints at a height of about $1/32$ of an inch.)

Border

Use the border element to define both borders and shading (in other words, foreground and background colors). To create a border, first select a setting: None, Box, or Custom. If you select Custom, you can create a border along any or all of the four sides of the block's rectangle. Select from a variety of border line styles, as well as border color and width, as illustrated in Figure 12-9. You can also dictate the padding between the border and the contents of the bordered element.

The Shading tab has options for background and foreground colors. You can also designate a background image in place of a color. Color Picker tools, like the one in the Fonts dialog box, abound in this tab.

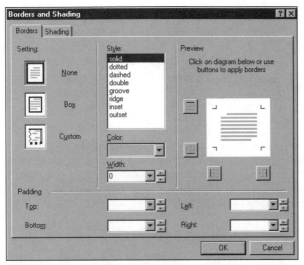

Figure 12-9: Select border formatting options in the Borders and Shading dialog box.

Numbering

The set of properties in the Bullets and Numbering dialog box, shown in Figure 12-10, is really for bullets and numbering. This set isn't applicable to anything other than list styles. Use this set of properties to designate a bullet style, choosing from a variety of numbering styles, HTML bullets, or custom-image bullets.

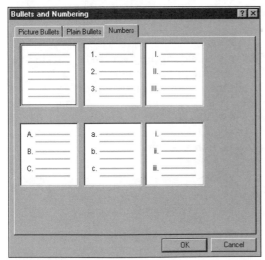

Figure 12-10: The style options for bulleted and numbered lists are found in the Bullets and Numbering dialog box.

Position

Selecting the position item opens the Position dialog box, the same dialog box that is accessed via the Position menu item or the Positioning toolbar (see "CSS Positioning," later in the chapter, for details on positioning). Specifying position information for a style enables you to apply consistent positioning to multiple elements.

Hyperlinks

FrontPage 2000 doesn't provide any direct way to control the style of hyperlinks. However, you can designate styles for hyperlinks by modifying the default style for the hyperlink <a> tag. See "Modifying existing styles" earlier in this chapter for details on how to modify existing styles. In addition, you can create specific style information on each of the following hyperlink states:

✦ **A:link**: Any hyperlink that has not been visited.

✦ **A:active**: The state of the hyperlink as it is being clicked.

✦ **A:visited**: The state of a hyperlink after the user has clicked the link (for example, after the user has "visited" the link).

For more information on these elements, see "Pseudo-classes and pseudo-elements," later in the chapter.

Tip You may be pleased (or horrified) to learn that you can use a style sheet reference to remove the underlining that is part of the default appearance of hyperlinks. Use the following style reference to accomplish this feat: a {text-decoration:none;}.

Style Sheets

As you have seen, with an embedded style sheet, applying a custom style to any element on your page is easy. This is a definite improvement over the inline style method, but it still doesn't serve the ultimate goal — consistent styles across *all* the pages of your Web. To accomplish this, you need to create an external style sheet and link it to any pages that you want governed by the style sheet.

Implementing style sheets in FrontPage is a three-step process:

1. Create a style sheet.

2. Define the styles in the style sheet.

3. Link the style sheet to HTML pages.

Featured Tool — Danere StyleMaker

FrontPage 2000 includes everything that you need to create style sheets for your Web pages. If you do much work with style sheets, however, you may want to use a dedicated tool for the project. The CD-ROM that accompanies this book includes an evaluation copy of Danere StyleMaker. This application has an easy-to-use graphical interface for creating and testing style sheets. Use it to experiment with styles and see the results as you make changes. You can switch between browser and HTML views with the click of a button. StyleMaker includes support for all the principal properties of both CSS1 and CSS2. It comes with numerous sample styles sheets to help you get started. It also includes several predefined filters, transitions, and other effects that were created by using style sheet definitions (see the demonstration page shown in the accompanying figure).

You can incorporate style sheets that you make with StyleMaker into FrontPage either by cutting and pasting from one application to the other or by saving the style sheet that you create and importing it into FrontPage. Alternatively, you can use StyleMaker's Web Applicator tool to link a style sheet to one page or every page in your Web site. With the same tool, you can designate separate style sheets to be displayed for different browsers.

Creating a new style sheet

To create a style sheet in FrontPage 2000, select File ➪ New ➪ Page and click the Style Sheets tab in the New dialog box, shown in Figure 12-11, to select a style sheet template. FrontPage comes with a representative selection of predefined style sheets. You can also create a blank style sheet.

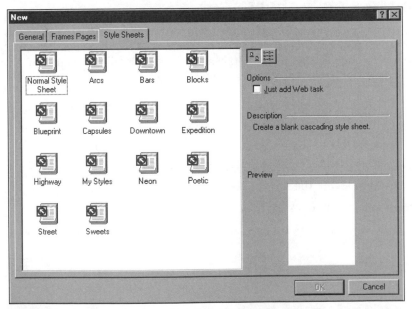

Figure 12-11: The style sheet templates in FrontPage 2000

Tip   Here's a big secret: a "blank style sheet" page is nothing more than an empty text file with a .css extension (which lets FrontPage know to treat it like a style sheet). When you open a CSS file in FrontPage 2000, notice that many of the standard page editing tools disappear. For example, no tabs appear for HTML or Preview, and all the toolbar drop-down menus and menu items are disabled. The only menu item that you really need to use to create your style sheet is the Styles item in the Format menu.

Defining style sheet styles

After you open a style sheet in FrontPage Page view, you can add and modify style definitions by using the same process that you used for embedded styles, as described in the previous section. To review, the procedure is as follows:

1. Select Format ⇨ Style.

2. Click New to create a new style definition; or, to modify an existing style, select either All HTML Tags or User-Defined Styles from the List drop-down menu.

3. Click the Format button and choose the formatting properties that you want to apply to this style.

4. Click OK on all open dialog boxes until you return to Page view, or continue to create additional styles.

When you return to Page view, FrontPage adds the appropriate CSS code to your style sheet. Save your style sheet to your Web, and you are ready to proceed to the final step: linking the style sheet to a Web page.

Linking to a style sheet

After you define and save your style sheet, you must associate it with any Web pages for which you want the styles to be in effect. Several ways exist to link style sheets to a Web page. FrontPage 2000 takes care of the details for you. You simply point and click. The basic steps are as follows:

1. Select the page or pages to which you want to link the style sheet.

2. Select Format ⇨ Stylesheet links to open the Link Stylesheet dialog box (see Figure 12-12).

3. Select either the All Pages or Selected Page(s) option.

4. Click Add to locate the style sheet file in your Web (or elsewhere).

5. After you locate it, click OK to return to the Link Stylesheet dialog box.

6. Click OK again to accept your changes and return to FrontPage Explorer.

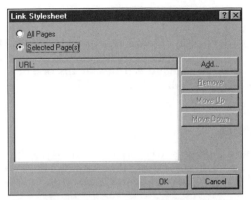

Figure 12-12: The Link Stylesheet dialog box enables you to link style sheets to your Web pages.

After you perform these steps, take a peek at the HTML source for your Web page. Near the top of the page, somewhere between the `<head>` and `</head>` tags, you should see a line that resembles this:

```
<link rel="stylesheet" type="text/css" href="mystyles.css">
```

This tag tells the Web browser that the HTML page in question is governed by the style sheet "mystyles.css".

Tip   The CSS standard also includes a mechanism for importing style sheets into an embedded style sheet. The syntax for this is `"@import mystyles.css"`. If you want to import rather than link your style sheets, you have to do it manually.

Linking to selected page(s)

You can select a page for the linking operation in either of two ways:

- ✦ Open the page in Page view.
- ✦ Select a page in Folder view.

Using Folder view is the only way to perform the linking operation on multiple Web pages simultaneously. To select more than one page in Folder view, hold down the Shift key and select the beginning and end of a range of files, or hold down the Ctrl key and click each file that you want to select.

Linking to all pages

To link a style sheet to all pages in your Web simultaneously, switch to Folder view and select the main Web folder. Now, when you select Format ➪ Link Stylesheets, only the All Pages option is enabled. Proceed as just described to link one or more style sheets to all HTML pages in the selected Web.

Using multiple style sheets

Occasionally, you may find that linking a Web page to more than one style sheet is useful. For example, you may create a generic style sheet that contains basic styles that apply to every page in your site, and then develop specialized style sheets for particular pages or sets of pages.

To link multiple style sheets to a page, use the same procedure previously described, but pay attention to the order of your style sheets. If the linked style sheets have overlapping style references (for example, if each has a style for H1 header levels), the style that is listed last dictates the style for that element.

Note It may seem counterintuitive that a style sheet listed lower on the list would have precedence over ones higher in the list. But, if you consider how the browser encounters the style information, this order makes sense. The browser reads the HTML page from top to bottom. When it encounters a LINK reference, it fetches the designated style sheet and reads through it. When it encounters a style reference for, say, H1, it records that as the current style for that element. It then goes on to the next LINK reference and repeats the process. When it encounters another H1 style reference, it discards the earlier one and replaces it with the current one. So, the last style always wins.

To adjust the order of linked style sheets in the Link Stylesheets dialog box, select the style sheet that you want to reorder, and then click the Move Up or Move Down buttons until the style is positioned where you want it.

In the following tutorial, you will create the first page of a newsletter, using a FrontPage template for the basic layout, and a custom style sheet for all of your formatting.

Tutorial 12.1: Create a Newsletter Style Sheet

1. Select New ➪ Page ➪ General tab and select the Two Column Body with Contents and Sidebar template.

2. Click OK to open the page in Page view.

3. Save the file as **pageone.htm**.

4. To import an existing style sheet, select New ➪ Page ➪ Style Sheets and select the Blueprint Style (or any other style sheet template) to open the style sheet in Page view.

5. Save the file as **pageone.css**.

6. Link the style sheet to the HTML page. Select Format ➪ Style Sheet Links, check the Selected Page(s) option, click Add, and select pageone.css. Click OK to return to the Link Stylesheet dialog box. Click OK again to apply the style sheet and return to Page view. You should notice that your page acquires a background color and a new text color. Save your changes.

7. Before going any further, you may want to make some changes to the content of the newsletter template. Figure 12-13 shows what our page looks like after a few minor adjustments. Most prominent is the fact that we added tables cells to contain the newsletter volume and date, and added headlines and hyperlinks to the two columns of featured content on the front page of our newsletter.

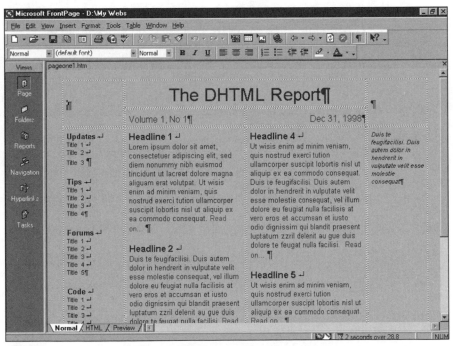

Figure 12-13: Our newsletter prior to any styling

You may have noticed that this page has several elements that lend themselves nicely to style sheets. At the moment, however, all the formatting details are contained in <font> tags. Your next task is to identify those elements and define styles for each.

8. Create the following styles:

   - **td.contents**   Formatting for the table of contents cell   •
   - **td.features**   Formatting for the main features content
   - **td.sidebar**   Formatting for the sidebar
   - **.headline**   Formatting for the headline
   - **.leadin**   Formatting for the lead-in title for each feature
   - **.section**   Formatting for the table of contents section names
   - **.item**   Formatting for the items under each section

9. After you identify the styles that you want to create, you can remove all the existing formatting, to avoid any conflicts between the style sheet and the existing formatting. (You could have done this to begin with, but defining the style elements is somewhat easier with the existing formatting intact.)

   Select the entire page either by choosing Edit ➪ Select All or by using the Ctrl+A shortcut. Select Format ➪ Remove Formatting. By the way, you can use this technique if you plan to convert an existing Web to use style sheets. The page should now resemble Figure 12-14.

10. Define the styles that you identified. To do this, return to the style sheet page, select Format ➪ Style, and create a series of New styles. The following code shows the styles as we have implemented them:

```
td.contents {
    background-color: #808000;
    color: #FFFFFF;
    border-right-style: solid;
    border-right-color: #FFFFFF
    }
td.features {
   font-size: 10pt
   }
td.sidebar {
   font-size: 10pt;
   font-style: italic;
   background-color: #FFFFCC
   }
.headline {
   font-size: 24pt;
   letter-spacing: 1pt;
```

```
color: #000080;
font-weight: bold
}
.leadin {
font-weight: bold
}
.section {
font-size: 10pt;
text-decoration: underline;
font-weight: bold
}
.item {
font-size: 8pt
}
```

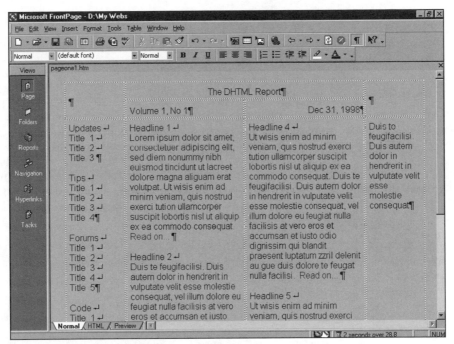

Figure 12-14: Our newsletter sans formatting

11. Apply the style names to the newsletter page. For the table cell styles, select the appropriate cell's properties, click the Style button, and designate the name of the appropriate style class (for example, contents, features, or sidebar), as illustrated in Figure 12-15.

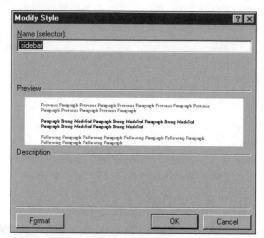

Figure 12-15: Adding style class selector
names to table cells

12. Applying style class names to the remaining elements is a bit trickier, because
many of the elements are divided only by a line break rather than a paragraph
block. To apply the class name, you first need to wrap the elements in a block
tag. We have used the `<span>` and `</span>` tags for this purpose (see
the later section "Span Versus Div" for an explanation of the `<span>` tag).
Currently, no way exists to add this tag in FrontPage other than by hand. As
you are adding the tag, also add the `class` attribute, as illustrated in the
following snippet of code from the contents section of the HTML page:

```
<td valign="top" width="15%" class="contents">
<span class="section">Updates</span><br>
<span class="item">Title 1</span><br>
<span class="item">Title 2</span><br>
<span class="item">Title 3</span><p>
<span class="section">Tips</span><br>
<span class="item">Title 1</span><br>
        <span class="item">Title 2</span><br>
        <span class="item">Title 3</span><br>
        <span class="item">Title  4</span></p><p>
<span class="section">Forums</span><br>
        <span class="item">Title  1</span><br>
        <span class="item">Title  2</span><br>
        <span class="item">Title  3</span><br>
        <span class="item">Title  4</span><br>
        <span class="item">Title 5</span></p><p>
<span class="section">Code</span><br>
        <span class="item">Title 1</span><br>
        <span class="item">Title  2</span><br>
```

```
        <span class="item">Title 3</span><br>
        <span class="item">Title  4</span><br>
        <span class="item">Title 5</span><br>
        <span class="item">Title 6</span><br>
   </td>
```

13. After you add all the style references to the HTML page, save and view the results. Our newsletter is shown in Figure 12-16. Pretty stylish, don't you think?

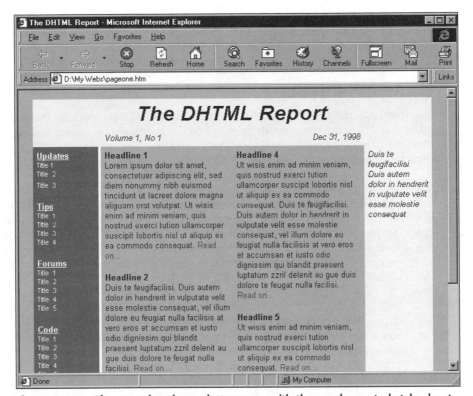

Figure 12-16: The completed newsletter page, with the newly created style sheet

Advanced Techniques

At this point in the chapter, you know enough about style sheets to create and use them effectively in FrontPage. The remaining sections of this chapter briefly discuss some of the subtler aspects of style sheets, culminating in an explanation of how to use FrontPage to position elements on the page.

Grouping styles

Frequently, you may want to apply the same style properties to several elements. For example, suppose that you want to use a special font called `my_cool_font` for all of your header levels. You could create a separate style for each element that repeats the same font designation, or you could create a grouping of elements. The grouping is just a comma-separated list of elements. For example:

```
h1, h2, h3, h4, h5, h6 {font-family: my_cool_font }
```

You can use the Style dialog box to create a group element. Simply select Format ⇨ Style and click the New button. In the Name field, type the comma-separated group and designate any formatting, as you normally would.

Using inheritance

Inheritance in the CSS world refers to the fact that HTML elements that contain additional elements pass on their styles to the contained element, unless that element has its own defined styles. In other words, the contained elements inherit the characteristics of the element that contains them.

Say, for example, that you have a line of text to which you apply the Header 1 style. One of the words in this line of text is italicized. By default, the italicized word inherits the characteristics of the Header 1 text: the same font size, font family, color, and so forth (the only difference being that it is italicized.) If you don't want the italicized text to inherit the characteristics of the Header 1 style, you need to create a specific style reference for italics, by modifying the <i> style. In this case, the italics style will override the Header 1 style.

Tip   One useful way to use inheritance is to create a generic <body> style that designates a standard font type, size, color, and so on. Because all other tags are contained within the <body> tag, they inherit its style, unless you dictate otherwise.

Contextual selectors

Okay, you think that you've mastered the concept of inheritance and overriding inherited style characteristics. Now, consider again the example used earlier: you have a line of text designated as a Header 1 style that contains an italicized word. You saw in the last section how you can give the italicized word a different style from the Header 1. But, what if you want italicized text in the context of a Header 1 line to have a different style from italicized text that appears elsewhere? You could create a separate class selector to handle this, but fortunately, an easier way is available.

You can use the *contextual selector* syntax to indicate a style that applies only in certain contexts. For example:

```
h1 i {font-color: #6699FF}
```

This style reference says that any italics that show up in the context of (in other words, is contained by) a Header 1 style should have the style indicated. Italics anywhere else unaffected by this style.

You can create this style reference in FrontPage 2000 by using the standard Style dialog box. Simply create a new style and name it by using the contextual selector syntax. Then, select the style properties by proceeding as you normally would.

Tip The concept of contextual selectors may strike you as somewhat esoteric. One context in which it may come in handy is the case of bulleted lists. Embedding a numbered or bulleted list in the context of another list isn't uncommon. You can use the contextual selector syntax to treat a standard list differently from one that appears embedded within another list.

Pseudo-classes and pseudo-elements

CSS introduces the concept of pseudo-classes and pseudo-elements as a way to gain stylistic control over some elements of an HTML page that don't directly correspond to strict tag elements. This section briefly identifies the most commonly supported pseudo-classes and elements.

Hyperlink pseudo-classes

Currently, the most commonly supported pseudo-classes are those associated with hyperlinks (first mentioned in the section on formatting hyperlinks, earlier in the chapter).

The three most prevalent elements are the following:

✦ **A:link**: Any unvisited hyperlinks.

✦ **A:active**: The state of the link as it is being clicked.

✦ **A:visited**: Any link that has been explored.

The pseudo-classes work just like any other selector. They just apply to the hyperlink under special user-event-based circumstances.

Note Microsoft also supports another hyperlink pseudo-class, a:hover, which defines the style for a hover button.

"First" pseudo-elements

The most commonly supported pseudo-elements are the "first line" element and the "first letter" element. The first line element (designated as `p:first-line`) is used to apply a special style to the first line of a paragraph of text. Similarly the first letter element (`p:first-letter`) enables you to create drop-caps and other fancy typographical flourishes.

Caution   Currently, neither of the two major browsers supports the `p:first-line` and `p:first-letter` pseudo-elements.

Style sheet comments

You can (and should) include comments in your style sheets, to help describe the purpose and effect of various style references. The syntax for CSS comments follows the C programming language conventions. The comment starts with `/*` and ends with `*/`, such as the following:

```
/* This is a sample CSS comment! */
```

CSS and Browser Compatibility

Throughout this chapter, the fact that browser support for CSS is less than perfect has been reiterated. The most recent versions of Netscape Navigator and Microsoft's Internet Explorer have implemented the majority of the CSS1 standard and some portions of CSS2 (see the earlier sidebar, "CSS Level 1 and Level 2," for details on the two levels of the CSS specification). What this means, in practice, is that some CSS techniques don't work as advertised anywhere, others work only on one or the other of the top two browsers, and some work on both browsers, but with slightly different results. Things only get worse when you try to incorporate CSS into a DHTML effect. If you want to know specifically which browsers support which features, check out Web Review's "Style Sheets Compatibility Chart" at http://style.webreviews.com/mastergrid.html.

The problem is critical enough to have spawned the creation of yet another acronym: XBDHTML, or *Cross-Browser Dynamic HTML*. XBDHTML refers to the subset of DHTML features, including CSS, that is supported by both browsers. Netscape has posted numerous technical documents on the subject and even some tools to make your pages cross-browser-compatible. Look for these items at http://developer.netscape.com/docs/technote/dynhtml/xbdhtml/xbdhtml.html.

CSS Positioning

If you have ever tried to create a Web page that involved even a small amount of page layout, you know how limited HTML is when it comes to positioning elements on a Web page. (For a thorough discussion of using tables for complex page layout, refer to Chapter 6.) Now, FrontPage 2000 makes it easy (well, relatively easy) to position text, graphics, form field inputs, or anything else exactly where you want them, by using the position property, as defined in the CSS2 specification.

Creating a position box

The following are the two ways to position an element on the page:

✦ **Relative positioning**: Maintains an element in a fixed relation to other elements on the page (see Figure 12-17). When the page is resized, the item is repositioned to retain its position relative to other elements.

✦ **Absolute positioning**: Fixes an element precisely on the page. It remains unchanged, even if the page is resized.

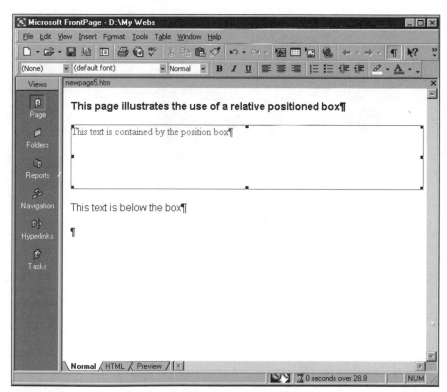

Figure 12-17: A box that is positioned relative to other elements on the page

The following are the three techniques for creating a position box around an element in FrontPage 2000; the steps for using each are then described:

✦ Use the Position formatting option in a style

✦ Format an element by using the Position command

✦ Use the Positioning toolbar

Inserting a position style

To create a position style, follow these steps:

1. Select Format ➪ Style.

2. Click the New button to create a new style.

3. Name the style, click the Format button, and then select the Position option.

4. Use the Position dialog box (see Figure 12-18) to define the Position attributes of your style.

5. Click OK three times to return to Page view.

6. Apply the Position style to an appropriate page element.

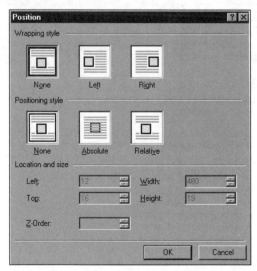

Figure 12-18: The Position dialog box, used to add position information to a custom style.

Formatting with the Position command

The second method of creating a position box is to use the Position formatting command. In this case, you should first add to the page the elements that you want to position. After you create those elements, follow these steps:

1. Select the element that you want to position.

2. Select Format ⇨ Position to open the Position dialog box (shown in Figure 12-18).

3. Select the desired positioning properties: choose a wrapping style or positioning style, and set any desired location and size values.

4. Click OK to return to Page view.

Using the Positioning toolbar

The third method of creating a position box is to use the Positioning toolbar. With this method, as with the Position dialog box, you should first create the element that you want to position. Then, select the element to position, and select View ⇨ Toolbars ⇨ Positioning to show the toolbar (see Figure 12-19).

Figure 12-19: The Positioning toolbar

To create an absolute position box around the selected element, click the Position icon at the left end of the toolbar. Use the other toolbar fields to specify the location and size values that you want to use, just as you did in the Position dialog box.

Positioning pictures

In addition to the methods just described, you can position a picture by using the Absolutely Positioned button on the Picture toolbar. To use this method:

1. Select the picture to position.

2. If the Picture toolbar is not visible, select View ⇨ Toolbars ⇨ Picture.

3. Click the Position button on the toolbar.

Advanced positioning properties

At this point, you know how to create and edit basic position properties for relative and absolute positioned elements. This section concludes by examining some of the finer points of working with CSS positioning.

Span versus Div

By default, when you create a position box, FrontPage places the positioned element inside `<div>` and `</div>` tags. `<div>`, short for "divider," is a logical tag that identifies a self-contained unit, separated from any elements that come before or after it. In most cases, this is fine, but occasionally, you may want the element to fit seamlessly between other elements. In this case, you need to use the `<span>` element in place of the `<div>` element. The difference is illustrated in Figure 12-20. The `<span>` element is used in the next tutorial.

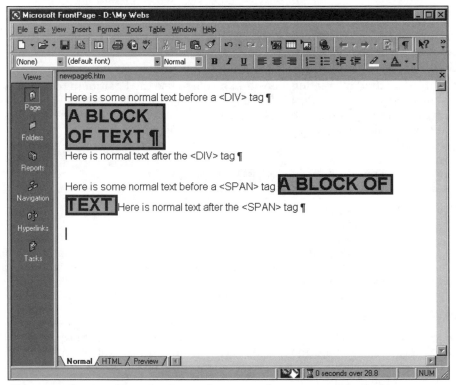

Figure 12-20: The effect of <div> and <span> elements on a block of text

Z-index

One of the side effects of being able to position page elements precisely is that they can overlap. If you overlap several elements, how do you know which one is "on top"? The answer is the `z-index` property. The smaller the `z-index` value, the closer to the top of the heap the element will be (in other words, an element with a `z-index` of 1 appears in front of an element with a `z-index` of 2). The `z-index` is a relative number: you can start with 1 or 100, it doesn't matter.

You can set the `z-index` by using either the Format ➪ Position dialog box or the Positioning toolbar.

Visibility

Another property that is useful with positioned elements is `visibility`. This property has three acceptable values: `visible`, `hidden`, and `inherit`. This property is of limited usefulness in a style sheet, but it is commonly used when scripting style properties. (You can learn more about this in Chapter 16 or Chapter 18.)

In the following tutorial, you use CSS positioning and formatting to create a colorful headline banner for the newsletter page that you developed earlier in the chapter.

Tutorial 12.2: Positioning Text

1. Start with a new blank page: Select File ➪ New ➪ Page and select the Normal Page template.

2. Save this page as **headline.htm** with the title **The DHTML Report**.

3. Define the formatting styles that you want to use to create the headline.

4. Create two paragraph classes — one for a block letter font and the other for a script font.

5. Select Format ➪ Style, click the New button, and name the first style **p.block**. Then, do the following:

   • Select Format ➪ Font and select Arial as the default font, a font size of 50pt, a font color of white, and a font style of bold.

   • Select Format ➪ Paragraph and set the Alignment to center.

   • Select Format ➪ Border and set the border color to navy blue and the border size to 2px.

6. Click OK to return to the Style dialog box. Click the New button and name the second style **p.script**. Then, select Format ➪ Font and select a script font, such as Brush Script MT, set the font size to 32 pt, the color to charcoal gray, and the font style to italic. Click OK to return to the Style dialog box.

7. Create a `div` class style to put a colored border around the `DIV` block. Click the New button and name this style **div.border**. Click the Format button and select Border. Set the border color to gray. Click OK to return to the Styles dialog box.

8. Create a series of `div` element IDs, one for each of five colored blocks that you are going to need. Select New and name the element **#lime** (the hash mark represents an ID designator). Select Format ➪ Border, select the Shading tab, and change the Background color to Lime. Click OK to return to the Style dialog box. Repeat the procedure for **#yellow**, **#cyan**, **#red**, and **#purple**. After you create all five background styles, click OK to return to Page view. Save your style work. If you check the results of your handiwork in the HTML tab, you should see an embedded style sheet that resembles the following code:

```
<style>
```

```
<!—
p.block          { font-family: Arial; font-size: 50pt; color:
#FFFFFF;
                  font-weight: bold; text-align: center;
border-style: solid;
                  border-color: #000080;border-width:2px; }
#purple          { background-color: #800080 }
#red             { background-color: #FF0000 }
div.border       { border-style: solid; border-color: #808080 }
#lime            { background-color: #00FF00 }
#yellow          { background-color: #FFFF00 }
#cyan            { background-color: #00FFFF }
p.script         { font-family: Brush Script MT; color: #808080;
font-size: 32pt;
                  font-style: italic }
—>
</style>
```

9. Create the text that you will use in your headline. At the top of the page, type **The**, click Enter, and then type **D**, **H**, **T**, **M**, **L**, clicking Enter to create a paragraph break after each letter. Finally, type **Report** and click Enter.

10. Place the cursor next to each element. Click the Absolute Position icon to create a box around the text of that paragraph. Then, set the following property values:

```
The: top: 15; left: 15; width:40; z-index: 2
D: top: 30; left: 70; width: 80; z-index: 1
H: top: 45; left: 135; width 80; z-index: 2
T: top: 60; left: 200; width: 80; z-index: 3
M: top: 75; left: 265; width 80; z-index: 4
L: top: 90; left: 340; width 80; z-index: 5
Report: top: 150; left: 405; width: 120; z-index: 6
```

11. Apply formatting styles to each paragraph of text. Locate the cursor after The and select the Normal.script style from the Styles drop-down menu. Repeat this process for Report. Select each of the letters D, H, T, M, and L in turn and apply the Normal.block style.

12. The final step requires some manual HTML work, because FrontPage 2000 doesn't provide a way to give an ID to a DIV element. Switch to the HTML tab, and for each DIV element associated with the letters D, H, T, M, and L, add an ID attribute (for example, id="lime"). Set the ID equal to lime, yellow, cyan, red, and purple, respectively.

13. Preview your results. They should resemble Figure 12-21.

Caution   Now for the bad news. The flashy headline that you just created looks great in Internet Explorer 4, but it doesn't look so hot in Netscape, which doesn't handle border styles as well as IE4 does. For more information on browser compatibility, see the "CSS and Browser Compatibility" sidebar, earlier in the chapter.

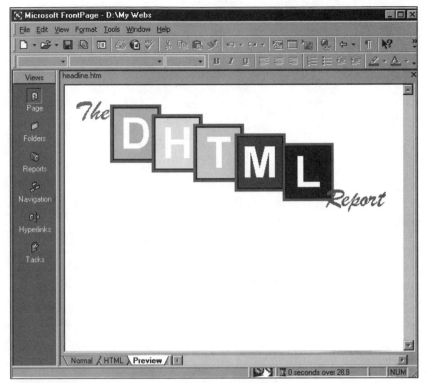

Figure 12-21: A newsletter headline banner, created entirely with styles

Summary

This chapter culminates the page layout and formatting techniques introduced throughout Part III. Now, using styles, you can create Web pages that are freed from the limitations of "old fashioned" HTML. FrontPage 2000 provides a WYSIWYG environment for creating and referencing style sheets, and, occasionally, manually editing styles in your HTML code is still necessary, or more efficient. Chapter 11 showed you how to use the HTML Source tab to work directly with Web page source code.

The next part of the book launches into the subject of adding interactivity to your Web pages. Chapter 13 explores the latest FrontPage Components — prebuilt functions that you can add to your Web page without a stitch of programming. Subsequent chapters demonstrate the creation and handling of forms, introduce some of the coolest ways to make your Web a multimedia experience, and show you how to create an online discussion forum.

✦   ✦   ✦

Activating the User Experience

Adding FrontPage Components

This chapter introduces FrontPage Components, the ready-to-use programs that are an integral part of FrontPage's operation. With these Components, you can easily add interactive functionality to your site—without taking a course in computer programming. This chapter provides an overview of the FrontPage Components.

Many of the FrontPage Components provide to your Web site interactive elements that respond to the actions of visitors. For example, a Hit Counter responds to a visit by changing the number of visitors displayed, and Search Boxes respond to a visitor's query with a list of matching pages.

Note   Prior to FrontPage 98, FrontPage Components were called *WebBots*. The HTML codes for FrontPage continue to refer to Components as WebBots. This same WebBot terminology is also used for HTML tags applied to other FrontPage elements that are not included in the Component submenu, such as Comments.

Defining and Using Components

FrontPage Components actually are small programs that are embedded in FrontPage. You don't need to know *how* FrontPage Components work to use them, but you should be aware of two particular attributes of Components:

✦ FrontPage Components enable you to use preprogrammed elements that normally require a scripting language to create.

✦ Most FrontPage Components work only after your Web is published to a Web server with FrontPage extensions.

FrontPage Components are programs

FrontPage Components are prebuilt programming modules that you can customize and insert into your Web pages. When you add a FrontPage Component to your Web page, FrontPage inserts HTML tags that reference it, much as HTML is used to reference a graphic, a sound file, or a Java applet.

Customization of Components is done through HTML attributes in the Component tag. Figure 13-1 shows an example of the HTML used to point to a Component; in this case, you can see WebBot tags for both a Substitution Component (near the top of the HTML page), and a Comment.

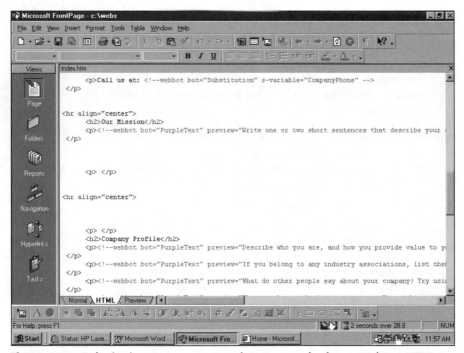

Figure 13-1: Substitution Components and Comments both use WebBot HTML tags.

When a user requests a Web page containing an embedded FrontPage Component, the server must activate the appropriate Component, enabling it to perform its magic before the page is sent. Components are closely tied to the operation of the server, which is why most Components work only on FrontPage-enabled Web servers. No special additions are required at the user's end. A Netscape browser will display Components as well as Microsoft's browser.

Note   The Comment Component is embedded by using a variant on a standard comment tag. This "hijacking" of HTML's comment tag is part of the reason that FrontPage does not support standard HTML comments.

FrontPage Components require FrontPage extensions

One other thing that you need to know about FrontPage Components is that, as mentioned earlier, they usually require that your Web site be published to a server with *FrontPage extensions*. These extension files provide the coded modules that enable the Components to work.

If you aren't publishing your Web to a server armed with FrontPage extensions, you can disable the Components that require extensions by selecting Tools ➪ Page Options and clicking the Compatibility tab. Then, deselect the Enable with Microsoft FrontPage Server Extensions check box. After you do that, only those Components that do *not* require FrontPage extensions will display. The rest are grayed out, as shown in Figure 13-2.

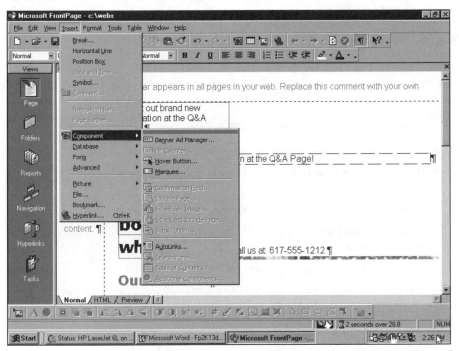

Figure 13-2: Without a FrontPage server, most FrontPage Components are not available.

Suppose that you are developing your Web site by using a drive-based Web or a server that doesn't have FrontPage extensions, but you plan eventually to publish your Web to a server that does have FrontPage extensions. In that case, do *not* disable Components. You can still place them on Web pages — you just can't test them or use them in a Web site, until you publish to a FrontPage-friendly Web server with FrontPage extensions.

Because Components require FrontPage-enabled servers, they are less portable than standard CGI applications or Java applets and are more akin to other Microsoft technologies, such as Active Server Pages, that are limited to servers supported by Microsoft. But, if you have access to a FrontPage-enabled Web server, the ease with which you can add Components makes using them hard to resist.

If you don't plan to publish your Web site to a FrontPage server, and you are inclined to do your own scripting and programming, you can jump ahead to Part V of this book, which introduces other programming components that you can use to create many of the same functions, with perhaps a bit more labor on your part.

The Component lineup

In addition to the Components listed in the Insert ⇨ Components submenu, the Insert menu includes a few miscellaneous but highly useful objects that work like Components, such as the Position Box, the Date and Time (which works like a time stamp), and Comments. These features are explored in this chapter, too, even though they aren't listed in the Component submenu.

The following is the lineup of features available from the FrontPage Components submenu, along with a description of the purpose of each feature:

✦ **Banner Ads Manager:** Rotates different images.

✦ **Hit Counter:** Tracks how many visitors have "hit" your page.

✦ **Hover Button**: Reacts when a visitor's cursor "hovers" over it, even without being clicked.

✦ **Marquee:** Scrolls text across your page.

✦ **Confirmation Field**: Works with input forms to create customized feedback after a form is submitted.

✦ **Include Page**: Embeds a page within your page.

✦ **Scheduled Image**: Embeds an image, but only for a set time period.

✦ **Scheduled Include Page**: Embeds a page, but only within a specified time period.

✦ **Substitution:** Updates pages instantly with embedded codes.

✦ **Autolinks:** Generates links automatically.

✦ **Search Form:** Enables visitors to search your site.

✦ **Table of Contents:** Generates a table of contents.

✦ **Additional Components:** Displays Components from third-party providers.

Inserting Components

You have two principal ways available to add a Component to your Web page:

✦ Insert the Component directly into your Web page (the primary method).

✦ Use one of the many Web page templates and wizards that come with preconfigured FrontPage Components (secondary method).

This section describes the primary method for inserting Components. You'll be able to recognize these same Components in sites that were generated by wizards or templates, and you can edit them just as if you had personally placed them in the page.

To insert a Component, open your Web page in Editor and position the cursor where you want the Component to appear. Select Insert ⇨ FrontPage ⇨ Component, or click the Insert FrontPage Component icon in the toolbar. The Insert ⇨ FrontPage Component submenu is detachable, and becomes the floating Insert Component toolbar when detached, as shown in Figure 13-3.

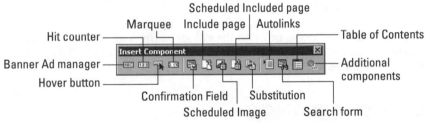

Figure 13-3: Components can be inserted from the floating Insert Component toolbar.

After you select the Component, additional dialog boxes may appear, enabling you to customize the Component's properties. After you add a Component to your Web page, you can edit it by double-clicking it. Alternatively, you can right-click the Component and select (*Component's Name*) Properties from the pop-up menu. Or, you can select the Component and select Edit ⇨ (*FrontPage Component*) Properties.

Using Date and Time and Comments

The Date and Time and Comments elements could have been put in the Components submenu, but they weren't. Nevertheless, they work like Components. When you insert a Date and Time code, you create a time stamp HotBot code in HTML. Comments also generate HotBot coding. Both of these elements require that you publish your Web to a FrontPage server before they will work.

Like the features in the Components submenu, these two cool elements are linked to coding in a FrontPage server that enables you to place little applets in your Web site without worrying about programming.

Date and Time

The Date and Time Component displays the modification time and date of the Web page on which the Component resides. In other words, you can tell visitors exactly when the page was last changed, so that they can quickly decide whether the material at your Web site is current enough for their needs.

Including a last-modified date on your Web pages is a courtesy to visitors, because it helps them judge whether the information on your site is up to date. Of course, if currency isn't that important to your Web page, you certainly aren't required to have a time stamp on it.

Every time that you resave your Web pages, the time stamp (Date and Time code) updates. So, the only "revising" reflected by your time stamp may simply be that you actively maintain the page. Manually updating the modification date by resaving a page is one way of indicating that you *are* maintaining the page, even if the content has not changed recently.

To add a Date and Time code, position the cursor at the location where you want the Component to appear. Select Insert ➪ Date and Time. The Date and Time Properties dialog box appears, as shown in Figure 13-4.

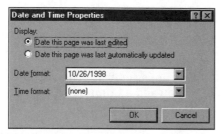

Figure 13-4: Date and Time options control the look of your time stamp.

The Date this Page Was Last Edited radio button revises the displayed date only when you actually change (or resave) the page. The Date this Page Was Updated Automatically radio button changes the Date and Time code if the page was changed by the action of a FrontPage Component or other applet. For example, if a page contains a Table of Contents that is subject to automatic updates, the displayed date changes whenever the Table of Contents recalculates.

Use the Date Format drop-down menu to select from a variety of date formats. Use the Time Format drop-down menu to select from a list of time formats.

After you make your selections, click OK to insert the Date and Time code in your page. The time stamp appears just as it will look in the Web page. You can format the date text. When you edit in Page view, you can distinguish the Date and Time data from regular text, because its code has an arrow over it rather than an insertion cursor, as shown in Figure 13-5.

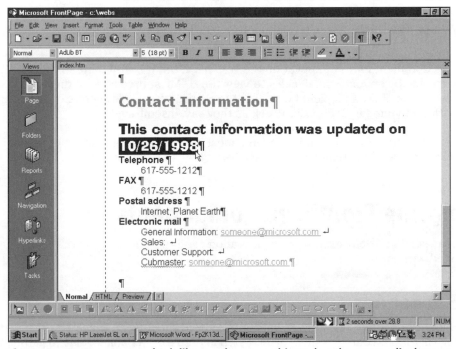

Figure 13-5: Components look like regular page objects, but the cursor displays as an arrow when you move over them.

Comment

To add a Comment, position the cursor where you want the Comment to appear in the Web page, and then select Insert ⇨ Comment. The dialog box shown in Figure 13-6 appears, enabling you to enter the text of your Comment.

Comments show up in FrontPage in the visited link color, which is purple by default (in fact, the actual name of this Component is *PurpleText*, as you can see if you look closely at the HTML). Comment text doesn't appear when the page is viewed by a Web browser, because the entire Component is enclosed in a standard HTML comment tag.

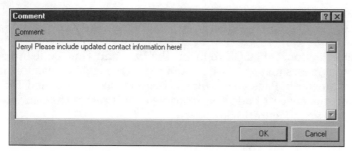

Figure 13-6: Comments are a good way to communicate with your co-developers or to leave yourself a reminder.

The Comment may not appear on the Web page, but it is still there in the HTML, viewable by anyone who decides to view the HTML source code of the page. As a result, use of the Comment Component to record your trade secrets or the combination of your safety deposit box is, as they say, discouraged!

The Comment Component is used in almost every template, to instruct you about the purpose of the template or to teach you how to customize it.

Exploring FrontPage Components

This section briefly examines the operation of all the Components that come packaged with FrontPage 2000.

Banner Ads

Banner Ads rotate two or more images in a space, creating an animated presentation for visitors to your Web site. The first step in preparing a Banner Ad is to gather some images that you want to display. You don't need to insert pictures into your page to include them in your Banner Ad, but you do need to have the pictures available in file form. With your images picked out, select Insert ➪ Component ➪ Banner Ad Manager. The Banner Ad Manager dialog box appears, as shown in Figure 13-7.

Adding images to a Banner

Use the Add button in the dialog box to add images to the list of those that will display in your Banner Ad. The Add Image for Banner Ad dialog box, shown in Figure 13-8, displays your image when you select it. You can either pick images from your Web site or use the Clip Art button to include clip art in your Banner Ad. You can also select the Use Your Web Browser button or the Select a File on Your Computer button in the lower-right corner of the dialog box to include files from the Web or your local computer.

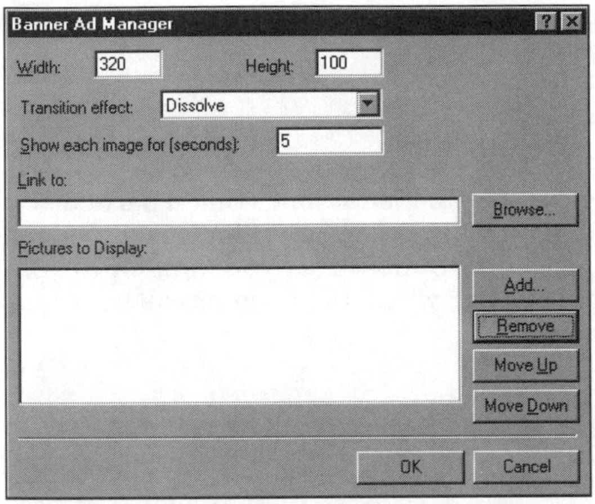

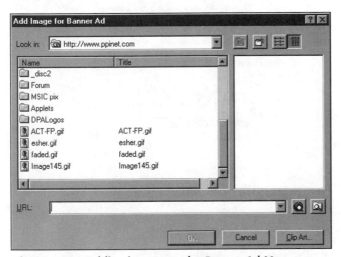

Figure 13-7: Defining a Banner Ad

Figure 13-8: Adding images to the Banner Ad Manager

You can edit your display list by using the Remove, Move Up, or Move Down buttons in the Banner Ad Manager dialog box. Define the size of your Banner Ad in the Width and Height fields. Choose a transition effect from the drop-down list. Then, select a number of seconds to display each image. After you define your Banner Ad, click OK in the dialog box.

Linking to Banners

Banner Ads function as a graphic hyperlink (although they don't have to). To define the page to which you want your banner to link, use the Browse button or enter a URL in the Link To field.

Banner Ads don't require FrontPage Server extensions. You can preview your Banner Ad in the Preview tab or in a browser.

Hit Counters

The Hit Counter Component displays the number of times that a particular page has been accessed, or "hit." To insert a Hit Counter, select Insert ➪ FrontPage Component ➪ Hit Counter. Then, select the options that you want for the display and click OK. A small placeholder indicates where the counter will be displayed on your page, as shown in Figure 13-9.

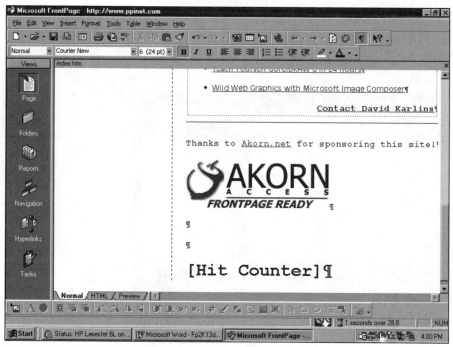

Figure 13-9: Hit Counters don't work in Page view.

Hit strategies

Hit Counters record how many "hits" your Web site has received. Hits pretty much correspond to visits (if a visitor refreshes his or her browser window, that counts as an additional hit). The following are the two basic approaches to using a Hit Counter:

✦ **Use it to show off how many hits your site is getting.** Of course, the credibility of a Hit Counter is somewhat suspect, because (as you'll soon see) you can set your own starting number. Still, sometimes a valid reason exists to display a count of how many folks have been to a site.

✦ **Use it for your own purposes, just to keep track of how effective your site is.** You can place a Hit Counter at the bottom of a page, where visitors are not likely to notice it.

Figure 13-10 shows a Hit Counter that is subtly stashed at the very bottom of a Web page, where it quietly keeps track of visitors.

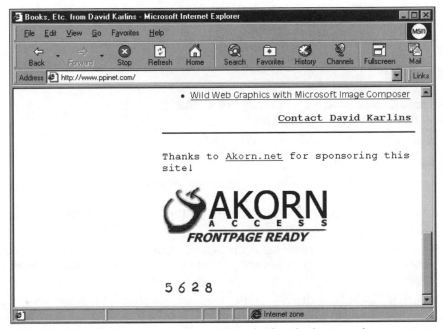

Figure 13-10: Hit Counters can be subtly stashed at the bottom of your page.

Defining a Hit Counter

In the Hit Counter dialog box, click a radio button to select a style for your Hit Counter. Use the Reset Counter To check box if you want to enter a starting number other than zero (which is the default). Use the Fixed Number of Digits check box to enter a set number of digits for your Hit Counter. After you define your Hit Counter, click the OK button in the dialog box. Your Hit Counter displays when you preview your Web page in your browser. You will see a code "Hit Counter" in Page view.

Hover Buttons

Hover Buttons display an effect when visitors to your page pass their cursor over the button. Hover Buttons provide a way to make boring buttons more interesting. Effects range from a glow, to color changes. You can even specify images and sounds to use for the button, to provide a more interactive look and feel to your pages.

To add a Hover Button, select Insert ➪ Component ➪ Hover Button. The Hover Button dialog box appears, as shown in Figure 13-11.

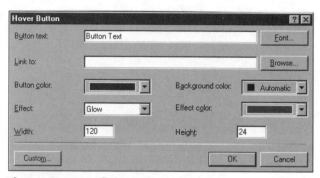

Figure 13-11: Defining a Hover Button

Hover Button options

You can make the following selections in the Hover Button dialog box:

✦ **Button Text:** The text that is displayed on the button's face. You can change the font, color, style, and size by clicking the Font button.

✦ **Link To:** The page or file that is opened when the button is clicked by visitors. Enter the URL directly in the text box, or click the Browse button to select a page.

✦ **Button Color:** The button's "static" color when you don't use an image; the color that displays when a visitor does not move his or her cursor over the button.

✦ **Background Color:** The color for the button's background. This color shows through even if you use a transparent GIF as a button image.

✦ **Effect:** You can choose between these effects:

• **Color Fill:** The entire button changes color.

• **Color Average:** The entire button changes to a color halfway between the button color and the effect color.

• **Glow:** The center of the button changes to the effect color, with the color fading toward the edges.

• **Reverse Glow:** The center of the button remains the button color, but it fades to the effect color at the outside edges.

• **Light Glow:** A muted version of Glow.

• **Bevel Out:** The button takes on a 3D appearance, as if it is protruding from the page. This effect works best with relatively light button colors.

✦ **Bevel In:** The reverse 3D appearance of Bevel Out, so that the button looks like it is indented into the screen.

✦ **Effect Color:** The button's "hover" color that displays when you don't use an image. When a visitor's cursor passes over the button, this color shows, in combination with the effect that you apply.

✦ **Width:** The button's width in pixels. It does not automatically change if you select a large font size or a large image; you have to change the size manually.

✦ **Height:** The button's height in pixels. It does not automatically change if you select a large font size or a large image; you have to change the size manually.

Adding sound effects

You can add sound effects to your Hover Buttons. To do this, click the Custom button in the Hover Button dialog box to open the Custom dialog box. This dialog box has two fields, for up to two different sounds. You can assign one sound to play when a visitor "hovers" over the button, and a different sound (or the same one) when a visitor clicks the button. The trick is that the sound files must be in the AU sound file format.

Note   You might expect that, being a FrontPage Component, Hover Buttons would support the WAV file format that is generally accepted in Microsoft Office applications. However, Hover Buttons generate Java code that requires sound files in the AU file format.

The following are the two sound options for a button:

✦ **On Click**: Plays a sound when a visitor clicks the Hover Button.

✦ **On Hover**: Plays a sound when a visitor passes the cursor over the Hover Button.

You can use the Browse buttons associated with each sound field to attach sounds to either of these two options. Just remember, you must attach a sound file in the AU file format.

Displaying custom images

The Custom dialog box also enables you to assign custom images that display when a visitor either moves his or her cursor over a Hover Button or clicks a Hover Button. The following two fields in the Custom dialog box represent your options for specifying custom images:

✦ **Button**: Displays the image when a visitor is not hovering over the button.

✦ **On Hover**: Displays the image when a visitor hovers over the button.

Again, you can use the Browse buttons associated with each image field to attach images to either of these two options.

Caution   The Hover Button does not resize to fit an image, so you have to do that manually.

Scrolling with Marquees

Scrolling Marquees present text scrolling across your screen. A scrolling Marquee is one FrontPage Component that doesn't require you to save your site to a Web server. You don't need to preview your Web page in a browser to see how your Marquees will look. You can test them in the Preview tab of Page view.

To create a scrolling Marquee, click in Page view to set the insertion point for the Marquee. Then, select Insert ➪ Component ➪ Marquee. The Marquee Properties dialog box displays, as shown in Figure 13-12.

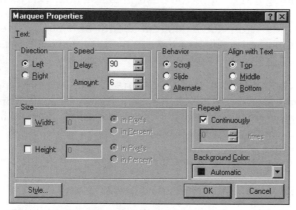

Figure 13-12: Creating a scrolling text Marquee.

Keep them simple

Many scrolling text properties exist that you can tweak. The Background Color drop-down menu lets you select a background for the scrolling text. Experimenting with the three radio buttons in the Behavior area is pretty safe. However, fiddling with the other options presents quite a bit of potential for disaster; you are advised to enter some text in the Text field and accept the default settings.

After you enter text in the Text field, click OK. You can see how your scrolling text will look in a browser by using the Preview tab of Page view. To resize your scrolling text Marquee, click and drag side or corner handles.

Experiment with Scroll Properties

For those of you determined to blaze the cutting edge of scrolling text displays, experiment away. Just remember that you can always delete a messed up Marquee and start from scratch with the default settings. The following are the available options in the Marquee Properties dialog box:

✦ **Scroll:** The text starts at the left (unless you have Right set under Direction) and moves to the right until all the text has moved off the screen, and then it repeats.

✦ **Slide:** Similar to Scroll, except that when the first letter hits the right edge of the Marquee, the text disappears and starts again at the left.

✦ **Alternate**: The text bounces back and forth between the left and right edges of the Marquee, like a ping-pong ball.

✦ **Align with Text:** Controls how the Marquee aligns with other (non-Marquee) text on the same line. These options work the same way as alignment options work for graphics.

✦ **Size:** The Height and Width check boxes enable you to define the height and/or width of the box, either in pixels or percent. You can also resize the box by clicking and dragging on handles in Page view.

✦ **Repeat:** Controls how many times the text scrolls across the screen. The default is Continuously, but if you deselect that check box, you can enter a set number of repeats.

✦ **Background Color:** By default, this is the background color of your page (or clear, if you use a background image). You can pick any other color, or create a custom color by using the color palette. If you change the background color, you may have to change the text color, so that they form a good, contrasting set of colors.

You edit many of the Marquee properties in Page view. For example, you can click the Marquee and select text size, color, and font, and apply attributes such as italics or boldface. You can also resize the Marquee in Page view by clicking and dragging the sizing handles.

Confirmation Fields

When you generate an input form and use FrontPage's built-in Form Handlers, FrontPage automatically generates a confirmation page that confirms the information that the visitor entered.

If you want to define your own customized confirmation page, you can use the Confirmation Field Component to insert those fields in a page. The Confirmation Field Properties dialog box has only one field: a blank in which you enter the Field name. This dialog box is shown in Figure 13-13.

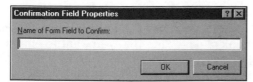

Figure 13-13: Inserting a Confirmation Field

How do Confirmation Fields work with input forms?

To use the Confirmation Field Component, you must create an input form. (Creating forms is the topic of Chapter 14.) As you create input forms, you'll also create input form fields, such as radio buttons, one-line text boxes, and scrolling text boxes. Each of these fields has a name, and each collects input. You need to record the names of all the fields in your form that you want to use in the confirmation page (the old-fashioned way, by writing them on a scratch pad).

After you create a Web page with an input form, you can assign a confirmation page for that form. The details are in Chapter 14, but, in short, right-click the form, select Form Properties from the context menu, click the Options button, and then click the Confirmation Page tab in the Options for Saving Results of a Form dialog box. Here, you can name a page that will act as a confirmation page, which is the page in which you place your Confirmation Fields.

For example, you might create a confirmation page called Confirm.htm. You would enter this page in the Confirmation Page tab, as described in the previous paragraph. Your page, Confirm.htm, could start with some text that said "Your form was successfully submitted. You told us your name was [*Name*]." This would work if you collected information in a field named "Name." If someone had entered David as their name, they would see a message that said "You told us your name was David."

Inserting Confirmation Fields

To add a Confirmation Field, position the cursor where you want the field input to appear. Select Insert ⇨ Component and choose Confirmation Field from the list of available Components.

Enter the name of the field whose input you want to appear. Click OK to insert the Component. (Unfortunately, FrontPage doesn't give you a list of available fields from the form—perhaps FrontPage 2001 will.) FrontPage inserts the field name in brackets (for instance, [*username*]) as a placeholder to indicate the presence of the Component. When the confirmation page is displayed, this placeholder is replaced with the actual input from the field.

Embedding included pages

The Include Page Component enables you to insert the contents of another file into your Web page. In some ways, this feature has been eclipsed by the ability to create shared borders. Creating a bottom shared border usually is easier than creating a new page to function as a footer (see Chapter 5 for more information on Web page navigation).

The Include Page Component is still useful as a way to include elements that are common to many pages, such as a chunk of page data that you want to embed in several different pages. By including these elements in a separate Web page, you can edit the included page, and the changes will be reflected on all pages.

To use the Include Page Component, first create a page to include in other pages. Then, select Insert ⇨ Component ⇨ Include Page and use the Browse button to find the page to embed. The Include Page Component Properties dialog box is shown in Figure 13-14.

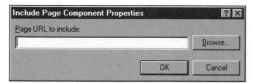

Figure 13-14: Embedding an Include Page

When FrontPage first creates a new Web, it creates a folder named __private. Contents of this folder are not directly accessible to visitors to the Web site, but it can be used to store objects that are part of the Web. This is a good place to put files that you want to include using the Include Page Component.

Scheduling images and scheduling included pages

With the Scheduled Image and Scheduled Include Page Components, you never again have to worry about your Web page advertising a fantastic offer that expires on June 1st, 1997. Scheduled Images and Scheduled Include Pages can be defined so that they vanish on a set date.

Scheduled Image and Scheduled Include Page Components are both variations on the Include Component just described. The difference is that the two Scheduled Components enable you to designate a particular time period during which a given image or other Web content is displayed. The time interval is indicated with a start time and an end time. The time range can be from one second to several years, with minutes, hours, days, and months as options in between.

By default, nothing is displayed by the Component until the scheduled starting time. Alternatively, you can include an alternative, default image to display before and after the time interval.

To add a Scheduled Image Component to your Web page, position the cursor on the Web page where you want the image to appear. Select Insert ⇨ Component and choose the Scheduled Image Component. In the Scheduled Image Properties dialog box (see Figure 13-15), indicate the image to include, the starting and ending times to display the image, and, optionally, an image to display before and after the scheduled time frame. Note that browsing for the image to include is limited to the current Web or the World Wide Web. Consequently, you will want to import the desired image into your Web prior to configuring the Component. Click OK to add the image to the current Web page.

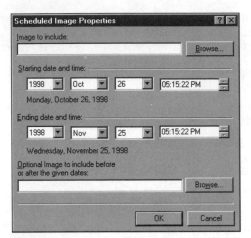

Figure 13-15: Indicate the image to include and its starting and ending times in the Scheduled Image Properties dialog box.

If the current time is within the range of the Scheduled Image time, the selected image displays in Editor. If not, it displays a bracketed message: "[Expired Scheduled Image]." This message is displayed even if the beginning time for the Scheduled Image hasn't been reached yet. Otherwise, if you have opted to include an alternative image, this image displays in lieu of the bracketed message.

You add a Scheduled Include Page by using the same technique. The only difference is that instead of specifying an image, you specify the URL of the page that you want to use for the Scheduled Include Page. You can designate an alternative URL to display before and after the scheduled time.

Substitution

The Substitution Component is one of the coolest, most underrated features of FrontPage. Scenario: You are responsible for a 28,000-page Web site, and the slogan of your corporation is on each of those pages. When you show up for work on Monday morning, you learn that the company motto has changed, and must be substituted on every page where it appears.

Yes, one option would be to search and replace, but that's pretty tedious, and requires that the text being searched for is a perfect match. The other option is to create a "parameter" called motto, and then simply change the definition of that parameter when you need to update your Web site.

By default, your Web's standard configuration consists of several predefined parameters. To view (and change) these parameters, select Tools ➭ Web Settings and click the Parameters tab. This tab displays your existing parameters, as shown in Figure 13-16.

You can add a new parameter by clicking the Add button and entering a name and value for your parameter, as shown in Figure 13-17.

Figure 13-16: Modify parameters in the FrontPage Web Settings dialog box.

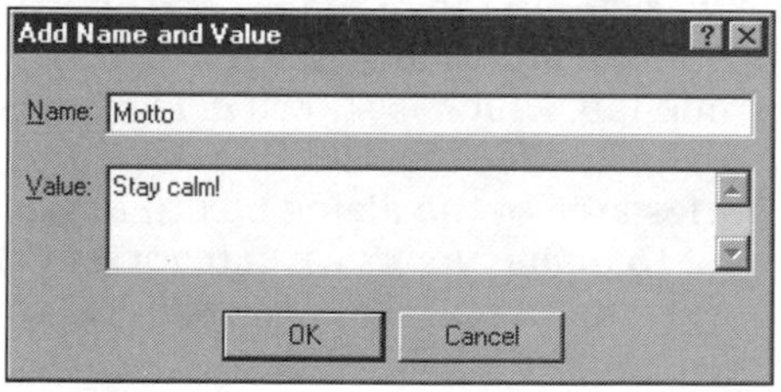

Figure 13-17: You can define parameters and values, and then update them at any time.

Use the Modify button to change a parameter value, or the Delete button to delete the parameter. After you define parameter names and values, click OK in the FrontPage Web Settings dialog box.

With your own parameters defined, you can insert them into any Web page. Just set your insertion point, and select Insert ⇨ Component ⇨ Substitution. Pull down the Substitute With list and select a field, as shown in Figure 13-18.

When you modify the Substitution parameter value, your Web pages are updated with the new value. Each time visitors view your Web page or refresh their browser window, they see the latest value for a Substitution Component.

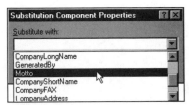

Figure 13-18: Inserting a Substitution field

Autolinks

Autolinks are used to automatically generate links on a page to other pages assigned to set categories. You can use categories to group your Web pages. For example, you might assign pages that have to do with the business aspects of your organization to the Business category, and assign pages related to upcoming events to the Schedule category.

You can also define your own categories. By assigning pages to categories, you can automatically create useful links beyond what is possible with navigation bars.

Assigning pages to categories

You can assign pages to categories in the Workgroup tab of the Page Properties dialog box. To do this, right-click in an open page and select Page Properties from the context menu. Then, click the Workgroup tab, which is shown in Figure 13-19.

Click check boxes in the Available Categories area of the dialog box to assign a page to one or more categories. If you want to define your own category, click the Categories button in the Workgroup tab and enter a new category name in the Master Category List dialog box, as shown in Figure 13-20.

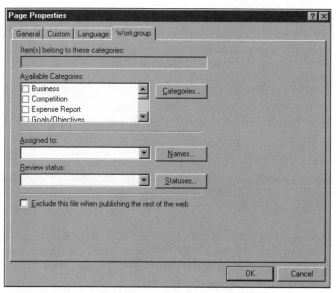

Figure 13-19: Categories are assigned in the Page Properties dialog box.

Figure 13-20: You can create your own categories in the Master Category List dialog box.

Note   One way to assign categories to all of your pages (or many of them) is to view your site in Reports or Folders view, and then right-click pages in the list of pages. You can open the Page Properties dialog box from Reports or Folders view, and assign Categories here, as well.

Using Comments with Autolinks

When you generate Autolinks, you also have the option of displaying a summary for each page to which you create a link. To define Comments for a page, right-click a page in Folders or Reports view, select Page Properties from the context menu, and click the Summary tab in the Properties dialog box.

In the Properties dialog box, enter Comments in the Comments field. Click OK. The Comments that you define will be available if you want to include them in Autolinks.

Generating Autolinks

After you assign categories to your pages, you're ready to create some Autolinks. Select Insert ⇨ Component ⇨ Autolink. The Categories dialog box appears, as shown in Figure 13-21.

Use the check boxes to select which categories you want to generate links to. Use the Sort Pages By drop-down menu to sort either by Document Title or by Date Last Modified. The two check boxes on the bottom of the dialog box allow you to include the date that each displayed, linked page was last modified, and the document's Comments.

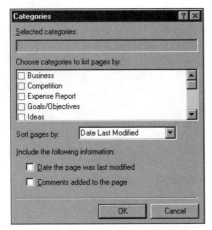

Figure 13-21: Inserting Autolinks

Search Forms

The Search Form Component is used to add a text-search component to your Web page. The Search Form Component enables users to search all or part of your Web for pages containing one or more text strings. Results of a search are displayed by listing the titles of matching pages, with each title hyperlinked to the actual page.

Details of the results page can also be controlled via the Search Form Component. If you have a content-rich Web and are looking for a relatively simple way to enhance the usability of your Web site, the Search Form Component could be just the thing.

To place a Search Form in your Web page, place your insertion point where the Search Box should appear, and select Insert ➪ Component Search Form. The Search Form Properties dialog box appears, as shown in Figure 13-22.

At this point, you can either click OK to insert a default Search Box, or you can adjust both the way the Search Box collects input and the results that it generates.

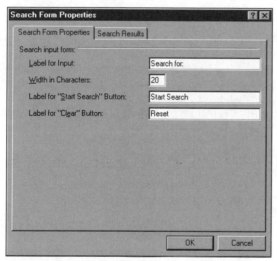

Figure 13-22: The Search Form Properties dialog box — the default settings often work fine for generating a Search Box.

Search Form Properties

The redundantly named Search Form Properties tab of the Search Form Properties dialog box enables you to define how your Search Form will look. You can change these options:

✦ **Label for Input:** Displays a label for your Search Box input field. You can change it to "Tell us what topic you are interested in" or "What are you looking for?" or some other label. Often, the default "Search For:" works fine.

✦ **Width in Characters:** Controls only how wide the *display* is of the input field, not how much users can input. Visitors can still enter 40 characters in a 20-character field.

✦ **Label for "Start Search" Button:** Displays a name for the button that starts the search. Keep the default, or create your own.

✦ **Label for "Clear" Button:** You can change the default name for the button that clears whatever a visitor has typed into the Search Box field.

Displaying Search Results

The Search Results tab in the Search Form Properties dialog box controls what kind of results are displayed for a search.

The three check boxes at the bottom of the dialog box define what information is displayed about the pages that are located:

✦ **Display Score (Closeness of Match):** Adds a number "score" to each page that matches the search criteria. Larger numbers indicate a closer match. The logic for this number is somewhat arbitrary, but visitors can elect to try pages with a "score" of 100 before trying a page with a "score" of 10. Even if you don't select this check box, results are still ordered by score.

✦ **Display File Date:** Adds to the list of results the date that the file was last changed.

✦ **Display File Size (in KB):** Adds the file size to the results list.

The three fields at the top of the Search Results tab control how results are displayed:

✦ **Word List to Search:** The default, "All," searches all folders in your Web site, except those that begin with an underscore, like _private or _borders. If you want to restrict your search to a specific folder, enter that folder name here.

✦ **Date Format:** If you selected the Display File Date check box, use this drop-down menu to choose a format for the date display.

✦ **Time Format:** If you selected the Display File Date check box and want to display both the date and the time that a matching file was created, use this drop-down menu to choose a format for the time display. Even in the age of microseconds, most folks won't need this much detail about when your Web page was created.

Figure 13-23 shows a Search Box in a Web page, with a Search Results list that includes the filename, date, file size, and score.

Table of Contents

If your Web site has navigation links, then, in a sense, it already has a table of contents. This section discusses the Table of Contents Component, which is a comprehensive list of all pages in your Web site, or at least all the publicly accessible ones.

Does your Web site need this kind of Table of Contents? Not necessarily. If you have provided useful navigational links, and perhaps a Search Box, a visitor might not need anything else to find exactly the information they are looking for. One downside of a Table of Contents is that if your Web site has 500 pages, you're looking at something more like an index than an easy-to-follow table of contents. Given these warnings, if you want to create a Table of Contents, you can generate one automatically.

Sometimes, creating a list of the contents of your Web or of a certain portion of your Web is useful, so that visitors can see what you have to offer, and can navigate easily from place to place. However, maintaining a Table of Contents can be tiresome if you have content that changes with any frequency. The FrontPage Table of Contents Component generates its table of contents automatically and updates it every time that you save the page.

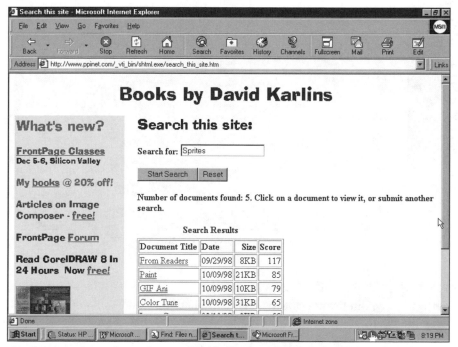

Figure 13-23: Search results can display file size, the date the file was last changed, and a "score" that somewhat randomly calculates how closely the page matches the search criteria.

Using the Table of Contents template

Numerous ways exist to generate a Table of Contents. The quickest way is to use the Table of Contents template to create a separate Table of Contents page. To use this template to create a list of pages in the Pedigree Pets Web, open Editor, select File ➪ New ➪ Page, and then choose the Table of Contents template. This opens a new page, as shown in Figure 13-24. (Note the use of the Date and Time code that was discussed earlier in this chapter — at the bottom of the page.)

The Table of Contents Component inserts a placeholder list of names, like that shown in Figure 13-24. The actual content of the file list only appears when you view the page in your browser.

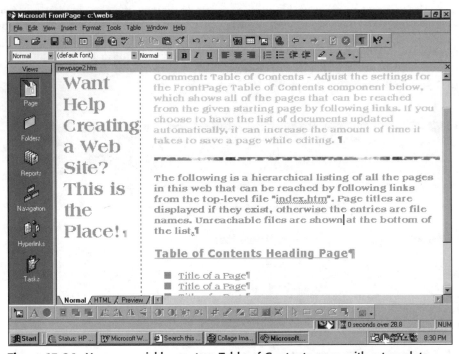

Figure 13-24: You can quickly create a Table of Contents page with a template.

Inserting a Table of Contents in a page

That was easy! But if you want to insert a Table of Contents in an existing Web page, that's almost as simple. Place your cursor where you want to insert the Table of Contents, and select Insert ➪ Component ➪ Table of Contents. This opens the Table of Contents Properties dialog box, shown in Figure 13-25. If you created your Table of Contents with the template, you can get to this dialog box by double-clicking the

Table of Contents. Alternatively, right-click the Component. Either way, the Table of Contents Properties dialog box appears.

The Table of Contents Properties dialog box contains several options. The most important is to choose the start page for the Table of Contents. This page serves as the starting point for the Component. It appears in the header of the Table of Contents, unless you specify None for the Heading Font Size.

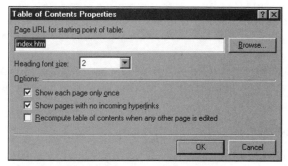

Figure 13-25: Editing a Table of Contents

The Heading Font Size refers to the size of the initial link, the title of which can serve as the main header for the list. Select the start file that you want to use. The title of this Web page appears in the header location. The check box options are as follows:

✦ **Show Each Page Only Once:** Usually a good choice, unless you really want to display the full hierarchy of your Web pages.

✦ **Show Pages with No Incoming Hyperlinks:** Deselect this box to weed out pages that are no longer referred to by other pages in the Web.

✦ **Recompute Table of Contents When Any Page Is Edited:** This option may be worth the extra time that it adds if you make frequent changes to the content.

Table of Contents challenges

The Table of Contents Component is useful, but implementing it can create some challenges. The Component works by reading the links from the start page, and following each of those to the next page, and so on. The Component works well when you want to display the structure of links on your pages. This produces a list of Web pages in the order of how they are linked to one another, which isn't the typical way to organize Web pages to present to visitors.

Here are a few challenges that you may encounter when implementing the Table of Contents Component:

✦ If you change the filename of a file on the local copy of your Web and then publish the Web to a remote server, FrontPage adds a new file with the updated name but doesn't delete the previous version of the file. Under normal circumstances, this adds some clutter to your file system, but it isn't a problem for users. However, if you have included a Table of Contents Component, you should be sure to uncheck the Component option Show Pages with No Incoming Links. Otherwise, your Table of Contents shows all the unlinked pages.

✦ If you use the Table of Contents Component to generate a separate page, and you are using this Table of Contents as the sole navigational element, the other pages will not be linked. If they are not linked, you can't check the No Orphans check box.

✦ The Table of Contents page doesn't work especially well with frames, because it generates links to both frame set documents and individual Component pages.

Additional Components

You can purchase additional FrontPage Components from third-party vendors, including J-Bots, who creates Java-based interactive Components for your Web site. If you do incorporate such third-party add-ons, they attach themselves to the Component submenu and appear when you select Insert ➪ Component ➪ Additional Components.

You can see a list of third-party add-ons for FrontPage at `http://www.ppinet.com /resource.htm`.

In the following tutorial, you will create a Web page with a scrolling text Marquee, Hover Buttons, a Hit Counter, and a Date and Time stamp.

Tutorial 13.1: Add FrontPage Components to a Web Page

1. Create a new FrontPage Web from the Personal Web template (select File ➪ New ➪ Web and then double-click Personal Web).

2. Open the file Index.htm in Page view.

3. Click at the end of the first line of text and press Enter to create a new line. Select Insert ➪ Component ➪ Marquee. Type **Welcome to the ultimate Web site** in the Text field and click OK in the dialog box.

4. Place your cursor at the end of the second paragraph and press Enter to create another blank line. Select Insert ➪ Component ➪ Hover Button. Type **Photos** in the Button Text field, and **Photo.htm** in the Link To field (or use the Browse button to find the file Photo.htm). Click OK. Create a few additional Hover Buttons linked to the Interests and Favorite pages.

5. Press Ctrl+End to move to the end of the page. Select Insert ➪ Component ➪ Hit Counter. In the Hit Counter Properties dialog box, click the radio button next to a Hit Counter that has a style you like. Click OK.

6. Note that the Web template generates a Date and Time field on the home page. Double-click the date to open the Date and Time Properties dialog box, and add a Time format from the drop-down menu. Click OK.

In Page view, your Web page should look something like the one in Figure 13-26.

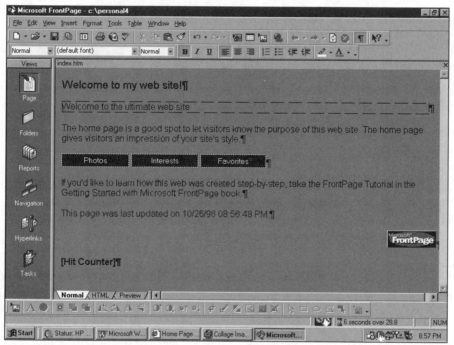

Figure 13-26: The scrolling text Marquee and Hover Buttons aren't that exciting in Page view.

If you preview your Web page in a browser, it should look a little like the one in Figure 13-27. You can keep your server clear of unwanted files by deleting this Web: Select File ➪ Delete Web, choose the top radio button in the dialog box, and then click OK.

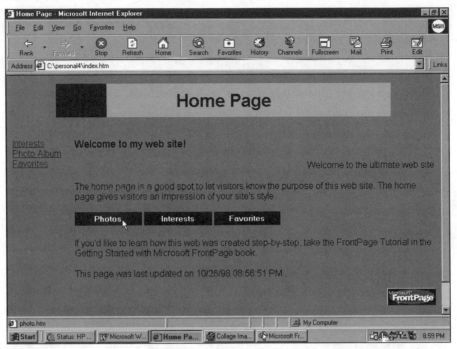

Figure 13-27: The scrolling text Marquee and Hover Buttons are more fun when viewed in a browser — and they don't require FrontPage extensions either.

Summary

This chapter introduced you to FrontPage Components and demonstrated how they work. You learned to implement coded programs without programming, enabling you to insert Components such as Hit Counters, Substitution Fields, and Search Forms. Although you don't need to know the underlying method behind these Components, you should remember that some of them only work if your Web site is published to a Web server that has FrontPage extension files. Some Components: scrolling text Marquees, Hover Buttons, Banner Ads, and Autolinks don't require a FrontPage-friendly server to operate.

In the next chapter, you will enter the interactive world of designing input forms. Input forms enable you to gather data from visitors. You'll learn to design forms that collect visitor input through text boxes, check boxes, options buttons, and drop-down menus.

✦   ✦   ✦

Designing Input Forms

In this chapter, you learn to create forms in FrontPage and to use built-in FrontPage Components that are available for processing and managing form input. You also learn to customize confirmation pages. This chapter provides a complete overview of the process of using forms to collect information from visitors to your site, including how to design forms, define input validation, collect form input, and display a result or confirmation page after the data is processed. This chapter also serves as the foundation for later chapters in this part and the next part of the book, which explain how to use programming elements that provide even more options for handling form input.

Discovering Interactive Forms

The Web pages that you learned how to build in earlier chapters have a limited ability to accept input from users. For example, including your e-mail address (and a link to it) in a Web page is a basic level of interactivity. A visitor can easily send you e-mail. However, e-mail links don't give you much control over the input that you receive.

Form elements open up a whole new level of interactive possibilities. By creating input form fields, you can frame the input that you get from visitors to your Web site. You can elect to collect names, addresses, and many types of text and data input. All of this is possible without any programming, by using built-in form handling components in FrontPage 2000. You can build on these same form elements to create applications that enable users to access and share information, conduct business, play games, and perform a variety of complex tasks. All of these things are possible because forms provide various means for users to add their input via a Web page and get back information based on that input.

Creating a Form

A Web page form is composed of one or more elements for accepting user input, and some means of submitting the input for processing. In general, the simplest form includes a single input field and a button to submit the results for processing.

Note You have probably seen search engines with a single input field and no Submit buttons. How is that done? It works because some browsers are designed such that if a form has only one input box, pressing the Enter key performs the same function as clicking a Submit button.

Forms can be used as a way to collect information from users, request feedback, initiate a database query, or facilitate a discussion.

Forms consist of two elements: form fields and push buttons. *Form fields* collect information. *Push buttons* (usually a Submit and a Reset button) are used to submit information to a Web server or clear a form. The significance of grouping form fields into forms is that all the contents of a single form are sent to the same destination, which can be a text file, a Web page, an e-mail message, or other, more-complex targets.

To create a form in FrontPage, you first position the form elements on the Web page and adjust the properties of each. The following two sections describe each of the basic form elements and its properties, as well as some of the basic properties of forms in general.

Working with Form Templates

FrontPage includes several templates that contain predesigned forms. If you are looking for a fairly standard form type, starting with one of these templates is likely to save you some time. A Form Wizard is also available, which is discussed toward the end of this chapter. The following are the form templates:

✦ **Feedback Form**: A simple form designed to solicit comments from users on a variety of company-related topics. It uses the Save Results Component to send input to a text file.

✦ **Guest Book**: A basic text-input form that enables site visitors to record a comment, much like the guest register of a small hotel or bed-and-breakfast inn. Although this form is more of a courtesy to users than anything else, a surprising number of people actually take the time to "sign" your guest book (especially if you let them read what they and others have written). The Guest Book form uses the Web Save Results Component to send comments to an HTML page that can be viewed by visitors to your Web site.

✦ **Search Form**: A simple one-field text-string search form used in conjunction with FrontPage's built-in text search engine. This form, which is part of the Search Component, is discussed in detail in Chapter 13.

✦ **User Registration**: Enables users to enter a username and password that gains them access to a designated access-controlled Web. This Component is restricted to certain Web servers and must be saved in a root Web. Results are processed by the Web Registration Component.

Dealing with Form Elements

All Web forms are composed of a handful of form elements: a one-line text box, a scrolling text box, check boxes, radio buttons, drop-down menus, and push buttons. In FrontPage, these elements can be inserted into your Web page either by selecting Insert ➪ Form and choosing the item to use or by using the Forms toolbar, which can be accessed by selecting View ➪ Forms Toolbar.

In addition to the form components previously described, you can use the Form menu option to insert a form, as well as to insert an image that can function as a push button, or a Form Label. The Form menu options are shown in Figure 14-1. Form Labels enable a visitor to select form input simply by clicking the text associated with that form field, as you will see later in this chapter.

Figure 14-1: The Form menu options

The easiest way to begin creating a form is to select Insert ➪ Form. Immediately, you see a dotted-line rectangle with a Submit and Reset button on your Web page. If you insert a form field into a location that doesn't already have a form defined, FrontPage generates a new form. If you insert a form element into an existing form, the new field is added to the existing form. A form is represented in Editor's Normal view by a dashed rectangle, which is not visible in Preview mode or in a browser. The next section identifies all the major form types, as well as the various options and parameters that each possesses.

Tip   Form fields display differently on different browsers. To keep your form looking nice and neat, you should consider using a table to line up its parts. After you insert your first form field (and create the form container), insert a table within the dashed container box. You can now drag the form items into the appropriate cell in the table. (See Chapter 9 for more information about constructing tables.)

Detaching the floating Form menu

The options in the Form submenu can be detached and made to float on your FrontPage Page editing window. To detach the Form menu (which then becomes a toolbar), select Insert ➪ Form and then move your cursor to the gray stripe at the top of the submenu. The tip "Drag to make this menu float" appears, as shown in Figure 14-2.

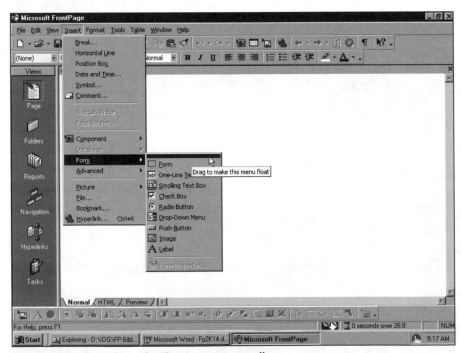

Figure 14-2: Detaching the floating Forms toolbar

Click and drag this bar to move the menu onto your Page editing window. The menu becomes a floating toolbar, whose tools are identified in Figure 14-3. Throughout the rest of this chapter, when you are asked to select a menu option from the Form submenu, you can alternatively click that tool in the floating Forms toolbar if you prefer.

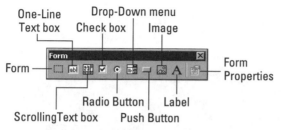

Figure 14-3: Options in the Form submenu are also available from the floating Forms toolbar.

When you are designing complex forms, you might find the floating toolbar a bit annoying. In that case, you can drag the toolbar's title bar and dock the toolbar in the Formatting menu. It takes a bit of trial and error, but after you stash the Forms toolbar at the end of the Formatting toolbar, it looks like the toolbar in Figure 14-4.

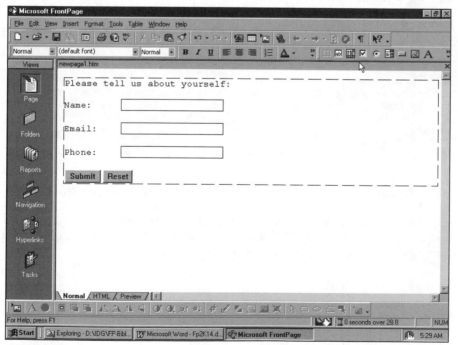

Figure 14-4: Docking the Forms toolbar

To keep things relatively simple, the following sections refer to the Form menu commands. But, as you explore the different components of form fields, remember that you can insert Form components from either the Form menu or the Forms toolbar.

One-line text boxes

The one-line text box is the staple of most online forms. It is suitable for short input, such as is shown in the Event Registration form in Figure 14-5.

Figure 14-5: Collecting input through one-line text form fields

To create a one-line text box, select Insert ➪ Form ➪ One-Line Text Box.

To resize the input box, select it and drag with the mouse on either side handle of the box, as shown in Figure 14-6. A one-line text box *can't* be resized vertically (in other words, it can be made wider or narrower, but not taller).

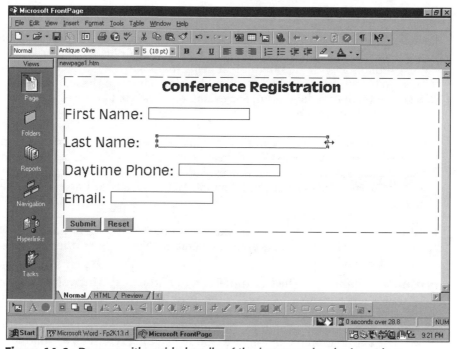

Figure 14-6: Drag on either side handle of the box to resize the input box.

Text box properties

To edit the text box properties, double-click the input box, or right-click the box and select Form Field Properties. The Text Box Properties dialog box is displayed, shown in Figure 14-7.

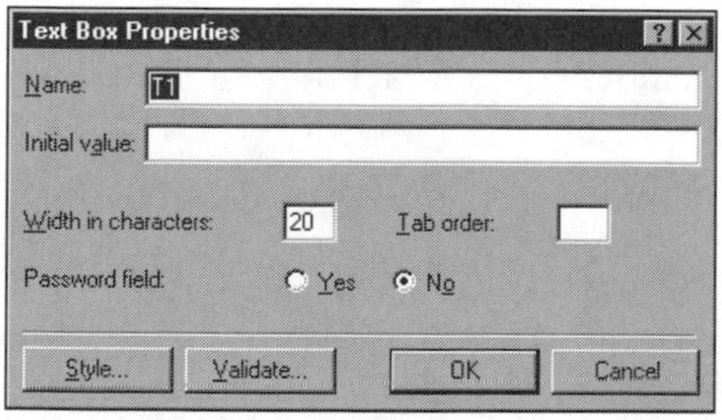

Figure 14-7: The Text Box Properties dialog box

You can edit the following properties in the Text Box Properties dialog box:

✦ **Name**: The name of the form field. This name is used internally when the form is processed. By default, the name of a text field is T plus a number corresponding to the number of text fields that have been placed on the form. To keep track of your input, you should assign names to these fields that describe the field's data input. For example, a field that collects last names could be called LName.

In the previous example, "LName" is used rather than "Last Name" because input form fields can contain only ASCII characters and numbers. Spaces are not permitted, because some scripting languages that handle input don't recognize these characters. FrontPage warns you if you attempt to create an unacceptable field name.

✦ **Initial Value**: Default text that appears when the form is first opened or when it is reset. The initial value is empty, by default. Normally, text input fields should be blank.

✦ **Width in Characters**: The horizontal length of the field. This value is adjusted automatically whenever you resize the form by using the mouse, as previously described (refer to Figure 14-6). This number designates the physical size of the text box. It does *not* limit the amount of text that can be entered in the box. For information on limiting text input, see the section on validating text input, later in this chapter.

You may find that the text-input box size that you define in FrontPage does not exactly match the size of the box when viewed in a Web browser. The only way to see exactly how fields will look is to view your input form in a browser. It does not display exactly in FrontPage.

✦ **Tab Order**: When filling out a form, your visitors can use the Tab key to switch between fields. By default, the order in which your users tab between fields is the order in which the fields appear onscreen. To change this order, enter a number in this text box (remember to give each field a different number, in sequence).

✦ **Password Field**: Generally, the text-input box echoes to the screen any characters that the user types into it. If the input box is created as a password field, by choosing the Yes radio button for the password property, placeholder characters are echoed instead. This feature provides a modicum of security for user passwords. For example, if you are collecting input that a visitor would not want someone to read over their shoulder, password fields hide that input, as shown in Figure 14-8. Recognize, however, that this property only governs the screen display. It does not provide any encryption of the input when it is sent back to the server.

Password field

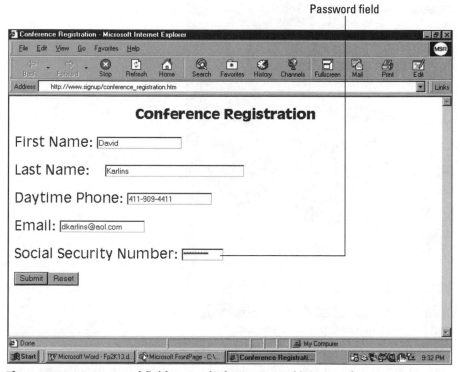

Figure 14-8: A password field conceals the content of input on the screen.

Formatting text box input

You can define font attributes, paragraph formatting, and borders for text fields. These formatting features are available through the Style button in the Form Field Properties dialog boxes. Font attributes can be applied to any input form field that displays text.

> **Tip** Formatting that is applied to input form fields is referred to as a *style*, and is a basic form of applying Cascading Style Sheets. For more discussion of higher levels of Cascading Style Sheets, see Chapter 12.

To add style attributes to a text box, click the Style button in the Text Box Properties dialog box and then click the Modify Style button. In the Modify Style dialog box that appears, click the Format button, and select one of the options discussed next to format your input field.

Format Font

When you select Font from the Format button drop-down list in the Text Box Properties dialog box, the Font dialog box appears, as shown in Figure 14-9.

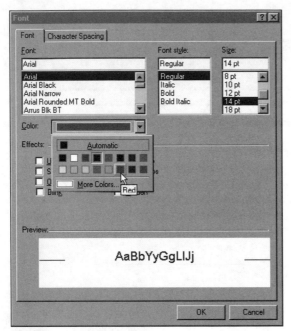

Figure 14-9: Defining input field text fonts

The font attributes that you define apply to text entered into the one-line text box. You can define text font (for example, Courier New or Arial), font size, font color, and font effects. In Figure 14-9, red, 14-point Arial font is being assigned to visitor input. In addition, you can define horizontal and vertical character spacing in the Character Spacing tab of the Font dialog box. Normally, irregular spacing is not useful in a one-line text box, especially where clear, readable text is the main goal.

Format Paragraph

When you select Paragraph from the Format Button list in the Text Box Properties dialog box, the Paragraph dialog box appears. Here, you can define paragraph alignment (default, left, right, centered, or full-justified). The default option applies the formatting that is applied to the text before the input field.

Indentation and spacing are not particularly useful for one-line input, which tends to be short and (by definition) no more than one line. These formatting options are explored in more detail later in the chapter, when scrolling text boxes are discussed. However, centered or right-aligned text might be appropriate for some one-line input.

Figure 14-10 shows an input form collecting text in one-line text boxes, where visitor input has been formatted in Courier font.

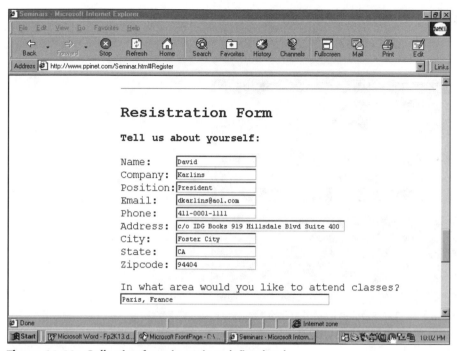

Figure 14-10: Collecting form input in a defined style

Format Borders and Shading

The Borders and Shading dialog box can be selected from the Format button drop-down menu in the Modify Style dialog box. The Border tab enables you to define border size, style, and the padding (space) between the border and the field input.

The three options in the Setting area of the dialog box enable you to choose no border, a box border, or a custom-drawn border. The Style List, the Color Palette, and the Width drop-down menus enable you to define the appearance of your border. And the four Padding drop-down menus enable you to define the padding between the border and the fields.

The Shading tab enables you to define either a fill color or an image for an input field. Normally, you will want to keep one-line text boxes clean and simple so that visitors can clearly read the text that they enter into a text box. However, you have the option to select background and foreground shading colors, or to use the Browse button in the Shading tab to select an image to use as a field background. If you do assign a background image, you can use the four pull-down menus at the bottom of the dialog box to define the position of the image. In a one-line text box, it is not usually helpful to clutter input fields with too much background noise, but a background shade may be appropriate.

After you define border and shading options, click OK in the dialog box. Your border and shading format is previewed in the Preview section of the Modify Style dialog box, as shown in Figure 14-11.

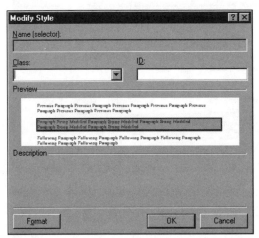

Figure 14-11: Previewing form input style

Format Numbering

The Format button drop-down menu in the Modify Style dialog box has a fourth style option available: Numbering. Because one-line input fields can collect only one line of text, numbering style attributes are not applicable to this type of field.

Validating text box input

In addition to its basic properties and style formatting, each form field type in FrontPage can be configured to limit its acceptable inputs, by using the form field's validation options. You access a form field's validation dialog box either via the Validate button on the Properties dialog box or by right-clicking the form field and then selecting Form Field Validation.

Tip   Any time that you specify validation options, be sure to alert your user to the presence of those options on the form itself, if the restrictions are not obvious ones. A good example is any fields that you designate as "required." Failing to alert users is likely to reduce the number of people who complete the form, and probably will result in some curt messages from users who do not appreciate surprises.

The Text Box Validation dialog box is shown in Figure 14-12. It includes several options for specifying what input is accepted by the form. By default, the form field's accepted Data Type option is set to No Constraints, meaning that any input is accepted, including no input. The data type constraints that you can place on fields in a form are explained next.

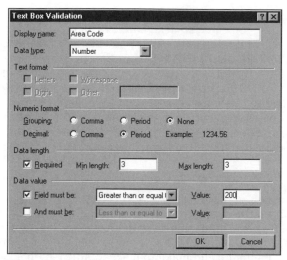

Figure 14-12: The Text Box Validation dialog box

Data type constraints

Besides No Constraints, you can choose to constrain the types of data that a form field accepts. Selecting one of the data type constraints activates additional validation options. The following are the options available in the Data Type drop-down list:

✦ **Text:** If you choose to constrain to text the data types that are accepted by a form field, the additional validation options in the Text Format area of the dialog box are activated. You can restrict the text that a field accepts to Letters, Digits, Whitespace (space, tab, carriage return, and line feed), and/or Other. To include one or more of these formats, check the box next to its name. If you select Other, you must also type the other characters that you want to permit, such as a comma, hyphen, dollar sign, or at (@) sign.

✦ **Integer:** If you choose to constrain to integers (in other words, whole numbers) the data types that are accepted by a form field, the Grouping radio buttons are activated in the Numeric Format area of the dialog box. You can designate how the digits of the number should be grouped. The options are Comma (for example, 1,234,567), Decimal (for example, 1.234.567), or None (for example, 1234567).

✦ **Number:** If you choose to constrain to numbers the data types that are accepted by a form field, the Decimal radio buttons are activated in the Numeric Format area of the dialog box. You can designate the decimal character by selecting either the Comma or Period radio button. Note that the Grouping character and the Decimal character can't be set to the same character.

Display Name

If you select a data type constraint, you can also designate a display name for the field, in the Display Name text box at the top of the Text Box Validation dialog box. This name is used to identify the field to users, in the event that they haven't entered valid data in the form field. By default, any error message uses the name of the field that is specified in the form field properties. Use the Display Name field if you are using shorthand field names (such as T1) and want to include a more recognizable name in any error messages. For example, if you have a field named Code in which you are collecting area codes, you can identify the nature of the input, so that visitors are told that they need to enter an area code to complete the form.

Data Length

Even if you don't want to constrain the data type (and choose the default, No Constraints), you can still constrain the data length. In the Data Length area of the Text Box Validation dialog box, you can stipulate that input in the field is required. In addition, you can designate a minimum and maximum acceptable length, in characters, for any input.

Tip   You should always designate a maximum length in any text field. This prevents potential misuse of the form. Give users a reasonable length limit, but no more than reasonably necessary.

Data Value

The Data Value section of the Text Box Validation dialog box enables you to restrict input to a range of acceptable values:

✦ If you constrain the data type to integers or numbers, FrontPage check results numerically.

✦ If you constrain the data type to text or don't set any constraints, input is compared by using alphabetic order.

Options in the drop-down box for limiting data values include: less than, greater than, less than or equal to, greater than or equal to, equal to, and not equal to. Use the second data value check box if you want to designate two range criteria, such as an upper- and lower-range limit.

Scrolling text boxes

A scrolling text box, called a *text area* in HTML, is used for data input that is longer than a few words. Typically, a scrolling text box is used when a paragraph of text is called for, such as comments or messages.

To create a scrolling text box, select Insert ➪ Form ➪ Scrolling Text Box, or click the corresponding icon on the Forms toolbar.

To resize the input box, select it and drag with the mouse from any side or corner of the box. A scrolling text box can be resized horizontally and/or vertically.

Scrolling text box properties

To edit the scrolling text box properties, either double-click the input box or right-click the box and select Form Field Properties. You can resize a scrolling text box both horizontally (make it wider or narrower) and vertically (make it taller or shorter) by dragging any of the eight corner or side handles that appear when the box is selected. Figure 14-13 shows a scrolling text box being enlarged in both height and width.

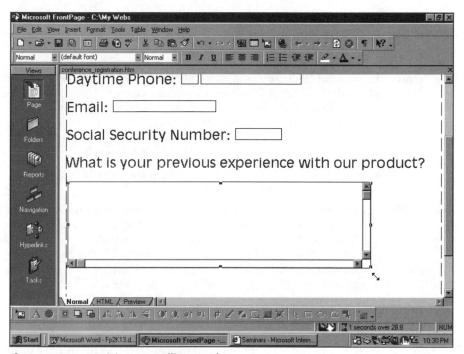

Figure 14-13: Resizing a scrolling text box

In addition to resizing a scrolling text box, you can define other properties by double-clicking the field to open the Properties dialog box. Or, you can right-click a scrolling text box and select Form Field Properties from the context menu. In either case, the Properties dialog box opens, as shown in Figure 14-14.

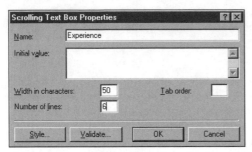

Figure 14-14: The Scrolling Text Box Properties
dialog box

You can edit the following properties in the Scrolling Text Box Properties dialog
box:

✦ **Name**: The name of the text box is used internally when the form is
  processed. By default, the field name is *S* plus a number corresponding to the
  number of scrolling text fields that have been placed on the form. You
  probably want to change this name to a field name that helps you to keep
  track of the data that you are collecting. For example, if you are collecting
  feedback on a product, you might call the field "Feedback."

✦ **Initial Value**: The default text that appears when the form is first opened or
  when it is reset. The Initial Value is empty by default.

✦ **Width in Characters**: The horizontal width of the field is adjusted
  automatically whenever you resize the form by using the mouse, as previously
  described. Note that this number designates the physical size of the text box.
  It does not limit the amount of text that can be entered in the box. For
  information on limiting text input, see "Validating Scrolling Text Box Input,"
  the next section in this chapter.

✦ **Number of Lines**: Designates the vertical height of the text box. This value is
  adjusted automatically whenever you resize the form by using the mouse, as
  previously described. Note that this number designates the physical size of
  the text box. It does not limit the amount of text that can be entered in the
  box. For information on limiting text input, see the next section, "Validating
  scrolling text box input."

✦ **Tab Order**: Enter the position number that you want this field to have when
  your visitors use the Tab key to move through the form's fields.

Tip

Wrapping text refers to the ability of text to start a new line automatically any time
that the text approaches the end of the text box. In Internet Explorer, scrolling text
boxes wrap by default. In Netscape Navigator, they do not. To enable text wrapping in all versions of Netscape, open the form page in Editor and select View ➪
HTML. Locate the `<TEXT AREA>` tag that corresponds to the scrolling text box.
Add the attribute `WRAP` inside the tag (`<TEXT AREA WRAP>`.) See Chapter 11 for
help on using the HTML view.

Validating scrolling text box input

To select validation options for a scrolling text box, either select the Validate button from the Properties dialog box or right-click the form field and select Form Field Validation. The validation options for a scrolling text box are the same as for a one-line text box, as described in the previous section.

Because scrolling text boxes tend to be a "free form" way to collect input from users, you are not likely to add strict validation rules to them. For example, if you are asking visitors to describe their opinion of your product, you probably would allow text and numbers as input, and not define a minimum number of characters for their input. However, you might elect to make the field a required field, so that visitors must enter something in the field to submit the form. Additionally, you might want to set a maximum number of characters that someone can enter into the field.

Formatting scrolling text box input

You can apply format styles to a scrolling text box in the same way that you apply them in one-line input boxes, as described in the previous section, "One-Line Text Boxes." However, some additional paragraph formatting attributes are available that can be applied to a scrolling text box that aren't useful in one-line text boxes.

You can select the paragraph attributes by clicking the Format button in the Modify Style dialog box, which presents the Paragraph dialog box, shown in Figure 14-15. The following are the Indentation options in the Paragraph dialog box for scrolling text box input:

✦ **Before Text:** Defines the indentation to the left of the paragraph, either as a value or percentage.

✦ **After Text:** Defines the indentation to the right of the paragraph, either as a value or percentage.

✦ **Indent First Line:** Defines indentation for the first line of the paragraph.

Paragraph spacing for scrolling text box input can be defined as a percentage of the screen, in pixels (px), percent, or other units. The following are the Spacing options in the Paragraph dialog box:

✦ **Before:** Defines spacing above the paragraph

✦ **After:** Defines spacing below the paragraph

✦ **Word:** Defines spacing between words in the paragraph

✦ **Line Spacing:** Defines spacing between the lines of the paragraph (such as double-spacing)

Absolute spacing can be defined in pixels, inches, points, picas (pc), centimeters (cm), or millimeters. *Relative spacing* is defined as a percentage. If you use absolute spacing, you should stick with pixels, because that is the unit of measurement used by computer monitors. The spacing that you define is illustrated in the Preview area of the dialog box, as shown in Figure 14-15.

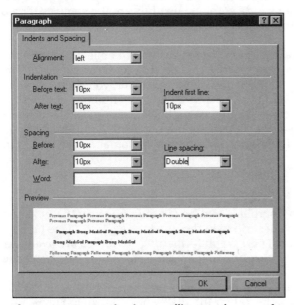

Figure 14-15: Previewing scrolling text box text formatting

Check boxes

Check boxes enable users to indicate a selection by clicking a small box. Selecting a check box typically marks it with an *x* or check mark. Check boxes are used for simple yes/no input. Although check boxes are often used for a group of options, they are *nonexclusive*, which means that checking one box does not restrict the user from checking another box in the same grouping. This is the chief difference between check boxes and radio buttons. Radio buttons are *exclusive*, which means visitors can select only one radio button in a group.

To create a check box, select Insert ⇨ Form ⇨ Check Box. To add some text next to the check box to describe what a visitor is selecting, click the check box.

Check box properties

To edit the check box properties, either double-click the check box or right-click the box and select Form Field Properties. The Check Box Properties dialog box, shown in Figure 14-16, is displayed. You can edit the following properties:

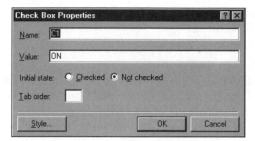

Figure 14-16: Check Box Properties dialog box

✦ **Name**: The name of the check box. This name is used internally when the form is processed. By default, the name is *C* plus a number corresponding to the number of check boxes that have been placed on the form.

✦ **Value**: The value that is sent by the check box if it is checked. By default, the Value is ON. This value is used internally, so unless you are writing your own program to process a form, few reasons exist to change the default. Typically, you'll want to create a more meaningful value, to aid you in interpreting the form's output.

✦ **Initial State**: Selecting the Checked option causes the check box to be checked already, by default, when the form is first accessed or when it is reset.

✦ **Tab Order**: Enter the position number that you want this field to have when your visitors use the Tab key to move through the form's fields.

Often, when you are creating check boxes, you are creating a list of items that your visitors can select from. For example, you might have a series of check boxes that are each labeled with a different type of animal, asking your visitors what types of pets they have. To help keep your form reply more manageable, you will find that it is easier to provide all the check boxes in this type of series with the same name, but different values — in other words, name all the check boxes "pet," and then assign each check box a different value, such as cat, dog, orangutan, and so on.

Why not validate check box input?

No mechanism exists for validating a check box. Why not? Primarily because a check box doesn't have much to validate. A visitor either selects a check box or doesn't.

If you want to ensure that users check a particular box on a form before they proceed (for example, a check box that asks users to acknowledge that they understand certain policies or restrictions pertaining to the form), you need to add some simple scripting to the check box. (Scripting languages are discussed in Chapter 18.)

Alternatively, you can use a single radio button for this purpose. See the next section for details on validating a radio button.

Attaching labels to check boxes

Attached labels enable a visitor to select a check box (or radio button) by clicking text associated with that check box. Check boxes are small, and label text makes it more convenient to select a check box. Figure 14-17 shows a check box being selected by clicking label text. The label text appears in a dotted rectangle when the associated check box is selected.

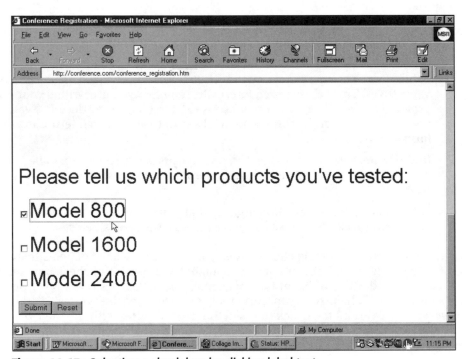

Figure 14-17: Selecting a check box by clicking label text

You can assign label text to a check box by typing text next to the check box. Then, click and drag to select the text and the check box, and select Insert ➪ Form ➪ Label. Figure 14-18 shows a label being assigned to a check box.

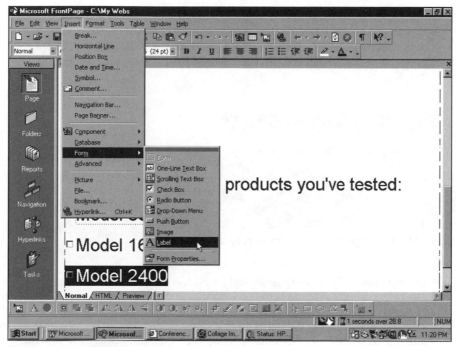

Figure 14-18: Defining a label

Caution Labels are supported by versions of Internet Explorer 4.0 and above. However, visitors viewing your forms with browsers that don't support labels are still able to make selections by clicking directly the associated check box or radio button.

Radio buttons

A radio button, also known as an *option button*, refers to a hollow, round circle that contains a smaller, solid-black circle when selected. Radio buttons are always used in an exclusive grouping, meaning that only one option in the group can be selected at a time. Selecting a new option automatically deselects any previous selection.

To create a radio button, select Insert ➪ Form ➪ Radio Button.

Although creating a single radio button is possible, in practice, radio buttons are usually grouped. Groups of radio buttons are analogous to a multiple choice question on a test. A visitor selects one, and only one, button in a group. By default, additional radio buttons that you create are grouped with any button(s) that precedes them. To change groupings, use the Radio Button Properties dialog box, as described in the next section.

Radio button properties

To edit the radio button properties, either double-click the radio button or right-click the button and select Form Field Properties. The Radio Button Properties dialog box, shown in Figure 14-19, is displayed. You can edit the following properties:

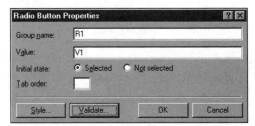

Figure 14-19: The Radio Button Properties dialog box

✦ **Group Name**: This name is shared by all radio buttons in the same group. Users can select only one option from the group. By default, the group name is *R* plus a number corresponding to the number of radio button groups that have been placed on the form. Every radio button in a group must have the same group name. The common group name ensures that only one of the radio buttons (within the group) can be selected.

Maintaining the exact same group name for each radio button in a group is important. The easiest way to make sure that all radio buttons have the same group name is to create a button, assign a group name, and then copy that button. Later, you can change the value for each button within the group. To create more than one group of radio buttons, create the first radio button of the second group, change its name to differentiate it from the first group, highlight it, press Ctrl+C, and then Ctrl+V to paste copies of it.

✦ **Value**: The value that is sent by the radio button if it is checked. A radio button value needs to be unique within its group, to distinguish responses. By default, the value is *V* plus a number corresponding to one more than the value of the preceding radio button. Typically, you will want to create a more meaningful value, to aid you in interpreting the form's output.

✦ **Initial State**: Choosing the Selected option causes the radio button to be selected by default when the form is first accessed or when it is reset. Note that only one radio button in a group can be selected, by default. Choosing Selected for a given button automatically causes any previously selected button to lose its default selection.

✦ **Tab Order**: Enter the position number that you want this field to have when your visitors use the Tab key to move through the form's fields.

Validating radio button input

You can use radio button validation to require that users select one of the options from a radio button grouping.

You access a radio button's validation dialog box either via the Validate button on the Properties dialog box or by right-clicking one of the radio buttons in a group and selecting Form Field Validation.

Tip

Radio buttons typically are designed so that a selection is required. After a button has been selected, it is difficult to deselect all buttons. If one of the options for a set of radio buttons is None, you should include this as an explicit choice and make it the default.

The Radio Button Validation dialog box is shown in Figure 14-20. Check the Data Required check box to require that users select one of the radio buttons in a grouping. Note that checking this option for one of the buttons in a group activates the validation for all buttons in the group. In addition, you can designate a display name to be used if it is necessary to prompt the user to select an option.

Figure 14-20: The Radio Button Validation dialog box

Caution

If you open the Radio Button Properties dialog box and change the group name associated with the radio button, the Validate button is temporarily grayed out. Close the dialog box and reopen it to reactivate the Validate button.

Drop-down menus

Drop-down menus are similar to check boxes or groups of radio buttons in that they enable a visitor to make selections from a group of options. The difference is mainly in the appearance of the form field. Most often, drop-down menus enable a visitor to choose one option from a list. Figure 14-21 shows a drop-down menu with four options.

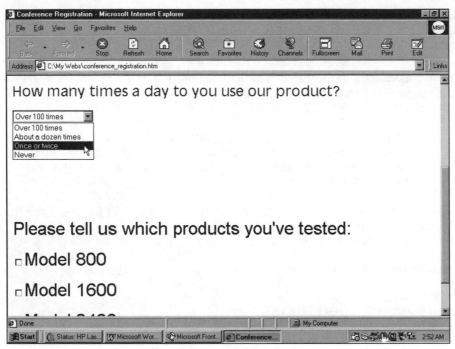

Figure 14-21: Collecting input through a drop-down menu

Drop-down menus can also be defined so that a visitor can select more than one option from the list. When you allow for more than one selection from a list, displaying multiple lines in the drop-down menu is helpful, as shown in Figure 14-22.

To create a drop-down menu list, select Insert ➪ Form ➪ Drop-Down Menu. This creates an empty drop-down menu, which is not very useful. To add items to the menu list, edit the drop-down menu properties, as described in the following section.

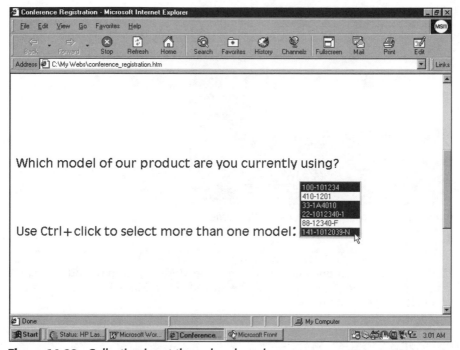

Figure 14-22: Collecting input through a drop-down menu

Drop-down menu properties

To edit the drop-down menu properties, either double-click the drop-down menu or right-click the drop-down menu and select Form Field Properties. The Drop-Down Menu Properties dialog box, shown in Figure 14-23, is displayed. You can edit the following properties:

✦ **Name**: The name of the drop-down menu field. This name is used internally when the form is processed. By default, the name of a drop-down menu is D plus a number corresponding to the number of drop-down menus that have been placed on the form.

✦ **Choice**: The location in which you create the list of items that appears in the drop-down menu. To add an item, select Add. This opens the Add Choice dialog box, as shown in Figure 14-24. Type the list item into the Choice input field. Optionally, check the Specify Value field and type a value to be sent when the form is submitted. Because the value is used internally, you don't need to specify a custom value unless you are writing your own program to handle the form. Select the Selected radio button to have this item selected by default.

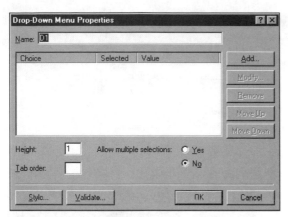

Figure 14-23: The Drop-Down Menu Properties
dialog box

After you add at least one choice item, use the Modify button to edit an item, the
Remove button to delete an item, or the Move Up and Move Down buttons to
change the order of items.

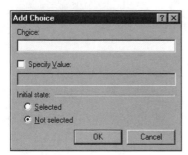

Figure 14-24: Use the Add Choice dialog
box to add items to a drop-down menu.

✦ **Height**: By default, the height of the drop-down menu is 1. You can edit this
number to display more items in the list simultaneously. Using any number
greater than 1 causes the menu list to change from a drop-down menu to a
menu list. If the number of items in the list is greater than the height, the
menu list will include a vertical scroll bar. If the number of items is less than
or equal to the height, the menu list simply displays all items. In Normal view,
Editor usually displays menu lists of more than one line with an extra line that
isn't visible in a browser.

✦ **Allow Multiple Selections**: If this option is checked, users can select more
than one choice by using a method appropriate to their browser and
operating system. (On a Windows system, hold down the Shift key to select a
range of items; hold down the Control key to select noncontiguous items.)

Validating drop-down menu input

You access a drop-down menu's Validation dialog box either via the Validate button on the Properties dialog box or by right-clicking the drop-down menu and selecting Form Field Validation.

The drop-down menu has two different validation menus, depending on whether the menu has been configured to accept one or multiple selections. The validation option for menus that allow only single selections is shown in Figure 14-25.

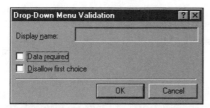

Figure 14-25: Validation dialog box for a drop-down menu that allows only one selection

Check the Data Required check box to require users to select an option from the menu. Select Disallow First Item if you want to place a direction, such as Select an Item, as the first item in the list and don't want this to be included as a valid selection. If you have made the menu required, you can optionally designate a name to be used to identify the menu field to the user if they fail to make a valid selection.

The Validation dialog box for menus that allow multiple selections has an additional option, as shown in Figure 14-26. In this case, you can stipulate a minimum and maximum number of allowable choices, using the Minimum Items and Maximum Items fields.

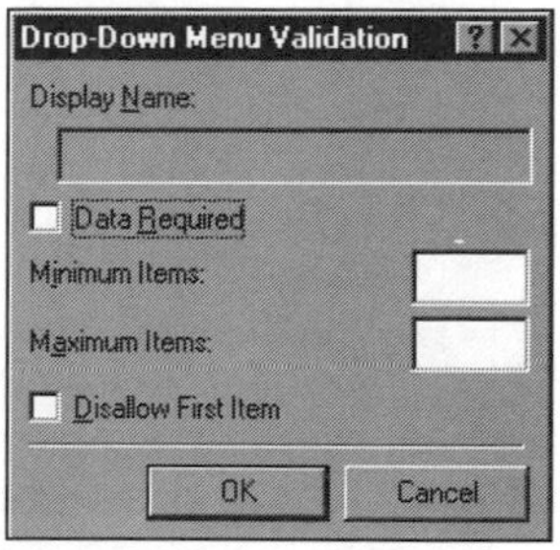

Figure 14-26: Validation dialog box for a drop-down menu that allows multiple selections

Push buttons

A form button is a special button that initiates some action in relation to a form. When users fill out a Web-based form, they are filling out a copy of the form that is resident on their computer. For the server to process the form input, it must be sent back to the server. Submitting data for processing is the primary function of a form button. Another function is to reset the form to its default state. Note that when you add the first field to a form, the Submit and Reset buttons are added automatically.

Other buttons can be defined and associated with custom actions, but that topic is beyond the scope of the present chapter. These buttons are discussed in Chapter 18, in conjunction with scripting in FrontPage.

Creating a form button

When you select Insert ➪ Form ➪ Form to create a new form, Submit and Reset push buttons are automatically inserted into the form. Without at least a Submit button, you won't be able to process the information that visitors enter into a form. In the next chapter, you'll learn how to handle form input, but for now, be aware that every form needs a Submit button.

If you want to insert a new push button, or if for some reason you deleted the Submit button that was generated automatically when you initiated your form, you can insert a push button into any form. To create a form button, select Insert ➪ Form ➪ Push Button.

Push button properties

By default, push buttons are created as Normal buttons, which require scripts to work. To edit the properties of your push button, either double-click the button or right-click the button and select Form Field Properties. The Push Button Properties dialog box, shown in Figure 14-27, is displayed. You can edit the following button properties:

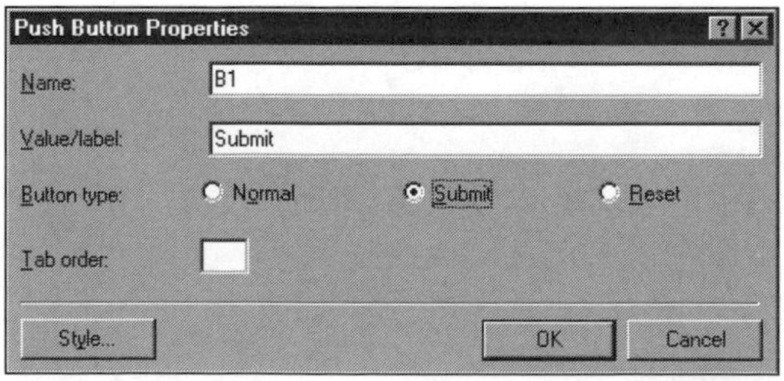

Figure 14-27: The Push Button Properties dialog box

✦ **Name**: The name of the button. This name is used internally when the form is processed. By default, the name of a button is *B* plus a number corresponding to the number of buttons that have been placed on the form.

✦ **Value**: Although it may seem counterintuitive, the value of the button is the descriptive text that appears on the button on the Web page. Type the text that you would like to appear on the button.

Tip

To center the text on the button and extend the length of the button, insert one or more spaces in front of the text and an equal number of spaces after the text.

✦ **Button Type**: A Submit button sends input from the form to the action designated in the Form Properties dialog box (discussed later in this chapter). A Reset button restores the form to its default form, without sending any data. A Normal button performs no inherent action and must be associated with a scripting function in order to be of any other than decorative use. (Scripting is discussed in Chapter 18.)

Form field images

An image used as a form button sends to the server the location where the user clicked the button, but this information is not used by any of the FrontPage Components. Custom scripting is required to make use of this feature. Form images are linked to the Scripting Wizard, which simplifies the task of creating functional buttons and other interactive image elements. (The Scripting Wizard feature is discussed in Chapter 18.)

To create an image form button, select Insert ➪ Form ➪ Image. The image form field is not accessible from the Forms toolbar. Images inserted in a form have the same properties as regular images.

Form field labels

All form fields should be labeled on the Web page form so that users recognize what to input into the field. HTML has no special provision for form field labels, but for some reason, FrontPage includes a special menu item for labeling form fields. To add a form field label, create a form field and type some text adjacent to it. Now, highlight both the field and the text and select Insert ➪ Form ➪ Label. A small, dashed box appears around the text, indicating that it is a field label.

Using the Form Page Wizard

In addition to the form templates described earlier in this chapter, FrontPage also includes a Form Page Wizard that can help you to construct a sophisticated form quickly.

To create a form page by using the Form Page Wizard, select File ➪ New and choose the Form Page Wizard from the New File template list. You are greeted with the first screen of the Wizard, as shown in Figure 14-28. Click Next to continue.

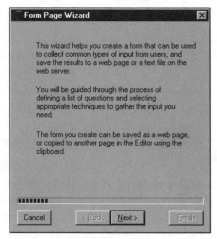

Figure 14-28: The opening screen of the Form Page Wizard

Naming the form

In the next dialog box, shown in Figure 14-29, give the page a title and URL. The title will appear in the title bar of a visitor's browser and can be more descriptive than the URL. The URL should have an .htm filename extension; for example, Survey.htm. Click Next to continue.

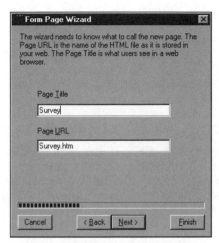

Figure 14-29: Naming your form by using the Form Page Wizard

Form input types

The Add button that appears in the next Wizard dialog box enables you to add input fields and text prompts to your form. The following are the many options to choose from:

✦ **Contact information**: Build form fields to capture name, affiliation, address, and phone number.

✦ **Account information**: Prompts for username and password.

✦ **Product information**: Asks for a product name, model, version, and serial number.

✦ **Ordering information**: Produces a form to take a sales order, including a list of products to order, billing details, and shipping information.

✦ **Personal information**: Form to collect information such as username, age, and other personal characteristics.

✦ **One of several options**: Form item that requires users to pick exactly one option.

✦ **Any of several options**: Form item that enables users to pick zero or more options.

✦ **Boolean**: Prompts to input a yes/no or true/false question.

✦ **Date**: Prompts to input a date format.

✦ **Time**: Prompts to input a time format.

✦ **Range**: Creates a rating scale from 1 to 5.

✦ **Number**: Creates an input box for a number.

✦ **String**: Creates a one-line text box.

✦ **Paragraph**: Creates a scrolling text box.

Adding an input type

After you select a question to ask in your form, click the Next button in the dialog box. You are prompted for details about the question that you are asking. For example, if you ask for contact information, you can use the check boxes in the dialog box shown in Figure 14-30 to define exactly what contact information you want to collect.

Figure 14-30: Selecting question details in the Form Page Wizard

After you define one question for your form, you can click the Next button to return to the dialog box that lists the questions that you've created. Click Add to place additional questions in your form.

After you create a list of questions to ask in your form, you can click any of those questions and use the Move Up or Move Down buttons to move a selected question up or down on the page. After you complete your list of questions, click the Next button to move to the Presentation Options dialog box in the Wizard.

Presentation Options

The Presentation Options dialog box, shown in Figure 14-31, enables you to define the look of your form page.

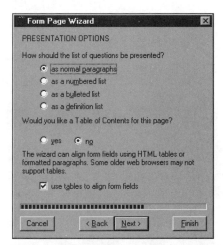

Figure 14-31: Defining page layout in the Form Page Wizard

The group of four radio buttons at the top of the dialog box enables you to lay out your questions as normal paragraphs, as a numbered list, as a bulleted list, or as a definition list. (Numbered lists, bulleted lists, and definitions lists are discussed in Chapter 6.) Select one of these options for organizing your form questions.

The yes and no radio buttons under "Would you like a Table of Contents for this page" enable you to place a table of contents on your form page. The table of contents generates links within the page to each question, so that a visitor can jump directly to a selected question. For a simple form, a table of contents usually isn't necessary. For input forms with many questions, a table of contents can be helpful. Click the Use Tables to Align Form Fields check box to let FrontPage organize your questions in table cells, for a more orderly layout (using tables for page design is covered in Chapter 9).

Figure 14-32 shows a generated form page with questions organized in a numbered list, a table of contents, and questions placed in table cells.

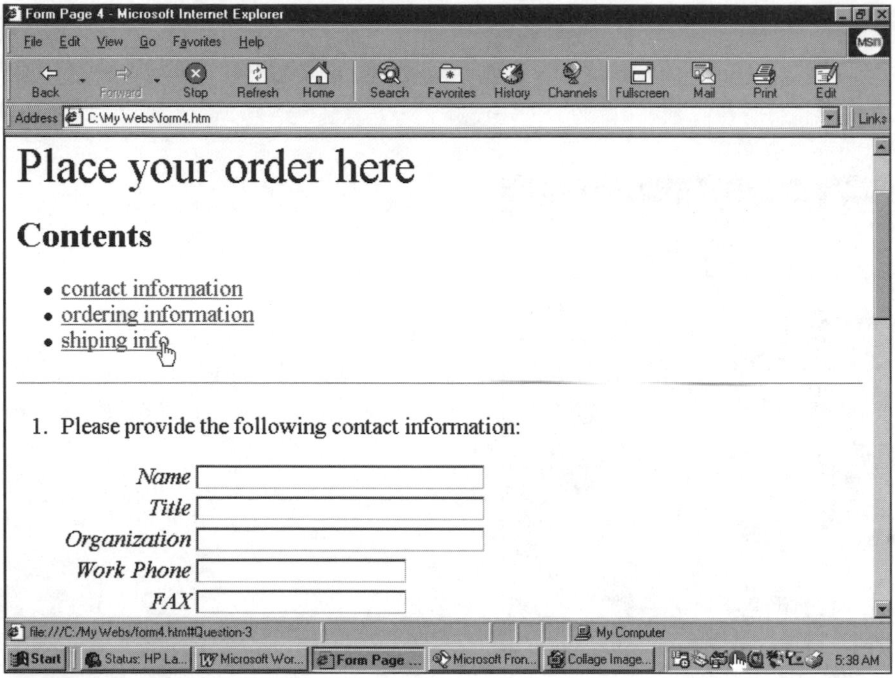

Figure 14-32: A generated form page with a table of contents — created with the Form Page Wizard.

After you define your presentation options, click the Next button to see output options.

Output options

Output options determine what happens to the data submitted in a form. The next chapter explores input-handling options in detail. For now, you can click either the Save Results to Web Page radio button, to send the input to a page that can be viewed in your browser, or the Save Results to Text File radio button, to send the results to a file that can be opened with a word processor. CGI scripts require programming, which is explained in the next chapter.

After you select an output option, click the Finish button to generate a Web page with your form. Chapter 15 explains how to view and manage information collected in forms.

Design Approaches

Well-designed input forms collect valuable information. The following approaches can be integrated into designing forms:

✦ Ask for specific information. If you want to find out what product a visitor has purchased, providing a list of radio buttons or a drop-down menu might yield more accurate information than a one-line text box.

✦ Explain to visitors why providing form information is in their interest. For example, explain to visitors who fill out a survey how their input will be used. Or, explain to visitors filling out an order form why it is important to collect all the information in the form.

✦ Keep forms as short as possible, but collect all the information that you need.

✦ Testing your own form is a good idea. After you create it, save your Web page and view it in a browser. Put yourself in the place of a visitor. Are your questions clear? Is your form design easy to follow? Does it have repetitious questions that can be avoided. In general, test, test, and test again to create a form that invites a visitor to fill it out.

In the following tutorial, you will create a feedback form that uses all five types of form fields.

Tutorial 14.1: Create a Form

1. Click the New Page tool (top-left button in the Standard toolbar) to create a new Web page.

2. Click the Save button, type **feedback.htm** in the filename field, and then click OK in the dialog box.

3. At the top of the page, type a title for the page: **Your comments on this Web site are appreciated!** Press Enter to create a new line.

4. Select Insert ➪ Form ➪ Form to create a form. Press Enter to create a line above the Submit and Reset buttons, as shown in Figure 14-33.

5. In the new, blank line in your form, type **Please rate this site**, and then type **Great**, and then press the Tab key. Type **Could Be Better**, press Tab, and then type **Poor**.

6. Click to place your insertion point right before the word Great and select Insert ➪ Form ➪ Radio Button to insert a radio button before the word Great, as shown in Figure 14-34.

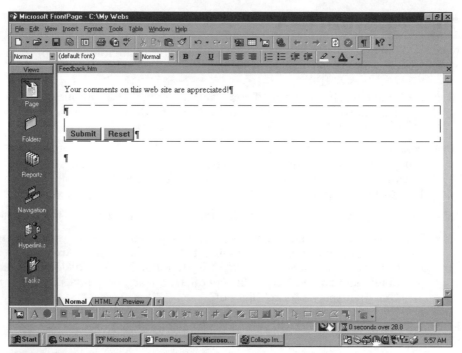

Figure 14-33: Creating a new input form

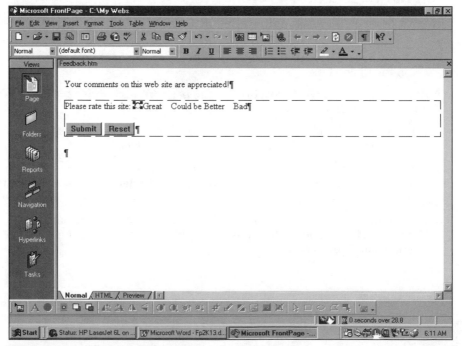

Figure 14-34: Placing a radio button

7. Double-click the radio button to open the Radio Button dialog box, and enter **Rating** in the Group Name field. Enter **3** in the Value field, and select the Not Selected radio button. You can leave the Tab Order field blank to use the default tab order, for visitors who use the Tab key to move between fields. The radio button dialog box is shown in Figure 14-35.

Figure 14-35: Defining a radio button

8. After you define the radio button, click the OK button and use the Copy and Paste tools in the toolbar to paste copies of the radio button before Could Be Better and Bad. Double-click the middle radio button and change the value to **2**. Change the value in the third radio button to **1**. Set all three radio buttons to Not Selected.

9. Place your insertion point after the word Bad, press Enter, and then type **How often do you visit this site?** Select Insert ➪ Form ➪ Drop-Down Menu from the menu bar, and double-click the (tiny) drop-down menu.

10. Type **Visits** in the Name field of the Drop-Down Menu Properties dialog box, and click the Add button. Enter **Daily** in the Choice Field and press Enter. Add **Weekly** and **Monthly** choices, as well. Leave the other options at their default settings. Your dialog box should look similar to the one in Figure 14-36. Click the OK button.

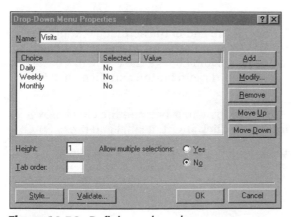

Figure 14-36: Defining a drop-down menu

11. Click to place your insertion point at the end of the drop-down menu and then press Enter. Type **Any Advice?** and then press the spacebar. Select Insert ➪ Form ➪ Scrolling Text box. Double-click the text box, change the Name to **Advice**, and press Enter. Click the right-top corner handle to stretch the box to the width of your page, so that the text box looks similar to the one in Figure 14-37.

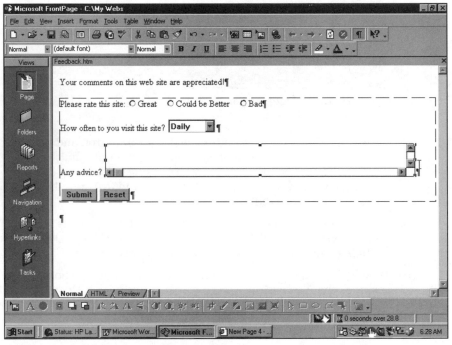

Figure 14-37: Resizing a scrolling text box

12. Place your insertion point at the end of the scrolling text box and press Enter. Select Insert ➪ Form ➪ Check Box. Press the spacebar and type **Please contact me**. Double-click the check box and change the Name to **Contact** and the Value to **Yes**. Select the Checked radio button and then click OK in the dialog box.

13. Click and drag to select both the check box and the check box text, and then select Insert ➪ Form ➪ Label. Click after the label and press Enter.

14. Type **E-mail Address** and select Insert ➪ Form ➪ One-line Text Box. Double-click the one-line text box and change the Name to **E-mail**. Click the Validate button and click the Required check box. In the Min Length field, enter **8**, because any legitimate e-mail address will be at least that long. Click the OK button in the Text Box Validation dialog box, and then in the Text Box Properties dialog box.

15. Your input form should look something like the one in Figure 14-38. Of course, if you customized the form or experimented with other options, that's fine! Apply some text formatting by selecting all the text in your form and choosing a font and font size. Save your page, and click the Preview in Browser button in the toolbar. Read and click OK in each of the dialog boxes that warn you that not all of your features are available in browsers other than IE 4.0, and that some of your features need to be published to work. In the next chapter, you'll explore how to publish forms, so that you can collect data.

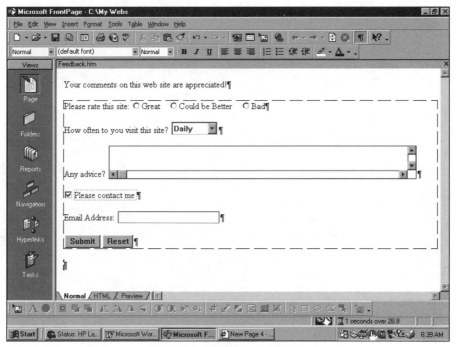

Figure 14-38: A custom-designed feedback form

16. You can experiment with entering data into your form in your browser, and using the Reset button to clear the form. In the next chapter, you'll learn to implement forms, so that you can actually collect form input.

Summary

In this chapter, you learned how to design input forms. By utilizing the different types of input fields and the different options associated with each type of field, you can enable visitors to input a wide variety of data.

In the next chapter, you'll learn to collect data that is placed in your input forms. This data can be sent to Web pages, to text documents, and to e-mail addresses. Chapter 15 also introduces some custom scripting techniques for managing input data.

✦   ✦   ✦

Working with Form Handlers

In the previous chapter, you learned to create attractive HTML input forms with FrontPage. Your form is only as useful as what you do with the information that users put in your form. This chapter looks at several methods of dealing with form input. After a brief overview of how HTML forms work, this chapter examines the built-in FrontPage form handlers, including the newly added Database handler. This chapter concludes by discussing ways that you can implement your own custom form handlers.

How HTML Forms Work

Any HTML form that you create has three basic parts:

✦ One or more input fields

✦ A means of submitting the results

✦ A program to receive, process, and record the submitted input

In the previous chapter, you learned how to create and configure the input fields in your form. You also learned how to create the special Submit button that sends the user's input back to the server. When the user clicks your Submit button, their browser packages up the form input into a series of paired values, one set for each form element. The first half of each pair is the name that you gave the form element. The second half is the value that the user entered for that element. Working with form handlers is mostly about what to do with the name/value pairs the browser sends back from your form.

In the beginning, the only real method of handling HTML form input was to attach the form to a Common Gateway Interface

(CGI) program. CGI is not a programming language. It is really no more than an agreed upon format for how a Web server can communicate with an external program. Although no longer the only way to handle forms, CGI remains a viable way to handle forms, and FrontPage enables you to link your forms to custom CGI programs.

Developing custom CGI programs is covered later in the chapter, but if you're a nonprogrammer, the good news is that FrontPage provides several standard form-handling options that you can use without having to learn CGI programming.

Form Properties

You configure your form handler by using the Form Properties dialog box. To access this dialog box, you first need a form. The Feedback Form template that comes with FrontPage is used in this section to illustrate how the Form Properties dialog box works. This form is a good example of a basic HTML form, partly because it includes an example of almost every possible HTML form element. The Feedback Form template shown in Figure 15-1 is used as-is, except for the addition of a theme and background to improve its visual appeal.

Note   For those interested, the Form Properties dialog box works by controlling the ACTION attribute of the <FORM> tag. If you insert a custom form handler (as described later in this chapter), FrontPage configures this tag in the standard fashion. All other predefined handlers are controlled by a FrontPage Component inserted in place of the standard ACTION attribute.

To designate a form handler, open the Web page containing a form, right-click anywhere inside the form and select the Form Properties item from the options menu, which displays the Form Properties dialog box (see Figure 15-2). Alternatively, you can select Insert ➪ Form ➪ Form Properties.

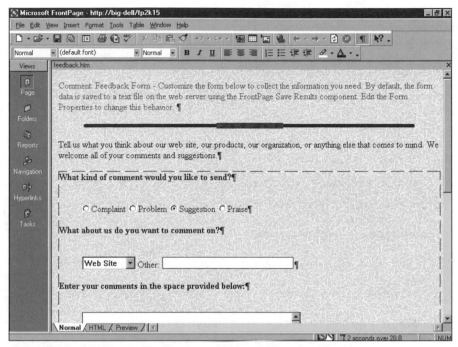

Figure 15-1: A basic Feedback Form awaiting its form handler

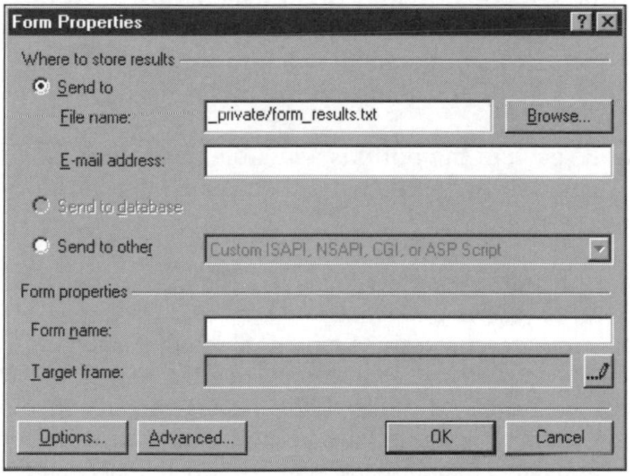

Figure 15-2: The default settings for the Feedback
Form's Form Properties dialog box

The Form Properties dialog box consists of two principal parts: a section to designate where to send the form results and a section to designate basic form properties. The Where to Store Results area of the dialog box includes:

✦ **Send To:** Click this button to send your results to either of the following:

  • **File Name:** The Feedback Form is preconfigured to send results to a text file, feedback.txt, that is created and stored in the _private folder of the current Web (see Figure 15-2).

  • **E-mail Address:** In addition to sending results to a file, you can send results to an e-mail address.

✦ **Send to Database:** New in FrontPage 2000, you can send results to a database.

✦ **Send to Other:** You can designate your own custom form handler. Selecting a form handler is as simple as clicking one of the three options and setting some basic option parameters.

The Form Properties area of the Form Properties dialog box includes:

✦ **Form Name:** Giving all of your page elements descriptive names is always a good practice. In many cases, you many never have need to use this name, but if you do any scripting of your Web pages, having the name references is helpful.

✦ **Target Frame:** You can specify a target frame for the page returned when the form is submitted (either a confirmation page or an error page). If your form page is not part of a frame set, you probably don't need to alter this property.

To learn more about frames and setting target names, refer to Chapter 10. Later in the chapter, you learn how to designate the confirmation and error pages.

The following sections describe each of the options available to you for handling form results automatically. Custom form handlers are discussed later in the chapter.

Tip   How do you know what kind of form handler to select? The answer depends on how much input you expect to receive and what you want to do with the results. Generally speaking, storing form results in some kind of file format is a good idea, if only for the purpose of logging activity to your form. Use the e-mail feature in combination with saving the results to a file if the results require an e-mail response (or if you simply want to be alerted each time that the form is submitted). Use a delimited file format or a database if you plan to do analysis of the data that is submitted. If the form results require any immediate processing, you have to create a custom form handler.

Sending results to a file

By default, all FrontPage Forms are configured to send results to a text file. This file records each field name and value in a comma-separated format. By using the Form Properties Options button, you can control the type of file to which the data is output and the quantity of information that is output. You can even save the results to two files, each with a different format.

The steps described in the following sections explain how to configure your results page.

Designate the results file

If the file already exists in the current Web, you can use the Browse button to locate the file. Otherwise, type the full path name to the file. If the file doesn't exist, FrontPage creates it the next time that you save your Web page.

Tip   Although FrontPage limits you to browsing for a results file within the current Web, the file doesn't have to reside within the Web. In fact, unless you want to make this file available for anyone to view, you are better off storing the file outside of your Web (using the _private directory, or another directory that isn't available from a Web browser).

Next, click the Options button to display the Options for Saving Results of Form dialog box. In this dialog box, you see the name of the results file that you indicated in the previous step (if you didn't provide a filename yet, you can do so here; otherwise, FrontPage will complain).

Now you are ready to configure various options for your results file.

Select a file format

FrontPage enables you to save the files either in a basic text file that is suitable for logging purposes, as an HTML file that can be made available to your Web site visitors, or in a text database file that can be imported into another application. Within these types, FrontPage allows various formatting style options. The following list describes the details of each of the available file formats:

✦ **HTML:** Displays the form input in an HTML page. If Include Field Names is checked, it creates a list of the input formatted, as follows:

> **Field_name**: Field_value

Input from scrolling text boxes is listed separately at the end of the results list. The Field name is formatted as a level-three header (<H3>), and the results are listed as a separate paragraph.

Currently, FrontPage provides limited control over where or how the HTML input is recorded on the page. (One can only hope that Microsoft gets around to implementing the HTML File function in the same way that the confirmation page works.) By default, FrontPage adds new responses to the bottom of the HTML page, making it difficult to create a page footer. However, a workaround to this exists. First, create your page without the footer. Then, test the page and submit some results. The first time that results are submitted, FrontPage adds a FormInsertHere FrontPage Component to the HTML page. Open the updated HTML page in FrontPage and add your footer after this Component. (Don't forget to remove your bogus input!)

✦ **HTML definition list:** Same as HTML just described, but formats results by using an HTML definition list. If Include Field Names is checked, results are listed as follows (note that some browsers may display definition lists differently):

>   **Field_name**
>   Field_value

✦ **HTML bulleted list:** Same as HTML, but formats results by using an HTML bulleted list. If Include Field Names is checked, results are listed as follows:

>   **Field_name**: Field_value

✦ **Formatted text within HTML:** In FrontPage terminology, "formatted text" refers to what HTML calls "preformatted text," text contained within a `<PRE>` tag. This tag was initially designed to represent text as-is, maintaining spacing, tabs, and so forth. It is typically displayed using Courier type, such as the following (note the wider tab):

```
Field_name:          Field value
```

You can use a style sheet to control the formatting of your HTML results page. For more information on using style sheets, refer to Chapter 12.

✦ **Formatted text:** Generates a text page that resembles the formatting of the HTML pages previously described. For each set of results submitted, FrontPage creates a "ruled line," composed of asterisks, and then lists elements, as with the formatted text within HTML; for example:

```
*****************************************
```

Field_name: Field_value

Note that if you inadvertently use this option within an HTML page, the elements display in one long line, because HTML ignores standard text line returns.

The Latest Results at End check box is disabled for all text file formats. (I'm sure there must be a good reason for this...)

✦ **Text Database using comma as a separator:** Records the results in a data file format that later can be imported into a spreadsheet or database application. Each result set is written in a single line, with individual fields separated by commas. All field values are marked by quotation marks (mainly so that a comma sent as part of the results is not confused for a comma separator). If the Include Field Names option is checked, the first record in the file indicates the field values. (Note that this line is written the first time that results are submitted from the form.)

✦ **Text Database using tab as a separator:** Just like the previous option, except that it uses tabs as field separators instead of commas.

✦ **Text Database using space as a separator:** Just like the previous two options, except that it uses spaces as field separators instead of commas or tabs.

Select additional file format options

Check Include Field Names to include both field names and values in your file. Uncheck this option to include only the values submitted.

If the Latest Results at End option is available, check it to append new records to the bottom of the page. Uncheck this option to have the most recent submissions appear at the top of the page. The latter format is appropriate for content that will be viewed by users, which is perhaps why this option is enabled only for the HTML formats.

Optional second file

You quite possibly might want to save the results in two different file formats. For example, you might want to log the results both to a tab-separated file that you can examine in Excel and as an HTML bulleted list that you (and, optionally, anyone else) can look at from the Web. Or, perhaps you just want to record the same information in the same format in two different files, just to be safe. You can use the Second File option to do this.

Caution

FrontPage happily lets you configure your form to submit results to the same file twice, which is great if that is what you want to do.

Sending form results via e-mail

In many instances, it is helpful to be alerted whenever anyone submits a form from your Web site. The classic example is a customer-support form, for which the expectation of a rapid response time (thanks to that old, outmoded device called a telephone) is fairly high. Assuming that FrontPage Server Extensions have been configured for your mail, sending results to an e-mail address is quite simple:

1. Right-click the form element and select Form Properties.

2. Type the e-mail address of the recipient in the E-mail Address field.

3. To specify e-mail options, click the Options button and select the E-mail Results tab.

E-mail options

As with the results file, you can specify the format of the e-mail message that is sent. All the file formats previously listed for the results file apply here as well. The chief difference is that an e-mail message always contains data for one record. Also remember that your e-mail reader must support HTML formatting if you want to receive the file in one of the HTML formats:

✦ **Include Field Names:** Check to send field names as well as the input values.

✦ **Subject Line:** Two ways exist to designate a subject line for the e-mail results:

- In the field provided, you can type what you want to appear in the subject line. For example, typing "Customer Service Web Form" causes this line to appear in the subject heading of every e-mail sent from this form.

- You can designate a form field whose contents you want to appear in the subject line. To do this, first check the Form Field check box just above the subject line and then type the field name in the subject line. When the e-mail is sent, it will contain the value of the field indicated.

✦ **Reply-to Line:** Similar to the Subject Line option, except that the default is to put a field name in the Reply-to field (assuming that you are most likely to reply to the e-mail address of the person who submitted the e-mail results). If this is what you want, leave the Form Field check box checked, and indicate the field name in the Reply-to input box. If you want to insert a static value into the Reply-to field, such as the e-mail address of the person to whom certain e-mail results get escalated, uncheck the Form Field check box and type the Reply-to value in the designated field.

When you are finished, click OK to return to Page view. If your server has not been configured to send e-mail, FrontPage warns you, as shown in Figure 15-3.

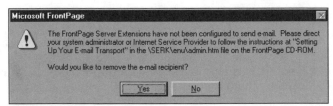

Figure 15-3: This warning appears if your server is not already configured to send e-mail.

How Do I Configure My Server Extensions to Send E-mail?

The answer to this question depends on which version of FrontPage Server Extensions you are using. If you have FrontPage 2000 Server Extensions installed, the steps required are as follows:

1. Open the Microsoft Management Console (MMC) by clicking Start ⇨ Programs ⇨ Configure Publishing Extensions.

2. Right-click the server for which you want to configure the mail server, and then select Properties from the options menu.

3. In the Options section of the Publishing tab, click the Settings button next to the item labeled Specify How Mail Should Be Sent.

4. Specify the mail server address. Optionally, indicate a Web server's mail address, which appears as the From line of any e-mail sent. The Contact address is listed in case any problems occur submitting a form via e-mail.

For more information on the MMC and how to use it, see Chapter 23 on administering server extensions.

Previous versions of FrontPage Server Extensions rely on a configuration file called frontpg.ini that, by default, resides in the Windows folder. Open this file in your favorite text editor. Entries in this configuration file are divided by port numbers.

To configure the server extensions to send e-mail, you need to add an entry to the section to specify a mail server for the particular port (or virtual server) that you are using. The line looks like this, substituting in the name of your mail server in the appropriate place:

```
SMTPHost=<name_of_your_mail_server>
```

Save the configuration file and restart your Web server. For details on other configuration options in this file, consult the Server Extension Resource Kit (SERK).

Creating a confirmation page

Recording users' input is all fine and well, but you can also reassure users that you have received their information by returning a confirmation message to them. FrontPage calls such a message a *confirmation page*.

To provide your visitors with feedback, you don't *have* to designate a confirmation page. FrontPage does this by default. As Figure 15-4 shows, the default confirmation page is adequate, although somewhat less than inspirational. Fortunately, you can easily create your own custom confirmation page that includes only the input field information that you select.

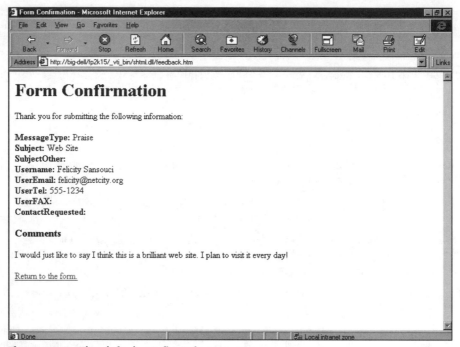

Figure 15-4: The default confirmation page

Creating a confirmation page is a simple three-step process:

1. Create the basic confirmation page, just as you would any HTML page. If you like, you can use the Confirmation Form template that FrontPage provides for this purpose (although this particular template is more useful as a sample confirmation page than as a template). Save a place for any results information that you plan to include on this page.

2. Insert any results fields that you want to include. To insert a result field, place the cursor where you want the field results to appear, and select Insert ⇨ Component ⇨ Confirmation Field. Type the name of the field whose value you want to appear on the page. Be careful to get the name correct, because FrontPage doesn't have any way to check with you. (If the name of the field rather than its value shows up on the confirmation page, you probably got the name wrong somewhere.) Save your results when you are done.

3. Attach your custom page to your form page. To do this, open the form page, select Form Properties (as described earlier), select the Confirmation Page tab, and type or select the name of your confirmation file. Does this file have to be in the current Web? You can designate a filename before you create the file, but in this case, FrontPage doesn't create a file. It simply creates the link to the file and complains that the file doesn't exist.

Tip

The Confirmation Page dialog box indicates that you should provide the file URL. However, you can also store the file outside of your Web site document directory and link to it by using the full path name of the file.

Creating a validation error page

In the previous chapter, you learned how to configure validation properties on HTML form fields. Here's a quick review. To set validation options for a given field, right-click the field and select Form Field Validation (you can also select Form Field Properties and click the Validate button in the properties dialog box). Select the validation options that you want, and click OK to return to Page view.

When you designate validation requirements, FrontPage adds a Validation Component to the page. When a visitor to your site requests the page, FrontPage replaces the Component with script functions (what kind of script depends on how you have configured your default scripting languages in the Advanced tab of Web Settings) that correspond to the requirements that you designated. If the visitor fails to complete a field validly, by default, the page displays a dialog box indicating the error.

But, what if the user doesn't have a JavaScript-enabled browser, or does but has disabled the use of JavaScript? This is where the Validation Error page comes into play. By default, FrontPage returns a page that indicates the nature of the validation error (see Figure 15-5).

Using the Confirmation tab, you can designate your own Validation Error page. You can use this option to include a somewhat more sophisticated Validation Error page.

Tip

You can include a special confirmation field to return the same bulleted list of validation errors that you see in the default Validation Error page. Select Insert ⇨ Component ⇨ Confirmation Field, and type **Validation-Error** as the name.

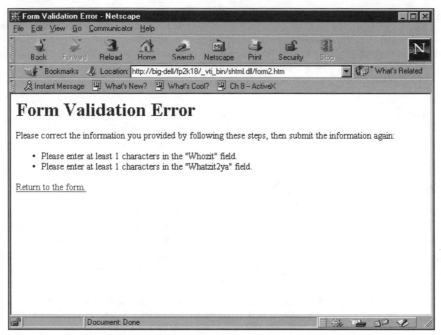

Figure 15-5: The default Validation Error page, showing error messages returned — bad grammar and all.

Selecting fields to save

The last tab in the Form Properties Options dialog box is the Saved Fields tab. You use this tab to customize which fields are recorded to a file or e-mailed to the designated recipient. You can also use this tab to include additional information in each response.

By default, FrontPage includes the name of every form element in the list of fields to record (with the exception of Reset buttons). This means that, by default, FrontPage records the value of the Submit button, which doesn't change under most circumstances. To add, edit, or delete a field name from the list, simply type the name as you would in a text field. Cut and Paste shortcut keys are enabled. Fields are recorded in the order that they appear in this list, so you can change the order to suit your needs.

The Saved Fields tab also enables you to add one or more informational fields to each record. These include:

✦ Date

✦ Time

✦ Remote Computer Name

✦ User Name

✦ Browser Type

Tip   One circumstance in which you might actually want to record the value of the Submit button is if you have several similar forms to submit to the same file. In this case, you could use different Submit button values to record which form has been submitted (of course, you could also use hidden fields to do this).

Creating a Multistep Form

Nobody likes to fill out a long form. In cases where developers have no alternative but to provide a long form, some developers prefer a long, scrolling form, divided into clear sections to guide the user through the input process. Others prefer to divide the form into multiple pages, something like the way wizards function in the Microsoft Windows world. If you are one of the latter, read on.

Because of a known bug in FrontPage's form handling, trying to set up a multiform submission process can be a little tricky. (Frankly, I think if you are savvy enough to understand the work-around to this problem, you can probably write your own custom form handler.)

Here's the problem. When the user submits the first form, the next page that you want them to see is the confirmation page, containing the second form. Unfortunately, when you try to set this up, FrontPage goes ahead and *submits* the form on the second page (which, of course, isn't completed) and returns instead the confirmation page of the second form. (If this also happens to have a form element, the process simply repeats.)

Microsoft's official work-around to this condition (notice that I am taking no responsibility for this) is to set up the confirmation page to do an automatic redirect to the second page of the form. Before the second page loads, the user first sees the real confirmation page, which might contain a cheerful message like, "One moment please while we process your information..." (which is *not* what you are doing, but is probably more palatable as an explanation than the truth, "One moment please while I work-around a known bug in FrontPage, to make you fill out yet another form page...").

This approach has two problems. First, this requires a modicum of scripting to pull off, which you might regard as counter to the reason why you are using the built-in form handler in the first place. Second, passing information from one page to the next using the Confirmation Field Component becomes somewhat trickier. It can be done, but my advice is to use a custom mechanism, if this is what you are trying to achieve.

Adding Results to a Database

The latest addition to FrontPage's automatic form handlers is the ability to send the results directly to a database file. This is a very useful handler, but if you are planning to connect your Web to a database, you probably are going to want to explore using Active Server Pages to help maximize your use of the data.

To activate this database-file option, right-click your form and select Form Properties. Select the Send to Database option and then click Options to configure the database connection.

Caution   To use the database handler, you must have the current version of FrontPage Server Extensions installed on your Web server. You also must have Active Server Pages extensions installed. If the database handler option is grayed out on your dialog box, you probably don't have one or the other of these installed. (See Chapter 23, "FrontPage Server Administration," for more information on FrontPage Server Extensions.)

Creating a database

If you don't have an existing database that you are working with, FrontPage will generate a simple database that corresponds to your form elements.

Click the Create Database button. FrontPage creates a new Access database, with an .mdb extension. By default, FrontPage stores the database in an fpbd folder of your Web. FrontPage then creates a table in the database, connecting fields with names that match the form fields you have created.

Updating a database

What happens if you make a change to your form after you create your database? You can use the Update Database button to modify your database to reflect any new fields that you have added.

Using an existing database

In most cases, after you design your form, letting FrontPage create your database is the simplest option. However, this isn't always an option, so FrontPage also lets you manually map your form fields to a database. This is a three-step process:

1. Create a connection to this database within FrontPage.

2. Connect this database to the form.

3. Designate a mapping between each form field that you want to capture and the field names in the database.

Caution I don't believe that fields can be saved to more than one table. If the fields that you need to save span multiple tables, you have to create a new table to store the data temporarily, and then use database functions to copy the data to its appropriate places.

Adding database connections

You can connect your form to one of three types of databases:

✦ A database that is located within the current Web

✦ A database that is already configured as an ODBC data source

✦ A network database

Testing Form Results

Configuring your form handler is so easy in FrontPage that you many be lulled into thinking that you don't need to worry about testing it. But plenty of things can go wrong, or at least produce unexpected results.

To test your form results handler, you need to use the File ➪ Preview in Browser feature. If you attempt to test the page in Preview mode, you will notice a message saying, "This page contains elements that may need to be saved or published to preview correctly." Translated, that message means that the Preview mode cannot handle form submission.

Before examining custom form handlers, the following tutorial reviews what you have learned thus far. In this tutorial, you create a standard guest book application by using the Guest Book template as your starting point. The Guest Book template is set up to record input to a separate file that is then included on the guest book page. Each time the page is reloaded, any newly submitted results are added to the page.

Tutorial 15.1: Create a Guest Book

1. Open FrontPage, select New ➪ Page, and select the Guest Book template (see Figure 15-6).

2. Add a Theme to your guest book page to give it a bit of life.

3. The template provides only a single input field for comments. You want to capture a bit more information from the user, so add a Name and an E-mail field.

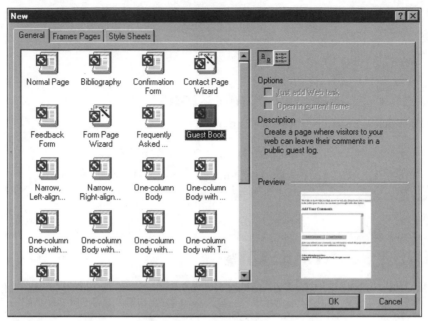

Figure 15-6: Starting a Guest Book template

4. To make sure that guests actually complete all fields, configure the Form Validation properties for each of the form fields. Set each of the text box fields to no constraints between 1 and 100 characters. Set the Comment field to no constraints and a required length between 1 and 500 characters. Give each validation element a Display Name, which is the name that appears in the error message when the form is not correctly completed.

5. Configure the results display. You want to display the field values without the field names. Right-click the form and select the Form Properties dialog box. Note that the template has already designated a filename, guestlog.htm, as the results page. Leave this as it is. Click Options, and in the File Results tab, select HTML as the file format, and uncheck both the Include Field Name and Latest Results at End options.

6. Click the Saved Fields tab. First, verify that all three fields — GuestName, GuestEmail, and Comments — are included in the list of fields to be recorded, as shown in Figure 15-7. Select a format to display the time and date that the guest comment was sent. Uncheck all other options.

7. Test your guest book.

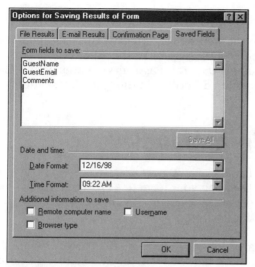

Figure 15-7: The Saved Fields tab, displayed in the Options for Saving Results of Form dialog box

Other Form Handlers

The Form Properties dialog box also enables you to select alternative form handlers for your results. To select an alternative form handler, check the Send To Other radio button in the Form Properties dialog box and pick the appropriate handler from the list. Three options are available, which are described next.

The Registration Component

The Registration Component serves the specialized purpose of allowing users to register with a username and a password, to enable them to access password-protected Webs. Forms that use the Registration Component must be saved to the root Web of a FrontPage Web server.

The Discussion Component

The FrontPage Discussion Component is also a specialized form handler, designed to store messages that are input from a discussion form. The Discussion Component stores each message as an HTML page, and adds the page to a discussion table of contents, arranged according to messages and their responses.

Custom scripts

Custom scripts, or programs, run on the Web server and can utilize form data in any number of ways (including replicating the actions of the other FrontPage form handlers for systems that are not running the FrontPage Server Extensions). The various types of custom form handlers are described in the following section.

Developing Custom Form Handlers

In case the built-in FrontPage form handlers don't meet your needs, you can also use the Form Properties dialog box to attach your form to a custom form handler. Several types of custom form handlers are available that you can use, the most common of which are discussed in this section.

Even though Microsoft has done a good job of anticipating the basic form-handling needs, the following are several situations in which you might consider a custom form handler:

✦ Your Web server doesn't have FrontPage Server Extensions, and you don't have the option of using the built-in form handling features.

✦ You need functionality that isn't provided by any of the built-in form handlers.

✦ You need functionality that can be used across multiple Web server platforms and configurations.

✦ You are the do-it-yourself type.

If any of the preceding fits your situation, then you probably need to keep reading. If not, you can safely move on to another chapter.

CGI form handlers

In the early days of the Web, writing a Common Gateway Interface (CGI) application was really the only way that you could add form-handling functionality to your Web.

CGI programming languages

CGI is not a programming language. It is a standard for how information should be passed from a Web server to an external program, and how the external program should pass information back to the server. CGI's name is derived as follows:

✦ **Common:** CGI is *common* not because it is low-class, but because it is a defined standard that uses a basic data-passing mechanism, one to which all good Web servers adhere.

✦ **Gateway:** CGI is a *gateway* interface because the program that you write serves as a gateway between the Web environment and any other application (a database, for instance) that you might want to send Web data to or return data from. In many cases, of course, the CGI application serves as an end unto itself.

✦ **Interface:** CGI is an *interface* because it defines how two separate entities — the Web server and your program — can communicate with one another.

A CGI application can be written in any programming language that can run on the same system as your Web server. Some of the more common programming languages used to create CGI applications include:

✦ **Perl:** Perhaps the most commonly used CGI programming language, Perl is an acronym for *Practical Extraction and Report Language*. Perl was originally written for UNIX and ported to Windows and Macintosh, and is perhaps the most portable CGI language (besides C). Perl is an *interpreted* language, which means that the source code is read and interpreted when the Perl program is run (as opposed to being *compiled*, like a C program, beforehand).

✦ **Visual Basic:** The most popular Windows programming language, VB applications are also fairly simple to implement.

✦ **C/C++:** C programming language are reputedly harder to learn than languages such as VB and Perl, and so you see fewer freely available C-based CGI programs. Because it is a compiled language, C typically produces faster CGI code than most other languages.

✦ **Java:** Although Java is more commonly used to write applets that run inside a Web page (see Chapter 20 for more detail), as a cross-platform programming language, Java is perfectly suitable for CGI programming as well.

CGI pros and cons

The choice of which programming language to use depends on several factors, including the scope and complexity of the task, time and budget constraints, and who you enlist to do the work and what their experience is. Ultimately, any one of the programming languages just listed produces serviceable CGI code.

The chief virtues of a CGI application are that it can be written in any of a variety of programming languages, and that the CGI interface specification itself is very easy to understand and use. As a standard, CGI is supported by practically all commercial Web servers.

One disadvantage of a CGI application is that it is relatively slow and can be a drag on system resources, particularly if you have a CGI application that is frequently invoked by many people simultaneously. The server has to start a separate instance of the CGI application for each user, pass the data back and forth, and then close the application when it is finished.

Another limitation of CGI is that it can only be invoked via the server. (Note that sometimes this is actually an advantage.) This means that to process any information, the CGI application must have the information submitted via an HTML form. As soon as the CGI application processes the information that it receives and returns its response, it is done. This creates a challenge for any application involving multiple transactions by a user, because as far as the CGI is concerned, each time that the user calls the application, it is the first time.

POST versus GET

A few simple CGI examples are coming up, but before you delve into the details, you need to understand the basic principles of how a Web server sends form input to a CGI application.

Basically, two methods exist by which the server can send form input to an external, "gateway" application. These two methods are called GET and POST.

Note GET and POST are part of the larger HTTP specification. If you are interested in the nitty-gritty details of this specification, check out `http://www.ics.uci.edu/pub/ietf/http/rfc1945.html`.

The POST method of submitting input is preferred. POST instructs the server to output the form data to *standard input (STDIN)*, a well-known repository that the CGI program can monitor and, when data comes in, from which it can pick up data. In addition, the POST method sets a variable called `CONTENT_LENGTH` that tells the CGI program how long the string of text is that it wants to pick up. One of the chief virtues of the POST method is that the data is passed "behind the scenes," transparent to the user. Only HTML forms are capable of invoking the POST method.

The GET method is more of a general-purpose method for handling data than is POST. GET is not as powerful or elegant as POST, perhaps, but it is serviceable in certain circumstances. GET can be used to send form data, or it can be invoked directly from a URL. For this reason, GET is limited to a maximum length of 255 characters.

With the GET method, form input data is attached to the URL itself before being sent to the server. The basic format for a GET URL is as follows:

```
http://www.myserver.com/cgi-bin/
myhandler.cgi?name=david&rank=101&serialno=345
```

Data is separated from the body of the URL by a question mark (?). Data elements are separated by ampersands (&), and each data element consists of a name/value pair, linked by an equals sign (=). The CGI application receives the data portion of this URL in a variable called QUERY_STRING.

Armed with the preceding information, you are ready to configure an HTML form to work with a custom form handler. But first you need a form handler, so you create one in the next section.

A simple Perl CGI

A typical CGI program performs several basic functions, including:

✦ Determines whether data is submitted via GET or POST

✦ Parses the data input into name/value pair variables

✦ Processes and/or stores the data input in a useful format

✦ Returns an appropriate response to the user via the Web server

Your Perl script, simplecgi.pl, doesn't do anything fancy, but it does illustrate each of these steps. A complete discussion of Perl is beyond the scope of this chapter, but the next four sections point out some of the salient parts of the program.

Note   You can find a copy of this script on the CD-ROM that comes with this book.

Parsing the data

This section of the script, contained in a subroutine called parseResults(), is the most complicated. parseResults() first determines whether the results have come from a GET or a POST method, and then obtains the results string from the appropriate place:

```
$contentLength  = $ENV{'CONTENT_LENGTH'};
$requestMethod = $ENV{'REQUEST_METHOD'};
    if ($requestMethod eq 'GET') {
      $resultString = $ENV{'QUERY_STRING'};
    }
  elsif ($requestMethod eq 'POST') {
    read(STDIN, $resultString, $contentLength);
    }
```

After this, parseResults() massages the results string, placing the data in an associative array (%results) that makes the data relatively easy to work with.

Running Perl on Windows

Before you can run a Perl script on your Windows 95 or NT Web server, you need to perform several preliminary steps (or have a system administrator perform them for you):

1. Obtain a copy of the Perl for Windows executable. The most commonly used version of Perl for Windows is available from ActiveState at its Web site, www.activestate.com.

2. Install Perl in an appropriate and secure location (see the section on scripting security in this chapter), not in a directory that is Web-accessible.

3. Configure your Web server to recognize Perl scripts and associate them with the Perl application.

Perl is a flexible and powerful programming language, and the one thing that you don't want to do is to put the executable someplace where any Web user could have access to it. Under no circumstances should you place the executable in the cgi-bin directory of your Web server or in any other directory that has been set up to execute CGI scripts. To do so would open a gaping security hole in your system.

Instead, you should place Perl executables in a location that isn't directly accessible from a Web browser, but is somewhere that the server can find the Perl when it needs to. Two approaches can be used to do this, mentioned next, with a focus on the second:

Option 1: Create a shell, or wrapper program, that sends the appropriate information to the Perl executable. This approach is safer because it filters out any of the nasty things that someone might do by accessing Perl directly. This wrapper program can be created as a batch file (a not-so-great idea) or as a Visual Basic or C program (a better idea). For more information on how to do this, see the LoboSoft site.

Option 2: Associate Perl scripts with perl.exe in the Windows Registry. This approach is the official Microsoft explanation for setting up Perl with Internet Information Server (IIS). An equivalent explanation isn't provided for PWS, but it seems to work just fine. This method requires making a change to your system registry information, so you should be comfortable with editing the registry before trying this. The basic steps:

1. Open the Registry database by using RegEdit.

2. Navigate to HKEY_LOCAL_MACHINE::System::CurrentControlSet::Services::W3Svc::Parameters::ScriptMap.

3. Right-click in the right side and select New ⇨ String value.

4. Enter **.pl**.

5. Right-click the string value that you just created and select Modify.

6. Enter the full path to the Perl executable; for example, **C:\perl\bin\perl.exe**.

7. Add a space and **%s** after the path name; for example, **C\perl\bin\perl.exe %s**.

8. Close the Registry.

Saving the data

After it has parsed the form input, simplecgi.pl proceeds to write the field values to a file. The path and name of this file are held in the variable $logfile, which you can configure to point to a valid file. The log writing is performed in the &saveResults() subroutine. This routine is not particularly flexible, although you can configure the field separator (a comma, by default) by changing the value of the $FS variable. Only field values are written to the file.

Returning the data

Finally, a simple confirmation page is returned. The HTML for this page is formulated by the Perl program. The data-results display is formatted in a separate subroutine, which makes changing the formatting relatively easy. Even if you are not familiar with Perl commands, you should recognize that this section of the &returnResults() subroutine is primarily standard HTML:

```
   $resultsHTML = <<"returnHTML";
<HTML>
<HEAD>
<TITLE>$title</TITLE>
</HEAD>
<BODY BGCOLOR=#FFFFFF>
<H1>$title</H1>
$fResults
</BODY>
</HTML>
returnHTML
```

Configuring a custom CGI handler

With your simple CGI form handler ready to go, it is finally time to create and configure a form to send data to your custom handler. Note that to make this work, you need to make sure that Perl is installed and running on your server, and that you have a scripts directory (typically either scripts or cgi-bin) that is configured to permit the execution of programs such as simplecgi.pl. (Even if you can't run the script, however, you can still follow the steps necessary to configure the form.)

1. Create a form. (Because simplecgi.pl is completely generic, you can create any number of form fields; see Figure 15-8 for an example.)

2. Right-click the form element and select Form Properties from the options menu.

3. Select the Send To Other option and select Custom ISAPI, NSAPI, CGI, or ASP script.

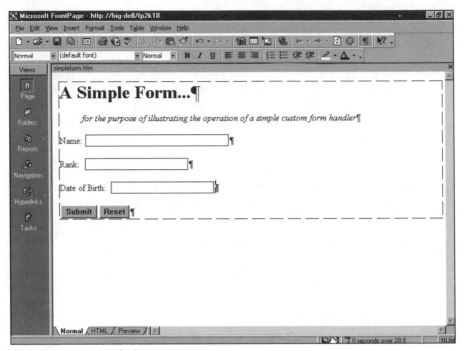

Figure 15-8: A simple form

4. Click the Options button to bring up the Options for Custom Form Handler dialog box.

5. Set the Action field to the URL for the script file; for example, **/scripts/simplecgi.pl**.

6. Set the Method field to POST (the default).

7. Leave the Encoding Type field blank (the default, application/x-www-form-urlencoded, is fine in most cases).

8. Click OK to return to the Form Properties dialog box. Click OK again to return to Page view.

9. Save the form and preview it. (Don't forget that you may need to change the name of the log file in the Perl script. To do this, open the script in your favorite text editor and adjust the $logfile variable to suit.) When you submit the form, you should see results that resemble Figure 15-9.

10. Check the log file to see whether the input values are recorded there as well.

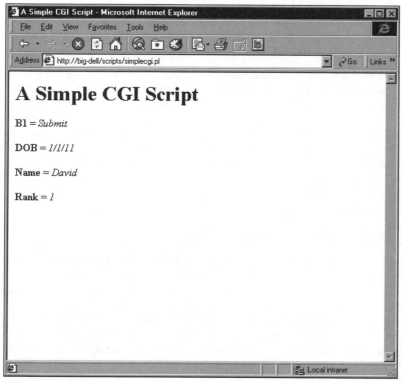

Figure 15-9: Results of a simple form, processed by your custom Perl script

Security precautions with CGI

If you plan to use any CGI programs on your Web site, you need to be aware of the potential security problems that running scripts can present. Any time that you introduce programming elements onto your site, you open up a potential entrance to your computer system. This is not intended to scare you away from using scripts — only to alert you to the need to take precautions. The following is general advice to help avoid problems. It applies as well to any type of custom form handlers.

✦ **Keep program executables out of public directories.** By definition, your scripts directory must allow general access to execute programming. For this reason, placing the Perl.exe interpreter in this, or any accessible directory, is incredibly dangerous. See the earlier sidebar, "Running Perl on Windows," for directions on how to avoid this.

✦ **Limit access to script directories.** For similar reasons, make sure that you or your system administrator has turned off Read access on your script directories. Visitors have no reason to browse this directory. It is enough that they can execute scripts.

✦ **Control the functionality of scripts.** Although the simplecgi.pl script that has been used to illustrate some basic CGI principles has nothing intrinsically dangerous about it, it isn't a particularly intelligent script, partly because it doesn't sufficiently trap for errors. Equally important, it doesn't sufficiently limit its own functionality. It has nothing to prevent someone with Web access to create a form with hundreds or thousands of fields, fill each field with volumes of text, and then point their form at your script. The result would probably not be amusing. A good CGI script should check the authenticity of the form that calls it.

NSAPI and ISAPI form handlers

CGI programs are relatively simple to create, and they function adequately under normal circumstances. Because CGI programs are separate programs from the server, however, they have several limitations. Each time that they are invoked, they have to be started. Likewise, when they finish their task, they have to be stopped. Also, because CGI programs run in their own memory space, if 100 people request a script simultaneously, the Web server has to start 100 copies of the program, which can quickly eat up system resources on heavily used sites. NSAPI and ISAPI form handlers are an attempt to overcome some of the limitations inherent in CGI.

NSAPI stands for *Netscape Application Programming Interface*. ISAPI, Microsoft's equivalent to NSAPI, stands for *Internet Server Application Programming Interface*. Although they differ in particulars, both of these entities define methods by which a programmer can construct a CGI-like application that is loaded within the memory space of the Web server. In this fashion, all the previously mentioned limitations of CGI programs are largely overcome.

Note   FrontPage Server Extensions for Internet Information Server are an example of ISAPI applications.

So, why doesn't everybody just use these API-based handlers if they are so great? In the first place, they are much more difficult to write than a standard CGI applications. In all but the most complex situations, the time and cost involved to create them isn't worth using them. Secondly, this type of handler is highly Web-server dependent, as witnessed by the fact that Netscape and Microsoft Web servers have separate APIs.

ASP form handlers

You can also use an Active Server Page to handle form processing and responses. ASP is covered in more detail in Chapter 18, so if you are unfamiliar with the ASP concept, you may want to take a look at some of the general information in Chapter 18 before you try to digest this section. This section, which assumes that you have some basic familiarity with ASP, simply illustrates two ways in which ASP can provide a relatively uncomplicated method of implementing custom form handlers.

Caution   To use Active Server Pages as form handlers, you first need to ensure that the ASP extension is installed on your Web server.

Using ASP in a confirmation page

If you have read the CGI section of this chapter, you know that form input comes to the server either via the GET method or the POST method. ASP has two constructions to access the data in each of these methods. Using one of these constructs, you can easily create a custom confirmation page that includes input from the submitted form, just as you did earlier with the help of the FrontPage Confirmation Field Component.

Accessing GET method input

Data from a GET request is stored in the ASP `Request.QueryString()` collection. To identify a particular GET request field, insert the field name as a parameter in this object. For example, if you want to retrieve the value of the Name field in your form, you would write **"Request.QueryString("Name")"**.

Accessing POST method input

Data from a POST request is stored in the ASP `Request.Form()` collection. As with the GET method request, you identify a particular form field value by inserting the field name as a parameter to this object. So, if you want to retrieve the value of the Name field in your form, you would write, **"Request.Form("Name")"**.

Accessing general input

ASP also supports a general-purpose way to identify request input, using the `Request()` collection. If, for example, you want to retrieve input from a Name field, but you are not sure whether the input will come from, you can use the use the `Request("Name")` syntax. This looks through each `Request` collection, in turn, until it finds a Name variable.

Creating a simple ASP confirmation page

Armed with the preceding information, you can fairly easily create an ASP page that handles either type of input, much as you did in the simplecgi.pl Perl script described earlier. The final confirmation page, used in conjunction with the simple form page that you developed in the CGI section, looks like this:

```
<HTML>
<HEAD>
<TITLE>A Simple ASP Program</TITLE>
</HEAD>
<BODY BGCOLOR=#FFFFFF>
<% method = Request.ServerVariables("REQUEST_METHOD")
name = Request ("Name")
 rank = Request ("Rank")
 dob = Request ("DOB")
%>
<%
 Response.Write("This is a "+ method + " request method.<P>")
 Response.Write("<B>Name</B> = <I>" + name + "</I><P>")
 Response.Write("<B>Rank</B> = <I>" + rank + "</I><P>")
 Response.Write("<B>DOB</B> = <I>" +dob + "</I><P>")
 %>
</BODY>
</HTML>
```

Although this ASP file doesn't have exactly the same general functionality as the earlier Perl script, you may be surprised by how much less code is required to accomplish effectively the same task.

Using ASP to read and write files

The capability to return to users the form data that they submitted is useful, but it isn't really sufficient to be considered form handling. To be complete, your ASP handler also needs to be able to write the data that it receives. Without going into detail, the following is sample ASP code that opens, appends text to, and then closes a log file:

```
<%
Dim fs, a
Set fs = CreateObject("Scripting.FileSystemObject")
Set a = fs.OpenTextFile("c:\temp\logfile.txt", 8, True)
a.writeLine("This is a test")
a.Close
%>
```

Summary

In this chapter and the previous one, you learned to design, create, and enable HTML forms. You have witnessed the capabilities of the built-in FrontPage form handlers, and you have caught a glimpse of the larger world of custom form handlers available with some amount of programming. The next chapter applies what you have learned about forms and form handling to a Web devoted to fostering interactive communication among users. Chapter 17 examines in detail the Discussion Web, shows you how to use the Discussion Web Wizard, and explains how to extend a Discussion Web beyond the basics. It also looks at another communication capability built into FrontPage channels.

✦　　✦　　✦

Animation and Multimedia

This chapter explores ways of adding multimedia to your Web page with FrontPage. As a side effect, it also serves as a primer in Web-based multimedia formats, from relatively simple GIF animations to more sophisticated animation, audio, and video techniques. A single chapter can't cover all the possible multimedia formats available, or even the major ones in great detail. The chapter is primarily an introduction to the possibilities. It won't turn you into an overnight multimedia developer, but it can help you to recognize the key types of multimedia currently available, and to understand what is involved in producing and delivering them.

Using Animated GIF Files

An *animated GIF file* is a sequence of GIF images that have been collected into a single GIF file. As mentioned in Chapter 7, the GIF image format is a convenient cross-platform format for transferring graphics. In its recent incarnations, the GIF format enables you to embed multiple images in a single file. It is this ability to include many images in a single file that enables the GIF file format to store *animated* images.

The set of images in an animated GIF file work like the frames in a movie. When displayed in sequence, they create the illusion of motion, or animation. When you create an animated GIF from many individual images, you define how long each single image displays, and what transition effects will occur when the next image appears. The effect is similar to what you get when you draw several images in the lower-right corner of a notebook and flip the pages.

How Animated GIFs Were Born

Initially, the main reason GIF files were designed to hold multiple images was *compressibility*. If you have five images that repeat much of the same graphical information, putting all five images in a single file, so that you can store the common information only once, is more efficient than storing them in five separate files. The GIF format was not initially intended for animations, but some smart folks soon realized that if the format was convenient for storing the information, that information also could be read out and the images played like a sequence of movie frames. Thus, more or less, the concept of GIF animation was born.

When animated GIF files display in normal Page view, you see only the first frame in the animation. When you place an animated GIF file in a Web site, and then view that site through your browser, the image becomes animated. You can also experience animated GIFs by using the Preview tab in Page view.

Note

Simple animations have become ubiquitous on the Web, thanks largely to the spread of advertising banners among commercial sites. Animations are a relatively simple, low-bandwidth way to add life to your Web pages and to draw a reader's attention to particular elements on the Web page.

Inserting animated GIFs

The easiest way to incorporate animated GIF files into your Web site is to use someone else's animated GIF file. FrontPage comes with several animated GIF files in the Clip Art Gallery, and Microsoft's online Clip Gallery Live has a much larger selection of animated GIFs. You can use files from either of these sources to include in your Web site, or to deconstruct to learn animation techniques.

To insert an animated GIF from Microsoft's Clip Art Gallery, follow these steps:

1. With a Web site open, in Page view, select Insert ➪ Picture ➪ Clip Art. The Clip Art Gallery appears.

2. If you are connected to the Internet, you can use the Clips Online button at the top of the Gallery to jump to Microsoft's online clip art collection, Clip Gallery Live. After reading the reasonable agreement (that allows you to use the images in your own Web site under most circumstances), click the Motion tab in the Clip Gallery Live. You'll see a large selection of animated GIFs dancing, moving, and putting on their show. These animated images can be saved to your local computer. Or, you can click the Motion Clips tab in the FrontPage Clip Art Gallery to choose from a selection of animated clip art on your computer. Insert clip art from the Gallery by clicking an image and then clicking the Insert Clip button in the pop-up menu, as shown in Figure 16-1.

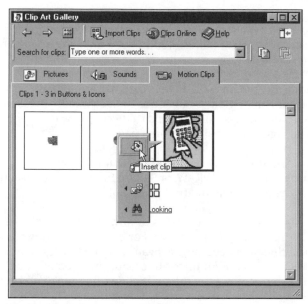

Figure 16-1: Inserting a GIF animation is as easy as inserting a standard image file.

3. You can preview your animation in the Preview tab of Page view.

4. Some, but not all, picture properties for an animated GIF can be edited in the Picture Properties dialog box. Right-click the image and select Picture Properties to open the dialog box. Picture type options are grayed out, because you can't change the file type of an animated GIF (JPEG images do not support animation).

Tip

Inserting multiple copies of the same graphic in a Web page, or even on the same Web, is a good way to conserve bandwidth. A given image is downloaded only once from the Web server. Any subsequent copy of the image is taken from your browser's local cache, resulting in negligible download times under reasonable circumstances.

Preparing images for animation

Animated images can range from a blinking bullet icon to an elaborate video production, the latter of course taking much more time and work, and adding much more download time to a page. In either case, creating an animated GIF is a two-step process:

1. Create one or more images to use in an animation.

2. Add the images as frames in an animated GIF. This procedure is explained in an upcoming section, "Adding Images to Frames."

Note   An animation can be constructed using just one image. By placing a single image in different locations in different frames, you can use an animation to create the illusion that the object is moving.

The first step in creating an animated GIF is to create the individual picture(s) that will combine to become an animation. Using fewer images results in a smaller, faster-loading animated GIF, whereas animations that compress dozens or hundreds of images into a GIF can significantly slow down a page.

The images that you create don't have to be in GIF file format. For example, you can use Microsoft Image Composer, CorelDRAW, or Adobe Photoshop to create images, and then simply copy them into an animation program.

One way to examine this process "in reverse" is to download one of the animated GIFs available at the Microsoft Clip Gallery Live. For example, we downloaded an animated GIF showing a duckling becoming a swan. The next section of this chapter explains how to use Microsoft's GIF Animator to create (or open existing) animated GIFs. But, for now, an examination of the different slides that make up this animated GIF should be helpful to you. The image is deconstructed into slides in Figure 16-2.

Figure 16-2: Animated GIFs are composed of two or more alternating images.

Tutorial 16.1, at the end of this section, examines one very simple trick for creating images to use in an animation.

Animating with GIF Animator

Microsoft GIF Animator, shown in Figure 16-3, is one of the easiest to use tools for packaging images into an animated GIF. GIF Animator is bundled with FrontPage 2000. Unfortunately, if you obtained FrontPage 2000 as part of Office 2000, your version of FrontPage may not include GIF Animator. However, Microsoft currently lets you download GIF Animator free. Links to download sites for GIF Animator can be found at

```
http://softseek.mdonline.net/Internet/Web_Publishing_Tools/Animatio
n_and_Drawing/Review_6764_index.html
```

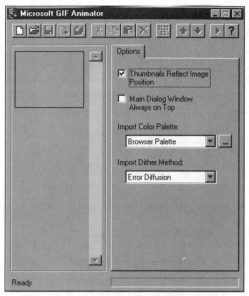

Figure 16-3: You can copy images into GIF
Animator to create an animated image.

Adding images to frames

With GIF Animator downloaded, you can copy any image into a frame. To do this,
split your screen into two windows, so that the program containing your images is
in one window, and GIF Animator is visible in another.

With both your source images and GIF Animator visible onscreen, drag images into
frames of GIF Animator, as shown in Figure 16-4.

After you place all of your images in GIF Animator frames (in the order in which
they will display), save the *entire set* of files as one animated GIF file. To save an
animated GIF in GIF Animator:

1. Click the Save button in the GIF Animator toolbar.

2. Use the Save In drop-down list to navigate to the folder in which you want to
   save your animated GIF.

3. Enter a filename in the File Name box. Note that the Save As Type drop-down
   list has but one option, CompuServe GIF (*.gif). Click Save.

Your animated GIF is now saved and ready to be placed in a Web page. However,
you first need to define and test transition attributes between slides, the subject of
the next several sections.

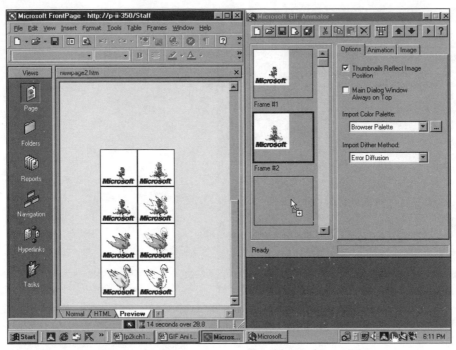

Figure 16-4: Dragging a third image into a GIF Animator frame

Defining Animation Options

The Options tab of the GIF Animator dialog box controls how the program itself displays, and how to handle image colors. The following describes the result of checking the two check boxes located on the top half of the Options tab:

✦ **Thumbnails Reflect Image Position:** Enables you to see your slides (thumbnails) with images located within the slides in the position they will assume as the animation is run. This is very helpful, for example, if your animation involves an image moving from right to left, or up to down, within the overall viewing area of the image.

✦ **Main Dialog Window Always on Top:** Keeps the GIF Animator window on "top" of any other program that you have open when both programs are sharing your screen. This prevents parts of the GIF Animator window from slipping behind other programs as you drag images into frames.

The following Import options, located on the bottom half of the Options tab, control how GIF Animator handles color palettes for the pictures that you drag into frames. GIF Animator converts images to GIF files, and assigns color palettes to them that are compatible with Web browsers.

✦ **Import Color Palette:** By default, set to generate a single Browser Palette for all of your slides. The Optimal option generates separate color palettes for each slide, which increases file size but maintains truer colors. Use this option only if your images have hundreds of colors that you want to maintain as precisely as possible, at the cost of slower download times. If you have a custom color palette in PAL file format, you can click the Open button next to the Import Color Palette drop-down list and assign that palette.

✦ **Import Dither Method:** Defines the way that GIF Animator reduces the total number of colors in an image that has more colors than the 216 available for most browsers. The default, Error Diffusion, compensates for missing colors by mixing pixels of different colors to simulate missing shades. Normally, Error Diffusion handles imported colors smoothly. The Solid option assigns solid colors, reducing color subtlety, but creating faster-loading images. The Pattern and Random options are a bit faster than Dithering, but do a poorer job of maintaining your original colors.

Even before you begin to assign animation attributes, you can preview your animation. To do this, click the Preview button (a right-pointing arrow) or press Ctrl+R. Your animation will run in the Preview window, as shown in Figure 16-5.

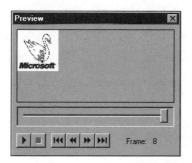

Figure 16-5: Preview an animation in GIF Animator to experiment with animation options.

Don't feel badly if your original settings don't produce a fun animation. You can play movie director and enhance the effect by changing settings in the Animation and Options tabs, explored next.

Controlling animation

The Animation Width and Animation Height spin boxes in the Animation tab define frame size. For example, if you want to create an animation in which a figure moves from right to left, you set the Animation Width at a value large enough that the image does not fill the entire frame. Aligning images within the frame is discussed in the next section.

The Looping check box enables you to repeat your animation. In most cases, you will want to *loop* (repeat) your sequence of slides. You can assign a number of loops in the Repeat Count spin box, or use the Repeat Forever check box to run your animation over and over.

The Comment field simply enables you to attach a note to yourself about this animated GIF. The Comment is not visible in a browser.

Image options for animated GIFs

Some attributes in your animation are assigned to particular images. For example, you can display one image for one second, and another for three seconds. Or, you can assign one transitional fade for some images, and a different transition to other images.

Attributes that are assignable to particular images or frames in your animated GIF are found in the Image tab of the GIF Animator window. To assign these images to *all* frames in your animation, click the Select All button in the GIF Animator toolbar, as shown in Figure 16-6. You can also select groups of contiguous frames by holding down the Shift key while selecting more than one frame. Selected frames are indicated by a blue outline in the frames display on the left side of the window.

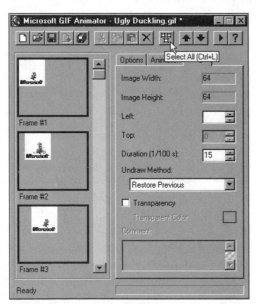

Figure 16-6: Many animation attributes can be assigned to individual frames, or to all frames.

With a frame or series of frames selected, you can apply the options described in the following sections.

Setting left and top displacement

If you set an Animation Width in the Animation tab that is wider than the images in your frames, you can define a distance (in pixels) from the left edge of the frame by using the Left spin box in the Image tab. And, if you define an Animation Height in the Animation tab that is higher than the frame size, you can define an offset distance from the top of the frame by using the Top spin box.

You can use these settings to make your images move around within an animation frame, like fish swimming around in an aquarium. Just as fish can't leave an aquarium, images can't move outside the defined animation frame size.

Figure 16-7 shows images defined with increasing top and left settings, to create the appearance of the objects moving down and to the right as the animation is played.

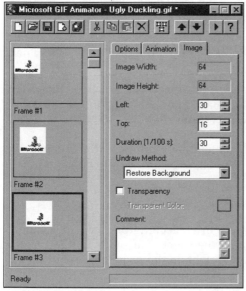

Figure 16-7: Objects can appear to move around within a defined animation frame.

Defining frame duration

You may notice that your animation plays very fast. To control the speed, use the Duration field on the Image tab. Transition speed is defined *only for selected frames*, so select frames before applying a duration.

Use the Duration spin box to change the time of display for each frame. If you use the Select All button, you assign this timing to all frames. To test your duration settings, run Preview.

Choosing Undraw Methods

Undraw Methods apply only to selected frames. You can use a design strategy of applying one Undraw Method to the whole animation, or you can spice things up by applying different Undraw Methods to different slides within an animation.

The Undraw Methods include the following:

✦ **Undefined:** Displays the following image with no effects applied. However, the Undraw technique often leaves "shadows" of previous frames. These shadows are displaced more elegantly when you use either Restore Background or Restore Previous.

✦ **Leave:** Sends to your visitor's browser a command to maintain the previous graphic image while the next image is being drawn. This technique leaves a frame in the browser window while the animation plays.

✦ **Restore Background:** Redraws the original background as the selected frame is displayed. This maintains a consistent background and eliminates the shadowing or continuous display of a frame produced by the Undefined or Leave transitions.

✦ **Restore Previous:** Redraws the previous image as the current image is drawn. The effect is similar to the Restore Background method insofar as the old image is wiped out as the new one is displayed.

You can create complex animations by combining Undraw Methods that leave a frame onscreen and methods (Restore Background or Restore Previous) that wipe out old frames.

Assigning transparency

You can assign transparency to one color in a selected frame or to all frames in an animation. Transparency often enhances the effect of an animation by making it appear that an image is bouncing around right on the page background.

To assign transparency, follow these steps:

1. Select one frame, or, to apply transparency to all frames, click the Select All button in the GIF Animator toolbar.

2. Click the Transparency check box to enable one transparent color for all selected frames.

3. Click the Transparency color swatch to open the palette for selected frames. Click in the palette on the color that you want to be transparent, and click OK.

4. Click the Preview button to view your animation with the assigned transparent color.

Note

The transparency color palette has several white squares. If your first attempt to assign white as your transparent color does not produce a completely transparent background, experiment with other white squares.

Additional GIF animation tools

Microsoft's GIF Animator is convenient because it works so nicely in conjunction with FrontPage and Image Composer. It comes free with FrontPage 2000 (except if you purchased FrontPage as part of Office 2000, in which case you can download it, as described earlier in the chapter). And, GIF Animator is one of the easier to use animation tools available.

GIF Animator is not the only GIF animation tool in town, however. This section closes with references to three other resources from which additional tools may be acquired. (All are shareware products, or can be purchased online.) The tools offered at the following sites provide more-robust animation control than GIF Animator.

✦ **MediaBuilder:** This Web site includes several free online image tools, including free sample animated GIFs, and a tool that transforms images into animated GIFs. You can check out the latest tools from MediaBuilder at `http://www.mediabuilder.com/`. The Animated Banner Maker tool allows users to create a simple GIF animation banner by using their own text and one of a long list of effects.

✦ **Ulead Systems:** This site offers a shareware version of PhotoImpact, a graphics package that includes the ability to generate animated GIFs. The Ulead site also offers a trial version of Ulead GIF Animator, with many custom animation effects. Ulead's GIF Animator also has very good optimization capabilities, leaving you with smaller animation files—always a good thing. Check out its product line at `http://www.ulead.com`.

✦ **Alchemy Mindworks:** Besides the obvious virtue of its having an original name, Alchemy Mindworks' GIF Construction Set is also a highly respected animation program that has been in use longer than the two previously mentioned products. You can use an animated GIF tutorial, or find out more about GIF Construction Set from the Alchemy Mindworks Web site, `http://www.mindworkshop.com/alchemy/alchemy.html`.

GIF animation can be quite complex. For one of our favorite animated GIF sites, check out Cat Hebert's Virtual Drama Society at `http://www.virtualdrama.com`.

While GIF animations can be quite complex and time-consuming, they can also be quite simple. You can create twinkling bullets, morphing icons, and transforming horizontal lines with very little work. In the following tutorial, you will learn a technique for creating all three effects, starting only with two clip art images available in FrontPage.

Tutorial 16.1: GIF Animation

1. Open a new or existing Web, and open a new page in Page view.

2. Select Insert ➪ Picture ➪ Clip Art. In the Search for Clips box, type **lake** and then press Enter to see a set of available lake images.

3. Select any of the lake images, and click the Insert Clip button in the pop-up toolbar. Before you insert your second clip art image, make sure that you click outside the lake image that you just imported. Otherwise, if one image is already selected, you will replace it when you try to add a second image.

4. Select Insert ➪ Picture ➪ Clip Art again. In the Search for Clips box, type **frog** and then press Enter to see a set of available frog images.

5. Select any of the frog images, and click the Insert Clip button in the pop-up toolbar. Click and drag a corner sizing handle to make the frog about half its original size. You should have a lake and a frog in your Web page, as shown in Figure 16.8.

6. Save your page, which also saves the embedded images.

7. Launch GIF Animator (if your version of FrontPage came without GIF Animator, refer to the download information in the section "Animating with GIF Animator," earlier in this chapter). In the Options tab, select the check boxes labeled Thumbnails Reflect Image Position and Main Dialog Window Always on Top. Choose Browser Palette in the Import Color Palette drop-down list, and Solid in the Import Dither Method drop-down list.

8. Click and drag the lake image from FrontPage into the Frame 1 in GIF Animator.

9. Click and drag the frog into Frame 2 in GIF Animator. Drag the frog into additional Frames 3 through 10. The lake should be in Frame 1, and the frog in Frames 2 through 10. In the Animation tab, select the Looping and Repeat Forever check boxes.

10. Click the Select All button in the GIF Animator toolbar, and enter a Duration of 15 ($\frac{15}{100}$ of a second) in the Duration spin box in the Image tab.

11. Choose the Restore Previous Undraw Method.

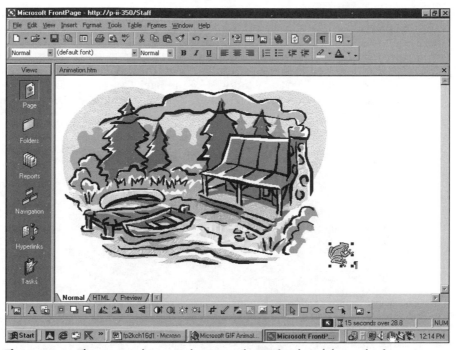

Figure 16-8: The two main actors in your animated epic: a lake and a frog.

12. Click the Transparency check box and click the Transparent Color swatch. In the Local Palette, choose a white square, and click OK. When you test your animation, if you find that the transparency is not satisfactory, you may have to experiment with other white swatches in the palette.

13. Click Frame 1 and choose Leave in the Undraw Method drop-down list. You will leave the lake image onscreen during the entire animation.

14. Your next step is to animate the frog to create the appearance of a jumping frog. To do this, you change the Animation Width and Height in the Image tab for each frog frame. Before you do, note the current Animation Width and Height. This is the size of the lake frame and defines the "screen" against which the frog can move.

15. Click the Image tab in the GIF Animator window. Defining the exact location of the frog in Frames 2 through 10 will take some experimenting. But, to have the frog begin to jump from the lower corner of the "screen," leave the Left spin box at 0 and start by entering 300 in the Top spin box, to offset the frog 300 pixels from the top of the frame. If the frog is too large to fit that far down from the top of the frame, GIF Animator adjusts the distance (makes it less) so that the frog still fits.

16. You have defined the first two frames of your animation. The first frame displays a lake that will appear as long as the animation runs. The second frame placed a small frog in the lower-left corner of the screen. You can view Frame 2 of your animation to check your progress by clicking the Preview button in the GIF Animator toolbar. Click the Stop button in the controls at the bottom of the Preview window. Use the Back One Frame or Forward One Frame buttons to move to Frame 2. This slide should look something like the one in Figure 16-9.

Figure 16-9: You can examine individual frames as you construct your animation.

17. Now comes the fun part. You have to define locations within the frame for the remaining frogs. Increase the Left offset and decrease the Top offset settings to have the frog appear to jump up and to the right. Increase the Top setting to have the frog jump down. Increase the Duration for frames in which you want the frog to appear to be sitting, and decrease the Duration for frames that should move by quickly. If you want some initial settings to start having fun with, you can try these, shown in Table 16-1:

	Table 16-1			
	Frame-by-Frame Settings for an Animated Frog			
Frame #	**Left**	**Top**	**Duration**	**Undraw Method**
1	(none)	(none)	300	Leave
2	0	280	12	Restore Previous
3	30	160	12	Restore Previous
4	70	200	120	Restore Previous
5	90	180	12	Restore Previous
6	125	190	240	Restore Previous
7	180	160	12	Restore Previous
8	275	260	180	Restore Previous
9	350	200	12	Restore Previous
10	436	250	12	Restore Previous

18. After you experiment with different settings for the different frog frames, save your animated GIF as **Frog**. Back in FrontPage Page view, select Insert ➪ Picture ➪ From File. Click the Select a File from Your Computer button (in the lower-right corner of the Picture dialog box). Navigate to your Frog file and click OK.

19. Preview your animation in the Preview tab of Page view. If you need to adjust your animation further, save changes in GIF Animator and then insert the changed animated GIF image again.

Working with DHTML Effects

DHTML, short for Dynamic HTML (which, of course, is short for Hypertext Markup Language), is a method of adding animation and other visual effects to a Web page. It combines the use of scripting languages (such as JavaScript) and the HTML Document Object Model (DOM) with Cascading Style Sheets (CSS). If you are interested in creating your own DHTML "effects" and want to learn how, check out Chapter 18 on scripting languages. If you couldn't care less how DHTML works, and just want to know how you can use the DHTML effects, FrontPage generously provides for your use — read on.

FrontPage DHTML Effects

FrontPage DHTML effects consist of numerous customizable animation effects that you can add to your Web pages without worrying about the technical details. All that you really need to understand is how to add an effect to your page. The basic process involves three simple steps:

1. Create one or more elements that you want to animate. These elements may be text or graphics, or a combination of the two.

2. Select the element(s).

3. Use the DHTML Effects toolbar to select and configure the effect that you want to apply to the element(s) in the Position Box.

These steps are demonstrated in the upcoming DHTML Effects tutorial. First, take a look at the DHTML Effects toolbar and what it offers.

Using the DHTML Effects toolbar

To see the DHTML Effects toolbar, select View ➪ Toolbars ➪ DHTML Effects. Unfortunately, the DHTML Effects toolbar by itself is not much to look at, because all of its elements are grayed out. To activate the toolbar, you first need to create a Position Box. To create a simple Position Box, select Insert ➪ Position Box. Select the Position Box (it is selected by default when you first create it), and the DHTML Effects toolbar comes to life, as illustrated in Figure 16-10.

The basic procedure for creating a DHTML effect is as follows:

1. **Choose an Event**: This is a technical way of saying you need to define what action will trigger the effect to do its thing. The *event* might be either something the user does, such as clicking the object with the mouse, or something the browser does, such as loading the page. Select an option from the drop-down menu to activate the Apply options.

2. **Choose an Effect:** The *effect* is what happens when the event occurs. For example, the object might change its appearance or move around. Different events have different effects that can be associated with them, so depending on what you select in the first step, you see a different set of options for this step. Select an effect from the drop-down menu to activate the settings options.

3. **Choose Settings:** The *settings* are the particular properties of the effect. Each effect has its own set of settings.

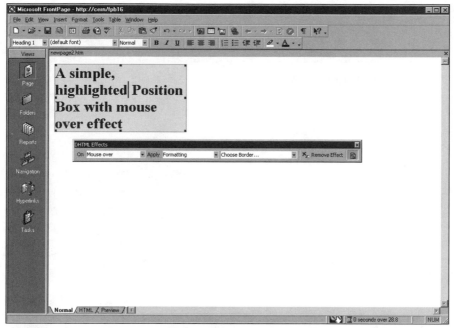

Figure 16-10: A simple Position Box and text, with the activated DHTML Effects toolbar.

In addition to the three main option menus, the toolbar has two other features:

✦ **Remove Effect:** This option is activated after you create an effect. It is always nice to have a way out!

✦ **Highlight DHTML Effects:** This option, represented by a page icon on the far right of the toolbar, adds a peaceful, aqua highlight to your effect in FrontPage. This is just a visual reminder to you that a DHTML effect is on the page (see Figure 16-11). The highlight doesn't show up on the Web page in a browser. This option is selected by default. Click the page icon to turn off highlighting.

The next several sections provide a brief description of the primary options available in the Events, Effects, and Settings option menus on the DHTML toolbar. If you are eager to try out DHTML, skip to the tutorial.

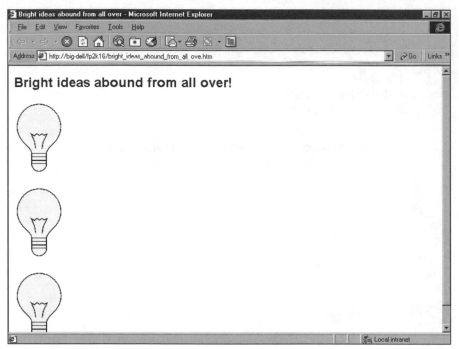

Figure 16-11: A text element with a DHTML effect highlighted. Use your imagination to add light-blue.

DHTML events

To create a DHTML effect, you first select one of the DHTML event options. The "event" is the action that initiates the effect. Most events are triggered by something that the user does, such as loading a particular page or clicking a particular page element. The following are the four events to choose from:

✦ **Click**: Triggered if the user clicks with any mouse button on the element contained within the Position Box. If the event involves a format change, clicking a second time undoes the effect (returns the element to its original state). Click events can trigger changes in the appearance (format) of the element or initiate a "fly out" that causes the element to move off the page.

✦ **Double-click:** Triggered if the user double-clicks the element in the Position Box.

✦ **Mouseover**: Triggered any time the user moves the mouse over the element within the Position Box.

✦ **Page load**: Trigged automatically when the page first loads. It is best suited for run-once animations, such as elements that move into place on the page.

DHTML effects and settings

Each of the four DHTML events has associated with it certain effects. After you select an event, you next choose one of the available effects for that event. The following list describes each of the available effects and, where appropriate, indicates which events have the effect as an option:

✦ **Formatting:** Enables you to change the appearance of an element when an event occurs. This effect is available for Click, Double-Click, and Mouseover events.

✦ **Choose Font:** Enables you to select a font change (typically a color change) to occur.

✦ **Choose Border:** Enables you to select a border change to occur.

Note

The formatting choices can be used in conjunction with one another (it is not an either/or choice, as is the case with the animation settings).

✦ **Swap Images:** Appears only on the Mouseover event when the element is an image. Replaces the original image with an alternate, providing the equivalent of a "two-state" image. The only setting is Choose Image.

✦ **Fly out:** Causes the affected element to disappear off the page in the direction designated by the setting option. Your choices are the following:

- To left
- To top
- To bottom left
- To bottom right
- To top right
- To top left
- To top right by word
- To bottom right by word

Formatting and fly out effects lend themselves nicely to effects initiated by the user after the page has loaded. Enabling these effects when the page loads wouldn't make sense, because you would never see the formatting change, nor the elements that flew off the page before it loaded.

The remaining effects are limited to the `On Page Load` event. They are all methods of moving elements onto the page with pizzazz.

✦ **Drop in by word:** Displays a string of text one word at a time.

✦ **Elastic:** Text flies in and bounces up and down before coming to a stop. You can elect to bounce text up from the bottom of the page or in from the right.

✦ **Fly in:** The opposite of fly out. Settings are similar to those for the fly out effect (except that they are prefaced with From rather than To), with the addition of Along corner, which causes the text to rise from the bottom and take an abrupt right turn to its final resting place.

✦ **Hop**: Causes a string of text to appear one word at a time, each word "hopping" in over the previous word.

✦ **Spiral**: Element appears in a sweeping arc from the upper-right corner of the page.

✦ **Wave**: Similar to Hop, except that each word does a loopy-de-loop (that's its technical name) when it appears.

✦ **Wipe**: Text reveals itself a line at a time. Setting are left to right, top to bottom, and from the middle.

✦ **Zoom**: Causes the element to grow or shrink to its final size. Settings are "in," in which case the element starts small and grows to its final size, and "out," which causes the element to start large and shrink down to its final size. Note that any size formatting you apply to this element is ignored.

In the following tutorial, you create a simple but bold statement, punctuated with the dramatic effects of Dynamic HTML.

Tutorial 16.2: DHTML Effect

1. Create a new Web page.

2. Type your message, **Bright ideas abound from all around!**

3. Now you bring this message to life. Select View ➪ Toolbars ➪ DHTML Effects and select the text message.

4. In the DHTML toolbar, select Page Load for On and select Hop for Apply. Now, the text will really "abound"!

5. Add some light bulbs to create a visual representation of the "bright ideas." Select Insert ➪ Picture ➪ Clip Art, select the Concepts category, and insert the light bulb picture. We have elected to add three light bulbs. You can add as many as you like.

6. Give each light bulb a different fly-in effect. If you need help here, try From bottom left, From top right, and From bottom right.

Now, preview the multiple effects in the Preview tab. Pretty dramatic stuff! Notice that the effects always fire in order from top to bottom down the page. One of the limits of using DHTML effects in this way is that you cannot really create "synchronized" effects.

DHTML Effects Behind the Scenes

This section takes a brief look at how DHTML effects are created. If you have no interest in this topic, skip ahead. If you want more details on how DHTML works, and even want to try your hand at some of your own "effects," check out Chapter 18.

As noted at the beginning of the chapter, DHTML is nothing more than the combination of CSS style information, a Document Object Model (DOM) that enables you to manipulate the styles, and a scripting language that gives you the ability to bring the elements to life. This section looks at how each of those elements comes into play in the simple example used earlier in the chapter.

When you add a DHTML effect, FrontPage adds style information, object identifiers, and some JavaScript events to the activated element. Here is the animated text, before and after adding the DHTML effect:

Before:

```
<h1>A simple, highlighted Position Box with Mouseover
effect.</h1>
```

After:

```
<h1 dynamicanimation="fpAnimformatRolloverFP1"
fprolloverstyle="color: #008000; border-style: solid; border-
color: #800000" onclick="clickSwapStyle(this)"
language="Javascript1.2">A simple, highlighted Position Box
with Mouseover effect.</h1>
```

The key elements of these additions are the alternative style designations in the fprolloverstyle and the onClick events.

The other important addition that FrontPage makes is to include a reference to a JavaScript file named animate.js. The actual file is added to your Web. This file contains all the functions used by the DHTML effects, including clickSwapStyle(), the function referenced by the onClick event.

Here is the clickSwapStyle() function from animate.js:

```
function clickSwapStyle(el)
{
    var ms = navigator.appVersion.indexOf("MSIE")
    ie4 = (ms>0) &&
(parseInt(navigator.appVersion.substring(ms+5, ms+6)) >= 4)
    if(ie4)
```

```
{
  ts=el.style.cssText
  el.style.cssText=el.fprolloverstyle
  el.fprolloverstyle=ts
}
```

This function takes as a parameter the element (el) from which it was called. It uses the IE DOM to reference the style properties of the object. The function sets the current style of the element to the alternative style, and sets the alternative style to the original style. This is how the effect toggles the styles each time that the user clicks the element.

DHTML and Browser Compatibility

DHTML effects are very slick and remarkably easy to produce using FrontPage. Before you start adding effects to all of your pages, however, you may want to reflect on some of the limitations of DHTML. (By the way, this topic is discussed in gory detail in the scripting chapter, Chapter 18.) DHTML effects basically have three drawbacks:

✦ Not all browsers are capable of supporting DHTML. If you can count on (or insist on) your user having a Netscape or Microsoft browser, version 4 or greater, you are fine (and among the lucky few). If not, you have to remember that not everyone will see your cool effects.

✦ Even browsers that do support DHTML don't have exactly the same support for it. This means that any good DHTML implementation must check for the browser type and deal with it appropriately.

✦ FrontPage's method of handling the preceding drawback is to enable the effects only for IE (this drawback is specific to the DHTML effects).

The bottom line on DHTML effects: they only work with Microsoft's browser.

Tip   The DHTML effects are controlled by an included JavaScript (or VBScript?) file called animate.js. You can also edit this file to deal with the Netscape browser.

GIF animation and DHTML effects are great ways to add visual spunk to your Web pages. Their repertoire is limited to text and images, however. What if you want to add bona fide multimedia to your Web? Well, you're in luck, because FrontPage provides support for this as well.

The next sections explore several multimedia technologies that FrontPage can assist you in adding to your site.

Page Transitions

You can apply transition effects to specific text and graphic elements of your Web pages by using DHTML. But, you can also apply dynamic effects to an entire page by assigning *page transitions*.

Caution　Page transitions work only with Internet Explorer.

Transitions assigned to a page can be activated when the page is first opened or exited. Alternatively, the transition effect can be set to activate only if the page is accessed when your site is first opened, or exited, in a browser.

To apply a transition to a page or a Web site, follow these steps:

1. Open the Web and view the page to which you are assigning a transition in Page view. Even if you are assigning a transition effect for when your site is opened or exited in a browser, you still need to have a Web page open in Page view.

2. Select Format ⇨ Page Transitions. The Page Transitions dialog box opens.

3. Define what event you want to trigger the transition effect by selecting Page Enter, Page Exit, Site Enter, or Site Exit from the Event drop-down list.

4. Set a duration for the effect in seconds by entering a value in the Durations box.

5. Choose one of the effects from the Transition Effect list. You can select a new event, and define another transition effect if you want. Then, click OK.

Caution　Contrary to what you might expect, if you define both a page and site transition effect on a page, the page transition effect takes precedence over the site effect.

Background Audio

As Web pages continue to evolve in the direction of multimedia titles and interactive television programming, the ability to add background audio has become an increasingly prevalent element of multimedia Web pages. FrontPage includes support for a Microsoft-specific HTML extension that enables developers to embed an audio file in a Web page. When the page is requested, this audio file loads and plays automatically.

Note　This feature is easy to implement, although it does not offer much in the way of user control. Remember, it is also Microsoft-specific, and it is not supported by all browsers.

A Primer on Digital Audio Formats

The background audio feature supports several digital audio formats. Without attempting to go into detail, here are the formats:

✦ **Wave Sound (WAV):** The Windows standard audio format.

✦ **AIFF Sound (AIF, AIFC, AIFF):** The Macintosh equivalent of WAV files.

✦ **AU Sound (AU, SND):** A Sun audio format that is widely used on the Web and that has gained limited cross-platform acceptance.

✦ **Musical Instrument Digital Interface (MIDI):** The format generated by synthesizers.

The first three formats are sampled audio, also known as *waveform audio*. Waveform audio formats record, or "sample," sounds, much as a tape recorder does. MIDI, unlike a sampled sound format, records a set of instructions about how to re-create, or "synthesize," a particular sound. As a result, MIDI has a more limited repertoire than waveform audio, which can copy any sound that you feed into a microphone. MIDI is, however, far more economical in the size of its files than is waveform audio. Most musical compositions are created in MIDI format.

Getting audio files

To add background audio to your Web page, you first need an audio file. You have two options: either create a digital audio file yourself or obtain a file from an existing source. Several sites on the Internet maintain sample sounds and music clips. Always be aware of any possible copyright issues before you download and use audio files from the Internet, however.

Fortunately, Microsoft has made available several audio samples on its Web site, at `http://www.microsoft.com/gallery/files/sounds/default.htm`. Select a nice little number from the Musical section called Caribbean, shown in Figure 16-12—just say no to door slams, cat screeches, and other audio samples commonly known as noise. Follow the directions on the Caribbean page to download and save this MIDI file (only 27K).

Caution   Turn down your stereo speaker before you check out the sound samples page listed here. It provides a good example of why unannounced sounds on Web pages is a bad idea. I jump out of my skin every time I go there.

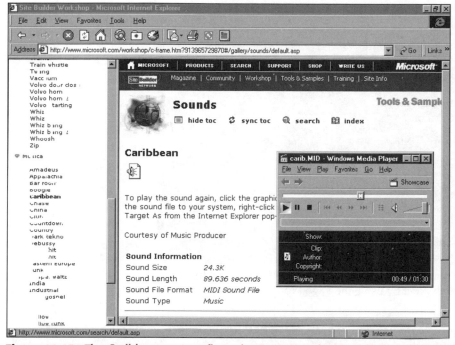

Figure 16-12: The Caribbean at your fingertips, courtesy of Microsoft's Sound Sample site.

Inserting audio files in your Web pages

After you copy the file to your local drive, you need to add it to your Web page. Add this file to the Pedigree Armadillo page, because it provides a complementary backdrop to your scuttling armadillo animation. To insert a background audio into a Web page:

1. Open the Web page in FrontPage.

2. Select File ➪ Page Properties. The dialog box shown in Figure 16-13 appears.

3. In the Location field of the Background Sound area, click the Browse button and locate the audio file to play when the page is loaded.

4. Click OK.

5. Save the Web page. You are prompted to add the sound file to your Web, if it is not already there.

6. Preview the sound in your Web browser and dance along with the armadillo. (Or just check it out in Figure 16-14.)

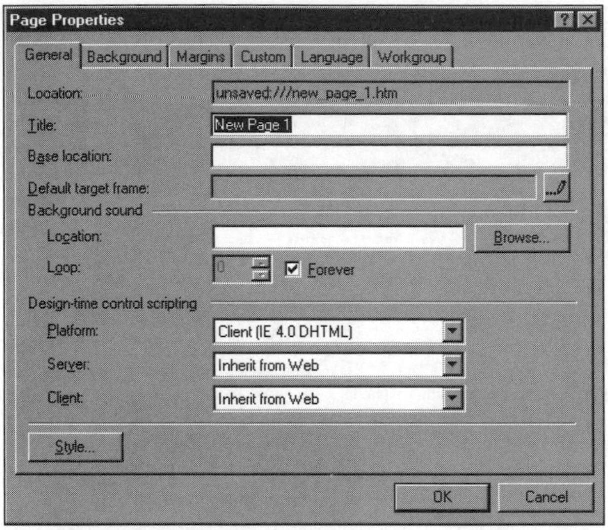

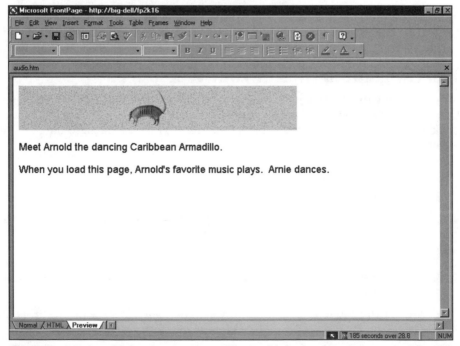

Figure 16-13: Inserting a background sound into your Web page by using the Page Properties dialog box

Figure 16-14: Arnold the dancing Armadillo (Hold the book to your ear to hear this background music playing.)

Available formats

FrontPage supports several popular audio formats, including:

✦ **WAV:** Waveform audio format

✦ **MIDI:** MIDI format

✦ **RA/RAM:** Real Audio file formats

✦ **AIFF:** A standard Apple audio file format

✦ **AU:** au format, principally a UNIX format

Setting audio properties

After you create a background sound, you can control a few properties. For instance, as with GIF animations, you can set the sound file to loop a designated number of times. To do this, select File ➪ Page Properties, and in the General tab, indicate the number of times to loop the sound file. You can also use the Page Properties dialog box to change the name of the background sound.

Inline Video

In addition to providing basic support for background sounds, FrontPage supports the ability to add video clips into your Web pages. This feature is easy to implement but limited in its flexibility. FrontPage supports inline video in AVI format, the standard Windows video format. Although players are available for the AVI video format on all major computer platforms, AVI is not considered a cross-platform standard. Nor does it have the best compression methods available. Even relatively short video clips are likely to be 300K and larger, more than the average user is going to want to confront unannounced on a Web page.

Inserting video clips in your Web pages

Select Insert ➪ Picture ➪ Video, locate the AVI file that you want to include, and click OK. A preview of the video appears in the Web page, showing the initial frame of the video clip.

You now have video in your Web page. When you save the page, you are prompted to save the video in the current Web. To preview it, select the Preview tab.

Additional Sound Ways and Means

If you are looking for sound bytes to add to your Web, or if you want to learn more about sound formats, the following are several Web resources that you may want to investigate:

✦ **WWW Virtual Library:** Maintains lists of Internet resources on a variety of topics. Each topic is maintained by a volunteer. The library's list of audio resources is located at `http://www.comlab.ox.ac.uk/archive/audio.html`. It contains links to sound archives, software, newsgroups, and online radio.

✦ **Harmony Central:** An excellent site for MIDI resources and information. Everything from MIDI forums to software and links to MIDI archives. `http://www.harmony-central.com/MIDI/`

✦ **The MIDI Farm:** Another full-service MIDI site with a well-organized potpourri of MIDI-related content. `http://www.midifarm.com/`

✦ **Webplaces Internet Search Guide:** This bare-bones site has links to all sorts of searches. The Audio Browser section has links to numerous sound file archives. `http://www.webplaces.com/html/sounds.htm`.

✦ **Internet Underground Music Archive (IUMA):** If you are looking for music on the Web, this should be your first stop. Lots of audio, and a way-cool, award-winning interface. `http://www.iuma.com`.

If you are serious about audio, you may want to investigate some of the other technologies for adding audio to your Web. Here are some of the leading contenders:

✦ **Netscape LiveAudio:** Netscape Navigator ships with an audio plug-in called LiveAudio. It is capable of playing audio in a variety of formats, including AIFF, MIDI, WAV, and AU. The LiveAudio plug-in can be controlled via JavaScript. Information on Netscape Navigator is available at `http://www.netscape.com`.

✦ **QuickTime Audio:** Apple Computer's video format can also be used to prepare audio only. QuickTime files can be saved for "fast-start," enabling the QuickTime video to begin playing as it downloads. For more information, see the QuickTime WebMaster's Page, `http://www.quicktime.com/dev/devweb.html`.

✦ **RealAudio:** The original streaming audio format, and still the most popular. Unlike the standard audio formats, which require users to download an entire file and then listen to it, streaming audio plays as it downloads. It can even be used to broadcast audio in real time. RealAudio has its own player application, available in free and Plus versions. `http://www.realaudio.com`.

✦ **Crescendo:** A MIDI plug-in from LiveUpdate, available in Netscape and Microsoft versions. It is available in a free version and a Plus version, which can provide streaming of MIDI files. `http://www.liveupdate.com`.

✦ **Liquid MusicPlayer from Liquid Audio:** Another plug-in format, designed to allow users to download and play CD-quality audio, as well as to view art, lyrics, and credits: `http://www.liquidaudio.com`.

Setting video properties

The properties for video clips are located on the Video tab in the Image Properties dialog box. Select the video to preview, and then select Edit ➪ Image Properties, or right-click the image and select Image Properties from the pop-up menu. The Video tab of the Image Properties dialog box is shown in Figure 16-15. You can control how the video is displayed with the following items on this tab:

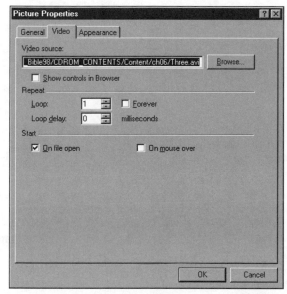

Figure 16-15: The video clip properties that you can control.

✦ **Video Source:** As with other inserted objects, you can alter the source name, effectively substituting another video for the current one.

✦ **Show Controls in Browser:** Enables you to insert simple playback controls into the Web page. Another way to see the controls is to insert the animation as a plug-in, using the same procedure as outlined earlier in the chapter for the PowerPoint presentation — an animation inserted as a plug-in automatically has the controls.

Caution

For some reason, when you elect to include the controls, FrontPage doesn't adjust the size of the space reserved to enable the video to compensate. If you don't enlarge the dimensions of the video, it is scrunched (that's a technical term) by the controls.

✦ **Repeat:** Just as with animation and sound, you can elect to loop the video clip as many times as you want to subject the poor user to the sequence.

✦ **Start:** By default, the video begins to play when the file loads. Alternatively, you can have it begin when the user passes the mouse over the video. If you use this option, you might want to prompt the user on what to do, unless you just want them to guess for themselves.

Video Viewing Alternatives

If you want to post your home movies for the world to enjoy, or broadcast your full-length documentary film, a variety of technologies are available that can help you do it. Internet video technologies have made great strides in the past few years, which means that the video they generate is almost watchable, even if you don't happen to have a T3 line or a cable modem.

Several of the technologies described earlier in the sidebar titled "Additional Sound Ways and Means" can be used to create and/or deliver video content. These include Netscape's MediaPlayer plug-in, RealAudio, which now includes streaming video, and Apple's QuickTime. In addition, the following other technologies merit investigating:

✦ **Microsoft NetShow Services:** The NetShow server is Microsoft's entry in the streaming multimedia category. (For a definition of streaming audio, see the discussion of RealAudio in the "Additional Sound Ways and Means" sidebar.) NetShow's content is created in ActiveX Streaming Format (ASF) or broadcast in real time from an audio/video source. NetShow can be used in conjunction with Internet Information Server (IIS), which is the Microsoft Windows NT Web server. For more information on NetShow or to download the free Windows Media Player, go to `http://www.microsoft.com/windows/windowsmedia/default.asp`.

✦ **VDOLive:** A streaming video technology from VDONet. It uses a separate VDOLive On-Demand server to deliver quality real-time video, even at dial-up connection speeds. For more information or to download the VDOLive plug-in for either Netscape or Microsoft, visit `http://www.vdo.net`.

✦ **VivoActive:** A serverless streaming video technology from Vivo Software, Inc. Use the VivoActive Producer to convert your video to VivoActive format, and then use a standard Web server to deliver the content. The VivoActive player is free for downloading from the VivoActive Web site, `http://www.vivo.com`.

Advanced Multimedia Technologies

The audio and video capabilities discussed in the previous section are fairly limited. They work reliably only in the IE browser, and they are very limited in what you can do with them. Watching a video clip or listening to a background audio track is entertaining, but it is a far cry from the kinds of multimedia experiences we have become accustomed to since the advent of CD-ROMs. Is this as good as it gets on the Web?

Fortunately, a lot of thought has been devoted to making full-out multimedia available via the Internet. You won't likely be watching movies via the Internet for quite a while, but much progress has been made in this field very quickly.

FrontPage does not have any particular support for streaming multimedia technologies. On the other hand, nothing prevents you from developing a streaming Web site using FrontPage. For the sake of completeness, we have surveyed some of the leading contenders in this arena. Don't be surprised if by the next revision, FrontPage incorporates more elaborate support for one or more of these technologies.

Macromedia Shockwave and Flash

Macromedia's Shockwave is one animation technology that deserves mention. Shockwave began as a simple plug-in for Macromedia Director applications. It has evolved into a family of plug-ins, supporting many of the Macromedia multimedia products, including Authorware and FreeHand.

The latest addition to the Shockwave family is Flash, a vector-based animation application that creates animations that download quickly and run smoothly. The Shockwave ActiveX control and plug-in are free for downloading. The Flash development application, of course, is a commercial product. However, you can download a trial version of the latest release, 2.0 as of this writing, from Macromedia's Web site, `http://www.macromedia.com`.

Microsoft DirectX

DirectX is Microsoft's name for a collection of multimedia technologies built into the Windows operating system. It includes services for graphics, 3D animation, sound, and video. The DirectX services support a wide variety of multimedia file formats, including Microsoft's Advanced Streaming Format (ASF), intended for Internet-based distribution of multimedia content. As of this writing, the current version of DirectX is 6.0.

Developer's can use DirectX technologies in a variety of ways, the simplest of which is through the use of ActiveX controls. The following are some of the principle DirectX controls. (Instructions on adding ActiveX controls to your Web pages is covered in Chapter 19.)

✦ **DirectAnimation:** The DirectX technology that provides streaming animation services, including 2D and 3D animation. DirectAnimation consists of a set of animation controls that you can add to your Web pages and manipulate by using a scripting language. Controls include a Path control, a Sequencer control, a Sprite control, and a Structure Graphics control.

✦ **DirectShow:** Formerly called ActiveMovie, a streaming technology that enables audio and video to be compressed and streamed to the user in a variety of formats.

✦ **DirectMusic:** A recent addition to the DirectX technology, designed for adding streaming audio tracks to your Web pages.

✦ **Windows Media Player:** Formerly known as NetShow Player, a user component for streaming DirectX multimedia content. Unlike the helper apps from days of yore, Media Player enables you to experience a wide range of multimedia formats by using a single application.

Real Networks, RealAudio, and RealVideo

Originally named Real Audio, Real Networks was one of the early promoters of streaming technology on the Web. It has progressed from pure audio streaming, to audio and video combined, including real-time streaming of content. Currently, the Real Networks technologies are some of the first to provide development support for the new SMIL standard, described in the next section.

SMIL

SMIL, pronounced "smile," stands for *Synchronized Multimedia Integration Language*, which is a fancy way of saying that it is a language for playing a bunch of multimedia elements together, making sure that they all come in at the right time and show up in the right place. The SMIL syntax looks very familiar to anyone who has seen HTML. In fact SMIL is an application of XML, or *Extended Markup Language*, the big brother of HTML.

Summary

This chapter has taken a whirlwind tour of the various ways that FrontPage simplifies the task of adding sound, action, and interactivity to your Web. It has focused on using additional Microsoft products to create animation and has called attention to other resources and methods that you can use to make you look like a multimedia guru (at least after you've had a chance to practice with them). The next chapter explains how you can use discussion forums as another way to create an interactive experience on your Web site.

✦   ✦   ✦

Discussion Webs and Channels

This chapter takes a practical look at implementing discussion forums. The focus is the multifaceted Discussion Web Wizard, which you can use to create a discussion forum with an automatically updating TOC, threaded messages, custom confirmations, and a search engine — all in a matter of minutes. This chapter walks you through each step in the creation of a Discussion Web. Following that, it explains how the Discussion Web is constructed, how it works, and how you can customize your forum (as well as how you can't).

Exploring Modes of Discussion

Discussion forums in a variety of modes have existed on the Internet for almost as long as the Internet has been in existence — much longer, certainly, than the upstart World Wide Web, which has really only been with us since the early 1990s. Most of these entities began as separate Internet services, just as the Web is one Internet service. So, each method of communicating has its own set of protocols and standards, as well as its own set of client applications (in other words, the programs that you use to interact with the particular service).

The early modes of Internet discussion break down into two categories:

✦ Asynchronous (nonreal-time) message systems, such as e-mail, mailing lists, and newsgroups

✦ Text-based, synchronous communication systems, such as Internet Relay Chat (IRC)

With the boom in Web popularity, an initial push was made to consolidate all Internet services in the browser. Web-based discussion forums, such as the one included with FrontPage, are one byproduct of this phenomenon. Another byproduct has been the intensive drive to consolidate multiple services under the umbrella of a single application (or at least a single brand name) — witness the transformation of Netscape's Navigator product into the current Communicator suite, and Microsoft's similarly aggressive production of Internet applications. A third driving force has been to create multimedia real-time communication: Internet phone, video conferencing, and 3D chat environments.

All of which is, of course, beyond the ken of the humble FrontPage Discussion Web Wizard. In the meantime, you can use the Discussion Web Wizard to create a very useful discussion forum that combines the convenience of a newsgroup with the Web's ease of use.

Discovering the Discussion Web Wizard

The Discussion Web Wizard is FrontPage's most full-featured wizard. In a matter of minutes, it can generate a fully functioning Web-based discussion forum, complete with the following:

✦ **Threaded messages and replies:** In the world of electronic messaging, a "thread" refers to a particular message and any replies generated from that message. In general, reading a group of messages that have a common thread is easier than simply reading messages in the order that they are posted to the forum, which is fairly haphazard. Organizing messages by threads is an optional feature of the Discussion Web Wizard.

✦ **Table of Contents:** The virtue of the Discussion Web Table of Contents (TOC) is that it updates automatically. From a management perspective, that is a godsend (imagine having to update the TOC by hand!). From the users' standpoint, the only drawback is that, thanks to your Web browser's ability to cache Web pages, refreshing the page sometimes is necessary to see new content.

Note

In Web browser lingo, as in computer lingo generally, a *cache* refers to files that the application stores in a readily available place, in anticipation of needing them again. Each time that you access a Web page, your browser stores a copy of the HTML file and any subsidiary files in its local cache on your hard drive. Then, if you return to the page, that tricky browser draws it from its cache, providing you with the momentary illusion of speed on the Internet.

✦ **Customizable Submission Form:** The Discussion Web Wizard offers you limited options for the discussion's Submission Form. Afterwards, however, you can add as many fields as you like — or as many as your users will tolerate.

✦ **Confirmation Pages with Confirmation Field Components:** As with other FrontPage forms, you can return a custom Confirmation Page to anyone who submits a message. By using the Confirmation Field Component, described in Chapter 11, the Confirmation Page can display any and all data submitted.

✦ **Searchable index:** A FrontPage Discussion Web can include the same text search engine discussed in Chapter 14. In this case, however, searching is confined to the posted messages.

✦ **Protected discussion messages:** You can configure a Discussion Web so that users are required to register before they can gain access to read or post to the discussion.

Although it has many steps, the Discussion Web Wizard actually is quite easy to complete. Many of the steps involve little more than including or excluding certain features. Because it is so easy, however, you should know what you are getting yourself into. Some features are worth including when you first create the discussion forum. Others, such as frames, may be implemented more easily and more flexibly later, should you choose to include them.

Creating a Discussion Web

Creating your Discussion Web is the easy part (easier than maintaining the discussion forum, for instance), because the wizard does all the hard work. However, planning ahead of time what you want to incorporate into your Discussion Web is a good idea. The Discussion Web Wizard is the most sophisticated of the wizards that accompanies FrontPage. Here are the issues to think about before you start:

✦ Will your forum be large enough to warrant a search engine in the beginning? (Nothing is sadder than a search that returns zero (0) matches.)

✦ Will your users benefit from using a frames environment to display the TOC and messages simultaneously? (Or, will they burn you in effigy for even thinking such a thought?)

✦ Does your Discussion Web need to have multiple discussion areas, or will a single forum suffice?

✦ Can anyone add messages to your forum, or do you need to restrict access with a Registration Form?

These are some of the major design-related questions that you may want to ponder before diving into the creation of your discussion forum.

Do You Really Want to Do This?

You should ponder one other, easy-to-overlook question before going any farther: Do you really have the time and resources to manage an active discussion forum? Even though FrontPage makes creating your Web easy, it requires work to maintain.

The TOC is going to swell to ungainly proportions, the search index is going to take longer and longer to perform its updates, messages are going to get corrupted and require attention. Am I scaring you sufficiently yet? The point is not to dissuade you from forging ahead — hey, there's a whole chapter to go here! — but don't make the decision to create a Discussion Web casually. Enough said.

Opening the Discussion Web Wizard

To create your Discussion Web, open Explorer, select File ➪ New, and choose the Discussion Web Wizard from the New FrontPage Web dialog box, as shown in Figure 17-1. In the first Discussion Web Wizard dialog box, identify the Web server or file location of your Discussion Web and give it a name. Like other Web names, this one is only used internally, so it can be short and simple. If you are following the example, call the Web **pettalk**, as shown in Figure 17-1. Click OK to continue.

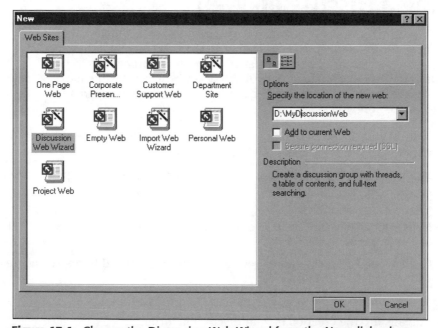

Figure 17-1: Choose the Discussion Web Wizard from the New dialog box.

The first Discussion Web Wizard screen describes its purpose and gives you an overview of the process. All very charming. Click Next to get on with it.

Selecting Discussion Web features

The next Wizard screen asks you to select the features that you want to include in your Web. Your answers here determine what additional questions the Wizard needs to ask. As illustrated in Figure 17-2, the options include:

✦ **Submission Form**: Used by folks who want to post a message to the discussion. Because a Discussion Web without any way to contribute is not very useful, this one is a required option (kind of an oxymoron, no?).

✦ **Table of Contents**: Lists all messages and their respective responses. This page is updated each time a new message is posted to the Web.

✦ **Search Form:** The same search engine explored in Chapter 16, but applied to the discussion messages.

✦ **Threaded Replies:** A *thread* refers to a message and all of its replies. Threaded messages are linked hierarchically, so that you can read messages as part of a conversation, rather than haphazardly in the order they happened to be posted.

Note

Personally, I have mixed feelings about the virtues of threaded forums as they are implemented in FrontPage. The Discussion Web considers any reply to be a new subthread under the original message. That means that if person A posts a message, person B replies to that message, A replies to B's reply, and B replies to A's reply, the messages will look like a series of nested threads, when, in fact, what most likely took place was a conversation sparked by the initial post. If your Discussion Web is fairly freeform, this may be okay. However, if you are planning a more topical Discussion Web, you may prefer to leave the messages unthreaded.

✦ **Confirmation Page:** After a person submits a message, it is nice to respond with a Confirmation Page that reassures the sender that you received the submission and that it hasn't simply been swallowed up in the virtual void.

For the purpose of this chapter's demonstration, select all the options. Why not have it all — it's so easy! When you are happy with your choices, click Next to continue.

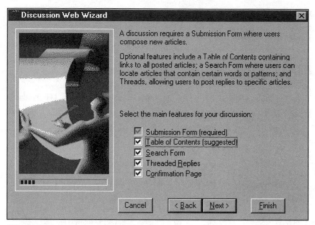

Figure 17-2: So many discussion features to choose from!

Naming the Web

The next screen asks you for the title of the Web. This is the information that visitors see at the top of each discussion page. The title should be descriptive without being overly long. The example Discussion Web for Pedigree Pets is entitled "Pet Talk."

The second item of information requested in this screen is the name of the folder in which discussion messages are kept. The folder is not visible directly to people who access your site. It is only accessed indirectly, typically via the TOC, which is why the folder name begins with the underscore character, FrontPage's way of marking private, system folders. To follow along with the example, name your folder in accordance with the title, **_pettalk**. Click OK to continue.

Selecting input fields

In this screen, you select the fields that you want to include in the Submission Form. These are the fields completed by anyone posting a message. At a minimum, you should have a Subject and a Comments field. Additionally, you can include a Category or Product list to select from. The example, shown in Figure 17-3, opts for the basics: Subject and Comments.

Caution

The problem with the Category and Product lists is that they have no impact on how messages are organized. The person's selection is simply recorded along with the rest of the message. If you really want to organize your discussion by categories or products, consider creating multiple Discussion Webs, one for each topic.

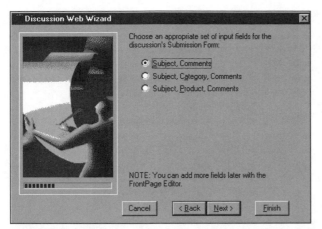

Figure 17-3: Selecting input fields for the Discussion Web Submission Form

This is a fairly meager set of options. Fortunately, you can customize the Submission Form later, and any additional fields that you add are saved along with the default fields. Click Next when you have made your choice.

Choosing Protected versus Open Discussions

The next screen asks whether you want to require users to be registered before they can participate in a discussion. Registration can be enforced in either of two ways:

✦ **Preregistration:** Only those users who are already registered can use the discussion forum. In this case, users need some way to request that they be added to the list of registered users.

✦ **Self-registration:** Users must still be registered to participate in the discussion, but they can register themselves. Thus, no time lag occurs between requesting admittance and gaining it. But, you have no chance to reject registrants. They fill out the form and are free to post messages.

Adding a Registration Component to a discussion forum is described later in the chapter. For now, stick to the basics. Select No, Anyone Can Post Articles (see Figure 17-4) and then click Next.

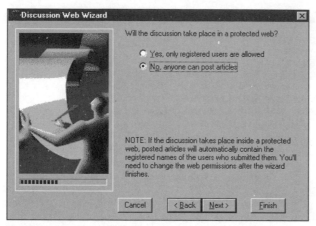

Figure 17-4: To register or not to register, that is the question.

Selecting the message sort order

The next screen poses a simple option. Do you want messages to appear with the oldest message first (at the top of the page) or with the newest message first? Putting the newest messages first is convenient for those users who just want current information without scrolling through last month's messages. If messages are not threaded, however, you frequently have to read replies to a message before you read the message itself. Because your current Web is threaded, select the Oldest to newest option, as shown in Figure 17-5. Click Next to forge ahead.

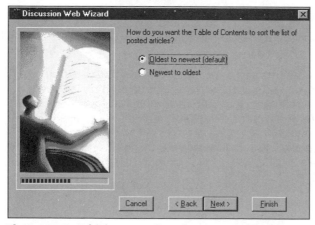

Figure 17-5: Which comes first, the new or the old?

Choosing the Table of Contents as the home page

This screen presents a simple Yes or No question: do you want the Table of Contents to be the home page? You can add a Discussion Web to an existing Web, but in this case, you are creating a new Web around the Discussion Component. Even so, you want to have an introductory page for your Web that leads to the Table of Contents. So, you just say No to a home page Table of Contents (see Figure 17-6). Click Next to proceed.

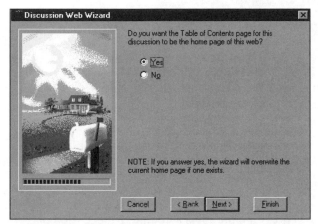

Figure 17-6: Opting to make the Table of Contents your Web's home page

Selecting the Search Results information

This screen sets the display options for the Discussion Web search results. The Search Results page is capable of displaying some combination of the subject, the match's score (which is a relative measure of how closely the file matches your search request), the file size, and the file date. The Wizard limits the choice of these options to four possible combinations.

Caution Does anybody know why this Wizard doesn't provide each of the four possible result fields as a check box option? As it is, no way exists to select only Subject and Score, for example.

Fortunately, you can edit the Search Results page later. For now, just select Subject, Size, and Date, as shown in Figure 17-7. Click Next to move along.

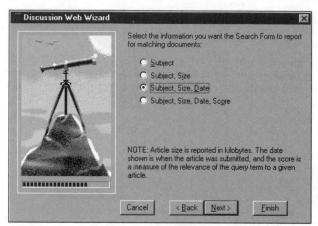

Figure 17-7: You can select some of the possible options for the Search Results page here. Later, you can edit these properties.

Choosing a Web Theme

To select a custom FrontPage Theme for your Discussion Web, click the Choose Web Theme button on the next screen. This brings up the standard Choose Theme dialog box, shown in Figure 17-8. (Chapter 5 has a complete discussion of implementing Themes.)

At the moment, you probably are too eager to finish your Web to think about interior decorating, so the customization of this page will be done later. Click Next to keep moving forward.

Tip   By default, the Discussion Web Wizard creates your Discussion Web using the Straight Edge Theme. If you prefer No Theme, click the Choose Web Theme button, select No Theme from the list of Themes, and click OK to return to the Wizard.

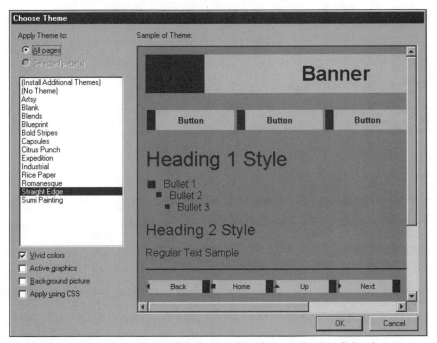

Figure 17-8: Dress up your Web by using the Choose Theme dialog box.

Framing your discussion

The next screen offers the following choices of frame and nonframe versions of the discussion Web:

✦ **No Frames:** Exactly what it says.

✦ **Dual Interface:** Uses a simple, two-frame frame set combined with a no-frames option.

✦ **Contents Above Current Article:** Same as the two-frame frame set in the Dual Interface, but with the addition of a banner frame and no option for no frames.

✦ **Contents Beside Current Article:** Puts the TOC in a vertical column on the left side of the frame set, and puts content on the right side. Includes a banner frame at the top, and no option for no frames.

To see how each of these frame options is laid out, click its radio button. The window on the left changes to reflect the currently selected arrangement (see Figure 17-9).

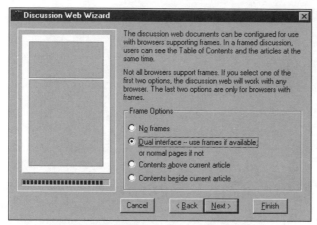

Figure 17-9: The frames selection screen of the
Discussion Web Wizard

If you select Dual Interface, the Discussion Web Wizard builds two versions of the
TOC, one designed for use in a frames environment, and the other as a standalone
page. For now, elect No Frames. Some of the advantages and disadvantages of using
frames for your Discussion Web are reviewed later in the chapter. For a more
complete treatment of using frames in FrontPage, refer to Chapter 10.

Tip   You can also wait and convert your Discussion Web later into a frame-based Web.
This gives you added flexibility, but is a bit trickier to do. Waiting until later is probably a good idea only if you want to create a custom frame set that is not among
the four options that the Discussion Web Wizard offers.

Click Next to continue to the final screen, which reiterates what you selected for
your Table of Contents page and the Submission Form. (What about those other
pages, you may be wondering?) Click Finish, and your Web is created. Figure 17-10
shows the Hyperlinks view of the newly created Web for Pet Talk. The next section
explores what you have created in greater detail.

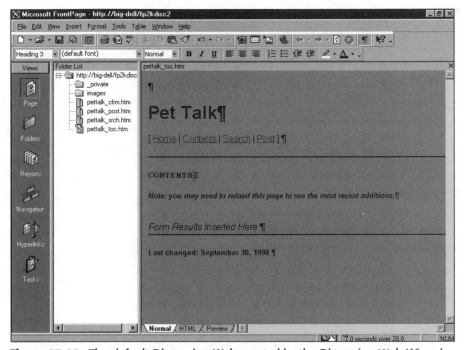

Figure 17-10: The default Discussion Web created by the Discussion Web Wizard

Using the Discussion Web

Now take a look at what the Discussion Web Wizard has wrought for you. To illustrate how a Discussion Web works from a user's standpoint, a somewhat revised version of the Pet Talk Discussion Web is used. After looking at the Web from the outside, the next section examines the files that make up the Discussion Web.

Figure 17-11 shows the home page created to put in front of the example Pet Talk Discussion Web.

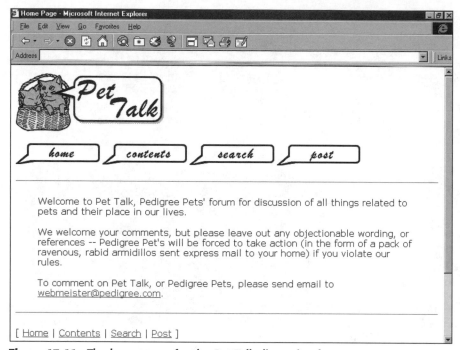

Figure 17-11: The home page for the Pet Talk discussion forum

Although the copy on the page illustrated in Figure 17-11 is somewhat facetious, this home page illustrates some principles that you might want to imitate when you set up your Discussion Web:

✦ First, it states the purpose of the discussion forum, clearly identifying what is and isn't permissible. This will not keep people on the topic, but it gives you a basis for removing content, if that should ever be necessary.

✦ Second, like the footer text mentioned earlier, it explains the limits of liability assumed by the operators of the discussion forum, and also emphasizes their conscientious efforts to make the forum an environment that is conducive to open discussion.

✦ Finally, it provides a feedback mechanism, so that users can contact the operators directly if they choose.

The discussion forum is not rocket science. One of its virtues is the fact that it is fairly intuitive to use. In case you don't have the forum in front of you, however, this section takes a quick tour of its main operations.

Table of Contents

The Table of Contents displays a constantly updated list of messages posted to the discussion Web. Figure 17-12 shows an example of the TOC from the Pet Talk Discussion Web. Note that this TOC is organized with the most recent messages at the top. Also note how the TOC page renders threaded messages, indented under the original message.

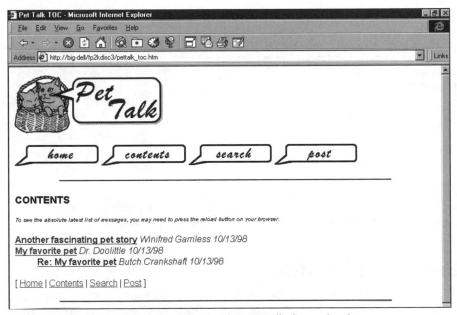

Figure 17-12: The Table of Contents for the Pet Talk discussion forum

The TOC is very straightforward from a user's standpoint. Simply click the hyperlinked subject heading of a message to read, and optionally respond, to that message.

Submitting a message

To add a message to the forum, simply click the Post button from any page. Note that clicking the Post button always creates a message at the top level of the message hierarchy. This is easy to forget when you are three levels down reading a message, and you click the Post button, thinking that you are responding to the message that you have been reading. Figure 17-13 shows a message in the process of creation.

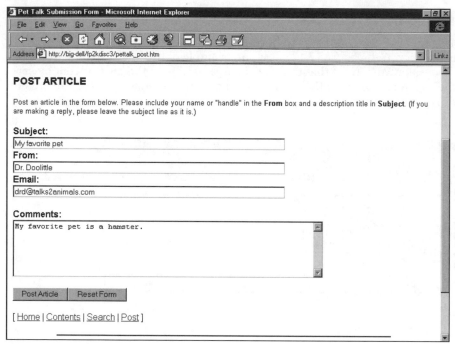

Figure 17-13: A Discussion Web message in the process of creation

Posting confirmation

After you post your message, the Discussion Web responds with a Confirmation Page, shown in Figure 17-14. The default Confirmation Page is very plain. You can edit this page to your liking, however. For more information on working with form results Confirmation Pages, see Chapter 15.

Replying to messages

You reply to a message after you have accessed its page. Clicking the Reply button on any message page takes you to a version of the Submission Form, but loads a default *RE: theoriginalsubject* line in the Subject header. Of course, this can lead to endless repetitions of this in the TOC, each one indented one level deeper in a threaded TOC.

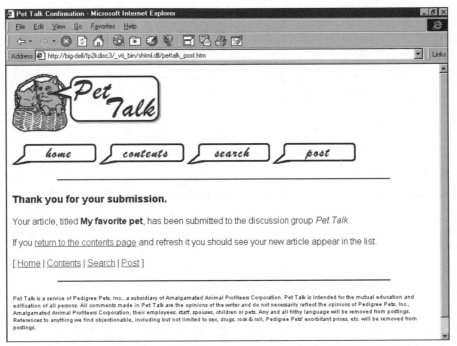

Figure 17-14: The Pet Talk Confirmation Page, returned when a user posts a message

Navigating

Sending and replying to messages is the main activity of the Web. Before you can reply to a message, however, you have to find an interesting one. You can either browse through messages, using the Next, Previous, and Up buttons, or you can go straight to the Search feature. The browse buttons work as you would expect: Next takes you to the next message in a sequence. It navigates down through a list of messages and replies, before moving on to the next messages. However, moving backward, messages are displayed at the top level (in other words, you are not forced to traverse backward through a series of messages and replies).

Search Form

The other way to find articles of interest is to use the Search Form, which has a simple text field entry form. Type a word or series of words and click the Start Search button. A page is returned showing a list of messages that contain the word requested. The results of a search are illustrated in Figure 17-15.

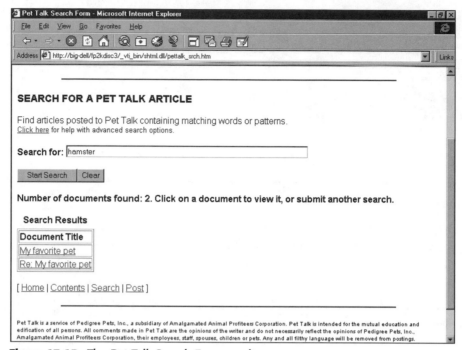

Figure 17-15: The Pet Talk Search Form results

Using the Search Form is a good way to find specific content that you might be looking for. Of course, searching for articles in this fashion may cause you to lose the thread of a conversation. After you find an interesting article, you can use the navigation buttons to get a better sense of the message's context.

Customizing a Discussion Web

This section returns to the Web created using the Discussion Web Wizard at the beginning of this chapter to find out what it includes and how it works. After you familiarize yourself with the terrain, you'll proceed to perform some "home improvement." The next several sections discuss each of the Discussion Web Components in a fair amount of detail, with an emphasis on customizing the forum to your needs. Following that, several more-advanced topics related to the Discussion Web are examined.

Hidden pages

By default, when FrontPage creates a new Web, it hides hidden files from view. A "hidden" file in FrontPage lingo refers to files in any directory whose name begins with an underscore character (_) — with the exception of the _private folder. This is all perfectly obvious, right?

If you want to see the rest of the files that the Wizard produces, you must first instruct FrontPage to show you the hidden directories. Select Tools ➪ Web Settings ➪ Advanced and check the Show Documents in Hidden Directories option. Note that this change affects this Web only.

When you refresh your Web, several new folders suddenly appear, as shown in Figure 17-16. The most important of these, for the moment, are the _pettalk folder, which you named during the Wizard process (earlier in the chapter), and the _borders folder, which contains standard header and footer elements that are included in the main files.

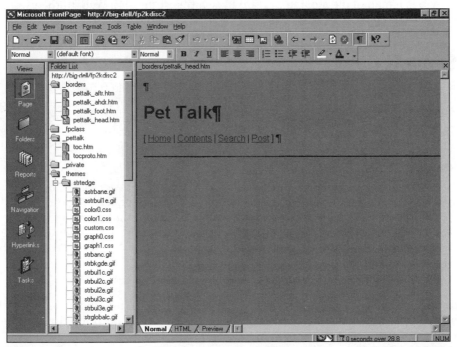

Figure 17-16: The directory structure of a Discussion Web after "unhiding" the hidden directories

What Goes on Behind the Curtain?

Magicians are told never to reveal the secrets of their black art. The FrontPage wizards seem to live by the same creed. They are very easy to use, but it is difficult to figure out what exactly they have done and where they store what they have created.

Why are wizards so secretive? Partly, I suspect, it is the *Wizard of Oz* syndrome: "Pay no attention to that man behind the curtain." The more mystery you can maintain, the more power you have over the mystified. Partly, too, FrontPage is not eager to have you mucking around in its files, because the less you know, the less likely you are to mess something up and then blame the creators of the application. Shame on you! On the other hand, knowing how the Discussion Web is assembled helps immensely, especially if you need to troubleshoot a problem.

Before you can readily customize your Discussion Web or make changes to it for maintenance purposes, you need to know what all of these files are. This section provides a map of the most important files in the Discussion Web, both system files and public HTML files.

Support files

A FrontPage Discussion Web is created with four supporting HTML files, which are stored in the _private folder of the Discussion Web — the main header, main footer, article header, and article footer — which are used and included on the main pages. This section describes how each of these HTML files functions.

Included Header

The Included Header file provides a consistent header for each of the main Web pages. The header file is located in the _private folder. It is named *yourweb*_head.htm, where *yourweb* represents the name that you gave your Discussion Web when you created it in the Discussion Web Wizard, and its complete title is Included Header for *YourWebTitle,* where *YourWebTitle* represents its title.

Open the Web header file from the pettalk1 Web in FrontPage. In this case, the default header consists of four text hyperlinks (the actual number of links may be less, depending on the selections you make in the Discussion Web Wizard). Your version is shown in Figure 17-17.

You want to replace the text hyperlinks with graphical buttons. This requires some care, however, to retain the links as they have been created. You add the graphics above the text links and then edit the links by using the View HTML feature. The next section moves the text links from the header to the footer.

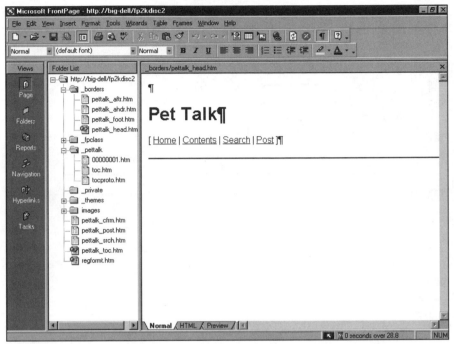

Figure 17-17: The bare-bones version of your Discussion Web header file

Tip

If you want your Web to be available to the widest possible audience, always provide a text link version of all site navigation. Not all Web browsers are graphical browsers, and some users who have browsers capable of viewing images choose to turn off the images, to speed the loading of pages.

Adding graphics

With the Included Header file open in Page view, select the text headline, Pet Talk, and delete it by using the Delete key or by selecting Edit ⇨ Delete. Position the cursor at the top of the page and select Insert ⇨ Image. Locate the _images folder for this chapter on the CD-ROM that is included in this book. Select the Pet Talk banner, ptbanner.gif. Click OK to add the banner to the page.

Next, insert the four graphical buttons for Home, Contents, Search, and Post. These images are located in the same folder as the banner graphic. They are named pthome.gif, pttoc.gif, ptsearch.gif, and ptpost.gif, respectively. To insert the images, first position the cursor on the line below the banner (press Enter to create a new line, if necessary). For each graphic, select Insert ⇨ Image, locate the image, and click OK. You may want to insert a space between each image (remember that multiple spaces are ignored). The results should resemble Figure 17-18.

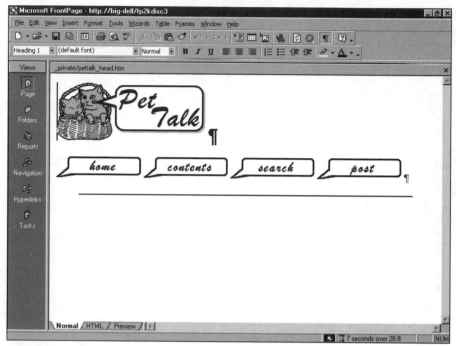

Figure 17-18: The Pet Talk Included Header with a new look

Editing graphic properties

For each of the newly inserted images, you should edit the image properties to add a text alternative and remove the border outline, as follows:

1. Select the image by clicking it once.

2. Select Edit ⇨ Image Properties.

3. In the General tab, add an appropriate text equivalent for the image in the Text input field of the Alternative Representations section.

4. In the Appearance tab, set the Border Thickness to zero.

5. Click OK to apply the changes.

Editing links

Using the standard method to add static hyperlinks to these graphics is possible (select the image, select Edit ⇨ Image Properties, and add the link to the Default Hyperlink field of the General tab), but you face a dilemma, because one of the default links includes Component information. Thus, rather than lose something important, you use the HTML Editor to copy the hyperlink information to the images.

With the Included Header file open, select the HTML tab. The page should resemble Figure 17-19.

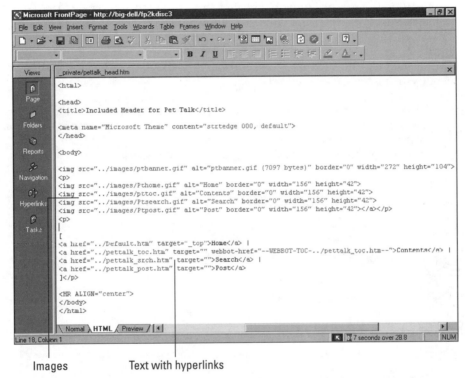

Images   Text with hyperlinks

Figure 17-19: The HTML text for the Include Header page before copying the hyperlinks to the images

Two sections, as indicated in the figure, are of particular interest. The first section consists of a series of four <IMG> tags. These are the buttons. The second section consists of the text links for Home, Contents, Search, and Post. Your mission is to copy the <A HREF> information from the text links to the buttons. The procedure is the same for all four buttons. For each, follow these steps:

1. Locate the text corresponding to the button. For example, for the first button, locate the Home text.

2. Select the <A HREF=...> tag immediately preceding this text, selecting everything between the <> brackets (including the brackets).

3. Use the keyboard shortcut Ctrl+C to copy this tag to the Clipboard.

4. Position the cursor immediately before the corresponding <IMG> tag (for example, <IMG SRC="pthome.gif">).

5. Use the keyboard shortcut Ctrl+V to paste the hyperlink tag in front of the <IMG> tag.

6. Position the cursor immediately after the <IMG> tag and type **</A>** to end the hyperlink tag. (Note that you could copy and paste this as well, if you prefer.)

Repeat this procedure for each of the four buttons. When you are finished, the HTML should resemble Figure 17-20. You can also check that the information copied correctly, using two other methods:

Tip   Notice that the page shown in Figure 17-20 breaks the <IMG> tag into two lines. This is perfectly legal. In fact, splitting a line in the middle of the tag is better than splitting it between the <A> and <IMG> tags. The latter method can cause stray underlining above or below your image in some browsers.

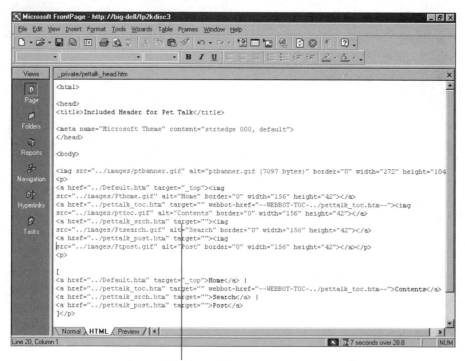

Images with hyperlinks

Figure 17-20: The revised header file HTML (with a little extra spacing for readability)

✦ **Pass the mouse cursor over each image.** The hyperlinked URL should appear in the status bar at the bottom of the Editor's window.

✦ **Open the Image Properties dialog box.** The correct hyperlink should appear in the Default Hyperlink field.

Caution If you edit the HTML in anything other than FrontPage's built-in HTML Editor, be aware that the various Components used in the Discussion Web add information to the file that is not seen in the FrontPage HTML Editor. Consequently, the HTML that you see in an external text editor looks slightly different.

If you are satisfied with the results (which you should be if you've followed the directions), save your changes.

Included Footer

The Included Footer file provides a consistent footer for each of the main Web pages. The footer file is located in the _private folder. It is named *yourweb*_foot.htm, where *yourweb* represents the name that you gave your Discussion Web when you created it in the Discussion Web Wizard, and its complete title is Included Footer for *YourWebTitle*, where *YourWebTitle* represents its title.

Open the Web footer file from the pettalk1 Web in Page view. The default footer consists of a simple horizontal rule with the TimeStamp Component underneath it.

You'll make two changes to this file: Move the text navigation from the header file to the footer file, and then add some additional identifying information to the end of the footer. The steps are as follows:

1. To move the text navigation, first open both the header and footer files in Editor. Switch to the header file, using the Window menu, and select the text navigation row. Select Edit ⇨ Cut, or use the keyboard shortcut Ctrl+X, to cut the text navigation from the header file and place it in the Clipboard. Switch back to the footer file. Position the cursor above the horizontal rule. Select Edit ⇨ Paste, or use the keyboard shortcut Ctrl+V, to paste the text navigation, including hyperlinks, into the footer. Save your changes.

Tip Sometimes, horizontal rules in FrontPage can be ornery about letting you insert the cursor in front of them. If you have trouble, try the following. Click the horizontal rule to select it so that it has a large, dark rectangle around it. Press the left-arrow key. The cursor moves one space before the horizontal rule.

2. Adding additional text is simply a matter of typing the text that you want. Figure 17-21 shows the completed footer and added text for the Pet Talk example, with a line identifying the owner of the Discussion Web, as well as a disclaimer (which probably has no legal validity, but at least sounds official). Save your changes.

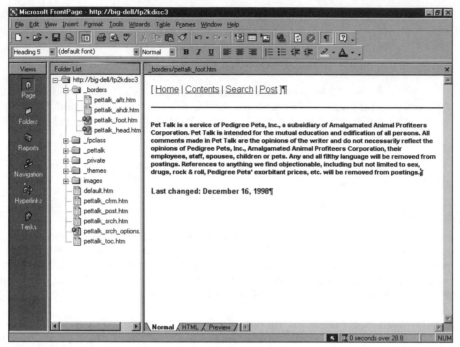

Figure 17-21: The Pet Talk Discussion Web footer, showing the added navigation and revised text

Included Article Header

The Included Article Header file provides a consistent header for messages posted to the Discussion Web. Similarly located in the _private folder, this article header is named *yourweb*_ahdr.htm, where *yourweb* represents the name that you gave your Discussion Web when you created it in the Discussion Web Wizard, and its complete title is Included Article Header for *YourWebTitle*, where *YourWebTitle* represents its title.

This header is very similar to the general header, with the addition of four new buttons:

✦ **Reply:** Opens a Submission Form with a standard "Re: *the original subject*" line placed in the subject header. Reply messages are listed directly under the original in the TOC.

✦ **Next:** Jumps to the next message in the same thread (at the same level of indentation in the TOC).

✦ **Previous:** Jumps to the previous message in the same thread.

✦ **Up:** Jumps to the "parent" of the current message (the original message to which the current message is related).

Your goal is to make the article header look like the general header. To do that, follow the directions previously provided in this section to do the following:

1. Add the graphical banner and navigational buttons.
2. Edit the properties of each graphic to add a text alternative and eliminate the border.
3. Copy the text hyperlinks to the buttons.

To add the Reply button, use the ptreply.gif; for the Next button, use ptnext.gif; for Previous, use ptprev.gif; and for Up, use ptup.gif. Do not delete the text navigation links, because you copy those to the article footer in the next section. Compare your results with Figure 17-22.

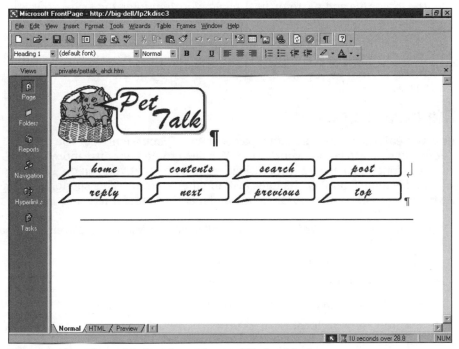

Figure 17-22: The article header with a multitude of buttons

Included Article Footer

The default article footer, also located in the _private folder, is named *yourweb*_aftr.htm, where *yourweb* represents the name that you gave your Discussion Web when you created it in the Discussion Web Wizard, and its complete title is Included Article Footer for *YourWebTitle*, where *YourWebTitle* represents its title.

Open the Web footer file from the pettalk1 Web in Page view. The default article footer looks exactly like the default Web footer. You want to add the same copy that you just added to the Web footer. You'll also move the article text navigation to this footer.

By now, if you have followed the earlier steps, you should be able to make these changes unprompted, but just in case, here are the basics:

1. To move the text navigation, first open both the article header and article footer files. Cut the text navigation from the article header file. Switch back to the footer file and paste the text navigation, including hyperlinks, into the footer. Save your changes.

2. To copy the footer text, open both the general footer and the article footer files. Copy the text. Switch back to the footer file and paste the text into the footer. Save your changes.

The main pages

After you edit the various included pages of your Discussion Web, you are practically ready to launch your forum. You need to do very little more to make your Web functional. In fact, very little more remains that you can do, even if you want to, because FrontPage handles just about everything. This section examines the main pages of your Discussion Web and readies them for a test run.

A FrontPage Discussion Web created with all available features has four main pages:

✦ A Table of Contents for listing messages

✦ A Submission Form for posting messages

✦ A Confirmation Page for responding to submissions

✦ A Search Form for locating messages

In addition, if you indicated during the Discussion Web Wizard that the TOC page is not this Web's home page, as you did earlier in the chapter, you need a home page. As you may have noticed when you were editing the Included Header files, the Discussion Web Wizard has assumed that you have a home page, default.htm, so you have actually added one already.

The Table of Contents

The Table of Contents page is named *yourweb*_toc.htm, where *yourweb* represents the name that you gave your Discussion Web when you created it in the Discussion Web Wizard. It is located in the main folder of your Discussion Web. The Discussion Web Wizard "suggests" but does not require that you include a TOC in your Discussion Web.

The default Table of Contents page is not much to look at, even with the included graphics, because you don't yet have any articles listed. FrontPage maintains this page automatically, so that, in principle, you never need to worry about it. If you have configured your discussion as a threaded forum, messages are arranged in outline fashion, with replies indented underneath the messages that prompted them. Figure 17-23 shows what the Table of Contents looks like after the forum is active.

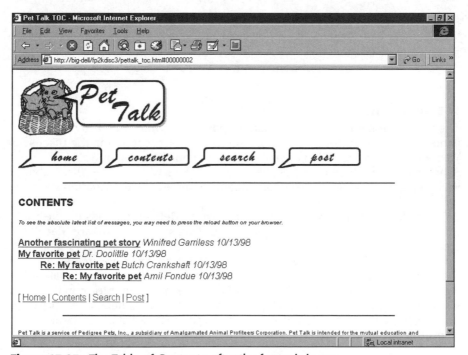

Figure 17-23: The Table of Contents, after the forum is in use

Introducing toc.htm and tocproto.htm

In addition to the Included files and the main pages that this section focus on, the Discussion Web Wizard also creates two crucial files, toc.htm and tocproto.htm, that it places in the _yourweb_ folder, where _yourweb_ represents the name that you assigned to the Discussion Web.

These two files are used by FrontPage to build the TOC. The tocproto.htm file is included in both toc.htm and the TOC file for the Discussion Web. The function of these two files is discussed later, in the section on managing your discussion forum. In general, you should leave these files alone.

Note that the _yourweb_ folder is initially hidden so that you can't see these pages. To view and edit these pages, you need to allow viewing of hidden folders: open the FrontPage Web Settings dialog box in Explorer (select Tools ⇨ Web Settings) and check the Show Documents in Hidden Directories check box, located on the Advanced tab.

You can make changes to the TOC by adding, deleting, or modifying text between the headline, CONTENTS, and the directions, "Note: you may need to reload this page to see the most recent additions."

The Submission Form

The Submission Form is named _yourweb_ post.htm, where _yourweb_ represents the name that you gave your Discussion Web when you created it in the Discussion Web Wizard. It is located in the main folder of your Discussion Web. The Submission Form is required, so, like it or not, your Web has one. The Submission Form uses the Discussion Web Component to process all information submitted.

Which fields appear in your Submission Form by default depends on the choices that you indicated when you completed the Discussion Web Wizard. Recall that you elected to include only Subject and Comments fields. The only other field included is the From field, which is included by default unless you have created a form that requires registration, in which case the Discussion Component automatically includes the username in the From input and doesn't prompt for it in this form. Had you opted to include either a Category field or a Products field, an empty drop-down menu would be included, enabling you to create a list of available categories or products.

Editing the Submission Form

You can edit the Submission Form in two places. The first place is the main copy, which has only a headline by default. This is a good place to put some directions. Be careful, however, because this same page is used to build the Reply Form (you likely have noticed that no separate page exists for this purpose). Any copy that you include here should be as applicable to a reply message as to a general, posted message. The solution used here is to provide directions for both cases. Not the most elegant method, but perhaps slightly better than nothing at all.

Editing and validating form fields

The second place that you can edit the Submission Form is in the form itself. You can edit any of the existing field properties: their labels, size, name, and so forth. Generally, these amount to cosmetic changes only. For example, as illustrated later in Figure 17-24, the name of the main text area is changed from "Article" to "Message." Also, the fields have been lengthened to be more in accordance with the graphic buttons.

One important change that you can make to the Submission Form is to provide validation requirements for the form fields. This may not prevent people from dumping junk into your forum, but it will at least put a cap on how much junk they can dump at one time. You can also use validation to require certain fields, so that you don't end up with a TOC with an empty row or, even worse, messages with no text.

At the very least, we recommend that you institute some limits on the length of messages. Figure 17-24 shows the Text Box Validation dialog box for the Message form field, in which the field is designated as Required, with a limit of 1000 characters. Even if you don't require a field, however, limiting its maximum length to a reasonable quantity is a good practice.

Note   The form field validation dialog box is accessible in either of two ways: right-click the form field and select Form Field Validation, or select Edit ⇨ Form Field Properties and click the Validate button in the Properties dialog box. For more information on form field validation properties, review Chapter 14.

Adding fields to the Submission Form

In addition to editing the existing form fields, you can add custom fields to the Submission Form. Input from these fields is added to the top of the message page, with the following format (where *FieldName* represents the Name property of the form field, and *InputValue* represents whatever the user submits in the field):

FieldName: *InputValue*

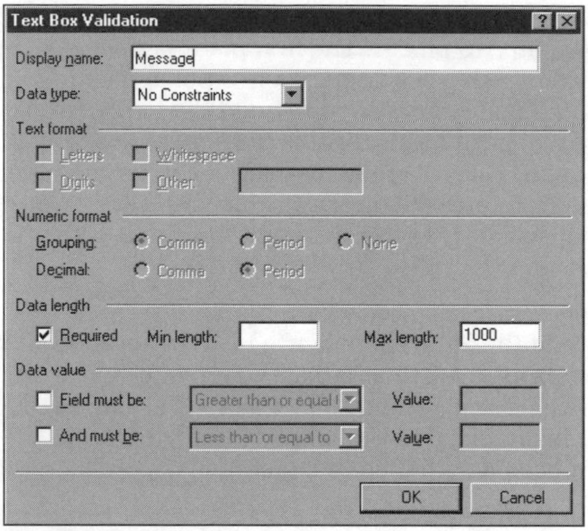

Figure 17-24: The Text Box Validation dialog box, showing validation parameters for the Message text box

To illustrate this, an Email field has been added to the form, enabling users to include an e-mail address if they want to receive personal responses directly. To add this field, position the cursor in front of the Comments box label and press Enter to create some space. In the line immediately below the From field, type **Email:** and insert a line break by pressing Shift+Enter. Select Insert ➪ Form Field ➪ One Line Text Box. Adjust the size and other properties of the Email field to your liking. Be sure to change the default field name (something like T1) to **Email**.

Your completed Submission Form page is shown in Figure 17-25.

Editing Submission Form handler settings

Every Web form has a *handler*, a program that processes and responds to the input from the form. (If this is news to you, you many want to review Chapter 15.) The form handler for the Discussion Web Submission Form is the Discussion Web Component. It is automatically associated with this form when you create your Discussion Web. It does have some optional settings that you can configure to your liking.

To access the form handler settings, right-click inside the dotted-line box that surrounds the form element, and select Form Properties. The dialog box indicates that the Discussion Web Component is, indeed, the selected form handler. Click the Options button below the Form Handler drop-down menu. The Settings for Discussion Form Handler dialog box appears, with the following three tabs:

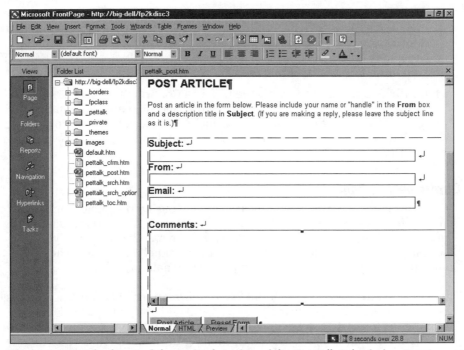

Figure 17-25: The heart of the revised version of the Pet Talk Submission Form

Caution

Somehow, the Discussion Web Wizard forgets to mention the fact that discussion folder names can be no more than eight characters, including the underscore (see the FrontPage Help entry for the Discussion tab of the Settings for Discussion Form Handler dialog box. I learned this one the hard way, when I tried to change the folder name manually, and it insisted on changing it back.

✦ **Discussion tab:** You can identify the Title of the Discussion Web, the Directory in which the discussion articles are stored, and the optional name of a styles page. These are all set by the Discussion Web Wizard. The more interesting options are in the section titled, Table of Contents Layout, in which you can indicate what fields to display for each record in the TOC. These fields can consist of any of the fields in the Submission Form, as well as the Time, Date, Remote Computer Name, and User Name fields, which are added to articles automatically. You can also select the order of the TOC entries from this tab. Check the Order Newest to Oldest check box to display entries in reverse chronological order. Leave it unchecked to display entries chronologically.

Caution

Of course, if you change the Table of Contents Layout options after your TOC already has contents, the new options take effect only at that point, and are not applied retroactively.

✦ **Article tab:** You can change the default name of the header and footer files to include on the article page. More important, you can select what automatic information to display for each article. Options are Time, Date, Remote Computer Name (or IP Number, if no name is available), and User Name (if the Web has a Registration Component).

✦ **Confirm tab:** You can identify the URL of a Confirmation Page as well as a Validation Failure page. The Confirmation Page is created automatically if you requested that option in the Discussion Web Wizard. You have to create the Validation Failure page on your own, although FrontPage provides a default error page.

Confirmation Page

The Confirmation Page displays a message to anyone who submits a message to the Discussion Web. It is located in the main folder of your Web and is named *yourweb*_cfm.htm, where *yourweb* represents the name that you gave your Discussion Web when you created it in the Discussion Web Wizard. The Confirmation Page is optional, but fairly conventional.

This Confirmation Page works like all form confirmations in FrontPage. The page consists of a general-purpose message with embedded Confirmation Field Components. In the default version of the Confirmation Page, the only field inserted in this fashion is the Subject. In general, limiting the confirmation fields to only those that you know the user has submitted is a good idea. Alternatively, you might use the Confirmation Page to parrot the information that the user has just submitted.

The Pet Talk Confirmation Page, with some minor cosmetic revisions, is shown in Figure 17-26.

Search Form

The Discussion Web uses the same Search Component that is used to index general-purpose Webs. The index for the Discussion Web search, however, is limited to the files contained in the *_yourweb* folder. The Search Form page is named *yourweb*_srch.htm and is located in the main folder of the Discussion Web.

The Pet Talk Search Form page, with minor revisions, is shown in Figure 17-27. The principle innovation introduced is the link to a Search Options page, for additional information on using the Search Form. Functionally, the Discussion Web search engine is exactly the same as the general-purpose Web search engine.

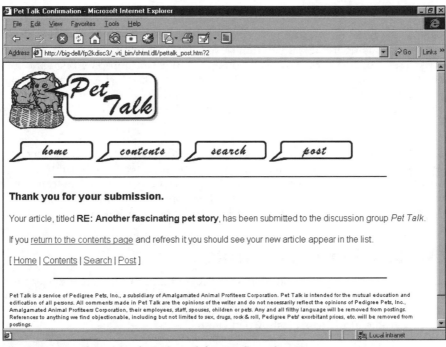

Figure 17-26: The revised version of the Confirmation Page

Figure 17-27: The Pet Talk Search Form

Tutorial 17.1: Add Frames to Your Forum

Recall that when you created your first Discussion Web, you chose not to build your Web by using frames. If you don't use frames, your Discussion Web will be accessible to more users. However, you may notice that jumping back and forth from the TOC to articles can become tiresome if you are trying to catch up on discussion postings. Using the Next, Previous, and Up navigation buttons can help, but you are operating on faith, because you can't see what you will get until you get there.

The chief advantage of using frames for your Discussion Web is that users can view the TOC while they read articles. Because the techniques for creating frames are covered in Chapter 10, this section provides a brief overview of the frame options available in the Discussion Web Wizard. These options include choosing whether your frame sets will have a vertical or horizontal orientation of the TOC.

A vertical Table of Contents

A frame set with the TOC located in a vertical column on the left is easily the most popular frames structure currently on the Web. If you use the Discussion Web Wizard, you can create a three-frame frame set that uses this structure and includes a banner frame at the top, as shown in Figure 17-28.

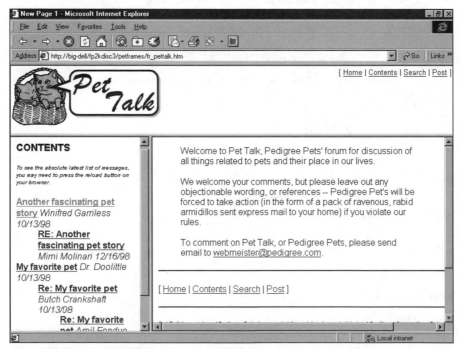

Figure 17-28: A vertical frame version of Pet Talk

This option may have the advantage of convention, but it can run into a small snag if you happen to have a deeply nested thread like the one pictured in Figure 17-28. You can minimize the problem by making the frames resizable (which is the default setting when you create them in the Discussion Web Wizard) so that users can expand the size of the Table of Contents window if they need to. Or, you can use a frame set with a horizontal orientation.

Keep in mind that if you create the vertical TOC frame set using the Discussion Web Wizard, you need to edit the frame set to add a provision for nonframes browsers.

A horizontal Table of Contents

The Discussion Web Wizard offers two variations of the horizontal TOC:

✦ A two-frame version that includes provision for nonframes browsers

✦ A three-frame version that adds a banner frame but doesn't provide an alternative for nonframes browsers

An example of the three-frame version is shown in Figure 17-29, with the same TOC that created problems for the vertical orientation described in the previous section. This is clearly a more readable TOC, although it is somewhat more difficult in this version to see the entire article (unless you happen to have a large monitor at high resolution). Again, making the frames resizable can help.

The Official Advice

For what it is worth, the official advice on managing content is this: If you need to delete or edit the content of the message, simply replace the content with a generic "[Deleted Article]" (personally, I think "Expletive Deleted" is a bit more colorful), but leave the message file intact. This way, you don't interfere with the Component's methods of keeping track of the number of messages and how they are related. Plus, everyone will be able to see what a censorious administrator you are.

The bottom line is that you should make any changes at your own risk. If you try to create any kind of serious discussion forum, however, you are likely to discover that the risk is unavoidable.

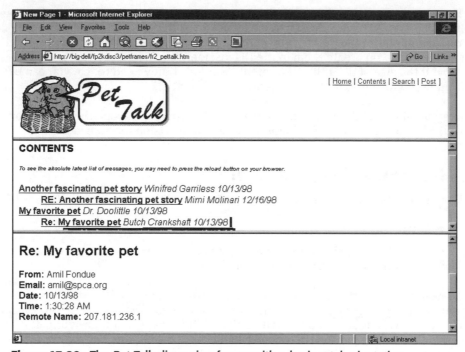

Figure 17-29: The Pet Talk discussion forum with a horizontal orientation

Managing Your Discussion Web

The FrontPage Discussion Web was designed to be configured once and then left alone. FrontPage offers no provision for editing the list of messages. In fact, the official documentation advises you not to touch the message files.

Not being able to edit the forum can be a rather major shortcoming, particularly if you happen to have a popular discussion forum. In this case, you may want to consider some method of archiving content.

Adding Registration to Your Discussion

When you use the Discussion Web Wizard to create your forum, among other things, it asks you, "Will the discussion take place in a protected Web?" This is the Wizard's gentle way of asking whether users need to register with a username and password to use the forum. If you answer, "Yes, only registered users can post articles," the Wizard creates a default Registration Form, which enables users to register themselves to use your Discussion Web. From that point, you are on your own.

A Sobering Tale from Real Life (Expletives Deleted)

The following is a true story (mostly). Never being one to take my own warnings too seriously, when I encountered a glitch due to changing filenames (see the Caution earlier in this chapter, in the section "Editing Submission Form Handler Settings"), I decided to attempt to repair the damage by boldly editing the Pet Talk TOC and message folder. I was able to move the files around and renumber them. By editing the tocproto.htm, I managed to get the messages to show up in the correct place in the TOC. I reset the article counter in the service.cnf file. I even got the messages linked to one another by changing a line in the _vti_cnf folder entry for each message file. But, I repaired the damage only after a very, very long time of messing around (and I only had *three* messages at the time). And even then, I was not convinced all was as it should be. In the end, even though it was sort of working, I decided it would be safer and faster to redo the whole thing. So I did.

Conclusion? I cannot recommend attempting to edit anything having to do with the messages or the TOC. Nor would I recommend manually changing the names of any of the files or folders created. FrontPage scatters information about these files all over the place, and it is easy to overlook one vital place where the information needs to be changed.

Note   What is the purpose of requiring a password if you then allow anyone to create one? Typically for marketing purposes, by forcing users to hand over some information about themselves if they want to participate. If you want to use passwords strictly for security, you should come up with another way of enabling users to receive a password—after you or someone else has qualified them. The topic of registration and security is addressed in Chapter 23.

Before you blithely answer Yes to this question, thinking that a protected discussion is probably a good idea, you need to ascertain that you, in fact, have the authority to implement the registration feature. What it takes and how to do it are the topics of this section.

So that you understand better what you are doing, how the registration system works from the user's perspective is examined first. When the users come to your Discussion Web, they are prompted to enter their username and password.

Do you have what it takes?

Before you can add a Registration Component to your Web (Discussion Web or otherwise), you need to have an appropriate system and an appropriate level of authority within FrontPage. To set up a Registration Component, you must have the following minimum requirements:

✦ Access to an NT or UNIX Web server that is capable of maintaining Web passwords, and that is running FrontPage Extensions (which are necessary for the Discussion Web anyway)

✦ The ability to add Web pages to the root FrontPage Web, which is where the Registration Form must reside

✦ Administrator-level authority within your own Web

If you are in one of the following situations, you can forget about registering users via the FrontPage Registration Component:

✦ You are using either Microsoft's Internet Information Server for Windows NT or Personal Web Server for Windows 95

✦ You use a FrontPage hosting service that provides you with access to a subweb but not to the root Web of the system

✦ You use a hosting service that doesn't permit customers to implement passwords on their Webs (which isn't uncommon)

✦ You are only a FrontPage author, without Administrator permissions

Note   You may feel that these exclusions rule out a fair number of circumstances. Indeed, they seem to leave only non-Microsoft Windows or UNIX servers for which Microsoft has published server extensions. For a list of available extensions, see Appendix C.

The Registration Form

If you have indicated that you plan to have a password-protected discussion forum, the Discussion Web Wizard automatically creates for you a general-purpose Registration Form. To use the Registration Form, you need to perform two steps:

1. Move the Registration Form to the root Web of your Web server.

2. Adjust the permissions for the Discussion Web to require user registration.

Moving the Registration Form

If you indicated that you want to require users to register to use your discussion forum, FrontPage automatically opens the Registration Form in Editor after it creates your new Web. At the top of the page is a long comment field that repeats the directions here (although in reverse order).

To save the Registration Form in the root Web, switch to Explorer and close the current Web. Open the root Web in the usual manner. Switch back to Editor and select File ➪ Save. The Save As dialog box opens, allowing you to save the Registration Form to the root Web with the default name of web_selfregistration_form.htm (or you can change the name to anything else that you want).

Setting Access Permissions

After you save the Registration Form to the root Web, you need to change the permissions on the Web so that users are required to provide a username and password before entering.

Note Notice that it is quite possible to set up limited access without providing a Registration Form that enables users to self-register.

How Registration works

First, make sure one concept is clear: The Registration Form is used by currently unregistered visitors to create a new username and password for themselves. This page is not the "login" page for users who already have a valid username and password. They should proceed directly to the protected Web.

When a user goes to your protected Web, they are confronted with a standard Web Password dialog box. If the user has already created a username and password, they can enter them and proceed on to the page that they requested. If they do not have a username or password, they receive a message indicating that their authorization has failed.

Note Some Web servers allow custom pages to be associated with failed authorization. If you have such an option, you can use it to send users directly to the Registration Form, if they fail to enter a valid username/password combination.

Visitors who don't yet have a username/password combination must proceed to the Registration Form to create one. After they complete the form, they receive a confirmation message, either the default or a custom one of your design. For more on the Registration Component and on security measures in general, see Chapter 23.

Note How do new visitors know that they need to register? Typically, you create the home page in an unprotected area — the root Web or some other Web — and direct users to that page. From there, you can create links to the protected discussion area for registered users and to the Registration Form for new users. The one catch in FrontPage is that password protection is Web-specific. You can't create a protected area within an unprotected Web, or vice versa. So, any initial pages need to be in a separate Web.

Implementing Multiple Discussions

One way to forestall the need to archive your Discussion Web is to create multiple Discussion Webs. For example, if your original Discussion Web focuses on pets, you might create spin-off, specialized Discussion Webs for the pets most often talked about, such as cats and dogs.

Customizing the Discussion Web Template Files

If you are planning to create multiple Discussion Webs with a similar appearance, you may want to give some thought to customizing the template files that the Discussion Web Wizard uses when it creates the default versions of the Discussion Web pages.

A full discussion of how to do this is beyond the scope of this chapter. The Discussion Web Wizard uses several HTX files as its templates for the various pages that it creates. These files are found in the vtdisc.wiz subfolder of the Webs folder in which you installed FrontPage (by default, in Program Files\Microsoft FrontPage). By editing these files, you can change the way that the Wizard builds its default Webs.

Note: Before you make any changes to the Wizard files, be sure to save a backup copy of the folder in a safe place.

If you have the ability to create multiple subwebs, this is probably the safest route, and it has the advantage of making it easier to upload changes to one discussion at a time. Alternatively, you can add additional Discussion Webs to your original Web. The method for doing this is essentially the same as that of creating your initial Discussion Web. The crucial difference comes right at the beginning. With the current Discussion Web open in Explorer, select New ➪ FrontPage Web. Select the Discussion Web Wizard and check the Add to the Current Web check box below the selection window. Besides this difference, just make sure to give the new Discussion Web a different title and folder name.

Note   For better or worse, each Discussion Web has its own search index, so cross-discussion searching is not possible.

Summary

This chapter explored the many components and features of the FrontPage Discussion Web Component, which wraps up your tour of FrontPage's Components. Part V raises the bar a notch higher, to examine the various ways in which FrontPage can work with programming languages to provide both simple and complex forms of interactivity. If you are not a programmer, don't panic. These chapters do not try to turn you into a code jockey in five easy lessons. Rather, the focus is on providing an understanding of the various (no, I did not say "nefarious"!) technologies that FrontPage is capable of working with, peppered with numerous examples that you can really use.

✦   ✦   ✦

Programming Elements

Scripting Languages

On the Web, all communication takes place between the Web browser that you use to access Web pages and one or more Web servers. Each time that you request a new page, your Web browser sends that request to a server, and the server responds. If you submit a form, your browser passes along the information to the server, which is responsible for processing and responding to your input, typically by using a CGI program (for more information on CGI, see "Developing Custom Form Handlers" in Chapter 15).

In many cases, having the server do all processing works very well, and it ensures that the developer does not have to worry about what particular browser you are using. Sometimes, however, it would be convenient to process a request the user has made, or input the user has submitted, without having to send the information all the way back to the server. Client-side scripting languages were created to address this need.

When you use a client-side scripting language, you embed programming directly into your Web page. When a user requests this page, the scripting is sent along with the rest of the page. The browser has to be savvy enough to interpret the scripting language and respond appropriately.

By using a client-side scripting language, you can increase the interactive character of your Web page without forcing the Web browser to send a request to the server and reload the page with a response. With scripting, for example, you can do the following:

✦ Have images on the page change when the user positions the mouse over them

✦ Perform calculations and automatically update form field information

✦ Pop up a message if the user enters invalid information into a form field

✦ Design your Web page to display different information to the user, depending on the type of browser he or she is using

Best of all, client-side scripting languages are easy to learn and use. Of course, having some experience with other programming languages helps, but even if you don't, you should be able to follow the example scripts provided in this chapter and adapt them to your own use. Scripting languages are not suited to large-scale applications, but they provide a quick way to increase the flexibility and interactivity of your Web pages.

To script or not to script

A scripting language gives you some powerful tools for adding functionality to your Web pages. You can manipulate the properties of page objects, such as the value of a form field, based on user-initiated actions. And, with a programming tool such as the Script Wizard, adding scripts is relatively simple.

Any time that you want to add simple functionality to your Web pages, you may want to consider using a scripting language. Remember that if you create script-based functionality that is essential to the operation of the page, you need to find a way to accommodate users who are using browsers that are not compatible with scripting languages. The following are some of the tasks that scripting languages are well-suited to do:

✦ Calculations

✦ Simple animation

✦ Window and frame control

✦ Pop-up messages

✦ Form field updating

✦ Form field validation

✦ Dynamic page control

✦ Browser detection

When not to use a script

Scripting languages are useful, fun, and easy to use (if you like that sort of thing), but they are not suited to every task. For one thing, scripts are not compiled, which makes them easy to appropriate. Another drawback of scripting languages is that they tend to be browser-dependent, thus complicating the choice of which browser to use under various conditions. (But, see the discussion of ECMAScript in the next section to hear good news on this front.) The following are reasons when *not* to use a script:

✦ If you need to access or process data

✦ If you need to record user input

✦ If you have a big project on a short timeframe

✦ If you need to protect your proprietary code

✦ If you need to support a lowest common denominator browser

A scripting example

Suppose that you have created a form that asks users to supply their name and e-mail address. You realize that a fair number of people are likely to input their e-mail address incorrectly. You would like to have a simple way to catch those who unintentionally mistype their e-mail address.

Using a CGI application, you could write a program that would do this. The user would need to submit the form to the server. The CGI application would read the e-mail address input by the user, and compose a reply message prompting the user to confirm his or her e-mail address. The user would then either successfully confirm his or her address, in which case the form would be resubmitted, or edit his or her e-mail address, in which case the original form would have to be reloaded with the existing data and the whole process repeated until the user got the e-mail address right.

This CGI solution has two main drawbacks:

✦ A fair amount of programming overhead is involved in building any CGI application, more overhead than you want for such a simple function.

✦ Your users are likely to find this function mildly distracting, if not annoying, particularly if they need to correct their e-mail address.

To effect this enhanced behavior more simply, you need some way to create a "smart" Web page, one that could perform this function without intervention from the server. That way involves using client-side scripting, a programming capability that resides in the Web page itself and that performs its work independent of the Web server, from within the Web client (in other words, the user's Web browser).

Now, imagine that instead of using a CGI program, you could simply pop up a message box with the same confirmation request when the form was about to be submitted. In this case, if the user makes a mistake, they are prompted to try again. No information is ever submitted until it is correct. This method is easy on the Web server and easy on the user. Plus, because no connections are made across the Internet, the confirmation process is blazingly fast, even on the slowest dial-up connection.

Creation of this script requires three simple steps:

1. Create the form (see Chapter 14 for details on building forms in FrontPage). Your example form is shown in Figure 18-1.

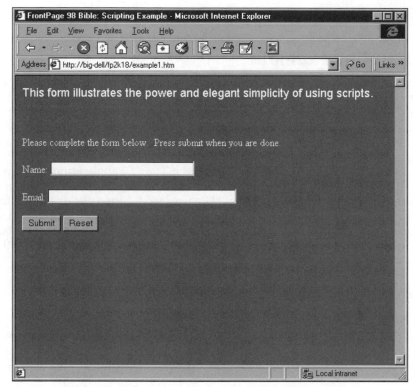

Figure 18-1: The beginning of your e-mail confirmation script

2. Switching to the HTML tab, insert the custom script function necessary to perform the confirmation. Later in the chapter, you learn how to use Microsoft Script Editor to add script. For now, just follow along. The script in question has a single function, called confirmEmail, which looks like this:

```
<script LANGUAGE="JavaScript">
<!-
function confirmEmail(name,email)
{
var confirmedEmail = window.prompt(name + ", Please retype
your email to confirm:","");
  if (confirmedEmail != null && confirmedEmail !="") {
    if (email==confirmedEmail) {
```

```
        document.ex1.submit();
        return true;
      }
      else {
        window.alert("First address (" + email + ") does not
match confirmation (" + confirmedEmail + "). Please try
again.");
        document.ex1.Email.value="";
        return false;
      }
    }
    else {
      return false;
    }
  }
//—>
</script>
```

3. After you construct your function, update the `button` tag to bind the `confirmEmail()` function to the button's `onClick` event handler. The `button` tag should resemble this:

```
<INPUT TYPE="button" VALUE="Submit"
ONCLICK="confirmEmail(ex1.Name.value,ex1.Email.value)"
NAME="B1">
```

When the user clicks the button, it executes the script, causing the `confirmEmail` function to spring into action, as shown in Figure 18-2.

Working with Microsoft Script Editor

FrontPage 2000 has incorporated a full-featured script editing application, Microsoft Script Editor (MSE). This editor replaces the Script Wizard in FrontPage 98. If you have used the Script Wizard, you initially may be disappointed at its disappearance. MSE can be daunting at first to the novice programmer who simply wants an easy way to add scripts to their Web pages. However, MSE is a much more robust, highly flexible, and powerful environment than the Script Wizard. MSE just takes a little getting used to.

Complete treatment of MSE is beyond the scope of this book. This section describes the basic MSE environment, after which four types of scripting (JavaScript, VBScript, DHTML, and ASP) that can be done in MSE are explored.

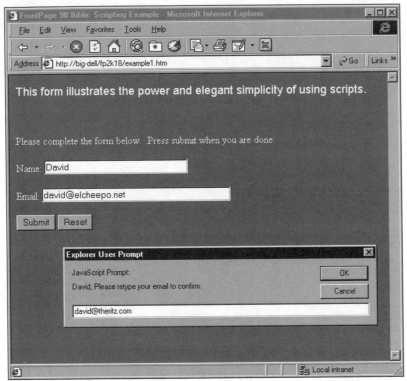

Figure 18-2: The confirmEmail script in action — no CGI required!

Starting Microsoft Script Editor

Microsoft Script Editor is designed for editing and debugging HTML, JavaScript (JScript), VBScript, DHTML, and Active Server Pages (server-side script).

Caution   If you have never used MSE and you didn't explicitly install it when you installed FrontPage 2000, you may receive a warning message "Microsoft FrontPage can't use Web Scripting. The feature is not currently installed. Would you like to install it now?" Select Yes, and have your installation CD-ROM handy.

To start MSE, open a Web page in FrontPage (MSE is not accessible without an open page) and select Tools ➪ Macro ➪ Microsoft Script Editor. The selected HTML page is opened in the Source tab of MSE's HTML Editor.

Working in the MSE environment

By default, MSE opens with the following windows, shown in Figure 18-3:

✦ A main HTML Editor window in the center

✦ A window on the left side, containing Document Outline view, Script Outline view, and HTML toolbox

✦ Two half-size windows on the right side, with the Project Explorer window on top and the Properties window on the bottom

In addition to the windows visible in the default layout, several other windows exist that you can work with in MSE. The next sections briefly describe each of the principle windows in the MSE environment and list some of the methods that you can use to customize the MSE environment to suit your needs.

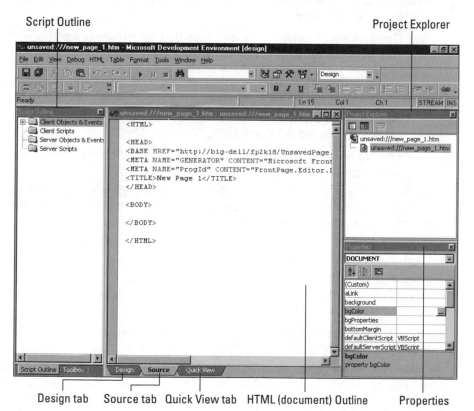

Figure 18-3: The default MSE environment, showing the HTML Editor, Script Outline, Project Explorer, and Properties windows

MSE windows

MSE contains a multitude of windows. Besides the HTML Editor window, in which you do most of your work, the other windows typically provide various views of the contents of the page that you are editing, lists of available objects to add to the page, or debugging information. The following are the main MSE windows, with a brief description of their function:

✦ **HTML Outline:** Displays a tree view of the HTML elements currently in the HTML document that you are editing. Double-click an item in the list to locate and select the item in the HTML Editor window.

✦ **Toolbox:** Contains a list of elements that you can add to the current HTML page. You can customize this toolbox by adding new elements to the list.

✦ **Script Outline:** Provides a tree-based view of scripting objects and events that you can add to your pages.

✦ **HTML Editor:** Enables you to edit the FrontPage HTML page. The HTML editor window consists of three views:

  • **Design View:** Available only for pages that are created directly in MSE. Any pages created using FrontPage 2000 have this view disabled. (In essence, FrontPage controls the Design view for its own pages.) When available, Design view functions as a WYSIWYG HTML editor, much like the Normal view in FrontPage.

  • **Source View:** The default view for the HTML editor, it displays the HTML source of the page for editing.

  • **Quick View:** Equivalent to FrontPage's Preview tab, this allows for quick previewing of the page you are editing.

✦ **Project Explorer:** Displays a hierarchical list of all MSE projects and the items contained in each project. Use this window to navigate through your projects, by selecting a project or item to make it active.

✦ **Properties:** Lists the properties of a selected object in the Editor. Use this window to edit an object's properties.

✦ **Object Browser:** Displays the various elements (classes, properties, methods, and events) available for use in your project. It is primarily a dictionary. Use it to find the syntax of objects and their elements.

✦ **Output**: Displays run-time messages when you run a script. It is typically used for debugging purposes.

✦ **Debug Windows**: Series of windows that provide information that is helpful in debugging scripts. Debug windows include: Immediates, Autos, Locals, Watch, Threads, Call Stack, and Running Documents. You can also access these windows from the Debug toolbar.

MSE toolbars

MSE provides the following toolbars for easy access to commonly used commands:

✦ **Standard:** Contains buttons to most of the basic file operations.

✦ **Debug:** Provides button access to the main debug features and windows.

✦ **Design:** Active only in Design view (which is unavailable from FrontPage, as previously indicated). It includes functions that affect how a page is displayed in Design view, and that enable you to add absolute-positioned elements to your HTML page.

✦ **HTML:** Contains HTML formatting elements to add to the page that you are editing. This toolbar is similar to the Formatting toolbar in FrontPage.

✦ **Window UI:** Provides shortcuts to manipulate the MSE windows and environment.

✦ **Fullscreen:** Single-item toolbar that toggles MSE between full and partial screen.

Customizing the environment

The MSE environment consists of a sophisticated set of windows and toolbars. After you are familiar with MSE's major features, you can customize the environment to suit your preferences. This section describes some of the general methods that you can use to alter the MSE environment to your liking:

✦ **Tab-linking windows:** Most of MSE can be superimposed in a single window with multiple tabs. To tab-link a window, click and drag the window on top of another existing window. MSE creates a single window with two tabs. You can tab-link additional windows to this window in the same way.

✦ **Dockable window and toolbars:** Many of the windows and toolbars can be fastened (or *docked*) to the top, bottom, left, or right side of the MSE environment. To dock or undock an item, click and drag it to the desired location.

✦ **Customizable toolbars:** You can add items to existing toolbars by using the Customize Toolbar feature. FrontPage has a similar feature. For details, see Chapter 22, "Customizing FrontPage."

✦ **Customizable toolbox:** You can also add elements to the various toolboxes. To customize a toolbox, right-click the toolbox and select Customize Toolbox. Select one or more items to add to the toolbox from the list of available elements.

✦ **Define Window Layout:** Use this command to define a custom layout that you want to be able to re-create. MSE has several default layouts (Debug, Design,

DevStudio, Edit HTML, Full Screen, and Visual Basic). To add your own layout, first arrange the layout as you want to save it. Select View ➪ Define Window Layout and give the layout a name. Select Add to add this name to the list of available layouts.

Editing an HTML page

As a preliminary example of how you can work with MSE, the following process creates a simple JavaScript form that prompts users to enter the year in which they were born, and then returns a message informing them which animal is associated with their birth date in the Chinese calendar:

1. Create a new, blank Web page in FrontPage.

2. Select Tools ➪ Macro @> Microsoft Script Editor to open the blank Web page in this application. Unless you have already reconfigured the MSE environment, the page opens in the Source tab of the Editing window, as previously illustrated in Figure 18-3.

   You need to create a form with one text-input box and a button. Of course, you could do this in FrontPage, but you need to practice your MSE skills. MSE includes a Design view, which is the equivalent of FrontPage Normal view, but it works only for pages that are first created in MSE. So, you work in Source view, the equivalent of FrontPage HTML view. Before continuing, make sure that you have open the Toolbox, Document Outline, Script Outline, and Properties windows. You can arrange these windows in any way that you like: my preference is to group together the first three windows, with tab links to the left of the main editing window, and then place the Properties window to the right. If you need details on how to customize the MSE environment, refer to that information earlier in the chapter.

3. Select your new page in the editing window. You should see the DOCUMENT properties displayed in the Properties window; select the Title property and change the text to **Your Birth Year Animal**. Note that the text between the <TITLE> and </TITLE> tags is updated in the Source tab.

4. In the Source tab of the main editing window, place the cursor inside the <BODY> tag of your blank HTML page. Notice that the Properties window changes to reflect the properties list for the selected tag. To change the color of the page, select the bgcolor property and click the three-dot [...] button to its right in the value field. Select the Safety Palette tab in the MSE Color Picker and select an attractive color for the background of your page (for example, #666699). Click OK to accept the color and update your page. Note that the color is registered in the <BODY> tag as well as in the Properties window (see Figure 18-4).

5. To preview your page color, select the Quick View tab in the main editing window. Voila! Alternatively, you can switch back to FrontPage and see that your page has been updated in Normal view.

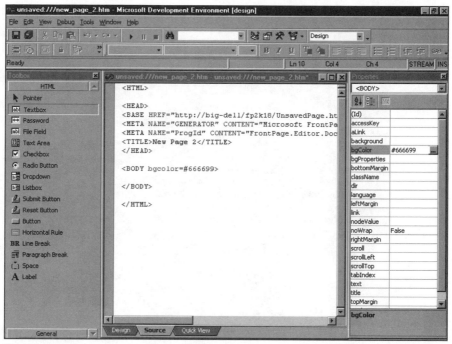

Figure 18-4: Your new page after adding a background color in the Properties sheet

6. Create your form. Place the cursor between the `<BODY>` and `</BODY>` tags. Select the HTML menu and Form to add a `<FORM>` tag set to the page. Select the Form element. You can do this as you previously did, by placing the cursor in the `<FORM>` tag element. Alternatively, select the Document Outline window. Two elements are listed: a `<BODY>` tag and a `<FORM>` element. Click the Form element to select it.

7. In the Properties dialog box, change the form name from the default "form1" to **birth_form**. (You also can change the `ID` attribute, although it isn't used in this example.) Because you are implementing a client-side script only, the `Action` attribute associated with this form isn't needed, so you can leave it blank.

8. Select the Toolbox window. Place the cursor between the `<FORM>` and `</FORM>` elements in the editing window and double-click the Textbox item to add a textbox to the form. Change the name of the Textbox from text1 to **byear**, using the method described in the previous step.

9. Repeat the preceding steps to add a form Button after the Textbox. Change its value to **Get Animal**. Figure 18-5 shows the form as it is shaping up in the Quick View tab.

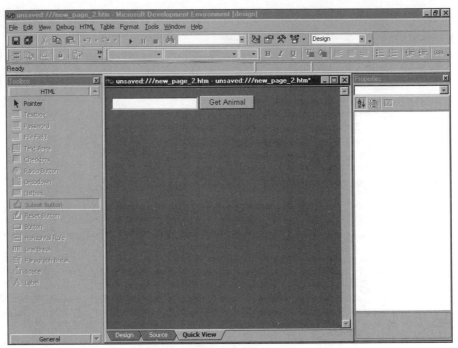

Figure 18-5: Your form page as it appears in the Quick View tab

It is time to add the scripting to your form, but first, this is a good time to save your work. Click the Save button on the MSE toolbar. Notice that MSE switches back to FrontPage momentarily to save the page, and then returns.

10. By default, MSE is configured to use VBScript as both the client and server scripting languages of choice (how surprising!). You want to use JavaScript (aka JScript), so you must first change the document properties to reflect this choice, which you can do in either of two ways:

   • Select the defaultClientScript property in the DOCUMENT properties window and change its value to JavaScript.

   • Select View ➪ Property Pages and change the Client Default Scripting Language to JavaScript.

Note MSE defaults to VBScript as the default client scripting language regardless of how you have configured your Web Settings in FrontPage (is this a bug or a feature?).

11. Select the Script Outline window and open the Client Objects and Events folder (if it isn't already open). In addition to the two default objects, Document and Window, you should see your form and, under it, the textbox and button objects.

Tip

You can hide/show the events available for each object by right-clicking any object in the Script Outline window and selecting Hide Events or Show Events.

Open the button object and show its events. Double-click the onClick event, which causes two things to happen to your Web page. First, MSE adds some stub JavaScript to the header section of your page:

```
<SCRIPT ID=clientEventHandlersJS LANGUAGE=javascript>
<!--

function button1_onclick() {

}

//-->
</SCRIPT>
```

This represents a script block with an empty function, called button1_onclick(), that is called when the button is clicked. To connect this code to the button, MSE also adds code to the <BUTTON> tag itself, so that the tag now looks like this:

```
<INPUT type="button" value="Get Animal!" id=button1
name=button1 LANGUAGE=javascript onclick="return
button1_onclick()">
```

Your task is to write the code that makes the page work to your specification. At this point, because you haven't yet learned how JavaScript works, concentrate more on how to use MSE to insert this code rather than on how the code works.

12. Basically, your goal is to take the year entered by the user, figure out which of the twelve animals of the Chinese calendar is associated with that year, and return a message informing the user which animal sign they were born under. When the form button is clicked, you need to take the value entered into the textbox and pass it to a function called get_sign(), the code for which follows:

```
function get_sign(yearoffset) {
  signs = new Array("Dragon","Snake",
"Horse","Sheep","Monkey","Rooster","Dog","Pig","Rat","Ox","Ti
ger","Hare");
  return signs[(yearoffset % 12)];
  }
```

Manually enter this code into the Source view window. Basically, this function takes a year that is offset from a baseline year that is known to be a year of the dragon (1880 is used, on the assumption that few people over 118 will use the form). The get_sign() function then divides the offset year by 12 and uses the remainder to figure out which of the twelve animals to return.

13. Add code to fill out the onclick function that MSE created for you. The bare-bones version of this function looks like this:

```
function button1_onclick() {
  var baseline = 1880;
  var byear = parseInt(document.birth_form.byear.value);
  var offsetyear = byear-baseline;
  window.alert("You were born in the year of the " +
get_sign(offsetyear) + "!");
  }
```

A couple of notable things happen as you type in this code. When you type **parseInt**, MSE reminds you of the proper syntax for this JavaScript function (see Figure 18-6). It is even smart enough to recognize your own get_sign() function and show you its syntax when you start to type it. Also, when you type the document object keyword and then the period, MSE pops up the valid completion of this object, including the form name. You can continue to type this object identifier or select it from the pop-up list.

Figure 18-6: MSE remembers proper JavaScript syntax, so you don't continually have to hunt for that JavaScript reference book.

Caution

If you keep the ID in the tag, MSE uses that as the only valid identifier, even though the name still works. The easiest way to circumvent this problem is to eliminate the id, unless you really need it.

14. At this point, your JavaScript works fine (see Figure 18-7), as long as you type something reasonable into the form. If you make a mistake and type a year before the baseline year or after the present year, or if you type your name instead of a year, bad things can happen. To trap some of the more obvious kinds of errors, add a more elaborate version of the `onclick` method, as follows:

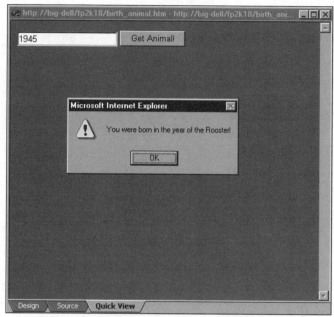

Figure 18-7: Signs of life from your JavaScript form!

```
function button1_onclick() {
  var baseline = 1880;
  var byear = parseInt(document.birth_form.byear.value);
  var today = new Date();
  var thisyear = 1900 + today.getYear();
  if (!isNaN(byear)) {
    if (parseInt(byear)> thisyear) {
      window.alert("Sorry, you are not yet among the living!");
      }
    else if (parseInt(byear) - baseline <0) {
      window.alert("You are too old to waste your time playing
frivolous games!");
      }
    else {
      var offsetyear = byear-baseline;
      window.alert("You were born in the year of the " +
get_sign(offsetyear) + "!");
      }
```

```
        }
   else {
     window.alert(document.birth_form.byear.value + " is not a
valid year!");
     }
   }
```

You can try out this code yourself, or use the version provided on the CD-ROM that accompanies this book.

The following several sections look at the major forms of scripting that you are likely to perform using MSE. These include JavaScript and VBScript, DHTML, and ASP.

Client-Side Scripting with JavaScript and VBScript

Scripts are written in a human-readable form and embedded into a Web page. When a Web browser receives a Web page containing a client-side script, the browser must be able to interpret the script. This means that a given Web browser must be able to translate and execute the script directly, making the scripting language very much browser-dependent.

Caution   Because scripts are embedded into Web pages, it is very difficult to protect your code from others. This is another reason that scripts tend to be relatively simple. It also means that most script developers are willing to allow others to use their scripts.

If you are going to use a scripting language, you need to know which browsers support which languages. You also need to know how to deal appropriately with browsers that do not support your scripts.

The first scripting language to hit the Web development world was Netscape's JavaScript. Contrary to what many people assume, Netscape's JavaScript, although it has some similarities in syntax to Java, is not directly related to the popular programming language developed at Sun Microsystems. JavaScript (as of this writing, currently in version 1.2) is also the basis of the recently defined standards-based scripting language, ECMA-262, also known as *ECMAScript*. ECMAScript is the work of ECMA (European Computer Manufacturer's Association), an international standards body. Both Microsoft and Netscape have announced their support for this standard, although both continue to support functionality that isn't contained in the standard. One way to ensure compatibility is to use only the standard functionality when developing, although this currently is somewhat difficult, due to a lack of ECMAScript-aware development tools.

Note Originally, JavaScript was known as LiveScript. The name was changed partly to signify that JavaScript syntax bore some similarity to Java, but mainly (one suspects) to capitalize on the rising popularity of the hot new programming language. Microsoft, on the other hand, while supporting JavaScript, calls its version JScript, for obvious reasons avoiding any clear associations with the Java name.

Microsoft, in its Internet Explorer browser, has developed support for a JavaScript-like language, which Microsoft refers to as JScript. Because of its support for JScript, Internet Explorer works correctly with many JavaScript scripts. You need to test any scripts that you develop in both Netscape and Microsoft browsers to ensure correct functionality in both environments.

Tip You can create support for VBScript in Netscape's browser by adding the NCompass ScriptActive plug-in.

In addition to its support for JScript, Microsoft has developed a second scripting language, called *VBScript*. VBScript, the full name of which is *Microsoft Visual Basic Scripting Edition*, is a subset of Microsoft's popular programming languages, Visual Basic and Visual Basic for Applications (VBA). If you already know how to program in Visual Basic, learning VBScript is a snap. Also, if you are planning to develop a Microsoft-based Web solution using ActiveX technologies, you may find some advantages to using VBScript. (See Chapter 19 for a discussion of ActiveX.) Remember, however, that only Internet Explorer contains support for VBScript. You need to either know that your users have this browser, or be prepared to deal with those who do not. For this reason, VBScript can be an appropriate choice for intranet developers, when a company has standardized on the Internet Explorer browser. It also works fine for server-side scripting languages, such as ASP (discussed in the last section of the chapter), for which browser support does not matter.

Note Both scripting languages now have server-side versions, so you can use the same programming environment to write scripts for both server- and client-side functionality.

Browser compatibility

As mentioned at the beginning of this chapter, one of the downsides of using client-side scripts is the lack of consistent browser support for various scripting languages. If you have more than one browser, try viewing the scripts in various browsers. Note that although JavaScript works in both Internet Explorer and Netscape Navigator, VBScript works only in Internet Explorer.

You need to consider two issues when trying to make your pages useable by as many browsers as possible:

✦ How to deal with browsers that don't support scripts at all

✦ How to deal with browsers that support one or the other type of script

Where to Find Scripts

Even if you have no plans to develop your own scripts, you can still make use of a scripting language by adapting existing scripts to your Web pages. A variety of scripting examples are presented later in this chapter, intended to spur you on to bigger and better things, as well as to give you some initial scripts to adapt to your own use.

In addition, you may have already added scripts to your Web page without knowing it. For example, if you have used FrontPage to add form validation rules to your form fields, FrontPage automatically creates JavaScript or VBScript to perform the validation functions.

You can also adapt preexisting scripts to use in your Web pages. Many sources offer freely available scripts, partly because they are easy to create and partly because they are difficult to protect. And remember, although by no means a requirement, crediting the source of any scripts that you borrow or adapt is always courteous.

One of the best places to look for scripting examples is the Gamelan site, at `www.developer.com`. For VBScripts, also check out Microsoft's site, `www.microsoft.com/vbscript` and `www.vbscripts.com`.

The no-script alternative

Believe it or not, not everyone uses the latest version of either Netscape's or Microsoft's browser (a pill that is very difficult for most developers to swallow). And even if they are using one of these browser versions, some users turn off their browser's support for active elements, such as Java, ActiveX, and scripting, primarily for security reasons.

For such users, you can prevent their browsers from displaying the script as if it were normal text. You also can define an alternative to the scripting functions that you include in your page.

Hiding scripts from old browsers

You can hide your scripts from older browsers by enclosing the script itself in a slightly modified comment tag. Comment tags begin with an exclamation point, followed by two hyphens `<!--`. The comment tag is closed with two hyphens, `-->`.

If you look back at the HTML created by Script Editor in the first two example scripts, you see that Script Editor automatically wraps your script in comment tags. In the JavaScript version, the end tag is preceded with a double slash, `//`, the JavaScript comment indicator. If your user's browser does not support scripting or if scripting is turned off, the browser interprets the script as a comment and ignores it. You should use a similar syntax any time that you insert a script manually. Note that the comment tag is placed inside the script tag—otherwise, even script-enabled browsers would ignore the scripts.

Alternatives for nonscripting browsers

Wrapping your scripts in comment tags ensures that incompatible browsers will not dump your code into your Web page, but this still leaves these users with a blank spot where useful information is meant to appear.

In most cases, you cannot provide these users with the same information (otherwise, why are you using scripts at all?). You can, however, inform these users that they are missing out on something. To include a message for nonscripting browsers, place the message in a `<NOSCRIPT>` tag.

Unfortunately, although both Netscape Navigator and Microsoft Internet Explorer support the `NOSCRIPT` syntax, FrontPage does not. Consequently, you have to insert this tag manually.

Return to the JavaScript example earlier in this chapter. Select the HTML tab to view the document source. Insert the following immediately after the end of the `<SCRIPT>` tag:

```
<NOSCRIPT>
<H6>Current time display requires a JavaScript compatible
browser with JavaScript currently enabled.</H6>
</NOSCRIPT>
```

Select the Normal tab to return to the WYSIWYG mode. Notice that FrontPage displays the comment tag icon around the inserted text, indicating that it does not recognize this `NOSCRIPT` tag. Not to worry. Select the Preview tab and you should see the appropriate display for a JavaScript-enabled browser.

To see the `NOSCRIPT` text displayed, select File ➪ Preview in Browser and select your favorite browser. Assuming that you have a JavaScript-compatible browser, you should see the current time displayed correctly.

To view the `NOSCRIPT` text in Internet Explorer, select View ➪ Options. In the Options property window, select the Security tab and uncheck the Run ActiveX Scripts check box. Return to the Web page and reload it, either by clicking the Refresh button or by selecting View ➪ Refresh. The current time should no longer be displayed. In its place is the alternative message.

To view the `NOSCRIPT` text in Netscape Navigator 4.x, select Edit ➪ Preferences. Select the Advanced item and uncheck the Enable JavaScript check box. Return to the Web page and reload the page, either by clicking the Reload button or by selecting View ➪ Reload. In Netscape 3.x, select Options ➪ Network Preferences, select the Languages tab, and then uncheck the Enable JavaScript check box. Return to the page and reload it as described for Netscape 4.x.

Working with More Examples

This section is devoted to an examination of several scripting examples that illustrate a range of the possible applications of client-side JavaScript and VBScript. These examples are meant to be useable as well as instructive. You can find the completed scripts on the CD-ROM that accompanies this book. The first example is discussed in some detail, to give you a good overview of the range of control possible with a scripting language. The remainder of the examples are described briefly, and then left to your perusal.

Interface controls (JavaScript)

The first script example serves as the interface for browsing the other scripts on the CD-ROM. It is a frames-based JavaScript application that controls various aspects of the user interface. It is made up of four files, located in the gui subfolder of the examples for Chapter 18. The main frameset file, guimain.htm, defines a three-frame interface. The top frame, guibanner.htm, displays a banner graphic. The main frame, whose start page is guicontent.htm, is used to display introductory descriptions of each of the other example scripts in this chapter. Each description page also has a button to launch the example.

If possible, you should view this example in Netscape Navigator or Internet Explorer 4, because its most prominent feature, the control of images, is not supported in Internet Explorer 3.

What it does

An important element of a good interface design is that it provides contextual feedback to users to help them understand what they are doing. Providing this kind of visual clue has been a staple feature of multimedia development, but accomplishing this in a Web page environment traditionally has been hard. The script presented here provides some simple ways to overcome that difficulty. It also illustrates ways that you can use a script to get beyond the one-page-after-another mentality of the Web browser.

When the user moves the mouse cursor over one of the buttons in the left frame, the button changes its state and displays a brief message in the window's status bar. Clicking a button causes it to remain depressed and become highlighted, indicating which page the user has selected. The button click also loads new pages into both of the other frames simultaneously. Each of the main content pages provides a brief description of the associated script. When the Demo button is clicked, it launches the script in its own browser window, which has been stripped of all the standard browser trappings. Figure 18-8 shows this script in action.

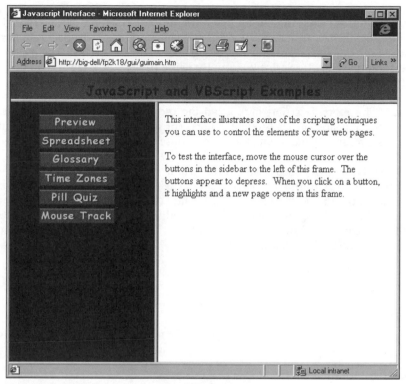

Figure 18-8: The scripting example interface

How it works

Some of the main features of this JavaScript example, and how they work, are examined next.

Browser detection

As previously mentioned, one of the main challenges of using scripts in your Web pages is insuring that the pages are well behaved in whatever browsers your site needs to support. In many cases, you can handle browser differences simply by providing an alternative page for those browsers that don't support scripting. This script, however, uses a method of altering the display of images that isn't supported in Internet Explorer 3, even though IE 3 is capable of recognizing client-side scripts. For that reason, this script contains a function, BrowserCheck, the purpose of which is to prevent IE 3 from running the portion of the script that it would not interpret correctly.

To see the BrowserCheck function, open the main file of the example, guimain.htm, in Editor and click to select the left frame containing the buttons. Notice that this frame has a blue border, indicating that it is the selected frame. To bring up Script Editor, either select Insert ➪ Advanced ➪ Scripts or click the Script icon in the Advanced toolbar. Click the Script Wizard. By using the Script Wizard, you can browse through the scripting procedures and variables used in each example.

> **Note**   Because the example scripts introduced the technique for browsing, this tech-nique isn't repeated in subsequent scripts. For more information on using the Script Wizard, see "Working with Microsoft Script Editor," earlier in the chapter.

To display the list of procedures used in this frame, first make sure that you have selected the Code View option at the bottom of the Script Wizard window. Click the plus sign next to the Procedures in the right frame of the Script Wizard (the frame labeled Insert Actions). Right-click the first procedure listed, browserCheck(), and select Edit from the drop-down menu. The browserCheck() function loads into the bottom frame of the Script Wizard window:

```
function browserCheck()
{
  if (document.images) {
    doIt = true;
  }
  else{
    doIt = false;
  }
}
```

This function has a simple purpose: it checks for the existence of an array of images and, if it finds one, sets a flag variable, doIt. This array is simply the collection of images loaded on the Web page. Because IE 3 doesn't support this object, it fails to set the tag. The key to using browserCheck() is to first check for this flag in any other function that involves the use of the image object. So, for example, the next function to run, initButtons(), first checks for the presence of doIt before building the array of Button objects, the purpose of which is described later in the chapter.

> **Note**   If you run this example in Internet Explorer 3, it functions correctly, but you miss the cool animated button feature.

Image control
The most prominent effect produced by this interface is its animated buttons. When you run the mouse over a button, it appears to depress. When you move the mouse away, the button returns to its original state. If you click the button, it remains depressed and the text is highlighted.

These effects are produced by manipulating the `src` property of the image object for each button. Each button is defined by a set of three separate GIF images, one for each possible state of the button. Any time that the user triggers a change in the state of the button, the appropriate image is loaded into the image's `src` property. This is an excellent example of the flexibility achieved by being able to control elements of the page. The next section describes the key functions that control the state of the image objects.

Note

If you are used to the slow download times that are typical for images, you may be wondering how this script loads the images instantaneously. The answer is that all the images for each button download when the page first opens, even though only one image per button is visible. Thus, when the image changes, it is drawn from the local cache. Using this technique does add to the initial download time of the page, so plan your images carefully.

Event handling

The image effects described in the previous section are controlled via the following set of JavaScript event handlers for images:

✦ **onMouseOver**: Triggers an event when the mouse cursor is over the object

✦ **onMouseOut**: Triggers an event when the mouse cursor leaves the object

✦ **onClick**: Triggers an event when the object is clicked by the mouse

These event handlers are added to the hyperlink tag for each image, as in this example, which has been broken into multiple lines for easier reading:

```
<a
href="../talk.htm"
target="main"
onMouseOver="mouseOverButton(0);
window.status=buttons[0].msg;
return true"
onMouseOut="mouseOffButton(0)"
onClick="mouseClicked(0)">
<img
NAME="0"
src="../images/gui/preview_up.gif"
border="0"
alt="Preview"
WIDTH="120"
HEIGHT="25">
</a>
```

This example is associated with a set of custom functions: `Mouseclicked()`, `MouseOffButton()`, `MouseOverButton()`, and `MouseOnButton()`, which are responsible for keeping track of the button states and displaying the appropriate images.

The onLoad handler

In addition to the mouse-related event handlers, this script makes use of one other useful handler: onLoad(). This method is called from the body tag (as is its cousin, onUnload(), which is not used in this script):

```
<body bgcolor="#000000" onLoad="initPage()">
```

Any functions associated with this method are run when the page is first loaded into the browser. In this script, the onLoad() method is used to call the browserCheck() function and initialize the Button objects, which are described in an upcoming section.

Status bar messages

As previously discussed, the buttons in this script change when you move the mouse over them. They aren't the only thing that changes, however. Watch carefully what happens to the text message at the bottom of your browser. The message should change to match the button that your cursor is over. This message area, called the Status line, is another window object that you can control. (You may have encountered one of those charming sites that put interminably scrolling text messages in your status bar, which is an example of using this object.) To see how to control this object, refer back to the code associated with the onMouseOver handler, described earlier under "Event Handling."

User-defined objects

The heart of this script is encapsulated in its array of Button objects. Button is a user-defined object that can be used just like the predefined JavaScript objects. The Button object consists of a constructor function that defines the object, and a series of instantiations of Button objects, using the New function. The Button constructor looks just like a regular JavaScript function:

```
function Button(w, h, offsrc, oversrc, onsrc, msg) {
   this.w=w;
   this.h=h;
   this.offImage= new Image(w,h);
   this.overImage = new Image(w,h);
   this.onImage= new Image(w,h);
   this.offImage.src=offsrc;
   this.overImage.src=oversrc;
   this.onImage.src=onsrc;
   this.state=0;
   this.msg = msg;
}
```

The purpose of the constructor function is to define the properties of the Button object. Each Button object has its own associated images and messages. When the button event handler is triggered, any of that button's properties can be identified and used, simply by knowing which button was affected.

To create a new `Button` object, an array is defined, and then each element of the array is instantiated as a new `Button` object. The following is one example from the `initButtons()` function, which creates the `Button` objects:

```
Button(120,25,"../images/gui/preview_up.gif","../images/gui/pre
view_over.gif","../images/gui/preview_down.gif", "Preview");
```

Using custom-defined objects is an excellent way to keep track of multiple properties in your script. In this example, the `Button` objects also help to manage what happens in the other frames when a button is clicked.

Frame control

Invariably, if you use frames in your Web pages, the time will come when you realize that you need to change the content of two or more frames when a single event occurs, such as a user clicking a button. JavaScript is the only way to make this happen.

When the user clicks one of the buttons, the normal `HREF` hyperlink goes into effect. This is what loads the new page into the main window of the frameset. In addition, as part of the function called by the `onClick` method, this line of JavaScript is executed:

```
window.parent.banner.location.href=buttons[i].bannerpage;
```

This line reads in the `bannerpage` property of the clicked button and loads that page into the URL of the banner frame. Using a similar method, you can control as many simultaneous frame changes as you like (and your user can tolerate).

Window control

Using JavaScript, you can also control the creation of new browser windows, by using the `window.open()` method. This method is called in the `newWindow()` function, which is stored in the frameset document. It is a simple function that takes one parameter, the text string name of the URL to open in the new window:

```
function newWindow(url)
{
window.open(url,"new","resizable=no,width=600,height=400,
status=yes");
}
```

Using the `open` method, you can dictate the size of the new window, as well as whether the window is resizable. In addition, you can show or hide various window components, including:

✦ **toolbar**: The row of buttons, including Back, Forward, and Stop

✦ **location**: The field for typing in new URLs

✦ **directories**: The row of buttons beneath the toolbar

✦ **status**: The status bar at the bottom of the browser window

✦ **menubar**

✦ **scrollbars**

By default, these items are hidden unless specified in the `open` method. To include one of these features, add a `[feature]=yes` item to the parameter list, as in the example of the status bar in the preceding example.

The interface script has been examined in detail, partly to give you some practice exploring scripts. The remainder of the scripts are for your enjoyment. You can experiment with them in the scripting interface, or look under the hood by using the FrontPage Scripting Wizard and the Editor's HTML Source tab.

An Investment Calculator (JavaScript)

The Investment Calculator illustrates the ability to create a working spreadsheet in a single Web page form, without recourse to CGI. The idea behind this Investment Calculator is to determine the overall percentage of your investments, given different investment ratios. (In case it isn't obvious, the values indicated for the various types of investments are entirely fictional. I don't advise making any investments based on this calculator.)

To see how this calculator works, try inserting different values into the percentages for the various investment types. After you allocate 100 percent of your assets, click the Calculate button. The calculator tells you what your overall return will be with this asset allocation. If, by chance, you try to evaluate more or less than 100 percent of your assets, the calculator does some simple error trapping and chides you to check your math (see Figure 18-9).

A Glossary (JavaScript)

The Glossary script, shown in Figure 18-10, illustrates two useful principles: the ability to update form input boxes without clicking a Submit button, and the ability to perform the equivalent of simple database functions within a Web page script.

To use the Glossary, first scroll through the list of terms. When you select a term, as illustrated in the figure, the definition of the term appears in the text area box on the right side of the page. Alternatively, type the name of a key word into the Find input box. When you click the Find button, it jumps to that term and displays its definition.

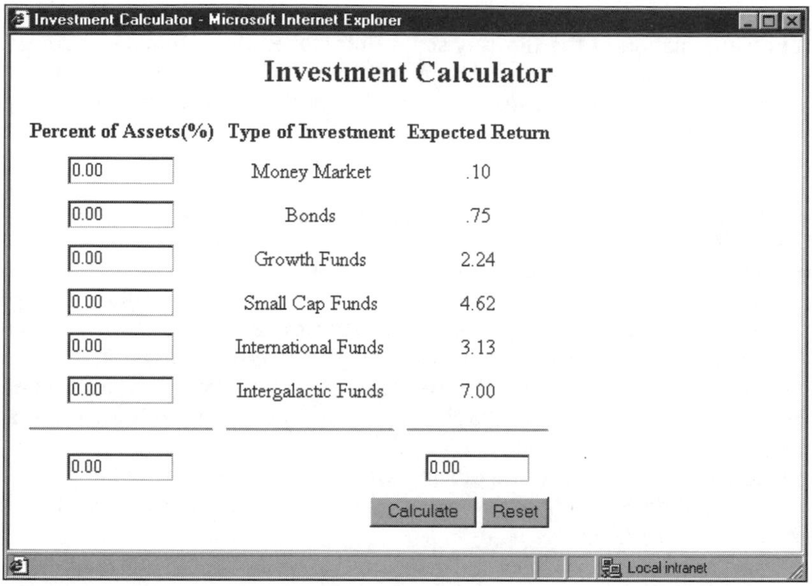

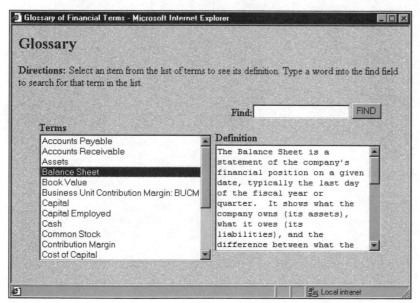

Figure 18-9: The Investment Calculator

Figure 18-10: The Glossary script provides a high-quality, interactive learning experience.

Netscape Navigator has a bug in the way that it handles the Find feature in the current implementation of the Glossary script (Internet Explorer handles it correctly). When you click the Find button in Navigator, the term is selected and its definition appears, but if the term happens to be out of view, the scrolling list does not scroll the term into view.

Displaying Time Zone Information (JavaScript)

The Time Zone page uses some of the same techniques used by the Glossary to update fields automatically when an item is selected. In addition, this script shows off some of the capabilities of scripts to work with time and date information and to update a page continuously. (It also shows some of the limitations of these techniques, because a client-side script depends for its information on the client-side system, which isn't always a reliable source of time and date information.)

To use this script, simply select one of the cities from the list by clicking its radio button. The current date and time, as well as the city name, are displayed in the textboxes (see Figure 18-11).

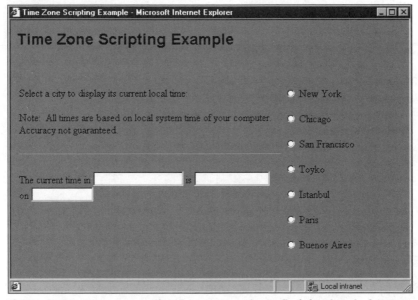

Figure 18-11: You can use the Time Zone script to find the time in faraway places.

Pill Quiz (JavaScript)

This script, shown in Figure 18-12, is an example of a hypothetical online training exercise. Mainly, though, it is intended to illustrate the variety of message boxes available to you in a scripting language. It also demonstrates a simple way of keeping track of user state information.

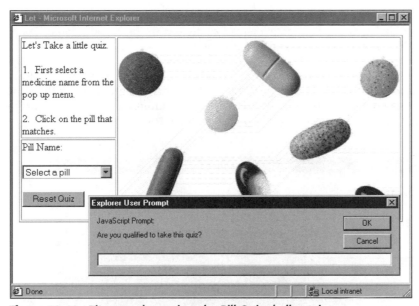

Figure 18-12: Pit your wits against the Pill Quiz challenge!

To take the quiz, first answer the initial question posed by the quiz. The correct and only acceptable answer, by the way, is Yes. Answer anything else and you won't be permitted to take the quiz. This authorizing question is posed via a Prompt box (called an InputBox in VBScript), which can capture and respond to user input.

Next, select a "pill" name from the list of available options. Then, guess which pill in the illustration corresponds to the name. Click the illustration that you think matches the name—if you are correct, you are congratulated. If wrong, you are exhorted to try again—up to a point. The messages are displayed in Alert boxes (called MsgBox in VBScript).

Mouse Tracking (VBScript)

This script, written in VBScript—which means that it can be run only on Internet Explorer—is intended as a simple game. Like most games, it is totally useless but oddly absorbing. It does have the virtue of illustrating some additional capabilities of scripting languages, namely:

✦ Random number generation

✦ Timing

✦ Automatic HTML generation

> **Note**   This game works by using frames, because of the limited ability of early versions of scripting languages to update a page's content. With the introduction of Dynamic HTML, this methodology is no longer necessary.

The object of the game is to locate the hidden "mouse" (use your imagination) somewhere in the green field. If you think that you have found it, click the spot — but don't dawdle, because you have only a limited amount of time to conduct your search. Figure 18-13 shows what happens if you are too slow.

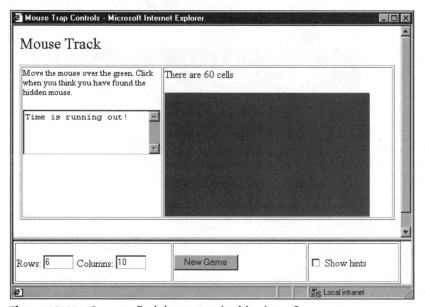

Figure 18-13: Can you find the mouse in this picture?

Several ways exist to improve your odds of winning this game. First, you can control the size of the playing field. Also, if you pass the mouse cursor over the field, the message area alerts you if you are getting warm. But this has a catch — the cursor movement actually advances the clock that keeps time in this game. The more that you move the mouse around, the sooner the game is over. (In addition, the length of time allotted to you is proportionate to the size of the field — the smaller the field, the less time that you get.) Finally, if you are really frustrated, you can check the Show Hints option. When you restart the game, it tells you which square the mouse is in.

Discovering DHTML

Dynamic HTML (DHTML) refers to Web page programming that manipulates page elements at the time that they are presented in the browser. DHTML makes the following possible: page-level animation, expandable navigation menus, drag and drop, and generally a more-sophisticated, dynamic Web page.

DHTML accomplishes all of this by combining a client-side scripting language, such as JavaScript or VBScript, with some means of accessing page elements. The programming interface that enables this interaction is called — by both Navigator and Internet Explorer — the *Document Object Model (DOM)*. Unfortunately, although the two major browsers have agreed on a name for this entity, they haven't agreed on an implementation. As a result, one of the chief difficulties of working with DHTML is dealing with browser compatibility issues.

A full account of the DOM and how it works is beyond the scope of this chapter. The goal here is to give you a general overview of the DOM, including some of the issues facing you if you take on a DHTML project. (You can find more information on adding DHTML effects to your pages in Chapter 16.)

 Note Fortunately, W3C has issued an initial DOM Level 1 specification, which means that, increasingly, browser vendors will move toward supporting the specification. In the interim, of course, you are left with the specification and various implementations that don't yet quite live up to the specification. But that's progress.

The Document Object Model

The Document Object Model is the terminology that defines how you can refer to elements of the HTML document. The purpose of the DOM is to enable programmers to interact with and make changes dynamically to HTML pages.

The W3C has recently released a specification for DOM Level 1, which includes the core objects that make up the DOM. This is good news in the near future for developers, but the reality is that, at the moment, Netscape and Microsoft have evolved separate DOMs that bear a resemblance to each other but use different syntax and give access to different elements of the HTML document. Presently, this means that the biggest challenge in using DHTML in a real-world application is making certain that the programming works in both browser worlds. (Of course, if you happen to work in an environment such as an intranet, in which you need to worry about only a single browser type, you are among the lucky minority.)

Note   As if worrying about DOMs isn't enough of a problem, you also need to know how to reference and manipulate style sheet elements via programming. The terminology for doing this sometimes is referred to as the *Style Sheet Object Model*.

Communicator versus IE

The main purpose of the DOM is to give programmers access to the elements of an HTML page. Netscape Communicator 4.x does this by exposing elements of the page that it refers to as *Layers*. This includes elements contained inside a `<LAYER>` tag, which is supported only by Netscape. It also includes elements that FrontPage calls *Position boxes*, namely `DIV` and `SPAN` elements. Because these are standard tags, you are probably best off to use these for any elements that you want to access via the DOM.

In addition, Netscape has developed in its version 4 browser a set of JavaScript elements to refer to style sheet elements that don't correspond to the CSS syntax. Look for this to change by version 5, but meanwhile, this babel of name differences used to refer to the same thing will very easily cause confusion. The example in the next section does a reasonable job of pointing out the degree of the headaches involved, and (fortunately) illustrates one approach to dealing with the problem.

Internet Explorer, in contrast, exposes all the tags on a given page, using a collection object named "all" as well as a set of "children" collections that refers to HTML tags contained within a specific tag. IE also exposes all the elements defined in `<STYLE>` tags, through the use of the styles collection associated with a particular element. Most importantly, IE allows for real-time updating of any element on the page. Netscape currently does not.

Note   This example assumes that you are familiar with JavaScript programming (refer to the previous section) and with CSS (refer to Chapter 12).

Developing a DHTML script

This section steps through the process of creating a relatively simple (from a conceptual standpoint) DHTML program, and then shows how it is complicated by the need to make it cross-browser compatible. The program that you create is a simple pop-up message box, similar in concept to Windows' ToolTips. Your program is called Pop-ups.

1. Create the pop-up message box. Open a new page in FrontPage and type something, to serve as temporary text for your pop-up box. Add a `DIV` element around the text. The simplest way to do this is by hand. (You can use the position box command in FrontPage to create this tag, but you will end up having to remove attributes manually. Alternatively, you can use MSE, which can insert `<DIV>` tags. Select HTML ⇨ Div and choose the Inline option.)

Switch to HTML view and type the following:

```
<DIV ID="popupbox">Our Sample Pop-up Text</DIV>
```

2. Create a local style for your position box. Select Format ➪ Style. Click the New button to create a new user-defined style. Name it **#popupbox** (the **#** designates a style ID) and click the Format button to set the following font, border, and position attributes:

```
#popupbox    {
    font-family: Arial;
    font-size: 10pt;
    color: #660033;
    background-color: #FFCC99;
position: absolute;
left: 50;
top: 40
    border: 1 solid #660033
}
```

The results are illustrated in Figure 18-14.

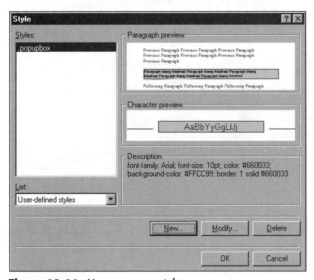

Figure 18-14: Your pop-up style

After you create this style, it should be applied to the DIV element that you made in Step 1. When you are satisfied with the way the box looks (disregard the fact that it's too long; you fix that in a moment), add the following line to the STYLE:

```
visibility: hidden
```

3. Before you leave HTML, you need to add some text with a hyperlink. When you pass the mouse over this link, you want it to pop up your message. To do this, you need to trap `mouseover` and `mouseout` events, using the following code:

```
<A ONMOUSEOVER="showPopUp()" ONMOUSEOUT="hidePopUp()">Here is
some text</A>
```

4. Create JavaScript routines to hide and show this element. For now, these functions are simple wrappers for methods to change the `visibility` attribute of the position box. However, you will need to add to these functions when you create cross-browser versions of your program.

Use MSE for your scripting work (more for the practice than from necessity — your scripting needs are fairly simple and could just as easily be done in the HTML tab). Select Macro ⇨ Microsoft Script Editor to open the HTML page in MSE. Select View ⇨ Property Pages and set the default client scripting language to JavaScript.

Right-click in the HTML source window at a location between the end of the `<TITLE>` tag and the end of the `<HEAD>` tag. Select Script Block ⇨ Client to insert an empty scripting block in the header of your page. Add the following functions:

```
<SCRIPT LANGUAGE=javascript>
<!--
function showPopUp() {

document.all.popupbox.style.setAttribute("visibility","visibl
e");
   }
function hidePopUp() {

document.all.popupbox.style.setAttribute("visibility","hidden
");
   }
//-->
</SCRIPT>
```

5. If you followed the directions accurately, you should see the text message pop up when you run the mouse over the hyperlink. When you remove the mouse button, the message disappears.

6. All you really need to add to this procedure are the capabilities to change the text message dynamically and to position the dialog box on the page.

Modifying the text is easy (until you begin to make the script Netscape-compatible). Simply pass a "text" parameter to the `showPopUp()` function and then add the custom text to the `ONMOUSEOVER=` event.

To position the pop-up message correctly, you need to find the location where the pop-up box is invoked. To do that, pass an event object to your function. Then, use the event object's `clientX` and `clientY` properties to get the necessary mouse coordinates. You relocate the top and left properties of the `popupbox` style relative to these mouse coordinates. When you are done, the `showPopUp()` function looks like this:

```
function showPopUp(e,text) {
  popupbox.innerHTML=text; //replace the text inside the DIV
tag

document.all.popupbox.style.setAttribute("left",e.clientX+15);
//x-offset
  document.all.popupbox.style.setAttribute("top",e.clientY+10);
//y-offset

document.all.popupbox.style.setAttribute("visibility","visible"
); //show popupbox
  }
```

The `MouseOver` event of the hyperlink tag should resemble the following (note the use of single quotes around the text string, to avoid clashing with the double quotes around the function call):

```
ONMOUSEOVER="showPopUp(event, 'This is a test...')"
```

That is it. You can even use this mechanism with an image map, to provide custom pop-up messages.

Adding non-DHTML support

If you were content with having your DHTML work only with IE 4 or greater, you would be done now. However, your page currently doesn't work in Netscape Navigator 4. To create cross-browser DHTML, you need to determine which browser specific users are using, and then build your DHTML accordingly.

The first (and frankly easier) step is to provide alternative functionality for those users who have pre-version 4 browsers. To do this, you set up three true/false variables: `IsIE`, `IsNav`, and `DoesDHTML`. Then, initialize them after checking the browser name and version. This code, listed here, is added to the top of the script block that you created in the previous section:

```
var IsIE = false;
var IsNN = false;
var DoesDHTML = false;

if (navigator.appName == "Netscape") {
```

```
      IsNN = true;
      }
else if (navigator.appName == "Microsoft Internet Explorer") {
   IsIE = true;
   }

if (parseInt(navigator.appVersion) >= 4) {
   DoesDHTML = true;
   }
```

Now, make two small changes to your showPopUp() function:

1. Wrap your current functionality in checks, to make sure that you perform them only if you have a version 4 or greater IE browser.

2. Add a generic function at the end of this function, to set the status bar with the text that you passed to your function.

In a version 3 browser (or any current non-IE browser), this is all that happens, as illustrated by the Netscape browser screen shot shown in Figure 18-15 — notice that it doesn't yet know what to do with the supposedly "hidden" position box text that it displays at the top of the page. You also need to add code to the hidePopUp() function, to set the status bar back to its default value. Here is the revised function:

> **Note** When you set the window.status property, you also add code to return a true value from your function. To accommodate this, you also update the ONMOUSEOVER call as follows:
>
> ```
> <A ONMOUSEOVER= "return showPopUp(event, 'This is a
> test')"
> ```
>
> A similar change is made to ONMOUSEOUT.

```
function showPopUp(e,text) {
  if (DoesDHTML) {
    if (IsIE) {
      popupbox.innerHTML=text;
document.all.popupbox.style.setAttribute("left",
  e.clientX+15);
document.all.popupbox.style.setAttribute("top",e.clientY+10);
document.all.popupbox.style.setAttribute("visibility",
  "visible");
      }
    }
  window.status = text;
  return true;
  }
```

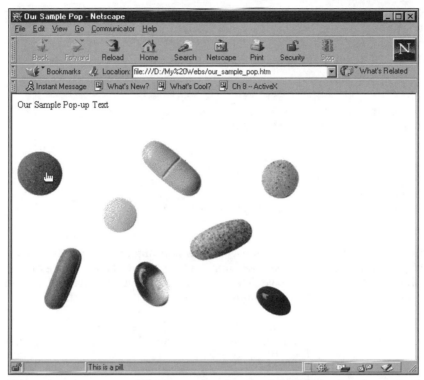

Figure 18-15: Netscape's browser, showing the default behavior of your DHTML script for non-IE browsers (notice the status bar!).

Adding cross-browser compatibility

The language used in this section's title requires some clarification. You actually have already made your script "cross-browser-compatible," but only if that means (as the marketing departments of the major browser companies mean) your script won't break in any browser. What you really want, though, is comparable behavior in both Navigator and IE. To get that, you have to work a bit harder.

The first question to address is why Netscape doesn't recognize the position box that you created. The answer is that Navigator chokes on the style information that FrontPage produces. Specifically, it does not like the way that FrontPage designates border information about the pop-up message (border: 1 solid #660033;). You can alleviate the problem by removing the offending line from the style designation and adding it into the showPopUp code for IE:

```
document.all.popup.style.setAttribute("border","1 solid
#660033");
```

Now, Netscape will hide the position box text, and you can add Netscape-specific code to render the text visible. Netscape's DOM has a very different way of referencing elements in the page. Here is the code to make Netscape show the position box at the appropriate location (added to the showPopUp routine):

```
else if (IsNN) {
   document.popupbox.visibility="visible";
   document.popupbox.top=e.pageY+10;
   document.popupbox.left=e.pageX+15;
   }
```

And here is the code added to hidePopUp:

```
else if (IsNN) {
   document.popupbox.visibility="hidden";
   }
```

You still have a couple differences to overcome. Although you have referenced the event object to find the mouse-cursor coordinates (note Netscape's use of pageX/Y rather than clientX/Y), you haven't yet added code to update the text of your pop-up message with the "text" variable that you pass to your function.

The challenge is that Netscape, unlike IE, doesn't update page elements automatically. It doesn't even have a way to reference the text inside a tag, in the way that you used the innerHTML property in your IE code.

The only way to update the text of a layer element (including DIV and SPAN elements, as well as the Netscape-specific LAYER element) is to call that layer's document.write() method. So, to change the text of the pop-up message in Netscape, use the following code (the second line is necessary to ensure that the next popupbox call does not simply append additional text to the existing text):

```
document.popupbox.document.write(text);
document.popupbox.document.close();
```

Now, you can update the text in your Netscape pop-up message. However, if you look closely at the results, you may notice that you have lost all the formatting of your position box, including font and border styles. Unfortunately, when Navigator calls the document.write() method, it overwrites everything that it knows about the popupbox element, including all of its styles. Are you starting to sense that this process takes you two steps forward and one step back? The next section offers a work-around to this new problem that actually solves several difficulties simultaneously.

One way to retain the style information when you rewrite the Netscape layer object (as just detailed) is to store that information in a separate class style and then write the class name back into the layer. This is easier to show than to describe. First create a new class style, called **.popup**, and give it the following styles (note that you need to create this style manually, because several of the style designations are Netscape-specific, and FrontPage cannot generate them using the Style dialog box):

```
.popup {
     font-family: Arial;
     ffont-size: 10pt;
     fcolor: #660033;
     fbackground-color: #FFCC99;
     fborder-color: #CC9966;
     fborder-width: 1px;
   }
```

Now, revise the original #popupbox style to include only the minimal style information needed:

```
#popupbox   {
   visibility: hidden;
   position: absolute;
       }
```

Finally, revise the Netscape document.write() line to read as follows:

```
document.popupbox.document.write("<SPAN class=popup>" + text +
"</SPAN>");
```

Admittedly, this last statement is a bit of a hack, because it requires writing a second layer element inside the original one. However, it works, and given the amount of fussing necessary just to get this far, I, personally, can live with this. Now, compare the final results in both Internet Explorer (Figure 18-16) and Netscape (Figure 18-17).

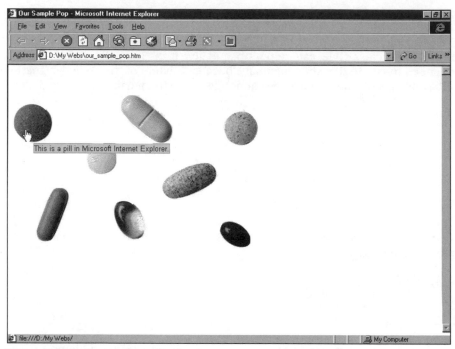

Figure 18-16: Your pop-up box in IE...

 Tip

In fact, one other adjustment was needed to get the Netscape pop-up box to fill in the background as shown in Figure 18-17. Prior to adding the extra line, Netscape insisted on creating a line of white between the border and the background color, which stubbornly resisted all efforts to go away. Adding the following line to the Netscape portion of showPopUp routine seemed do the trick, although I can't explain why and haven't seen this documented anywhere:

```
document.popupbox.bgColor="#FFCC99"
```

If you look closely, you'll notice that it still retains the extra padding around the text, but at least it is filled with color.

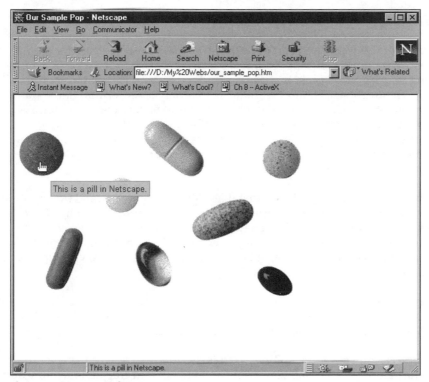

Figure 18-17: ...and Netscape.

Browser compatibility

Your DHTML example has gone beyond simply demonstrating what is required to create a DHTML script in FrontPage; it has demonstrated what is required to create a *real-world* DHTML script using FrontPage. Most of the challenges involved have little to do with FrontPage and everything to do with the disparate state of the various DOMs still in the process of coalescing around a standard. However, you may also notice that FrontPage does not provide much assistance for creating cross-browser scripts. FrontPage is more helpful if you decide to develop to the lowest common denominator (in other words, to use only those capabilities that are common to both browser environments). You may suspect that in the current state of DHTML, that fact leaves precious little to work with.

Server-Side Scripting with Active Server Pages

The last form of scripting examined in this chapter is Active Server Pages (ASP). In contrast to the other scripting techniques previously discussed, ASP is a *server-side* scripting language. ASP code is processed at the server before it is sent to the Web browser. The drawback to this technique is that only a server that understands and can interpret ASP code is capable of presenting ASP pages. The good news is that after you have an ASP-enabled server, your ASP code is entirely browser-independent. Also, you have less need to worry about proprietary code being stolen by users poking around in the HTML source code, because your ASP code is processed before it gets to the user.

The other good news about ASP is that, basically, it is simply standard scripting that is processed by the server rather than by the Web browser. Thus, if you are familiar with VBScript — and if you have read the earlier part of this chapter for an introduction — you are already halfway over the ASP learning curve. You can even use JavaScript instead if you like, although, practically speaking, VBScript turns out to be more convenient in the ASP world.

The main difference between client-side VBScript and server-side ASP is that ASP has access to additional resources (for example, objects) at the server side that are beyond the reach of your standard VBScript. These additional resources include:

✦ **Application and Session Objects:** Objects that help you to manage user state information by enabling your application to set and track application- and session-specific information about a user. These objects are managed by using a configuration script called global.asa.

✦ **Request Object:** A set of collections that provides access to information submitted by a user via a standard POST or GET command. Enables use of ASP as an alternative to CGI scripts.

✦ **Response Object:** Deals with responses back to the browser from the server.

✦ **ServerVariables Collection:** Retrieves a set of headers (elsewhere known as *CGI environment variables*) passed from the browser to the server.

✦ **Cookies Collection:** Cookies enable you to store in the browser data that can then be retrieved later by your ASP application.

✦ **FileSystemObject Object:** Provides access to file system information and server-side file objects.

✦ **Additional Server Components:** Built in to the Internet Information Server (IIS) as well as third-party components.

✦ **Database Access Components:** Provide connectivity between the Web server and databases.

✦ **Collaboration Data Object:** Provides support for messaging, calendaring, workflow, and collaboration applications.

ASP can also be augmented by writing Active Server Components that extend the functionality of a particular server — somewhat analogous to the extended client-side functionality that an ActiveX Component combined with VBScripting adds to the client side.

If you do not have a server that is capable of supporting ASP, you can disable ASP. To do so, select Tools ➪ Page Options, select the Compatibility tab, and uncheck the ASP support check box. (Check out the trial version of ChiliASP that adds ASP support to several non-Microsoft Web servers.)

Tutorial 18.1: Form Processing with ASP

As with the other scripting languages presented in this chapter, not enough space is available to provide a crash course in ASP programming. Instead, this tutorial provides a relatively simple example to give you a taste of what ASP is about, and to illustrate the process that you can use to create ASP pages in FrontPage.

You will create two ASP pages in this tutorial: a simple form that asks you to input some of your favorite things, and the form response page. The most interesting aspect of the two pages is that they remember what you have input, within the confines of a particular user session. Along the way, a few ASP basics are illustrated.

Create the form (FavThings.asp)

1. Create a simple form, as pictured in Figure 18-18. The main consideration is that you need a form element with two input elements: a scrolling textbox for entering new "favorite things," and a scrolling list input, created by inserting a drop-down menu and setting its `Height` to **6** in the form field properties dialog box. Name the scrolling textbox **NewThings**. Name the drop-down menu **OldThings**.

If you need help creating forms, refer to Chapter 14.

2. Right-click the form element and select Form Properties from the option menu. Choose the Send to Other option and click the Options button. Enter **FTResults.asp** as the Action. Click OK twice to return to the form.

3. Save the form as **FavThings.asp**. (Don't forget the asp ending rather than htm!)

4. Make sure that the folder that contains this ASP page is set to enable scripts to run. Even though you haven't added any ASP script to your form yet, it is still designated an ASP page and needs scripting permission to run. You will know that your folder does not have ASP enabled if it tries to save the page rather than display it when you Preview in Browser.

5. To enable scripts to run, click the Folder icon in FrontPage Folder view and select Properties from the option menu. Check the box labeled Allow Scripts of Programs to Be Run.

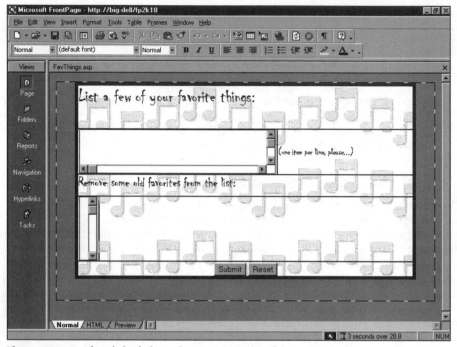

Figure 18-18: The default form for your Favorite Things ASP script

Create the Form Response (FTResults.asp)

Now create the results page, in which you get to add your first ASP scripting:

1. Create a new page in FrontPage and design the form results. Include a placeholder for newly added favorite things, removed favorite things, and a counter (see Figure 18-19).

2. Save the results page as **FTResults.asp**. With the new file open, select Tools ➪ Macro ➪ Microsoft Script Editor.

3. Create a script block for your main ASP. Place the cursor somewhere in the header of the HTML page and right-click. Select Script Block ➪ Server from the option menu to insert an empty server-side script block into your page.

4. This script block will contain the main script elements to be run when the page is loaded. It also contains functions that you will call from within the HTML results. When the results page is called, it needs to do the following:

   • Show the list of newly added favorite things

   • Show the list of items removed in this session

   • Update the list of current favorites

   • Update a simple page counter

   • Configure the return button to return to the page that called it

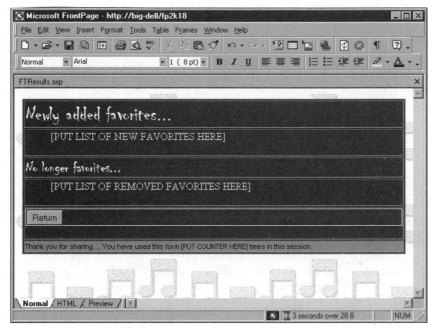

Figure 18-19: The initial template for your Favorite Things results page

5. You get the list of newly added favorites from the `NewThings` field in your FavThings.asp form. In ASP, form elements are passed in a `Request.Form` collection, in which the value of each form element is referenced as `Request.Form("fieldname")`. Create a simple function called `getNewFavorites` that returns the list of `NewThings` from the `Request.Form`. Your function takes one parameter, a string delimiter that enables you to change how the list is displayed in the results page. If no `NewThings` have been added, return a generic message.

After you add the function, simply reference it from the appropriate place in your HTML page. To do that, use a shorter syntax to designate an ASP script block to display text:

```
<%= getNewFavorites("<BR>") %>
```

which is short for

```
  <SCRIPT LANGUAGE=vbscript RUNAT=Server>
Response.Write(getNewFavorites("<BR>") </SCRIPT>
```

6. Add the Counter next, simply because it provides a simple example of using `Session` variables, which you will also use to store the `currentFavorites` and `oldFavorites` lists. Your counter simply counts accesses to this page from a specific user during a specific session. When you first access an ASP page within a particular application on your Web server, the server starts an ASP session for you, which it maintains by sending you a session ID cookie.

You can create custom session variables that are retained during the lifetime of a session, simply by invoking a new item in the Session collection.

Take your counter as an example. You create a simple counter function called updateCounter(). This function takes no input parameters and returns the current counter value, after first incrementing the value by one:

```
Function updateCounter()
Session("Counter") = Session("Counter" )+ 1
updateCounter = Session("Counter")
End Function
```

You call the function in the appropriate spot in your HTML with the following:

```
<% = updateCounter() %>
```

If you experiment with this, you will discover that the counter resets any time that you quit your browser and restart, or if you sit long enough that the session times out (by default, 20 minutes).

7. Create a session variable to hold all the current favorites and to add any new items to that list. This is the list that you eventually display in the initial FavThings.asp form.

First, create a subroutine called updateCurrentFavorites(). The job of this routine is to both add new items and delete any old ones. In this step, you deal with adding new items. The next step addresses deleting old items.

```
Sub updateCurrentFavorites ()
  'This adds new favorites to current list
  aList = split(Request.Form("NewThings"),chr(13)&chr(10))
  For Each strItem in aList
    If Not checkMatches(strItem, Session("CurrentFavorites"))
Then
      AddCurrentFavorite(strItem)
    End If
  Next
End Sub
```

To perform the adding of new favorites, you create two utility routines:

- **checkMatches():** Designed to compare a string against a list of strings to see whether the particular string is in the list. It returns a true/false value.

- **addCurrentFavorite():** This subroutine takes a new string to be added and adds it to the CurrentFavorites list. (Note that you elect to store your Session variable as a delimited string rather than as an array or collection, which means that each time you make changes, you have to convert the list to an array and then back to a delimited string.)

The two routines look like this:

```
Function checkMatches(tmpItem, tmpList)
```

```
  bMatch = false
  aList = split(tmpList,"$")
  For Each strItem in aList
    If StrComp(strItem,tmpItem) = 0 Then
      bMatch = true
    End If
  Next
  checkMatches= bMatch
End Function

Sub AddCurrentFavorite(tmpItem)
  If Not StrComp(Session("CurrentFavorites"),"") = 0 Then
    Session("CurrentFavorites") = Session("CurrentFavorites")
& "$"
  End If
  Session("CurrentFavorites") = Session("CurrentFavorites") &
tmpItem
End Sub
```

8. You also want to be able to list all the removed favorites during a given session, which requires adding any newly removed items to the list of accumulated removed items. Simultaneously, you want to remove any newly removed items from the list of current items. The process is analogous to Step 7. `GetOldFavorites()` first updates the list of removed items and then returns the updated list. `UpdateOldFavorites` is responsible for the updating, and `AddOldFavorite` adds a deleted item to the list of `OldFavorites`. Here are the new routines in their entirety:

```
Function getOldFavorites(delimiter)
  updateOldFavorites()
  getOldFavorites =
Replace(Session("OldFavorites"),"$",delimiter)
End Function

Sub updateOldFavorites()
'This is the list of newly removed items from FavThings.asp
aList = split(Request.Form("OldThings"),",")
For Each strOldItem in aList
    If Not checkMatches(strOldItem, Session("OldFavorites"))
Then
      AddOldFavorite(strOldItem)
    End If
Next
End Sub

Sub AddOldFavorite(tmpItem)
  If Not StrComp(Session("OldFavorites"),"") = 0 Then
    Session("OldFavorites") = Session("OldFavorites") & "$"
  End If
  Session("OldFavorites") = Session("OldFavorites") &
tmpItem
End Sub
```

Simultaneously, you want to remove any old items from the list of current favorites. To do this, you first create a RemoveCurrentFavorites() routine and then add a call to it in your updateCurrentFavorites routine. The new routine looks like this:

```
Sub RemoveCurrentFavorite(tmpItem)
  aTmpList = split(Session("CurrentFavorites"),"$")
  For Each strItem in aTmpList
    'add back any non-matches
    If Not StrComp(strItem,tmpItem)=0 Then
      If Not StrComp(NewList,"")=0 Then
        NewList = NewList & "$"
      End If
      NewList = NewList & strItem
    End If
  Next
  Session("CurrentFavorites") = NewList
End Sub
```

The additional code in UpdateCurrentFavorites() — added to the end of the preceding routine — looks like this:

```
'This removes any old favorites
aList2 = split(Request.Form("OldThings"),",")
For Each strItem2 in aList2
  RemoveCurrentFavorite(strItem2)
Next
```

9. Add a return button that returns to the page that called the results page. This is not a necessary part of the script, but it does show how ASP accesses system variables via the Request.ServerVariables collection.

One of the system variables, or cgi environment variables, that the server and the client typically pass is HTTP_REFERER. This designates the name of the page that referenced the current page. Armed with this piece of information, scripting the button is fairly simple. The code looks like this:

```
<%= Request.ServerVariables("HTTP_REFERER") %>
```

10. The final step is to return to the FavThings.asp form and update the code for the list box, so that it displays the current list of favorites, enabling the user to select ones to remove from the list. Because you created this form as an ASP page initially, you can simply add the requisite code to build the list of items in the appropriate place within the HTML page. Switch to HTML view and enter the following between the <SELECT...> and </SELECT> tags for the list box:

```
<%
      If Not StrComp(Session("CurrentFavorites"),"") = 0
Then
            aList = split(Session("CurrentFavorites"),"$")
            For Each strItem in aList
```

```
                        Response.Write("<OPTION VALUE=""" &
strItem & """>" & strItem)
                Next
        Else
                        Response.Write("<OPTION VALUE="""">No
current favorites")
        End If
%>
```

Now you have a complete Favorite Things Tracking System. Figure 18-20 shows the system in action. Within a session, you can add and delete favorite things, and ASP remembers both the total list of deleted items and the list of current items. Of course, if you really want to make this system functional, you need to connect it to a database. (For information on database programming using FrontPage, see Chapter 21.)

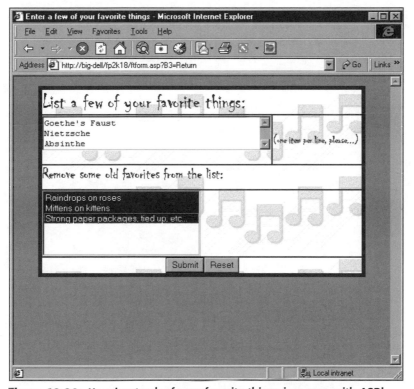

Figure 18-20: Keeping track of your favorite things is a snap with ASP!

Who knows, perhaps you will soon be adding ASP programming to your list of favorite things?

Summary

This chapter introduced you to the concept of scripting, and demonstrated how to use FrontPage to create and edit simple scripts using Microsoft Script Editor. This chapter called attention to some of the pros and cons of scripting use, and described what to expect from scripting in the near future. It introduced a veritable alphabet soup of scripting technologies: JavaScript, VBScript, DHTML, and ASP. It even offered several fascinating scripts for your amusement and edification. This has been a long chapter. Take a breather, and then head on to the next chapters, in which the big guns of the Web programming world are explored: ActiveX and Java.

✦   ✦   ✦

Plug-ins and ActiveX Controls

This chapter discusses plug-ins and ActiveX controls — advanced programming techniques that enable Web developers to insert interactive functionality into a Web page. This chapter introduces you to each of these elements, explains how they interact with a Web page, and then demonstrates how to add them to your page by using FrontPage. The chapter provides a general introduction to each of these technologies and plenty of examples to help you understand the particular strengths and weaknesses of each approach.

The Quest for Active Content

When the HTML standard was first defined, it was fairly limited in terms of the kinds of content that could be incorporated into a Web page. In fact, the only provision was for inline GIF images. To allow for the inclusion of other kinds of content, browsers were designed to work with *helper applications* — separate programs designed to display certain kinds of nontext content.

The helper application scenario works like this. Suppose that you want to enable your site's visitors to listen to an audio recording of your garage band. You could save the audio file in a fairly standard format, such as AU format, and name the file with an extension that indicated its format; for example, gband.au. Then, you could simply point to it with a standard HTML hyperlink reference. For the browser to identify and deal with this file correctly, however, another step is necessary. The file extension has to be mapped to a content type. This is done by using a standard known as *MIME*, for *Multimedia Internet Mail Extensions*.

MIME Types

The MIME type specification was first devised to address another problem: how to transmit binary (nontext) data via e-mail, a transport mechanism that was designed to transfer only text characters. Occasionally, depending on what e-mail circles you travel in, you may still encounter e-mail attachments that have been sent to you MIME-encoded.

MIME types also turn out to be a convenient way of identifying different data types for a Web browser. In this context, you don't need all the details about how MIME works. You can recognize a MIME type by the fact that it consists of a general type name, such as application, image, text, audio, or video, and a subtype name, separated by a forward slash (/).

These days, most browsers come preconfigured to recognize a long list of MIME types. However, you can add new types to the list. In Netscape 4.x, select Edit ⇨ Preferences, click to expand the navigation item in the Category list, and select Applications, as illustrated in Figure 19-1. You can use this interface to add new items, edit existing ones, or remove old and unwanted MIME types.

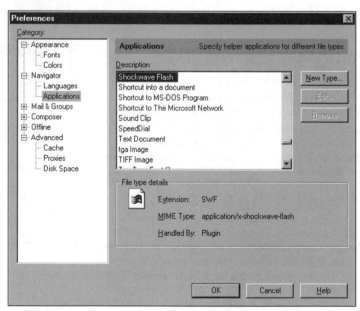

Figure 19-1: Viewing MIME types in Netscape Communicator

In Microsoft IE 4, MIME type information is gleaned from the Windows file type information. This can be accessed by opening My Computer, selecting View ⇨ Options, and then selecting the File Types tab; one portion of its contents is shown in Figure 19-2.

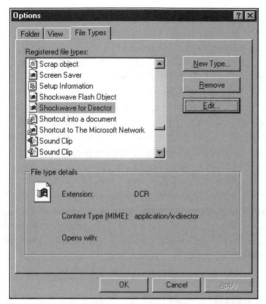

Figure 19-2: File type designations in Windows

Beyond the helper application

The helper application method is perhaps better than nothing, but it is not particularly user-friendly or useful. With a helper application, every content file must be viewed separately, so any possibility of a complete "multimedia" experience is lost. Not to mention the fact that you have to locate, download, install, and maintain a separate utility for every application.

Note   Although the goal of providing active content seamlessly within your Web experience is a noble one, adhering to the helper application model sometimes makes more sense. Consider, for example, the use of streaming audio. Click the link to an audio stream and you can listen to an hour rebroadcast of the evening news. In this case, you may find it convenient to have the news broadcast running in a separate application, freeing you to continue Web browsing as you listen.

One of the main virtues of the helper application approach is that it makes life for a developer blissfully easy. All you have to do to make your content file available to users via a helper application is to create a hyperlink to it, just as you would to any standard Web page. The rest of the work (making sure they have a proper helper app, and configuring their list of MIME types) is up to the users.

Unfortunately, making life easy for developers is not what drives innovation on the Internet. Making life easy for users is what counts.

What Is a Plug-in?

The next stage in the evolution of active content via the Web was Netscape's development of the plug-in, which was first unveiled in the Netscape 2.x Navigator browser. The best way to characterize a plug-in is to say that it is a "smarter" helper application that lives inside a Web page. When the user selects content to be displayed in a plug-in, the content downloads to the user, just as in the helper application scenario. With the plug-in, however, the content is handled by an application that works in conjunction with the Web browser. The browser opens the application, which displays itself *inline*, just as graphical images typically appear (in a sense, the browser's ability to display graphics in this fashion is just the first instance of a plug-in).

Note   Plug-ins remain principally a Netscape phenomenon, although Internet Explorer has also had the ability to display plug-ins since version 3.0. In practice, IE developers typically use ActiveX controls instead, which have some advantages over plug-ins and provide the developer with more flexibility.

Inserting plug-ins with FrontPage

Adding a reference to a plug-in is relatively straightforward, and FrontPage makes the task even easier. This section describes a simple example of how to do this, using a document in Adobe *Portable Document Format (PDF)*. You can find this sample file in the Chapter 19 folder on the CD-ROM that accompanies this book.

To use the file, first import it into the Web by selecting File ➪ Import. To insert the reference to the plug-in, simply select Insert ➪ Advanced ➪ Plug-in, opening the Plug-in Properties dialog box, shown in Figure 19-3. The most important element of this dialog box is the Data Source. Click the browse button to locate the file that you want to have displayed via a plug-in. In addition to the Data Source field in this database, you can configure several other options:

✦ **Message for Browsers Without Plug-in Support:** Insert text and/or HTML to be displayed by browsers that do not recognize the plug-in tag.

✦ **Size (Height and Width):** Indicates the dimensions of the plug-in, in pixels. You can also adjust the height and width of the plug-in by dragging and moving the plug-in icon.

✦ **Hide Plug-in:** Check this box to render the plug-in invisible. This normally is used with audio or other plug-ins for which a visible component to the plug-in isn't needed.

✦ **Layout (Alignment, Border Thickness, Horizontal Spacing, Vertical Spacing):** Designates various aspects of the location of the plug-in on the page.

When you are happy with your changes, click OK to return to the Editor window.

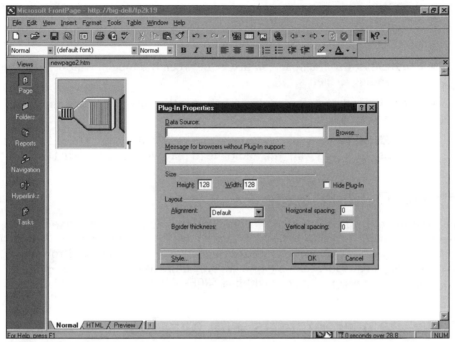

Figure 19-3: Inserting a plug-in using the Plug-in Properties dialog box

As illustrated in Figure 19-3, FrontPage puts a placeholder plug image in your page to represent the plug-in. You can preview your plug-in either by using the Preview tab or by selecting File ➪ Preview in Browser. If you click the plug-in image to select it, you can then drag a corner to resize the plug-in window. Double-clicking the plug-in image brings up its Properties dialog box for additional editing.

The plug-in <EMBED> tag

When you issue the Insert Plug-in command, FrontPage creates an `<EMBED>` tag for the plug-in, as shown in the following code:

```
<embed width="489" height="384" src="http://big-
dell/ch17/hvh2005.pdf">
```

FrontPage supports the following `<EMBED>` tag attributes via the Plug-in Properties dialog box:

✦ **SRC**: Identifies the URL of the file to be displayed by the plug-in. Its type is identified by its filename extension.

✦ **HEIGHT**: The height of the plug-in window, in pixels.

✦ **WIDTH**: The width of the plug-in window, in pixels.

✦ **BORDER**: Places a border around the plug-in window with the designated thickness, in pixels.

✦ **ALIGN**: Alignment of the plug-in window.

✦ **HSPACE**: Horizontal space, in pixels, between the plug-in window and the surrounding elements.

✦ **VSPACE**: Vertical space, in pixels, between the plug-in window and the surrounding elements.

✦ **HIDDEN**: Hides the plug-in element from view. This is most useful for audio plug-ins, when you want the audio file to play without any visual elements.

The <NOEMBED> tag

In addition to the properties (or attributes) of the plug-in, you can use the plug-in dialog box to create a simple text message to display for users with browsers that don't support the `<EMBED>` tag. Any text placed in the Message for Browsers Without Plug-in Support textbox appears only if the user has an incompatible browser. This message is placed within a `<NOEMBED></NOEMBED>` tag set.

How the user interacts with plug-ins

From the user's perspective, setting up to use plug-ins is very much like using a helper application. To use a plug-in, it must be downloaded and installed in the browser before encountering a page that requires it. To illustrate the ease of installing a new plug-in, imagine that you come upon a site that contains an Adobe PDF format document that you would really like to view. Here are the steps to follow to do so:

1. Locate the source of the plug-in. Frequently, developers kindly place a handy Get Plug-in XYZ Now! button on the page that contains a link to the content. In this case, assume that you see the Adobe Acrobat button and click it.

Caution

In practice, this "handy" button can turn out to be more confusing than convenient, because some plug-in makers require developers to link only to their home page, rather than to the plug-in download page. Most new Web users find the whole plug-in concept arcane enough. Sending them to a page with little or no visible connection to their mission is usually disorienting and annoying.

2. Assuming that you can find the location from which to download the plug-in, the next step typically is to fill out a registration form. Most plug-ins are distributed freely. How is this possible, you ask? Plug-ins essentially are viewers for content files that typically are proprietary in form. Software companies make money from people who develop content by using their software. The more people who want to view content in this form, the more people who buy the development software. In other words, free plug-ins generate demand for the products the software company sells.

However, for obvious marketing reasons, the plug-in developers like to know who is downloading their plug-ins. So, in effect, you trade your e-mail address and/or phone number for the opportunity to use their plug-in.

Note   On the topic of registration forms, two of the most widely used plug-in technologies, Macromedia's Shockwave and RealNetwork's RealPlayer (formerly RealAudio), have minimal, unobtrusive registration forms. Coincidence? You be the judge.

3. After filling out the form, you are directed to a download page. Assuming that you can find the plug-in version that you want on this page, select it and watch it download. (Plug-ins typically range from about 300K to 1.5MB in size.)

4. After the file downloads, run the installation program. Installation is usually fairly painless. The setup program copies the pertinent files into the plug-in directory of your Web browser and makes some changes to the Windows Registry.

5. Assuming that you kept open your Web browser during this process (remember that you initiated this process because you saw a file that you want to view), you must now shut down the Web browser and restart. Why? Because when the browser starts, it looks into its plug-in directory to see what is in there. The only way to get the browser to detect a recent addition is to restart it.

6. Now, if you can remember where you saw that document that you wanted to view, return to the site and click the file. Assuming that the plug-in installed correctly, the content opens in your Web page, as illustrated in Figure 19-4.

Tip   You can check on the status of your plug-ins in Netscape by selecting Help ⇨ About Plug-ins. This displays an internal HTML page listing all known plug-ins. An example of the About Plug-ins page is shown in Figure 19-5. If the plug-in is on the list, it should work (but see the cautionary tale below before you bank on this).

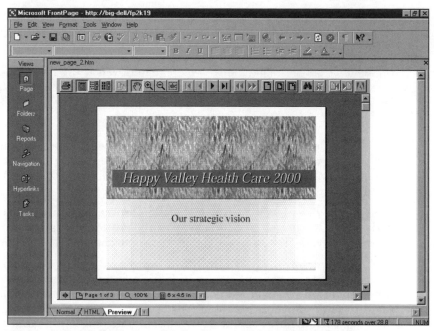

Figure 19-4: Displaying a PDF inline by using the Acrobat Plug-in

Figure 19-5: Everything you ever wanted to know about your Netscape plug-ins in the About Plug-ins page

Plug-in Woes: A Cautionary Tale

Here is another tale from the cross-platform compatibility frontlines.

When I first attempted to install the Netscape plug-in for Macromedia Shockwave for Director, I went to the Macromedia site and dutifully downloaded and installed the plug-in.

Every time that I attempted to access a Shockwave for Director file, however, I received an error message, indicating that the plug-in was not correctly installed, in spite of the fact that a quick check of the About Plug-ins page in Netscape indicated that all was fine.

After snooping around and noticing that the Registry entry for the Shockwave for Director MIME type did not have a `CLSID`, on a hunch, I decided to check out IE's ability to view these files. It couldn't, and neither did it want to download the control automatically.

Finally, I reinstalled IE 4 and installed its Shockwave controls at the same time. After this, not only did the IE controls work flawlessly, so did Netscape's plug-in (and you thought these guys were in competition).

Popular plug-ins

When Netscape first introduced the plug-in concept and made available the resources for developers to build their own plug-ins, dozens of companies who had proprietary file formats rushed to create plug-ins for their file types. This has resulted in nearly 200 plug-ins listed on Netscape's site (see the upcoming reference, "Where to Find Plug-ins"). In practice, however, only a handful of plug-ins have achieved any real acceptance. Most of these also exist as ActiveX controls. This section profiles some of the major "players," so to speak, organized by common categories.

Animation

The hands-down leader in this category has been Macromedia, who was one of the first to capitalize on the plug-in format. It developed a viewer for its Director file format, rechristened Shockwave for the Web community. Since this humble beginning, Macromedia has released versions of Shockwave to run Authorware applications and Freehand presentations. Its most recent entry is Flash, a vector-based animation program that produces compact animations geared toward bandwidth-limited media.

Audio/video/streaming media

The early leaders in this category included Apple's QuickTime, and the streaming audio technology originally called RealAudio, the product of RealSystems (formerly Progressive Networks), now expanded to include streaming video and renamed RealVideo. Other popular contenders include VivoActive and VDOLive. In the world of MIDI music, the Crescendo plug-in is frequently used, although many options are available. Of course, Netscape has released its own A/V plug-in modules that work with most standard, nonproprietary formats.

VRML

VRML, short for *Virtual Reality Markup Language*, and often pronounced "vermel" (isn't that a little North American rodent?), is a programming language for creating 3D "worlds," or spaces through which you can navigate by using the mouse pointer. The issue of whether VRML is a cool technology that has come and gone or is still just a little ahead of its time is still unclear. It has never quite lived up to its promise, although with the release of VRML 2, it has become more flexible and interactive.

The prominent VRML plug-ins are Silicon Graphics' Cosmo browser, VReam's WIRL, and Intervista's WorldView.

Interactive chat

Like VRML, chat plug-ins represent an attempt to put inside a Web browser not just different file formats but whole new services. The Web is particularly poorly suited to chat functionality. The leader in this category is iChat. Another interesting contributor in this category is Onlive! Traveler, a 3D chat environment.

Formatted documents

No question here, Adobe's Acrobat reader for its own PDF format is the hands-down favorite, although other products are available that perform similar functions.

Where to find plug-ins

Because the plug-in is a Netscape phenomenon, not surprisingly, the main source for plug-ins is the Netscape plug-in site, located at

```
http://home.netscape.com/comprod/products/navigator/version_2.0/plu
gins/index.html
```

At last count, this site has 176 registered plug-ins available, in a variety of categories.

Tip   You can access this site quickly by opening the About Plug-ins page (as described earlier) and clicking the hyperlink at the top of the page.

In addition to the Netscape site, several other good sources for plug-ins exist (although, frankly, Netscape's site is the largest, easiest to use, and best maintained), including:

✦ **Browserwatch Plug-in Site:** `http://browserwatch.internet.com/plug-in.html`

✦ **Plug-in Gallery:** `http://www2.gol.com/users/oyamada/`

The problem with plug-ins

Although plug-ins have the advantage over helper applications of being able to run inside the Web browser, it is still just too much of a hassle and has too many ways for things to go wrong. The plug-in model is also relatively inflexible. Plug-ins tend to be large, static applications that typically aren't accessed or manipulated by the Web developer.

Tip You really can do much more with plug-ins than they have been given credit for here. Several plug-in elements are supported by FrontPage. In addition, plug-ins written to the Netscape LiveConnect specification can communicate with the HTML page and the user via JavaScript. This functionality is not supported by Internet Explorer. For more information on plug-ins, visit Netscape's plug-in guide http://developer.netscape.com/library/documentation/communi-cator/plugin/index.htm.

Note An increasing number of companies with plug-ins are developing Java-based versions of their viewer applications. These work much like plug-ins, but don't require installation and can be downloaded in advance of the content automatically.

Discovering ActiveX

About the time that Netscape was introducing the plug-in innovation, Microsoft (the non-Internet company) was waking up to realize that it needed to remake itself and simultaneously remake the nature of the Internet, to avoid being left in the virtual exhaust dust of the information superhighway. The introduction of the ActiveX technologies is characteristic of Microsoft's efforts to put itself back in the driver's seat.

ActiveX is Microsoft's answer to Netscape plug-ins (as well as to Sun Microsystems' Java programming language, described in the last section of the chapter). To a large degree, the ActiveX name is really just a repackaging of preexisting Microsoft technologies (most notably, the Object Linking and Embedding specifications, or OLE), fine-tuned a bit for their new role on the global Internet. These technologies make possible the reuse of application components and enable applications to communicate with one another and even embed parts of themselves in other applications.

Note Although ActiveX usually is associated with the Internet, it really is just a general-purpose set of technologies that happens to include the Internet. This is both its power — in its ability to render practically seamless the computer system, its local and any remote resources on the Internet — and its drawback — because all of this is platform-dependent and operating system-dependent.

A Brief, Acronym-Cluttered History of ActiveX

First came Visual Basic Extensions (VBE), custom controls that can be accessed using the popular Visual Basic programming language. Then came Object Linking and Embedding (OLE) and OLE Controls (OCXs). OLE technology essentially enabled developers to put one document type inside another. You have experienced OLE if you have ever embedded, say, a spreadsheet in your word processing document.

When Microsoft first discovered the Internet, it quickly extended the OLE technology to operate via the Internet. Then it gave OLE a catchy marketing name. Voila! ActiveX was born.

For a time, Microsoft tried using the term "ActiveX" as the umbrella brand name for all of its Internet programming technologies, but the term has fallen out of vogue in the past six months. The latest marketing terminology is *DNA*, which is meant to stand for *Distributed interNet Application*. Today, ActiveX is used primarily in connection with ActiveX controls, as discussed in this chapter.

In somewhat more formal terms, *ActiveX* refers to any of several technologies that use the Microsoft Component Object Model (COM) specification to create programming entities that can be combined, reused, scripted, and delivered via a network such as the Internet. The term "ActiveX" encompasses an array of applications that use the core concepts of OLE and COM.

ActiveX controls

An *ActiveX control* is simply a reusable, modular programming component. It can be inserted into another application, such as a Web browser's Web page, and it can be configured or scripted to perform a variety of tasks. It can range in size from something as simple as an option button to a sophisticated spreadsheet application.

ActiveX controls are really just one segment of the larger ActiveX picture, but they are entities that can be used relatively easily, even by nonprogrammers (although a little programming knowledge never hurts). Because ActiveX controls tend to be easier to use than to explain, the next section provides an example of how to add an ActiveX control to your Web page.

Inserting an ActiveX Control

To insert an ActiveX control, select Insert ➪ Advanced ➪ ActiveX Control to bring up the Insert ActiveX Control dialog box, shown in Figure 19-6, which lists all the ActiveX controls currently registered on your computer.

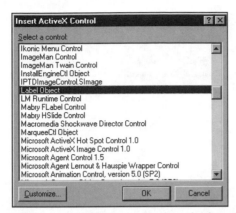

Figure 19-6: FrontPage displays the list of available ActiveX controls.

Caution

Chances are that the list of available controls is relatively long. How did all of those controls get there? (Spooky, isn't it?) Some are from Windows itself, others have come to you via Web pages, and still others are from other applications that you have installed on your computer.

The main purpose of this dialog box is to select the control that you want to insert into your Web page. You can also customize this dialog box so that it lists only the controls that you might actually want to use. To customize the list, click the Customize button and deselect any items that you don't want to appear on the list. (Don't worry, if you change your mind later, you can always return and recheck any items that you remove from the list.)

Tip

Each time a control is registered on your computer, a reference is created in your System Registry file. Many of the controls listed by FrontPage likely no longer exist. You can remove them from sight by using the Customize button. (Or, get a utility to remove the reference completely from your Registry.)

After you select a control from the list, click OK. For the purposes of demonstration, a simple ActiveX control, the Label Object, has been selected. Figure 19-7 illustrates what the Label Object control looks like when it is first inserted. Not particularly exciting, unless you have been looking for a way to get a big "Default" on your page. The next section examines how to manipulate your control to serve a better purpose.

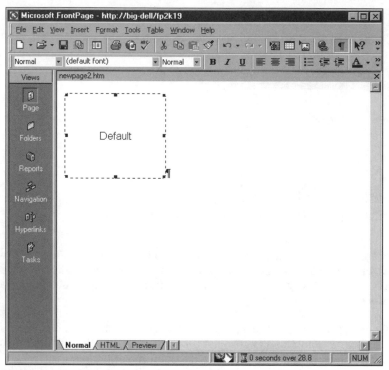

Figure 19-7: A basic ActiveX control icon inserted in Normal view

Editing Control Properties

Being able to use an ActiveX control like a plug-in is useful, but the real power of ActiveX begins to be more apparent when you configure a control to your liking. In many ways, ActiveX controls are much like any other HTML object. They have properties that you define to change how the controls look and/or behave. FrontPage gives you easy access to these properties.

The Label Object control enables you to take a string of text and manipulate it in one of several possible ways. This section describes how to modify the Label Object's properties.

To edit the properties of an ActiveX control that you have inserted into your page, double-click the object. Alternatively, you can right-click the object and select ActiveX Control Properties from the options menu, or you can select the object and select Format ➪ Properties from the main menu. The Properties dialog box for the Label Object control is shown in Figure 19-8.

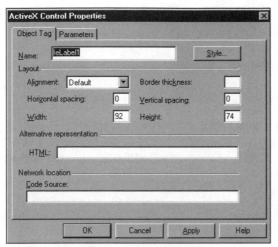

Figure 19-8: The Properties dialog box for the ActiveX Label Object control

The Properties dialog box for the Label Object control has two tabs: Object Tags and Parameters. The number of available tabs and their names vary from control to control. The options available for the Label Object control are representative of many basic controls.

Object Tag

The Label Object control's Object Tag tab enables you to define the control's general placement and appearance on the page. It does not affect how the control functions (which you define by using the control's parameters in the next section). The following are the options available on the Object Tag tab:

✦ **Name:** The control's name is used to reference it when using a client-side scripting language, such as VBScript or JavaScript. The name cannot contain spaces and must begin with either a letter or an underscore.

✦ **Layout section:** Contains properties that affect how the control appears on the page:

- **Alignment:** Like an image, an ActiveX control can be positioned in various ways relative to the elements around it.

- **Border Thickness:** By default, the border attribute is 0. Set this to a positive number to indicate the thickness of the border, in pixels.

- **Horizontal Spacing:** The spacing, in pixels, between the control and any elements to its left and right.

- **Vertical Spacing:** Spacing, in pixels, between the control and elements above and below it.

- **Width:** The width of the control, in pixels. Typically, you adjust the width and height by dragging and moving the ActiveX icon to an appropriate size. Use these fields for fine-tuning.

- **Height:** The height of the control, in pixels.

✦ **Alternative Representation:** Enter any text, including HTML, that you want presented to users with browsers that don't support ActiveX.

Tip

You can place HTML into the Alternate Representation, including <EMBED> and <NOEMBED> tags. This way, if the browser can display ActiveX controls, it will. If it can't display ActiveX but can display a plug-in, it will. Otherwise it displays the text contained within the <NOEMBED> command.

✦ **Code Source:** Indicates the URL to which users should go to download the ActiveX control when the page is loaded, if the user does not already have the control.

Parameters tab

The Label Object control also has a Parameters tab, shown in Figure 19-9, which contains a list of user-configurable parameters that the control recognizes. The parameters of an object enable you to change the behavior and/or appearance of an ActiveX control. As the next section describes, these parameters are stored in the HTML as part of the <OBJECT> tag.

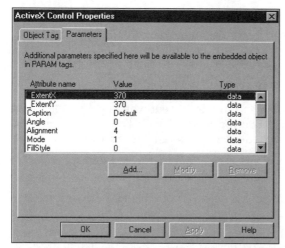

Figure 19-9: The Parameters tab for the ActiveX Label Object control

The following is the list of the principal parameters available for the Label Object:

✦ **Caption:** The text that the control displays

✦ **Angle:** The angle of the text (0 is horizontal)

✦ **Alignment:** Options are as follows:

0 left top
1 centered top
2 right top
3 left centered
4 centered
5 right centered
6 left bottom
7 centered bottom
8 right bottom

✦ **Mode:** Options are as follows:

0 simple no rotation
1 simple rotation
2 user-defined no rotation
3 user-defined rotation

✦ **Fillstyle:** 0-solid, 1-outline

✦ **ForeColor:** An integer representing the foreground (the text) color

✦ **BackColor:** An integer representing the background color

✦ **FontName:** Any valid font

✦ **FontSize:** An integer representing the pixel size of the font

✦ **FontItalic:** True/false

✦ **FontBold:** True/false

✦ **FontUnderline**: True/false

✦ **FontStrikeout:** True/false

Adding or modifying parameters

From the Parameters tab, you can add, modify, or remove parameters from the parameter list. You can add a parameter to the list or remove an existing parameter. Keep in mind that you are only adding and removing parameters from the list included in the HTML. You cannot change the functionality of the control itself with this dialog box.

To add a parameter, click the Add button to open the Edit Object Parameter dialog box (see Figure 19-10), select a new parameter from the list of available component properties, and configure the other options as described in the next section. To modify a parameter, select it from the list in the Parameters tab and click the Modify button to open the Edit Object Parameter dialog box with the current configuration of this parameter displayed. Make changes to this configuration as described in the next section. To remove a parameter, click the Remove button (FrontPage does not prompt you before eliminating the parameter).

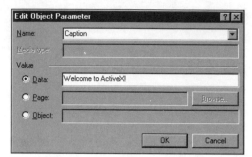

Figure 19-10: The Edit Object Parameter dialog box

Using the Edit Object parameter dialog box

The Name field in this dialog box shows the parameter that you selected. You can select a different parameter from the drop-down menu. The dialog box offers three options for how values are provided to the control:

✦ **Data:** The most common (and the default) option. Use this option whenever you want to enter the value directly to the parameter as an alphanumeric character string.

✦ **Page:** Enables you to enter a value that is a URL reference to another resource. This is typically used when the control incorporates external media, such as graphics, sounds, video, and so forth. Note that selecting this option also enables the Media Type field under the Name field.

✦ **Object:** Enables you to enter a value that references the ID of an `OBJECT` declaration in the same page.

Modifying the Label Object

The following steps walk you through the process of editing a control's parameters:

1. Open the Properties dialog box for the Label Object that you created earlier in this section. Select the Parameters tab.

2. Make the following changes:

    Caption = "Welcome to ActiveX!"

    ForeColor = #FF0000 (this is red)

    Angle = 45

    FontBold = True

3. Click OK to apply your changes and return to Normal view (see Figure 19-11).

4. Switch to Preview to see the changes take effect.

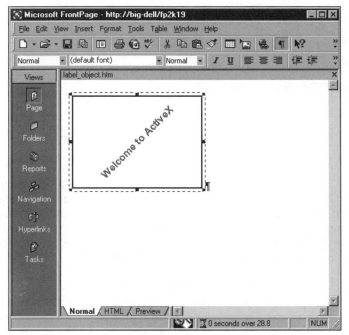

Figure 19-11: The Label Object after some parameter changes

You may discover that when you update the caption, it creates a small problem in the size of the control. To change the size of the control, select the control icon in Normal view and drag a corner of the control to increase its size, until you can read the entire caption message. If you watch carefully when you do this, you will notice that the width and height properties update to match your adjustments.

Examining the Object Tag

You have now successfully inserted and configured an ActiveX control, all without a stitch of programming. Just to show you what you have accomplished, take a look at the HTML that FrontPage generates for your control. When FrontPage inserts an ActiveX control into a Web page, it creates an instance of the `<OBJECT>` tag, an example of which is shown here:

```
<OBJECT CLASSID="clsid:99B42120-6EC7-11CF-A6C7-00AA00A47DD2"
ID="MyLabelControl"
WIDTH="199" HEIGHT="140" BORDER="2">
    <PARAM NAME="_ExtentX" VALUE="5265">
    <PARAM NAME="_ExtentY" VALUE="3704">
    <PARAM NAME="Caption" VALUE="Welcome to ActiveX">
    <PARAM NAME="Angle" VALUE="45">
    <PARAM NAME="Alignment" VALUE="4">
    <PARAM NAME="FontBold" VALUE="1">
    <PARAM NAME="FillStyle" VALUE="0">
```

```
            <PARAM NAME="ForeColor" VALUE="#FF0000">
            <PARAM NAME="BackColor" VALUE="#000000">
            <PARAM NAME="FontName" VALUE="Arial">
            <PARAM NAME="FontSize" VALUE="12">
            <PARAM NAME="FontItalic" VALUE="0">
            <PARAM NAME="FontBold" VALUE="0">
            <PARAM NAME="FontUnderline" VALUE="0">
            <PARAM NAME="FontStrikeout" VALUE="0">
            <PARAM NAME="TopPoints" VALUE="0">
            <PARAM NAME="BotPoints" VALUE="0">
            <PARAM NAME="Mode" VALUE="1">
Sorry, your browser does not support ActiveX.
</OBJECT>
```

The <OBJECT> tag set contains several attributes. The most important of these is
CLASSID (CLSID). This is the unique key stored in the Registry that identifies the
control. Entering this string by hand is both time-consuming and error-prone (and
memorizing too many of these numbers is tough). So, in this case, FrontPage does
you a favor by automatically inserting the correct ID number.

In addition, the <OBJECT> tag includes an ID attribute, which is the name used to
identify the object within the HTML page. The HEIGHT and WIDTH attributes define
the size of the object on the page. The BORDER attribute indicates that this object
has a 2-pixel border around it.

Within the beginning and ending <OBJECT> tags are two elements:

✦ A series of <PARAM> tags that correspond to the parameters that you
    configured earlier using the FrontPage ActiveX Properties dialog box.

✦ Optional text displayed by browsers that don't support the <OBJECT> tag.
    How to deal with browser compatibility issues is the subject of the next
    section.

Dealing with browser compatibility

One of the chief drawbacks of using ActiveX controls is the fact that only
Microsoft's Internet Explorer browser currently supports them. If you are
developing in a controlled environment, such as an intranet, in which you know
that your users have a certain browser, this may not be a concern. Otherwise, you
have a tough choice to make. These are your leading options:

1. Ignore the non-Microsoft browsers. If you do nothing, they will never know
   what they missed.

2. Use the HTML Alternative option to display an apologetic message and let the
   user know what they are missing.

3. Use the HTML Alternative option to display a functionally equivalent option
   for the non-Microsoft crowd. For example, you might embed a Netscape

plug-in that provides the same functionality (and within the plug-in code, you can embed a non-Netscape/non-Microsoft alternative!).

4. Use a scripting language to perform browser checking and act accordingly (see Chapter 18, "Scripting Languages," for an example of how to do this).

5. Recommend that your users obtain a Netscape plug-in capable of displaying ActiveX controls.

Scripting a Control

In addition to controlling the properties of an ActiveX control at design time, you can access your control via client-side scripting. This enables you to create sophisticated Web pages and ActiveX controls with minimal effort.

This section illustrates the process of scripting the Label Object control used in the earlier example. Following this simple example are two more-detailed tutorials. The first tutorial demonstrates one method for using ActiveX controls in place of standard HTML form elements. The second builds the beginnings of an online calendar page, using the Calendar Control. This chapter assumes that you are familiar with basic client-side scripting techniques. If you are not, you may want to peek at Chapter 18 before tackling this section.

Scripting the Label Object control

In this example, you add some additional ActiveX controls to the Label Object control example that you constructed earlier in the chapter. These new controls enable you to change the appearance of the label interactively. To follow this example, you need to have the Microsoft Forms 2 ActiveX controls registered on your computer. If you do not, you can substitute standard HTML form elements and obtain similar results.

Start with a new Web page and insert a Label Object control, as previously described. Using the ActiveX Control Properties dialog box, name the control **MyLabelControl** and make it 200 x 200 pixels square. Modify the Caption parameter to suit your tastes (and the size of the control).

Adding Form controls

You are going to add a series of ActiveX Form controls. These are similar to the standard HTML form elements, only much more versatile.

1. Create a table to hold the Form controls. You are going to add a Form control to modify the label caption, height, width, style, angle, and color. You can use Figure 19-12, which shows the Form control labels already inserted, as a guide to create the table.

Figure 19-12: The table structure for the Forms controls, complete with labels

2. Add the necessary Form Label controls. Place the cursor in the first table cell and select Insert ⇨ Advanced ⇨ ActiveX Control. Select the Microsoft Forms 2.0 Label control. Edit the Form Label properties by double-clicking the label. Name the first control **lblCaption**, change its Height value to **20**, and modify its Caption parameter value to **Caption:**. Repeat this step for the other Label controls, as indicated in Figure 19-12.

3. Add the remaining Form controls. You may have noticed that the Microsoft Forms 2.0 controls include a long list of Form controls. You are going to use only three: the TextBox control, CheckBox control, and SpinButton control. Of these, only the SpinButton control has no standard HTML equivalent (and, if you are really clever, you can probably imagine a way that you could emulate this control by using standard HTML form buttons and some additional scripting).

4. To add a TextBox control, select Insert ⇨ Advanced ⇨ ActiveX Control and select the Microsoft Forms 2.0 TextBox control from the list. Name this control **tbCaption** and insert it next to the Caption Label control. Adjust the size, as needed. Repeat the same process to create TextBox controls for Height, Width, and Angle. Create three boxes for the RGB color values. See Figure 19-13 for layout possibilities.

5. To add a CheckBox control, select Insert ➪ Advanced ➪ ActiveX Control and select the Microsoft Forms 2.0 CheckBox control. Name this control **cbFontBold**. Click the Parameters tab and modify the Caption parameter to **Bold**. Set the value of this check box to **0** (the default is 2). This makes the check box not selected by default. Repeat for Italics and Underline.

6. To add a SpinButton control, select Insert ➪ Advanced ➪ ActiveX Control and select the Microsoft Forms 2.0 SpinButton control. Name it **sbAngle**. Place this control next to the Angle textbox control.

7. You also need a button control. Select Insert ➪ Advanced ➪ ActiveX Control and select the Microsoft Forms 2.0 Command Button control. Name it **btnUpdate** and modify the Caption parameter to **Update**.

You now have a nifty Web page Control Panel, shown in Figure 19-13, for your Label Object control. In the next section, you hook up the control to the Control Panel.

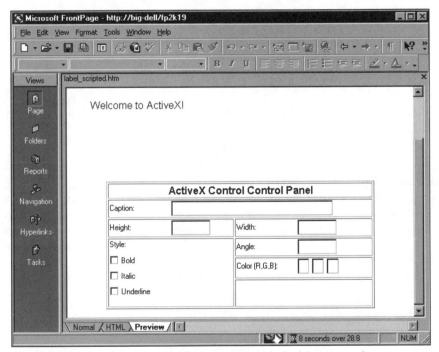

Figure 19-13: A custom Control Panel for the Label Object control

Scripting the Form controls

The idea is simple. You want to be able to edit the values of any of the available Form controls and click the Update button to register the changes with the Label Object control. To do this, you must write a few simple scripts.

Creating Event subroutines

To write these simple scripts, you use VBScript, mainly because VBScript has built-in support for ActiveX control events. The Command Button includes a `Click` event method. To script that event, you create a subroutine called `btnUpdate_Click`:

```
Sub btnUpdate_Click
   'Our code will go here
End Sub
```

You also need an event subroutine for the SpinButton control. Each time that the top spin button is clicked, you want the value of the Angle textbox to increase, and each time the bottom spin button is clicked, you want the value of the Angle textbox to decrease. The SpinButton control has two events, `SpinUp` and `SpinDown`, to handle these events. The code that you add here is relatively straightforward:

```
Sub sbAngle_SpinUp
   If (tbAngle="") Then
          tbAngle=0
   End If
   tbAngle=tbAngle+1
End Sub

Sub sbAngle_SpinDown
   If (tbAngle="") Then
          tbAngle=0
   End If
   tbAngle=tbAngle-1
End Sub
```

Completing the update event code

When the Update button is clicked, you need scripting that checks the status of each update element and then makes any necessary changes to the parameters of your Label Object control. This is a relatively straightforward matter of setting each of the parameters in the Label Object (`MyLabelControl`) to the value of the Form control. Here is the code:

```
Sub btnUpdate_Click
   MyLabelControl.Caption=tbCaption
   MyLabelControl.Height=tbHeight
   MyLabelControl.Width=tbWidth
   MyLabelControl.Angle=tbAngle
   MyLabelControl.FontBold=cbFontBold
   MyLabelControl.FontItalic=cbFontItalic
   MyLabelControl.FontUnderline=cbFontUnderline
   MyLabelControl.ForeColor = setColor(tbR,tbG,tbB)
End Sub
```

Dealing with color values

The one complication to the update routine in the previous section is the color designation. Although FrontPage allows you to designate a color by using hexadecimal notation (such as #FF0000), the scripting object doesn't accept this format. Instead, it requires a packed integer notation. The good news is that the script includes a conversion function, setColor(r,g,b), that accepts color values from 0 to 255 for red, green, and blue. It translates this into the requisite packed integer and sends it along to the Label Object control. The following is the code for this function:

```
Function setColor (r,g,b)
    'converts RGB values to packed integer
    Dim iColor
    If StrComp(r,"")=0 Then
            r=0
    Else
            If cInt(r)> 255 Then
                    r=255
            End If
    End If
    If StrComp(g,"")=0 Then
            g=0
    Else
            If cInt(g)> 255 Then
                    g=255
            End If
    End If
    If StrComp(b,"")=0 Then
            b=0
    Else
            If cInt(b)> 255 Then
                    b=255
            End If
    End If
    iColor = (b * 65536) + (g * 256) + r
    setColor = iColor
End Function
```

Setting the default values

At this point, you have everything in place to use the Label Object Control Panel. Try it out! Compare your results with those in Figure 19-14.

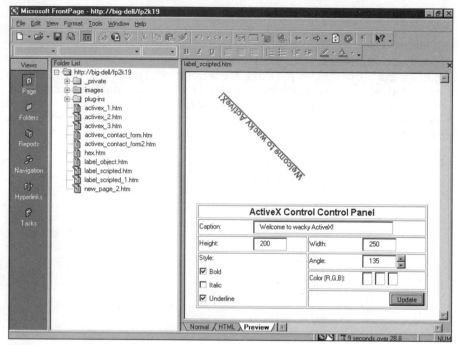

Figure 19-14: Updating the Label Object control with your ActiveX Control Panel

In this section, you make one last refinement to your Control Panel. You need to add a routine to set the Control Panel fields to the default value of the Label Object control.

Note   Why add this routine? Well, mainly because the first time I tested the update routine, I forgot to put in values for the height and width. When I clicked the Update button, poof! the control was gone. Or, rather, it was still there, it was just 0-pixels wide by 0-pixels high. Thus, the value of setting the defaults.

Create a subroutine called onPageLoad. Create a series of assignments that are the reverse of the ones in the update routine. The code is listed here:

```
Sub onPageLoad
   tbCaption=MyLabelControl.Caption
   tbHeight=MyLabelControl.Height
   tbWidth=MyLabelControl.Width
   tbAngle=MyLabelControl.Angle
   cbFontBold=MyLabelControl.FontBold
   cbFontItalic=MyLabelControl.FontItalic
   cbFontUnderline=MyLabelControl.FontUnderline
End Sub
```

You want to call this routine when the page first loads. To do this, update the <BODY> tag of the Web page to the following:

```
<BODY ONLOAD="onPageLoad">
```

Now, the initial values of all the Form controls are set when you initialize the page.

Tutorial 19.1: Submit an ActiveX Form

In your first scripting example, you were introduced to the Microsoft Forms 2.0 controls. These are highly versatile alternatives to the standard HTML form elements. Having gotten a taste of these controls, you might be thinking, "Why would I ever use the standard form elements again?" Two reasons. The first is the compatibility problems discussed earlier in the chapter. Not everybody is going to be able to use your ActiveX form.

The second reason is that the ActiveX elements don't have any built-in way of communicating back to the server. This is a rather serious limitation if you want to capture a user's input, a fairly standard practice with forms. This tutorial demonstrates one way to work around these problems.

Create a form

The purpose of this tutorial is to focus on how to submit a form from ActiveX. Consequently, the form itself is kept fairly simple. Using the Microsoft Forms 2.0 controls, as in the previous example, create a form with three TextBox controls.

Create the labels

1. Locate your cursor at the insertion point and select Insert ⇨ Advanced ⇨ ActiveX Control.

2. Select Microsoft Forms 2.0 Label control from the list of controls.

3. Click OK to insert the Label control.

4. Double-click the control to open the Properties dialog box. Modify the label name to **lblName**. Adjust the height to 20 pixels.

5. Select the Parameters tab and select the Caption parameter. Click Modify and change the caption data value to **Name:**. Click OK to return to the Web page.

6. Repeat these steps for the second and third labels. Name them **Email:** and **Your Message:**, respectively. Use Figure 19-15 as a guide.

Create the basic text boxes

1. Locate your cursor at the insertion point and select Insert ⇨ Advanced ⇨ ActiveX Control.

2. Select the Microsoft Forms 2.0 TextBox control from the list of controls.

3. Click OK to insert the TextBox control.

4. Double-click the control to open the Properties dialog box. Modify the textbox name to **Name**. Set the width to 340 pixels and the height to 24 pixels. Click OK to return to the Web page.

5. Repeat for the e-mail textbox. Name this control **Email:** and set the width and height to similar values. Use Figure 19-15 as a guide.

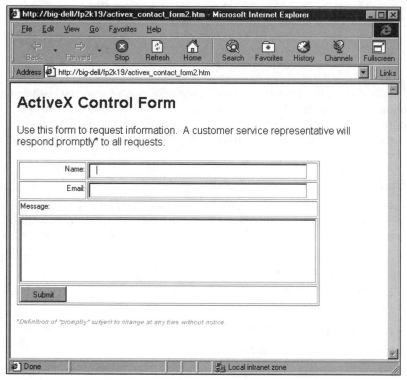

Figure 19-15: Basic interface for your ActiveX Submission Form

Create a scrolling text box

You may recall that among the standard form elements are two textboxes: a one-line box and a scrolling box. However, the Microsoft Forms 2.0 set of controls has only one TextBox control. To create a scrolling box, you simply edit parameters of the standard TextBox control, as follows:

1. Insert a TextBox control, as described in the previous section.

2. Double-click the control to open its Properties dialog box. Name the control **Message** and set its width to 460 and height to 100 (or whatever values you prefer).

3. Select the Parameters tab and modify the following parameters:

VariousPropertyBits = 2894088219 (this enables WordWrap)

ScrollBars = 2 (this adds a vertical scroll bar)

MaxLength = 500 (this prevents someone from sending an inordinately long message)

4. Click OK to return to the Web page.

Create the Command Button

1. Place the cursor at the insertion point and select Insert ➪ Advanced ➪ ActiveX Control. Select the Microsoft Forms 2.0 Comand Button control. Click OK to return to the page.

2. Double-click the control to open the Properties dialog box. Name the button **btnSubmit**. Set the width to 72 pixels and the height to 24 pixels.

3. Select the Parameters tab. Modify the Caption value to **Submit**.

4. Click OK to return to the Web page.

Non-ActiveX version

The form looks great (refer to Figure 19-15), but it doesn't do much yet, and it does even less if you don't happen to have Internet Explorer or an ActiveX-compatible browser. Your next step is to create a parallel version of the form, which will work for anyone else. Then, you will be ready to hook up both versions to the Form Submission programming.

Add Form Element

1. Select Insert ➪ Form ➪ Form to create a form element with a Submit and Reset button. Remove the buttons.

2. Select the table that contains your ActiveX controls (you can do this from the menu by using Table ➪ Select ➪ Table).

3. Cut the table.

4. Paste the table inside the form. The main reason for this step is to enable the alternative form elements that you create in the next section.

Caution Interestingly, although the ActiveX controls are not part of the form — in other words, they are not considered part of the normal form input — they must be referenced in the scripting language as if they were part of the form.

Create Alternative form elements

1. Open the Properties dialog box for the ActiveX lblName control by double-clicking its icon. In the Alternative Representation section, enter the text **Name:**. This text will appear instead of the Label Object control in all non-ActiveX browsers.

2. Open the Properties dialog box for the ActiveX Name textbox by double-clicking its icon. In the Alternative Representation section, enter the following HTML:

```
<INPUT TYPE="TEXT" NAME="NameHTML" SIZE="50" MAXLENGTH="50">
```

This is a standard HTML textbox form element. It will appear instead of the TextBox control in all non-ActiveX browsers.

3. Repeat the alternative representation for each control in the form. When you are finished, you should have a set of alternative components that produce a form very much like the ActiveX version (see Figure 19-16).

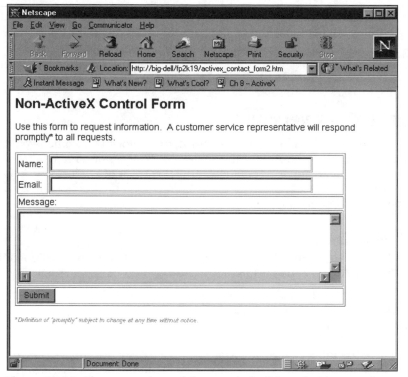

Figure 19-16: The appearance of the non-ActiveX form in Netscape browser — hard to tell the difference!

Create a dynamic title

This last step is really just gravy. You create a dynamic title that changes to reflect whether the form you see is an ActiveX form.

Tip You could also do this by using another ActiveX control and a non-ActiveX alternative, but there is always more than one way to do things!

The key to the dynamic title is detecting the user's browser. This can be done in JavaScript reference:

```
myBrowser = navigator.userAgent;
```

The userAgent property returns a string that the browser sends to the server to identify itself. Basically, the string identifies the browser name, version, and platform. Unfortunately, the format of the userAgent string is somewhat free-wheeling. Compare, for example, Netscape Navigator to Internet Explorer:

```
Navigator returns: "Mozilla/4.06 [en] (Win95; I)"
IE returns: "Mozilla/4.0 (compatible; MSIE 4.01; Windows 95) "
```

Tip Why is the Navigator browser named "Mozilla"? That is a vestige from the early Netscape days. The original Netscape team was composed of several renegades from the original "Mosaic" browser team. They invented a green monster whose name, Mozilla, combined Mosaic with Godzilla. As Netscape has grown up, the monster has faded from prominence, but its name remains as part of the "official" browser name.

Navigator returns the browser name and version, as well as a language version, and platform. IE, oddly, returns as the official browser name the Navigator name and version with which it is compatible. Then, it gives its own identifier and platform, with Windows completely spelled out rather than abbreviated, as it is in the Netscape version.

Determining whether you are dealing with an IE browser is fairly simple. You create a function called IsActive() and use it to check the userAgent to see whether it contains the MSIE indicator. If not, you know that you have a non-ActiveX-compatible browser.

```
if (myBrowser.indexOf("MSIE") = = -1) {
     return false;
     }
```

After you know that you are dealing with an IE browser, though, you also want to make sure that you have at least a 3.0 version. To do this, you split the version string into pieces, find the piece that contains the MSIE version number, and then evaluate that number. The scripting to do this looks like this:

```
browserParts = new Array();
  browserParts = myBrowser.split("; ");
  subParts = new Array();
  for (p in browserParts) {
        if (browserParts[p].indexOf("MSIE") == -1) {
              continue;
              }
```

```
subParts = browserParts[p].split(' ');
if (parseInt(parts[1]) >= 3.0) {
            return true;
        }
    }
```

With this function in hand, you simply have to create a script section in the body of the page that checks your IsActive() function and displays the appropriate title:

```
if (isActive()) {
   document.writeln("ActiveX Control Form");
   }
else {
   document.writeln("Non-ActiveX Control Form");
   }
```

You can compare the two versions in Figures 19.15 and 19.16.

Script the form submission

You now have a form that displays equally well in both ActiveX-compatible and noncompatible browsers. This section ties both versions to a standard FrontPage Submission Component.

Prepare the form responder

1. Select the Form Properties dialog box by right-clicking the form and selecting Form Properties.

2. Select Send to: File Name.

3. Click the Options button to open the Options dialog box.

4. Select a text database file format to save the results and keep the default filename (or create a new file if you want).

5. Click OK to return to the page.

Create hidden fields

The key to getting the ActiveX controls to submit their results via a standard CGI form back to the server is to pass the input values to hidden fields in the standard form. You need to create one hidden field for each control whose value you want to pass. In this case, that means you need to create three hidden fields: Name, Email, and Message:

1. Open the Form Properties dialog box, as you previously did.

2. Click the Advanced button to open the Hidden Fields dialog box.

3. Click Add, and add a hidden field named **hName**.

4. FrontPage insists that you provide a value for this field, so record something. It doesn't matter what, because you will replace it anyway. (You can always edit the HTML directly and remove whatever you enter here.)

5. Repeat for two additional hidden fields, **hEmail** and **hMessage**. The results are shown in Figure 19-17.

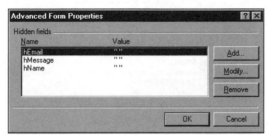

Figure 19-17: Adding hidden fields to your form

Note   The capability to pass ActiveX control values directly to the standard HTML form elements would be nice, instead of passing them to some additional hidden fields. Unfortunately, as far as Internet Explorer is concerned, the alternative representations don't exist. Consequently, no way exists to reference those elements.

Script the Submit Button

In this section, you create a VBScript subroutine to map the inputs from the ActiveX controls to the hidden fields, and then submit the HTML form:

1. Create a VBScript subroutine for the `Click` event of the ActiveX Command Button:

```
Sub btnSubmitX_Click
      MessageForm.hName.value=MessageForm.NameX
      MessageForm.hEmail.value=MessageForm.EmailX
      MessageForm.hMessage.value=MessageForm.MessageX
      MessageForm.Submit()
End Sub
```

2. Test the form in both IE and a non-IE browser. In IE, the results are recorded in the hidden field values. In any non-ActiveX browser, the results are submitted in the normal input fields. Default confirmation results for each are shown in Figure 19-18.

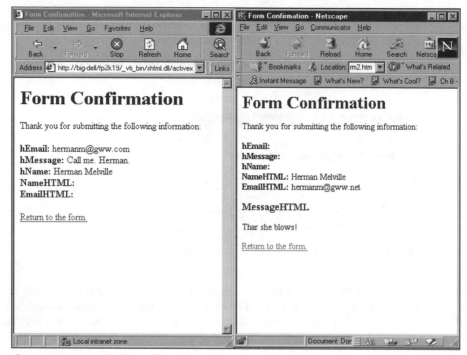

Figure 19-18: Default Confirmation Pages for your two-in-one form submission page

> **Tip** This method of passing the data through hidden fields has one small problem — the input isn't always recorded in the same fields. This makes it somewhat cumbersome to import the results file into a database. It also complicates the confirmation process, because you never know which fields to display back to the user. One solution is to write another routine that runs when the standard form is submitted, to transfer the standard form input into the hidden fields as well.

The Script Editor and ActiveX

This section describes the use of the Script Editor in conjunction with ActiveX controls. This discussion assumes that you already have read about the Script Editor in Chapter 18, "Scripting Languages," so this discussion focuses on an example of how you can use the Script Editor to configure your control.

The following tutorial illustrates the basic use of the Script Editor in conjunction with a more sophisticated control, the Microsoft Calendar Control. In this tutorial, you focus on using the Script Editor to modify ActiveX control parameters. To use this control effectively, you will want to add some scripting to the page that displays the calendar — a topic that is beyond the scope of this chapter.

Tutorial 19.2: Calendar Scripting

1. Open a new Web page and insert the Calendar Component by selecting Insert ➪ Advanced ➪ ActiveX Component and selecting the Calendar Component (this example uses version 8). If the Calendar Component is not listed, click the Customize button and check the Component in the list of registered ActiveX Components. Click OK the requisite number of times to return to Page view.

Note
The Calendar Component installs with FrontPage 2000. If you don't see the Calendar Component in the Customize list, that means that it isn't registered on your system for some reason.

2. Select Tools ➪ Macro ➪ Microsoft Script Editor to open the Calendar page in the Script Editor.

3. Click the Calendar Component in the editing window to view its properties in the Properties Explorer (see Figure 19-19).

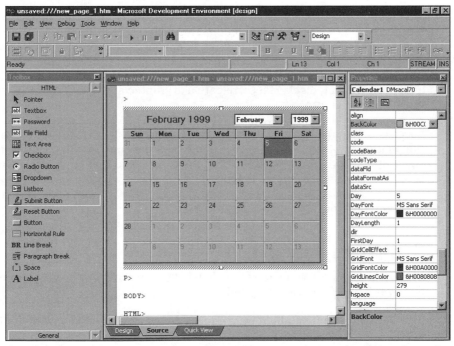

Figure 19-19: The Calendar Component and its properties, as shown in Microsoft Script Editor.

4. The Properties Explorer lists all available properties for this component, as well as showing all available options for each property.

5. For example, suppose that you want to adjust the `BackColor` property — the value that determines the color of the calendar background. Select the `BackColor` property in the Properties Explorer. This enables a drop-down Color Picker, from which you can select the background color that you want.

6. After you adjust the Calendar Component properties to your liking, return to FrontPage. You will notice that all the parameters have been updated.

ActiveX Security

When you allow a remote computer to send a program to you to be run on your local computer, as is the case with both ActiveX controls and Java, you open up the possibility of security problems. What is to stop someone from sending you a "malicious" program that wreaks havoc with your computer system? The question is always how to safeguard your computer to a reasonable degree of certainty from such attacks without completely foregoing the advantages that the ability to send programming across the Internet affords.

Microsoft has addressed security issues with its ActiveX technologies by creating a method of digitally signing their code. This digital signature technology is called *Authenticode*. When the user arrives at a Web page that contains active content requiring a control that isn't currently resident on the user's system, the page issues a request to download the software. It checks the sender's digital signature and, if it's correct, displays a certificate-like graphic and asks you for permission to download the control.

Success of this method relies on several assumptions — that the entity who signs the digital certificate is trustworthy and would not cause any harm; that the digital signature has been generated by its actual owner; and that the person receiving the programming can make a reasonable decision about whether or not the owner is deserving of trust. After you determine that the entity is legitimate and safe, you grant the program license to do as it pleases.

Setting security in IE 3

In Internet Explorer, you can set the level of security of your browser. Internet Explorer 3.x has three security options:

✦ **High:** Any potentially unsafe content is not downloaded, and a warning is issued to this effect.

✦ **Medium:** You are warned when unsafe content is about to be downloaded, and choose whether to allow the download.

✦ **Low:** No safety measures are enacted. All content downloads.

Setting security in IE 4

In Internet Explorer 4, you can set a similar range of general security levels. In addition, you can customize security options by setting the level of numerous potential security risks.

Select View ⇨ Internet Options and click the Security tab, as shown in Figure 19-20.

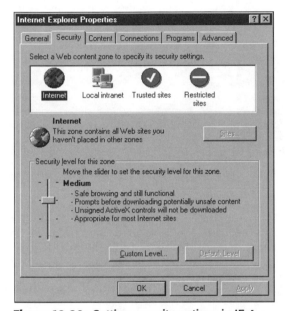

Figure 19-20: Setting security options in IE 4

Select one of four zones: Local Intranet Zone, Trusted Sites Zone, Internet Zone, or Restricted Sites Zone. The Internet zone is the default zone for any location not specified as being part of one of the other zones. To add a location to a zone, select that zone and click the Add Sites button.

Select a security level option: High, Medium, Low, or Custom. The first three levels are the same as in IE 3. The last gives you very fine-grained control over your security choices, as shown in Figure 19-21.

All of these options may help to make you feel safe, but if you happen to allow a bad piece of code through, no physical layer of security protects the computer system from this code. This is the main difference between security as it is implemented by Microsoft in its ActiveX technologies and Sun in Java, the topic of the next chapter.

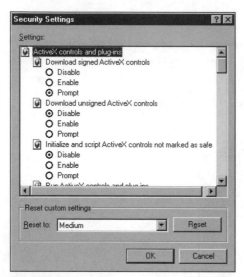

Figure 19-21: So many security choices, so little time!

Locating controls

For a time, after Microsoft first introduced Internet Explorer 3, it maintained a very useful and informative ActiveX gallery on its Web site. Unfortunately, this gallery has been replaced with a short list of other sites that now maintain repositories of ActiveX controls. You can find the list of third-party repositories at www.microsoft.com/com/gallery/. You can also find information on ActiveX at www.microsoft.com/activex/.

Two other sites worthy of mention are

> ✦ **C/Net's ActiveX site:** www.activex.com
> ✦ **Browserwatch ActiveX Arena:** www.browserwatch.com/activex.html

Summary

This chapter showed you how to insert plug-ins and ActiveX controls into your Web page using FrontPage. After reading this chapter, you should be able to make decisions about what kind of active content to include in your pages and how to get that content into the page correctly. You have seen how to enhance your use of these advanced elements with client-side scripting. The next chapter introduces another advanced element, Java programming. Just as in this chapter, Chapter 20 shows you the information and basic techniques that you need to incorporate cool Java applets in your Web pages.

✦　　✦　　✦

Java Programming

This chapter explores what you need to know to use FrontPage to add Java applets to your Web pages. Java is another of the advanced programming elements that FrontPage supports and makes easy to incorporate into a Web page — even if you're not a programmer. This chapter focuses on explaining the basic details of Java that you need to understand to use it effectively.

What Is Java?

OK, you've heard the hype, but what is Java, exactly? Java is a programming language: no more, no less. In that respect, it is no different than C, C++, Visual Basic, or COBOL. You can write regular applications in Java (these are starting to appear on the market as we write) that operate just like other applications. However, Java is a special kind of programming language, because it is designed for a multiplatform, networked environment, such as the Internet. Several aspects of the Java programming language make it well-suited for Internet use:

- ✦ **Object-oriented**: Helps to make Java code modular, extensible, and highly reusable, especially with the introduction of *Java Beans*, Java components that are roughly the equivalent of ActiveX controls.

- ✦ **Multithreaded**: Describes applications that can perform several actions simultaneously. This is good in an environment in which download times are a factor.

- ✦ **Portable**: Java's claim to fame is that the same programming instructions can be run on a variety of computer platforms without having to redo the code.

✦ **Automatic garbage collection**: A Java program can take itself out of memory when it's no longer in use, which is just one prominent example of Java's ability to keep track internally of some of the aspects of programming that normally the developer has to worry about. This helps to make Java a relatively easy language to use.

✦ **Security restrictions**: Java's security methodology is designed for "untrusted" environments, such as the Internet. Java has had security holes, but, in general, more people have complained about Java's overly rigorous security than about the lack thereof.

The Java Virtual Machine

The key element that distinguishes Java from other programming languages is that, from a developer's standpoint, it is entirely platform-neutral. In other words, a developer should be able to write his or her program, give it to someone using a Windows-based PC, Sun UNIX system, or Macintosh (I haven't heard of an implementation for the Commodore 64 yet...), and the application should run without requiring any "porting" of the code. (Notice the use of "should" — this refers to the real world, in which the ideal situation isn't always 100 percent in line with marketing promises.)

How can a programming language perform this miracle? Elves? Well, not exactly, but the Java programming language does depend on some helpers to do the hard work. Typically, when a computer program is *compiled*, a set of instructions, written in human-readable form, is converted into specific instructions that the computer understands. In Java, when the developer compiles a program, the compiler only "semicompiles" the program into *bytecode*, which can't be understood directly by any operating system and thus must be interpreted by the *Java Virtual Machine (JVM)*. The JVM, which must reside on your computer system, knows how to read Java bytecode, and it also knows how to speak directly to your computer, translating the nonplatform-specific Java bytecode into something that your computer can understand.

You need a JVM to run Java programs, whether those are full-fledged applications or a Java applet that comes to you as part of a Web page. In the case of the applet, when you happen upon a Web page with a Java applet embedded in it, the Web server sends the applet's bytecode to your browser. The browser, an expert at delegating, knows to pass the bytecode to the JVM, where it undergoes some last-minute compiling for your machine and then performs its applet magic. The topic of Java applets is picked up again momentarily.

Note You may be wondering how you got the JVM on your computer in the first place? Browsers that support the display of Java applets typically install a version of the JVM.

The Java class library

The other Java "helper" is the set of fundamental Java classes that provides the basic Java functionality. These base classes are used by developers when they build their Java applets and applications, and the classes come to you as part of the Java-enabled character of your Web browser. (If these classes weren't present, they would have to be downloaded to you each time that you tried to run an applet.) These base classes perform numerous critical programming functions.

Caution One of Java's detractions is that these base classes are still evolving, which means that the set of Java base classes that you previously downloaded with your new Web browser aren't necessarily the current set of base classes in use among Java programmers.

In the first version (1.0.2) of Java, these classes were broken into the following six major *packages* (a collection of Java classes put together in a file system's subdirectory):

✦ **Java.Applet**: Contains the classes that generate the foundation of all Java applets.

✦ **Java.Awt (Abstract Window Toolkit)**: Contains the classes that produce the Java user interface elements (buttons, lists, scroll bars) and graphical elements (rectangles, images, and so on).

✦ **Java.Io**: Contains the classes that enable Java to perform basic I/O operations — reading and writing files. Note that applets, because of their security restrictions, cannot read or write local files.

✦ **Java.Lang**: Contains the classes that include many of the elements essential to the Java language itself — classes related to data types, string functions, multithreading, error trapping, and so forth.

✦ **Java.Net**: Contains the classes that perform basic network operations, including the ability of a Java applet to read and understand URLs.

✦ **Java.Util**: Contains the classes that are used for various purposes, usually associated with some kind of data manipulation.

As of the writing of this book, the current release of the Java base classes is version 1.2. In addition to significant enhancements to the packages in the preceding list, recent versions have added the following major components:

✦ **Java Beans**: Reusable Java components, similar in concept to Microsoft's ActiveX components.

✦ **Remote Method Invocation (RMI) classes**: Enable a Java application to call other Java classes that reside on other computers.

✦ **Java Archive (JAR) format**: Enables developers to compress the class files for faster downloading over the Internet.

✦ **Java Native Interface (JNI) classes**: Connect Java applications to "native" programming (programming written in languages that are machine-specific, such as C++).

✦ **Java Database Classes (JDBC) classes**: Used to write Java applications that connect to databases.

✦ **Java Interface Definition Language (Java IDL)**: Adds CORBA (Common Object Request Broker Architecture) capability to Java. CORBA, which has its own defined IDL, is an industry-standard method of invoking remote objects across the network.

✦ **Security**: Enhancements to the Java security model give developers fine-tuned control over how security policies are defined and how access permissions are enforced.

✦ **Swing classes**: No, Java doesn't include lessons in ballroom dancing... Swing is Java's set of interface components that enables developers to create applications with the "look and feel" of particular operating systems (Macintosh, Windows, Linux, and so on) without writing multiple versions of their program.

Tip   If you look for these Java classes on your computer, you may find them stored in a ZIP file (if you are using a PC) called classes.zip.

What is an applet?

First, you need to understand that Java isn't just a programming language for building applets. Java is quite capable of creating full-scale applications (although some arguments persist about how capable "quite capable" is). A Java applet is only one specialized kind of Java application, designed especially to operate within a Web browser environment — embedded in a Web page — rather than as a standalone application. Usually, an applet is smaller and simpler than a Web application, and it is limited in its operations by the security restrictions that Java places on remotely accessed applets. The main difference between an applet and a Java application, however, is that the applet has some special characteristics associated with starting and stopping the applet. This is because an applet is not "run" in directly the same way as a standard application is run. An applet must be able to start when it downloads with a Web page. Likewise, it must respond intelligently when a user stops the Web page from loading, clicks the Back button to return to the page it is on, and so on.

The next section illustrates the process of adding Java applets to your Web pages in FrontPage. The simple Java applets that are used in the examples are freely available on the Internet. You will not be writing any of your own applets in this chapter, but you will explore three examples:

✦ The first example focuses on inserting an applet into a FrontPage Web page and configuring the applet.

✦ The second example goes a step further, demonstrating ways that you can control how an applet operates from a scripting language, such as JavaScript.

✦ The third example, provided as a tutorial, explains how to work with Java source code to compile it into a working Java applet.

Inserting a Java Applet with FrontPage

This section starts by inserting a simple but eye-catching applet, called Fireworks, into a Web page. As you might guess, it produces an animated display of fireworks on your screen. It is easy to work with and provides a good sense of some of the animation capabilities that Java offers for a Web page.

Note　The two Fireworks classes, Firework.class and Rocket.class, are available on the CD-ROM that accompanies this book.

Before you can insert the applet into a Web page, you must import into your Web the two required classes for this applet, Firework.class and Rocket.class. Select File ➪ Import and locate the two classes on the CD-ROM. Alternatively, you can download this free applet from the Java Boutique Web site, www.javaboutique.com.

Inserting the Java applet

To add the Fireworks applet to your Web page, open the page and place the mouse cursor at the spot where you want the applet to appear. Select Insert ➪ Advanced ➪ Java Applet, which opens the Java Applet Properties dialog box, shown in Figure 20-1.

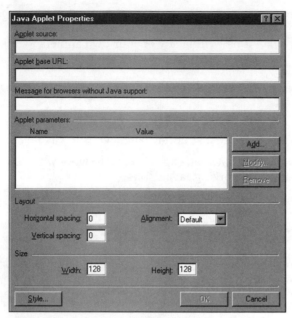

Figure 20-1: The Java Applet Properties dialog box

This dialog box has the following options:

✦ **Applet Source:** The name of the applet class file (in this case, Firework.class).

✦ **Applet Base URL:** The path name of the directory that contains the class files for this applet. (In this case, the two Java class files, Firework.class and Rocket.class, are placed in a Fireworks directory, so type **Fireworks** in the Base URL field.)

✦ **Message for Browsers Without Java Support:** You can include an optional message that displays only when a user's browser isn't capable of displaying a Java applet. This message also displays if the user has turned off Java support in their browser. This message can include HTML tags.

✦ **Applet Parameters:** An applet may have one or more parameters that you can configure. Use this dialog box to add, modify, and remove parameter names and values (this is examined in more detail momentarily).

✦ **Layout**: You can set the following attributes, which work for applets in the same way that they work for images:

  • **Horizontal Spacing:** Dictates the amount of space between the applet and any page elements on either side of it.

- **Vertical Spacing:** Dictates the amount of space between the applet and any page elements above or below it.

- **Alignment:** Determines how the applet is oriented relative to other elements on the page.

✦ **Size:** Adjust the Width and Height attributes. It is easier to modify these visually by dragging the applet icon in Normal view.

Adding parameters to an applet

If you set the applet source and base URL for the Fireworks applet, as previously indicated, and then attempt to preview it in FrontPage, you'll notice that the applet appears to load, but then nothing happens. Not much of a fireworks display, is it? Nothing happens because you need to provide the Fireworks applet with some information about how to display the fireworks. You communicate this information to the applet via parameters.

> **Tip**
>
> How do you know what parameters the Java applet accepts? In contrast to ActiveX components, FrontPage has no idea what parameters are available for any specific Java applet. You must rely on documentation from the applet itself for this information.

The Fireworks applet accepts the following parameters:

✦ **AnimationSpeed**: Used to adjust how rapidly the fireworks explode.

✦ **RocketSoundtrack**: You can include an audio file (in AU format) that accompanies the pyrotechnic display.

✦ **RocketStyleVariability**: Affects the range of variation of the fireworks displayed.

✦ **MaxRocketNumber**: Defines the maximum number of fireworks displayed at one time.

✦ **MaxRocketExplosionEnergy**: Affects the size of the fireworks.

✦ **Gravity**: Affects how quickly the fireworks fall.

To add parameters to the applet, double-click the big *J* Java applet icon in Normal view (see Figure 20-2) to open the Java Applet Properties dialog box.

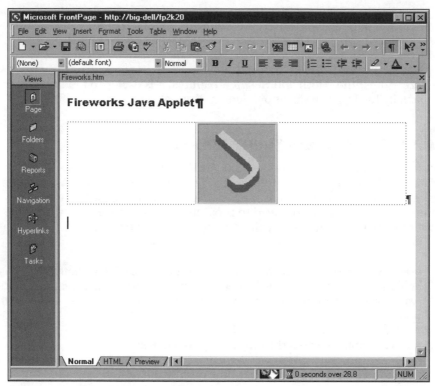

Figure 20-2: FrontPage Normal view represents your Java applet as a big *J* icon.

In the Applet Parameters section of the dialog box, click the Add button to open the Set Attribute Value dialog box, shown in Figure 20-3. Type the name of one of the fireworks parameters in the Name field and add an appropriate value to the Value field. Click OK to return to the Java Applet Properties dialog box. You should see the parameter information added to the parameter list.

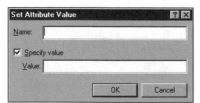

Figure 20-3: The Set Attribute Value dialog box for adding parameters to your Java applet

To edit or remove a parameter from the list, first select the parameter from the list in the Properties dialog box. To edit the parameter's name and/or value, click the Modify button. This opens the Set Attribute Value dialog box with the parameter information. To remove a selected item from the list, click the Remove button. One example of a complete configuration is shown in Figure 20-4.

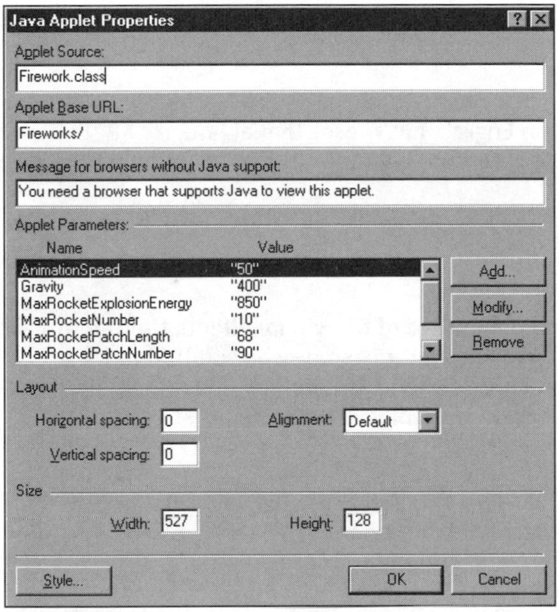

Figure 20-4: Configuration for the Fireworks applet

Java applets in HTML

You have learned the basics of adding a Java applet to your Web page. Now, take a look at what FrontPage has created for you behind the scenes. A Java applet is added to an HTML page by using the <APPLET> tag. The following is the HTML for the Fireworks applet:

```
<APPLET WIDTH="527" HEIGHT="128" CODE="Firework.class"
CODEBASE="Fireworks">
    <PARAM NAME="AnimationSpeed" VALUE="50">
    <PARAM NAME="Gravity" VALUE="400">
    <PARAM NAME="MaxRocketExplosionEnergy" VALUE="850">
    <PARAM NAME="MaxRocketNumber" VALUE="10">
    <PARAM NAME="MaxRocketPatchLength" VALUE="68">
    <PARAM NAME="MaxRocketPatchNumber" VALUE="90">
    <PARAM NAME="RocketSoundTrack" VALUE="fire.au">
```

```
<PARAM NAME="RocketStyleVariability" VALUE="10">
You need a browser that supports Java to view this applet.
</APPLET>
```

The source filename for the applet is designated by using the CODE attribute. The directory path to the Java classes is contained in "CODEBASE". Each of the parameters that you used is contained in a separate <PARAM> tag, with attributes for the name and value of the tag. The alternative text for non-Java-enabled browsers is indicated within the <APPLET> tag, as well.

Caution   At this point, the <APPLET> tag, which FrontPage uses here, has been *deprecated* as an HTML standard. In plain English, this means that although <APPLET> is still recognized as a valid way to insert an applet in your HTML, it is not the recommended approach.

A second example

The Fireworks applet is a splendid example of the visual effects that are possible in a Java applet. You might feel, however, that it is somewhat limited in its functionality. The next example is more useful. It displays a scrolling message in the applet. It is a variation of a "ticker tape" applet, one of the most popular Java applets.

The name of this applet is TinyScroller. It is freely available from www.javaboutique.com. It is also available on the CD-ROM that accompanies this book.

Inserting the applet

The TinyScroller applet is designed to scroll a series of text messages vertically across the screen. It can scroll the message up (the default) or down. You can adjust the background color and foreground text color, as well as the font and spacing. This applet is only 4K in size, which means that it loads quickly.

Start by importing the TinyScroller.class file into your Web. Next, open the Web page where you want the applet to appear. Select Insert ⇨ Advanced ⇨ Java Applet to open the Java Applet Properties dialog box. Designate the Applet Source name as **TinyScroller.class** and the Applet Base URL as the path within your Web to the applet. You can add a text message to display for non-Java browsers. Adjust the size and alignment of your applet to suit your circumstances.

The TinyScroller applet recognizes several parameters, but the only required parameters are the ones that indicate the lines of text to scroll. These are indicated with a series of LINE parameters, beginning with LINE1 up to as high as LINE100. You need to define only as many lines as you want, but you should use consecutive numbering, because the applet stops looking for lines after the first sequential number that is missing. For example, define the following lines:

```
LINE1 = "Welcome to our web site!"
LINE2 = "We hope you like all the cool features"
LINE3 = "you will find here...."
LINE4 = ""
LINE5 = "Like this cool scrolling applet, for instance!"
```

Notice that in LINE2 and LINE3, the text is manually "wrapped," because the applet doesn't automatically wrap a long line of text. Alternatively, you can make the applet wider. Also note how LINE4 is used to include a blank line between lines of text.

Now, test your applet. Your results, with formatting added but scrolling missing, unfortunately, are shown in Figure 20-5.

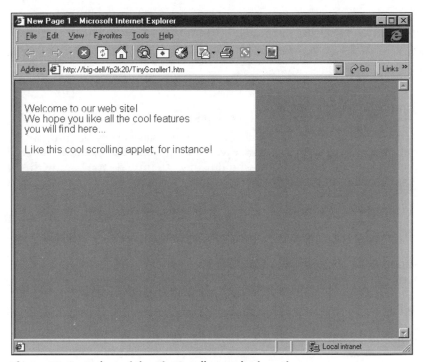

Figure 20-5: A shot of the TinyScroller applet in action

Additional parameters

In addition to the LINE parameter, the TinyScroll applet includes numerous optional parameters, which include:

✦ **BGRED, BGGREEN, BGBLUE**: Use to define the background color (white is the default). Each parameter can have a value between 0 and 255.

✦ **FGRED, FGGREEN, FGBLUE**: Use to define the foreground (text) color (black is the default). Each parameter can have a value between 0 and 255.

✦ **FONTNAME, FONTSIZE**: Use to define the font typeface and size. If you use one of these, you must use both.

✦ **SPACING**: Defines the line spacing between lines (12 is the default).

✦ **DELAY**: Dictates the time delay between line movements (100 milliseconds is the default).

✦ **XPOS**: Controls the horizontal position of the lines in the applet (5 is the default).

✦ **DIRECTION**: To scroll up, choose 0 (the default); to scroll down, choose 1.

✦ **BACKGROUND**: Designate an image to display in the background, in either JPEG or GIF format.

Communicating with your applet

The ability to configure an applet by using <PARAM> tags is very helpful, but what if you want the user to be able to interact with your applet? For example, a scrolling message window is very nice, but it would be nice to provide the user with a way to stop the applet if they have seen it enough times. Even better, wouldn't it be fun if the user could change the text displayed? This section examines how you can achieve these effects without becoming a Java programmer. All it takes is a recent version (4.0 or better) of either Netscape's or Microsoft's browser.

Controlling your applet with scripting

Any browser that is capable of displaying a Java applet must have access to a JVM (as discussed earlier in the chapter). More recent browsers have taken this a step further, enabling you to control the applet from either JavaScript or VBScript. This requires only that the applet have methods or properties that are declared public (in other words, accessible from outside the applet itself).

Because all applets derive from a generic Applet class that is defined by the Java base classes, you can guarantee that any applet will have a minimum set of methods that are public. The fine points of this are beyond the scope of this book. What is important to you is that two of those public methods are the methods that start and stop an applet.

To add Start and Stop buttons to your TinyScroller applet, perform the following steps:

1. Open the TinyScroller example created in the previous section.

2. Add a name identifier to the `<APPLET>` tag. Because the Java Applet Properties dialog box does not include a Name field, you have two ways to add a name identifier:

   - Switch to the HTML tab and add a `NAME=YourAppletName` attribute to the `<APPLET>` tag by hand, substituting the actual name of your applet for *YourAppletName*.

   - Double-click the Java applet icon (*J*) in Normal view to open the Java Applet Properties dialog box, click Style to open the Style dialog box for the Applet, and then type *YourAppletName* in the ID field.

3. Create the form buttons. Select Insert Form ⇨ Push Button to create a form element with a Push button. (FrontPage also adds a Submit and Reset button by default. You can delete these.) Double-click the Push button to open its Properties dialog box. Change its name to **StartButton** and its value to **Start**. Be sure to keep the Normal option selected. Repeat the process for a second button, named **StopButton** with a value **Stop**.

4. Script the Start and Stop buttons. To call any public method of the applet, you first identify the applet, using the object name that you created in Step 2, followed by the method name. For example, the call to the stop method of an applet, *YourAppletName*, would look like this:

```
document.YourAppletName.stop()
```

You can add this to the `ONCLICK` event for each button. Switch to HTML view and add the following to the `<INPUT>` tag for the Stop button (remember to substitute the actual name of your applet for *YourAppletName*):

```
ONCLICK="document.YourAppletName.stop()"
```

Repeat for the Start button, using

```
ONCLICK="document.YourAppletName.start()"
```

Your page should now resemble Figure 20-6 when displayed in the browser. Test the Stop and Start buttons.

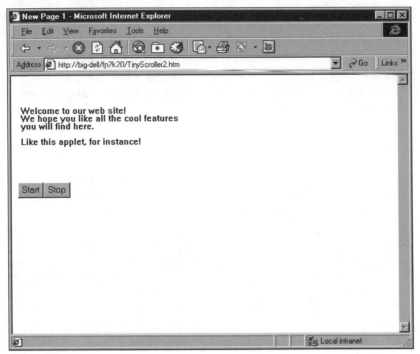

Figure 20-6: The TinyScroller applet with JavaScript-enabled Start and Stop buttons

Controlling parameter settings

Ideally, if you are writing your own applet that you want to control from a scripting language, you create public methods within the applet itself that enable you to change parameter settings on the fly. Unfortunately, your TinyScroller class doesn't contain any such methods. However, you can devise a workaround to this by using a scripting function to write the `<APPLET>` tag and then rewrite the tag after updating parameter values. It is not as elegant a solution, but it works. It can even be written to work for version 3 browsers, although it requires the use of frames to manage the rewriting. The remainder of this section describes the steps necessary to complete this version of the applet:

1. Create a two-frame frame set. Select File ➪ New ➪ Page, select the Frames Pages tab, and select a two-frame template, such as Footnotes.

   For each frame, click the New Page button to create a new, blank frames page in the top and bottom frames. Save the three HTML pages (the example uses ts_fr.htm, ts_main.htm, and ts_panel.htm).

   Your frame set before adding any functionality is shown in Figure 20-7.

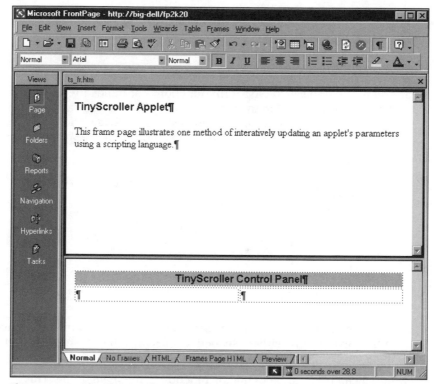

Figure 20-7: The TinyScroller applet frame set

2. Create JavaScript variables to hold the message information.

   Your goal is to create five LINE parameters for your TinyScroller applet. To do that, create an array with a length of 5 (you can make it more or less later, if you so choose). After you have your array, you need two functions to handle the array text: one function to populate the array initially, and one to enable you to set the array values from another frame. Here is the code for the array and the two functions:

```
var tsLength = 5;
var tsLines;
tsLines = new Array(tsLength);
initLines();

function initLines() {
        for (i=0;i<tsLines.length;i++) {
                tsLines[i]="This is a test";
                }
        }
```

```
function setLine(l,txt) {
        //note: no error checking on array range!
        tsLines[l]=txt;
        }
```

This code should be added to the frame set page.

3. Add to the frame set a JavaScript function that builds the `<APPLET>` tag, using the variables defined in the previous step. The easiest way to do this is to create the `<APPLET>` tag information using FrontPage, and then move the text into a variable. This is illustrated in the following `buildApplet` function:

```
function writeApplet() {
        var appletHTML;
        appletHTML="<APPLET NAME=\"TS\" WIDTH=\"371\"
HEIGHT=\"71\" CODE=\"tinyScroller.class\"
CODEBASE=\"TinyScroller/\">";
        for (i=0;i<tsLines.length;i++) {
                appletHTML= appletHTML + "<PARAM NAME=\"LINE" +
(i+1) + "\" VALUE=\"" + tsLines[i] + "\">";
                }
        appletHTML= appletHTML + "</APPLET>";
        return appletHTML;
        }
```

This code is added to the frame set page. Note that any quotation marks used in this text must be either escaped, by placing a backward slash(\) in front of them, or changed to single quotation marks (').

4. Add a call to the applet-building function in the main frame. This is a simple matter of adding a `document.write()` method in the body of the page and passing it to the text returned by your `buildApplet` function. Here is the code snippet for this operation, which should be placed in the main (upper) frame within the body of the page:

```
<SCRIPT language="javascript">
document.write(top.writeApplet());
</SCRIPT>
```

This is a good time to test and debug your applet, just to make sure that you have set up this portion correctly. At this point, the frame set should load and run the TinyScroller applet with the default lines of text.

5. Add a form to update the variables and reload the applet. Name the form **frm** if you are planning to use the code snippet provided in Step 6. We have created one text box for each line of text that you want to add (alternatively, you could use a scrolling text box and parse the input into lines). Name the text boxes **T1**, **T2**, **T3**, **T4**, and **T5**. This simplifies the code that you have to write in the next step. We have also added an Update Applet button to use to update the applet. (Check the illustration in Figure 20-8 to see the example.)

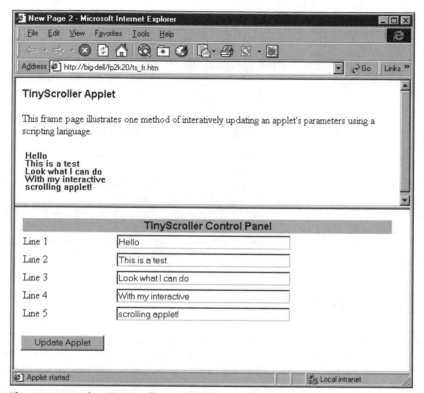

Figure 20-8: The TinyScroller applet frame set with a form for updating the scrolling message text

6. Add a function to the panel frame that is called when the user clicks the Update Applet button. This function calls the setLine function for each line and then reloads the applet page in its frame. The code is listed as follows:

```
function B1_OnClick() {
      for (i=0;i<top.tsLines.length;i++) {

top.setLine(i,eval("document.frm.T"+(i+1)+".value"));
            }
      parent.main.document.location="ts_main.htm";
}
```

This code assumes that you have created the appropriate number of text input boxes and named them T1 through T5. Anything else generates a JavaScript error.

7. Finally, call the function written in the previous step from the `ONCLICK` attribute of the Update button. Add `ONCLICK="B1_OnClick()"` to the button's `<INPUT>` tag.

Now, try it out. After the applet loads the first time, type some text into each of the input boxes and click the Update Applet button. The top frame should reload and restart the applet, this time with your text.

Tutorial 20.1: Compile and Run a Java Applet

So far, this chapter has demonstrated how to insert a Java applet into a Web page by using FrontPage, and has looked at a more advanced example that adds scripting control to your Java applet. Now, this tutorial describes the steps required to get a Java applet up and running when you have only the Java source code, rather than the compiled class file. This is as close as you will come to creating a Java applet in this book. If you are game, forge ahead. If not, you may proceed on to the next section of the chapter, which describes the use of Microsoft's Liquid Motion.

Preparing Java applets

If you want to follow the Java examples in the next sections, you need to do some preparation. Before you can insert a Java applet into your Web page, you need to locate an applet, compile it (if it comes in its source code format), and then import it into your FrontPage Web. This section details the steps necessary to perform these preparations. If you already have your Java applet class file ready to go and are itching to try it out in FrontPage, you can jump to the next section, "Inserting Your Java Applet."

Java Development Kit (JDK)

If you are going to do any work with Java, you first need to download the JavaSoft JDK. This contains all that you need to get started programming with Java. It includes the base Java classes, described earlier, and a set of tools that includes the Java source compiler, javac.exe, and an applet viewer, appletviewer.exe. It also contains valuable documentation and Java examples. The JDK is available from JavaSoft at `http://java.sun.com/products/jdk/`. Three versions are available at the time of this writing:

✦ **JDK 1.0.2**: The baseline standard for Java development, released in May 1996. Many applets are still written to the 1.0 release.

✦ **JDK 1.1.7**: The last version of the 1.1 release. A majority of Java applications currently under development are being written to the 1.1 release.

✦ **JDK 1.2**: The current release as of this writing.

After you obtain the JDK, follow the directions for installing it. Once installed, you will find in the bin subfolder of the main Java folder the tools that are described next.

Using the Javac compiler

When a Java program is first created, whether an applet or an application, it exists as source code that is just a plain text file with a .java extension. To execute the program, you must compile the source code into a bytecode class file (with a .class extension). If you purchase premade Java applets, or even download the latest free applet from a site on the Internet, you are likely to receive a class file that already is compiled for you. However, many of the Java examples that come with the JDK must be compiled before they can be added to your Web page.

To compile a Java source file by using the javac compiler, first locate the compiler (usually in /java/bin/javac.exe) and your Java source file (identified as .java). Open an MS-DOS window by selecting Start ⇨ Programs ⇨ MS DOS Prompt. Change to the directory that contains the javac compiler. Use the following syntax, substituting the appropriate source code reference, to run the compiler and compile your source code:

```
javac <</full/path/toyour/sourcecode.java>
```

If the compiler returns successfully, you should now have a file, <<sourcecode.class>, in the same directory with the .java extension file. This class file is a ready-to-run Java applet.

Using the Appletviewer

The appletviewer utility that comes with the Java JDK enables you to run Java applets without recourse to a Web browser. Appletviewer is a command-line utility, so to use it, you must first open an MS-DOS window, which you can do by selecting Start ⇨ Programs ⇨ MS DOS Prompt.

Change to the bin directory of your Java JDK (c:\java\bin). To start appletviewer, you use the following command syntax:

```
appletviewer <<URL of Web page containing applet>
```

Appletviewer doesn't run class files directly. You must first create a Web page and insert the Java applet in it, before you can use appletviewer. (You may want to skip to the section on inserting Java applets in FrontPage.) Replace <<URL of Web page containing applet> with the full URL to the appropriate Web page, (www.myserver.com/coolapplet.html). Appletviewer starts, loads, and runs the applet contained in this page. (Note that when you start appletviewer for the first time, it displays licensing information that you must acknowledge before you see your applet.)

Now, you are armed with enough tools and information to make inserting a Java applet into your FrontPage Web a breeze.

Tic-Tac-Toe

The third example of a Java applet is a classic version of Tic-Tac-Toe. This applet displays a 3x3 square playing area. You click a section to record your move, and then the applet counters with its move, accompanied by appropriate sounds.

The source code for this applet is available from the JavaSoft Web site in the Applet section. The complete list of available applets is located at `www.javasoft.com/applets/js-applets.html`. The TicTacToe example is located at `www.javasoft.com/applets/TicTacToe/1.0.2/example1.html`

The TicTacToe.java example is available as source code. Save this file as TicTacToe.java and compile it using javac, as described in the previous section. Next, you need to import the Java file. Select File ➪ Import, locate the class file, and add it to your Web.

Create a new Web page in Editor. Select Insert ➪ Advanced ➪ Java Applet to open the Java Applet Properties dialog box, shown in Figure 20-9. Unfortunately, you must type the class filename in the Applet Source text field. You can use the Applet Base URL field to record the URL page to the folder in which the Java applet is stored. Other options include:

✦ **Message for Browsers Without Java Support**: As with the previous types of active content, you can use this field to display a message, including HTML, for any users who do not have a Java-enabled browser.

✦ **Applet parameters**: Like the ActiveX controls discussed in Chapter 19, Java applets can be configured by using parameters that are specific to a particular applet. The TicTacToe applet doesn't require any parameters to be set. An applet that does require parameters to be set is examined in the next section.

✦ **Size**: Set the width and height of the space allotted to the applet (this does not change the size of the applet itself).

✦ **Layout**: Set the horizontal spacing, vertical spacing, and alignment of the applet on the page.

After you set the parameters to your liking, click OK to return to the Editor page. FrontPage inserts a large, aquamarine *J* in your page, indicating the presence of a Java applet.

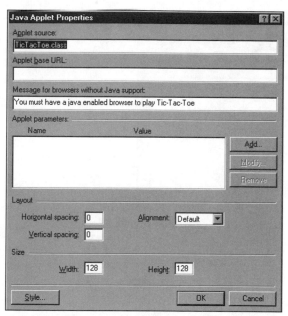

Figure 20-9: The Java Applet Properties dialog box, set for the TicTacToe applet

Before your TicTacToe game works, however, you need to add some support files. Create (or import from the examples from Chapter 20 on the CD-ROM that accompanies this book) two small GIF images, called **not.gif** (the *O*) and **cross.gif** (the *X*). Place these files in a subfolder called **images**. If you want your version of TicTacToe to have sound effects, you need to create those as well. The sound files need to be saved in AU format and named **yahoo1.au** (the sound made when you win), **yahoo2.au** (the sound made when you lose), **return.au** (the sound made for a tie), **ding.au**, and **beep.au**, the last two of which are pretty self-explanatory and are heard during the normal course of taking turns. These sound files need to be placed in an audio subfolder.

Tip

The filenames given in the directions are the ones hard-coded into the TicTacToe.java file. If you want, you can change the names of the files in the source code and then name them anything that you like.

After you assemble at least the graphic files (otherwise, not much will happen when you run your applet), you are ready to preview. You can preview your Java applet either in the Preview tab or by selecting File ➪ Preview and opening the page in your favorite Java-enabled Web browser (don't forget to save the page first). If you are savvy enough to outwit the computer, your applet might resemble the one shown in Figure 20-10.

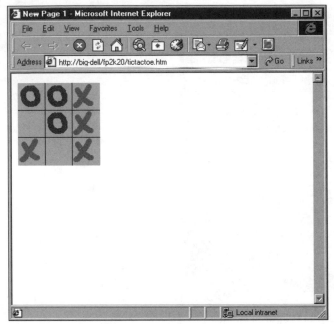

Figure 20-10: A hard-fought victory in the Java version of Tic-Tac-Toe

The Java <APPLET> tag

When you insert a Java applet into your Web page, FrontPage generates an
<APPLET> tag for this element. The following is the <APPLET> tag for the
TicTacToe.class created in the previous section:

```
<applet width="128" height="128" code="TicTacToe.class">
You need a java enabled browser to view this Java applet.
</applet>
```

Caution FrontPage 2000 continues to use the old-style <APPLET> tag for Java. This is currently deprecated in favor of using the more general <OBJECT> tag for Java, as
well as other kinds of active content.

Configuring a Java applet

The Java applet example in this section demonstrates how you can configure some
applets by using the parameter settings in the Java Applet Properties dialog box.
The example used here is called NervousText. It is provided with JDK 1.1 and also
can be found at www.javasoft.com/products/jdk/1.1/docs/relnotes/
demos.html.

This applet takes a text string and, well, makes it look nervous. The text string is passed to the applet via a parameter. To insert this applet by using FrontPage, first compile the applet NervousText.java, as described in previous sections, and import it into the current FrontPage Web.

Select Insert ➪ Advanced ➪ Java Applet to open the Java Applet Properties dialog box. Designate the Applet Source as **NervousText.class**. To add the text parameter, click the Add button next to the Parameters list box. In the Set Attribute Value dialog box, type **Text** in the Name field and a text string of your choice in the Value field. Click OK to return to the Java Applet Properties dialog box. Check to make sure that the text string appears in the Parameters section, as illustrated in Figure 20-11.

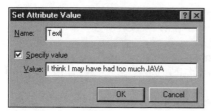

Figure 20-11: Adding a text string to the parameter list for your NervousText applet

That's all there is to it. Now you can preview the results, either in the Preview tab or by using the Preview in Browser function. If you have not adjusted the size parameters, which are 128x128 pixels by default, you may need to resize the applet space to see your entire text string. To do this, you can select the applet in the Normal tab of the Editor window and drag a corner to resize.

Java security

Java uses a different security methodology than Microsoft's ActiveX, discussed in Chapter 19. Java is essentially paranoid. It assumes that any code is potentially vicious, and therefore limits the capabilities of certain kinds of activities. In Java lingo, the code is said to run in a "sandbox" — it can play with all the toys in the sandbox, but it cannot get out of the sandbox to get at your computer. This is a good idea insofar as it doesn't rely on the user to make appropriate choices about which software to allow and which to deny (although you can still do this by using the facilities provided by your Web browser). However, the sandbox also limits (some would say unduly limits) an applet from doing things that could otherwise be productive. For example, a Java applet under normal circumstances cannot read files or write files.

As a result, Sun has begun to make adjustments to the sandbox methodology to allow developers and systems administrators, working in a "trusted environment," to be able to enable more functions within their Java code.

Using Microsoft Liquid Motion

Liquid Motion is an application that enables nonprogrammers to create eye-catching Java animations, button effects, and other applets. The program is designed to integrate smoothly with FrontPage. This section explores how Liquid Motion works, and provides a simple example demonstrating a few of LM's leading features.

Note   You can obtain an evaluation copy of Liquid Motion from Microsoft's Web site. (Information on obtaining a "Try & Buy" evaluation version of Liquid Motion can be found on Microsoft's Web site at www.microsoft.com/liquidmotion/shop/ Default.htm.) This copy is fully functional, but does not include a full set of templates and sample applets to get you started. It is valid for a 45-day trial period.

When you start Liquid Motion, it presents you with a Getting Started dialog box with three options (see Figure 20-12):

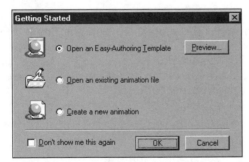

Figure 20-12: The Getting Started dialog box greets you when you first start Liquid Motion.

✦ **Open an Easy-Authoring Template**: These templates are prebuilt animations that you can easily and quickly customize.

✦ **Open an Existing Animation File:** Enables you to continue working on animations that you began in an earlier session.

✦ **Create a New Animation:** Choose this command to create an animation from scratch.

Select the last option, Create a New Animation, which creates a blank animation screen, as shown in Figure 20-13.

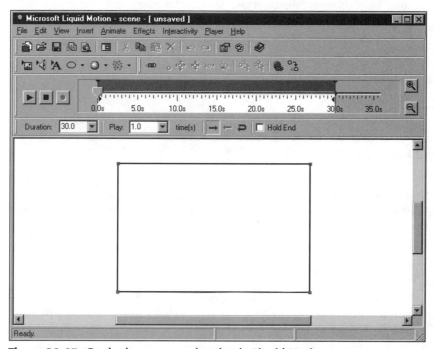

Figure 20-13: Beginning a new animation in Liquid Motion

Working with Liquid Motion

The Liquid Motion interface consists of several toolbars and a main window in which you build and preview your animation. To create a new Liquid Motion Java animation, you use the toolbars to add objects and then animate them. You can also add a variety of automated animations, filters, and effects. You can configure the properties of objects by using Property dialog boxes.

The main view consists of a window with a resizable rectangle that represents the visible portion of the applet (objects may sometimes be placed outside the box). You can use the corner handles to resize the rectangle. You can also switch to Structure view, which provides a handy tree view of the elements that you have added to the animation.

As shown in Figure 20-14, Liquid Motion has four principal toolbars:

Timing toolbar   Standard toolbar   Behavior toolbar   Object toolbar

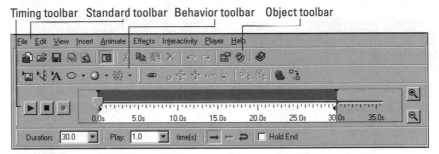

Figure 20-14: Liquid Motion's toolbars

> ✦ **Standard toolbar:** Provides buttons for basic operations — creating a new animation, saving an animation, previewing in a browser, publishing, and so on.
>
> ✦ **Object toolbar:** Enables you to select and insert a wide variety of object types, including 2D and 3D shapes, text, images, and audio, as well as LiquidMotion AutoEffect (described later in this section).
>
> ✦ **Behavior toolbar:** Enables you to add a predefined action, or behavior, to a selected object. Options include animate, color, jump, grow, shrink, spin, rotate 3D, follow, and avoid.
>
> ✦ **Timing toolbar:** Includes Duration, Play, Times, Play Forward and/or Backward, and Hold End. Also includes the timeline and playback buttons (Play, Stop, Pause), which are always visible.

Inserting elements

The first step in creating a Liquid Motion animation is to add one or more objects to the applet. To insert an element, click the down arrow beside one of the object icons in the Object toolbar. This drops down a menu of available objects to choose from (see Figure 20-15).

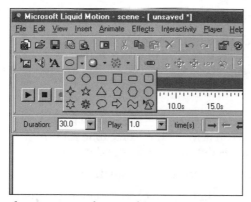

Figure 20-15: The 2D object menu used to insert an element into the animation

Select a star and insert it into your banner animation. The result, after three stars, is shown in Figure 20-16. After you create an element, you can resize or rotate it by using its handles. You can change its color (from the default aqua) and any effects that you have added to the element.

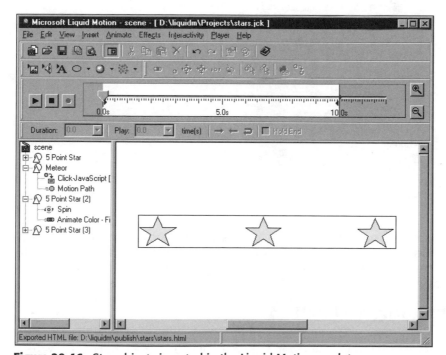

Figure 20-16: Star objects inserted in the Liquid Motion applet

The object Properties dialog box, illustrated in Figure 20-17, consists of four tabs:

✦ **Shape**: Change the Line (foreground) and Fill (background) colors of the object. If you click the Edit as Freeform button in this dialog box, you can also flip the object on its horizontal and vertical axes and change the method used to resize the object (Reshape is the default; Bezier and Stretchy are the other choices).

✦ **Timing**: Select options to play once for a certain duration or to repeat a designated number of times. You can also set the exact time that the animation begins (the ending time is determined by the duration).

✦ **TimeEffects**: Use to alter the relative speed of the animation.

✦ **Details**: Miscellaneous properties, including the object's name, a comment field, and the exact dimensions of the object.

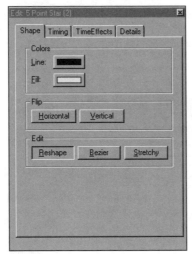

Figure 20-17: The Liquid Motion object Properties dialog box

Tip
You can also edit the Properties for the scene. The easiest way to do this is to right-click an empty portion of the scene window and select Properties. Alternatively, open Structure view and double-click the scene icon at the top of the tree.

Animating elements

You can animate an object either by adding a predefined behavior to the element or by recording a custom animation sequence. (If you are patient enough, you can also manually construct a frame-by-frame animation sequence.)

The principal animation options are the following:

✦ **Color**: Cycles through color changes

✦ **Jump**: Object appears to jump from one point to another

✦ **Grow**: Increases the size of the object

✦ **Shrink**: Similar to Grow, only backwards

✦ **Spin**: Object turns around, clockwise or counterclockwise

To apply an animation, click the element to select it and then select the animation. If you have Auto Preview enabled on the View menu, the animation automatically plays when it is first selected. To replay the animation, click the Play button in the Timeline toolbar.

Animations can be superimposed on one another. For example, you could make your stars spin and change colors simultaneously. Animations can also be sequential. You could make your stars spin for ten seconds and then begin to change colors. Or, make them spin in one direction and then the other. You can adjust the duration of a particular animation either by dragging its end point in the timeline or by using the Timing tab of the object's Properties dialog box.

Record Motion

The Record Motion option enables you to easily create a custom animation for an object. Select an object whose motion you want to record, and then select Animation ⇨ Record Motion. Next, drag the object to the spot where you want it to go. Liquid Motion writes a trail so that you can see where you have been (this doesn't display when the animation runs). Release the object to finish recording. As an example, we have added a wandering meteor to our spinning stars animation.

Tip

If you drag the timeline pointer to a new time, the scene is changed to reflect its state at that moment in time. Any properties that you configure will be in effect at that moment. This enables you to add subtle effects. If you forget, it could cause you to misconfigure your animation.

Adding effects

Liquid Motion enables you to add sophisticated filters and transitions to your animation with a few clicks of the mouse. These effects can give your animation a professional touch — but they use IE 4-specific capabilities, so all of your hard work is lost on users of other browsers (your animation still runs, but without the effects).

Caution

These effects do not appear in the Liquid Motion Preview window. You must preview them in IE 4 or greater to see the results.

The following are the various types of filters and transitions available:

✦ **Filters**: A variety of effects applied to the animation scene as a whole, including:

- **Drop Shadow**: Adds a colored shadow to the animation. If the background is transparent, adds the shadow to all objects in the animation.

- **Glow**: Adds a halo effect around the animation, or around objects in the animation when the background is transparent.

- **Gray**: Turns a color image into grayscale.

- **Negative**: Shows an image in reverse colors.

- **Transparency**: Can add partial or total invisibility to the animation, or if background is transparent, to objects in the animation.

- **Wave**: Adds a ripple effect to the animation.

✦ **Transitions**: Can be a transition in (brings an object into view) or out (removes the object from view), including:

- **Dissolve**: Causes the animation to appear or disappear gradually, a few pixels at time.

- **Random**: Performs the transition in or out using a randomly selected transition.

- **Fade In/Out**: Fade In causes the animation to go from very faint to its full color; Fade Out does the reverse.

- **Blinds**: The animation (or objects in the animation, if background is transparent) enters or leaves the scene like a window blind being opened. Can be horizontal or vertical.

- **Box In/Out**: Box In starts as a tiny square in the center of the animation and grows to its proper size; the Box Out shrinks to a tiny square.

- **Checkerboard**: Animation appears or disappears in a checkerboard pattern.

- **Circle In/Out**: Animation grows from a tiny circle (Circle In) or shrinks down to a tiny circle (Circle Out), like the zoom on a telescope lens.

- **Random Bar**: Transitions the animation in or out in horizontal or vertical lines of random width.

- **Split**: Causes the animation to open or close like sliding doors.

- **Strips**: Animation appears or disappears in a diagonal stripe.
- **Wipe**: Causes the animation to appear or disappear from one of four directions.

Adding interactivity

You can also choose to add various types of interactivity to your animation. As with the filters and transitions, interactivity is designed for IE 4 only. Interactive options include:

✦ **URL Link**: Links an object to a URL, triggered when you click it.

✦ **Trigger**: Another name for an event that causes an action to take place. When you add a trigger to the animation, the Trigger Properties dialog box opens. Select the trigger action, the result of the action, and the target object for the action. You can also indicate whether the trigger should happen on every occurrence of the event or just on the first occurrence.

✦ **Script Trigger**: Similar to the regular trigger, except that you can write your own scripts as the results of the trigger action.

✦ **Avoid**: Causes the object to move away from the mouse when it is moved toward the object.

✦ **Follow**: Causes the object to follow any mouse movement in the animation.

Viewing and publishing your animation

While you are developing your animation, you can preview it in Liquid Motion, using the Play button. To really see how the animation performs in a browser, you will want to publish the animation to a browser.

Publishing options

You can publish your animation to one of several locations:

✦ **Publish to local disk**: For viewing on your local system without the aid of a Web server.

✦ **Publish to FTP:** Allows you to upload animation files to a remote server via FTP.

✦ **Publish to FrontPage Web:** Allows you to add your animation directly to a FrontPage Web. By using this option, you can either publish the animation to an open page in FrontPage or allow Liquid Motion to create a new folder with the animation files.

To publish the animation, follow the simple directions in the Liquid Motion Publishing Wizard. Liquid Motion compiles all the necessary files for the animation, including a default HTML page. After this page is generated, you can easily edit the HTML page by using FrontPage.

Summary

This chapter covers the basics (and a bit more) of working with Java applets in FrontPage. After reading this chapter, you should be able to add a Java applet to your Web page and configure it. In addition, you have learned how to control an applet with scripting and use the Java JDK to compile an applet. You have learned how to use Microsoft's Liquid Motion to create cool Java animations without needing to be a programmer. The next chapter takes you through the process of yet another variation of creating dynamic Web pages — building pages on the fly from data drawn from a database.

✦   ✦   ✦

Database Connectivity

Some of the largest and most used Web sites on the Internet today are built on top of powerful databases. These Web database applications can seem quite daunting to set up and maintain. FrontPage 2000 has added improved support for creating a Web database application, which can take some of the pain out of the process of connecting your Web pages to a database. This chapter focuses on using FrontPage to create relatively simple, but useful, online resources. It demonstrates the basics of using the FrontPage 2000 Database Results Wizard to create a database-driven site without requiring programming. This chapter also explores some simple ways to customize your database application. If you are looking for more information on building database applications, you should also check out the section on using Active Server Pages (ASP) in Chapter 18.

Note   Although FrontPage 2000 has improved the Database Results Wizard introduced in FrontPage 98, if you have database pages created in FrontPage 98, you have to either update them or protect them from FrontPage 2000, which will try to make changes to them. Also, in FrontPage 2000, you no longer can create new database records or update or remove existing ones. The FrontPage 2000 Wizard only allows views of existing data.

Understanding Web Database Applications

Web sites connected to databases are among the most useful and exciting resources on the Internet. They enable users to access information and add to the share of information in ways simply not possible before the Web took the world by storm. Everything from libraries and galleries to catalog services, job recruiters, travel agencies, real estate and investment brokers, and health care providers are increasingly looking for ways to grant users access to the information that they need.

The term "online databases" typically conjures up images of vast, intricate systems overseen by swarms of database administrators tending to the system like ants to their queen. Such systems do exist, but the Web now enables anyone to create a database and make it available to whoever might be interested. If you run a small business with a catalog of products, maintain a directory of contacts or customers, or even simply want to keep track of your family tree, keep your online resume up to date, or find a place to store all of your favorite quotations, a database could help you to manage your own information and make it available to others.

The upside

What are some of the advantages of a database-driven Web site over traditional, static Web pages?

✦ Real-time updating of information, so users always see up-to-date information

✦ Flexible, customizable presentation of information

✦ Secure and controllable remote access to existing data, including the ability of remote users, where appropriate, to add to as well as view data

Caution   Be forewarned: the secret agenda of this chapter is to convince you that connecting a database to your Web site is within your reach.

The downside

Although databases are powerful tools, they are not necessarily for everyone. They require care and feeding, not to mention a certain level of technical expertise. Some of the reasons not to embark on a database-related project?

✦ An online database requires more resources, more software, and thus more money

✦ The increased number of connections means more overhead and maintenance

✦ With more parts involved, more can go wrong

In sum, most of the potential disadvantages can be mitigated, so you don't need to be scared off from a database project because you think it is too hard, too expensive, or too much work. But, like any useful project, a database project often entails more work up front to reap the bigger rewards down the line. Thus, you have to ask yourself whether the commitment is worthwhile. You should be realistic about the fact that, to be successful, a database system requires a higher level of commitment than does a handful of pretty Web pages.

Note If you have an existing database with information that you want to make available on the Web, but aren't sure that you want to embark on a full-out database application, a compromise does exist. Both Access 97 and MS SQL Server have Web publishing tools that enable you to export your data as static HTML pages. They are static presentations of the data, but they are easy to generate, so you can republish as frequently as you need to, and you don't need a database connected to your Web server to do it.

Getting ready

Creating a Web database application isn't difficult, but it can be a little confusing because of the many pieces of the puzzle that are necessary to enable a Web page to communicate with a database. Before you get too charged up planning all the ways that you can use a database on your Web site, you need to think through what is required to implement such a system:

✦ **What database do I need?** Using FrontPage, you are going to build Web pages that access your database via *Open Database Connectivity (ODBC),* a standard means of connecting to a database. ODBC is supported by virtually all major databases, and even many minor databases. The important thing is that you must have the appropriate ODBC drivers for your database. (Typically, this isn't a problem, because any database that supports ODBC comes with the necessary drivers. Most come with the Windows operating system, as does the ODBC Manager that you use to set up your ODBC data source.) If you are operating on Windows NT or Windows 95, the most likely candidates are Excel for spreadsheet data, Access for small to medium-sized projects, and SQL Server for medium to large undertakings. All the examples in this chapter use an Access database.

✦ **What Web server can I use?** Assuming that you want to use FrontPage's database capabilities, you need to have a Web server that is capable of processing Active Server Pages (ASP), the technology FrontPage uses to build its database connectivity. If you use the services of a Web hosting provider, check to see whether it supports database services. Not all do. If you are running your own Web site, you can use Microsoft's Internet Information Server (IIS) or O'Reilly's WebSite Pro. You can even use the Personal Web Server (PWS) that comes with Windows 98 (or is available for download from the Microsoft Web site).

To review, if you want to build a database application using FrontPage 2000, you need the following:

✦ An ODBC-compliant database system

✦ The appropriate ODBC drivers and an ODBC Management utility

✦ A Web server with ASP and FrontPage 2000 Server Extensions installed

✦ FrontPage 2000

If you have all of these items, you are ready to get started.

Adding Active Server Extensions to PWS

To use ASP with PWS, you must install Active Server Extensions (ASE). You can check whether you have them in either of two ways:

✦ **Run a database query in FrontPage**. If what you see in your browser looks like gibberish, then the server hasn't translated the ASP code into recognizable HTML, and you probably don't have ASE installed.

✦ **Check for their presence in the Windows Registry, but only if you know what you are doing.** Tampering with the Registry, even if you are only looking, is potentially dangerous (there, you've been warned). Open the Registry to HKEY_LOCAL_MACHINE\SYSTEM\CurrentControlSet\Services\ W3SVC. If no ASP folder exists in the W3SVC folder, then you don't have ASE installed.

So, you simply have to get ASE, right? The catch (this *is* Microsoft we are talking about here) is that the only way to get ASE is to download it with Microsoft's IIS. As of this writing, Microsoft has placed IIS 4 online for downloading, but only via the mega-megabyte download of NT 4 Option Pack. If you have lots of extra time on your hands, I highly recommend this as a way to kill a great deal of it.

A somewhat more feasible option for most people is to download the IIS 3 Server. It is smaller overall, and because you are interested in ASE only, not the server itself, smaller is better. More important, you can actually configure the download of IIS 3 to install only ASE and not all the other bells and whistles that you aren't interested in.

However, finding IIS 3 is no easy task, because Microsoft has buried it deep in the virtual bowels of its Web site (and, by the time that you read this, Microsoft may well have removed IIS 3 altogether). Look for IIS 3 at www.microsoft.com/ msdownload/iis3. If it's not there, do a search for IIS 3 or try searching for Active Server Extensions.

If you get IIS 3 downloaded, run the installation program, ignoring the fact that you appear to be about to install an NT application on your Windows 95 system. Do a custom installation, adding only ASE. Unlike the ordeal of trying to find ASE, the installation is relatively straightforward. ASE even comes with a fairly thorough set of documentation, called *The Active Server Pages Roadmap*.

Using the Database Results Wizard

FrontPage 2000 uses ASP to communicate with an ODBC data source. When you use the Database Results Wizard to guide you through the process, it takes care of the messy programming and configuration issues for you.

To use the Database Results Wizard (DRW), follow these steps:

1. Open an existing Web page or create a new Web page to contain the database results.

2. Select Insert ⇨ Database ⇨ Results to bring up the first screen of the DRW.

The DRW consists of a series of five screens. The following sections walk you through the steps of the Wizard, with a simple example to get you started. Subsequent sections examine the advanced DRW options in more detail.

Note

First it was called *Database Connection Wizard*, emphasizing the fact that it helped create the connection between the Web page and a database. In FrontPage 98, it was renamed *Database Region Wizard*, suggesting that it helped to define the region that displayed database results. In FrontPage 2000, it is called *Database Results Wizard*, highlighting the fact that it helps you to formulate the query that gets data from a data source *and* formats the results for the user.

Step 1: Connecting to a database

The first step in creating a Database Results page is to create a connection to the database that you are working with. As shown in Figure 21-1, the DRW presents you with three basic options:

Database Results Wizard - Step 1 of 5   ? X

This five-step wizard creates a database results region that displays information from a database. The wizard can also create a search form on the same page to let site visitors look up specific information.

You can:

○ Use a *s*ample database connection (Northwind)

● Use an *e*xisting database connection

    | FPNorthwind ▼ |

○ Use a ne*w* database connection

    | Create... |

| Cancel | < *B*ack | *N*ext > | *F*inish |

Figure 21-1: The first screen of the Database Results Wizard — selecting a database connection.

✦ **Use a Sample Database Connection (Northwind):** FrontPage's sample Northwind Traders database is good for practice and to test your setup.

✦ **Use an Existing Database Connection:** If you haven't set up a database connection yet in this Web, no items are listed in this drop-down menu.

Tip

You can also check the list of previously created database connections by selecting Tools ⇨ Web Settings and clicking the Database tab.

✦ **Use a New Database Connection:** Use this option to create a new database connection to an existing database.

The Right Stuff

To use the DRW, you need to have FrontPage 2000 Server Extensions installed on the server that contains the database Web. That server also needs to have the ASP extensions installed. You know that you have what it takes if you select Insert ⇨ Database and see that Results is enabled. (Don't worry if the Column Value option is grayed out. It is enabled only under special circumstances after you create a Database Results page.) If the database option is grayed out, follow these steps to ascertain whether you can use FrontPage's database features:

1. Check that you have opened or created on the server a Web that is enabled for database connections. If you start FrontPage without opening a Web, or if you open a Web that isn't connected to a Web server, the database features are disabled. Open an existing Web or create a new Web on the appropriate server. If you need to install a Web server, see Chapter 23.

2. If you opened a Web on your Web server and the database features still aren't enabled, you are missing either FrontPage 2000 Server Extensions or ASP, both of which are required. If your Web server is IIS 4 or greater or PWS 4 or greater, chances are that ASP is installed and that you need to upgrade FrontPage Server Extensions. (See Chapter 23, "FrontPage Server Administration," for details on upgrading FrontPage Server Extensions.)

3. If you are unsure whether your server has ASP capabilities, you can use one of several methods to check this. If you have administrative privileges and are familiar with the Registry, you can use RegEdit (or an equivalent) to check for ASP functionality. If you have only user access to the server, the simplest test is to create a basic ASP page and see whether it works. See the ASP chapter for details on creating a simple ASP test page.

4. If your current Web server doesn't have ASP functionality, you can upgrade to IIS 3 or better if you are using Windows NT, upgrade to PWS 4 if you are using an earlier version of PWS, or add ASP capability to an earlier version of PWS.

For the purpose of your first example, use the sample Northwind database. If you want to learn how to create a new connection, skip ahead to the next section, "Establishing Database Connections." Select the radio button labeled Use a Sample Database Connection (Northwind) and then click Next.

Note

When you select the sample database, FrontPage creates a new data source, named Sample, and uses it as the data source.

Step 2: Select a data record source or custom query

In the next DRW screen (Figure 21-2), you select a record source to use in the query. Typically, a *record source* is a table in the database, but it may also be a stored query in the database application. The DRW provides you with a list of available record source names. Select one from the list. If you want to retrieve results from multiple tables, you need to create a custom query (see "Creating Database Queries," later in this chapter).

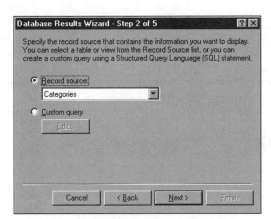

Figure 21-2: The Database Results Wizard — selecting a record source

For now, select Products from the drop-down list. Click Next to continue.

Step 3: Designate fields to Display and advanced query options

Having selected a database and record source, you can now indicate which fields to include in the results. The third screen of the DRW (Figure 21-3) lists the fields currently slated to be returned. By default, all fields are displayed.

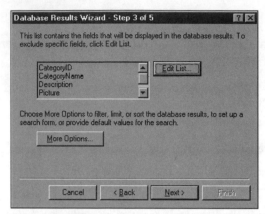

Figure 21-3: The Database Results Wizard — selecting fields to display

To edit the list of fields, click the Edit List button to display the Displayed Fields dialog box (see Figure 21-4). To add a new field to the list, select the field name from the Available Fields list and click the Add button. To remove a field, select a field from the Displayed Fields list and click the Remove button. To change the order in which the fields are displayed, select a field and click the Move Up or Move Down button to change its relative order in the display. Click OK to return to the main Wizard screen after you finish editing the Displayed Fields list.

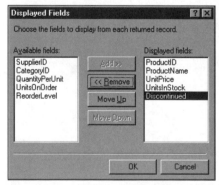

Figure 21-4: Editing the Displayed Fields list in database query results

In this example, you want to display the ProductID, ProductName, UnitPrice, UnitsInStock, and Discontinued fields, so you select the other fields from the Displayed Fields list (to select multiple fields, hold down the Control key and select each field) and click the Remove button. The removed fields are transferred to the Available Fields list. Click OK to return to the main DRW screen.

You can also use this DRW screen to designate advanced query options. These options are examined in detail in the later section, "Setting Advanced Query Options." For this example, you are ready to proceed to the next step. Click Next to continue.

Step 4: Select results formatting options

You have now completed the database query setup. In the final two steps of the DRW, you select options regarding how results from the query will be displayed.

In this DRW screen, you can choose to display the results in a table format, with or without the field names as column headers, or as lists in a variety of formats. When you choose Table – One Record Per Row from the drop-down list, the following options are available (see Figure 21-5):

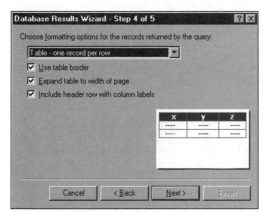

Figure 21-5: The Database Results Wizard — options for displaying results in a table

✦ **Use Table Border:** Check if you want the border to appear. If you uncheck this option, the table border is turned off.

✦ **Expand Table to Width of Page:** Check to create a table that resizes itself to the full width of the browser window. If this option is not checked, the table cells are sized to the width of the widest column value.

✦ **Include Header Row with Column Labels:** Check to include the field names in a header field in the first row of the table.

When you choose List – One Record Per List from the drop-down list, the following options are available (see Figure 21-6):

Figure 21-6: The Database Results Wizard — options for displaying results in a list

✦ **Add Labels for All Field Values:** Check to include the field name before each value.

✦ **Place Horizontal Separator Between Records:** Check to include a horizontal line between records.

✦ **List Options:** Select a format for the list of field values.

Select Table – One Record Per Row and check all three available options. Click Next to continue.

Step 5: Select grouping options

The final step of the DRW is in some ways its most valuable contribution, and the simplest to select. Use this screen (Figure 21-7) either to split records into groups of a designated number of records or to display all results together. If you elect to group the results, FrontPage automatically adds to the Web page a set of four buttons: First, Next, Previous, and Last, as illustrated in Figure 21-8. These buttons enable the user to page through the data one group at a time. FrontPage automatically adds the programming necessary to keep track of which group is currently being viewed, and reloads the data accordingly.

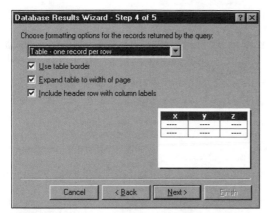

Figure 21-7: The Database Results Wizard — you can show all records or group them into separate pages.

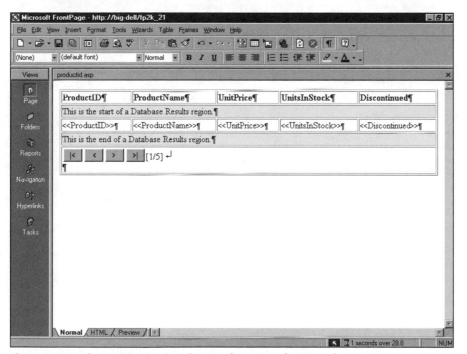

Figure 21-8: The result of using the Database Results Wizard

If you have included input parameters, this Wizard screen also offers you the option of generating a Submission Form, to collect inputs on the same page as the search results. In most cases, you collect that input on a prior page, but this feature can be useful for situations in which the user may need to reenter the input values. When it is available, the option is a simple check box.

Click Finish to complete the DRW and return to the Web page.

Previewing the results

The results of the DRW are shown in Figure 21-9. To preview the Database Results page, first save the page and then select File ⇨ Preview in Browser. If you attempt to use the Preview tab, you are warned that it is unable to display database results. Figure 21-9 shows a sample page, after some revision, as it should look when viewed in a Web browser.

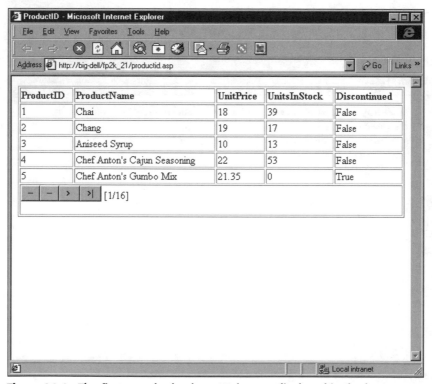

Figure 21-9: The first sample database Web page displayed in the browser

This section has demonstrated the basic steps necessary to create a database connection. The next section looks at some of the ways to customize the process.

Caution

FrontPage manages its database connections by using application variables in the global.asa file in the root directory of the Web. Application variables are read by the server the first time that the global.asa file is accessed, which means that the following sequence will fail: 1. Create a database connection in FrontPage; 2. Create a Database Results page; 3. Preview the Results page in your browser; 4. Repeat the same steps for a second database connection in the same Web. To preview the second connection results, you must first restart the server.

Editing an existing database results page

You can modify the query and results configuration of an existing Database Results page by double-clicking the start or end indicators of the database region (shown in neon yellow in Normal view). When you pass the mouse over the database region, the cursor changes to a hand holding a piece of paper. Alternatively, you can right-click in this region and select Database Results Properties from the option menu.

Modifying column values

In addition to modifying the query results, you can alter the selected column value components displayed in the Database Results page. Column value components are indicated in Normal view by double tag brackets (<<*ColumnValue*>). You can add additional column values, edit the names of existing values, and delete values from the Database Results page.

To add a new column value, place the cursor somewhere between the yellow database region's start and end indicators on the page (otherwise, the Column Value menu option is disabled). Select Insert ➪ Database ➪ Column Value to open the Database Column Value dialog box (see Figure 21-10), which consists of a single pop-up menu, showing all available column names. Select a column name from the available list. Click OK to return to the Database Results page.

Tip

If the column that you want to include is not listed in the Database Column Value dialog box, you may need to modify your query to include this column.

To modify an existing column, double-click the Column Value region to open the Database Column Value dialog box. Alternatively, right-click the existing column value and select Database Column Values Properties from the options menu. Select the alternative column name that you want to use. Click OK to return to the Database Results page.

To delete an existing column, select the Column Value region and click the delete button.

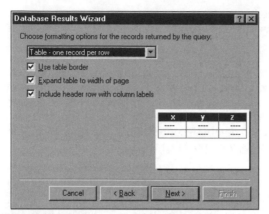

Figure 21-10: The Database Results Wizard —
options for displaying results in a table.

Establishing Database Connections

The initial example used the FrontPage 2000 sample Northwind database as the
source for your Database Results page. This is a handy way to test that your
database access is working correctly, and to practice using the DRW, but you won't
likely use this method very often to connect to a database. This section describes
the standard methods of connecting your FrontPage Web to a database.

Add a database

Two ways exist to add a new database connection to your FrontPage Web:

✦ Use the DRW, as previously described, and select Create New Database
   Connection in the first step of the Wizard.

✦ Select Tools ➪ Web Settings, click the Database tab, and click the Add button
   to create a new database source.

If you use the DRW, it opens the Web Settings dialog box to its Database tab (see
Figure 21-11), enabling you to click the Add button.

Note   Use the Database tab of the Web Settings dialog box to remove any unwanted
              database connections from the Web.

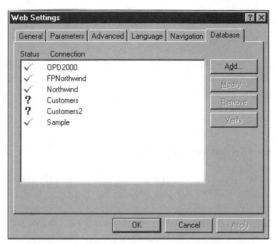

Figure 21-11: The Database tab. Use this tab to create database connections in your FrontPage Web.

In either case, you can click the Add button on the Database tab to open the New Database Connection dialog box (see Figure 21-12). You can select one of three ways in which to designate a database connection. In each case, you select the appropriate option, indicate a name for the data source that you are creating, and then click the Browse button.

Figure 21-12: Adding a new database connection to your FrontPage Web

✦ **File or Folder in Current Web:** Click the Browse button to locate the database file in the current Web. (See the next section for details on importing a database file into your Web.)

✦ **Data Source on Web Server:** Click the Browse button to select from the list of available ODBC data sources. (See "Creating an ODBC Data Source," later in the chapter, for details.)

✦ **Other Database Server on the Network:** Click the Browse button to select the type of database server that you are using, designate the server's URL in the Server Name field, and designate the name of the database in the Database Name field.

Importing a database file into the current Web

If your database is an Access or Excel file, the simplest method of identifying the data source in FrontPage is to import the file into your Web. To import a database:

1. Open Folder view in FrontPage. Select the folder into which you want to import the database.

2. Select File ➪ Import and click the Add File button.

3. Locate the database file and click Open to return to the Import dialog box. Click OK to import the file.

4. When you import a database file, FrontPage prompts you to provide a name for the database. If you elect to name the database when you import it, FrontPage adds it to the list of available databases. You can then use the DRW to create a query to access this database.

5. If you elect not to provide a name for the database when you import it, you need to use the Database tab of the Web Settings dialog box to name the database and add it to the list of available databases, before you use the DRW.

Working with ODBC data sources

Importing a database into FrontPage is a simple procedure of establishing a connection between your Web server and the database application. In many cases, moving an existing database isn't feasible. In this case, you need an alternative way to identify it to FrontPage. One standard method is to set up the database as an ODBC data source.

When you select the Database on Web Server option in the New Database Connection dialog box, you are given a list of existing ODBC data sources on the Web server to select from. If your database is already configured, simply select it from the list. If you need to configure the data source, read on.

Creating an ODBC data source

To identify to FrontPage a database outside the current Web, you need to register your database as an ODBC data source. ODBC is an industry standard for accessing database information. It is supported by most database systems, and it is the means — directly or indirectly — that ASP uses to communicate with a database.

To create your ODBC data source, use the ODBC Data Source Administrator (see Figure 21-13) found in the Windows Control Panels. To locate this utility, select Start ➪ Settings ➪ Control Panels. Double-click the icon named 32bit ODBC (or perhaps just ODBC).

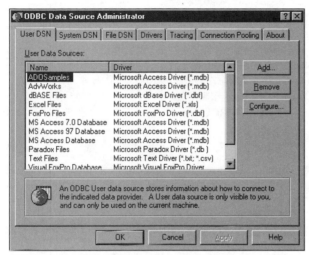

Figure 21-13: The ODBC Data Source Administrator is used to configure your database as an ODBC data source.

The utility contains several tabs:

✦ **User DSN (Data Source Name):** A data source visible only to you, the current user.

✦ **System DSN:** A data source visible to local users of this computer. The key is that this includes services running on the computer (such as a Web server).

✦ **File DSN:** Used to access remote data sources.

To create a DSN for your application, select the Add button and choose the appropriate ODBC driver for your application (for example, Excel or Access). Figure 21-14 shows the Microsoft Access Driver being selected. Click Finish to continue setting up the data source.

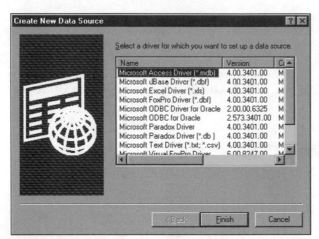

Figure 21-14: Selecting the appropriate ODBC driver in the ODBC Administrator

Next, you need to configure your data source, using the screen shown in Figure 21-15. Designate a Data Source Name for your data source (use the example name **OPD**) and provide a short description of the database. Next, configure the data source to use your newly created database. Click Select, locate your database file (for example, opd.mdb), and click OK three times to save your configuration and exit. This database is now accessible to FrontPage by using its DSN, OPD.

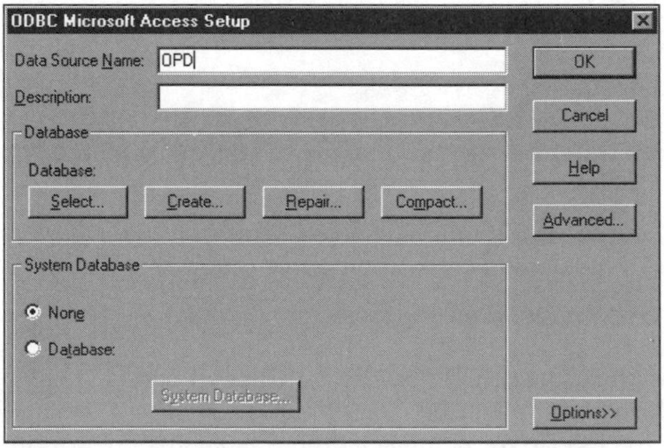

Figure 21-15: Naming and locating your ODBC data source

Working with a network database

Your Web also can access a database on another networked server, a fairly typical scenario if you happen to have a large Web site or are working on a corporate intranet application. The first requirement is that you have a database application that is networkable: Microsoft SQL Server or Oracle, for example. In addition to knowing the type of database server being used, you need to know the identify of the server (typically a host name or IP address) and the database name. Identify these three pieces of information in the Network Database Connection dialog box, shown in Figure 21-16.

Figure 21-16: Creating a connection to a network database server

Using the Web Settings Database tab

In addition to providing a way to add new database connections to your Web, the Web Settings dialog box's Database tab (refer to Figure 21-11) enables you to make changes to and test those connections. From the Database tab, you can perform the following functions:

✦ **Modify a database connection:** Select an existing connection name, click the Modify button, and make any changes that you want to the Database Connection Properties.

✦ **Remove a database connection:** Select an existing connection name, click the Remove button, and confirm that you really want to delete this connection. (You aren't deleting the database itself, just the currently defined connection to the database.)

✦ **Verify a database connection:** Select an existing connection name and click the Verify button. Database connections that have been verified are listed with a green check mark icon next to their name.

✦ **Configure advanced database connection options:** Select an existing connection, or click Add to create a new connection. In the Database Connection Properties dialog box, click the Advanced button to bring up the Advanced Properties dialog box. Use this to configure any required username and password for the database, set timeouts, and add any additional parameters that are necessary for connecting to the database.

Creating Database Queries

In the earlier example, you used the DRW to create a simple database query, without having to worry about how that query was formulated. This is fine for simple queries, but for most real-world applications, you will want to have a bit more control over how your data requests are formulated. This section explores the mechanisms that you can use to designate various kinds of data queries.

Setting advanced query options

One of the easiest ways to customize a query is to use the Advanced Options button in Step 3 of the DRW. Clicking this button opens the Advanced Options dialog box, as shown in Figure 21-17, which has the following options:

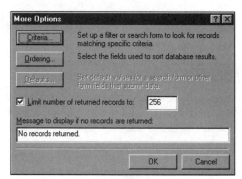

Figure 21-17: Setting Advanced Options in the Database Results Wizard

✦ **Criteria:** Click to open the Criteria dialog box, in which you can specify for designated fields the conditions that you want to use to limit the records returned by the query. By default, all records are returned. Click Add to add a new criteria in the Add Criteria dialog box, shown in Figure 21-18, which offers these options:

   • **Field Name:** Select a name from the drop-down menu of available fields.

   • **Comparison:** Select a comparison from the drop-down list of available options. The comparison options vary with the type of data contained in the field.

- **Value:** Indicate a static value for the comparison, or check the Get Value from This Query Parameter option and indicate the name of the field from which to obtain the comparison value.

- **And/Or:** Select And if all criteria must be true for the comparison to be true. Select Or if any one of the criteria may satisfy the comparison.

If you include input criteria from query parameters, the DRW gives you the option of including form elements on the Database Results page to collect these inputs.

✦ **Ordering:** Click to open the Ordering dialog box (see Figure 21-19), in which you can select fields to use to sort the records returned. You can select multiple sort order fields, and you can indicate what kind of sort to perform, either ascending or descending. The order of the fields makes a difference when, for example, you have a list of names that you want to sort based on Last Name and First Name fields. If you sort on first name and then last, you group all "Toms" together, for example, arranged alphabetically by their last names. If you sort on last name and then first names, you put all "Smiths" together, arranged alphabetically by first names — probably more like what you want. The buttons in the Ordering dialog box are used to do the following:

  - **Add:** Click to add the selected field to the list of Sort Order fields.

  - **Remove:** Click to remove the selected field from the list of Sort Order fields.

  - **Change Sort:** By default, the sort order on a field is ascending, from lowest to highest for numbers, and from 0 to 9 and a to z for alphanumerics. To change the sort order to descending, select the Sort Order field and click the Change Sort button.

  - **Move Up or Move Down:** If you sort on multiple fields, you can change the order of the sort by selecting one of the Sort Order fields and clicking either of these buttons.

✦ **Limit Number of Returned Records To:** Set a maximum number of records to return. You may want to limit the number of records that can be returned for such reasons as to protect your interest in proprietary data that you don't want to give away to every passing Web surfer, or to improve the performance of your Database Results page. If you have a large database, and users are accessing many fields, your Web server resources can be drained, particularly if you have numerous visitors.

✦ **Message to Display if No Records Are Returned:** Use this unfortunately small text field to indicate the message to present to the user when no records are returned by the query. This message may contain embedded HTML.

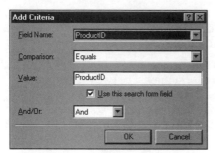

Figure 21-18: Use the Add Criteria dialog box to add new criteria to your database query.

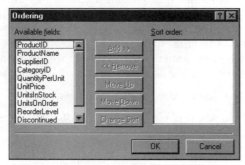

Figure 21-19: Designating the sort order on query results

Creating a custom query

Using the Advanced Options dialog box in the DRW, you can create a variety of sophisticated queries without worrying about the database programming required to formulate the query. The DRW doesn't handle all circumstances, however, so if you need to create a query that it doesn't support, you can use one of several approaches:

✦ **Use the DRW to create a custom query.** Involves knowledge of *Standard Query Language (SQL)*, the general-purpose programming language that is used to query a database. The next section examines a relatively simple example, combining results from two tables. If you don't know how to construct SQL statements, you may want to consider one of the other two methods in this list.

✦ **Use a prepared query stored in the database.** Requires understanding of, and access to, the application used to create the database (such as Access or

SQL Server). This approach is particularly effective if you are working in a team environment, with database experts maintaining the database and Web authors creating the Database Results pages. In this scenario, the database developers can write queries that can be accessed via the DRW for use by nonprogrammers. An example of this approach is provided later in the chapter.

✦ **Create in the database a new table that contains the joined records.** Provides the easiest approach, in some ways, assuming that you have the ability to add tables to your database. The chief advantage of this approach is that it keeps the query simple, which improves your application's performance. If your database changes with any frequency, however, maintaining this table so that it remains in synch with the original tables can become a challenge.

Creating custom queries

To insert a custom query in the DRW, select Insert ➪ Database ➪ Results, select a database source in the first screen, and click Next to go to the second Wizard screen.

Select the Custom Query radio button to enable the Edit button. Click the Edit button to open the Custom Query dialog box, shown in Figure 21-20. You can type a valid SQL `SELECT` statement in the text field. Other query types (insert, update, delete, and so forth) are not supported. In addition, you can click the following Custom Query dialog box buttons to select the actions described:

Figure 21-20: Use the Custom Query dialog box to create a custom database query.

✦ **Insert Parameter**. The same function performed automatically by the DRW when you define query criteria by using the Advanced Options button, previously described. To insert a parameter field, create the criteria clause of your SQL statement. Place the cursor at the point where you want to insert the parameter value. Click the Insert button to open the Insert Form Field Parameter dialog box. Type the name of the form field that contains the value to insert (do *not* include the double percentage-sign identifiers — that is the dialog box's job). Click OK. FrontPage inserts the field name, including the proper parameter identifiers (double percentage signs) into your SQL statement. (Of course, you can always just type this identifier yourself.)

✦ **Paste from Clipboard**. Use to cut and paste into the SQL Statement box an SQL query statement that you create with another application, such as Microsoft Access. (You can also use the Paste shortcut, Ctrl+V.) An example is described later in the chapter.

✦ **Verify Query**. Use to verify that the SQL statement you typed is valid. FrontPage tests the SQL statement and returns a success or error message. Oddly, the Wizard attempts to verify the SQL statement anyway, when you click OK.

Caution   As of B2, the Verify Query function returns success even if you create a SQL statement containing mismatched type information.

Joining results from multiple tables

The DRW supports queries on a single record source. In most cases, this record source is a single table in the database. For relatively simple databases, this may be adequate. However, many databases store related information in multiple tables, mainly to eliminate the need to repeat information in multiple records.

For example, imagine that you have a Customer database in which you want to store addresses for your customers. A given customer may have several addresses, for home, work, shipping, billing, and so forth. You could construct your database with a single Customer table, with separate fields for each of the various types of address, including street, city, state, and zip fields for each type. Or, you could create several records for each customer, each with a different address.

As a third alternative, you could create a separate Customer table and a separate Address table. In the Address table, you would have a field containing the customer ID number, keyed to the customer record in the Customer table. You also would have a field that indicates what kind of address the particular record is. In this scenario, every customer has one record in the Customer table and one or more records in the Address table.

This method of structuring data is called *normalizing* the data. It produces a relatively efficient database, with little repetition of information. It does require a little more work on your part to retrieve a particular customer's address. Suppose that you want to create a Query Form that prompts the customer for their first and last name and returns a detailed list of their known addresses. (Of course, your task would be much simpler if you could prompt the customer for their customer ID, but customers typically are better at remembering their name than an ID number.) The query that you want should find all the addresses for a specific customer name. To achieve this query, you need to join together the Customer and Address tables. The query to do this looks something like the following:

```
SELECT * FROM Customer, Address
WHERE Customer.customerid=Address.customerid
AND Customer.FirstName = '%%FirstName%%'
AND Customer.LastName = '%%LastName%%'
ORDER BY Address.AddressType
```

The first WHERE clause in this SELECT statement links together the Customer and Address table records. The last two criteria provide a match on the database. Note that when you create a custom query, several of the DRW's Advanced Options, such as Criteria, Ordering, and Defaults, are disabled, regardless of whether you include criteria statements.

Tip   You may find that using the PivotTable Component serves your needs in this case. See Chapter 4 for details on using the PivotTable Component.

Using access to create a custom query

The previous section assumes that you have some familiarity with SQL statements and are comfortable creating your own by hand. Even if you aren't a SQL guru, you can create custom SQL statements by using a visual query-design tool, such as the one provided with Access, and then paste the resulting SQL statement into the DRW. This section discusses two methods that you can use to create queries in Access 2000: The Simple Query Wizard and the Query Design tool.

Simple Query Wizard

To use the Simple Query Wizard in Access 2000, open your database, select Queries from the Objects list, and select the Create Query by Using Wizard item.

Before you start the Simple Query Wizard, however, first make sure that you have defined any necessary relationships between the tables that you plan to use in this query. To define relationships between tables, select Tools ⇨ Relationships to open the Relationships layout window. If prompted, add both the Customer and Address tables to the Relationships layout by using the Show Table dialog box, shown in Figure 21-21. If you are not prompted, right-click the Relationships layout window and select Show Table to open this dialog box.

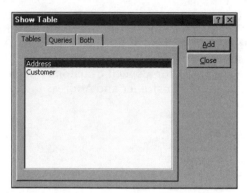

Figure 21-21: In Access, select the tables that are part of the relationship that you want to define.

After you add both tables to the Relationships layout, select CustomerID from the Customer table and drag it across to the Address table. The mouse cursor changes to a long, thin rectangle, representing the field; when you release the mouse button, the Relationships dialog box opens, with the link between the two fields defined. Click Create to create the relationship, illustrated as a line connecting the CustomerID field in the Customer table to the CustomerID field in the Address table (see Figure 21-22.)

After you define all necessary table relationships, you can begin the Simple Query Wizard (SQW). The first SQW screen, illustrated in Figure 21-23, prompts you to indicate which fields you plan to include in your query. You must include at least one field from each table that is part of the query. For this example, select all fields from both the Customer and Address tables. Click Next to continue.

If you haven't defined the relationship between the Customer and Address fields in your database, the SQW prompts you to do so before you can continue (in fact, you have to start over, so it's best to do this first).

If you have defined the necessary table relationships, you are next prompted to select either a Detail query, which returns all the selected fields for every record in the database, or a Summary query, which enables you to create some simple grouping of data, based on the kind of data in your database. Select Detail and click Next.

In the final SQW screen, give the query a name. Note that the SQW can't insert query parameters or sort order information. You have to add this manually, using the Design view described in the next section. But for simple joins, the SQW is an easy tool to use. Click Finish to complete the SQW.

To copy the query statement to the Clipboard, open the query in Design view and then switch to SQL view by selecting View ➪ SQL View. Select all and copy.

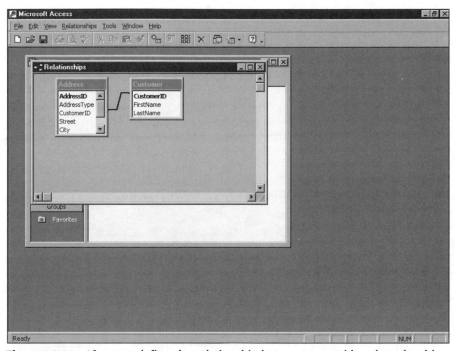

Figure 21-22: After you define the relationship between two tables, they should look like this.

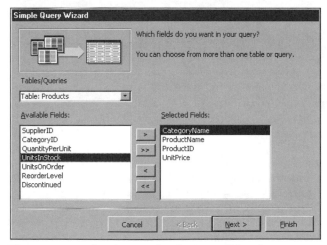

Figure 21-23: The Access Simple Query Wizard

Query Design tool

The Query Design tool provides a more sophisticated way to define a query without manually constructing the SQL statement. To use the Query Design tool, open your database, select Queries from the Objects list, and select the Create Query in Design View item.

The Query Design view window, as shown in Figure 21-24, appears and prompts you to add the tables that you want to include in the query. Using the earlier example, select and add the Customer and Address tables. Click Close to close the Show Table dialog box.

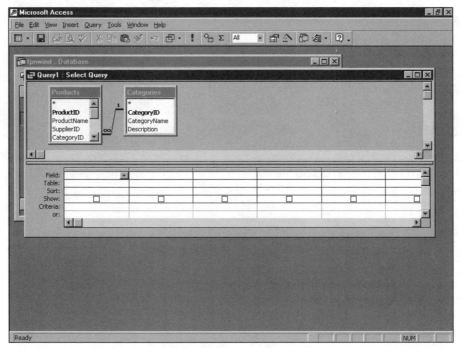

Figure 21-24: Access Query Design tool

The next step is to add the fields that you want to return in the columns of the Query Design tool. Select each field that you want to include, one at a time, and drag the field into the top row of an empty column in Query Design view. (Alternatively, you can double-click the field name to have it appear in the next available column.) As a shortcut, to include all fields, you can select the star (*) items at the top of each table.

At this point, you may be finished, or you can continue to refine the query in several ways. You may have noticed that when you added the tables initially, Access created a relationship between the two tables. You can edit this relationship by right-clicking the line that connects the two tables.

You can designate criteria for the query by using the Criteria row for each column. If your query includes multiple criteria, use the And row to indicate whether multiple criteria should be linked as And or Or clauses. Similarly, you can use the Sort row to indicate sort order instructions.

After you finish designing your query, test it in Access and save it with an appropriate name (use **Get All Customers** for this example). Then, switch to SQL view by selecting View ⇨ SQL View (see Figure 21-25). Select the entire text of the SQL statement (it is selected by default) and select Edit ⇨ Copy. Switch back to FrontPage and use the Custom Query option of the DRW to paste in the SQL statement.

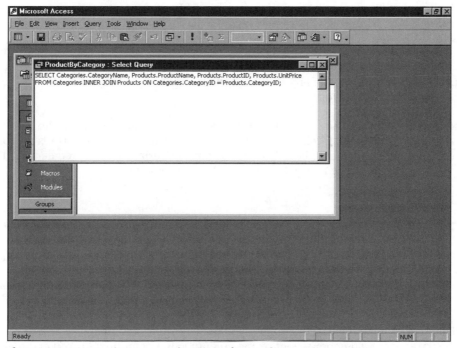

Figure 21-25: Creating a query in Access for use in FrontPage 2000

Accessing an access query in FrontPage

In the previous section, you created in Access a database query called Get All Customers, which you then pasted into your FrontPage Database Results page. Alternatively, you can access the query directly from the FrontPage DRW and save yourself the trouble of creating the custom query in two places. After you create a query in Access 2000, it becomes available to the DRW as a record set, in the same way that all the database tables are presented. (This is true only of `SELECT` statement queries — or what FrontPage 2000 terms "database views.")

To demonstrate this, create a query with either the Access SQW or Design Query tool and save the query in Access. Then, return to FrontPage and launch the DRW. Select the appropriate database source and, in the second screen of the DRW, you should see the query name in the list of available record sources.

Passing parameters to an access query

Chapter 18 looks at methods for adding input parameters to a database query. But, if you are neither a database designer nor an ASP programmer, you can create a query in Access and pass parameters to it from FrontPage, a method that is fairly straightforward.

First, create a general-purpose query in Access, using the method described in the previous section. Include any static criteria (criteria that always remains the same), but omit any variable criteria.

Return to FrontPage and start the DRW. Select the Access query from the list of available record sets. Click Next to continue. Click the Advanced Options button to access the Criteria dialog box. Add any variable criteria, as described earlier in the chapter. Complete the rest of the DRW and save the page.

Customizing the Database Results Page

After you use the DRW to create a basic Database Results page, you can use the FrontPage page editing features to adjust the appearance of the page. Of course, you can create the basic design of the page first, before you run the DRW, but you still need to make some formatting changes to the data results section itself.

The main thing to be careful about if you make formatting changes is not to disrupt the database region component or the column value components. You can make changes to a column value's font by selecting the column value component and then applying formatting. If you are careful, you can even cut and paste these elements to different locations on the page (as long as you don't move a column value component outside the database region). Keep in mind that any page elements that you add inside the database region will be repeated for each record returned by the query.

Caution You should save any formatting of the database region itself until you are fairly confident that you won't need to edit the query. Any time that you rerun the DRW, it regenerates the database region, undoing any formatting changes that you may have made.

Passing Parameters via Hyperlinks

One of the most common uses of database applications is to display a summarized list of results and then to link each item in the list to detailed information about it. Consider, for example, a catalog search form that enables users to search for keywords in the catalog descriptions. The results of the search might be displayed in list form, arranged by product name. The product name is then linked to another database function that returns the detailed product information regarding the designated item.

The key to making this application work is the ability to pass to the second database function a parameter that identifies the product. FrontPage 2000 includes a new parameter feature in its Hyperlink dialog box that makes setting this up a breeze.

To illustrate, use the sample Northwind database that accompanies FrontPage 2000. First, you need to create the initial database search:

1. Create a new page and select Insert ➪ Database ➪ Results.

2. Using the DRW, create a connection to the FrontPage Northwind sample database (select Use a Sample Database Connection). Click Next to continue.

3. Select Products from the Record Source drop-down list. Click Next to continue.

4. In the Displayed Fields screen, click the Edit List button. Remove all fields except ProductName and UnitPrice. Click OK to return to the main DRW screen. Click Next to continue.

5. In the formatting screen, select Table -- One Record Per Row. Check Include Header Row with Column Labels. Uncheck the other boxes. Click Next to continue.

6. Select Display All Records Together. Click Finish.

   The results should resemble Figure 21-26.

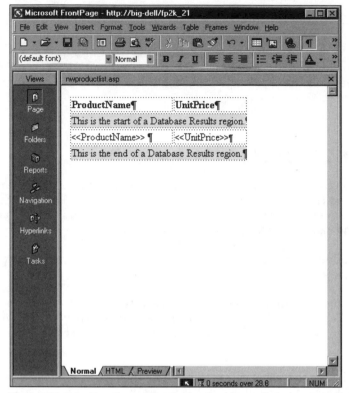

Figure 21-26: Creating a simple product list to link to a Detail view

Now, you create the second database function, which expects to be passed a ProductID, and returns detailed information on the product (the Northwind database doesn't include product descriptions, but it does include a lot of additional information about the product).

7. Create a new page. Select Insert ➪ Database ➪ Results to start the DRW.

8. Select the Sample Northwind database, as in Step 2. Click Next to continue.

9. Select Products from the Record Source drop-down list. Click Next to continue.

10. This time, you want to display every field in the Product record, so you can leave the Displayed Fields list as is. Click the Advanced Options button.

11. In the Advanced Options dialog box (refer to Figure 21-17), select Criteria. Click Add. In the Add Criteria dialog box (refer to Figure 21-18), select ProductID as the Field Name, select Equals as the Comparison, check Get Value from This Query Parameter, and then type **ProductID** in the Value textbox. Click OK to return to the Criteria dialog box. Click OK again to return to the Advanced Options dialog box.

12. In the Advanced Options dialog box, check Limit Number of Returned Records To and type **1** in the input field. Click OK again to return to the main DRW screen. Click Next to continue.

13. In the results formatting screen, select List –One Record Per List, and then select a Table list from the List Options drop-down list. Check Add Labels for All Field Values. Do not check Place Horizontal Separator Between Records. Click Next to continue.

14. In the last DRW screen, select Display All Records Together. Don't check Generate Form to Collect Input Parameters. Click Finish to view the completed page.

15. Save this page, shown in Figure 21-27, with an appropriate name (such as **ProductName.asp**).

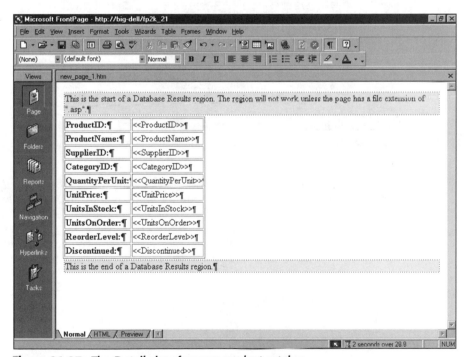

Figure 21-27: The Detail view for your product catalog

Now you can join the two database lookups by using a hyperlink that passes the appropriate parameter.

16. Return to the first database page. Select the <<ProductName> column value component. Either click the Hyperlinks icon in the toolbar, select Insert ⇨ Hyperlink, or right-click the column value and select Hyperlink from the option menu.

17. In the Hyperlink dialog box, select the productdetail.asp file as the URL. Click the Parameters button to open the Hyperlink Parameters dialog box (see Figure 21-28).

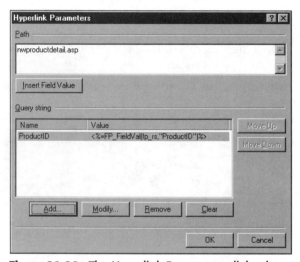

Figure 21-28: The Hyperlink Parameters dialog box

18. Click the Add button underneath the Query String input area. In the Add Parameter dialog box, type the parameter name, **ProductID**, and select the ProductID field from the drop-down list as the parameter value. FrontPage inserts some ASP code, as shown in Figure 21-29. Click OK to return to the Parameter dialog box. Click OK again to return to the Hyperlink dialog box, and click OK a third time to return to the Database Results page.

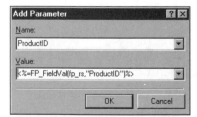

Figure 21-29: Creating a simple product list to link to a Detail view

19. At this point, the ProductName column value component should be hyperlinked.

20. Preview this page. Click one of the hyperlinked product names in the initial list. You should get a second page showing details (although, frankly, not very interesting details) for that record.

Supporting Existing Database Applications

In each of its last two revisions, FrontPage has undergone fairly significant changes in its support for database applications. Prior to FrontPage 98, support was provided through the use of IDC and HTX files. In FrontPage 98, support was shifted to ASP, although marginal support was still provided for users with installed IDC/HTX applications. In FrontPage 2000, the use of ASP has changed and no direct support of IDC exists any longer.

If you have upgraded to FrontPage 2000 but still have an application built in an earlier version, you have to decide which is less painful — keeping the existing application and trying to maintain it in FrontPage 2000, or going to the trouble of updating everything. (Another alternative — in some ways, the least likely to cause you to tear out your hair — is to continue to use an older version of FrontPage to maintain your older application, and use the newer version for everything else.)

Upgrading a FrontPage 98 ASP application to FrontPage 2000

When you open in FrontPage 2000 an ASP file created in FrontPage 98, FrontPage 2000 automatically updates the behind-the-scenes ASP to be compatible with the newer version. Be warned that if you save the page at this point, your FrontPage 98 version will be gone forever.

Unfortunately, the fact that FrontPage 2000 automatically (without asking your permission) revises the ASP page doesn't mean that the database query built into the page will automatically work. To update the page completely, you need to open the DRW and redo the query. Of course, when you do this, any formatting of the results that you have done will be overwritten.

Tutorial 21.1: Create a Web Database Application

Note

The basic steps in this tutorial are adapted from examples first written for the *FrontPage 98 Bible*. Part of the motivation for reproducing them here is to see how much improvement has been made in the FrontPage database support. In general, this application is much easier to generate in FrontPage 2000. The bad news is that you no longer can use the DRW to add, modify, or delete database records.

The scenario

You are going to create a simple phone directory search interface. All users can search the phone directory for listings. By clicking the entry, they can view detailed information about the person listed.

In addition, users can update their own information by clicking the Modify hyperlink next to their name in the phone directory. (Users can't add new records or delete existing records.) When a user clicks the Modify hyperlink, they are first prompted for a username and password, which is linked to the record they want to edit. If they can't provide the correct authorization information, they can't update the record. (In this tutorial, you can only go so far as creating the editing form. To update the database requires some custom ASP. See Chapter 18, "Scripting Languages," for more on custom ASP.)

The database

This application uses a simple online phone directory database, opd.mdb. Start by importing the database into your Web and creating a data connection for it:

1. Select File ⇨ Import, click the Add File button, and locate the opd.mdb database file.

2. When you import the file, FrontPage prompts you to give the database a name. Call it **OPD** and click Yes to finish adding the database to the Web.

Create the search form interface

The first step is to create a basic phone directory search interface:

1. Create a new Web page, **opd.asp**.

2. Select Insert ⇨ Database ⇨ Results and select the OPD database. Click Next to continue.

3. Select the Contact table and click Next to continue.

4. You want to display an initial list of search results, so edit the list of fields returned to limit it to Last Name, First Name, and Phone Number. Click the Edit List button and remove all other fields. Click OK to return to the DRW screen.

5. Click Advanced Options and then click the Criteria button to designate search criteria. Click Add and select LastName as the Field Name, select Begins With as the Comparison, check the Get Value from This Parameter box, and type **LastName** as the form input name. Click OK twice to return to the Advanced Options dialog box.

6. Click Ordering and select the LastName and FirstName fields for an ascending sort order. Click OK to return to the Advanced Options dialog box.

7. In the text field provided at the bottom of the dialog box, indicate a message to display if no records are returned. Click OK to return to the DRW screen. Click Next to continue.

8. Select the Table display format and check Include Header Row with Column Labels. Click Next.

9. Select Display All Records Together and check the option to create a Search Form on the Results page. Click Finish.

Next, you tidy up the display a bit. Add some color, a more pleasing font, and so on. The results are displayed in Figure 21-30.

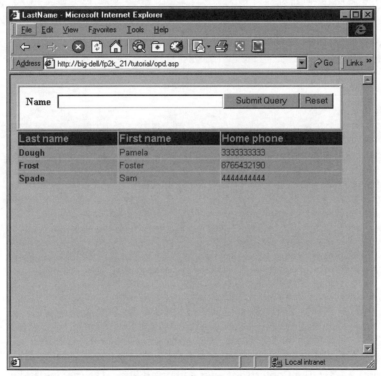

Figure 21-30: The initial Contacts list after some sprucing up

These results have a few problems. One is the phone number. Another is the lack of any link to additional information. The formatting problem is easily fixed, but it requires some hands-on work with the database query generated by the DRW.

10. Double-click the Database Results region to open the DRW. Click the Custom Query button. The current query opens in an editing box. To format the telephone number, make the following change (indicated in italics) to the SQL statement:

```
SELECT *, Format(HomePhone, '(000) 000-0000') as fHomePhone
FROM Contacts WHERE (LastName LIKE '%%LastName%%') ORDER BY
LastName ASC,FirstName ASC
```

Next, add a visual interface, using letters of the alphabet, as shown in Figure 21-31.

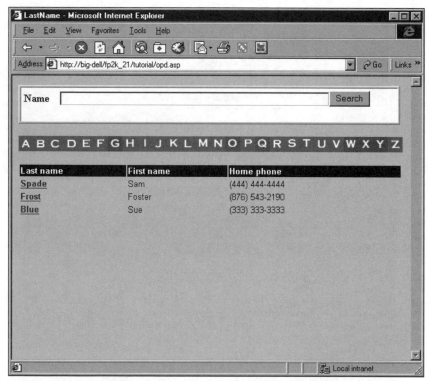

Figure 21-31: The Contacts list after adding additional formatting and an alphabet lookup interface

11. Add the alphabet images from the CD-ROM that accompanies this book (or make your own).

12. For each letter, select the image and click the Hyperlink toolbar icon to open the Hyperlink dialog box. Alternatively, right-click the image and select Hyperlink from the option menu.

13. In the Hyperlink dialog box, select the same page, opd.asp, as the URL.

14. Click the Parameters button at the bottom of the dialog box. Click Add, and in the Name field of the Add Parameter dialog box, type **LastName**. In the Value field, type the appropriate letter of the alphabet, (for example, *A*). Close all dialog boxes. Now, try clicking a letter of the alphabet. The query should return all database entries that begin with the corresponding letter.

Note

Any time that you redo the DRW search results, it prompts you to re-create the output. This means that if you revise your query, as you are doing here, after you format the output, you have to reformat the page. For this reason, you usually should save formatting until you are sure you are done.

Create the Detail view

In this section, you create a Detail view and link it to the Database Results page via the phone directory record ID:

1. Create a new Web page and save it as **opddetail.asp**.

2. Select Insert ➪ Database ➪ Results and select the OPD database. Click Next.

3. Select the Contacts table as the record source. Click Next to continue.

4. Select Advanced Options. Click Criteria, click Add, and select ContactID as the Field name, Equals as the Comparison, and a form field Value of **ContactID**. Click OK twice to return to the Advanced Options dialog box. You want to include all available fields in this detailed view, so you don't need to edit the list of displayed fields. Check Limit Number of Returned Records To and designate **1** as the maximum. An occasion to display more than one record shouldn't arise, but it never hurts to be sure.

5. Before you leave the Advanced Options dialog box, you also need to set a default value for ContactID. Again, in theory, you will always pass a value via a hyperlink parameter. But what if someone tries to access the page directly? The page shouldn't display a record, but if you don't define a default value, it will generate an ASP error.

   Click the Defaults button in the Advance Options dialog box. The Defaults dialog box shows the ContactID parameter. Click Edit and set the default value to **-1**. Click OK to leave this dialog box, and click OK again to return to the main DRW screen. Click Next to continue.

6. In the formatting options screen, select List – One Record Per List, and choose the Table format from the List Options drop-down list. Check the Add Labels

for All Field Values box (you will edit these labels to make them a bit more user-friendly, but you might as well let FrontPage do as much of the work as possible). Click Next.

7. Select the Display All Records Together option, and don't check the Generate Form to Collect Input Parameter option, because you will pass the ID as a query string parameter from a hyperlink. Click Finish.

Figure 21-32 shows your Detail Results page after some cleanup work. Next, you link the List Results page to the Detail Results page.

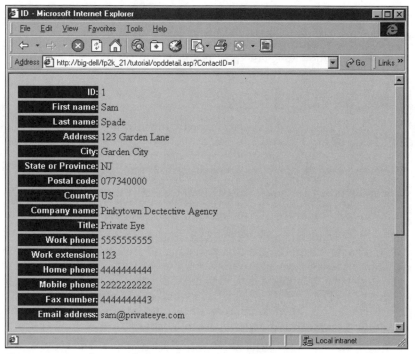

Figure 21-32: The Detail view of your phone directory.

8. Open the List Results page, opd.asp, and select the <<LastName> column value component. Click the Hyperlink icon in the toolbar or use one of the other ways to open the Hyperlink dialog box. Locate opddetail.asp and identify it as the target URL. Click the Parameters button. Click Add and select ContactID from the drop-down Parameter Name list. FrontPage automatically writes the ASP code to include the appropriate field value as the parameter value. Click OK twice to return to the main page.

9. Save your work and preview. You should be able to click a last name in the search results and bring up the detail record for that record.

Create the Edit Login page

After you have the Search Form, List Results page, and Detailed Results page, you have a complete, working phone directory. Wouldn't it be nice, though, if you could let users update their own records in the database, so that you don't have to pay anyone to maintain the database?

Your plan is to issue to every user a username and password that enables them to edit their own record. You will also create administrative passwords for users who are permitted to edit any record in the database. The idea is to put a Login Form at the bottom of the Detail Results page. If a user wants to edit their record, they retrieve the Detail view, input the correct username and password, and then edit their record.

To create the Login Form:

1. Open opddetail.asp. Place the cursor at the bottom of the page, before the end of the database region. Select Insert ⇨ Form ⇨ One-line Text Box to generate a textbox and Submit and Reset buttons. Double-click the textbox and change its name to **Username**. Click OK. Insert a second one-line textbox. Name it **Password** and check Yes for Is Password.

2. Now, for a small piece of magic. You want to pass along the ID number of the record as part of the parameter string sent to the login validation. To do this, you use a hidden field. Right-click the form and open the Form Properties dialog box. Click the Advanced button at the bottom of the dialog box. In the Hidden Field dialog box, click Add. Name the hidden field **ContactID**. For the Value, type <%= **Request("ContactID")** %>. This is ASP terminology for "put the contact ID returned with the record on this page please."

Note If you want to learn more about ASP, see Chapter 18. To learn more about creating HTML forms, see Chapter 14.

In the next section, you create the login validation query that you will attach to this form.

Create the Edit page

The rule that you have created is that a user can edit a record only if they have a valid username and password that are associated with that record. In the database, this is managed by creating a second table, called Editors. This table consists of three fields: Username, Password, and EditRecord (which contains the ContactID of the record that this person can edit; for system administrators, the EditRecord field contains a zero, meaning that they can edit any records).

When the user submits their username and password along with the ContactID for their record, you have to check that all of these items match a record in the Editors table. If they do not, you return an error message.

You could do this in two steps: first, check to see whether a match exists in the Editors table. If a match exists, then return the directory information in a form. However, you can combine both of these steps into a single query. If it returns a record, you know that the user is valid, and vice versa.

1. Create a new page and save it as **editopd.asp**.

2. Select Insert ⇨ Database ⇨ Results and select the OPD database.

3. Select Custom Query. Enter the following query:

```
SELECT * FROM Contacts
WHERE ContactID=%%ContactID%% AND
(SELECT Count(*) FROM Editors
WHERE Username='%%Username%%' and Password='%%Password%%' and
(EditRecord=%%ContactID%% Or EditRecord=0))>0
```

Caution   This SQL includes two elements that may not work in all circumstances: the Count(*) function, which returns a count of the number of rows matched by the query, and the embedded SELECT statement within a WHERE clause. These two shortcuts enable the two queries to be combined efficiently into one query. If they don't work in your circumstances, you may need to break the login verification and edit page into two steps.

Note the places where parameters have been entered in this custom SQL statement. You can add them either manually or use the Insert Parameter button to assist you.

4. In the Advanced Options dialog box, add an appropriate message for the user if no records are returned. For example: "The username and password that you submitted do not allow you to edit this record. Use the Back button to return to the Login Form. If you experience repeated problems, contact your system administrator."

5. Select all fields to include in the results, as in the previous example, opddetail.asp.

6. Select List – One Record Per List, and format the results in a Table format.

You may want to test this page before you go to the next step of inserting all the field values into textboxes for editing. To test it, return to the form element in opddetail.asp. Right-click the form and select Form Properties. Select the Send to Other option, and click the Options button. Enter the name of the edit form, **editopd.asp**, in the Action field. Click OK and save your results. Try it out, entering a valid username and password combination.

7. After you are sure that you have everything working, you are ready to go back to the edit form and insert the field values into form fields. The process is essentially the same for each form field. The steps for the LastName field are described next.

8. Place the results table inside a form element. Many approaches exist to doing this, but my favorite is as follows:

 a. Select Table ➪ Select ➪ Table.

 b. Select Edit ➪ Cut to move the table into the Clipboard.

 c. Select Insert ➪ Form ➪ Form to create a blank form element.

 d. Place the cursor inside the form and select Edit ➪ Paste to return the table to the page, inside the form.

9. Next, remove the <<LastName> column value component from the table. Place the cursor in its table cell and select Insert ➪ Form ➪ One-line Text Box. Double-click the textbox to open its Properties dialog box. Change the name of the textbox to **LastName**. For its Value, enter the following ASP code:

```
<%= FP_FieldVal(fp_rs, "LastName")%>
```

This snippet uses a library function that extracts the field value of a given field from the rowset returned by the query.

10. Save everything and test. You should see the field element populated with the current value.

11. Repeat the process for each field value.

Create the Update page

After the user makes their editing changes, they submit the page to an Update Query page. As noted earlier in the chapter, FrontPage really isn't designed to handle *action queries* (queries that perform some action that changes the database). The problem is that you have no good way to verify that the record actually updated. Your solution is to tack on an additional query that retrieves the record that was just updated and displays it back to the user. If any problem exists, they will at least be alerted by the fact that the data doesn't match what they expect. (The better solution is to use ASP to handle the update query rather than FrontPage, but that is saved for another chapter...)

Summary

This chapter has introduced you to the basics — and a few of the finer points — of developing database applications using FrontPage 2000's support for ASP. You have learned how to use the Database Results Wizard, including all of its advanced features. You have created examples of database queries, linked a list of search results to detail views, and devised a form for editing database records. Not bad for one chapter!

This is the last of the programming chapters. The final part of this book describes how you can use FrontPage as part of a development or maintenance project, and what system administrators need to know to integrate FrontPage into their Web server environment.

✦   ✦   ✦

Advanced Topics

Customizing FrontPage

This chapter offers an overview of the many ways that you can customize FrontPage to suit your needs. The first half of the chapter focuses on relatively simple, nonprogramming customizations: customizing the FrontPage environment, creating Themes and templates, and using macros. The last half of the chapter is aimed more at developers: using Visual Basic Editor (VBE) to create FrontPage macros and using Visual Basic to create design-time controls and wizards (with a brief glance at add-ins). The development section is designed to explore the basic possibilities for customization. A full-scale discussion of programming is beyond the scope of this book.

This chapter in its entirety is not for everyone. If you are a novice FrontPage user, I recommend that you read this chapter's initial section on creating your own templates and Themes. These are easy to do and don't require programming skills. You may also want to look over the sections on macros, design-time controls, wizards, and add-ins, just to familiarize yourself with the terminology. Even if you are unlikely to create any of these yourself, understanding what they are and how they work is helpful, in the event that you use controls that someone else has created.

On the other hand, this chapter is highly practical. It does not try to give you a full-blown course in programming. This chapter is for you if you are the kind of person who says, "Gee, FrontPage is a swell Web development tool, but if only it could do X..." or, "I have done these same tedious commands 20 times in the last week. I sure wish I could automate this!" If this doesn't describe you, well, maybe this chapter will give you a spark of inspiration!

Working with Custom Templates

Creating custom templates requires no programming. It is as simple as creating an HTML page and converting it to the template format. FrontPage recognizes three template types:

✦ **Page:** A single page template, located in the pages subfolder of the FrontPage main folder

✦ **Frame set:** A frame set and all frames, located in the frames subfolder of the FrontPage main folder

✦ **Web:** A collection of interconnected pages, stored in the Webs subfolder of the FrontPage main folder

Creating a page template

To create a page template:

1. Create the HTML page. If you have not yet saved the file, select File ⇨ Save. Otherwise, select File ⇨ Save As.

2. Select FrontPage Template (*.tem) from the Save As Type drop-down menu.

3. Enter a name for the template file and click the Save button, which opens the Save As Template dialog box. Enter a title, name, and description for the template. Click the Browse button if you want to select the title and name from a list of existing templates.

4. Click OK to save your template.

Creating a frame set or style sheet template

You create a frame set or style sheet template much as you do a page template:

1. Define the layout of the frame set or the style sheet styles.

2. Select File ⇨ Save or File ⇨ Save As, and select FrontPage Template (*.tem) from the Save As Type drop-down list.

3. Complete the template information, as described in the previous section for a page template. Your new frame set template appears in the Frames Pages tab of the New Page dialog box. Your new style sheet template appears in the Style Sheets tab of the New Page dialog box.

Creating shared templates

In FrontPage 2000, you can create a template to be shared among all authors of a given Web. To do this, check the Save Template in Current Web option when you create your template. FrontPage creates a hidden folder, called _sharedtemplates, and stores your shared template there.

Note   Unfortunately, you can't share a template across multiple Webs.

Editing templates

To edit an existing template, you must open the existing template as a new page, edit the page, and resave it as a template with the same name as the existing template. The steps are as follows:

1. Select File ➪ New ➪ Page.

2. Select the template to edit from the General, Frames Pages, or StyleSheets tab. Click OK to open a new page using the selected template.

3. Make changes to the template in the new pages.

4. Select File ➪ Save As and select FrontPage Template (*.tem) from the Save As Type drop-down list.

5. Resave the template using its existing name.

Deleting templates

To delete a shared template, first show hidden folders in your Web by selecting Tools ➪ Web Settings and checking the Show Documents in Hidden Directories option in the Advanced tab. Switch to Folders view, select the _sharedtemplates folder, select the template to delete, and select Edit ➪ Delete, or right-click the template and select Delete from the options menu.

Creating Web templates

You can create Web templates manually or, if you are using the Microsoft Personal Web Server, you can use the Web Template Maker utility (webtmpl.exe) that is part of the FrontPage SDK.

To create a Web template manually:

1. Create a folder called *myweb*.tem, where *myweb* is the name of the Web template, and place this folder in the Webs subfolder, located in the main FrontPage folder (\Program Files\Microsoft FrontPage, by default).

2. Create the Web to be used as the basis for the template.

3. Locate the Web files and copy to the *myweb*.tem folder. If your Web contains files in private or images subfolders, these must be copied as well.

4. Create a *myweb*.inf file, as described in the next section.

To create a Web template using the webtmpl.exe utility, follow these steps:

1. Launch the utility.

2. Select the Web to use from the available Webs list.

3. Indicate template information.

4. Click Make Web Template.

The template INF file

When you create a template, FrontPage saves all the necessary files in the appropriate template directory. In addition, it creates an INF file for the template. The INF file is simply a standard Windows INI format text file that stores configuration information about the template. This file can have several sections:

✦ **Info:** Contains information on the templates title, description, Theme, and any shared borders.

✦ **FileList**: Enables you to map files in a template directory to explicit URLs within the Web that is created. This is the only way to create a Web template with subdirectories.

✦ **MetaInfo**: Store meta information variables that can be used in the Web, typically in conjunction with the Substitution Component.

✦ **TaskList**: Store information about initial tasks for your Web template, using the TaskList section of the INF file. A task has six attributes: TaskName, Priority (1-3), CreatedBy, URL, Cookie, and Comment.

For more information on the format of the INF file, consult the FrontPage SDK.

Customizing Your Workspace

FrontPage 2000, like the other Office 2000 applications, enables you to modify the commands available on the menus and toolbars. You can even create your own toolbars. This section describes the basic toolbar- and menu-customization features. Later in the chapter, after you learn how to create macros, you find out how to add your macros to a custom toolbar by using the methods outlined here.

Customizing toolbars

You can customize toolbars by using either of two methods:

✦ Use the Customize dialog box, described next in "Using the Customize Dialog Box."

✦ Use the Add or Remove Buttons option available on each toolbar (this option is not available on custom toolbars), described here.

To access the Add or Remove Buttons option, click the small downward-pointing arrow at the right end of a toolbar. This brings up a list of the current buttons, as shown in Figure 22-1. To remove a button, deselect it from the list. To add it back, select it.

You can also access the Customize dialog box from this option menu by selecting Customize, which is the last item on the list.

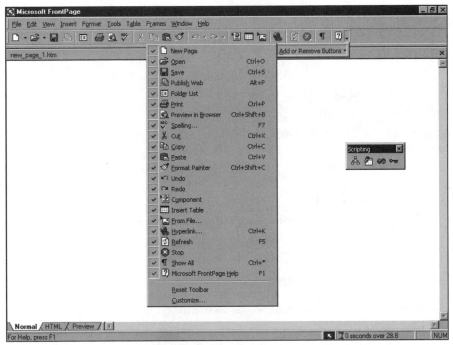

Figure 22-1: Adding or removing buttons from a toolbar

Moving command items

To move a command from one toolbar to another, press Alt+Ctrl and drag the toolbar command to a new toolbar. If you release the Alt and Ctrl keys and drop the command anywhere other than on another toolbar, it deletes the command from the original toolbar. If you drop it accidentally, you can always add it back by using the Add or Remove Buttons menu, as previously described.

Using the Customize Dialog Box

All of the FrontPage customization features are accessible from the Customize dialog box. To open this dialog box, select Tools ➪ Customize (see Figure 22-2).

Figure 22-2: The Customize dialog box enables you to create your personal FrontPage interface.

Creating toolbars

Using the Toolbars tab, you can designate which toolbars you want to have visible. To show a particular toolbar, simply select it to check the box next to its name. To hide the toolbar, select it again to uncheck the box.

The Toolbars tab has four buttons:

✦ **New**: Use to add a custom toolbar to the list

✦ **Rename**: Change the name of a custom toolbar that you have added by using the New button

✦ **Delete**: Delete a custom toolbar that you have added by using the New button

✦ **Reset**: Reset a standard toolbar to its default state if you have made changes to it.

When you select one of the built-in toolbars, the only other function available to you — besides the New button — is the Reset button. The other buttons are reserved for any custom toolbars that you create.

As an example, create a new toolbar:

1. Click the New button and type the name of the new toolbar; call it **Scripting**, because your plan is to add the buttons needed to access the macro functionality that you use repeatedly in this chapter.

2. Click OK to create your Scripting toolbar (see Figure 22-3). This toolbar isn't much to look at yet, but in the next section, you learn how to add commands to it.

Figure 22-3: Your custom Scripting toolbar, without commands

Tip

Opening the Customize menu performs a bit of magic on the FrontPage interface itself. Unlike most dialog boxes, when you open the Customize dialog box, you can still access menu lists. And, when you do so, a strange and marvelous thing happens: If you drag an item from a menu item, a menu list name (File, Edit, View, and so on), or a toolbar item, you can move it to another location and drop it into place.

Using the Commands option menu

If you right-click an item, you see the option menu list, shown in Figure 22-4. This is the same menu accessed when you select an item in the Commands toolbar and click the Modify button. Use this menu to remove, rename, or designate a new icon for an item.

Figure 22-4: The Commands option menu

The Commands tab

The Commands tab enables you to customize the commands available to you on a given menu list or toolbar.

To access the Commands tab, select Tools ➪ Customize and click the Commands tab, illustrated in Figure 22-5. This tab lists all the commands that are available to be added to or removed from toolbars or menu lists. For example, if you select the Tools item in the Categories list on the left side, the list of current commands for Tools appears on the right.

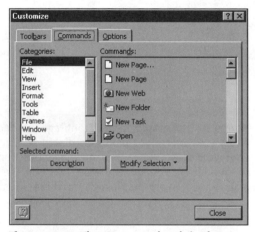

Figure 22-5: The Commands tab in the Customize dialog box

Scroll down the list of commands on the Tools menu until you come to Macros. Click and drag this item onto your Scripting toolbar. Repeat this procedure for Visual Basic Editor and Microsoft Script Editor. Now you have your own toolbar. You can hide/view it by using the standard View ➪ Toolbars mechanism. You can even dock and undock your toolbar.

To remove your toolbar, simply return to the Toolbars tab, select the toolbar that you want to delete, and click the Delete button.

As an example, suppose that you have used earlier versions of FrontPage and are accustomed to inserting scripts via the Insert ➪ Advanced menu item. (See Chapter 18 for details on how to insert scripts in FrontPage 2000.) To re-create this functionality:

1. Select Tools ➪ Customize to open the Customize dialog box. Click the Commands tab and select Tools from the Categories list.

2. Scroll down the Commands list to locate the Microsoft Script Editor command. Drag this item to the FrontPage menu bar and pause over the Insert menu item, keeping your mouse button depressed the entire time. The Insert menu expands.

3. Drag the Script command down the Insert menu until it is over the Advanced menu item, which expands the Advanced submenu. Drag the Script command over the submenu and drop it into this submenu by releasing the mouse button, as shown in Figure 22-6.

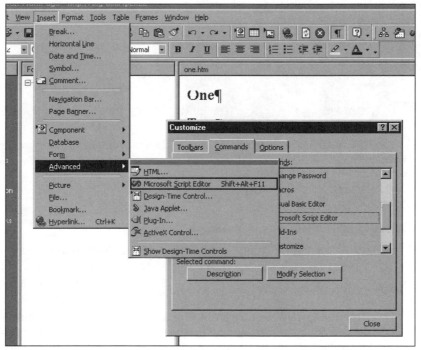

Figure 22-6: Customizing a toolbar

To change the name of this new item, right-click it and type a new name in the Name Property textbox. To define a shortcut key, place an ampersand (&) in front of the shortcut character. For example, to designate the letter *C* as the shortcut key for a command called My Command, give its name as **My &Command**. Shortcut key characters are underlined in the menu bar. They can be accessed by pressing the Alt key and the shortcut key simultaneously.

To remove this new item, right-click it and select Delete.

Options

The Options tab of the Customize dialog box (see Figure 22-7) contains miscellaneous options that you can control, including the following miscellaneous customization options:

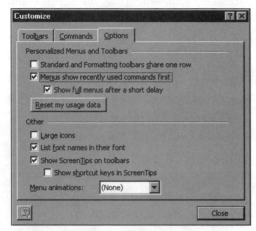

Figure 22-7: The Options tab of the Customize dialog box

✦ **Personalized Menus and Toolbars:**

- **Standard and Formatting Toolbars Share One Row:** Check to cause the two primary FrontPage toolbars to occupy a single row. Good for conserving space if you have a large enough monitor. Otherwise, you have to scroll the single row to access all toolbar items.

- **Menus Show Recently Used Commands First:** Check to limit menu lists to recently used commands. This is one of the options available for reorganizing menu items in various ways, a great feature of Office 2000 applications.

- **Show Full Menus After a Short Delay:** Works in conjunction with the previous option to minimize menu clutter. When checked, shows you all menu items if you don't select one of the recently used items.

- **Reset My Usage Data:** Wipes out FrontPage's memory of your recently used commands, enabling you to reset which menu items appear by default.

✦ **Other:**

- **Large Icons:** Check to make the toolbar icons bigger.

- **List Fonts in Their Font:** Check to cause each font name in the Fonts menu list to display using that font's typeface.

- **Show ScreenTips on Toolbars:** Turns on ScreenTips, the little yellow boxes that show up when you place the cursor over an item on the toolbar.

- **Show Shortcut Keys in ScreenTips:** Adds to the ScreenTip a reminder about a command's shortcut key.

- **Menu Animations (None, Random, Unfold, Slide):** Enables you to control how menu lists appear. Select None to have them appear as they have always done—all at once. Select Unfold to have the menu appear from top to bottom. Select Slide to have the menu appear from top to bottom and from left to right. Select Random to enable FrontPage to select at random which type of animation to use each time you access a menu list.

Adding custom menu items

To add a custom menu item to the main menu bar, select Tools ⇨ Customize and select the command that you want to add. This can either be an existing command or a custom menu item. To add a custom item, select Macros from the Categories list and select the Custom Menu Item command.

You can add menu commands to any existing submenu. You can even add a Menu command to the menu bar. However, you cannot create a top-level menu command with its own submenus.

Caution   You can delete a default menu item from the menu bar. If you do this, and then want to undo the delete, select the Toolbars tab of the Customize dialog box, select Menu Bar, and click the Reset button. If you really get stuck and accidentally delete the Tools menu and the Insert menus, you can always get back to the Customize dialog box by right-clicking the menu bar. You cannot remove the menu bar.

If you really want to create a custom menu item and add commands to it, you can use the method described in the FrontPage SDK (the question of whether a FrontPage 2000 SDK will be released still isn't clear, nor is it clear whether such a release would still support this procedure). The problem with editing the Registry is that you can't add commands to a menu item initialized this way by using the Customize dialog box (which is one sign that this method is no longer fully supported). See the FrontPage SDK for more details.

Using Macros

In the computer programming world, a *macro* is a shortcut, a way to encapsulate a set of tasks or commands into a single step. In FrontPage 2000, you can create time-saving macros by using VBE. You can create macros to automate tasks that you perform in Webs or tasks associated with individual Web pages.

The nitty-gritty of how you create a macro using VBE is discussed in a moment, but first a word on how you invoke a macro after you have one. To run an existing macro, select Tools ➪ Macro ➪ Macros to open the Macro dialog box (which looks similar to the one shown in Figure 22-8), which lists all existing macros. To run a particular macro, either double-click it or select it and click the Run button.

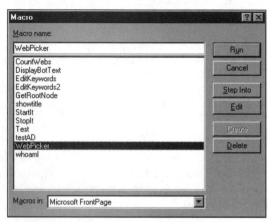

Figure 22-8: The Macro dialog box

Creating and editing macros

You use VBE to create a macro. You can access VBE in either of two ways:

✦ Select Tools ➪ Macro ➪ Macros, select a macro, and click Edit

✦ Select Tools ➪ Macro ➪ Visual Basic Editor to open the editor directly

Exploring Visual Basic Editor

FrontPage 2000 includes Visual Basic Editor for the purpose of creating FrontPage macros. These macros are intended for use when designing Web pages or administering Web sites. They are not part of the Web pages viewed by users. For information on programming that can be added to Web pages, such as JavaScript, VBScript, DHTML, and ASP, refer to Chapter 18, "Scripting Languages."

VBE exposes three object models that developers can use in their macros:

✦ **Application Object Model:** The top level of the FrontPage programming model. Provides access to Add-ins, System information, CommandBars, and the FrontPage Application object, which contains a pointer to Webs and the Web Object Model.

✦ **Web Object Model:** This set of objects enables macros to operate on FrontPage Webs — including folders, navigation nodes, and Themes.

✦ **FrontPage Document Object Model:** Parallels the DHTML Document Object Model (discussed in Chapter 18). It exposes design-time document objects within FrontPage.

These three object models are contained in two class libraries, FrontPage and FrontPage_Editor, which you can peruse by using VBE. To browse these libraries, open VBE and select View ➪ Object Browser. VBE's Object Browser window provides a brief description of each class, its methods, and its properties, as shown in Figure 22-9.

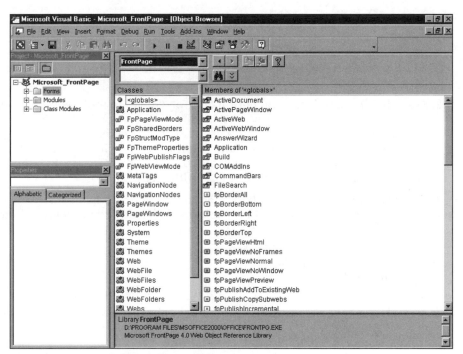

Figure 22-9: Visual Basic Editor's Object Browser

A complete description of the FrontPage programmable interfaces is beyond the scope of this book. The tutorials that follow illustrate two simple macros, one demonstrating how to interact with Webs, and the other showing how to use a macro to make changes to a Web page. The discussion assumes that you are familiar enough with VB programming — perhaps you have created macros in Visual Basic for Applications before — to be able to use VBE.

Tutorial 22.1: Create a Web Switcher Macro

A great feature of FrontPage 2000 is that you can now have multiple Webs open simultaneously. Unfortunately, no list of the open Webs is maintained. In this tutorial, you create a simple macro that enables you to switch among open Webs. This macro does not do all that it might, but it does serve to illustrate some of the basic principles of macro creation within the Web Object Model.

The goal is to create a macro that, when run, displays a form containing a list box control that lists the names of the currently open Webs. When the user double-clicks one of the Webs, it is activated.

Create the basic form

1. Create a new userform. Open VBE and select Insert ➪ UserForm to create a new default UserForm object. In the Properties sheet for this form, change the name to **frmWebPicker**, enter **Web Picker** for the caption, and adjust the size as shown in Figure 22-10.

2. Add a list box and command button control. Open the toolbox control by selecting View ➪ Toolbox or by clicking the toolbox icon in the toolbar. Add a label element, name it **lblWebPicker**, and enter **Available Webs:** as the caption. Select a list box control and add it to the userform element. Name the list box **lstWebList**. Add a command button control, name it **cbCancel**, and set its caption to **Cancel** (compare with Figure 22-10).

3. Script the button. The Cancel button has a simple role: when clicked, it hides the form element. To add the event script, double-click the Command button and enter the following code in its `Click` function:

```
Private Sub cbCancel_Click()
    frmWebPicker.Hide
  lstWebList.Clear
End Sub
```

4. Script the double-click event for the list box. The list box contains a list of the names of Webs currently open in the FrontPage application (that code is examined momentarily). When the user double-clicks an item in the list box, it should open the Web that has the corresponding name. To add a double-click event, select the list box name (for example, lstWebList) from the object list on the left side of the code window. Then, select Double-Click from the event list on the right. VB automatically creates the correct function syntax. You simply need to supply the code. Use the following:

```
Private Sub lstWebList_DblClick(ByVal Cancel As
MSForms.ReturnBoolean)
    Dim fp_Webs As Webs
    Dim fp_OpenWeb As Web
    Set fp_Webs = Webs

    For Each fp_OpenWeb In fp_Webs
```

```
            If StrComp(fp_OpenWeb.Title,
    lstWebList.List(lstWebList.ListIndex)) = 0 Then
                fp_OpenWeb.Activate
            End If
        Next
    lstWebList.Clear
        Unload frmWebPicker
End Sub
```

This function gets the collection of Webs currently open in FrontPage and then
loops through them, looking for one that has a name that matches the currently
selected list item. When it finds one, it activates it. Then it unloads itself.

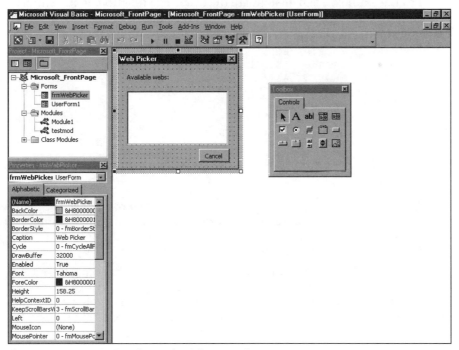

Figure 22-10: Creating the Web Picker user form

Caution
This code doesn't add an error-checking routine to handle the case when the user
tries to run this macro without any Webs open. For an example of such error handling, see the next tutorial.

You have now completed the form, but how do you get it to show up in FrontPage?
That is the task for the next section of the tutorial.

Create the macro procedure

For your macro to work properly, you need to create a function in a FrontPage module that instantiates the form and populates it with a list of the names of the open Webs:

1. Get the collection of open Webs—much as you did in the earlier code. Use the Web collection, which is a property of the Application object—the default FrontPage object (which means that you don't need to identify it explicitly; in essence, however, the object Application.Webs is identical to saying Webs).

2. Loop through the Webs collection, extracting the title of each Web and adding it to the list box. Then, instantiate the form. The function, in its entirety, is shown here:

```
Public Sub WebPicker()
    Dim fp_Webs As Webs
    Dim fp_OpenWeb As Web
    Dim fp_WebList As String
    fp_WebList = ""
    Set fp_Webs = Webs

    For Each fp_OpenWeb In fp_Webs
        frmWebPicker.lstWebList.AddItem (fp_OpenWeb.Title)
    Next
    frmWebPicker.Show
End Sub
```

3. Try it out. Open three or four Webs and run the macro as described earlier. Figure 22-11 shows the Web Picker form next to the custom Scripting toolbar that you created, for easy access to your macros (read the next tutorial for directions on how to add a macro to a custom toolbar).

The following exercise demonstrates one basic method of handling the editing of HTML within a Web page by using a macro. Specifically, you write a macro that supports the simple entry and editing of Meta tag keywords, which are commonly used by search engines to index pages. The end of the exercise shows how to add this macro to a custom toolbar, for easy access.

Tutorial 22.2: Create a Keyword Meta Tag Macro

1. Open FrontPage and access VBE by selecting Tools ➪ Macro ➪ Visual Basic Editor. In the Editor, select Insert ➪ Procedure, enter **EditKeywords** as the Name, choose Sub for Type, and choose Public for Scope. Click OK to create the basic subroutine block:

```
Public Sub EditKeywords()
End Sub
```

2. To work with the HTML of a FrontPage Web page, you use the FrontPage Document Object Model (DOM). The first step is to isolate the <HEAD> object in the open page. To do this, use the collection of 'all' elements in the ActiveDocument:

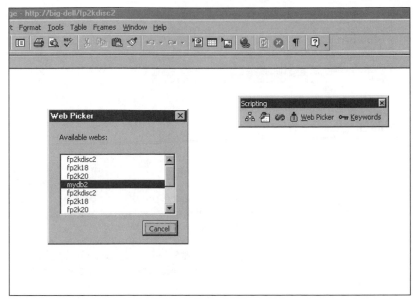

Figure 22-11: The Web Picker in action

Tip   For details on the FrontPage DOM, open VBE and select View ➪ Object Browser. This is a good reference source for all the supported object classes and their methods and properties.

```
For Each oHTMLTag In ActiveDocument.all
    If StrComp(UCase(oHTMLTag.tagName), "HEAD") = 0 Then
        Set oHeadTag = oHTMLTag
'remove message box after testing
        MsgBox ("Current Header: " & oHeadTag.innerHTML)
Exit For
    End If
Next
```

The `For` loop checks each tag element in the active document until it finds one that has a tag name that matches `"HEAD"`. It then saves that element and exits the loop, after displaying the contents of the header tag to demonstrate that you found the right one.

3. Add an input box to collect the keywords to add to the `<META>` tag:

```
sKeywords = InputBox("Enter a comma-separated list of
keywords:", "Add Keywords")
sKeyWordTag = "<META NAME=""keywords"" CONTENT=""" &
sKeywords & """>"
```

The first line presents the user with an input dialog box and stores the input in the string variable `sKeywords`. Note that this code assumes that the user correctly inputs the keywords. The second line takes the input and creates the `<META>` tag that you plan to insert. This input box in action is shown in Figure 22-12.

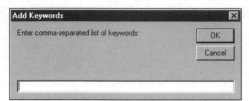

Figure 22-12: A standard VB input box for collecting keywords

4. Collecting keywords is fine, but you really want to add them to a keyword `<META>` tag and then add the tag to the page. The goal is to add this tag at the end of any existing `<META>` tags, which typically are placed before the `<TITLE>` tag. If no `<META>` tags are in the current document, then you place this tag at the beginning of the `HEAD` element.

Note   You really don't need precise placement of the keyword `<META>` tag, as long as it is somewhere in the `<HEAD>` tag. The motive for placement is simply to try to create cleaner HTML.

This step has two keys:

- **Use of the `children` collection of the `<HEAD>` tag.** The `<HEAD>` tag also has an `all` collection, but using the `children` collection is better, because it returns only the tags that are direct children of the named tag. The `all` collection returns every tag, even if the tag is two or three levels deep in the tag structure.

- **Use of the `innerHTML` property of the `<HEAD>` tag object.** In the FrontPage DOM, tags have two HTML string properties: `innerHTML` and `outerHTML`. `InnerHTML` refers to the text between the beginning and ending tags. `OuterHTML` refers to `InnerHTML` plus the tags themselves.

The following code loops through the children of the `<HEAD>` tag, each time adding back the HTML of the current tag to the new `HEAD` element. When the loop finds a `<META>` tag, it sets a `True/False` flag to `True`. When the next tag that isn't a `<META>` tag is encountered, it adds in the keyword tag and then finishes out the loop. If the loop never encounters a `<META>` tag, it places the keyword tag at the beginning of the `<HEAD>` tag. If the loop never encounters anything after the `<META>` tag, it places the new tag at the end of the `<HEAD>` tag.

```
For Each oChildTag In oHeadTag.Children
        If StrComp(UCase(oChildTag.tagName), "META") = 0 Then
            hasMeta = True
        Else
            If hasMeta = True Then
                'we have come to the end of the meta tags
                newInnerHTML = newInnerHTML & newMetaTag
                hasMetaNew = True
            End If
        End If
        newInnerHTML = newInnerHTML & oChildTag.outerHTML
```

```
Next
If hasMetaNew = False Then
    oHeadTag.innerHTML = newMetaTag & newInnerHTML
Else
    If hasMeta = False Then
        oHeadTag.innerHTML = newInnerHTML & newMetaTag
    End If
End If
```

Caution

For some reason, the DOM wants to add an extra CRLF to each tag as it is added back to the HEAD element. The following code can be added to correct the problem, if you encounter it:

```
oHeadTag.innerHTML = Replace(newInnerHTML, Chr(10) &
Chr(13), "Chr(10)")
```

Note that you should use the Replace function for all three of the statements that set the oHeadTag.innerHTML at the end of this subroutine.

5. This macro adds keywords nicely to any Web page that does not already have them. Unfortunately, it doesn't yet recognize pages that already have keywords. Until you fix this, the macro adds new keyword tags to the header of the page each time that the script is rerun.

The fix requires two additions to your code. First, you need to check before you show the user the Keyword input box. If a keyword tag already exists, you want to load in the existing keywords and allow the user to edit them. Then, you want to replace the existing keyword tag with your new one. If no keyword tag exists, then you let the user add a new one. The following code performs this check:

```
For Each oChildTag In oHeadTag.Children
        If StrComp(UCase(oChildTag.tagName), "META") = 0 Then
            If StrComp(UCase(oChildTag.getAttribute("NAME")),
"KEYWORDS") = 0 Then
                sKeyword = oChildTag.getAttribute("CONTENT")
                sKeyword = InputBox("Enter comma-separated
list of keywords:", "Edit Keywords", sKeyword)
                oChildTag.setAttribute "CONTENT", sKeyword
                isDirty = True
            End If
        End If
    Next
```

The key here is the use of another property of the Tag element object: getAttribute and setAttribute. These enable you to identify keyword <META> tags and then put their current content in the input box for editing.

Notice that another flag, IsDirty, also is set, indicating that the page has already been edited. You need to add a check for this before you start adding the code that adds a new keyword tag. To do this, you add the following code around the block of code discussed in Step 4:

```
If Not IsDirty Then
....code...
End If
```

Now you have a fairly functional macro. You can use it to add keywords quickly to your Web pages (see the sample results in Figure 22-13). Now, if only you had a feature to add the keywords to every page...

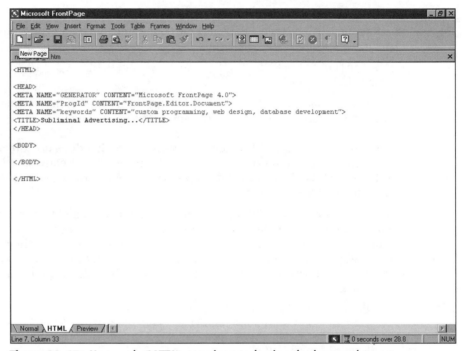

Figure 22-13: Keyword <META> tags inserted using the keyword macro

6. This keyword macro isn't meant to provide comprehensive error checking, but one error that is fairly important to check for is that you actually have an active document to work with. Presently, if you try to run this macro with no open document, FrontPage returns an Operation Failed message. This isn't particularly informative to the user, and if you try to run the macro from within VBE, it does not even run.

A better solution is to trap for errors yourself, and then return a more informative message to the user. To do this, first add an On Error Resume Next statement near the beginning of the subroutine. This ensures that the program will carry on, even after an error is encountered. Trapping any errors and reporting them back is your responsibility.

For now, you'll do this when you first begin to work with the ActiveDocument element. If no active document exists, you need to stop the macro and alert the user. Here is the code that traps an error:

```
If Err.Number > 0 Then
        MsgBox ("You must open a Web page document before
using this macro.")
        End
    End If
```

Place this code right after the beginning of the `For` loop that identifies the `all` collection of the `ActiveDocument` element. This is the line that fails if no `ActiveDocument` element is present. Now, try it by closing all documents.

7. Now that you have this time-saving macro, you can use the following steps to access it with a single click of a button, rather than selecting Tools ⇨ Macro ⇨ Macros, choosing the correct Macro, and then clicking the Run button:

   a. Select Tools ⇨ Customize and click the Commands tab. Scroll through the Categories list and select Macros. Drag the Custom Button icon from the Commands list to the location on the toolbar where you want the custom button to appear. (Alternatively, drag the Custom Menu Item from the Commands list and drop it on a menu.)

   b. Right-click the custom button to bring up its Options menu. Change the name of the button to **&Keywords**, select a new button icon (the key works nicely, I think), select Assign Macro from the options, and choose the EditKeywords macro. Click OK to close the Customize dialog box. Now, you can access your favorite macros with a single click.

Creating Design-Time Controls

A *design-time control (DTC)* is an ActiveX control inserted into FrontPage 2000 that enables simplified development of some aspect of a Web page. In essence, DTCs work much like the FrontPage Components discussed in Chapter 13. The main difference is that the FrontPage Components are designed exclusively for use by FrontPage, whereas DTCs are intended more as general-purpose tools and are built by using the same ActiveX standards that apply to run-time ActiveX controls.

Basically, a DTC presents the Web page designer with a list of properties that they can configure for the control. The control itself produces HTML text that is added to the page at run time, for example, when the page is viewed by a browser. The viewer never sees the control, only the text that it generated (or, more precisely, they see the HTML page generated by the text that was generated by the DTC).

Note If the DTC option is disabled, you probably don't have any controls registered yet. (It can also mean that you don't have a server-based Web open.)

Using Design-Time Controls

To add an existing DTC to your Web page, follow these steps (see the next section, "Creating Design-Time Controls," to find out how to make and register your own DTCs):

1. Open the Web page into which you want to insert the control, and locate the cursor at the desired location.

2. Select Insert ⇨ Advanced ⇨ Design-Time Control to open the Insert Design-Time Control dialog box.

3. If the control that you want to use is listed in this dialog box, select it and click OK to add it to the page.

4. If the control is not listed, click the Customize button to see a list of all registered controls. Check the item that you want to add to the Insert list and click OK to return to the Insert DTC dialog box. Select the DTC and click OK to add it to the page. Note that you can remove items from the list by unchecking a checked item in the Customize dialog box.

Creating Design-Time Controls

DTCs can't be created in VBE, the macro development tool discussed in the previous examples. (Why not, you ask? Mainly because VBE is not capable of creating executable code.) You can create DTCs in any programming language capable of creating COM objects (aka ActiveX controls). To follow the next tutorial, you need two things: the DTC SDK, available for download from Microsoft's Web site, and Visual Basic.

Note   To create a DTC, you can use either the version 1 DTC SDK, or the version 6 SDK that accompanies Visual Studio 6. The following example is created with the older SDK that is available (as of this writing) from Microsoft's Web site.

In the following tutorial you are going to generate a control that is a simple illustration of the method used to create a DTC. The goal is to create an easy way to insert simple ASP code into your Web page without invoking Microsoft Script Editor.

Tutorial 22.3: Create an ASP DTC

1. Download and install the SDK, if you don't already have it. The SDK includes the Type Library webdc.tlb, samples and documentation, and a utility, Regsvrdc.exe, for registering your control as a DTC. The SDK is available from Microsoft's Web site.

2. Create a new DTC project. Start VB 5 and create an ActiveX control project by selecting File ⇨ New Project and selecting the Active X control in the New tab. Select Project ⇨ Project1 Properties from the menu bar and rename the project **SimpleASP**.

   VB has automatically created a UserControl for you. This control has no real functionality in a DTC. It is, however, displayed in the Normal view of FrontPage when you insert the DTC into a Web page. It is not displayed when the page is viewed in a browser.

Select the UserControl and change its Name Property to **ASPDTC**. Add a Label control and change its Caption to **ASPDTC**. You can change other properties if you like to make the control more aesthetically pleasing (or not, it's up to you). For example, see Figure 22-14.

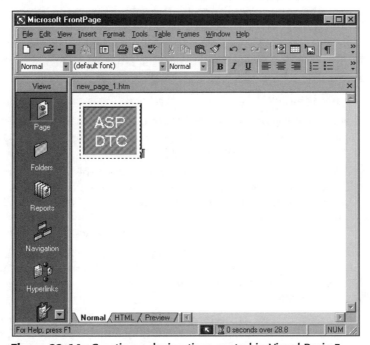

Figure 22-14: Creating a design-time control in Visual Basic 5

3. Add a reference to the DTC Type Library. This step converts your ActiveX control from a standard control to a DTC. Select Project ⇨ References from the menu bar. If you have not yet added the DTC Type Library to VB's list, select Browse and locate the webdc.tlb file. The SDK installation puts it in Samples \VB\Common folder in the installation directory that you selected. Select Open to add a reference to Microsoft Web Design-Time Control Type Library to the list. Click this item to select it, and click OK to return to your control.

Note that after this Type Library is loaded, it remains in the list, but you still have to select it each time that you create a new DTC.

4. Add a custom property member. Next, you create a Properties dialog box that is accessed by double-clicking the DTC UserControl. To create this interface, you use the ActiveX Control Interface Wizard. Select Add-Ins from the menu. If VB ActiveX Control Interface Wizard is listed as one of the loaded add-ins, select it. If it is not, select Add-Ins Manager and select the Wizard from the list. Click OK to return and then select the add-in.

The first screen of the Wizard is informational only, so click Next to begin using the Wizard. In the Select Interface Members screen, remove all members from the Selected Names list by clicking the Remove All button (indicated by double left-pointing arrows, <<). Click Next.

In the Create Custom Interface Members screen, click New. Enter **AspCode** in the Name textbox and select Property (the default) from the Type options. Click OK to return to the Wizard. Continue to the next screen.

In the Set Mapping screen, select UserControl in the Control list in the Maps To section. Click Next. In the Set Attributes screen, select String as the Data Type and add

```
= ""Put ASP code here!""
```

as the Default Value (note the double set of quotation marks to avoid syntax problems later on). Click Finish to complete the Wizard. Click Close to close the summary information provided by the Wizard.

5. Select Project ➪ Add Property Page and double-click the VB Property Page Wizard. Click Add and enter **ppgAspCode** as the name of the Property Page. Click OK and then click Next. Select the custom property, AspCode, from the list of available properties to place on this page, and then click the single right arrow (>) to add it to the Property Page. Click Finish to complete the Wizard.

   You can edit the layout of the Property Page (see Figure 22-15) by clicking the ppgAspCode form. You may want to enlarge the textbox area for inputting ASP code, and edit the label caption and the Property Page caption (which becomes the tab label).

6. Select Tools ➪ Procedure Attributes. Select the AspCode property from the Name list and click the Advanced button. Choose ppgAspCode from the Use This Page in Property Browser list. Click OK to close the dialog box.

7. Code the Text procedure. Open the code window for the UserControl. Add the following line to the general declarations section at the top of the code:

   Implements IProvideRuntimeText

   Select the IProvideRuntimeText item from the object list and add the following to the IProvideRuntimeText_GetRuntimeText() function:

```
Private Function IProvideRuntimeText_GetRuntimeText() As
String
Dim sDTCStr As String
Dim sCRLF As String
sCRLF = Chr$(13)
sDTCStr = "<% " & m_AspCode & " %>" & sCRLF
IProvideRuntimeText_GetRuntimeText = sDTCStr
End Function
```

8. Register the control and the DTC. Save the project. Select File ➪ Make SimpleASP.ocx to compile the control. Open a DOS window and change to the directory in which you saved the OCX files. Register the control by issuing the following command at the DOS prompt:

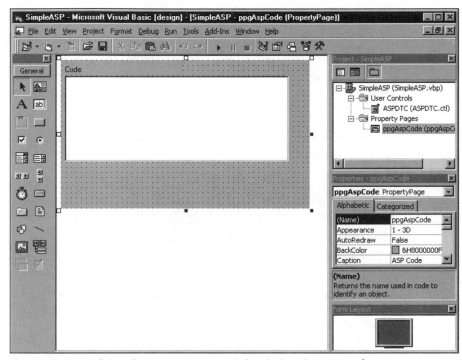

Figure 22-15: Editing the Property Page of the design-time control

```
Regsvr32 SimpleASP.ocx
```

Regsvr32 should return a message box indicating "DLLRegisterService in SimpleASP.ocx succeeded."

> **Tip**
>
> At this point, you can adjust the default name of the control using the Registry.

This command registers the control as an ActiveX control. In addition, you need to register your control as a DTC. To do this, you need to use the tool provided in the version 1 SDK. To use this DOS command, change directories to the folder in which this executable is stored and issue the following command at the DOS prompt:

```
regsvrdc SimpleASP.ASPDTC
```

This command should respond with a DOS response: "Successfully registered SimpleASP.ASPDTC."

9. Test the control.

Open FrontPage, and open a new Web page. Select Insert ➪ Advanced ➪ Design Time Controls. In the Design-Time Control dialog box, select Customize. SimpleASP.ASPDTC should appear in the list of registered DTCs (see Figure 22-16). Select it to check the box next to it, and click OK to add it to the list of loaded controls.

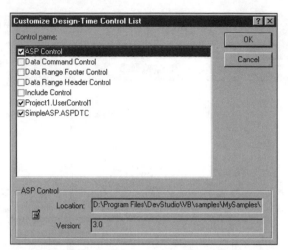

Figure 22-16: Loading your new DTC into FrontPage

Select your new DTC in the DTC dialog box and click OK to insert the control into your Web page. This inserts the UserControl interface as you designed it. Double-click the user control to open the Property Page with the default text. You can leave it as is or insert some other valid ASP code.

Save the page to a folder that has permissions set to run ASP code (see Chapter 18 for details on how to set up a folder to run ASP). Test the page by previewing it in a browser.

Creating Custom Page and Web Wizards

In the Windows world, a *wizard* refers to an application that helps you perform a particular task by walking you through a series of simple steps. FrontPage comes with numerous wizards that can simplify the task of creating a new Web page or a new Web.

You can also create your own wizards. This is particularly useful if you find yourself repeatedly creating the same type of page — or set of pages — with some minor modifications. Of course, you can also create your own wizard just to prove that you are a wizard yourself.

FrontPage supports two kinds of wizards:

✦ **Page wizards:** Create a single Web page. These wizards are accessed when you select File ➪ New ➪ Page. An example is the Form Page Wizard.

✦ **Web wizards:** Create a multipage Web. These wizards are accessed when you select File ➪ New ➪ Web. Examples include the Corporate Presence Wizard and the Discussion Web Wizard.

At the time this book was going to press, Microsoft had not yet released an updated SDK for wizard development. As a consequence, the following examples discuss the Wizard SDK examples distributed with FrontPage 98. These examples use a legacy object model rather than the FrontPage 2000 Object Model described earlier in this chapter.

Creating custom wizards

Creating your own wizards involves real programming, and it is not for everyone. However, Microsoft has released a Software Development Kit for FrontPage that includes some examples and code libraries that you can use to simplify the task. This section illustrates the process of creating a wizard by using these examples.

To create your own wizard, you need to have Visual Basic 5 or greater. Unfortunately, you can't use the Visual Basic Editor that comes with FrontPage. The FrontPage Web wizards are standalone executables, which VBE is not capable of generating.

The FrontPage SDK

The FrontPage SDK includes the following sample wizards, including both compiled versions and source code for Visual Basic:

✦ **Hello Wizard:** A simple page wizard

✦ **Calendar Wizard:** A more sophisticated page wizard that produces a calendar page

✦ **Hello Web Wizard:** A simple Web wizard

✦ **Real Estate Wizard:** A more advanced Web wizard that produces a real estate Web

In addition to these samples, the SDK provides three Visual Basic modules:

All three of these modules contain legacy code. Although they are still supported in FrontPage 2000, they have been replaced by the Object Model, discussed earlier in this chapter.

✦ **Botgen.bas:** Procedures related to creating FrontPage Components

✦ **HTMLgen.bas:** Procedures for creating HTML text

✦ **Wizutil.bas:** Procedures for initializing FrontPage Webs and Web pages

Note   The SDK also includes detailed instructions on creating wizards in a word document, FPDevkit.doc.

Note   If you have a copy of FrontPage 98, you will find the Hello Wizard on the CD-ROM, in SDK/Wizards/Pages. You can also download the SDK from the Microsoft FrontPage Web site.

Using the Hello Wizard

Using the example wizard source files and utility files provided in the SDK greatly simplifies the task of creating a FrontPage wizard. To illustrate how easy it is to create a customized wizard, you will make some minor modifications to the Hello Wizard, a simple wizard written in Visual Basic that is part of the SDK, to create a Contact Page Wizard.

Start Visual Basic and open the Hello Wizard project file, hello.vbp. The project file consists of a form, hello.frm, and a programming module, wizutil.bas. Open the form, as shown in Figure 22-17. In general, wizard forms consist of a single form object and multiple frame objects that comprise the wizard panels. The Hello Wizard contains three frames. You can see them all if you increase the size of the form and then move the frames so that they are not on top of one another.

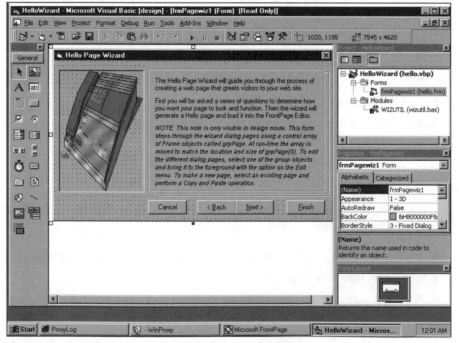

Figure 22-17: Editing the Hello Wizard in Visual Basic 5

The first screen simply introduces the Hello Wizard. The second screen takes useful (or potentially useful) information from the user and turns it into Web page content. The third screen identifies the name and location of the page to be created.

Editing the wizard form

To explore the Hello Wizard, you will make a few simple changes to the wizard form. To that end, you will add a panel to the Wizard to collect contact information to put into your Web page. This panel enables users to enter their name, phone number, and e-mail address, with an option to hyperlink their e-mail address automatically.

Step one of the Wizard is to add a new Frame control and then add the input controls needed to collect contact information. Add name, phone, and e-mail labels and call them **lblName**, **lblPhone**, and **lblEmail**. Add textbox controls for each, as well, calling them **txtName**, **txtPhone**, and **txtEmail**. Add an inner frame control and enter **E-mail Hyperlink** as its caption. Add two radio buttons with **Yes** and **No** captions. Set the default value of the Yes button to **True** and the No button to **False**.

You need to change the name of the new frame control so that it appears in the right order in the wizard (after the greeting frame and before the URL frame). To do this, you need to adjust the indexes on the grpPage array that constitutes the collection of frame elements. Select the last frame, originally grpPage(2) and change its Index property to **3**. Rename the new frame that you just created to **grpPage** and set its Index property to **2**.

You now need to make a few minor code adjustments to accommodate your new panel. Double-click the form to open its code page. Select the Form object and go to the Form_Load subroutine. This is the procedure that is called when the form is loaded. It contains a variable, maxpage, that is set to 2. Change it so that maxpage is set to **3**.

While you are in the Form_Load subroutine, you need to comment out a conditional statement that does not work properly in FrontPage 2000. The section to remove contains the following code:

```
If Len(WizardPageURL) > 0 Then
   'do not include the page/url dialog
   maxpage = 1
   txtURL = WizardPageURL
End If
```

You can delete these lines completely or comment them out by placing a single quotation mark (') in front of each.

The last step is to revise the output generated when the user clicks the Finish button at the end of the wizard. When this happens, the wizard calls a subroutine, GeneratePage, whose job it is to create the new HTML page. Select General from the object list in the form code page and select GeneratePage from the procedure list. This routine creates the file through several Print statements to a newly created file. You can edit this page in any way that you like. At least, you need to add lines that use the new inputs that you have added to the wizard.

> **Tip**
> You may sense that the method the Hello Wizard uses to generate HTML is not the most efficient. To see an example of a somewhat more efficient method, take a look at the more sophisticated SDK samples, the Calendar Page Wizard and the Real Estate Web Wizard.

The following code creates a contact page:

```
Print #fn, "<B>Name:</B> " & txtName.Text & "<P>"
Print #fn, "<B>Phone:</B> " & txtPhone.Text & "<P>"
If optEmail(0) Then
    Print #fn, "<A HREF=""mailto:" & txtEmail.Text & """>"
End If
Print #fn, "<B>Email:</B> " & txtEmail.Text & "<P>"
If optEmail(0) Then
    Print #fn, "</A>"
End If
```

After you make these changes, save and recompile the wizard code as **contact.exe** and place it in the contact.wiz subfolder of the pages folder.

To test your wizard, open FrontPage and select File ➪ New ➪ Page. You should see a new wizard, Contact Wizard, listed. Double-click it to start the wizard (see Figure 22-18).

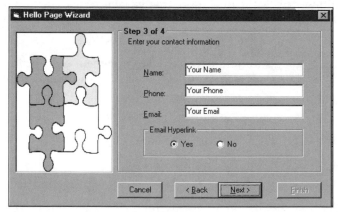

Figure 22-18: A new wizard is born.

Using Add-Ins

Add-ins, a new feature in FrontPage 2000, are programs, typically supplied by third-party developers, that extend the capabilities of FrontPage. You can also write your own custom add-ins, using Visual Basic or Visual C++. Creation of add-ins is beyond the scope of this book, but if you are curious, Visual Basic includes both an Add-in template and documentation on this topic.

Most users encounter add-ins only when installing and using a commercially developed add-in. The remainder of this section focuses on using add-ins in FrontPage 2000. Typically, an add-in comes with an installation program. After installing the add-in, you need to load or unload the add-in into FrontPage.

Ad-ins are loaded and unloaded by using the Add-in Manager, accessible from the Add-in item in the Tools menu.

To load an add-in, select Tools ➪ Add-ins, select it from the list of available add-ins, and then select the Loaded/unloaded check box. To load an add-in automatically when you start FrontPage, click it in the list of available add-ins and then select the Load on Startup check box. To load an add-in from the command prompt or from a script, click it in the list of available add-ins, and then select the Command Line check box. To unload an add-in, click it in the list of available add-ins and then deselect its Loaded/unloaded check box.

Summary

This chapter has looked at a variety of ways to customize how FrontPage works for you, ranging from nonprogramming customizations to some fairly sophisticated components that you can add to FrontPage to make it work for you. The final chapter discusses issues related to setting up, configuring, and maintaining Web servers that support FrontPage.

✦   ✦   ✦

FrontPage Server Administration

This chapter explains how FrontPage interacts with Web servers. The focus of attention is on FrontPage Server Extensions (FSE)—what they do, how they do it, and how you install and configure them using Microsoft Personal Web Server (PWS) and Internet Information Server (IIS). The chapter also describes the FrontPage security model and how it integrates with Windows NT security.

Note This chapter is intended for those who have the job of setting up and maintaining Web servers to work with FrontPage. See Chapter 3 for detailed information on how to publish Webs and Web pages to a Web server with FrontPage.

FrontPage Server Extensions

For FrontPage to manage Webs, permit Web page authoring, and provide the enhanced Web page Component functionality, it needs some means of communicating with a Web server. If you have read Chapter 3 on publishing FrontPage Webs, you realize that FrontPage is capable of sending Web pages to any server that is using standard FTP protocols. In this scenario, however, FrontPage functionality is limited to standard Web page authoring. To take advantage of the enhanced FrontPage features, you need to install and configure FrontPage Server Extensions (FSE) on your Web server.

The following section provides a quick tour of FSE. The information presented here is largely excerpted from Microsoft's *FrontPage Server Extension Resource Kit (SERK)*. If you are planning to install and use FSE, you should obtain the current copy of the SERK and read it carefully. The current version of the SERK is available from Microsoft's Web site at `www.microsoft.com/frontpage/wpp/serk`.

Exploring server extensions

FSE is a set of lightweight executable programs that are added to the Web server to enable the FrontPage application to communicate with the Web server. FrontPage Server Extensions come in two basic varieties: the versions designed for Windows platforms are written as *Dynamic Link Libraries (DLLs)*; the UNIX versions are written as standard C program executables CGI applications. When you install FSE on your Web server, the installation creates a Root FrontPage Web on each virtual server managed by the Web server, and then installs these executables (as well as administrative information) in that Web. Each subsequent Web (or subweb) that you create in turn creates a separate stub copy of these applications in the new Web.

The installation process creates several administrative folders in each Web, all having names that begin with _vti. The most significant folders and their content are identified as follows:

✦ **_vti_bin:** Contains the main FSE executables that perform key FrontPage functions.

✦ **Web Page Authoring (*author.dll/author.exe*):** Keeps track of the location, hyperlinks, and other aspects of Web pages.

✦ **Web Administration (*admin.dll/admin.exe*):** Handles user permissions and passwords.

✦ **FrontPage Components (*shtml.dll/shtml.exe*):** Provides run-time functionality to the Web page, substituting the Component tags with valid HTML.

Note In IIS, these executables are written as ISAPI DLLs and are stored, by default, in Common Files\Microsoft Shared\Web Server Extensions\version4.0\isapi.

✦ **_vti_cnf:** Contains configuration files, one per Web page, containing information that FrontPage uses for file management and other tasks. These files have identical names to the Web pages that they describe.

✦ **_vti_pvt:** Contains miscellaneous files that FrontPage uses to manage Web and file operations.

Note Are you curious about why all of these folders start with _vti? Before Microsoft acquired FrontPage, it was a product developed by Vermeer Technologies, Inc. The company has long since been absorbed into the Microsoft juggernaut, but VTI has left its stamp on the FSE naming conventions.

Note   FSE is provided on the FrontPage CD-ROM. The Windows versions are in the ServExt subfolder. UNIX versions are in the UNIX subfolder. Current versions of FSE can be downloaded from the FrontPage section of the Microsoft Web site, at www.microsoft.com/frontpage/wpp/serk.

Communicating with the server

The FrontPage client communicates with a server via standard HTTP POST requests sent to the extension executables. Because all communication takes place via standard HTTP protocols, FrontPage is able to work across a firewall. So, for example, you can develop content inside the company firewall and publish it to a public Web server, or work on your company intranet from home (provided the firewall permits HTTP traffic). (See "FrontPage Security," later in the chapter, for more information on this topic.)

Supported platforms and servers

Because FrontPage Server Extensions are standard CGI programs, they work with any Web server that supports the CGI standard (which means virtually all Web servers). When you install a Microsoft Web server, such as PWS (described later in this chapter) or IIS, FSE is automatically installed. On other platforms and/or servers, you must install FSE manually. Two flavors of FSE exist: Those that run on Windows operating systems are DLLs, and the UNIX varieties are standard C executables. Table 23-1 shows the list of supported platforms and servers.

Table 23-1	
Servers Supported by UNIX and Windows	
Operating Systems	**Web Servers**
UNIX	Digital UNIX 3.2c, 4 (Alpha)
	BSD/OS 2.1 (Intel x86)
	BSD/OS 3 (Intel x86)
	Linux 3.03 (Red Hat Software) (Intel x86)
	HP/UX 9.03, 10.01 (PA-RISC)
	IRIX 5.3, 6.2 (Silicon Graphics)
	Solaris 2.4, 2.5 (SPARC)
	SunOS 4.1.3, 4.1.4 (SPARC)
	AIX 3.2.5, 4.1, 4.2 (RS6000, PowerPC)
	SCO OpenServer 5 (Intel X86)

Continued

Table 23-1 (continued)	
Operating Systems	**Web Servers**
UNIX (continued)	Apache 1.1.3, 1.2
	CERN 3
	NCSA 1.5.2
	Netscape Commerce Server 1.12
	Netscape Communications Server 1.12
	Netscape Enterprise Server 2, 3
	Netscape FastTrack 2
Windows NT Server, Intel x86	IIS 2 or higher, including IIS 4
Windows NT Workstation, Intel x86	Netscape Commerce Server 1.12
	Netscape Communications Server 1.12
	Netscape Enterprise Server 2, 3
	Netscape FastTrack 2
	O'Reilly WebSite
	FrontPage Personal Web Server
Windows NT Server, Alpha	IIS 2 or higher, including IIS 4
Windows NT Workstation, Alpha	Peer Web Services (on NT Workstation)
Windows 95	Personal Web Server (on Windows 95)
	FrontPage Personal Web Server
	Netscape FastTrack 2
	O'Reilly WebSite

Note   Although not mentioned in this list, Microsoft also has available a Macintosh version of the PWS for those who want to use FrontPage with a Macintosh Web server. No set of server extensions currently exists for the popular WebStar Web server, however.

Supported features

Many of FrontPage 2000's Web management and Web page authoring features require the presence of FSE to function. These features are unavailable to FrontPage users who don't have access to a Web server with FSE installed. The following are FrontPage's Web features:

✦ **Hyperlink mapping:** Provides graphical mapping of all hyperlinks on a given Web page.

✦ **Full text indexing:** Enables the search engine functionality.

✦ **Persistent structure:** The structure of Webs is related to, but distinct from, the Web server file system structure.

✦ **Web Themes:** Associates a set of graphical images, buttons, backgrounds, banners, and so on, with a Web

✦ **Task list:** Maintains the tasks to be performed for a Web.

✦ **Security settings:** Enable separate Webs to be configured for use by different users or groups.

✦ **FrontPage Components:** Includes, but is not limited to, the Search Form handler, e-mail handler, Discussion Form handler, and Database Form handler.

Installing FrontPage Server Extensions

Several ways exist to install FSE. When you install FrontPage, you can install or upgrade your Web server's server extensions automatically. You can also install FSE if you subsequently install either PWS 4 or IIS 4. In this case, too, FSE is added automatically during installation of the server. The last alternative is to download the latest version of FSE from Microsoft's Web site.

Using older versions of the extensions

FrontPage 2000 can be used with a Web server that has an older version of FSE. The most likely scenario is one in which you don't control the server that you use to host your Web site. In this case, FrontPage works compatibly with the older version of FSE, but you can't use the newer features of FrontPage 2000 that depend on the FrontPage 2000 Server Extensions. Likewise, you can use FrontPage 98 with a Web server that has the FrontPage 2000 Server Extensions, although you will only have FrontPage 98 functionality available to you.

Caution According to the SERK, IIS 4 is not compatible with versions of FSE prior to FrontPage 98.

Converting disk-based Webs

In most cases, you install FrontPage and FSE after you install your Web server. However, you may have previously used FrontPage without a server, by creating disk-based Webs. If and when you do bring up a server, you can convert your disk-based Webs to server-based Webs. The basic procedure is as follows:

1. Open the disk-based Web that you want to convert.

2. Select File ➪ Publish Web.

3. Enter the URL of the server as the destination.

Administering FrontPage Server Extensions

After you install FSE and have FrontPage configured and running, FSE requires very little maintenance. In fact, FSE includes utilities for installing, updating, removing, and checking the Server Extensions in both the root Web and all subwebs.

This section describes several of the most commonly encountered methods of administering FSE, beginning with a historical look at the server administrator utility that is used with FrontPage 98 Server Extensions.

The FrontPage MMC snap-in

Previous versions of FrontPage used an administrative utility called fpsrvwin. In FrontPage 2000, this utility has been replaced by a FrontPage snap-in to Microsoft Management Console (MMC).

MMC is a "shell" application intended to provide a consistent interface for administration of Windows services. Administration programs are written as *snap-ins* to MMC, meaning that their functionality gets added to the MMC shell. When you start an MMC snap-in, it loads into MMC.

You may interact with the FrontPage snap-in as a standalone utility if you are using FrontPage with a Window 95/98 Web server or with a non-IIS server on Windows NT. If you are using Microsoft IIS 4, the FrontPage snap-in simply adds its functionality to the existing IIS snap-in, and you access it by starting the IIS snap-in.

Using the FrontPage snap-in

This section describes the basic procedure for accessing the FrontPage snap-in functionality for an IIS server. After this section, some of the operations that you can perform by using the FrontPage snap-in are listed.

To access the FrontPage snap-in, start Internet Service Manager. MMC starts, as shown in Figure 23-1.

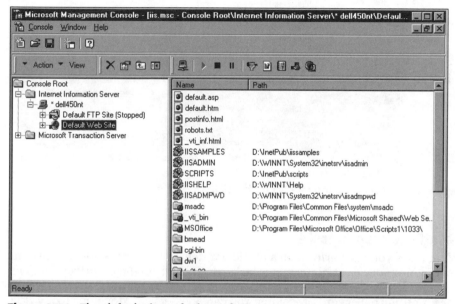

Figure 23-1: The default view of Microsoft Management Console with the IIS snap-in

MMC shows a tree directory of the Webs and folders in the Web server's document directory. To perform a FrontPage-related task, select a Web or folder, select Action ⇨ Task from the toolbar at the top of MMC, and then select the desired task. Alternatively, as shown in Figure 23-2, you can right-click an item in MMC, select Task, and then choose from among the available tasks.

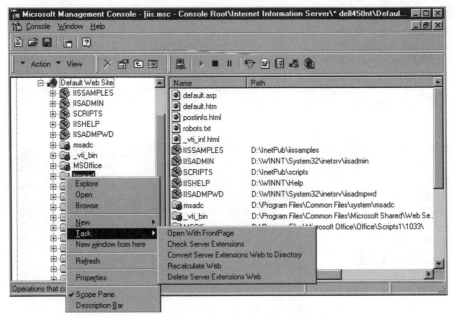

Figure 23-2: Accessing the task list in the IIS MMC

FrontPage snap-in tasks

What tasks you can perform on a particular item in MMC depends on the item. This section provides a list of the major tasks available from the FrontPage snap-in:

✦ **Configure Server Extensions:** You can add Server Extensions to a virtual server or subweb. Select Task ➪ Configure Server Extensions.

✦ **Remove Server Extensions:** You can remove Server Extensions from a Web or subweb by selecting Task ➪ Remove Server Extensions.

✦ **Check and fix Server Extensions:** Occasionally, FrontPage gets out of synch with the files in a Web. Use this function to find and repair the problem. This function can also be used to check on the permission settings on the files in a Web. Select Task ➪ Check Server Extensions.

✦ **Upgrade Server Extensions:** If a FrontPage upgrade is available, select Task ➪ Upgrade Extensions.

✦ **Create a subweb:** Select New ➪ Server Extensions Web.

✦ **Delete a subweb:** Select Task ➪ Delete Publishing Web to delete both the Web and its content.

✦ **Add an administrator to a Web or subweb:** Select New ➪ Server Extensions Administrator.

✦ **Convert folders and subwebs:** You can convert folders to subwebs and vice versa. Select either Task ➪ Convert Directory to Web or Task ➪ Convert Web to Directory, as relevant.

✦ **Open a Web in FrontPage:** If FrontPage is available on the Web server, you can use this task to launch a Web. Select Task ➪ Open Web in FrontPage.

Setting Web properties

In addition to the FrontPage functions available via the Task menu, you can set a variety of Web properties by using the Properties menu. To access the Properties dialog box for a Web or subweb, select the item and click Action ➪ Properties, or right-click the item and select Properties from the option menu. Select the Server Extensions tab, as shown in Figure 23-3, which includes the following options:

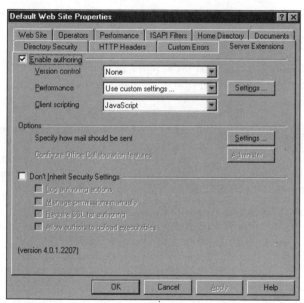

Figure 23-3: The FrontPage Server Extensions tab in the MMC Properties dialog box

✦ **Enable Authoring:** Uncheck this item to disable authoring from a Web.

✦ **Version Control:** Select an available version control utility from the drop-down list.

✦ **Performance:** Choose a performance selection from the drop-down list or click the Settings button to configure manually.

✦ **Client Scripting:** Select a default client scripting language (JavaScript or VBScript).

✦ **Configure E-mail:** Click Settings to enable e-mail on this Web or subweb.

✦ **Configure Security Settings:** By default, subwebs inherit security settings from the parent Web. Check Don't Inherit Security Settings to configure settings separately for a Web or subweb. Security settings that you can configure include:

- Log authoring actions

- Manage permissions manually

- Require SSL for authoring

- Allow authors to upload executables

Other Administrative Tools

If you are running a server that can't use MMC, you can use three other mechanisms to perform administrative tasks (detailed descriptions are available in the SERK):

✦ **Fpsrvadm utility:** For local, command-line functions; the main application for administering FSE. It is a command-line program on both UNIX and Windows NT. Use this utility to install, update, remove, and repair Server Extensions on FrontPage Webs. For specifics on the command-line operations and options available for fpsrvadm, consult the SERK.

✦ **Fpremadm utility:** Enables remote access to Windows servers. Like the fpsrvadm utility, fpremadm is used to install, update, remove, and repair FSE, and it is intended specifically for remote administration of FSE in a Windows environment. (If you need to be able to perform remote administration of a non-Windows server, you can use HTML Administration Forms, described next.) For details on the command-line operations and options available for fpremadm, consult the SERK. To use fpremadm, you must first enable HTML Administration Forms, because both use the same CGI (or DLL) applications.

✦ **HTML Administrative Forms:** Enable remote access to Web server administration via a Web browser. For security reasons, these forms are not installed by default. You should read and understand the security implications in the SERK before electing to install and use these forms. For details on installing and using HTML Administration Forms, consult the SERK.

FrontPage Security

The issue of security is one of the main reasons for hesitation by companies looking to add FSE to their Web servers, especially for use in Internet applications. As in most security-related matters, the key question that you need to ask is whether FrontPage is secure enough. The fact that it seamlessly updates files between FrontPage and the Web server is a large bonus. However, the ease with which this can be done is accomplished only by means of some openness in the flow of data.

One advantage of having FrontPage transfer files via HTTP is that FrontPage works with a secure server using Secure Socket Layers (SSL) to encrypt all content. In this case, not only is the content between Web server and users encrypted, but the same is true for content passed between the FrontPage client and the Web server.

Windows NT security

If you are using IIS on Windows NT, FrontPage uses NTFS Access Control Lists (ACLs) as the basis for setting permissions. Users can't be created in FrontPage. You add users to a FrontPage Web by selecting them from a list of valid NT users. When the user initiates an action that requires permission, FrontPage sends the username and password that the user logged in with.

If you are using Microsoft PWS 4, you can't set permissions for your Webs. All users on the network — whether an intranet or the Internet — can browse to your Webs. Authoring and administering Webs must be performed from the computer that is running the Web server. PWS 4 thus isn't a good option if you are working on a development site that you don't want to be accessible for general viewing.

Note   Earlier versions of PWS are capable of working with user lists if they are connected to a network server that can provide a list of valid users.

UNIX and Non-IIS security

The standard means of maintaining security on a Web server is through the use of ACLs. Typically, these ACLs are maintained separately from the list of user accounts on the system. For most non-IIS servers, FrontPage uses this ACL mechanism to create and authenticate users, authors, and administrators. The steps required to add and remove users, set user permission levels, and change passwords are described later in the chapter.

Using FrontPage with a proxy server

Many networks use a firewall to protect internal information from the prying eyes of the outside world. A *firewall* is a generic term for any mechanism — whether hardware, software, or both — that restricts the flow of bytes (sometimes referred to as *network traffic*) across a network. How firewalls do this varies, but one common method is to filter out certain protocols while allowing other protocols. For example, a firewall might permit outward-bound Web traffic, but prohibit FTP or telnet. Another example is the case in which the firewall permits outbound traffic only to a specific list of destinations.

In most cases, networks that have a firewall in place also use *proxy servers* to enable basic network services, such as HTTP, without compromising the security of their network. In this scenario, all requests go to the proxy server, which determines whether to let the requests through. It then collects any responses and returns those to the requestor.

If you are working with a proxy server, you need to instruct FrontPage to use it. To configure FrontPage, select Options and click the Proxy Settings button in the General tab (see Figure 23-4).

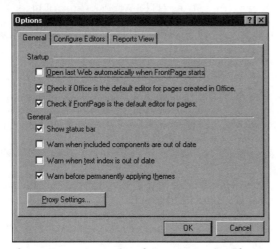

Figure 23-4: Accessing the Proxy Settings button in the Options dialog box

Clicking the Proxy Settings button opens the Internet Explorer Internet Properties dialog box, in which general information about network connections is kept. If you are accessing your Web server via a LAN, click the LAN Settings button. If you access your Web server via a dial-up account (in this scenario, you most likely are outside the firewall and the server is inside), click the Settings button in the Dial-Up Settings section.

In the Connection Settings dialog box, shown in Figure 23-5, check the Use a Proxy Server option and type the complete domain name or IP number of the proxy server. Include the port number (the default for HTTP services is 80). If you need to configure the proxy server for multiple services, click the Advanced button.

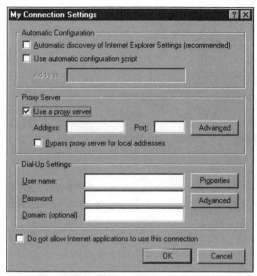

Figure 23-5: Setting a proxy server to use with FrontPage

FrontPage User Administration

FrontPage includes tools for configuring user levels in FrontPage Webs at either the root Web level or the level of individual subwebs. In either scenario, you can set three levels of control:

✦ **Browser Access:** Allows users to view Web pages

✦ **Author Access:** Allows users to create, edit, delete, and view pages

✦ **Administrator Access:** Allows users to change settings, add new Webs, and perform other administrative tasks, in addition to having full Author and Browser Access permissions

Note

For IIS Web servers running on Windows NT, administrators are given Administrator Access to FrontPage by default.

To control permissions, you must either have administrator-level authority or use a site with no active access controls in place. Using FrontPage, you can add new users, add new groups, and modify or delete either users or groups.

Adding users and groups

If you are using PWS 4, your security option is disabled. Likewise, if you do not have a server-based Web open, security is turned off.

In FrontPage, select Tools ➪ Security ➪ Permissions to display the Permissions dialog box. The tabs on this dialog box vary, depending on whether you are in the current Web. The root Web, shown in Figure 23-6, has three tabs:

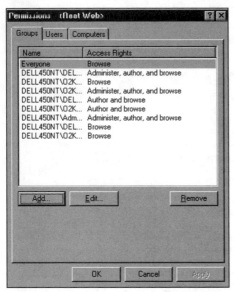

Figure 23-6: Setting permissions for the root Web

✦ **Groups:** Lists the names and access rights of any existing groups

✦ **Users:** Defines a list of users who have access to the Web server and can make changes on it

✦ **Computers**: Defines who can and cannot use the service, by referring to the IP number, domain name, or the computer used to access the Web

Within each tab, you can add, modify, and delete entries. Users and groups can be granted permission either to browse the Web, to browse and author Web pages, or to browse, author, and administer the Web. Access to a Web can be restricted by using either or both users and groups.

To add a user or group, select the appropriate tab, click the Add button, choose a server or domain from the Obtain List From pull-down menu, and then add one or more groups from the Names list to the Add Names list. For each set of groups that you add, you can select the level of access that you want to assign to them. Designate whether all users or only specified users have Browse Access of the Web. If you don't grant Browse Access to all users, users will be asked to enter a username and password when they browse the Web site (see Figure 23-7). When you are satisfied with your additions, click OK to complete the task.

Figure 23-7: User authentication dialog box in FrontPage

Editing an existing user or group

After you add a user or group to FrontPage, you can modify their permission level. Open the Permissions dialog box by selecting Tools ➪ Security ➪ Permissions and then select the user or group from the appropriate tab. Select Edit and then select a new user level from the dialog box provided. Click OK.

Deleting a user or group

To delete a user or group, open the Permissions tab and select the user or group to be deleted. Click Remove.

Caution

Before you click Remove, make sure that you want to remove the group or user, because FrontPage does *not* prompt you to confirm this option.

Limiting access to particular computers

In addition to being able to specify certain users who have permission to author and administer FrontPage, you can restrict access based on individual computers or on a group of computers. To do this, use the computer's IP number. Select the Computers tab and click Add. Using the Add Computer dialog box, shown in Figure 23-8, you can specify individual computers by IP, or a range of computers by using wildcard characters.

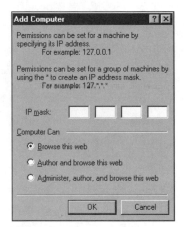

Figure 23-8: Restricting access by computer

Working with subweb permissions

Subwebs have a slightly different interface. When you select Tools ➪ Security ➪ Permissions for a subweb, it displays an initial Settings tab, shown in Figure 23-9. This additional tab enables the current Web to either use the same password system as the parent Web (the default) or keep a list of distinct users on a per-Web basis. If you elect to use the same usernames and passwords as the parent Web, you can view, but not modify, users and groups in the additional tabs.

To enable the buttons for adding, editing, and removing users, you should select the Use Unique Permissions for this Web option.

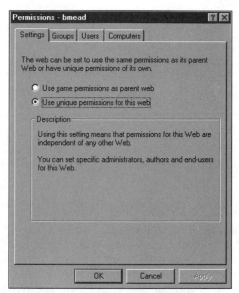

Figure 23-9: For a FrontPage subweb, you can elect to use the same permissions in effect for the root or parent Web, or create an independent set of users and groups.

Changing Your Password

If you are using IIS on Windows NT, you don't have access to change your password by using FrontPage. Users and passwords can be administered only from the standard user account administrative tool.

If you are using FSE with UNIX or with a non-IIS (and non-PWS) server, you can change the password that was initially created for you.

To change your password, select Tools ➪ Security ➪ Change Password (see Figure 23-10). In the Change Password for fpadmin dialog box, type the current password in the Old Password box. Type the new password twice, once in each the New Password box and the Confirm Password box. Click OK. Assuming that you accurately typed the same thing twice, your new password is effective. Note that if passwords are not in effect on the current Web, the Change Password menu item is unavailable.

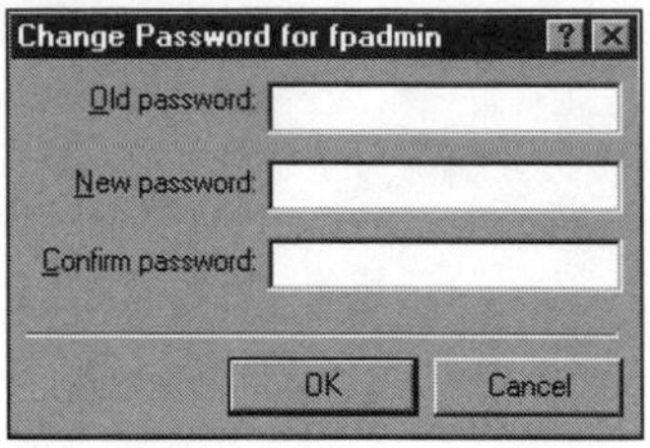

Figure 23-10: Changing a
password in FrontPage 2000

Summary

This chapter has offered a basic overview of the configuration and administration
of FrontPage Web servers using FrontPage Server Extensions. The chapter has
explained how FrontPage works with Web servers, with an emphasis on the two
Microsoft servers, Personal Web Server and Internet Information Server. The
chapter provides enough information to help you manage your FrontPage Webs at
the server. This chapter doesn't claim to provide a complete course on Web server
administration. For that, you need to find another book, because you have come to
the end of this one.

✦   ✦   ✦

Using the CD-ROM

The CD-ROM that accompanies this book contains content files and completed Web pages for all the examples used in the book. In addition, it contains numerous applications and helpful utilities for Web developers.

About the Directories

The CD-ROM contains two main directories:

✦ **Tools:** Contains the installation files for several useful applications and utilities.

✦ **Examples:** Contains completed HTML versions of the examples described in the book. Examples are organized on the CD-ROM by the chapters in which they appear in the book.

What's on the CD-ROM

The following list briefly describes the main applications and utilities found on the CD-ROM. For detailed information and installation instructions, consult the README files that accompany each application on the CD-ROM. Web addresses are also listed for further information and surfing satisfaction.

HTML editing and validation

✦ **LinkBot Pro (Tetranet Software):** An industrial-strength tool for validating and updating Web site hyperlinks (http://www.tetranetsoftware.com)

✦ **CSE HTML Validator (AI Internet Solutions)**: A tool for checking the syntax of your HTML programming (http://www.htmlvalidator.com)

Graphics and multimedia

✦ **Liquid Motion trial (Microsoft)**: Microsoft's visual tool for creating sophisticated Web animations without requiring programming knowledge. (One time Internet access required to use this trial.) (http://www.microsoft.com/)

✦ **ThemePak Themes (Matrix Productions)**: Sample Themes from Matrix Production's collection of professional FrontPage Themes (http://www.themepak.com/)

Programming tools and components

✦ **J-Bots Plus 2000 Demo (WebsUnlimited)**: Provides a dozen useful components to the FrontPage menu, making it easy to add such features as Browser Detection, Forward/Back buttons, Play Music, and Random Image (http://www.websunlimited.com/)

Server log analyzer

✦ **WebTrends Log Analyzer (WebTrends Software)**: A powerful, professional log analyzer that creates reports and graphs of your Web site activity in a variety of formats (http://www.webtrends.com)

Utilities

✦ **Acrobat Reader 3.0 (Adobe Systems, Inc.)**: A viewing tool used to share information electronically across platforms (http://www.adobe.com)

✦ **WS-FTP Pro (Ipswitch)**: A professional FTP client for transferring files between computers on the Internet (http://www.ipswitch.com)

✦   ✦   ✦

Index

continued

continued

F

continued

H

continued

continued

continued

Z

NOTES

NOTES

NOTES

NOTES

IDG BOOKS WORLDWIDE, INC. END-USER LICENSE AGREEMENT

<u>READ THIS.</u> You should carefully read these terms and conditions before opening the software packet(s) included with this book ("Book"). This is a license agreement ("Agreement") between you and IDG Books Worldwide, Inc. ("IDGB"). By opening the accompanying software packet(s), you acknowledge that you have read and accept the following terms and conditions. If you do not agree and do not want to be bound by such terms and conditions, promptly return the Book and the unopened software packet(s) to the place you obtained them for a full refund.

1. <u>License Grant.</u> IDGB grants to you (either an individual or entity) a nonexclusive license to use one copy of the enclosed software program(s) (collectively, the "Software") solely for your own personal or business purposes on a single computer (whether a standard computer or a workstation component of a multiuser network). The Software is in use on a computer when it is loaded into temporary memory (RAM) or installed into permanent memory (hard disk, CD-ROM, or other storage device). IDGB reserves all rights not expressly granted herein.

2. <u>Ownership.</u> IDGB is the owner of all right, title, and interest, including copyright, in and to the compilation of the Software recorded on the disk(s) or CD-ROM ("Software Media"). Copyright to the individual programs recorded on the Software Media is owned by the author or other authorized copyright owner of each program. Ownership of the Software and all proprietary rights relating thereto remain with IDGB and its licensers.

3. <u>Restrictions On Use and Transfer.</u>

   (a) You may only (i) make one copy of the Software for backup or archival purposes, or (ii) transfer the Software to a single hard disk, provided that you keep the original for backup or archival purposes. You may not (i) rent or lease the Software, (ii) copy or reproduce the Software through a LAN or other network system or through any computer subscriber system or bulletin-board system, or (iii) modify, adapt, or create derivative works based on the Software.

   (b) You may not reverse engineer, decompile, or disassemble the Software. You may transfer the Software and user documentation on a permanent basis, provided that the transferee agrees to accept the terms and conditions of this Agreement and you retain no copies. If the Software is an update or has been updated, any transfer must include the most recent update and all prior versions.

4. <u>Restrictions On Use of Individual Programs.</u> You must follow the individual requirements and restrictions detailed for each individual program in the "Using the CD-ROM" appendix of this Book. These limitations are also

contained in the individual license agreements recorded on the Software Media. These limitations may include a requirement that after using the program for a specified period of time, the user must pay a registration fee or discontinue use. By opening the Software packet(s), you will be agreeing to abide by the licenses and restrictions for these individual programs that are detailed in the "Using the CD-ROM" appendix and on the Software Media. None of the material on this Software Media or listed in this Book may ever be redistributed, in original or modified form, for commercial purposes.

5. <u>**Limited Warranty**</u>.

   (a) IDGB warrants that the Software and Software Media are free from defects in materials and workmanship under normal use for a period of sixty (60) days from the date of purchase of this Book. If IDGB receives notification within the warranty period of defects in materials or workmanship, IDGB will replace the defective Software Media.

   (b) IDGB AND THE AUTHORS OF THE BOOK DISCLAIM ALL OTHER WARRANTIES, EXPRESS OR IMPLIED, INCLUDING WITHOUT LIMITATION IMPLIED WARRANTIES OF MERCHANTABILITY AND FITNESS FOR A PARTICULAR PURPOSE, WITH RESPECT TO THE SOFTWARE, THE PROGRAMS, THE SOURCE CODE CONTAINED THEREIN, AND/OR THE TECHNIQUES DESCRIBED IN THIS BOOK. IDGB DOES NOT WARRANT THAT THE FUNCTIONS CONTAINED IN THE SOFTWARE WILL MEET YOUR REQUIREMENTS OR THAT THE OPERATION OF THE SOFTWARE WILL BE ERROR FREE.

   (c) This limited warranty gives you specific legal rights, and you may have other rights that vary from jurisdiction to jurisdiction.

6. <u>**Remedies**</u>.

   (a) IDGB's entire liability and your exclusive remedy for defects in materials and workmanship shall be limited to replacement of the Software Media, which may be returned to IDGB with a copy of your receipt at the following address: Software Media Fulfillment Department, Attn.: *Microsoft FrontPage 2000 Bible*, IDG Books Worldwide, Inc., 7260 Shadeland Station, Ste. 100, Indianapolis, IN 46256, or call 1-800-762-2974. Please allow three to four weeks for delivery. This Limited Warranty is void if failure of the Software Media has resulted from accident, abuse, or misapplication. Any replacement Software Media will be warranted for the remainder of the original warranty period or thirty (30) days, whichever is longer.

   (b) In no event shall IDGB or the authors be liable for any damages whatsoever (including without limitation damages for loss of business profits, business interruption, loss of business information, or any other pecuniary loss) arising from the use of or inability to use the Book or the Software, even if IDGB has been advised of the possibility of such damages.

(c) Because some jurisdictions do not allow the exclusion or limitation of liability for consequential or incidental damages, the above limitation or exclusion may not apply to you.

7. **U.S. Government Restricted Rights.** Use, duplication, or disclosure of the Software by the U.S. Government is subject to restrictions stated in paragraph (c)(1)(ii) of the Rights in Technical Data and Computer Software clause of DFARS 252.227-7013, and in subparagraphs (a) through (d) of the Commercial Computer — Restricted Rights clause at FAR 52.227-19, and in similar clauses in the NASA FAR supplement, when applicable.

8. **General.** This Agreement constitutes the entire understanding of the parties and revokes and supersedes all prior agreements, oral or written, between them and may not be modified or amended except in a writing signed by both parties hereto that specifically refers to this Agreement. This Agreement shall take precedence over any other documents that may be in conflict herewith. If any one or more provisions contained in this Agreement are held by any court or tribunal to be invalid, illegal, or otherwise unenforceable, each and every other provision shall remain in full force and effect.

my2cents.idgbooks.com

Register This Book — And Win!

Visit **http://my2cents.idgbooks.com** to register this book and we'll automatically enter you in our fantastic monthly prize giveaway. It's also your opportunity to give us feedback: let us know what you thought of this book and how you would like to see other topics covered.

Discover IDG Books Online!

The IDG Books Online Web site is your online resource for tackling technology — at home and at the office. Frequently updated, the IDG Books Online Web site features exclusive software, insider information, online books, and live events!

10 Productive & Career-Enhancing Things You Can Do at www.idgbooks.com

- Nab source code for your own programming projects.

- Download software.

- Read Web exclusives: special articles and book excerpts by IDG Books Worldwide authors.

- Take advantage of resources to help you advance your career as a Novell or Microsoft professional.

- Buy IDG Books Worldwide titles or find a convenient bookstore that carries them.

- Register your book and win a prize.

- Chat live online with authors.

- Sign up for regular e-mail updates about our latest books.

- Suggest a book you'd like to read or write.

- Give us your 2¢ about our books and about our Web site.

You say you're not on the Web yet? It's easy to get started with IDG Books' *Discover the Internet,* available at local retailers everywhere.

CD-ROM Installation Instructions

The CD-ROM that accompanies this book contains content files and completed Web pages for all of the examples used in the book. It also has numerous applications and helpful utilities for Web developers.

The CD-ROM has two main directories:

+ The **Tools** directory holds the installation files for several useful applications and utilities.

+ The **Examples** directory contains completed HTML versions of the examples described in the book. Examples are organized on the CD-ROM by the chapters in which they appear in the book.

Place the CD-ROM in your CD-ROM drive. Consult the README files for specific instructions on how to install and run each individual program. For more information about the contents of the CD-ROM, see the Appendix.

Microsoft Product Warranty and Support Disclaimer

The Microsoft program was reproduced by IDG Books Worldwide, Inc., under a special arrangement with Microsoft Corporation. For this reason, IDG Books Worldwide, Inc., is responsible for the product warranty and for support. If your CD-ROM is defective, please return it to IDG Books Worldwide, Inc., which will arrange for its replacement. PLEASE DO NOT RETURN IT TO MICROSOFT CORPORATION. Any product support will be provided, if at all, by IDG Books Worldwide, Inc. PLEASE DO NOT CONTACT MICROSOFT CORPORATION FOR PRODUCT SUPPORT. End users of this Microsoft program shall not be considered "registered owners" of a Microsoft product and therefore shall not be eligible for upgrades, promotions or other benefits available to "registered owners" of Microsoft products.